Readings in Modern Jewish History

*From the American Revolution
to the Present*

Department of Religious Studies
Moore Reading Room
University of Kansas

Readings in Modern Jewish History

From the American Revolution
to the Present

SOURCES

Selected and Introduced

by

Eliezer L. Ehrmann

Published for the
BOARD OF JEWISH EDUCATION
OF METROPOLITAN CHICAGO

by

KTAV PUBLISHING HOUSE, INC., NEW YORK
1977

Library of Congress Cataloging in Publication Data
Main entry under title:

Readings in modern Jewish history, from the American
Revolution to the present.

Includes bibliographies and index.
1. Jews — History — 1789-1945 — Sources. 2. Jews —
History—1945-   —Sources. I. Ehrmann, Eliezer L.,
1903-   II. Board of Jewish Education of Metropolitan
Chicago. III. Title: Modern Jewish history.
DS125.R42   909'.04'924   77-13474
ISBN 0-87068-447-7

MANUFACTURED IN THE UNITED STATES OF AMERICA

For
MARLI
and
FRANK

CONTENTS

vii

Preface

The use of source material in the teaching of history is recommended in the professional literature and considered good educational practice. Sources provide a direct encounter with the past, challenge the student's judgment and imagination, arouse interest for additional reading, supplement textbooks as well as lectures, and evoke wide-ranging discussion.

Encounter with the sources is likely to make the study of history more authentic. The reading of sources adds depth to the learning process and enables the students, in some small degree, to *experience* the past.

Regrettably, there is a dearth of collections of suitable and sufficiently varied source materials for the study of Jewish history comparable to those available in the field of general history. This book, covering modern Jewish history from the American Revolution to the present, endeavors to meet this need. Students are introduced to a variety of source materials— primary, secondary, and interpretative. A range in the level of understanding of the selections offered will allow the instructor to choose what is most suitable to his particular age group.

In the matter of determining when to begin the *modern* period in Jewish history there is no such consensus as exists among general historians in deciding on the beginning date of modern European history. This book of modern Jewish history begins with the era of revolutions, American and French, when the Jews became enfranchised in America and first gained political emancipation in Europe. It is the period when, chiefly in Western Europe and the United States, the Jews were challenged by the encounter with the modern world.

For our purposes seven topics have been chosen for the study of modern Jewish history: Revolution and Emancipation, New Religious Movements, Oppression in Eastern Europe, the Jews in Soviet Russia, the Holocaust, Zionism and the State of Israel, and the Jews in the United States.

The selection of sources to be included in a book of this nature is necessarily a difficult process, circumscribed as it is by the limitations of space and by the judgment of the individual author. The book is not limited to the sequence of political events. Memoirs, autobiographies, newspaper reports, theoretical discussions and intellectual treatises, literary and artistic sources will be found, along with the usual political documents. They are all necessary to convey a picture of a historical epoch and a cultural milieu.

Each chapter of the book is preceded by an introduction that provides the necessary historical information for the understanding of the topic and places the selected sources in a proper setting and perspective. These introductions vary in length and detail, depending on the nature of the chapter and how much background information was deemed necessary.

A prefatory note of explanation has been added to each selection. Subtitles have been supplied for some lengthy selections to facilitate the reading and understanding. Omissions have been indicated by three dots [. . .]. When condensing a selection, care has been exercised not to disrupt the sequence of thought.

The division of books for students and for teachers in the listing of suggested readings supplied for each chapter should not be too strictly followed. There are many books listed for teachers which advanced readers among the students can read with benefit.

The sources of the selections edited and quoted in the text are listed on the page of acknowledgments.

I am indebted to many historians upon whose work I have drawn to an extent which cannot be acknowledged by quotations and footnotes.

I am grateful to various people who have given generously of their labor and talents in the preparation of this volume. These include:

Mrs. Dolly Ballogg and Ms. Toni Alberti of the Chicago Board of Jewish Education, who both pursued the difficult task of securing publishers' and authors' permissions for use of their copyrighted materials.

Ms. Judy Kadish, librarian of the Chicago Board of Jewish Education, and Mrs. Edith Hart of Los Angeles supplied me with needed books which were otherwise not available to me.

Edward A. Nudeman, former superintendent of the Chicago Board of Jewish Education, gave the manuscript the meticulous reading which has been so valuable to many of his former colleagues. Abraham Pannitch, a valued friend, offered helpful suggestions which have improved the text.

I am appreciative of the advice of Mrs. Helen Davidson of the High School of Jewish Studies of the Board of Jewish Education of Metropolitan Chicago, who read some of the chapters of the manuscript.

Finally, I want to express my gratitude to Dr. Irving Barkan, superintendent of the Board of Jewish Education of Metropolitan Chicago, who encouraged me in this endeavor and made possible the publication of this work by the Board of Jewish Education.

E.L.E.
April 1976

I. Revolution and Emancipation

Western and Central Europe, the United States of America

Introduction

I. Jewish Society during the Pre-Emancipation Era

It might be helpful to sketch briefly some aspects of Jewish life in Central and West European countries in the years 1650–1789, which constitute essentially the century preceding the French Revolution. The sketch which follows will serve as background information for a better understanding of the struggle for emancipation.*

Countries

The largest centers of Jewish population in Central and Western Europe at this time existed in Germany and Austria. Smaller numbers were found in France, Holland, England and Italy. Thus France had in the south a small community of Sephardic Jews, who had come as Marranos from Spain and Portugal. A larger Ashkenazic group lived in Alsace-Lorraine, which France had acquired in the seventeenth century through annexation as a result of the wars with Germany. Similarly, Holland and England also had Sephardic and Ashkenazic elements. The Jews living in England were the result of immigration that started in Cromwell's time (seventeenth century). The Sephardic Jews of Holland, among them Marranos, had escaped the Spanish and Portuguese inquisitions. The Ashkenazim came during the seventeenth century from Germany and Poland, seeking refuge either from the Thirty Years' War or the Chmielnicki massacres.

Rights of Residence

In the European setting Jews were considered aliens who had neither political nor legal claims to acceptance or toleration. They, therefore, had no residential rights unless specifically granted them by the political authorities. If they were allowed to settle, it was on the basis of a contract between the Jews and the political authority involved. Such permission could be granted to an individual and his household or to a larger unit.

---

*Much of the information here supplied has been drawn from *Out of the Ghetto* by Jacob Katz (Cambridge, Mass.: Harvard University Press, 1973).

3

Holland

The same condition prevailed even in Holland, considered a country of refuge, where Jews felt freer and economically less hampered than in other European countries. There the contributing factors to the more favorable status of the Jews were the expanding Dutch economy and the atmosphere of religious tolerance which followed a period of religious strife. But legally the status of the Jews in Holland was not different from that of Jews in other countries. They had to secure the right of residence from some district or municipality, and such right was not always granted.

Germany

In Germany the situation was rather complex, since no central authority existed after the religious wars and the Peace of Westphalia in 1648. The supremacy of the emperor existed in name only; all actual power and sovereignty were exercised by some three hundred governmental units of varying sizes. Permission to reside in any locality depended upon the good will of the local authorities, and many districts and towns remained closed to the Jews.

England

England presented a situation different from the European pattern existing at the time. Although the legal status of Jews admitted since Cromwell's time remained unclarified, permission to remain in the country meant freedom to live in any part of it. A Jew born in England was a British subject, while a Jew who came from abroad remained an alien. Political and occupational disabilities from which Jews suffered were a consequence of restrictions against all non-Anglican Christians and not the result of special anti-Jewish legislation.

Theological Reasoning

From medieval times, Christian theological reasoning allowed Jews to continue to exist but only in a degraded state so that they might serve as witnesses to the truth of Christianity. This acceptance, however, did not necessarily imply the right to live in any particular locality. Even in countries where Jews were admitted, they were not allowed to settle where they pleased. It is hard to find a rational explanation in economic or other terms for the presence or absence of Jews in particular places. Much depended on the history of a specific community.

Influence of Ideas

In the case of Cromwell's England, for example, some of the Puritan groups, because of their identification with the Israelites of the Bible, created an atmosphere which was more favorable to Jews.

Economic Needs

As to economic factors, there were several. Thus the developing centralized state had a need for money. Jews with money were, therefore, more readily admitted in such places. After the middle of the seventeenth century, the court Jew in German principalities served as an agent, purveyor, contractor, mediator, and banker. But city burghers would as a rule be suspicious of Jewish economic activities, which might present competition with their crafts and trades, and, consequently, often objected to the acceptance of Jews. The question of admitting Jews was never a simple issue and could even produce conflicts between the central and the local authorities.

Migrant Jews

The right and retention of residence and the ability to establish a family were a source of concern to every Jew. Of similar concern were the efforts to procure such rights for those who had none. Even when some did, a great many Jews did not enjoy this fundamental right. Lacking a place of residence in their own right, they might be employed in a Jewish household or serve as a teacher or a beadle and could thus gain residence. Others, who could not find an occupation, led a kind of migrant existence, going from community to community. They relied on the charity of Jews, often becoming a burden on their fellow-Jews and a liability to Jewish and non-Jewish society alike.

Occupations

Occupational choices were limited even for those who were privileged to have the right of residence. This right usually included permission to pursue certain occupations but exclusion from others. Jews have been active in trade since their dispersion among other nations. But commerce became their characteristic occupation only during the Middle Ages, when they were dislodged from almost all other occupations with the exception of trade and the lending of money. During the sixteenth and seventeenth centuries, the money-based economy expanded and offered new opportunities to Jews in this field. Such commercial ventures might range from that of an agent to the king to the menial activity of a peddler who might even have to borrow money for himself. However, Bohemia and especially Poland, with its density of Jewish settlements, constituted exceptions in that opportunities for pursuing various handicrafts also existed.

In the struggle for emancipation Christian adversaries pointed to the preference of the Jews for trade rather than for occupations which required physical labor. This contention was made especially in Germany. Ignored was the anti-Jewish legislation of previous centuries when Jews were systematically debarred from other occupations. In this context Moses Mendelssohn formulated his famous epigram: "They bind our hands and then reproach us for not using them."

Autonomy

Since the political and legal authorities did not take cognizance of Jews as individuals, they accepted the preference of the Jews for maintaining a community organization of their own. The Jewish community concerned itself with various aspects of the life of the individual Jew. Personal matters like marriage, divorce, inheritance, etc., came under the jurisdiction of the Jewish institutions and were dealt with according to Jewish law based on the Talmud. Marriage contracts often required the special permission of the Christian authorities since they were interested in limiting Jewish population growth. Jewish courts dealt with litigation between Jews and Jews on the basis of Jewish law, although non-Jewish courts were also available to Jews.

The community leadership, elected by the Jews who constituted its members or by a privileged number of them, exercised the powers granted to the community by the non-Jewish authority, as, for example, the power of taxation, which included payments due to the Christian authorities and the monies required for the maintenance of Jewish institutions. The Jewish leadership also had the authority to control the religious and social behavior of its members and the right to inflict punishment, such as fines, imprisonment, and religiously sanctioned bans.

Uniting Small Units

When, because of limited numbers, it was not feasible to form a proper community organization, the Jews of a given political district would join in establishing a combined Jewish community. Such was at times the case in German states where Jews lived dispersed in small groups in villages and townlets.

Contacts with Jews in Other Communities

The Jewish community was not self-sufficient in a provincial way. The upper class, the bankers, court agents, and purveyors, were able to rely on business contacts, personal and by letter, with Jewish communities in distant cities and foreign countries. Even humble businessmen, retailers, and peddlers, although they did not travel great distances, still visited neighborhoods other than their own. Then, too, youths often left their hometowns to study in famous yeshivot (talmudical academies) of other communities. For the students and the learned, exchanges among Poland,

Austria, Germany, England, Holland, and France were not uncommon. The Sephardic communities of England, southern France, Holland, and northern Germany maintained similar cultural and business contacts with their sister communities in Italy and the Levant. This mobility and these contacts broadened the scope of Jewish society beyond the local boundaries and helped to develop the consciousness of a Jewish nation to which every Jew belonged. The individual Jew felt committed to the more local community in which he lived as well as the broader Jewish society, to the Jewish tradition and its religious tenets. He identified himself with the people to which he belonged by birth and religious obligation and a consciousness of mutual responsibility.

Contacts with Non-Jews. Beginning Changes

Contacts with non-Jews were limited to business activities and negotiations with the political authorities.

The static picture of pre-emancipation Jewish society as sketched above underwent changes in the course of the eighteenth century, and more especially during its second half. The Christian society began to be secularized and the way was opened for Jews to enter the general society. The great upheaval caused by the French Revolution shook European society to its very foundations. As a result of the French Revolution, the emancipation of the Jews was launched in the Western world; it went on, gradually advancing, despite repeated reverses.

II. The Struggle for Emancipation

A Turn in Jewish History

Starting in the last third of the eighteenth century, Jewish communities in Western Europe and America underwent a transformation that changed their legal status, their occupational distribution, their cultural habits, and their religious outlook and behavior. This transformation, which covered approximately a hundred years, was caused by the emancipation of the Jews. The entrance of Jews into European as well as American society represents a turn in Jewish history. Modern Jewish history begins with the period of emancipation.

Meaning

Emancipation means the liberation of individuals or groups from slavery and political and social disabilities. Jewish emancipation involved the abolition of discrimination and the lifting of the limitations and handicaps from which Jews had suffered for centuries, the recognition of

Jews as the equals of other citizens, and the formal grant to them of the rights and privileges of citizenship.

Rights of Man

The philosophers of the eighteenth century questioned traditional doctrines and values and emphasized humanitarian ideas and universal human progress. The same century was a period of industrial and economic changes. All these developments in economics, politics, social structure, and ideologies led to the French Revolution and its Declaration of the Rights of Man, and put an end to the feudal society evolved during the Middle Ages. A new basis, a structure of society based on equality, came into being.

Debate About the Status of the Jews

The revolutionary slogans of liberty and equality, the assumption that all men had definite rights which no government could abrogate, would ultimately affect the status of the Jews and afford them the enjoyment of the same rights and privileges as other citizens. The Jew had long been considered a social outcast. After centuries of religious and social hostility, the antipathy to Jews which had developed in host nations could not be readily or quickly obliterated. Anti-Jewish sentiment hampered the full realization of equality even after the latter had been proclaimed by the state and included under the law.

In the discussion on the subject of granting emancipation to Jews, the opponents pointed to the "defects" of the Jews, which they proclaimed to be innate. Even those who favored emancipation answered that these "defects" were a natural result of the degrading status and the legal disabilities from which Jews had suffered for centuries. They contended, further, that the "civic improvement of the Jews" would result from the alleviation of their prejudiced situation, by the removal of all forms of discrimination and disability.

It should be borne in mind that even the liberal French and German philosophers and statesmen who proposed the emancipation of the Jew had a decidedly negative image of him and harbored a strong antipathy toward his religion. Some of them may even have nurtured the expectation and hope that as a result of emancipation and equal status the Jewish community would dissolve and merge with the surrounding society.

France and the United States

In the course of the French Revolution, France became the first European country where Jewish emancipation was accomplished and became a political and legal fact. In the United States the principle had been accepted a few years earlier.

The French armies carried the slogans of the revolution to other parts of Europe and established new republics on the principle of liberty and equality. Keeping the Jews in a politically limited and socially inferior status seemed at variance with the principle of civic equality. With this type of thinking and with the Napoleonic conquests, the Jews gained emancipation in neighboring countries.

After the Napoleonic wars, during the years of reaction following the Congress of Vienna, cities and countries formerly conquered by the French armies tried to reestablish the old pre-revolutionary order and to abolish the gains made by the Jews as a result of the emancipation which had been granted.

Germany

In France and England emancipation had been obtained with comparative ease. But it took decades of debate and struggle in Germany, in which Jewish spokesmen vigorously participated, to gain some measure of political equality. Modern Germany continued to discriminate against Jews in public administration and military service until the Weimar Constitution, enacted after the First World War, established a full-fledged democratic republican order in 1919.

What happened to the Jews in Western countries during the period discussed became a pattern later followed by Jews in other parts of the world. In Eastern Europe, which is discussed in a separate chapter of this volume, emancipation was not achieved before the twentieth century.

Science of Judaism

The battle for emancipation in German countries, beginning in the first half of the nineteenth century, and the accusations hurled against Jews by the opponents of emancipation, resulted in research and study by Jews into the nature and history of Judaism and the Jewish group and gave rise to the modern "Science of Judaism." The scholarship that resulted, the historical-critical study of the Jewish heritage by Jews, may be considered a positive gain of this period.

Emancipation and Its Price

Emancipation strengthened the position of individual Jews, who entered every area of life in modern society and due to their talents contributed to virtually every field of contemporary endeavor. Besides, emancipation made life more tolerable and less hazardous for all Jews.

Advantageous as emancipation was, the Jews had to pay a substantial price for it. Their greatest loss was in the sharp curtailment of their ethnic-religious autonomy. Rights and privileges, such as autonomous community administration and jurisdiction, which they had enjoyed in the pre-emancipation period, were sacrificed. The Jewish community, which constituted a cohesive ethnic and cultural group, and which in the past had united all Jews and concerned itself with every aspect of Jewish life, lost its cohesion. The process of cultural assimilation and religious adaptation tended to diminish the specifically Jewish content of the individual Jew's life.

The Jews of that time accepted these developments as inevitable. Besides, they could not foresee conflicts which might later arise. For example, the affirmative answer given to one of Napoleon's questions that the Jews consider France as their home country and Frenchmen as their brothers became the pattern for similar declarations in other countries (see selections no. 7, 8). Such thinking implied that the Jewish community was split into French Jews and German Jews, or into Frenchmen and Germans of the Mosaic persuasion. But the Jews, however identified they are with the nations of which they are members, somehow have ties, however defined, which transcend the boundaries of the nations of which they are members. How declarations such as first expressed by the Notables in Paris and later followed by other Jews harmonized with a feeling of Jewish group identity, and with the institutions, customs, and international connections, seemed to be of no concern to this generation of Central and West European Jews, who were filled with optimism and looked forward only to unlimited progress.

Different Experience in the United States

Due to the immigration from a great variety of countries, the Jewish experience in America was quite different. For it should be borne in mind that even though the early immigrants to America were mainly English, at the time of the American Revolution half of the population south of New England was non-English. By 1850 only 12 percent of the foreign-born were of English origin. As regards religion, in 1790 the largest Christian denomination in the country included only one-fifth of the nation's churches. As time passed, religious, ethnic, and regional group differences increased considerably. Under the conditions that existed, Jews were not expected to abandon their communal ties in order to become citizens.

The Documents

The documents selected for our chapter begin with the United States, the first country in which emancipation took place. The importance of the Virginia Act is described in a letter of Thomas Jefferson (no. 1), followed by relevant articles of the United States Constitution (no. 2) and a letter of George Washington pointing to the example set by the United States (no. 3).

France, the first European country which granted Jewish emancipation is represented by Isaiah Berr-Bing, a Jewish spokesman before the Revolution (no. 4), the famous and oft-quoted remarks of Count Clermont-Tonnerre in the debate of the French National Assembly (no. 5), the proclamation of emancipation by the National Assembly (no. 6), and Napoleon's dealings with the Assembly of Jewish Notables and the Sanhedrin bearing on the civic role of the Jews in the modern state (nos. 7 and 8).

The ideas of the Enlightenment, the example set by the French Revolution and the defeat of Napoleon, led to an upsurge of reform in Prussia. Wilhelm von Humboldt, scholar and diplomat, prepared a draft on the principles of a projected emancipation (no. 9), and in 1812 a royal edict outlined the new civic status of the Jews in Prussia (no. 10). In the decades following the Congress of Vienna, the debate about Jewish emancipation was taken up again, and the voice of an eloquent Jewish spokesman, Gabriel Riesser, was heard among others (no. 11). Full political and social emancipation was proclaimed in the German constitution of 1919 (no. 12).

In England, where emancipation did not face the obstacles encountered in other European countries, the speech of the historian Macaulay on "Jewish Disabilities" is noteworthy (no. 13).

The chapter concludes with an excerpt from the writings of Leopold Zunz, one of the founders of the "Science of Judaism." Zunz called for the study of Judaism and the Jews as a corollary of Jewish emancipation (no. 14).

1. THE VIRGINIA ACT

THOMAS JEFFERSON

Thomas Jefferson (1743–1826), author of the Declaration of Independence and president of the United States (1801–9), drafted a statute in 1785 which proclaimed it "to be a natural right of mankind that religious opinions shall never offset civil capacities, and that no man can be compelled to support any religious worship." This statute was adopted in Virginia in 1786. It greatly furthered Jewish emancipation in the United States, but also profoundly influenced the French Revolution, as can be seen from the following letter by Jefferson, the American minister to France, addressed to James Madison.

... The Virginia Act for religious freedom has been received with infinite approbation in Europe, and propagated with enthusiasm. I do not mean by the governments, but by the individuals who compose them. It has been translated into French and Italian, has been sent to most of the courts of Europe, and has been the best evidence of the falsehoods of those reports which stated us to be in anarchy. It is inserted in the new Encyclopedia, and is appearing in most of the publications respecting America. In fact, it is comfortable to see the standard of reason at length erected, after so many ages during which the human mind has been held in vassalage by kings, priests and nobles; and it is honorable for us to have produced the first legislature who had the courage to declare that the reason of men may be trusted with the formation of his own opinions. . . .

2. RELIGIOUS FREEDOM IN THE CONSTITUTION OF THE UNITED STATES

The Virginia Act of 1785 was reflected in the new Constitution of the United States. Thus the United States became the first country to inaugurate Jewish emancipation.

Article VI. Section 3 (1788). No religious test shall ever be required as a qualification to any office or public trust under the United States.
First Amendment to the Constitution (1791). Congress shall make no law respecting an establishment of religion, or prohibiting the free exercise thereof.

13

3. AN EXAMPLE WORTHY OF IMITATION

GEORGE WASHINGTON

Washington's statements in his letter to the Hebrew Congregation of Newport, Rhode Island (1790), can be considered as premature to some degree, as not all states followed the religious-freedom articles of the Constitution but required religious qualifications or a religious oath for office-holders. In the course of the nineteenth century, however, such requirements were abolished by those states.

. . . The citizens of the United States of America have the right to applaud themselves for having given to mankind examples of an enlarged and liberal policy worthy of imitation. All possess alike liberty of conscience and immunities of citizenship. It is now no more that toleration is spoken of as if it were by the indulgence of one class of people that another enjoyed the exercise of their inherent natural rights, for happily the Government of the United States, which gives to bigotry no sanction, to persecution no assistance, requires only that they who live under its protection should demean themselves as good citizens in giving it on all occasions their effectual support.

4. FRANCE: DEMAND FOR EQUAL RIGHTS

ISAIAH BERR-BING

Isaiah Berr-Bing (1759–1805), a Jew in Alsace, France, responded to an anti-Semitic pamphlet in 1787 and included the following demands.

We do not ask for favors or special privileges. We demand a law which will admit us to the natural rights which all men, without exception, should enjoy. We demand that the humiliating wall which separates us from all other citizens be removed. . . . that everybody be permitted to choose his place of domicile as he sees fit, be allowed to pursue any occupation or trade. . . . We demand that educational institutions be open to us as to any other citizen. . . .

5. RIGHTS FOR INDIVIDUALS

STANISLAUS DE CLERMONT-TONNERRE

Clermont-Tonnerre's words in the French National Assembly on December 23, 1789 have been often quoted and interpreted in various ways. In accordance with the new principles of civic equality, the Jews were to be treated as individual citizens on their own merits, on the same basis as everyone else but not as a "nation within a nation." Some interpreters have seen in Clermont-Tonnerre's words an unwillingness to accord Jews their own recognition as a group.

All should be refused the Jews as a nation, but everything should be granted to them as individuals. (Literal translation: to Jews, everything, to Judaism nothing).

6. PROCLAMATION OF JEWISH EMANCIPATION

FRENCH NATIONAL ASSEMBLY, SEPTEMBER 28, 1791

France became the first European country to proclaim Jewish emancipation and to accept the Jews as equal citizens.

Whereas the conditions under which French citizenship is granted are set forth in the Constitution and whereas every person accepting those conditions and obliging himself by oath of citizenship to fulfill such conditions is entitled to the enjoyment of all rights guaranteed in the Constitution, the National Assembly herewith abrogates all earlier decrees.

The Jews by taking the oath of citizenship forego the right to any previously granted privileges and special legislation.

7. QUESTIONS SUBMITTED BY NAPOLEON TO THE ASSEMBLY OF JEWISH NOTABLES IN PARIS

In 1806, Napoleon summoned an Assembly of Jewish Notables selected by the prefects, or chief administrative officials, of the departments (districts) of France. Napoleon put twelve questions before the Notables. The main purpose was apparently to clarify the relationship between the Jewish religious law and the civil law of France with a view to eliminating any remnant of Jewish "corporateness."

The Jews had little choice but to answer yes to the questions, as expected by Napoleon. Only in one respect did they stand their ground—namely, on the question of mixed marriages. All they were prepared to grant was a declaration that intermarriage, if legalized by the civil authorities, would be respected by the Jewish community.

In his grandiose manner Napoleon called for a Sanhedrin, modeled after the ancient Jewish institution, to ratify the answers of the Notables which he found satisfactory so that they might be considered by the Jews as binding laws. Napoleon later lost interest in the matter and even enacted some restrictive legislation affecting Jews.

1. Is it lawful for Jews to have more than one wife?
2. Is divorce allowed by the Jewish religion? Is divorce valid, although pronounced not by courts of justice but by virtue of laws in contradiction to the French code?
3. May a Jewess marry a Christian, or a Jew a Christian woman? or does Jewish Law order that the Jews should only intermarry among themselves?
4. In the eyes of Jews are Frenchmen not of the Jewish religion considered as brethren or as strangers?*
5. What conduct does Jewish law prescribe toward Frenchmen not of the Jewish religion?
6. Do the Jews born in France, and treated by the law as French citizens, acknowledge France as their country?* Are they bound to defend it? Are they bound to obey the laws and follow the directions of the civil code?
7. Who elects the rabbis?
8. What kind of police jurisdiction do the rabbis exercise over the Jews? What judicial power do they exercise over them?
9. Are the police jurisdiction of the rabbis and the forms of the election regulated by Jewish law, or are they only sanctioned by custom?
10. Are there professions from which the Jews are excluded by their law?
11. Does Jewish law forbid the Jews to take usury from their brethren?
12. Does it forbid, or does it allow usury in dealing with strangers?

8. THE ANSWERS

The decisions of the Sanhedrin, which were based on the answers of the Notables, were formulated in nine articles and drawn up in French and in Hebrew.

1. In conformity with the Decree of R. Gershom, polygamy is forbidden to the Israelites.
2. Divorce by the Jewish law is valid only after previous decision of the civil authorities.
3. The religious act of marriage must be preceded by a civil contract.
4. Marriages between Israelites and Christians are binding, although they can not be celebrated with religious forms.
5. Every Israelite is religiously bound to consider his non-Jewish fellow citizens as brothers, and to aid, protect, and love them as though they were coreligionists.

---

*See the Introduction to this chapter for comments on these questions.

6. The Israelite is required to consider the land of his birth or adoption as his fatherland, and shall love and defend it when called upon.
7. Judaism does not forbid any kind of handicraft or occupation.
8. It is commendable for Israelites to engage in agriculture, manual labor, and the arts, as their ancestors in Palestine were wont to do.
9. Finally, Israelites are forbidden to exact usury from Jew or Christian.

9. PRUSSIA: NEW LEGISLATION PROPOSED

WILHELM VON HUMBOLDT

Wilhelm von Humboldt (1767–1835), scholar and statesman, became Prussian minister of education and in 1809 drafted principles for the legislation to be enacted granting emancipation to the Jews, which he strongly supported. The excerpt is reprinted here in abridged form.

As regards religious ideas, the contrast between Jew and Christian will inevitably continue as long as the notion that Christianity is the opposite of Judaism is not universally dissipated. . . . Only an immediate concession of full and equal rights is just politic and consistent. . . . We must abandon inhuman and prejudiced ways of thinking, by which a man is judged not by his actual characteristics but by his origin of religion, and he is regarded not as an individual but as a part of a race, whose attributes he necessarily possesses. The state is not an educational but a political institution. No legislative system in favor of the Jew will achieve its end if it uses the word "Jewish" otherwise than in its religious connotation. . . . If the Jews will not readily accept the obligations imposed on every citizen I would prefer that, if all remedial measures to this end had been exhausted, they be rather expelled from the country entirely. For to endure persons within a state who would countenance the manifestation of so little confidence in them would be detrimental to the morality of the entire nation. . . . Loss of citizenship should be imposed on Jews only in cases where the same penalty would be imposed on Christians. . . .

10. CITIZENS OF PRUSSIA

ROYAL EDICT, MARCH 11, 1812

After its defeat by Napoleon, various political reforms were introduced by the Prussian government. During this period of reform, Jews became citizens of the state in 1812 and were granted free choice of residence and occupation. The improved civil status was withheld from the Jews in Posen, a province which had been annexed by Prussia after the partitions of Poland by Russia, Austria and Prussia at the end of the eighteenth century. More than 40 percent of the Jews of Prussia lived in Posen.

The contemplated advances did not all materialize in the decades following the Napoleonic wars. Nor did naturalization automatically secure for the Jews the same rights that were enjoyed by Christian citizens. But the royal edict of 1812 made possible the political integration of Prussian Jewry, the culturally most advanced community of Jews in Western Europe. This achievement was considered a turning point in the history of the Jews of Germany. The stage had been set for the struggle for full equality.

The Jews in the ancient Prussian states are considered natives and Prussian citizens, on condition that they shall adopt family names, and, in all transactions, make use of the German or some other living language.

They shall enjoy equal rights and privileges with the Christians.

They shall be eligible to academical, and also to parochial offices.

They shall be at liberty to live in any part of the state, acquire landed property, exercise any lawful trade, and follow any lawful business. The Jews shall have to pay no additional taxes, but must bear all the charges and duties alike with other citizens. They are subject to military service.

Their marriages are not liable to any impediments, only a foreigner cannot acquire the right of citizenship by marrying a citizen.

They are not to have any separate laws, except in matters of divine worship and ritual usages; but without a retroactive force. They shall not be allowed a jurisdiction of their own.

Finally the government reserves to itself the necessary determinations about the conditions of the church, and improving education amongst the Jews, in considering of which, it shall avail itself of the assistance of confessors of the Jewish religion, known for ability and integrity, and hear their opinion.

11. CONTINUING THE STRUGGLE FOR FULL EQUALITY

GABRIEL RIESSER

In the continuous struggle for full equality, the Jews of Germany found a most eloquent champion in Gabriel Riesser (1806–63). Although a doctor of law, he was denied a university post and refused admittance to the bar on account of his Jewish faith. He refused conversion as a way out, as accepted by some of his contemporaries. He was widely respected for his uprightness, his literary abilities, and great eloquence. In 1860 he was appointed a district judge in Frankfort. The selection is taken from his "Open Letter Concerning the Position of the Adherents of the Mosaic Faith in Germany," published in 1831.

Religious Freedom

The time for martyrs to the faith is gone; the problem of religious freedom today is more one of right, honour, liberty, than of faith. But confidence in a just cause is also faith; it can inspire to efforts and sacrifices; though these may not be crowned with immediate success, they will plant fertile seeds for the future. . . .

Conversion

My objection to a "lucrative" conversion to the dominant faith in our days, and the rejection of such an act by the right-thinking among both the adherents of the dominant and of the oppressed religion, as well as the unmistakable opposition of public opinion—these attitudes are due not to a principle of fanaticism, but to the fundamental tenet of truth and equity, that what is strange to one's heart should not be professed by one's lips.

All our intention and power should be directed towards the realization of the one aim: to strive for the obtaining of human and civil rights which are so unjustly withheld from us; but we must not obtain them through lies. . .

12. EQUAL STATUS IN GERMANY

FROM THE CONSTITUTION OF THE GERMAN REICH, 1919

After the years of reaction following the Congress of Vienna in 1815, and after the abortive Revolution of 1848, the Jews in the German states achieved improved status of citizenship in successive stages. Although undoubtedly recognized as citizens, the Jews labored under discriminatory restrictions. The fight against such restrictions went on during the decades following the Congress of Vienna (see also no. 11). A radical change as regards discrimination came about when, through the unification of the northern states, a new constitution for the North German Federation in 1869 promulgated the principle that "all limitations of civic and citizenship rights deriving from differences of religion which are still in force are hereby abolished." This law was later extended over the newly founded German Empire in 1871.

Yet the army and the political administration continued to practice discrimination. Strictly speaking, there was also no legal recognition of Judaism as a religion. Full equality for the Jews of Germany was achieved in the Constitution of 1919, after the First World War.

Article 135. All inhabitants of the Commonwealth enjoy complete liberty of belief and conscience. The free exercise of religion is assured by the Constitution and is under public protection.

Article 136. Civil and political rights are neither conditioned upon nor limited by the exercise of religious liberty. The enjoyment of civil and political rights as well as eligiblity to public office is independent of religious belief.

13. LET US FIGHT THE BATTLE OF TRUTH

LORD MACAULAY

Political and occupational disabilities from which Jews in England suffered were a consequence of restrictions against all those who did not belong to the Church of England. When these restrictions were abolished and the emancipation of the dissenters and the Catholics was carried out in 1829, the grant of similar rights was expected by the Jews. The Tories, however, continued to cling to the concept of the Christian character of the state. All members of Parliament, for example, as well as public officials and university teachers, had to take the oath on "the true faith of a Christian." A Jew who was elected to Parliament, Baron Lionel de Rothschild, could not take his seat because he refused to take such an oath.

The Liberals fought for the admission of Jews. The battle was joined by Thomas Babington Macaulay (1800–1859), statesman, historian, and essayist, who was a champion of Jewish emancipation. He contributed to the *Edinburgh Review* a masterly essay on this question in "Civil Disabilities of the Jews." Similar arguments were advanced by him in a speech delivered before the House of Commons on April 17, 1833. Finally, in 1858, a compromise proposal was carried by which each house was permitted to formulate the oath according to its own decision.

The selection from Macaulay's speech follows (abridged).

. . . The honorable member of Oldham* tells us that the Jews are naturally a mean race, a sordid race, a money-getting race; that they . . . are averse to all honourable callings; that they neither sow nor reap; that they have neither flocks nor herds; that usury is the only pursuit for which they are fit; that they are destitute of all elevated and amiable sentiments. Such, Sir, has in every age been the reasoning of bigots. They never fail to plead in justification of persecution the vices which persecution has engendered. England has been to the Jews less than half a country; and we revile them because they do not feel for England more than a half patriotism. We treat them as slaves, and wonder that they do not regard us as brethren. We drive them to mean occupations, and then reproach them for not embracing honourable professions. We long forbade them to possess land; and we complain that they chiefly occupy themselves in trade. We shut them out

---

*An adversary of Jewish emancipation. (Ed.)

from all the paths of ambition; and then we despise them for taking refuge in avarice. During many ages we have, in all our dealings with them, abused our immense superiority of force; and then we are disgusted because they have recourse to that cunning which is the natural and universal defence of the weak against the violence of the strong. But were they always a mere money-changing, money-getting, money-hoarding race? Nobody knows better than my honourable friend the member for the University of Oxford that there is nothing in their national character which unfits them for the highest duties of citizens. He knows that, in the infancy of civilisation, when our island was as savage as New Guinea, when letters and arts were still unknown to Athens, when scarcely a thatched hut stood on what was afterwards the site of Rome, this contemned people had their fenced cities and cedar palaces, their splendid Temple, their fleets of merchant ships, their schools of sacred learning, their great statesmen and soldiers, their natural philosophers, their historians and their poets. What nation ever contended more manfully against overwhelming odds for its independence and religion? What nation ever, in its last agonies, gave such signal proofs of what may be accomplished by a brave despair? And if, in the course of many centuries, the oppressed descendants of warriors and sages have degenerated from the qualities of their fathers, if, while excluded from the blessings of law, and bowed down under the yoke of slavery, they have contracted some of the vices of outlaws and of slaves, shall we consider this as matter of reproach to them? Shall we not rather consider it as matter of shame and remorse to ourselves? Let us do justice to them. Let us open to them the door of the House of Commons. Let us open to them every career in which ability and energy can be displayed. Till we have done this, let us not presume to say that there is no genius among the countrymen of Isaiah, no heroism among the descendants of the Maccabees. . . .

. . . Let us not fight the battle of truth with the weapons of error, and endeavor to support by oppression that religion which first taught the human race the great lesson of universal charity.

14. SCHOLARSHIP AND EMANCIPATION: THE NEED FOR JEWISH SCHOLARSHIP

LEOPOLD ZUNZ

Leopold Zunz (1794–1886), one of the founders of the "Science of Judaism" movement, is considered one of the greatest Jewish scholars of the modern era. Zunz called for the cultivation of modern historical research, one function of which would be to acquaint the Christian world and its leaders with the true

nature of Judaism and thus help to promote civic equality. His books are works
of objective, painstaking scholarship. Zunz took an active interest in the
political events in Germany in his time and was a passionate spokesman for
democracy and liberalism.

. . . It is high time that the Jews of Europe, particularly those of Germany, be
granted right and liberty rather than rights and liberties-not some paltry,
humiliating privileges, but complete and uplifting civil rights. . . . The
neglect of Jewish scholarship goes hand in hand with civil discrimination
against the Jews. Through a higher intellectual level and a more thorough
knowledge of their own affairs the Jews could have achieved a greater
degree of recognition and thus more justice. Furthermore, much bad
legislation, many a prejudice against Jewish antiquity, much condemnation of new endeavors are a direct consequence of the state of neglect in
which Jewish literature and Jewish scholarship have been for about
seventy years, particularly in Germany. And even though writings about
the Talmud and against the Jews mushroomed overnight and several
dozen Solons offered themselves to us as reformers, there was no book of
any consequence which the statesmen could have consulted, no professor
lectured about Judaism and Jewish literature, no German learned society
offered prizes in this field, no philanthropist went traveling for this
purpose. . . . Religion and scholarship, civil liberty, and intellectual
progress require schools, seminaries, and synagogues; they must enlist the
efforts of capable community leaders, competent teachers, well-trained
rabbis. If emancipation and scholarship are not to be mere words, not some
tawdry bit of fancy goods for sale, but the fountainhead of morality which
we have found again after a long period of wandering in the wilderness,
then they must fecundate institutions—high-ranking educational institutions, religious instruction for everyone, dignified religious services,
suitable sermons. Such institutions are indispensable for the needs of the
congregational totality of the Jews; but to establish them we need religious
zeal and scholarly activity, enthusiastic participation in the entire project,
benevolent recognition from the outside. . . .

QUESTIONS FOR THOUGHT AND DISCUSSION

1. What is meant by the "feudal society" of the Middle Ages? What was the status of the Jews in medieval society?

2. In what way does a modern democratic society differ from the feudal structure of the Middle Ages? How does the situation of the Jews differ in each of them?

3. Find out about the Declaration of the Rights of Man adopted during the French Revolution. How did it contribute to the emancipation of the Jews?

4. What is the historical significance of the twelve questions put by Napoleon to the Assembly of Jewish Notables and their answers?

5. In what way was the American experience of Jewish emancipation different from the European? Why?

6. Why have certain forms of anti-Jewish discrimination survived even in countries which granted Jews full civic equality?

7. The Versailles peace treaties after the First World War provided national minority rights for Jews in some East European countries, such as Poland and Lithuania. Find out what these provisions implied and how successful they were in safeguarding the rights of Jewish citizens.

8. Some historians of the twentieth century have spoken of the "crisis of emancipation." What is meant by the term "crisis" as used in this connection?

SUGGESTED READING

Note: Books suggested in more than one chapter are here listed by the
name of the author only. A key to such listings will be found at the
end of the book.

A paperback edition is indicated by the letters PB.

Books for the Student

Charry-Segal, chap. 18.
Elbogen, chap. 1.
Graetz, vol. 5, chaps. 11–13.
Grayzel, pp. 567–99.
Learsi, chap. 3.
Margolis-Marx, chaps. 80–81, 83–85, 88. PB.

Books for the Teacher

Berlin, Isaiah. *The Age of Enlightenment*, New York, 1956. PB
Duker, Abraham G., and Meir Ben-Horin, eds. *Emancipation and
Counter-Emancipation.* New York, 1976.
Hertzberg, Arthur. *The French Enlightenment and the Jews.* New York,
1968.
Janowsky, Oscar. *Jews and Minority Rights, 1898–1919.* New York, 1933.
Katz, Jacob. *Out of the Ghetto: The Social Background of Jewish
Emancipation.* Cambridge, Mass., 1974.
Marcus, Jacob R. *The Rise and Destiny of the German Jew.* Cincinnati,
1936.
Meyer, Michael A. *The Origins of the Modern Jews: Jewish Identity and
European Culture in Germany, 1794–1824.* Detroit, 1967.
Sachar, chaps. 1–3, 5, 8.
Schwarz, chap. 13.

II. NEW RELIGIOUS MOVEMENTS

Introduction

The Need for New Interpretations

Emancipation created a crisis within Judaism. As long as Jews lived in a closed Jewish society, separated from the surrounding non-Jewish society by medieval laws that were still in force, the task of remaining Jewish presented no problem. However, the new status of the Jews in a non-Jewish society, their entry into the secular life of modern Western nations, and the efforts of individual Jews to become a part of this life constituted influences that forced the Jews to reexamine their religious beliefs and practices and to adjust their ways of living to those of the surrounding culture. In response to the changed political, social, and cultural conditions, modern interpretations of Judaism emerged in the course of the nineteenth century. These reevaluations started in Germany and resulted in the Reform, Neo-Orthodox, and Conservative movements.

Reform Judaism

Reform Judaism was the first of the movements that developed from the efforts to rethink the principles of the Jewish religion and to adapt its practices to the secular character of the modern world. Reform Judaism is also at times called Liberal or Progressive Judaism.

The Reform movement started at the beginning of the nineteenth century, and the first Reform Jews were lay people, not rabbis. Jewish learning had already declined. There were Jews who were no longer following the traditional religious practices, and there were even defections from Judaism by wealthy Jews. Some Jews compared the informality of Orthodox congregations with the services conducted in Christian churches and became very critical of the lack of decorum at synagogue services. The reformers introduced such changes as reducing the number of prayers, giving the sermon in German, and including German prayers along with the Hebrew prayers to which services in the synagogue had been previously limited. The use of German in the service was considered a radical change. But even more radical was the introduction of the organ. To traditional Jews, the use of the organ on the Sabbath and the festivals was a very serious breach, a genuine desecration of the holiness of the day.

The esthetic improvement of worship was not, however, the sole aim or

27

motivation of the early reformers. The traditional prayers for a return to Zion and the restoration of the Temple in Jerusalem were regarded as objectionable and were either changed or omitted altogether. Moreover, the strictly traditional observance of the Sabbath and many other Jewish practices seemed to the reformers to constitute obstacles to the acceptance of the Jew as a part of Western society.

Rabbinical Conferences

At the same time, a new generation of rabbis and scholars, with university education in addition to traditional learning, had risen who in many instances were sympathetic to the cause of Reform. In the 1840s rabbinical conferences were held in Brunswick, Frankfort, and Breslau with the aim of bringing together the various adherents of the newer approaches to Judaism. There were practical matters to be solved— changes in the services, in the traditional severity of Sabbath observance, in the laws of marriage and divorce, etc. By seeking a legitimate way to ease the "yoke of the law" for the modern Jew, Reform made possible close social and cultural relations with the Gentile world and thus promoted political as well as cultural emancipation. But it would be wrong to regard Reform only as having such practical goals. There was, in addition, a sincere religious striving to develop an all-inclusive view of Judaism that would be in harmony with the status of the modern Jew as a citizen of a country like Germany and as a member of a non-Jewish society.

Abraham Geiger

A leading figure among the rabbis advocating Reform was Abraham Geiger (1810–1874), who was also an outstanding scholar. He laid the intellectual foundations for Reform Judaism. On the basis of his research, he concluded that change and adaptation have been characteristic of Judaism. To Geiger the spirit of Judaism was sacred while the forms, customs, and ceremonies were subject to change. He believed that Judaism had within it the capacity for new development.

Geiger valued the teachings of the prophets, monotheism, and the moral law as the constant elements of Judaism. He regarded the dispersion of the Jews as a means for them to carry out their "mission" of spreading faith in the One God and His moral law.

Geiger considered the Jewish people no longer a nation but only a religious community. He omitted all references to the return to Zion from the prayerbook which he published in 1854. He interpreted the messianic hope as not involving the national restoration of the Jewish people but rather as an age of universal brotherhood.

In his later life Geiger's approach became more understanding of Jewish historical experience as a basis for Reform. Thus he introduced the second day of the festivals, which he had previously abolished.

Liberal Not Reform

Many Jewish communities in Germany adopted revised liturgies and introduced organ accompaniment. Yet there was a marked difference between these congregations in Germany and the Reform movement in other countries, especially in the United States. German Reform Judaism was more traditional in character as contrasted with Reform in the United States. It called itself "Liberal" rather than "Reform." The latter term was restricted to the extremist Berlin *Reformgemeinde* (Reform community), the only congregation in Germany with an all-German service, bareheaded worship, and services on Sunday instead of Saturday.

Reform in America

Reform Judaism achieved its greatest success in America. The dominant Protestant character of Christianity in the United States and the tradition of multiple and independent religious denominations influenced the organizational structure and activity of other faiths in America. This type of religious organization, which encouraged any religious group willing and able to band together, without the need for concurrence on the part of a governmental or religious body, influenced the Jewish immigrants. Any Jewish group was able to set up its own congregation as it saw fit without fear or interference from the organized Jewish community (*kehillah*)* or from the government, as might be the case in Europe. Congregationalism and congregational autonomy became the rule in Jewish religious organization. It was, then, through trial and error that American Jewry developed the national synagogue unions, which by the twentieth century became the prevailing pattern.

The first Reform group in America was founded in 1824 by twelve members of the congregation in Charleston, South Carolina. They seceded from the congregation when their petition for reform in the ritual was rebuked by the elders. The Reformed Society of Israelites, which they formed, was short-lived. With the large immigration of Jews from Germany in the 1840s, many congregations which adopted a Reform ritual were established. It was due largely to the organizing talent of Isaac Mayer Wise (see below, no. 16) that all those congregations with a variety of

---

Kehillah: the Hebrew word for the Jewish community in many European countries and its autonomous government in pre-emancipatory times. Also used for the framework of Jewish community institutions in the nineteenth and twentieth centuries. (Ed.)

interpretations avoided the danger of anarchy and found a center and direction in the Union of American Hebrew Congregations, established in 1873, and a seminary for the education of rabbis, the Hebrew Union College, established in Cincinnati in 1875. The American Reform movement has not remained static but has been able to adjust to changing conditions.

In Germany Reform Judaism called forth counter-movements, which came to be known as Neo-Orthodoxy and Conservative Judaism.

Neo-Orthodoxy

From the very beginning of the movement there were Orthodox opponents of early reformers, both rabbis and laymen. However, it was only later, during the second half of the nineteenth century, that Neo-Orthodoxy, as it was called, took definite shape and developed its institutions. The leader both in formulating the thinking and promoting the organization of Neo-Orthodoxy was Samson Raphael Hirsch (no. 19), who became the rabbi of an Orthodox separatist group in Frankfort in 1851. There he found a favorable setting in which to realize his ideals and plans.

Hirsch, too, recognized that Judaism had entered a new period and needed new emphases. He spoke of Torah im derekh eretz—"Torah along with a worldly occupation,"* reinterpreted as secular culture. Hirsch himself had studied at a university. He aimed at a combination of traditional Orthodoxy and European culture, and joined the struggle for emancipation and secular education. At the same time he considered biblical-talmudic Judaism as indivisible, to be accepted in its entirety without compromise and with strict adherence to the Law (halakhah) in all its minute details.

The national character of Israel is of a purely spiritual nature according to Hirsch. Israel "was introduced into the ranks of the nations" that "through its history and life, [it] should declare that God is the only creative cause of experience, and that the fulfillment of His will is the only goal of life." Israel's mission is to proclaim "these great truths." This mission does not depend on land and soil. Israel's most cherished "ideal is that of the universal brotherhood of mankind."

Hirsch was uncompromising in his opposition to Reform Judaism. In his opinion the Jews, rather than Judaism, were in need of reform. "The reform that is needed is education of the present generation in the Torah and not lowering the level of the Torah to the need and spirit of the present day."

---

*Sayings of the Fathers 2:2. Study of Torah along with a "worldly occupation" is traditionally understood as an occupation for purposes of earning a living. (Ed.)

Day Schools

To achieve his educational goals, Hirsch organized three schools in Frankfort: a primary school, a secondary school, and a high school for girls. Besides the Hebrew language and the Jewish subjects, the curriculum included studies in the customary secular subjects, such as German, foreign languages, mathematics, and the natural sciences. These schools became the pattern for similar Orthodox day schools in other places and countries.

Split Among the Orthodox

In 1876 a German "Law of Secession" was passed which enabled individuals to secede from a church or religious community even when they retained their religion. This law made possible the secession of Orthodox members from the established Jewish communities when they regarded coexistence with the Liberal or Reform leadership as intolerable. To Hirsch, secession became a necessary and supreme religious principle which was to be acted on; he, therefore, became an advocate of "separatist Orthodoxy." In a few German cities small groups of the Orthodox seceded and formed independent and separate Orthodox congregations. But the large majority of Orthodox Jews in Germany remained within the framework of the organized community (kehillah) which provided for their religious needs. Thus Orthodoxy in Germany was split into two groups.

Another later split concerned the attitude to Zionism. There were Orthodox Jews who joined the religious wing of the Zionist movement known as Mizrachi. The leaders of the separatist Orthodoxy in Frankfort, on the other hand, provided the thinking that led to the world organization of Orthodox Jews, Agudat Israel, founded in 1912, to counter both Zionism and Reform Judaism. Although opposed at first, Agudat Israel after the Holocaust revised its position on Zionism.

Neo-Orthodoxy in the United States

With the mass immigration of East European Jews to the United States, beginning in the 1880s, Neo-Orthodoxy found a fruitful field amidst changed political, social, and cultural conditions necessitating changed emphases. Yeshiva University in New York has become the center of modern Orthodoxy in America.

Conservative Judaism

When the rabbinic conference held in Frankfort in 1845 tended to accept radical changes as suggested by the Reform elements, Zacharias Frankel (1801–1875), rabbi in Dresden and an eminent scholar, registered his protest by withdrawing from the conference. He considered the retention of Hebrew in the worship as essential, and not merely advisable as the conference had voted. Frankel did not object to the idea of reform; he pleaded for a "middle position," for "moderate reform," and insisted on historic continuity. He reached the conclusion that the bulk of the ritual and of the Law (halakhah) had to be retained.

Frankel became the head of the Jewish Theological Seminary in Breslau, founded in 1854. Its curriculum became the pattern for other rabbinical seminaries of the "positive-historical school" which Zacharias Frankel represented. The historical school later influenced the Conservative movement in the United States, which struck roots in this country. While opposing extreme changes in traditional observances, the movement permits certain modifications in response to the changing life of the Jewish people. Conservative Judaism has become a leading religious movement in the United States. Its center is the Jewish Theological Seminary in New York, founded in 1887 and reorganized by Solomon Schechter in 1902 (see nos. 21 and 22).

Reconstructionism

It has been pointed out that American Judaism has produced the greatest variety of interpretations of what it means to be a Jew under modern conditions. Reconstructionism is a genuine American attempt at the reinterpretation of Judaism by Mordecai M. Kaplan, professor at the Conservative Jewish Theological Seminary in New York. Kaplan considers Judaism as not just a faith but an "evolving religious civilization" comprising a history, a language, a religion, a social organization, standards of conduct, spiritual and social ideals. Although allowing freedom to modify the existing ritual, Kaplan and his associates revere traditional institutions. A full Jewish life means participation in cultural and communal activity as well as adherence to ethical conduct and moral principles. It demands the cultivation of the Hebrew language and its literature and the recognition of Eretz Israel as a cultural center.

The movement published *A New Haggadah* (1941) and the *Sabbath Prayer Book* (1945), both of which introduced changes in the traditional texts. A Reconstructionist Rabbinical College was established in 1967 in Philadelphia.

Kaplan's Reconstructionism goes beyond existing party lines and has influenced the thought of some leaders of various religious groupings in the United States.

Sources

Reflecting the diverse religious developments and movements sketched above, our selection of sources begins with a call for reform by a group of lay Jews in Berlin in 1845 (no. 15). Reform in the United States found its spokesman and organizer in Isaac Mayer Wise (no. 16). Its ideology and its ability to adjust to needed changes are found in the Pittsburgh and Columbus Platforms of 1885 and 1937 (nos. 17 and 18).

The attitude of Orthodoxy to the efforts for emancipation in Germany and the nature of Israel's mission are discussed by Samson Raphael Hirsch, who became the founder and leader of Neo-Orthodoxy (no. 19). The process of rabbinic law-making as faced by an Orthodox rabbi is presented by Immanuel Jakobovits, chief rabbi of the United Hebrew Congregations of the British Commonwealth (no. 20).

The aims of the middle position, the "positive-historical school," which led to the development of Conservative Judaism in America, are formulated by Alexander Kohut, rabbi and scholar and Solomon Schechter, the first president of the United Synagogue of America (nos. 21 and 22).

The principles of Reconstructionism are explained by Rabbi Ira Eisenstein, a leader of the movement, president of its Rabbinical College, and editor of the *Reconstructionist* magazine (no. 23).

15. A CALL FOR REFORM

BERLIN REFORMERS, 1845

The changed political, economic, and cultural conditions of the nineteenth century and the nature of the modern secular state of which the Jew became a citizen called for changes in the interpretation of Judaism, its traditional practices and institutions. The most radical changes were initiated by the Reform movement, which began in Germany. An appeal of a group of Jewish laymen was published in various Berlin newspapers in April 1845. It led to the establishment of an extremist Reform congregation in Berlin. See the introduction to this chapter.

The Conflict

From the time that we ceased to suffer from political oppression in our German fatherland and the soaring spirit cast off its fetters; from the time that we became identified with our surroundings in culture and custom, our religion failed gradually to give us that satisfaction which was the comfort and the happiness of our ancestors. Our religion clung to the forms and prescriptions that had been handed down for centuries, but our convictions and our sentiments, our *inner* religion, is no longer in harmony with this interpretation. Hence we are in a state of conflict with ourselves, and there is a contradiction between our inner life and faith and the external life, the given law.

Confusion and Indifference

True, our savants and teachers are engaged in a combat in the field of theology for and against a reconciliation of this contradiction; but how long has this been the case! and the end of the combat is not in sight. In the meantime, however, life has superseded science; in the meantime the overwhelming majority of the cultured members of our community has renounced the grestest portion of our religious prescriptions, and even those which they still keep are observed without belief and without enthusiasm. The confusion is great. Nowhere union, nowhere a support, nowhere a limit. The old rabbinical Judaism with its firm basis has no basis any longer in us. In vain are the efforts of those who aim to preserve it artificially. The petrified doctrine and our life are divorced forever. The doubt which has begun to negate threatens to transgress all limits. It begets indifference and unbelief and delivers us over to a state of helplessness in which we are compelled to witness with pain how, together with the antiquated forms, the eternal holy kernel of true Judaism threatens to be lost for our descendants.

Necessity of Change

These are facts which speak for themselves, which only those do not see who will not see—facts which fill our hearts with glowing zeal, which call forth all our energy and embolden us to issue the call to you, our German coreligionists who feel as do we, who feel that it is incumbent on us not to view idly the ruin and the vain artificial varnishing of the breath but to take steps together after coming to a mutual understanding, to save out of the chaos what can continue to exist in our spiritual development and in our German life, and to repudiate openly what has died in us.

With this sentiment we have come together, feeling our justification to declare openly and decidedly the necessity of a change, a justification which we assume and may assume because our holiest interests are threatened with immediate danger, although we are conscious at the same time that we are not the elect who are to carry out this change. Therefore we wish to assure ourselves of the sympathy and agreement of our German coreligionists and in conjunction with them convene a synod in order to fix that aspect of Judaism which corresponds with our age and the sentiments of our heart.

Our Goal

We desire: *Faith*; we desire: *Positive Religion*; we desire: *Judaism*. We hold fast to the spirit of Sacred Scripture, which we recognize as a testimony of divine revelation by which the spirit of our fathers was illumined. We hold fast to everything which is necessary for the true worship of God, rooted in the spirit of our religion. We hold fast to the conviction that Judaism's doctrine of God is eternally true and to the prediction that the knowledge of God as proclaimed by Judaism will at some time become the possession of all mankind. But we desire to interpret Holy Writ according to its divine spirit; we cannot sacrifice our divine freedom to the tyranny of the dead letter. We cannot pray sincerely for an earthly Messianic dominion which is to lead us to the home of our ancestors out of the fatherland to which we cling with all the bonds of love as though this were a strange land to us. We can no longer observe commands which have no spiritual hold on us and can no longer recognize a code as immutable lawbook according to which the essence and the mission of Judaism consist in blind adherence to forms and prescriptions which owe their origin to a time long past and forever vanished.

A New Structure

Permeated with the holy content of our religion we cannot preserve it in the bequeathed form, much less bequeath it in this form to our descendants and so, placed between the graves of our ancestors and the cradles of our children, the cornet-call of the age thrills us, the *latest* recipients of a great heritage in its antiquated form to be also the *first* who, with undaunted courage, with true fraternization by word and act, lay the foundation of this new structure for ourselves and the generations which come after us.

No Schism

However, we do not wish to dissociate ourselves by this step from the community to which we belong; nay, we extend the hand of brotherhood in love and tolerance to all, also to those of our coreligionists who differ with us. We desire no schism. But upon you, who sympathize with us, we call confidently for the closest union that shall make for truth within, indulgence without, endurance in the fight with others and faithfulness towards ourselves.

And thus our appeal goes forth to you, German coreligionists, far and near,

That you associate yourselves with us by name and assure us by word and act of your support and aid in order that we in great number can convene a synod which shall renew and establish Judaism in the form in which it is capable and worthy of continuing as a living force for us and our children.

16. INTELLIGENT RELIGION

ISAAC MAYER WISE

Isaac Mayer Wise (1819–1900) was born in Bohemia, migrated to America in 1846, and became the pioneer of Reform Judaism in this country. Starting in 1854 he served as rabbi in Cincinnati. He published a prayerbook for Reform congregations and introduced such reforms as mixed pews, choral singing, and confirmation. He succeeded in bringing together congregations with a variety of Reform interpretations and practices in a central organization, the Union of American Hebrew Congregations, founded in 1873. He established the Hebrew Union College in 1875, a seminary for educating rabbis. In 1889 Wise organized the Central Conference of American Rabbis, the association of Reform rabbis, and became its first president. "For him American Judaism represented a new phase in the history of the ancestral faith" (David Philipson).

The following selection is taken from an article written in 1854.

What Preserved Jewish Religion

Our religion contains better elements than a mere controversial rabbinism, and these better elements must be considered the primary cause of its self-preservation. The Jew had the consciousness that he alone possesses the most philosophical views of the existence and nature of the deity; of the nature, duties, and hopes of mankind; of justice, equity, and charity; of the several relations between God and his creatures, and between man and his fellow-man. . . .

The Jew felt conscious of the verities of his religion, and therefore he loved them better than his life and worldly interests; he saw himself alone in the world, alone with his sublime ideas, and therefore he lived in his faith and for it, and the thousand forms which he observed only led him to his sublime ideas. It was this elevating and inspiring consciousness, and not rabbinism, which preserved Judaism. But now the idea, the sublime cardinal elements, are almost lost sight of in the multitude of thoughtless observances of rabbinical forms. . . .

Judaism has become a set of unmeaning practices, and the intelligent Jew either mourns for the fallen daughter of Zion or has adopted a course of frivolity or indifference. Therefore we demand reforms. All unmeaning forms must be laid aside as outworn garments. The internal spirit of Judaism must be expanded, illustrated, and made dear again to the Jew. We must inform our friends and opponents that there is a Judaism independent of its forms, and that this is Judaism emphatically.

Principles of Reform

It is therefore our principle of reform: "All forms to which no meaning is attached any longer are an impediment to our religion, and must be done away with." Before we propose to abolish anything we should inquire: What is its practical benefit? If there is none it is time to renounce it, for one dead limb injures the whole body. Another principle of reform is this: "Whatever makes us ridiculous before the world as it now is, may safely be and should be abolished," for we are in possession of an intelligent religion, and the nations from our precept and example should be led to say, "This is a wise and intelligent people" (Deuteronomy 4:6).

A third principle of reform is this, "Whatever tends to the elevation of the divine service, to inspire the heart of the worshipper and attract him, should be done without any unnecessary delay," for the value of divine service must be estimated according to its effect upon the heart and understanding.

A fourth principle of reform is this, "Whenever religious observances and the just demands of civilized society exclude each other, the former have lost their power"; for religion was taught for the purpose "to live therein and not to die therein";* our religion makes us active members of civilized society, hence we must give full satisfaction to its just demands.

Last, or rather first, it must be remarked, the leading star of reform must be the maxim. "Religion is intended to make man happy, good, just, active, charitable, and intelligent." Whatever tends to this end is truly religious, and must be retained or introduced if it does not yet exist. Whatever has an effect contrary to the above must be abolished as soon as possible.

17. FROM THE PITTSBURGH PLATFORM

1885

A basic statement of principles or policy which guided the Reform movement for almost half a century was adopted at a rabbinical conference in Pittsburgh in 1885. It came to be known as the Pittsburgh Platform and was later approved by the Central Conference of American Rabbis, the Reform rabbinical organization. The following excerpt presents the paragraphs of the platform which were the basic principles of Reform Judaism; they should be compared with the 1937 revision of the platform (no. 18).

God

... We hold that Judaism presents the highest conception of the God idea as taught in our holy Scriptures and developed and spiritualized by the Jewish teachers, in accordance with the moral and philosophical progress of their respective ages. We maintain that Judaism preserved and

---

*Referring to the traditional interpretation of Leviticus 18:5. (Ed.)

defended, midst continual struggles and trials and under enforced isolation, this God idea as the central religious truth for the human race.

Bible

We recognize in the Bible the record of the consecration of the Jewish people to its mission as priest of the one God, and value it as the most potent instrument of religious and moral instruction. . . .

Moral Laws

We recognize in the Mosaic legislation a system of training the Jewish people for its mission during its national life in Palestine, and to-day we accept as binding only the moral laws, and maintain only such ceremonies as elevate and sanctify our lives, but reject all such as are not adapted to the views and habits of modern civilization.

Laws No Longer Valid

We hold that all such Mosaic and rabbinical laws as regulate diet, priestly purity, and dress, originated in ages and under the influence of ideas altogether foreign to our present mental and spiritual state. They fail to impress the modern Jew with a spirit of priestly holiness; their observance in our days is apt rather to obstruct than to further modern spiritual elevation.

No Longer a Nation

We recognize, in the modern era of universal culture of heart and intellect, the approaching of the realization of Israel's great Messianic hope for the establishment of the kingdom of truth, justice, and peace among all men. We consider ourselves no longer a nation, but a religious community and therefore expect neither a return to Palestine, nor a sacrificial worship under the sons of Aaron, nor the restoration of any of the laws concerning the Jewish state.

A Progressive Religion

We recognize in Judaism a progressive religion, ever striving to be in accord with the postulates of reason. We are convinced of the utmost necessity of preserving the historical identity with our great past. . . .

Social Justice

In full accordance with the spirit of Mosaic legislation, which strives to regulate the relation between rich and poor, we deem it our duty to participate in the great task of modern times, to solve on the basis of justice and righteousness the problems presented by the contrasts and evils of the present organization of society.

18. FROM THE COLUMBUS PLATFORM

1937

When the Reform rabbis met for their conference in Columbus, Ohio, fifty years after the Pittsburgh meeting, they faced a world which had changed considerably. America had become the center of the Diaspora; Zionism had grown in numbers and strength; Hitler had come to power and another world war was in the making. The membership of Reform congregations, which now included Jews of East European background, had undergone changes, and most Reform Jews had abandoned their anti-Zionist position. At this meeting of the Central Conference of American Rabbis in 1937, a declaration entitled "Guilding Principles of Reform Judaism" was adopted to replace the Pittsburgh Platform. The new Columbus Platform reflected the new thinking. "The Jewish people and its traditional ways had once again become significant factors in the ideology of the movement" (W. Gunther Plaut).

In the excerpt which follows, statements have been selected which facilitate a comparison with the Pittsburgh Platform (no. 17) and demonstrate the changes that were made.

Nature of Judaism

Judaism is the historical religious experience of the Jewish people. Though growing out of Jewish life, its message is universal, aiming at the union and perfection of mankind under the sovereignty of God. . . .

Torah

God reveals Himself not only in the majesty, beauty and orderliness of nature, but also in the vision and moral striving of the human spirit. Revelation is a continuous process, confined to no one group and to no one age. Yet the people of Israel, through its prophets and sages, achieved unique insight in the realm of religious truth. The Torah, both written and oral, enshrines Israel's ever-growing consciousness of God and of the moral law. It preserves the historical precedents, sanctions and norms of Jewish life, and seeks to mould it in the patterns of goodness and of holiness. Being products of historical processes, certain of its laws have lost their binding force with the passing of the conditions that called them forth. But as a depository of permanent spiritual ideals, the Torah remains the dynamic source of the life of Israel. Each age has the obligation to adapt the teachings of the Torah to its basic needs in consonance with the genius of Judaism.

A Jewish Homeland

In all lands where our people live, they assume and seek to share loyally the full duties and responsibilities of citizenship and to create seats of Jewish knowledge and religion. In the rehabilitation of Palestine, the land hallowed by memories and hopes, we behold the promise of renewed life for many of our brethren. We affirm the obligation of all Jewry to aid in its upbuilding as a Jewish homeland by endeavoring to make it not only a haven of refuge for the oppressed but also a center of Jewish culture and spiritual life.

Messianic Goal

Throughout the ages it has been Israel's mission to witness to the Divine in the face of every form of paganism and materialism. We regard it as our historic task to cooperate with all men in the establishment of the kingdom of God, of universal brotherhood, justice, truth and peace on earth. This is our Messianic goal.

Religious Practice and Education

Jewish life is marked by consecration to the ideals of Judaism. It calls for faithful participation in the life of the Jewish community as it finds expression in home, synagog and school and in all other agencies that enrich Jewish life and promote its welfare.

The perpetuation of Judaism as a living force depends upon religious knowledge and upon the Education of each new generation in our rich cultural and spiritual heritage.

Judaism as a way of life requires in addition to its moral and spiritual demands, the preservation of the Sabbath, festivals and Holy Days, the retention and development of such customs, symbols and ceremonies as possess inspirational value, the cultivation of distinctive forms of religious art and music and the use of Hebrew, together with the vernacular, in our worship and instruction.

19. NEO-ORTHODOXY

SAMSON RAPHAEL HIRSCH

Reform in Germany called forth a counter-movement by Orthodoxy which found a vigorous and brilliant interpreter in Samson Raphael Hirsch (1808–88). He represented a new type of Orthodox Jew who had studied at a university and was as much at home in European culture as in traditional Judaism. He stressed the need to combine both. Opposing all religious reform, he stood for strict adherence to the Torah and to all commandments of traditional Judaism. He became rabbi of the separatist Orthodox congregation in Frankfort, and through him Frankfort became the focus of Jewish Orthodoxy in Germany. (See the introduction to this chapter for more details.)

In the Nineteen Letters of Ben Uziel (pseudonym), published in 1836, Hirsch outlined his program, which was elaborated systematically and in detail in subsequent works. He translated the Pentateuch into German, was the author of commentaries on the Pentateuch, the Psalms, the Hebrew prayerbook, and of numerous essays.

The excerpt which follows is taken from the sixteenth of his *Nineteen Letters* and deals with Hirsch's attitude to emancipation and the nature of the exile status of the Jews.

You ask me for my opinion on the question which at present so greatly agitates the minds of men; namely emancipation. You wish to know whether I consider it feasible and desirable according to the spirit of Judaism. . . .

When Israel began its great wandering through the ages and among the nations, Jeremiah proclaimed it as Israel's duty to:

"Build houses and dwell therein; plant gardens and eat the fruit thereof; take wives unto yourselves, and beget sons and daughters and take wives for your sons and give your daughters in marriage that they bear sons and daughters, and that you multiply there, and diminish not. And seek the peace of the city whither I have exiled you, and pray for it to the Lord, for in its peace there will be unto you peace."

(Jeremiah 29:5–7)

To be pushed back and limited upon the path of life is, therefore, not an essential condition of the *Galuth*, Israel's exile among the nations. On the contrary, it is our duty to join ourselves as closely as possible to the state which receives us into its midst, to promote its welfare and not to consider our own well-being as in any way separate from that of the state to which we belong.

This close connection with states everywhere is not at all in contradiction to the spirit of Judaism, for the independent national life of Israel was never the essence or purpose of our existence as a nation, but only a means of fulfilling our spiritual mission.

Land and soil were never Israel's bond of union. That function was always fulfilled solely by the common task set by the Torah. Therefore the people of Israel still forms a united body, though it is separated from a national soil. Nor does this unity lose any of its reality though Israel accept everywhere the citizenship of the nations among which it is dispersed. This spiritual unity (which may be designated by the Hebrew terms *am* and *goy*, but not by the term "nation," unless we are able to separate from that word the inherent concept of common territory and political power) is the only communal bond we possess, or ever expect to possess, until that great day shall arrive when the Almighty shall see fit in His inscrutable wisdom to unite again His scattered servants in one land, and the Torah shall be the guiding principle of a state, a model of the meaning of Divine Revelation and the mission of humanity.

For this future, which is promised us in the glorious predictions of the inspired prophets as a goal of the Galuth, we hope and pray, but actively to accelerate its coming is prohibited to us. The entire purpose of the Messianic age is that we may, in prosperity, exhibit to mankind a better example of "Israel" than did our ancestors the first time, while, hand in hand with us, the entire race will be joined in universal brotherhood through the recognition of God, the All-One.

It is on account of this the purely spiritual nature of its national character that Israel is capable of the most intimate union with states, with, perhaps, this difference. While others seek in the state only the material benefits which it secures, considering possessions and pleasures as the highest good, Israel can regard it only as a means of fulfilling the mission of mankind.

Summon up before your mental vision the picture of such an Israel, dwelling in freedom among the nations, and striving to attain its ideal. Picture every son of Israel a respected and influential priest of righteousness and love, disseminating among the nations not specific Judaism—for proselytism is forbidden—but pure humanity. What a mighty impulse to progress, what a luminary and staff in the gloomy days of the Middle Ages would Israel have been then, if its own sin and the insanity of the nations had not rendered such a Galuth impossible. How impressive, how sublime it would have been if, in the midst of a race that adored only power, possessions and enjoyment, there had lived quietly and publicly human beings of a different sort, who beheld in material possessions only the means for practicing justice and love towards all, a people whose minds, imbued with the wisdom and truth of the Law, maintained simple, straightforward views, and emphasized them for themselves and others in expressive, vivid symbolic acts.

But it would seem as though Israel first had to be fitted, through the endurance of the harsh and cruel aspects of exile, for proper appreciation and utilization of the milder and gentler aspects of dispersion.

When Galuth will be understood and accepted as it should be, when, in suffering, the service of God and His Torah will be understood as the only task of life, when, even in misery, God will be served, and material abundance esteemed only as a means for this service, then, perhaps, Israel will be ready for the far greater temptations of prosperity and happiness in dispersion. Thus the answer to our question is quite obvious. Just as it is our duty to endeavor to obtain those material possessions which are the fundamental condition of life, so also is it the duty of every one to take advantage of every alleviation and improvement of his condition open to him in an honest way. For, the more means, the more opportunity is given to him to fulfill his mission in its broadest sense; and it is the duty of the community no less than that of the individual to obtain for all its members the opportunities and privileges of citizenship and liberty. Do I consider this desirable? I bless emancipation when I see how the excess of oppression drove Israel away from a normal life, limited the free development of its noble character, and compelled many individuals to enter, for the sake of self-preservation, upon paths which they were too weak to refuse to enter.

I bless emancipation when I notice that no spiritual principle, not even one of foolish fanaticism, stands in its way, but that it is opposed only by those passions which are degrading to humanity, namely, greed for gain and narrow selfishness. I rejoice when I perceive that in this concession of emancipation, regard for the natural rights of men to live as equals among equals is freely extended without force or compulsion, but purely through the power of their own inner truth. I welcome the sacrifice of the base passions wherever it is offered, as the dawn of reviving humanity in mankind, and as a preliminary step to the universal recognition of God as the sole Lord and Father, and of all human beings as the children of the All-One.

But for Israel I only bless it if, at the same time, there will awaken in Israel the true spirit which strives to fulfill the mission of Israel regardless of whether or not there is to be emancipation, to elevate and ennoble ourselves, to implant the spirit of Judaism in our souls, in order that it may generate a life in which that spirit shall be reflected and realized. I bless it, if Israel will regard emancipation not as the goal of its vocation, but only as a new condition of its mission, and as a new test, much severer than the trial of oppression. But I should grieve if Israel understood itself so little, and had so little comprehension of its own spirit that it would welcome emancipation as the end of the *Galuth*, and as the highest goal of its historic mission. If Israel should regard this glorious concession merely as a means of securing a greater degree of comfort in life, and greater opportunities for the acquisition of wealth and enjoyment, it would show that Israel had not comprehended the spirit of its own Law, nor learned anything from exile. And sorrowfully indeed would I mourn if Israel were so far to forget itself as to deem emancipation not too dearly purchased through capricious curtailment of the Torah, capricious abandonment of the chief element of our very being. We must become Jews, Jews in the true sense of the word, imbued with the spirit of the Law, accepting it as the fountain of spiritual and ethical life. Then Judaism will gladly welcome emancipation as affording a greater opportunity for the fulfillment of its task, the realization of a noble and ideal life.

20. RABBINIC LAW-MAKING

IMMANUEL JAKOBOVITS

How do Orthodox rabbis apply the rules of the Law (*halakhah*) to modern problems? How do new rabbinical rulings come about? By what methods do such rulings command the assent of Orthodox rabbis and laymen? These questions are discussed by Immanuel Jakobovits, formerly rabbi of the Fifth Avenue Synagogue in New York, and from 1966 chief rabbi of the United Hebrew Congregations of the British Commonwealth. The following excerpt is taken from his essay "Jewish Law Faces Modern Problems."

Jewish Law

Judaism expresses its beliefs, its philosophy and its ethics as well as its religious teachings primarily in terms of laws. It defines its ideals neither as human rights nor as human goals, but as a collection of duties, as positive and negative commandments legally incumbent on the individual and society alike. These precepts are as diverse and comprehensive as life itself; representing "a path of life," they seek to direct every aspect of human existence.

The criterion of the relevance of Judaism to the conditions and challenges of any given age lies, therefore, in the capacity of its legislation to evolve a response to such conditions and challenges. For an appraisal of the contemporary significance of Jewish thought one must look above all to contemporary rulings of Jewish law.

Responsa

Such rulings, in the form of rabbinical responsa, have been issued and published in great profusion in recent times. They reflect the authentic views of Judaism on a vast range of modern problems thrown up by the revolutionary changes of our age—from the European holocaust to the rise of Israel, from automation and the expansion of electric appliances to advances in medicine, from space travel to the increasing incidence of adoption and illegitimacy.

Legislator and Judge

In the jurisprudence of Judaism, the legislature and judiciary are fused together. Rabbis are charged to determine as well as to administer the law. They serve as judges in applying the rulings of existing laws to cases in doubt or under dispute; and when faced with situations lacking any precise precedents, they act as legislators by issuing new rulings.

In the exercise of both functions, rabbis are subject to a "constitutional" system, as presently practiced, which is altogether unique. Unlike any other national or religious legal system, Judaism does not vest the authority to make or adjudicate laws in any clearly defined individual or group. It has neither a supreme court nor a hierarchy, neither a chief justice nor a supreme pontiff to lay down the law with finality. In fact, there is no formal office or official appointment at all which would automatically authorize its incumbent to demand universal submission to his rulings. Even a Chief Rabbi of Israel—tenant of the highest ecclesiastical office in Jewry—may readily defer to the judgment of some superior scholar who holds no official position altogether, and any duly qualified rabbi may presume to challenge a decision rendered by others if his interpretation of the law conflicts with theirs.

How then does the juridical process of Judaism operate? Under such conditions of apparent licence and individual independence, how can order be joined to law? By what methods do rabbinical rulings eventually command the assent of rabbis and religious laymen the world over? Who and whose decisions enjoy final and binding authority?

In contrast to all other legal systems, whether on a state or church level, the administration of Jewish law is highly decentralized and yet subject to universal sanctions, and it is uniquely democratic whilst at the same time acknowledging the supremacy of individual authority. Thus it operates on three principal levels:

1. *Local Autonomy*. The authority of the local rabbinical head (the *Mara d'Atra*) of a congregation or community (e.g., the chief rabbi of a city or country) is traditionally binding for the members of such congregation or community, and it cannot be challenged by any other rabbinate, however superior its rank or area of jurisdiction. But such authority can only be exercised on a strictly local level; it does not extend beyond the confines of the individual rabbi's official jurisdiction.

2. *Consensus of Opinion*. When the principles of Jewish law have to be applied to new problems, a verdict one way or another is not usually accepted as authentic until it is endorsed by a number of leading rabbis constituting the majority of those consulted. As a rule, such problems are submitted quite independently to the judgment of various rabbinical authorities. As the replies accumulate, often in the form of printed responsa, a trend of opinion gradually becomes crystalized, and this is then accepted as the binding norm of the law, against any minority views of dissent, by virtue of the numerically superior weight of its endorsement.

3. *Individual Authority by Popular Acclaim*. A rabbinical ruling may also enjoy unquestioned validity by reason of the supreme excellence of the scholar who issued it. Such authority is quite informally, and solely as an expression of religious public opinion, bestowed on one or more of the *gedolei ha-dor*—the Sages of the Generation—purely because of the

popular recognition of their pre-eminent scholarship and saintliness. Their word is law, but it is their public esteem which makes it unchallenged and absolute.

With the exception, then, of the first category, which is strictly limited in scope and therefore immaterial as a general guide to rabbinic law-making, all new decisions of law derive their validity ultimately from their implicit or explicit assent by the majority. This system insures that:

1. the development of Jewish law, by virtue of its strongly democratic direction, will always be a dynamic and organic process commanding the indispensable sanction of public endorsement;

2. by vesting authority with duly qualified individuals rather than impersonal offices, legislative power will never be abused or exploited by unscrupulous and unworthy persons seizing control of such offices by political manipulation or the patronage of vested interests; and

3. the door is left open to individual dissent, based on a scholar's conscientious objection to the consensus of the majority, thus allowing for the possibility of the law's constant re-examination and revision in the continous study and debate among scholars.

21. THE MIDDLE WAY

ALEXANDER KOHUT

When radical Reform stated its position in the Pittsburgh Platform (no. 17), some rabbis and lay leaders looked for ways to meet this new challenge. Although they favored modern reform, they were inclined to more traditional views. The basis for a middle position between Orthodoxy and Reform had been proposed in Germany in 1845 by Zacharias Frankel, the founder of the "positive-historical school," which aimed at a combination of tradition and modernity (see the introduction to this chapter). In America Frankel's ideas became the foundation on which the middle position could grow into a major religious movement, Conservative Judaism.

The substance of Conservative thought was defined in a coherent way by Alexander Kohut (1842–92), Hungarian-born rabbi and scholar, who accepted a pulpit in New York in 1885 and became professor of Talmud at the Jewish Theological Seminary when it was founded.

Is Judaism definitely closed for all time, or is it capable of and in need of continuous development? I answer both Yes and No. I answer Yes, *because Religion has been given to man*; and as it is the duty of man to grow in perfection as long as he lives, he must modify the forms which yield him religious satisfaction, in accordance with the spirit of the times. I answer No, in so far as it concerns the Word of God, which cannot be imperfect. . . . You Israelite, imperfect as you are, strive to perfect yourself in the image of your perfect God. Hold in honor His unchangeable Law and let it be your earnest task to put new life into the outward form of our religion . . .

Our religious guide is the Torah, the Law of Moses, interpreted and applied in the light of tradition. But inasmuch as individual opinion cannot be valid for the whole community, it behooves individuals and communities to appoint only recognized authorities as teachers; such men, that is to say, as acknowledge belief in authority, and who, at the same time, with comprehension and tact, are willing to consider what may be permitted in view of the exigencies of the times, and what may be discarded, without changing the nature and character of the foundations of the faith.

A Reform which seeks to progress without the Mosaic-rabbinical tradition is a deformity—a skeleton without flesh and sinew, without spirit and heart. It is suicide; and suicide is not reform. We desire a Judaism full of life. We desire to worship the living God in forms full of life and beauty; Jewish, yet breathing the modern spirit. Only a Judaism true to itself and its past, yet receptive of the ideas of the present, accepting the good and the beautiful from whatever source it may come, can command respect and recognition. . . .

I do not know whether it will be my good fortune to have your sympathy in my religious attitude—that of Mosaic-rabbinical Judaism, freshened with the spirit of progress, a Judaism of the healthy golden mean. I hope I shall. . . .

22. CONSERVATIVE JUDAISM

SOLOMON SCHECHTER

Solomon Schechter (1847–1915), born in Rumania, rabbinic scholar, taught in England from 1892 to 1901 and in 1902 was invited to head the Jewish Theological Seminary in New York, which he reorganized. Under his leadership the seminary became a respected scholarly institution and the center of Conservative Judaism. Schechter's personality had a decisive influence on the growth of the Conservative movement. His watchword was "Catholic Israel," an all-embracing Judaism. "In its basic concept Judaism was to feel its indissoluble bond with Judaism of all ages and all countries; it could sustain differences of opinion in its midst; it did not require absolute conformity or exert the coercion of a system, but it presupposed continuity" (Ismar Elbogen).

In 1913 Schechter founded the United Synagogue of America, the association of Conservative synagogues in the United States and Canada. The selection which follows is taken from his address at the founding of the United Synagogue and discusses the principles of the movement.

No New Party

Indeed, what we intend to accomplish is not to create a new party, but to consolidate an old one, which has always existed in this country, but was never conscious of its own strength nor perhaps realized the need of organization. I refer to the large number of Jews, who, thoroughly American in habits of life and mode of thinking and, in many cases imbued with the best of culture of the day, have always maintained conservative principles and remained aloof from the Reform movement, which swept over the country. They are sometimes stigmatized as the Neo-Orthodox. This is not correct. Their Orthodoxy is not new. It is as old as the hills, and the taunt "new" can only be accounted for by the ignorance of those who took it into their heads that an observant Jew, who has taken a degree in a college is a new phenomenon representing a mere paradox.

East European Immigration

This Conservative, or if you prefer so to call it, this Orthodox tendency, represented by some of the noblest minds of American Jewry, to which several of the oldest synagogues bear witness, received a fresh impetus by the immigration from the Eastern part of Europe, begun some thirty years ago. This immigration brought hundreds and thousands, mostly from countries which were never touched by the Reform movement that had its birth in Germany. . . .

These our brethren are, undoubtedly, much stronger in numbers than the Reformers. But chaos reigns supreme among them, and just by this want of organization, they are subject to a process of constant attrition which must become dangerous if the tide of immigration should by more favorable conditions in the East, for which we hope and pray, be stopped for a few years. This is the condition of affairs which cannot be permitted to go on without making an effort to step into the breach and to create a Conservative Union.

Needed Changes

I am very reluctant to denounce any party in existence. But close observation for ten years and more has convinced me that, unless we succeed in effecting an organization which, while loyal to the Torah, to the teachings of our sages, to the traditions of our fathers, to the usages and customs of Israel, shall at the same time introduce the English sermon, and adopt scientific methods in our seminaries, in our training of rabbis and school-masters for our synagogues and Talmud Torahs, and bring order and decorum into our synagogues; unless this is done I declare unhesitatingly that traditional Judaism will not survive another generation in this country. Those of us advanced in years may be saved, but the younger generation will be swept away in a ruthless radicalism which even disquiets the better reformed minds. . . .

We must labor and work. And it is for this purpose that this Union has been created. Its scope is broad enough to admit of the cooperation of all synagogues that are devoted to the cause of the conservation of traditional Judaism, whether they style themselves Conservative or Orthodox. Yes, in view of the dangers threatening the historic faith dear to Conservative and Orthodox alike, we regard it as a sacred duty that all such forces unite, irrespective of the differences which otherwise divide them. . . .

23. RECONSTRUCTIONISM

IRA EISENSTEIN

Mordecai M. Kaplan, born in 1881, professor at the Conservative Jewish Theological Seminary and dean of its Teachers Institute, developed the philosophy of Reconstructionism and became the founder and leader of this movement. Among the modern interpretations of Judaism, Kaplan's has been described as "the most typically American." "America's democracy, . . . notions of tolerance, and readiness to change are reflected in his conception of Judaism as an evolving religious civilization" (Nahum N. Glatzer). See also the introduction to this chapter for a discussion of this philosophy.

The following selection is taken from *Creative Judaism* by Rabbi Ira Eisenstein, a disciple of Kaplan, a leader of the movement, editor of its magazine, the *Reconstructionist*, and president of the Reconstructionist Rabbinical College.

What must be done to render Judaism creative?

I. *Rediscover Judaism by learning to know its true scope and character:*

We must not regard it as a revealed religion which so transcends all laws of social life as to be completely unaffected by them; nor must we consider the Jews as a religious community bound together only by a mission of promulgating the truth about the unity of God and the brotherhood of man. Equally erroneous is the view that would eliminate religion from Jewish collective life and stake the future of the Jewish people upon the spirit of nationalism.

We must recognize Judaism to be nothing less than a civilization, containing all the elements of a civilization: the social framework of national unity, centering on a particular land, a continuing history, a living language and literature, religious folkways, mores, laws and art. Jewish civilization must so function that, through it, the Jewish people will help to make the life of the Jew creative and capable of self-fulfillment.

It must work through social institutions that answer to vital needs, and articulate itself in terms of ideals which are vital and relevant.

Jewish civilization must be able to assimilate the best in contemporary civilizations, in a deliberate and planned fashion, not in the spirit of yielding to their force or prestige, but in the spirit of cooperation.

Whatever changes in ideology, sanctions, practices or social organization such a development in Judaism involves must be evaluated by the extent to which such changes help Judaism to retain its continuity, its individuality and its organic character.

2. *Redefine the status and reorganize the communal life of the Jews:*

We are a people, by virtue of our consciousness of a common past, our aspiration toward a common future and our will-to-cooperate in the achievement of common ends.

Israel is essential if Judaism is to maintain its character as a civilization, for it serves as the symbol of the Jewish renaissance and as the center where essential Jewish creativeness will express itself in Hebraic forms.

Jewish communal life is essential for cooperation among Jews, organized in such a manner that all the activities of Jews shall be integrated into an organic unity. To such an organization, all Jews who feel physical or spiritual kinship with the Jewish people should belong no matter what their personal philosophy may be.

Units in the communal organization should include, not only congregations, but groups centered about literary, artistic and social activities. The Jewish community should establish centers dealing with religious, philanthropic, social and educational problems, institute arbitration courts, record births, marriages, divorces and deaths, represent Jews before the non-Jewish community and defend Jewish rights.

The Jewish community should direct Jewish education for children and adults, from elementary levels to the levels of higher learning, and foster intensive Jewish home life.

3. *Reinterpret and vitalize our tradition:*

Jewish tradition must be viewed not as a series of fixed and static ideas, requiring conformity in thought and action, but as the story of the past of the Jew which he is made to feel is in a deep and true sense *his* story, in which certain events, persons, places, objects, in brief, certain *sancta* come to possess a vital interest for him.

The ideology of a people comprises its interpretation of these *sancta;* but in our day Jewish unity may be attained by the general reference to these *sancta,* and does not depend upon one uniform interpretation of them.

Whatever interpretations are given, however, if they are to bridge the gap between tradition and modernism, they must reenforce the highest social and spiritual strivings of our day. As expression of the highest needs of the Jewish people and the spiritual reaction of Jews to the vicissitudes of life, such interpretations constitute Jewish religion for our day.

Customs and rites of a religious character comprise folk religion, the common spiritual denominator of the people, as distinguished from personal religion, which is essentially the world outlook which each person should achieve for himself. Folk religion can invest our daily habits with spiritual significance by rendering them beautiful and meaningful. Folk religion, expressed in public worship, which is related to the ideology of the modern Jew, yet based upon traditional forms, may become a source of spiritual power.

QUESTIONS FOR THOUGHT AND DISCUSSION

1. Why did it become necessary for Jews in the period of emancipation to rethink their approach to Jewish tradition?

2. What were the aims of the reformers in Germany?

3. Explain why the Reform movement has become most successful in the United States.

4. Compare the Pittsburgh and Columbus Platforms and point out changes which seem significant.

5. Both the Reform movement and Samson Raphael Hirsch, the leader of Neo-Orthodoxy, speak of a "mission" of Israel. Is the meaning of this term the same for both movements? If not, where do you see the difference?

6. What would have been Hirsch's attitude to Herzl if he had been a contemporary of Herzl? Which passage in the sixteenth of his *Nineteen Letters* (no. 19) bears on this question?

7. What is meant by the term "positive-historical school"?

8. Describe Solomon Schechter's aims for Conservative Judaism.

9. The founder of Reconstructionism speaks of "creative Judaism." What is meant by this term?

10. What does Kaplan mean by "sancta"?

11. Explain what you would consider as binding for your life if you were an Orthodox, Conservative, Reform Jew, or a follower of Reconstructionism.

SUGGESTED READING

Note: Books suggested in more than one chapter are here listed by the name of the author only, A key to such listings will be found at the end of the book.

A paperback edition is indicated by the letters PB.

Books for the Student

Charry-Segal, chap. 21.

Eisenstein, Ira. *Creative Judaism.* New York, 1953.

Elbogen, pp. 92–103, 121–31, 343–52, 441–44.

Graetz, vol. 5, chaps. 15–16 and 18.

Grayzel, pp. 583–89, 629–32, 696–98, 778–79.

Learsi, chap. 8.

Margolis-Marx, chaps. 83, 86, 91, 96. PB.

Parzen, Herbert. *Architects of Conservative Judaism.* New York, 1964.

Schwartzman, Sylvan D. *Reform Judaism in the Making.* New York, 1962.

———. *Reform Judaism Then and Now.* New York, 1971.

Books for the Teacher

Blau, Joseph L. *Modern Varieties of Judaism.* New York, 1966.

Belkin, Samuel. *In His Image.* New York, 1960.

Davis, Moshe. *The Emergence of Conservative Judaism; the Historical School in 19th Century America.* Philadelphia, 1963.

Herberg, Will. *Protestant, Catholic, Jew.* Garden City, N.Y., 1960.

Kaplan, Mordecai M. *Judaism as a Civilization.* New York, 1967. PB.

Martin, Bernard, ed. *Contemporary Reform Jewish Thought.* Chicago, 1968.

Philipson, David. *The Reform Movement in Judaism.* Rev. ed. New York, 1967.

Sklare, Marshall. *Conservative Judaism.* New York, 1972.

Stitskin, Leon D. *Studies in Torah Judaism.* New York, 1969.

Waxman, Mordecai, ed. *Tradition and Change.* New York, 1958.

Wiener, Max, ed. *Abraham Geiger and Liberal Judaism.* Philadelphia, 1962.

III. OPPRESSION IN EASTERN EUROPE

Introduction

While emancipation in Western and Central Europe was progressing in the course of the nineteenth century, the Jews in much of Eastern Europe remained separated from their non-Jewish neighbors and suffered anti-Jewish prejudice, discrimination, and outright hatred and persecution. In Western Europe the old forms of Jewish life were breaking up. But in Eastern Europe the cultural development of the Jewish masses took a turn quite different from that in the West.

Russia

In discussing Eastern Europe we limit ourselves to Russia. During the period under consideration in this chapter, like that in the remainder of the source book, namely, from the French Revolution to the present, the great majority of European Jews lived under Russian rule. For this time space of almost two centuries, Poland and some of the Baltic states existed as independent states for only a limited number of years. How it happened that such large numbers of Polish Jews came under Russian rule is explained by the partitions of Poland in the last three decades of the eighteenth century, when Russia, Austria, and Prussia divided Poland between them, with Russia receiving by far the lion's share.

Early Settlements

Jewish settlements already existed in southern Russia (Caucasus, Georgia) in classical times. By the thirteenth century settlements of Jews could also be found along the banks of the rivers Don, Dnieper, and Volga. But the rulers in these territories never favored having Jews in their midst and, therefore, subjected them to persecution. The attitude of the government and the Orthodox Church, to which the vast majority of the people belonged, was hostile, and the Jews were at times expelled from the territories in which they were living.

Partition of Poland

The partitions of Poland brought one million Jews, then one-half of the world's Jewish population, under Russian control. The government of the tsars wished to keep old Russia free of Jews and, therefore, forced the Jews, with only a few exceptions, to reside in the western and southern provinces in what was formerly Poland, a region which became known as the "Pale of Settlement" (selection no. 23). The movements of most Jews were restricted, and until 1915 they were forced to live only in the region of the Pale. The Pale was soon extended to encompass all of Russian Poland, Lithuania, Byelorussia, most of the Ukraine, the Crimea, and Bessarabia. In the latter half of the nineteenth century, certain categories of Jews, such as the wealthier merchants, Jews with higher education, and a number of other groups, were permitted to live in places outside the Pale.

Hostile Attitude

The hostile and repressive attitude of government and church obviously influenced the attitude of the Russian people to the Jews. In culture and education the masses of the people, who were mainly peasants, were backward. The government did little or nothing to reduce their ignorance. As a result, they could easily be influenced by any dishonest ruler or official. Sometimes Christian competitors of the Jews urged their expulsion from a city, in spite of the useful function which the Jews performed (no. 24).

Military Service

The height of despotic rule was reached under Tsar Nicholas I (1825–55). He considered the Jews a very undesirable element and aimed to have them become assimilated in the larger Russian population. To Nicholas assimilation meant conversion. In 1827, as one means of bringing about such assimilation and conversion, Nicholas introduced military service for the Jews. The military service lasted twenty-five years but was not even accompanied by the granting of citizens' rights to the Jews. Service in the army normally began at the age of eighteen. But for the Jews Nicholas conceived the idea of conscripting even Jewish children of twelve years and younger, with the hope that by exposing them early to Christian influences, conversion would be easy. Such child-soldiers were called "cantonists."* The tragic suffering of these children, taken early, sometimes even kidnapped from their parents, and exposed to brutal treatment, often in a faraway part of Russia, was remembered in stories and memoirs (nos. 25, 26). Many of them died under the harsh treatment. Some were converted, but others remained faithful to their religion.

In the Pale

Because of the greatly increased Jewish population, the cities of the Pale were overcrowded. The overwhelming majority of the Jews were artisans and unskilled laborers. There were tailors, shoemakers, glaziers, smiths,

*From "canton," a word applied to a recruiting district. (Ed.)

carpenters, stonemasons, and the like (no. 34). Trade was sparse, artisans were too numerous for the needy and poorly paid population. Although the Jewish artisans were considered the most skillful in the country, it was impossible for them to sustain themselves and their families. Poverty was widespread. The government, which had a hostile attitude toward the Jews, refused to make use of their constructive capacities.

Education and Haskalah

In contrast to the Russian population, the Jews tolerated no illiteracy in their midst. They maintained an extensive system of education although the scope of education was limited and antiquated, often carried on by teachers who were inadequately prepared. Secular studies were shunned. It was against this exclusiveness and one-sidedness that some Jews, influenced by the ideas of the Western Jews, took a stand. They were followers of Haskalah, a Hebrew word or description that is usually translated as "enlightenment." But the Haskalah was really broader in its meaning. Its goal was a complete revolution, a transformation in education: the teaching of the European languages, especially the official languages of the countries in which the Jews lived; vocational training aimed at changing and introducing variety in the ways in which Jews earned their living; and converting Jewish ways and manners of living so that they resembled more closely those of their European neighbors. Haskalah writers were guided by naive assumptions of "progress," by the belief that the medieval bigotry and prejudice of Christian society had vanished, that non-Jews had changed their attitude toward the Jews. They believed that if only the Jews in Eastern Europe were willing to change their ghetto ways, they would automatically be granted full equality.

The Haskalah writers, who usually wrote in Hebrew, discovered to their great dismay that often it was the emancipated Jew who became the indifferent Jew or even, as had happened in Western Europe, completely lost to Judaism. Among East European Jews such tendencies were far less extreme. The deep rootedness in Jewish tradition and the rich soil of a folk-life proved to be a potent barrier that a de-Judaized enlightenment found it hard to penetrate. In addition, the repressive measures of the tsarist government throughout the nineteenth century, aided by a cruel anti-Jewish attitude on the part of Russian Christian society, greatly contributed to the deep antagonism of the Jewish masses in Russia and Poland to the cultural changes advocated by the Haskalah.

The Jews reckoned with the realities of their situation. Even with the reforms of Alexander II, the great majority of Russian Jews continued to live in misery in the congested Pale of Settlement. Excluded by law not only from agriculture, but from the trades and crafts as well, and often denied admission to schools of higher education except in pitifully small numbers, the Jews had every reason to remain skeptical about the Haskalah writers' proposed solutions which were to lead to a happier life.

In the first half of the nineteenth century, changes in the educational system with the aim of improvement were initiated by some Jewish groups. In cities like Odessa in the south and Riga in the north, modern Jewish schools were established which proved very successful. The school in Riga was headed by Dr. Max Lilienthal, a young German rabbi, who had been invited to serve as its principal.

Lilienthal

Now the Russian government turned to Lilienthal and asked him to help in the establishment of government schools for Jews with a curriculum of Jewish and secular studies. Lilienthal traveled through cities of the Pale and tried to persuade the Jews to accept the school system proposed by the government (no. 27). He soon found among the Jews considerable skepticism about the true intentions of the government. They believed that the schools would be used to bring about the conversion of Jews rather than for any other purpose. Lilienthal himself lost confidence when he was approached with proposals for conversion, hurriedly resigned his post, and, in 1848, left Russia. He emigrated to America, where he became prominent in the early Reform movement. As a result of his experience in Russia, Lilienthal was deeply impressed with the religious faith of Russian Jewry (no. 28).

Liberal Reforms

Alexander II (1855–81), who succeeded Tsar Nicholas, introduced various liberal reforms, some of them affecting the Jews. The Crimean war (1854–55) had demonstrated the need for improved highways and railroads. Jewish entrepreneurs and financiers who would undertake these constructions and establish industries were, therefore, welcomed. Admission of Jewish students to secondary schools was no longer restricted. The right of residence was extended, and new Jewish communities were established in St. Petersburg and Moscow as well as places in the interior of Russia. This right of residence was limited mainly to wholesale merchants, financiers and their employees, academicians, and discharged veterans. These elements were, as a rule, ready for Russification and assimilation. Departures from Judaism proceeded fast among these groups and even conversions took place (no. 29).

Political Unrest and Reaction

Political unrest characterized the last decades of the nineteenth century in Russia. The incompetence of the government and its officials became more and more obvious. Cries for constitutional reform were heard and revolutionary circles were formed. In 1881 Tsar Alexander II was killed by bombs thrown by a group of terrorists. Under his successor reaction and despotism became the rule of the day.

Many of the reforms introduced by Alexander II and affecting the Jews were repealed. Only a percentage of Jewish students, from 5 to 10 percent, were henceforth admitted to high schools and universities. In the pursuit of a brutal and senseless anti-Jewish policy, a variety of new restrictions applying to Jews was enacted. The masses of Jews confined to the Pale found it more and more difficult to make a living.

Hate Propaganda and Pogroms

In desperation some Jewish youths joined revolutionary groups with the hope that the fall of the tsarist regime would eliminate all restrictions. This action, too, was used by the government as an excuse for declaring the Jews to be enemies of Russia. "Official propaganda of church and state, strongly supported by much of the press and the theater, created in the minds of the Russian people a stereotype of Jews as crafty, wily, greedy, parasitical money-grabbers" (Harry G. Shaffer).

Jews were blamed for all the ills that beset tsarist Russia. A hate propaganda accused the Jews even of ritual murder and other crimes perpetrated on non-Jews. But worse was to follow. Beginning in 1871, a wave of pogroms during the next decades was tolerated and even encouraged (nos. 30, 31, 33). Thousands of Jewish men, women, and children were brutally slaughtered, their houses burned, and their property pilfered or destroyed. In some cities the Jews organized for self-defense (no. 32).

Migration

A high Russian official expressed government policy toward the Jews in a statement that one-third of the Jewish population was to convert to Christianity, one-third was to perish, and one-third would be compelled to emigrate. Indeed, between 1871 and 1914 close to two million Jews emigrated from Russia, about one-third of the Jewish population. Most of them turned to the United States, some to England, and a few to Palestine. A whole people was in motion. Jewish aid societies in Europe and the United States organized help for the emigrants.

Revolution in 1917

The Revolution of 1917 during the First World War put an end to the rule of the tsars and their despotism. David Lloyd George, a British statesman and ally of the Russians during the war, called the Russian government "brutal, tyrannical, corrupt, rotten to the core." The new constitution abolished all discriminatory laws and granted full equality to the Jews.

Civil War

The leaders of the extreme left, the Bolsheviks, displaced the new government of 1917 and in the same year carried out their own revolution. In the next few years of civil war between the Bolsheviks and the armies of the right, the Jews underwent great suffering. They were exposed to massacres by the warring factions, especially those of the right. The pogroms in the Ukraine reached untold proportions. Hundreds of Jewish communities were wiped out.

With the establishment of Soviet rule in Russia, a new period in the history of the Russian Jews began. Another chapter of this book will deal with the Jews in Soviet Russia.

National Reawakening

The oppression of the tsars, and their efforts to make the life of the Jews intolerable, did not break the Jewish spirit. Every effort was made to maintain community institutions like schools, *yeshivot* (talmudical academies), and charitable organizations, and even to establish new ones. Tsarist oppression strengthened the Jewish will to survive, which drew on its inner strength and self-defense. The will for creative survival took various forms. A national reawakening led some groups to think of building a Jewish life in the land of Israel, Eretz Yisrael, even before the time of Theodor Herzl. The establishment of the Zionist organization by Herzl, therefore, found in Russia fertile soil for winning many loyal adherents (no. 36). At the same time a modern Hebrew literature had developed which was seeking new ways of expression and paving the way for the use of Hebrew as a living tongue. This literature also reflected the historic changes of how the Jew emerged from ghetto conditions and entered the modern world (no. 37).

Jewish Workers

Vast changes were also taking place in the ways of living and thinking of the masses of Jewish workers. The Jewish workers joined socialist parties. In time they discovered that they had particular concerns as a Jewish group with which the general socialist parties they had joined did not reckon. In 1897, therefore, they formed the Jewish Labor Alliance of Russia, Poland and Lithuania, which subsequently became an important party known under the abbreviation *Bund*, meaning "alliance" (no. 35). The Bund was somewhat more than an organization for the improvement of the conditions of the Jewish working class. In the course of time it became interested in improving the lot of the entire Jewish population, in broadening its cultural interests, and in adding to its civil rights. But its socialist goals were to have priority.

Yiddish, the language of the Jewish masses in Eastern Europe, and held in contempt by some as a "jargon," also had its staunch advocates and like Hebrew developed a modern literature (no. 38).

Jewish Self-Liberation

Russian Jewry, living amidst a hostile population and facing the brutal despotism of an anti-Jewish government and its officialdom, developed a creativity which is most impressive. With the exception of a minority of assimilationists, all factions and groups were guided by passionate attachment to the Jewish people and its fate. Within the Zionist and labor movements new voices were heard. The Jewish masses, as Weizmann explains (no. 36), were rising against the paternalism of their "notables," the men of wealth and influence who had always taken it on themselves to represent the needs of the Jews before the government. "Shaken to the foundations by the pogroms of the eighties, Russian Jewry . . . began to organize its own awakening forces. The spirit of rebellion was at last astir. This revolt found expression in the double phenomenon of the Jewish labor movement and the Jewish national movement . . . the setting in of a new epoch, perhaps the epoch of greatest Jewish activity in all the history of the Diaspora. . . . For the first time in the history of their struggle for human rights, the Jews spoke as a national entity."*

The Jewish people owes a historical debt to Russian Jewry (no. 30).

24. THE JEWS UNDER THE TSARS

MICHAEL DAVITT

Michael Davitt (1846–1906) was an Irish revolutionary and a member of the British Parliament (1895–99). He visited the United States and in 1903 went to Russia to report on the pogroms and the situation of the Jews for the newspapers of William Randolph Hearst. As a result of his observations and study, he wrote the book *Within the Pale*, from which the following excerpts are taken. Davitt tried to "find both sides of the anti-Semitic question" in Russia and often quotes from Russian sources.

The Pale

Jews in Russia are compelled by law to reside inside a Pale of Settlement,

---

*Shmarya Levin, The Arena, pp. 7–9.

or territory comprising some fifteen governments, or provinces, of western and southern Russia, extending south from the coast of the southern Baltic to the Crimea, and westward from Charkov and Smolensk to the borders of Roumania, Galicia, and Prussian Poland. The area thus embraced in the Jewish Pale is about equal to that of France, and the number of people of this section of Russia is upward of 27,000,000.

Under the ukase of 1882, which compelled Jews to leave the villages and live within the towns, these centres became crowded inside of what thus became virtual economic concentration camps.

Within these limits of legal domicile the density of Hebrew population is at the rate of some 2800 per square mile. In the non-Jewish towns of Russia the average is about 60 of urban to 1000 of rural population. Within the fifteen provinces included in the Jewish Pale, the average is close upon 230 of urban to every 1000 of country population.

The effects of this crowding of Jews into the towns of the Pale are as obvious as they are inevitable. There is a dense population, restricted by necessity and disposition to certain pursuits and occupations, in places where the economic conditions do not provide opportunities for the healthy exercise of one-fourth of the industry or abilities which could under normal conditions find opportunities for profitable employment.

No Friends

The Jew has no friend outside his own race in Russia, while not infrequently those of his own household are the worst paymasters of his talent and industry. The peasant dislikes him for his race, his religion. . . . The artisan and labourer in urban centres of the crowded Pale look upon him as an economic black-leg, because he is compelled to work at anything for the wages of bare subsistence, in order to live. He is, by the cruel decree of his fate, and not by choice, the cause of low wages. This is one reason why a great number of the sanguinary rioters at Kishineff were Russian and Moldavian workingmen.

The shop-keeper and petty dealer see in their Hebrew rival a competitor . . . who can succeed where the business capacity of the Slavonic gentile is wanting in perseverance and resource. Here hatred is born of a sordid jealousy.

As rich merchant and banker he is tolerated. The wealthy Russian Jew is, at present, a Russian necessity. Odessa, one of the richest cities of the Empire, is "run" by the superior abilities of the proscribed race. Its commercial prosperity would collapse to-morrow if they were expelled; just as the business and progress of Kishineff have been all but paralysed by the outbreak against them at Easter.

Growth of Prejudice

Anti-Semitic prejudices grow as we proceed from the rivalries of economic pursuits to the classes and interests associated with the administration of the Empire. The policeman knows the Jew is made an alien by law, and that the necessity he is under to evade the legal disabilities to which he is subject renders him a profitable source of blackmail. Where his poverty repels the exercise of this corruption, the guardian of the peace looks upon the Jew with all the mixed antipathy—racial, religious, and economic—of the superstitious, uninformed Mujik.

In the lower and middle grades of the civil service the Jew is feared as well as disliked. He is known to be far more intellectual, more industrious, and more capable than the average Russian, and there is a dread lest employment in the innumerable posts of a vast administration should, at some future period, be thrown open to a race so versatile, so sober, and so ambitious to succeed. In every Royal School or Gymnasium to which a Jewish youth is admitted—the number must never exceed 10 per cent of the whole attendance, in some schools not 5 per cent—the son of Abraham is certain to eclipse his rivals, and to walk off with whatever honours are to be won.

I have already indicated the feeling, candidly expressed, of the higher branches of the public service on the subject of the Jew as a possible rival in that department of the state. An equality of opportunity would mean a monopoly of posts by sheer force of mental and general equipment.

The Russian officer is not averse to the Jew as a soldier, but he must never be—a Russian officer.

The Government

Finally, the Government of Russia looks upon the Jew as the most dangerous of disturbing factors in the rapid development of the industrial life of the Empire, and as a political enemy within the ambit of its most vulnerable western frontier. He is believed to be the active propagandist of Socialism, and he is known to have powerful political and financial allies among the pressmen and financiers of France, England, and Germany—allies who can strike at Russia's financial credit, external policies, and moral prestige, in retaliation for the legal outlawry of their race within the dominions of the Tsar.

Against these governmental, religious, industrial, social, and national forces of a huge empire combined, what chance has a proscribed race, alienised by law, of obtaining redress? It is a hopeless struggle, look at it how we may.

25. A STATEMENT OF THE GOVERNOR OF KIEV

MICHAEL DAVITT

In 1833, General Levashoff, governor of Kiev, reported to the government on a petition of Christian merchants asking for the expulsion of Jews from that city. The governor's report, quoted by Davitt, explains the real motives of the petitioners.

"It is desirable on the ground of public utility to allow the Jews to remain in Kiev, where, by the simplicity and moderation of their mode of life, they are able to sell commodities at a cheap rate. It may positively be asserted that their expulsion would not only lead to an enhancement of prices of many products and articles, but that it will not be possible to obtain these at all. Under these circumstances the interests of the mass of the inhabitants must be preferred to the personal advantages which the Christian trading class would derive by the ejection of the Jews."

26. JEWISH CANTONISTS UNDER TSAR NICHOLAS I

ALEXANDER HERZEN

Alexander Herzen (1812–70) was a Russian journalist and political agitator. He developed a socialist philosophy that provided the basis for much of the revolutionary activity in Russia.

About cantonists see the introduction to this chapter. Herzen happened to meet a group of cantonists on a journey. He describes the dialogue which he had with the escorting officer.

"Whom do you carry and to what place?"

"Well, sir, you see, they got together a bunch of these accursed Jewish youngsters between the age of eight and nine. I suppose they are meant for the fleet, but how should I know? At first the command was to drive them to Perm. Now there is a change. We are told to drive them to Kazan. I have had them on my hands for a hundred versts or thereabouts. The officer that turned them over to me told me they were an awful nuisance. A third of them remained on the road (at this the officer pointed with his finger to the ground). Half of them will not get to their destination," he added.

"Epidemics, I suppose?", I inquired, stirred to the very core.

"No, not exactly epidemics; but they just fall like flies. Well, you know, these Jewish boys are so puny and delicate. They can't stand mixing dirt for ten hours, with dry biscuits to live on. Again everywhere strange folks, no father, no mother, no caresses. Well then, you just hear a cough and the youngster is dead. Hello, corporal, get out the small fry!"

The little ones were assembled and arrayed in a military line. It was one of the most terrible spectacles I have ever witnessed. Poor, poor children! The boys of twelve or thirteen managed somehow to stand up, but the little ones of eight and ten. . . . No brush, however black, could convey the terror of this scene on the canvas.

Pale, worn out, with scared looks, this is the way they stood in their uncomfortable, rough soldier uniforms, with their starched, turned-up collars, fixing an inexpressibly helpless and pitiful gaze upon the garrisoned soldiers, who were handling them rudely. White lips, blue lines under the eyes betokened either fever or cold. And these poor children, without care, without a caress, exposed to the wind which blows unhindered from the Arctic Ocean, were marching to their death. I seized the officer's hand, and, with the words: "Take good care of them!", threw myself into my carriage. I felt like sobbing, and I knew I could not master myself.

27. A FOLKSONG

Every Jewish community was assigned a quota of youngsters for this kind of military service. Sometimes a community used agents to kidnap orphans and children of the poor to make up the required quota. The impoverished masses resented that the community authorities favored members of the educated and wealthy classes and tended to shift the burden of the draft on the shoulders of the poor. The cantonist system was in force from 1827 to 1856 and left bitter memories in the minds of the Jewish people.

The following folksong, translated from Yiddish, expresses the resentment and anger of the poor.

> Tots from school they tear away
> And dress them up in soldier's gray.
> And our leaders, and our rabbis,
> Do naught but deepen the abyss.
> Rich Mr. Rockover has seven sons,
> Not a one a uniform dons;
> But poor widow Leah has an only child,
> And they hunt him down as if he were wild.
> It is right to draft the hard-working masses;
> Shoe makers or tailors—they're only asses!
> But the children of the idle rich
> Must carry on, without a hitch.

28. MODERN SCHOOLS BY GOVERNMENT DECREE

MAX LILIENTHAL

About Max Lilienthal (1814–1882) and how he was used by the Russian government, see the introduction to this chapter. The selection is taken from his *My Travels in Russia*.

Vilna, the Metropolis of Israel

Toward the end of the year 1841, I received a communication, addressed to me by Prince Shirinski-Shikhmatov, the Director of the Department of Public Instruction, informing me that Nisan Rosenthal of Vilna having represented to the minister the possibility of establishing another flourishing Jewish school in the city, His Excellency ordered me to accompany him thither as soon as Rosenthal would call on me, and then to report to him on the progress I had attained. A week afterward, Rosenthal, a modernized Polish Jew, a very handsome man indeed, entered my room. He had just been decorated by the emperor with the golden medal for some services rendered to the crown, and tried, like the politicians in this country, to gain some distinction and to make a living by all kinds of schemes and plans. He stood not in the best graces of his coreligionists, being considered as one of the new lights or Berliners, as the reformers, adjudged to be the followers of Mendelssohn in Berlin, are called in Vilna. . . . Vilna, even in Poland, is called *ir ve-em be-yisrael*, the metropolis of Israel! And when Napoleon I, on a Friday afternoon in 1812, having entered the gates of this city rode through its streets, he exclaimed to his marshals: "Gentlemen, I think we are in Jerusalem." Coming from Germany, where in all cities the Jews are in the minority, entirely disappearing amongst the larger majority of their Christian fellow citizens, I did not know what to make out of this swarming beehive of Jews. I, too, believed myself to be in Palestine instead of in Russia, so entirely and thoroughly Jewish appeared to me the city of Vilna. . . .

Meeting with Jewish Representatives

On Thursday night an assembly of the representatives of the congregation was convened in order to hear the propositions I had to make to them by order of the government. A committee led me into the vestry, where I found some hundred men assembled, all dressed in their *shubetze* (coat) and their fur caps. I felt so lonesome in the midst of these strange faces—the only *datshel* (German) in the crowd of Polish Jews. The president of the congregation, a wealthy man, but of a very insignificant appearance, a great Talmudist, but without any other education, who, on account of his riches and his fanatically orthodox ideas exercised a great influence, welcomed me in the name of the illustrious congregation, gave me his chair, and requested me to state the purpose of my visit with which I had honored them.

I stated to the meeting that my visit was of no official character. They were well aware that the emperor had appointed a special committee of ministers to take into consideration the affairs of the Jews from a religious as well as from a political and educational point of view, that the imperial government was determined upon introducing a wholesome change and that its intentions could not be eluded this time. Minister Uvarov, a friend of the Jews, had ordered me to tell my coreligionists that they should not let the opportunity presented to them escape as they had done in the time of the late Emperor Alexander, when delegates called to the capital were dismissed with the greatest disgrace to themselves as well as to their constituents; that His Excellency wished the Jews to establish schools in accordance with the spirit of the time and the demands of the age before the government would order and compel them to do so. By such a procedure, they would dispose the government in their favor, and being aware what an immense influence the Jewish metropolis of Vilna exercised upon the Russian Jews in general, he hoped that by setting a glorious example they would take the whole matter into their hands, thereby becoming the benefactors and regenerators of their race.

I had been listened to silently. The younger generation in Vilna, imbued with the progressive spirit of our age and well versed in the Hebrew, Russian, Polish, German, and partly French languages, were enthused by my short address; they hoped to see their favorite dreams and hopes fulfilled at last. . . .

But the elders sat there absorbed in deep contemplation. Some of them, leaning on their silver-adorned staffs or smoothing their long beards, seemed as if agitated by earnest thoughts and justifiable suspicions; others were engaging in a lively but quiet discussion on the principles involved; such put to me the ominous question: "Doctor, are you fully acquainted with the leading principles of our government? You are a stranger; do you know what you are undertaking? The course pursued against all denominations but the Greeks proves clearly that the government intends to have but one church in the whole empire; that it has in view only its own future strength and greatness and not our own future prosperity. We are sorry to state that we put no confidence in the new measures proposed by the ministerial council, and that we look with gloomy foreboding into the future."

"I am well aware of your apprehensions," I answered the respectable old man who had been the interpreter of the feelings of the gray-headed and silver bearded assembly, "and was well informed of all that is going on during my sojourn in Riga. The question we have to consider is this: Can we avoid the threatening danger by the useless answer that we do not want to have anything to do with it? I am convinced that the Jewish affairs are now in such hands that they surely will be acted upon. What will we gain by a wilful resistance? We will draw the dissatisfaction of the government upon ourselves, will provoke justifiable ill feeling and merely expose ourselves to dangers still more discouraging. I have pondered upon this subject carefully; but after mature and serious consideration, I have found it best to take this matter at once in our hands, and having established schools according to our plans, our means and under our own superintendency, we will anticipate the measures of the government. By thus presenting our intentions and views in a favorable light, I entertain not the least doubt that our schools will be sanctioned and our plans ratified by the department of public instruction."

"But what guarantee," asked another gentleman, "can you offer us that our religion will not be encroached upon?"

"Gentlemen," I replied, "born in Russia, you know a great deal better than I that I am unable to offer you any guarantee on the part of the department. The emperor's will reigns supreme and autocratic; he can recall today what he has promised yesterday; he changes his officers and their systems whenever he pleases. How should I, an humble stranger, be able to offer you a guarantee? I am not empowered to do it. All that I can promise you as your coreligionist is that I shall not go a step further in promoting the plans of the government before having obtained the assurance that nothing will be undertaken against our holy religion, that I shall lay down my office as soon as I shall become convinced of the contrary, and that no offense on the part of my brethren shall excuse me for breaking this promise I am giving you in this solemn hour."

This assurance was received with general satisfaction. Some of the members present hurried up to me and shook my hands heartily; others welcomed me in the most friendly manner, and the confidence and good understanding seemed to be restored. . . .

Talking to a Rabbinic Leader

After having passed the whole day examining the schools, I received in the evening an invitation from the *stadt-magid* (chief preacher) of the city to visit him at ten o'clock the same evening. The late hour of the appointment indicated to me that the rabbi wished to know the result of the examination in order to prevent me from making to the government a one-sided or too hasty report. I repaired to his humble rooms at the fixed time. He received me very kindly, and after having entertained me for about half an hour with some Torah, brandy, and cakes, he left the room, inquiring whether all his housemates were already asleep. Being assured that he was safe from all listeners, he took his seat at the oak table opposite my chair and in a low voice began to ask me:

"Well, doctor, you are firmly resolved upon introducing a change in our school system?"

"It is the will of the emperor and the order of the government, rabbi."

"Are you also aware of all the consequences that this change will effect in our religious views?"

"You see specters, rabbi, where there are none. I come from Germany where no one dreams anymore of such an opposition as the Russian Jews make to the establishment of better schools; and having quenched our thirst at the fountain of universal science and knowledge, we feel ourselves as good Jews as you do". . .

"You must not suppose, doctor, that I am entirely opposed to the introduction of your sciences. I have studied too frequently the immortal works of Maimonides, Ibn Ezra, and their successors not to be impressed with the importance, usefulness, and necessity of acquiring the knowledge of profane literature; yea, the Talmud itself recommends it highly unto us, and you know that the members of the Sanhedrin must be well versed even in seventy languages. But we are informed by our merchants visiting the large fair at Leipzig that your brethren in Germany deal very slightly with religion, and that the religious commands are not as strictly observed as in this country."

"Rabbi, for all that we have not as many converted Jews as there are in this country. Besides, I have already heard that if a Polish Jew puts off his shubetze, he treats religion with more disdain and disregard than is customary in Germany. But both our arguments lack a solid foundation; there are good and bad men amongst every nation, in every climate and under all circumstances. But granted even that the reform begun in Germany by the great Mendelssohn has led to some lamentable extremes, the false steps taken in the beginning have been remedied long ago, and you may profit by our experience to avoid all injurious extravagances."

"Doctor, I will tell you; we are ashes, all ashes; and as soon as anyone touches us, the whole edifice will crumble to pieces!"

He looked uneasily about after having uttered that gloomy sentence, whilst I stared in his face at this bold and thoughtful expression.

"You are wrong, rabbi, entirely wrong," I continued, interrupting the uncomfortable silence. "Our religion is not ashes; you confound the eternal truth contained in our doctrines with outworn and antiquated ceremonies. They, indeed, are ashes, and whether we touch them or not, time will destroy them, as in Western Europe it has already destroyed a great deal of them. Put those ashes away, and the jewel of our creed shall shine forth in all its brilliancy. We and mankind will be benefited by the removal of these your ashes.''

"But the whole mass of the people will not know how to discern between the ashes and the jewel, dear doctor. If you remove the ashes they will throw away the jewel, and then what will become of our creed for which our ancestors have suffered so much, for which we ourselves undergo such endless tortures, such awful agonies? It will be surrendered in course of time, and will you be the instrument for such a calamitous and sinful destruction?''

"My dear rabbi, I have too high an idea of the eternal truth of our creed to be in the least afraid of such gloomy consequences. Our creed and our people have outlived and outlasted quite other periods than that of a desirable reconciliation with the advancement and enlightenment of our age. I, on my part, consider it a sin to believe and to assert that our creed is not compatible with science and knowledge itself; its principles are light and nothing but undimmed light; its doctrines are true and eternal as God is; how can you suppose for a moment that by the reconciliation with the irrefutable demands of our age the existence of our sacred creed will be endangered? Your Polish rabbis excommunicated the immortal Mendelssohn, when first he published his German translation of the Pentateuch; you cried 'Murder!' when the pious reformer began the immense task of introducing his isolated brethren into the active arena of life; could you stop the onward march of the bold reformer? Could you bring back our brethren in Western Europe to the spirit of bigotry, darkness and isolation which you considered the only safeguard of our creed? His name stands in bold relief before posterity, and the names of all these Jewish inquisitors are forgotten. Are you resolved upon repeating the same fruitless transaction?''

The rabbi sighed and kept silent for some time, absorbed in deep meditation. "But his pupils," he continued, "have become apostates to our creed. Some members of his own family, I have been told, have become converts to Christianity. If apostasy should be the consequence of your proposed reform I, in the name of all my Jewish brethren, protest against it, and prefer our isolated position to all the allurements of civilization.''

"Rabbi, you again confound the levity and frivolity of a few with the good and importance of the cause. The mischief, committed at the first outburst of inexperienced and unbridled wantonness and presumptuousness, has been remedied in Germany long ago. A sincere attachment to the creed of our ancestors, a profound knowledge of science and the arts; a readiness to support every good institution, unbounded and unexampled charity, the dear heirloom of Israel, are the principal virtues making our blunders at present, and there is not the least apprehension that the old blunders will be committed again and again! And the schools we are proposing are the medium by which our brethren in Russia will avoid the reproaches you are making to Mendelssohn's school. Draw up a perfect plan for the proposed schools we intend to establish; appoint such teachers in whose religious views you can put implicit confidence; impress upon the susceptible mind of the young the doctrines of our faith, and you may instruct them afterward in any science you please—there will be no danger to the religion. And if men of your stamp would take the subject of reform into your own hands, men whose orthodoxy no one dares to doubt, men whose profound Talmudical learning fits them for this responsible and enormous task, the people, fully confiding in your integrity, will gladly abide by your decisions. You will lay the cornerstone for the glorious edifice that the future generations will erect. While your present system is unable to stop the wheels of human progress, the course I propose to you will enable you to direct its motions and become the benefactors of your people."

The clock struck midnight. The rabbi rose from his seat. "He sleeps not and slumbers not, the Guardian of Israel," he said. "Into His hands I confide the future of my brethren. He knows best how to accomplish His end." And shaking my hand heartily, he bade me good-night.

29. A SABBATH IN VILNA

MAX LILIENTHAL

Lilienthal was deeply impressed with the religious faith of the Jews in Russia. "He who has not seen Russian Jewry has no concept of what traditional authentic Judaism once was." The following selection is taken from his memoirs, *My Travels in Russia*, and describes a Friday night, the eve of Sabbath, when he visited Vilna in 1841.

. . . The synagogue was richly illuminated with wax candles; the celebrated *chazan* [cantor] . . . officiated with his assistants in a most dignified manner, and having received many a hearty "Good Shabbos," I left more than pleased with the service.

When I reentered the streets all was still and quiet. For the first time in my life I had an idea of a Sabbath as celebrated by our ancestors in the holy land in times of yore. Heaven and earth, moon and stars, houses and streets, all preached: "It is the Sabbath, the day consecrated by the Lord." All the stores were closed; no cart was moving in the street; a holy tranquility reigned anywhere. The men excepted, who returned from the

service, no person was to be seen in the wide and empty streets. The high
five-story houses were illuminated from the deep cellar up to the garret
rooms. It was as if the whole city had put on its holiday attire to receive
in a dignified manner the heavenly bride of the Sabbath. I stood full of
amazement in the midst of this spectacle, sunk in deep revery, disturbed
only now and then by a "Good Shabbos" addressed to me by the men who
passed by and quietly disappeared into their different homes.

I followed some of them, and through the cleft of a window shutter
looked into the front room anxious to observe how the Sabbath was
celebrated in the circle of these families.

How clean, how tidy looked the room! The floor, neatly scrubbed, was
strewn with sand; the walls were adorned with many lighted candlesticks;
in the middle of the room stood a large table covered with snow white
linen on which were several pairs of *chalos* (Sabbath-bread) and a bottle of
wine with several silver cups. In one nook of the room in a large leathern
armchair sat the grandmother, the head covered with a gold embroidered
cap, the breast adorned with a kind of richly gilded shield; she played with
a little grandson sitting on her lap. The mother, the head covered with a
turban, and the neck adorned with a golden chain and medal, sat with
folded arms engaged in a quiet conversation with one of her daughters-in-
law. All were nicely dressed and sat around the walls; the married ones
had their hair hidden beneath the turban; the single ones showed their
long, raven black tresses. They waited for their husbands, and none would
dare to disturb the holy peace of the Sabbath by loud conversation before
the men had returned with the sweet and charming greeting of a "Good
Shabbos" . . .

I again looked through the windows into the rooms where many men
were singing their *zemirot* (Sabbath songs), or engaged in a friendly
conversation either with the members of their families or with some
visitors. All had a different appearance—the gloomy, care-worn faces had
disappeared; everybody seemed reconciled with his God and the troubles
of life; the mitigating hand of religion had laid its balm upon the wounded
hearts; the agonies of the past and the cares of the future seemed to be
forgotten; confidence in the ever-living God of Israel, in his kindness and
bounty having taken their place, all enjoyed the presence and the blessings
of religion.

But soon the lights began to be extinguished. While passing several
houses I perceived wife and children already asleep, but the men still
sitting over a Hebrew book, enjoying the study of a commentary of a
chapter read on the following morning. Half an hour more and Vilna, that
beehive of Jews, being quiet and still, I returned to my hotel really
delighted with the spectacle I had observed for the first time, and with the

holiness with which the Sabbath is still kept among our coreligionists in Russia.

30. ANTI-SEMITISM AND ASSIMILATION

PAULINE WENGEROFF

Pauline Wengeroff (1835–1916) was the daughter of a wealthy Russian Jewish merchant and the wife of a banker. She became known for her memoirs, which reflect the life of a wealthy Jewish family in the second half of the nineteenth century in Russia. She describes the gradual destruction of the old way of life as it occurred in her home and in that of many families of the same class. The selection is taken from her memoirs.

Russification

In the sixties the government had begun its policy of russifying the Jews. After the Polish uprising of 1863, Russian was made compulsory in the Jewish schools in Poland and Lithuania. Then, the subject matter began to be regulated. Gradually, Jewish studies were shortened to make more time for the general curriculum. But the government's policy articulated the unspoken wish among the young generation, and especially their Jewish teachers, that general education be given priority. No wonder, then, that in the cold, dark and stormy eighties and nineties, our children in their frail boats, tossed on the raging waves of life, wanted to bring their little boats to safety. A safe harbor to them was baptism.

Nihilism

So this terrible word comes like a plague. The word has rarely crossed my lips for it was too close, piercing a mother's bleeding heart. After the terrible events, I never spoke of them, and confided only to my diary, damp with tears, and preserved them deep, deep in my memory—until today.

In those transitional seventies, all sorts of high-flown words become current: nihilism, materialism, assimilation, antisemitism, decadence. "Nihilism" made its appearance in Turgenev's *Fathers and Sons*. Our young people responded enthusiastically to the book and its hero, with whom they identified. Conflict between parents and their children became more embittered, and the young people became more alienated from their parents, often ashamed of them. They viewed in their parents only a purse which enabled them to satisfy their desires. But there was no respect. After all, one could only respect a person of high culture. If the relations between parents and children in the forties and fifties were tragicomic, these relations in the eighties and nineties were pure tragedy.

Jewish youth abandoned itself to total assimilation. Then came March 1, 1881, and the sun which had risen on Jewish life in the fifties suddenly set. Alexander II was killed by a bomb on the bank of the Catherine Canal in St. Petersburg. The hand that had freed sixty million serfs was stilled. The lips which had pronounced the great word of liberation were forever silenced. The City Council of Minsk sent two delegates to St. Petersburg to place a wreath on his fresh grave. The mayor of Minsk and my husband were chosen. It was the first time in Russian history that Jews had participated in a demonstration of mourning.

But different times came. The reptiles that had shunned the light emerged. Antisemitism erupted; the Jews were forced back into the ghetto. Without ceremony, the gateways to education were closed. The jubilation of the fifties and sixties turned into lamentation.

The few rights Jews had enjoyed were withdrawn. Disabilities began to pile up. Rights of residence for Jews in the cities became ever more restricted. An academic education became more and more difficult for Jews to attain, for only a very small Jewish quota was admitted to the gymnasium and even fewer were admitted to the universities.

Pogrom was a new word, coined in the eighties. The Jews of Kiev, Romny, Konotop were among the first to experience the savage assault of the local mobs.

That was the beginning.

Choices Left for Jews

In the eighties, with antisemitism raging all over Russia, a Jew had two choices. He could, in the name of Judaism, renounce everything that had become indispensable to him, or he could choose freedom with its offers of education and career—through baptism. Hundreds of enlightened Jews chose the latter. These apostates were not converts out of conviction, nor were they like the Marranos of an earlier age. These apostates disbelieved in all religions: they were nihilists.

31. POGROMS IN SOUTH RUSSIA

AN EYEWITNESS

This is an eyewitness account of the pogrom in Kiev in April 1881, one of a series of pogroms in various cities in southern Russia. About the role of the government in encouraging these outbreaks, see the introduction to this chapter.

At twelve o'clock at noon, the air suddenly resounded with wild shouts, whistling, jeering, hooting, and laughing. An immense crowd of young boys, artisans, and laborers was on the march. The whole city was obstructed by the "bare-footed brigade."* The destruction of Jewish houses began. Window-panes and doors began to fly about, and shortly thereafter the mob, having gained access to the houses and stores, began to throw upon the streets absolutely everything that fell into their hands. Clouds of feathers began to whirl in the air. The din of broken windowpanes and frames, the crying, shouting, and despair on the one hand, and the terrible yelling and jeering on the other, completed the picture which reminded many of those who had participated in the last Russo-Turkish war of the manner in which the Bashibuzuks† had attacked Bulgarian villages. Soon afterwards the mob threw itself upon the Jewish synagogue, which, despite its strong bars, locks and shutters, was wrecked in a moment. One should have seen the fury with which the riff-raff fell upon the [Torah] scrolls, of which there were many in the synagogue. The scrolls were torn to shreds, trampled in the dirt, and destroyed with incredible passion. The streets were soon crammed with the trophies of destruction. Everywhere fragments of dishes, furniture, household utensils, and other articles lay scattered about. Barely two hours after the beginning of the pogrom, the majority of the "bare-footed brigade" were transformed into well-dressed gentlemen, many of them having grown excessively stout in the meantime. The reason for this sudden change was simple enough. Those that had looted the stores of ready-made clothes put on three or four suits, and, not yet satisfied, took under their arms all they could lay their hands on. Others drove off in vehicles, carrying with them bags filled with loot. . . . The Christian population saved itself from the ruinous operations of the crowd by placing holy ikons in their windows and painting crosses on the gates of their houses. . . .

Here and there army officers would pass through, among them generals and high civil officials. The cavalry would hasten to a place whence the noise came. Having arrived there, it would surround the mob and order it to disperse, but the mob would only move to another place. Thus, the work of destruction proceeded undisturbed until three o'clock in the morning.

32. ON THE SLAUGHTER

CHAIM NACHMAN BIALIK

Chaim Nachman Bialik (1873–1934), born in Russia, is considered the greatest modern Hebrew poet, the poet of national reawakening, who deeply

---

*The Russian nickname for a crowd of tramps.
†Name of the Turkish irregular troops noted for their ferocity.

influenced Hebrew literature. He was a poet, storyteller, essayist, translator, and editor. He left Russia after the Bolshevick revolution and ultimately settled in what was then Palestine.

The bloody pogrom in Kishineff in 1903, which eclipsed all previous Russian excesses, shocked the world. Bialik reacted to this event in two poems expressing anger and pain, a longer one, "The City of Slaughter," and a shorter one, "On the Slaughter" reprinted here. His poems encouraged self-defense.

Heavenly spheres, beg mercy for me!
If truly God dwells in your orbit and round,
And in your space is His pathway that I have not found,—
Then you pray for me!
For my own heart is dead; no prayer on my tongue;
And strength has failed, and hope has passed:
O until when? For how much more? How long?

Ho, headsman, bared the neck—come, cleave it through!
Nape me this cur's nape! Yours is the axe unbaffled!
The whole wide world—my scaffold!
And rest you easy: we are weak and few.
My blood is outlaw. Strike, then; the skull dissever!
Let blood of babe and graybeard stain your garb—
Stain to endure forever!

If Right there be,—why, let it shine forth now!
For if when I have perished from the earth
The Right shine forth,
Then let its Throne be shattered, and laid low!
Then let the heavens, wrong-racked, be no more!
—While you, O murderers, on your murder thrive!

Who cries Revenge! Revenge!—accursed be he!
Fit vengeance for the spilt blood of a child
The devil has not yet compiled.
No, let that blood seep through the abyss,
There eat its way in darkness, there undo,
Undo the rotted earth's foundations!

33. BEGINNING OF SELF-DEFENSE

SHNEUR ZALMAN SHAZAR

Shneur Zalman Rubaschov (1868–1974), who hebraized his name to Shazar, was born in Russia and became the third president of the State of Israel. He was a scholar, writer, and socialist Zionist. The selection is taken from his memoirs.

Stolpce, city of my childhood! Pride of my youth! I still do not believe that you were led like sheep to slaughter. For did I not know your young heroes, reared on the banks of the Niemen and skilled in border fights? I remember your brave butchers and coachmen, ships' caulkers and river raftsmen, the tough peddlers who used to take on drunken peasants, and the Jews from the nearby villages nurtured on hard labor, and the young men at the markets experienced in handling weapons.

Aye, that handful of partisans who came to Palestine through the seven divisions of hell from the forests of Polesia across the border of Rumania and Italy are witness that also in that calamity, your heroism did not fail you. But I was a witness at the start, when first the spirit of resistance and defense was kindled in you. I remember well when first that powerful igniting word "self-defense" fell among your young people, when the self-defense movement had barely begun to be organized.

Self-defense itself was older than its formal organization. The town, surrounded by villages, lived by trade and handiwork. Sunday was market day and a day of misfortunes. On market days a crowd used to collect around the town inn and in front of the homes of Jonah and Mordecai Isaac, the vintners, scaring everyone. Jonah and Mordecai, devout and learned Jews, used to make raisin wine for *kiddush* and *havdala* for the townsfolk on Fridays, and on Sundays they sold vodka to the village peasants. Ever since liquor had become a government monopoly, the peasants used to line up every Sunday afternoon in the market place in front of the liquor store. There they left all the profit from the produce which they had brought to town. With extraordinary virtuosity, they used to pop the corks out of the bottles and swill one flask of vodka after another. That always boded danger. When Easter approached or Christmas Eve, when the town priest had duly inflamed the peasants' fantasy, after the long procession wound around town and passed the gates of the liquor store, the stirred-up peasants released their piety and their hostility in government liquor. Panic seized the Jewish households. Schoolboys used to tell stories that in such days Reuvele the coachman used to keep an iron rod in the leg of his boots—for any trouble that might come.

Reuvele the coachman was the eldest son of Moyshke the coachman.

Moyshke in his younger days used to drive his coach as far as Smolensk and Nizhny-Novgorod, carrying the town's merchants to the trade fairs. I knew him only when he was getting on in years. Once a year he drove us, my mother and the children, to see the doctor in a village five hours' drive from Stolpce. En route he kept reciting Psalms, in a sweet voice and a marvelous intonation, until in the course of the trip, while sitting on his coachbox, he recited from memory all the Psalms, and between one book of Psalms and the next he instructed me in how to write a most flowery Hebrew letter. Reuvele, his eldest son, was the first of the town's defenders. He would never take orders from an organization, mocking the help he could get from friends, certain that by himself he could drive off all the enemies of the whole town. At first sight, one could see nothing at all valorous in him. He was thin, not tall, but he was fearless, and all the villages spread the fame of his heroism. Once, it was told, seven peasants attacked him, one alone. He clobbered them all, laid them out cold, and came running back to town with a knife in his belly. Without organizations and without a special election, the town knew Reuvele was its protector.

The other strong man was Shmuel Tunik. In appearance he was just the opposite of Reuvele. Head and shoulders, he towered over Jews and Gentiles in town. He was a giant and a handsome man too. The ends of his thick blond mustache were pointed like spears. When he strode at the head of a unit of firefighters, whose commandant he was, with his copper helmet and the brass trumpet at his lips, the ground beneath him trembled. I do not recall that he really ever fought with a Gentile, but every drunken peasant feared even his glance. He had only to stroll around the market grounds to assure the townsfolk no harm would come to them.

Both these defenders had sufficed so long as times were normal. But then came the days of the first revolution, and the Black Hundreds were organized. Came the massacre at Kishenev, and the pogroms in Homel, and the dark clouds lowered also over the area of Stolpce. Since January 9, 1905, the wave of agitation against the Jews had not subsided. The newspapers were filled with news about pogroms. Suspicious characters turned up in town, neither buying nor selling, but loitering among the peasants and stirring them up. The peasants came out of church all keyed up. Decent, friendly peasants told us that agitators came to the villages and that the day and even the hour had been set. . . . In town, a clandestine labor movement had already come into being. The Bund had been in existence for some years. In 1905, a Labor Zionist group was organized, attached to the Minsk region. At one Zionist meeting, a speaker described the events of Troyanov. A group of young people had set out from Chudnov to bring help to the endangered Jews of Zhitomir. They passed the town of Troyanov, but its Jewish inhabitants were afraid to shelter the young people. As a result, seven were murdered on the road. A writ of excommunication was issued against the Jews of Troyanov. We, in our youthful rage, recited the age-old verse:

"Curse ye Meroz," said the angel of the Lord,
"Curse ye bitterly the inhabitants thereof,
Because they came not to the help of the Lord,
To the help of the Lord against the mighty."

The thought ripened among the Labor Zionists that we too ought to form a self-defense unit at Stolpce. To buy arms we needed money, and we had to approach the townspeople. We decided to hold a meeting in the synagogue. Organization of the meeting was put in the hands of Pinye Kushnir, a baker's son and a nephew of the Cherikover rabbi, one of the first supporters of the Mizrachi whom I had heard speak out in town on behalf of Zionism. I was assigned to make the speech in the synagogue. The panic that seized me before speaking could not be stilled—I was only a boy, a month in the party; it was my first political speech at a public meeting. The meeting was held in the old prayer house after evening services. Pinye ascended the pulpit, rapped the lectern, and announced that no one had better try to leave. Besides bolting the door, two of our comrades guarded the exit.

Surrounded by my "bodyguards," I went up to the pulpit and began to speak. I started out with some Talmudic quotations, proceeded to call on the young people to enroll in the self-defense group, and urged the well-to-do townspeople to provide us with funds. Then Pinye began to announce the donations.

A week later we received instructions from the regional party committee in Minsk that our branch was to organize the self-defense in the nearby villages. On this assignment Pinye and I visited Swierzna, Horodziej, Baranowicze, Musz, Lachowicze. It was our first propaganda tour. We initially approached the local Labor Zionists, but the assembly was always public, held in the synagogue. As for the self-defense organization, that was always nonpartisan; whenever possible we saw to it that a local leader, Zionist or Bundist, also addressed the meeting. Soon the police found out about our trips and the solid citizens became afraid to go to the synagogue. Even Pinye's threats and bolting the door did not always help. There were even such heroic types who, out of fear for the illegal meeting, leaped out of the window and fled. Yet when we came later to their homes, they received us well. I remember especially the assistance of a Zionist in Lachowicze, a son-in-law of one of the town's rich men. Though he refused to join us on the pulpit, he accompanied us to the homes of the rich, spoke sharply to the well-to-do, and got decent contributions from them. We used to assemble the young people separately, in the women's gallery of the synagogue. Pinye used to divide the volunteers into units of tens and appoint their commandants.

When we returned to Stolpce, we found it engulfed in fear. We decided to call a meeting in the old synagogue on the Great Sabbath, following the rabbi's sermon. Speaking with me was the leader of the Bund in Stolpce, once my fellow pupil in heder. Then we had a surprise: After we had both finished speaking, my uncle, Joel Ginzberg, warden of the burial society, ascended the pulpit. I was afraid he would castigate us for having dared to have invaded the synagogue, especially on the Great Sabbath. But his words astonished us:

"I am no preacher, neither am I a preacher's son. I have nothing to do with any of these parties. But this time the boys are right. It is God's commandment to help with money and with muscle, for the situation is bitter indeed."

After the Sabbath, the most distinguished townspeople brought my uncle their contributions. The next morning Pinye went to Minsk to get spitters, as we called revolvers. At our next meeting, held late at night in the hasidic prayer house, our organization counted about a hundred registered and armed members.

Twice during that period we used our organized strength. The first time, we were alerted to come to the aid of the nearby town Swierzna, across the Niemen. A town smaller than ours, it was renowned for its Jews who leased the orchards from the landowners. They used to guard the fruit trees all week until the fruit ripened; then they sold the apples and pears at the nearby markets. No prayer-house types, these Jews had been brought up in the outdoors, always had business with tough peasants, and knew the craft of self-defense. But at that time, the pogrom panic had seized everyone and fear confused even the bravest. Early in the morning we heard the news that "it" had begun in Swierzna. Friendly peasants came to Stolpce to tell us that their young people had set out to loot and terrorize Swierzna.

We assembled our self-defense unit and set out to aid Swierzna. It just happened to be the thaw, when the Niemen was rising. Normally, the trip from Stolpce to Swierzna took twenty minutes, but with the Niemen overflowing its banks we had to go roundabout and cross swampy streams. The wagon in which we had our weapons—iron rods with round lead ends and iron prongs—could not traverse the marshes. We had to haul the weapons ourselves, crawling over the mud. That procession took us, defenders of Stolpce, six hours. When we arrived at Swierzna toward evening, fatigued and battered, but ready to fight, we found a ghost town. All the shops were barricaded, the streets silent and empty; one could not see a living soul in the houses. We learned that the Jews, frightened at the oncoming peasants, had locked homes and stores and hid in the cellars. We went from cellar to cellar, with our commandant Pinye leading, informing the Jews in hiding that the danger was over, their defenders had arrived. After having spent a whole day in terror in dark cellars, they regarded us as saviors from heaven. I remember how the young rabbi of the town, out of deep gratitude, kissed Pinye on the forehead. The women brought jugs of sour milk out of the cellars and briny pickles to refresh us. Then we learned that the thaw and the perilous roads that had not deterred the Stolpce defenders had dissolved the determination of the peasant pogromists. They changed their minds en route and returned home empty handed.

Some days later we heard that "it" was coming to Stolpce itself the following Sunday. This time we were ready. We knew that agitators had come from afar. We saw peasant women coming into town with empty wagons, and we knew they were coming to loot and wanted to be able to take the stolen goods home. In the morning, our comrades were on the street ready with iron rods, lead bars, and whips with rounded pieces of lead at their tips. The commandants of the units of ten, armed with revolvers, stationed themselves at many points in the marketplace. At noon, when the peasants poured out of the white church, rabid and worked up, ready to assault the Jews, one of the outside agitators gave the signal and started to lead the peasants to break into the shops. Then all at once our unit commanders fired their revolvers—in the air, not hurting anyone. The shots came from all sides of the marketplace, creating panic and confusion among the crowd of attackers. The horses broke wild, the peasant women began screaming as though they were being slaughtered. One wagon collided with another. With what seemed their last gasp, the peasants ran in fear from the Jews firing all over the marketplace. It took only a few minutes before the marketplace was emptied of the aroused pogromists.

No, Stolpce, pride of my youth, I cannot believe that you were led like sheep to slaughter.

34. SHAME AND INDIGNATION

MAXIM GORKY

Maxim Gorky (1868–1936), famous Russian author of novels and dramas, was an opponent of the tsarist government and the capitalist system. Under the Soviet government he was engaged in many cultural activities. The following letter was written by Gorky to the Kishineff Relief Committee after the pogrom in 1903.

"Russia has been disgraced more and more frequently of recent years by dark deeds, but the most disgraceful of all is the horrible Jewish massacre at Kishineff, which has awakened our horror, shame, and indignation. People who regard themselves as Christians, who claim to believe in God's mercy and sympathy, these people, on the day consecrated to the resurrection of their God from the dead, occupy the time in murdering children and aged people, ravishing women, and martyring the men of the race that gave them Christ.

The Blame for the Crime

"Who bears the blame of this base crime, which will remain on us like a bloody blot for ages? We shall be unable to wash this blot from the sad history of our dark country. It would be unjust and too simple to condemn the mob. The latter was merely the hand which was guided by a corrupt conscience, driving it to murder and robbery. For it is well known that the mob at Kishineff was led by men of cultured society. But cultivated society in Russia is really much worse than the people, who are goaded by their sad life and blinded and enthralled by artificial darkness created around them.

The Cultured Classes

"The cultivated classes are a crowd of cowardly slaves, without feeling of personal dignity, ready to accept every lie to save their ease and comfort; a weak and lawless element almost without conscience and without shame, in spite of its elegant exterior. Cultivated society is not less guilty of the disgraceful and horrible deeds committed in Kishineff than the actual murderers and ravishers. Its members' guilt consists in the fact that not merely did they not protect the victims, but that they rejoiced over the murders; it consists chiefly in committing themselves for long years to be corrupted by man-haters and persons who have long enjoyed the disgusting glory of being the lackeys of power and the glorifiers of lies, like the editor of *Bessarabetz* of Kishineff and other publicists. These are the real authors of the disgraceful and awful crime of Kishineff. To all the shameful names hitherto given to these repulsive men must be added another, and the well-deserved one, of 'instigators of pillage and murder.' These hypocrites, with the name of God on their lips, who preach in Russian society hatred of the Jews, Armenians, and Finns, to-day heap base and cowardly calumnies upon the corpses of those killed through their influence, and they shamelessly continue their hateful work of poisoning the mind and feeling of the weak-willed Russian society.

"Shame upon their wicked heads! May the fire of conscience consume their decayed hearts, covetous only of lackey-like honours and slavishly obsequious to power!

Duty to Help the Jews

"It is now the duty of Russian society that is not yet wholly ruined by these bandits, to prove that it is not identified with these instigators of pillage and murder. Russian society must clear its conscience of part of the shame and disgrace by helping the orphaned and desolated Jews and assisting these members of the race which has given to the world many really great men and which still continues to produce teachers of truth and beauty in spite of its oppressed condition in the world.

"Come, therefore, all who do not want themselves to be regarded as the lackeys of the lackeys, and who still retain their self-respect; come and help the Jews!"

35. PORTRAIT OF A "SHTETL" IN RUSSIA

ABRAHAM AIN

Abraham Ain (1888–1959) was a communal leader in Eastern Europe. The translation is by Shlomo Noble.

I. GENERAL ASPECTS

Population and Appearance

Swislocz (Yiddish name: *Sislevich*) was considered one of the larger towns (*shtetl*) in the district of Grodno. According to the census of 1847, there were 997 Jews in Swislocz. Fifty years later, the town numbered 3,099 persons, of whom 2,086 were Jews. In the beginning of the present century the population again increased substantially. A leather industry of considerable size sprang up and a railway was built, linking the town with the industrial centers of Western Russia. Jews and non-Jews from surrounding villages flocked to the town. In 1906 it had some 600 families, of whom 400 were Jewish.

The town consisted of a market, five large and a dozen small streets and alleys, and a synagogue yard. The market covered an area of about two city blocks in the center of the town. It housed all the town's business places. All larger streets, which extended on the average to three or four city blocks, began in the market and terminated in the suburbs. These streets were known after the towns to which they led. Thus the Grodno Street led to the Grodno highway. Two of the larger streets, the market, and the synagogue yard were inhabited by Jews. The other large and most of the small streets were inhabited by both Jews and non-Jews. The non-Jews consisted of White Russians, Poles, a score of Russian civil servants and a dozen or so Moslem Tartars. . . .

Three of the large streets had cobblestone pavement; the other streets and the market were unpaved. On rainy days the mud was ankle-deep and crossing the market was no pleasant undertaking. In 1904, the chief of police ordered every property owner in the market to pave the street fronting his property to a depth of twelve feet. This was the sidewalk of the market. . . .

. . . Conflagrations were no rare events in the towns. In the course of the nineteenth century the town burned down to the ground twice. In 1910 half of the town was destroyed by fire again. Hence, the town was continually being rebuilt anew and its external aspect improved. Many of the houses were substantial two-story brick structures, adorned with balconies. Some of the newer houses had hardwood floors and papered walls. . . .

How Old Was the Town?

There were no records to indicate the age of the town, or the age of its Jewish community. The Holy Burial Association (*Khevre Kadishe*) formerly had a *pinkes*, a minute-book, but it was destroyed in one of the periodical fires, and no other source for the history of the Jews in town was left.

The Jewish cemetery was divided into a new and an old burial ground. On the old cemetery, near the entrance, the tombstones had collapsed, so that it was difficult to tell that the place had once been a burial ground. Farther down, the tombstones protruded half-way from the ground, but the inscriptions on them were obliterated. On the new cemetery the graves and tombstones were in better condition. But even the new cemetery had probably been used for centuries, for in the first World War it was filled up and ground was broken for another cemetery.

In 1903, when a railway was being built through the town, a large number of human skeletons was unearthed. These skeletons were laid out in rows, close to one another, at a depth of about three feet. There was no clue for closer identification of the skeletons, nor was there any real interest in them. Apparently, the town had a long history, which was completely obliterated from the memory of the inhabitants.

The Vicinity

The immediate surroundings of the town were dotted with villages. Their inhabitants, chiefly White Russians, were, in the main, poor peasants who had to supplement their meager incomes by doing chores in town or laboring in the forests. Some of them worked in the leather factories in town; others were engaged in hauling timber from the forests to the railway depot. In the villages close to the forest skillful peasants carved all sorts of articles out of wood: pails, kneading troughs, felloes, yokes, and shingles. These articles they brought to town for sale, and with the money thus realized they purchased not only farm implements, but occasionally also flour and barley, for some peasants had so little land that they could not raise enough food for their families. There were also in the vicinity several large and small estates that belonged to Polish landlords.

Nearly every village and estate had a Jewish family, engaged as millers or lessees. On the eve of the first World War there were practically no more Jewish millers in the villages, for two Jews, former millers in a village, by installing two motor mills in town rendered the village miller superfluous.

Administrative Authorities

Administratively and juridically the town was linked with Wolkowysk, the county seat, which was at a distance of some twenty-eight versts. Economically, however, the town was closely bound up with Bialystok, some seventy versts away. In 1906, the railway through our town was completed, and a closer contact was established with Wolkowysk and other nearby towns.

To maintain order the town had a chief of police and a constable (uryadnik). In 1905 this force was augmented by eight policemen. The chief of police (stanovoy pristav) was the ruler of the town; his word was law. Frequently, this official would tyrannize over the town, but a way was always found to placate him. As a rule, he was not averse to a little gift. . . . In 1903, a new chief of police came to our town. Forthwith he launched a vigorous campaign against "subversive" elements, particularly among the young people. His zeal knew no bounds. Once, encountering on the outskirts of the town two young men reading a book, he had them arrested and questioned for two weeks. Subsequently, they were released. Another time, he raided a meeting of the clandestine Jewish Labor Organization "Bund" in the forest and arrested ten young men and three girls. The arrested maintained that their gathering was in the nature of a harmless outing and as no forbidden literature was found on them, they were released. The young bloods of the town decided to teach the chief of police a lesson. On a dark night they set fire to the woodshed of a school on the outskirts of the town. The regulations called for the chief of police to be present at a fire. A group of young people lay in wait for him and gave him a thrashing. This experience considerably diminished his zeal for discovering conspiracies. The constable, too, who began to peer into closed shutters, was given a beating, while in a somewhat intoxicated state.

The town had, moreover, a justice of the peace (zemski nachalnik), who adjudicated minor litigations of the rural population, and three excisemen, who supervised the manufacture and sale of alcoholic beverages.

Controversies in Town

The town, consisting exclusively of *misnagdim* (opponents of Hasidism), had a Synagogue and three Houses of Study, in which services were conducted three times a day. The Houses of Study possessed rich collections of books, and at dusk, between the *minkhe* (late afternoon) and the *mayriv* (evening) services, numerous groups could be seen busily pursuing their studies of the Scriptures, the Talmud, or some ethical text. The untutored had a teacher who instructed them in the weekly portion of the Bible on Friday evenings and Saturdays. The older folks were pious but tolerant toward the young generation, which was largely heterodox in its religious views. The young people, in turn, refrained from publicly offending the religious sensibilities of the orthodox.

On one occasion, however, a sharp conflict broke out between the young and the old generations. An itinerant preacher came to town. He was a man of eloquence and power and opposed to the "progressives," whom he attacked in his sermons. These sermons led to strained relations between some of the parents and their children. Once several young people entered the House of Study and interrupted one of the preacher's customary diatribes against them with catcalls. Some of the older people rose to the defense of the preacher and a fight ensued. During the altercation a butcher called out that the young people were justified in deriding the preacher because he was sowing discord in the community. The older folks avenged the slight to the preacher by prohibiting the butcher from selling kosher meat. The prohibition would have ruined the butcher, had not the Jewish Labor Organization or "Bund" sent an ultimatum to the trustees of the Houses of Study to repeal the prohibition, or it would adopt strong measures. The trustees were frightened and complied with the request. . . .

The Community Council

The Community Council administered all religious and community affairs. It gave financial aid to the various religious and charitable associations, paid the salaries of the rabbi and other functionaries, and maintained the ritual bathhouse (*mikve*) and the poorhouse (*hekdesh*). The budget for these activities came from the tax on kosher meat known in our parts as *korobke*. The *korobke* was usually leased by one person, or by several partners, called the tax lessees. The *shokhtim* (ritual slaughterers) could not slaughter an animal or a fowl without a permit from the tax lessee. The permit for a chicken cost three kopeks; it was somewhat higher for a duck, goose, and turkey. The permit for a calf was sixty kopeks. For slaughtering a cow or an ox there was a certain tax, and an additional tax was levied on the meat, exclusive of the lungs, liver, head, and legs. To guard against the importation of meat from nearby towns, the rabbis prohibited the sale and consumption of such meat. In cases where this prohibition proved ineffective, recourse was had to the police.

Some twenty or twenty-five prominent members in the community, who were the trustees of the Houses of Study and the various associations, constituted the Community Council and ruled the community. They were the choosers and the chosen. The elections took place in the following way. By order of the rabbi a meeting was called, to which the Houses of Study sent delegates. The delegates were chosen in this manner. The trustee of the House of Study told the sexton to call out the name of the delegate. The sexton called out: "Rabbi Shmuel, son of Rabbi Mendel, first delegate! Will anybody second the motion?" The prominent members chorused, "Second." The sexton then called out: "Rabbi Mendel, son of Shmuel, second delegate! Will anybody second the motion?" The same members responded again, "Second." And so on, till the required number of delegates were "elected." The delegates met and elected the Community Council or passed upon matters of policy under discussion. Popular dissatisfaction with their decisions did not affect them.

Thus the Community Council ruled the town up to the first World War. During the German occupation of the town, the tax on meat was abolished. After the war, the Community Council was elected in a more democratic manner.

Associations

The Holy Burial Association (*Khevre Kadishe*) played a leading role among communal institutions in town. Its membership consisted of old and pious Jews. Membership in the Holy Burial Association was restricted. Admission took place in one of the following ways: first, members could enroll their children or grandchildren as minors and upon attaining maturity they became full-fledged members; or, second, an adult wishing to be admitted to the association had to serve for a year as a sexton, whose duties were the calling of the membership to meetings and attendance at funerals. The association purchased the site for the cemetery and took care of the surrounding moat (the cemetery had no fence). It obtained the necessary funds from the families of the deceased, in accordance with their financial abilities. To the credit of the association be it said that it never wronged these families. It was fair and reasonable in its demands and always conciliatory in its dealings.

The most popular of the organizations in town was the Nursing Association (*Khevra Line*). The function of this association was to provide nursing service for cases of prolonged illness. Constant attendance on the patient, in these instances, would leave the other members of the family exhausted, and this service would give them an opportunity for a brief rest.

The association sent two members—to a male, two men, and to a female, one man and one woman—to attend the patient from ten o'clock in the evening to seven o'clock in the morning. The association had its medical supply department that lent thermometers, icebags, heating pads, and similar sick-room needs to poor patients. The very poor were also supplied with medicine and nourishing food. The association obtained its funds from weekly dues paid by practically every adult in town, from special pledges in the synagogue, from the collection on the eve of the Day of Atonement, and from grants of the Community Council.

• Two types of visitors came to town frequently: poor Jews who went begging from door to door and itinerant preachers. The former were lodged in the poorhouse and the latter in a specially provided guest house (hakhnoses orkhim), consisting of a large room with several beds in it. The sexton would arrange for their meals in some household. The more distinguished preachers and the collectors for charitable organizations (meshulokhim) usually stayed at the inn.

The small merchants were always short of money and in need of a loan. Most of them had to resort to a private lender who charged usurious rates. For a loan of twenty-five rubles for a period of a half-year he charged four rubles interest, which he deducted initially. Repayments had to be made from the first week, at the rate of one ruble a week. There was in a town a traditional loan association, Gmiles Khasodim, granting loans up to twenty-five rubles without interest. But many people refused to apply to the Gmiles Khasodim, for they regarded such a loan as a form of charity.

In 1908–1909, a cooperative savings and loan association was established with the aid of the Jewish Colonization Association in St. Petersburg. The members of the association could borrow money at the rate of 8%. The state bank gave the association a loan of several thousand rubles. People had confidence in the association and instead of depositing their savings in the savings bank, they deposited them in the association, which paid 6% interest. Even the non-Jewish population did business with the association. In time the private lender with his usurious rates was banished from the scene.

Sanitary and Hygienic Conditions

Sanitary conditions in town were far from satisfactory. Some inhabitants had to attend to their needs in the open. The wells were not covered, and dust and dirt would find their way into them. Before the war some wells were covered, and water was obtained by means of a pump.

The Jewish community had a bathhouse, too small for the needs of the population. On Fridays it was badly overcrowded, particularly in the winter. In the summer conditions in the bathhouse were better, since a number of people bathed in the river. All types of disease were prevalent in town, though they rarely attained epidemic proportions. Only during the German occupation in the first World War and immediately thereafter, epidemics of dysentery and typhus raged in town.

The economic situation of the town was fair; the people were well-fed and well-dressed. As a rule, they had adequate medical attention. The town had a municipal hospital, with one physician, one assistant (*felcher*), and a midwife. Hospital service was free to all, and the non-Jewish population made use of it. The Jews, as a rule, avoided the hospital, although they occasionally used the services of the physician and the assistant in the capacity of private patients. In addition there were two physicians (Poles, who had estates in the vicinity), an assistant (a Jew), and two Jewish midwives in private practice. The physicians enjoyed an excellent reputation in the entire district. One of them, a surgeon and gynecologist, attracted patients from points hundreds of miles away.

Education

At the age of five, a boy was sent to a school (*kheyder*) where he was taught the alphabet and reading. In the *kheyder* the boy usually spent a year or a year and a half, and was then promoted to a higher grade, where he took up the study of the Pentateuch and the rest of the Bible. The next step in his education was the study of the Talmud. Some teachers (*melamdim*) also instructed their pupils in writing and in the elements of arithmetic. Thus, at the age of ten, a Jewish boy knew a little of the Bible, could write Yiddish, had a smattering of elementary arithmetic, and was studying the Talmud.

For the study of Russian there was a special teacher. Some boys studied in *kheyder* only part of the time and devoted several hours daily to the study of Russian, arithmetic, and writing.

Ordinarily the *kheyder* was in the home of the teacher. Study hours, except for beginners, were from nine in the morning to nine in the evening, with an hour for lunch.

For children whose parents could not afford the fee, there was a Talmud Torah, in which the fee was very low or tuition was altogether free. The Talmud Torah had three classes. In the first class instruction was given in reading, the Pentateuch, and the rest of the Bible; in the second class, in Bible, Talmud, and in writing Yiddish and Russian; in the third class, in Talmud, writing Yiddish and Russian, and in arithmetic. Instruction in the secular studies was given by two teachers who came for that purpose to the Talmud Torah for two hours daily, except Friday and Saturday. One teacher taught Yiddish writing and arithmetic and the other, Russian.

The years between twelve and fourteen were years of decision for the boys. Most of them entered at that age the leather factories, or were apprenticed to artisans. A small number of ambitious and promising boys left for the Yeshivas. Boys from the wealthier homes helped their parents in their factories or stores and simultaneously continued their education with a private tutor.

As for girls, their education was delayed to the age of seven or eight. It began with instruction in reading Hebrew and Yiddish, after which came instruction in writing Yiddish and Russian, and in the elements of arithmetic. At the age of thirteen or fourteen girls were usually apprenticed to seamstresses. The poorest became domestics. Some girls worked as saleswomen in their parents' stores part of the time and continued their education.

At the turn of the century a general public school, of four grades, and a modern Hebrew school were opened in town. These schools gave the foundation of a systematic education to a number of Jewish children. Moreover, some of the well-to-do parents began sending their children to secondary schools in the larger cities. At the time of the first World War, under German occupation, a secular Yiddish school was opened. After the war the old-fashioned type of kheyder became practically extinct. It was replaced by a net of Yiddish and Hebrew schools, which existed till the second World War.

Educational facilities for the non-Jewish population were provided by the Russian government. It maintained two elementary schools, one for boys and one for girls, and a seminary for the training of teachers for the elementary schools in the villages. The seminary had some 300 students. These students came from the entire district of Grodno and were provided with board and lodging by the school. Together with the faculty and staff the seminary population comprised some 350 people, who were a considerable economic factor in town.

Political Parties

The first political party in our town was the Zionist organization. On a winter eve, some time in 1898 or 1899, the Jews were summoned to the House of Study, where an out-of-town preacher and some local men addressed them and Hebrew songs were sung. As far as I recall, the speakers appealed to the audience to become members in the Zionist organization, and the response was good. The work of the organization consisted mainly in collecting money for the Jewish National Fund. Before every Zionist congress there was some activity in town in connection with the election of delegates. The Zionist organization also opened and maintained the Hebrew school in town.

From 1905 to 1907 the town had an organization of Zionist Socialists, known by the abbreviated Russianized name of S.S. The leadership of the group consisted of some temporary residents: a teacher and several workmen. Upon their departure, the group dissolved. The town also had an anarchist club, with a leader who also came from out of town. Upon his departure, the club closed its doors.

The Jewish Labor Organization or "Bund" had its beginnings in our town about 1900. By 1905 it had grown into a powerful organization. Its membership was drawn from all classes of the Jewish population. The organization conducted strikes in the leather factories and in the shops. It helped elect to the first Duma a "Bund" representative, who received some 80% of the Jewish votes cast in our town. But the years 1907 and 1908, the period of political reaction in Russia, saw a decline of the organization in our town. Some active members left town; others became disillusioned and gave up political activity. In 1909, the group was reorganized, concentrating mainly on cultural activities: symposia, lectures, discussions.

The heroic period in the history of the "Bund" in Swislocz was the year 1905. In the fall of that year a peculiar tension was felt in town. People awaited eagerly the arrival of the mail to obtain the latest news. Rumors of pogroms spread and there was talk of organizing a Jewish self-defense. Money was needed for the procurement of arms; and the following way of obtaining the required sum was decided upon, although the organization was in principle opposed to confiscation.

The town had two government stores for the sale of liquor. It was decided to stage an attack on one of these and to take its money. Once a month there was a fair in town, to which peasants and merchants from the neighboring villages and towns would come. During the fair the government stores took in considerable sums of money. The day of the fair was, therefore, deemed ideal for such an enterprise. Some time in October, 1905, in the evening following the day of the fair, as soon as the front door was closed, several of the most active members of the organization entered the store and, intimidating the salesgirls, departed with the money. Although the street was full of people and police (the chief of police summoned for the fair the police forces of the neighboring towns), no one noticed what had happened. When the salesgirls raised an alarm that they had been held up, no one believed them. Rumor had it that they embezzled the money and that the story of the burglary was an invention. It was only after the "Bund" published a proclamation taking responsibility for the act that suspicion of the salesgirls was allayed.

The attack was well organized, save for one serious slip. The participants entered the store undisguised, and the salesgirls identified two of them. One fled abroad; the other was arrested, and faced a long term

at hard labor. After several months' imprisonment, he was freed on bail of
five hundred rubles and likewise fled abroad. With the aid of the chief of
police a false death certificate of the arrested was secured. The certificate
was submitted to the district attorney and he released the bail. In the final
analysis, the affair cost considerably more than it brought in.

Theatre

Formerly, Joseph and Esther plays were given in Yiddish during the Purim
season. The actors, who were young men, took the parts of both men and
women. Some time in 1905 or 1906 the first Yiddish play was given in
which women, too, acted. This play was sponsored by the "Bund"; it was
followed by several Yiddish plays given by the Zionist Socialist group.

Great difficulties were involved in these dramatic presentations, mainly
in securing the requisite permission, which the chief of police was very
reluctant to grant. Another difficulty was finding a suitable place. For a
time a large barn was used, later on, a vacant factory loft. Under the
German occupation and thereafter, dramatic presentations in Yiddish
were given more frequently, with the dramas of Jacob Gordin enjoying
great popularity.

Folkways

At the ceremony announcing the engagement of a couple to be married,
plates were broken. After the engagement the bride and groom were
invited to the houses of their future in-laws for a holiday or a weekend. On
such occasions relatives and friends would send wine to the house
entertaining the guest, with a greeting, "Welcome to your guest!" (*Mit lib
aykh ayer gast.*)

Wedding festivities began on the Saturday night prior to the wedding.
The bride's girl friends would gather in her house for dancing and
merrymaking. This gathering was called the prelude (*forshpil*). At dusk,
the wedding proper commenced with a reception for the bridegroom, in
which, as a rule, the older people participated, and with the ceremony of
"seating" the bride (*bazetsn*), at which the young folks danced. After the
reception, the bridegroom was led to the house in which the bride was
"seated," where he performed the ceremony of veiling the bride.

The wedding ceremony was usually performed in the synagogue
courtyard. The bride and groom were led to the ceremony to the
accompaniment of music. First, the musicians led the bridegroom under
the canopy and afterwards the bride was brought. After the bridegroom
pronounced the marriage formula and the appropriate benedictions were
recited, the young couple were taken back to the house where the bride

was "seated." At the entrance of the house the couple were met by someone holding a tray with wine and cake. Since both bride and groom fasted on their wedding day, they were taken into a separate room, where they were given a light repast.

After the ceremony the older folks sat down to the wedding supper. Wedding gifts were announced by the sexton or the jester (badkhn) in the traditional formula: "A gift from the bride's [or groom's] relative!" When the elders finished their meal, the young folks had theirs and afterwards continued dancing.

On the following morning, the bridegroom served brandy and cake. On the Sabbath following the wedding, the traditional "seven benedictions" were pronounced three times: Friday night, Saturday morning, and Saturday afternoon. Saturday morning the bridegroom was led by a group of men to the synagogue, with the bride similarly led by a group of women. A bride and a lying-in woman were not permitted to be alone in the house or on the street. After the bride had been led to the synagogue and the lying-in woman had gone to religious services, the restriction was lifted. On the walls of the room in which there was a lying-in woman, talismans, known as shir hamaylesn, after their opening words, were hung, containing psalm 121 and a number of incantations.

At the birth of a child, for the first seven days of confinement, the beginners in kheyder would come at sunset to the house of the lying-in woman and recite in unison several passages from the Bible, for which they were rewarded with sweets. If the newborn infant was a boy, a celebration called the sholem zokher was held on the Friday night following his birth, at which the guests were served boiled peas and broad beans. Some considered it particularly beneficial to have the child circumcised in the House of Study.

In case of death, the Khevre Kadishe was notified, and its representatives came and "lifted" the deceased, that is, strewed a little straw on the floor and placed him with his feet at the door. The grave digger was ordered to bring the coffin and dig the grave. Female members of the Khevre Kadishe sewed the shrouds. The sexton was sent to call out through the town, "mes mitsve!" implying that attendance at the funeral was requested. While these preparations were going on, a group of men would recite psalms in the house of the deceased. The Khevre Kadishe then washed the body, dressed it in a shroud, placed it in the coffin, covered it with a black cover, and carried it to the cemetery. One of the members of the Khevre Kadishe descended into the grave and put away the body, placed potsherds over the eyelids, two forked twigs in the hands, and boards over the body.

On the eve of Sabbath or holidays the people were summoned to the synagogue by the sexton. His summons served to indicate to the women that it was time to kindle the Sabbath candles. As soon as his powerful baritone voice was heard thundering. "To the synagogue!" the trades-women quickly closed their shops and rushed home to usher in the Sabbath. The people were also summoned to the synagogue when a preacher came to deliver a discourse. . . .

Daily Fare

Like every other town, Swislocz, too, had a nickname: *sislevicher krupnik*. The town fully deserved that nickname. For there was not a day, except the Sabbath and the holidays, when *krupnik* was not on the menu of every Jewish home in town. What is *krupnik*? It is a thick soup of barley or groats mixed with potatoes. In the winter time, when meat was cheap, a slice of lamb or veal was added to the mixture. In the summer time, when meat was expensive, only the wealthy could afford to season their *krupnik* with meat. Most people had to be content with a little beef fat in their *krupnik*, to which onions were added as a preservative.

For the Friday breakfast the *krupnik* was prepared differently, as a rule with stuffed gut. It was eaten with fresh rolls, which nearly all Jewish women baked on Friday. Friday was also graced with potato pudding. Advantage was taken of the fact that the oven was kindled for the baking of Sabbath bread (*khale*). Some families had potato pudding twice on Friday.

Another popular dish was *lekshlekh bulve*, peeled potatoes, thinly sliced and boiled with meat. The dish was prepared in the morning, placed in the oven, and eaten for lunch or for supper. Likewise popular were potatoes boiled in their jackets (*sholekhts bulve*). The wealthy ate the potatoes with herring; the rest, with herring sauce. On the whole, potatoes were a staple in the diet of our district, both among Jews and non-Jews. It was not without a measure of justification that the district of Grodno was known in Russia as "the Grodno potato."

II. ECONOMIC ASPECTS

Occupationally, the Jews of the town were divided, in the main, into three categories: leather manufacturers and workers, merchants, and artisans.

The Leather Industry

Some 70% of the Jewish population were directly or indirectly connected with the leather industry. Its beginnings date from the 1870's, when Pinkhes Bereznitski opened a factory, in charge of a German master craftsman. Thereafter a number of other Jewish employers established factories. From 1900 to the German occupation (1915), the leather industry was the decisive factor in the general economic life of the town. At the beginning of this century the town numbered eight leather factories employing between forty and fifty workers each, and a dozen or so smaller shops employing from six to twelve workers.

The factories were divided into wet tanneries and dry shops. They produced leather from horse hides, which was used in the making of leggings and uppers for shoes and boots. The process of converting a raw hide into leather took about three months. The hide was taken into the wet tannery, soaked, scoured, and set out ready for the dry factory. These several steps took some ten weeks. In the wet tanneries the work was mainly unskilled, and most of the workingmen were non-Jews. In the dry factories it took another three weeks or so to curry, grain, wash, and otherwise make the leather ready for the use of the cobbler. Here the work was entirely skilled, and most of the workers were Jews. In both the wet tannery and the dry shop the work was done without machinery. It was hard work, the lighter tasks being performed by boys fourteen or fifteen years old. The big employers owned both wet tanneries and dry shops, with capital invested from twenty to forty thousand rubles. The business was conducted in a modern way. The raw hides were purchased in Bialystok with payments by drafts made out to a Bialystok bank. The leather was sent by freight to the leather merchants and the receipts for it were discounted in the Bialystok banks.

Practically all the manufacturers had to resort in part to borrowed capital. Some they obtained in the banks and some from private individuals on promissory notes. The interest private people charged on such loans ranged from eight to ten per cent. Every big employer went once a week to Bialystok to purchase raw hides and to settle his accounts with his banker. The smaller operators had no wet tanneries, but purchased half-finished hides in town or in nearby towns and finished them. The capital involved in such a business was between two and three thousand rubles.

Earnings of factory workers were good. From 1904 to 1908 earnings were the highest. An apprentice earned from two to four rubles a week; a semi-skilled worker, from eight to twelve rubles; skilled workers from sixteen to twenty-five rubles. In 1908 and 1909 earnings declined about one-third. This lower level of earnings obtained up to the first World War. From 1904 to the first World War the working-day was eight hours: from eight o'clock to twelve o'clock and from one o'clock to five o'clock, with the exception of Friday, when the workers quit at three. Jewish workingmen did not work on Saturdays. Since the workers in the leather industry earned good wages, their standard of living was comparatively high. They were well-fed, well-clothed, and contributed freely to many a charitable cause. Frequently they extended loans of small amounts to hardpressed merchants.

Merchants

There were some sixty stores in town, mostly small establishments, whose stock was worth fifty to a hundred rubles. A dozen or so were operated by women, with the husbands engaged in another occupation, such as tailoring or bricklaying. However, most of the merchants drew their entire sustenance from their stores. A few stores whose stock was valued at ten thousand rubles enjoyed the patronage of the landowners, officials, and leather manufacturers.

The big merchants took several business trips in the course of the year to Bialystok or Warsaw, where they purchased some of their stock. Otherwise, they purchased what they needed through a kind of commission merchant who did a two-way business. These commission merchants brought to town such farm products as butter, eggs, and mushrooms and shipped them to Bialystok on hired peasants' carts, usually on a Monday. Simultaneously, they took from the merchants in town orders for their immediate needs. On Tuesday mornings they would leave by train for Bialystok, attend to the orders given them, and sell the farm products that had in the meantime arrived in the city. On Thursday they would dispatch the carts back to town laden with merchandise and then go home the same evening by train. There, usually with the aid of wife and children, they delivered the merchandise to those who ordered it. Several of the more enterprising purchased some wares on their own account and sold them later on to the local business people.

Up to 1898 there were in town a dozen or so tavern keepers. After 1898, when the sale of liquor became a state monopoly, there were no more Jewish taverns. Several Jews obtained a license for a beer-hall (*raspivochno*), where bottled beer, tea, and a light bite were sold. Several Jews were grain dealers, buying from the landowners and the rich peasants. Part of the grain they ground to flour and sold to the bakers, and part they sold to wholesale merchants.

The district around the town abounded in forests; some were state owned and others the property of Polish landowners. (The Bialowiez forest, the property of the Czar, was a distance of fourteen verst from town.) A number of Jews were engaged in the timber business, some on a very large scale. The big timber merchants employed managers to supervise the work; the small merchants, who bought strips of forests (*otdelianka*), usually did all the work themselves. Occasionally, two or three small merchants formed a partnership. The better types of logs were floated down the Narew to the saw mills or to Germany. The others were used for railway ties. Defective logs were cut into fire-wood.

Artisans

There were two types of men's tailors in town: those that catered to the town's trade and those that worked for the peasants in the vicinity. The former were generally proficient in their trade and comparatively well-paid. Frequently, they employed two or three apprentices. The latter were less fortunate. In the summer time, when the peasants were busy in the fields, the tailors depending on them had a slack season. They had to resort to supplementary occupations, such as orchard-keeping and selling fruit. (The latter was usually the task of the wife.) Even in the winter time, when these tailors were fully employed, their earnings were meager. The materials they received from the peasants were home-made rough cloth, or sheepskins for coats. These materials could not be sewn by machine, but for the most part had to be stitched by hand.

The town had several women's tailors. Some employed one or two apprentice seamstresses. These tailors sewed bridal wardrobes, ladies' coats, or worked on orders for the wives of the landowners. They were proficient and well paid. There were, furthermore, a few seamstresses who sewed blouses and skirts for the town women. Other women sewed blouses or jackets (kurtka) for the peasant women. The remuneration for this work was very low: twenty or twenty-five kopeks per blouse. In addition, a few women were engaged in sewing underwear, pillowcases, and the like.

The shoemakers catered almost exclusively to the town population. Because the peasant went barefoot in the summer, a pair of boots lasted many years. The shoemakers made their wares to order. The uppers were cut according to measurement by the cutter (zagotovshchik). The soles, shanks, and heels were purchased in a store. The well-to-do shoemakers would purchase these supplies in larger quantities, and the poor, for each pair of shoes individually. A few wealthy shoemakers purchased leather for both uppers and soles in large quantities. These shoemakers employed several apprentices. During slack times, when orders were few, they kept on working, preparing a stock of shoes, and selling them later on, in the preholiday season. Before the first World War, when two merchants began to import shoes from Warsaw, the local shoemakers saw in this step a threat to their existence. They banded together and declared a boycott on the imported shoes: they refused to repair them. Some of the shoemakers were truly masters of their trade. They made a pair of shoes that vied in attractiveness with any displayed in the stores of the large cities.

The few blacksmiths in town catered, in the main, to the village population. They put rims on wheels, hammered out plows, and sharpened scythes. In the winter time, work fell off. It was practically limited to putting iron runners on sleds or shoeing horses. Some blacksmiths would purchase wheels in the winter time, put rims on them and sell the finished wheels in the summer, when there was great demand for them.

The town had eleven bakers. Two baked black bread, four baked both black and white bread, rolls, and khale for the Sabbath. Five baked cake, cracknels, and pastries.

The town also had a number of Jews without a definite occupation, shifting from one calling to another, or engaging simultaneously in two or more. Such a man would own one or two cows and sell milk, bake bread for sale, fatten geese, and bake matza for Passover. These tasks were carried out by the women. The men would go to the market, buy a measure or two of grain, and resell it to an export merchant. In the winter time, some of them would buy a calf or a lamb, have it slaughtered and sell the skin and the meat, retaining the head and the legs and other minor parts. Others would buy from the peasants skins of foxes and martens, wool, bristles, mushrooms, and berries, and resell them to export merchants.

These Jews without a definite calling were indirectly engaged in agriculture. The Jews who kept cows or horses had manure. The peasants in the vicinity were always short of manure. Those who owned fields near the town would sublet a strip of land for two years to a Jew who had manure. The Jew would hire laborers to strew the manure on the field and plant potatoes. The following year, he would plant barley, oats, or buckwheat. On the third year the field was returned to the peasant in a fertile state, ready for planting rye. The Jew, in turn, would have enough potatoes and barley, or any other cereal planted, for his use, and even a small quantity for sale. The straw, chaff, and very small potatoes served as food for the cattle.

Strikes and Lockouts

Until the turn of the century, working conditions in the leather industry were very bad. The working-day was fourteen or fifteen hours and even more; wages were very low. Gradually, conditions improved. The number of factories increased and some of the smaller establishments expanded. More workers were needed, and wages rose. The higher wages attracted a number of young people from well-to-do homes, who deemed it below their dignity to become artisans. (These usually entered the more specialized branches of the trade, such as trimming and cutting, which were better paid.) Also young people from the vicinity came to work in the leather factories.

In 1900–1901 the "Bund" called the first strike in the leather factories. Members of the organization assembled a large number of workers and together formulated their demands: a raise of wages, and a twelve-hour working-day, from seven to seven, with one and a half hours for breakfast and one hour for lunch. Thereafter, a general assembly of the workers was called, at which these demands were discussed. A strike committee was appointed and a resolution adopted that no one should resume work until all demands were granted by the factory owners. This resolution was confirmed by an oath taken on a pair of phylacteries by each worker.

When the strike committee presented the demands to the factory owners, the latter remained unimpressed. They were inclined to regard the entire affair as a boyish prank. On the following day, however, when not a single worker reported for work, the factory owners began to take a serious view of the strike. They attempted to break the solidarity of the workers by promising higher wages to the older workers. Some of these workers remained unmoved by the tempting offers and in the case of others, the oath on the phylacteries acted as a powerful deterrent. The strike lasted only a short time and ended in complete victory for the workers.

A second strike in the leather factories took place in the summer of 1904. This was during the Russo-Japanese war, when the profits of the factory owners were high and the cost of living had gone up. By then the "Bund" was firmly entrenched in town, conducting systematic organizational and educational activities among the workers. The "Bund" called a general assembly of leather workers in a forest one verst and a half from town. To impress the assembly, a speaker from the neighboring town of Wolkowysk was invited. The speaker presented the demands formulated by the "Bund": 1) a raise of about 35% in wages; 2) a working-day of nine hours, from eight to five; 3) job tenure, no worker to be discharged without sufficient cause; 4) medical aid, the employer to pay the medical bills of the ill employee.

That evening the demands were presented to the factory owners. They were ready to negotiate a reduction in working hours and a raise of wages, but would not consider the other two demands. They were particularly incensed by the demand for job tenure, which to them appeared highly arbitrary. The strike committee refused to negotiate their demands piecemeal, and a strike was called. It lasted three weeks and again ended in a victory for the workers. The newly acquired working conditions were in effect till the end of 1907.

The political reaction, which set in after 1905, began to show its effects in the economic sphere. In November, 1907, the factory owners called a general assembly of their workers and put before them the following conditions: 1) a reduction of 35-40% in wages; 2) discontinuance of medical aid; 3) abolition of tenure. Refusal to accept these conditions, they threatened, would be answered with the closure of all factories. The workers rejected these conditions and countered with a strike. Although the "Bund" was then considerably weakened, it took over the direction of the strike.

In the first weeks of the strike it became evident that the developments had more than a local character. The leather factory owners of the entire district were anxious for a victory of their fellows, in which instance they would follow suit and put before their workers similar conditions. On the other hand, the workers of the entire region were hoping for the success of the strikers in Swislocz. The Tanners Union of the district sent a professional organizer to advise and guide the strikers. He was an energetic young man and an eloquent orator, who inspired confidence. He also traveled throughout the district to collect funds for the strikers. The Tanners Union also enlisted the interests of the union in the district of Vilna and there, too, collections were made for the benefit of the Swislocz strikers.

Most of the strikers did not require aid. Before the strike, they had earned decent wages and had managed to accumulate some savings. The few less skilled workers whose earnings were in need of aid, were given one and a half rubles per week, if single, and three, if married. To keep up the spirit of the strikers, daily meetings were called. Since it was the winter and assemblies in the open were impossible, the strikers met daily, with the exception of Saturday, in the House of Study. The trustees of the House of Study raised no objection, for the majority of the Jewish population was in sympathy with the strikers.

At first there were no difficulties with the police. At the time of the strike the chief of police was a quiet and liberal man who gave assurances that as long as the strike was conducted peacefully, he would not interfere. It was difficult, however, to conduct the strike peacefully, and a clash between the strikers and the police occurred. The strikers had pinned their hope on the factory owners' need for money to cover their outstanding notes. When these notes became due, the factory owners decided to raise cash through the sale of half-finished leather. This transaction led to the clash. In the seventh or eighth week of the strike, the strikers were told that a factory was shipping half-finished leather to other towns. A group of strikers left for the factory to prevent the loading of the leather. At the entrance to the factory yard several policemen denied entry to the strikers. When they attempted to force their way into the yard, the police fired a salvo in the air. The strikers retired and marched to the homes of the factory owners, demanding that the police be withdrawn from the factories. In the altercation that ensued, a factory owner was beaten up. The chief of police took a grave view of the situation and called for soldiers to patrol the streets. Tension mounted steadily.

Fortunately, the strike committee kept cool heads. An ultimatum was presented to the factory owners to withdraw the police and the military from the factories and the streets, or they would bear responsibility for the consequences. The police and military were soon recalled, and the strike again assumed a peaceful character.

The strike continued into the ninth and tenth week. Some strikers began to feel discouraged. At the meetings of the strikers in the House of Study demands were made for opening negotiations with the owners. The strike committee decided to call a conference of the Tanners Union of the Bialystok and Vilna districts. The conference met in Swislocz in the twelfth week of the strike. (The chief of police might have known of the conference, for it met in the neighborhood of his office.) It lasted two or three days and was attended by delegates from a number of towns. After prolonged discussions, it was decided to continue the strike. Following the conference, a general meeting of the strikers was called at the House of Study. Several delegates addressed the strikers, moving the audience to tears.

When the strike entered its fifteenth week, the spirits of the workers flagged. Aid from the neighboring towns came irregularly. The Passover festival was approaching, and the needs of the strikers were great. The demands for a settlement became more urgent, and the factory owners, too, were in a conciliatory mood. A week later the strike was settled with a compromise on wages. The workers won on the other points.

The Leather Industry from 1908 to 1919

A few weeks after the strike, the factory owners renewed their demands for the abolition of tenure of job under the threat of a new lockout. When the workers refused their demands, they carried out their threat. The "Bund" was then weak and the workers were exhausted by the previous strike. After three weeks of lockout, the workers capitulated and accepted all the demands of the owners.

The workers were quite demoralized. Since several factories had closed, a number of them were unemployed. Furthermore, the large factories began selling their product in half-finished form, which meant that the workers in the dry factories were left without work. Dry factories that had previously employed forty and fifty workers reduced the number to fifteen or ten. In these factories the percentage of Jewish employees was very high, and the growing unemployment affected chiefly the Jewish workers.

Some of the unemployed workers opened their own shops. Two workers would usually go into business in partnership. For about two thousand rubles they could rent a shop, hire a couple of workers, buy a quantity of half-finished leather and finish it. The small shops paid lower wages than the factories. Thus, a worker who had received before the strike some sixteen rubles a week in the factory, was paid for the same work in the small shop ten or nine rubles. Even at their best these small shops could give employment to only a small fraction of those who were out of work. A large number of workers then decided on immigration to the United States and Canada.

36. BECOMING A LEADER OF JEWISH LABOR

VLADIMIR MEDEM

Vladimir Medem (1879–1923) was the son of an army medical officer. His parents were assimilated Russian Jews who baptized their son at birth in the Orthodox Church. The son returned to Judaism and devoted his life wholly to the cause of Jewish labor. In 1921 he migrated to the United States. His tombstone in New York City bears the inscription "Vladimir Medem, legend of the Jewish Labor Movement."

The selection is taken from his Yiddish autobiography. The translation is by Lucy S. Dawidowicz.

Our Home

My mother sits in the dining room. Before her stands a little old woman. I remember her name was Leyeh or, as she was called in our house, Leyke. My mother sits, Leyke stands, and they don't stop talking for a moment. I don't remember what they talked about, but I do remember that they spoke Yiddish.

I, a child of six or seven, hover near my mother. I hear Leyke calling her "dear Madame," I hear my mother replying in "jargon" (Yiddish), and I am beside myself with anger. Who ever heard of such a thing: an intelligent, educated woman, the wife of a Russian general, speaking "jargon"? I can hardly wait for my father to come home. Such goings-on aren't allowed in his presence. And indeed, when my father is heard coming, Leyke disappears hastily into the kitchen. I breathe more freely. Our home is once again truly Russian.

Leyke used to come to our house every Friday to make Jewish-style fish. True, it wasn't for Friday night suppers as in Jewish homes, but for Friday dinner. Nevertheless, it was a relic of old Jewish times, a trace of vanished Jewishness. Such traces became less and less frequent from year to year. Our house was increasingly becoming really Russian, not only in language, but in the full content of our lives.

Conversions

Both my parents were Jews by birth, real honest-to-goodness Jews. I think that my father was even a *kohen*. He came from Shavli (Kovno region) and had settled in Minsk; my mother came from Vilna. I never met my paternal grandparents, but I know that my father's generation was stricken by conversion, as was my mother's family. Practically all my uncles and aunts were Christians, and some of their children did not even know of their Jewish origin.

To understand this, we must remember that this epidemic of conversion began much earlier. My father, for example, was born in 1836. As a boy he studied in a Russian gymnasium and later attended the St. Petersburg military medical academy. When he was graduated, he became an army doctor and established himself in a Russian environment. He had left traditional Jewishness very early, if he had ever known it. Insofar as he had any contact with Jewish life, it was permeated with assimilationist leanings. In the sixties, the springtide of Alexander II's regime, the attitude toward Jews was liberal, and the Jewish community responded ardently in its desire to fuse with the Russian people.

Then came a shift in events. The political honeymoon ended and was replaced by years of reaction, pogroms, and antisemitism, especially when Alexander III ascended the throne. With political persecution also went social rejection of the Jews. The situation had changed. No matter how hard one had tried to forget one's former Jewishness, the outside world refused to allow it. "You are a Jew" became an insult, a detraction. And the Jew then began to feel ashamed of his Jewishness.

Denying One's Jewishness

This shame about Jewishness and the desire to conceal one's Jewish origin were typical for our milieu. I remember how, in my childhood, my family was speaking about someone: Is it known or not known that he is a Jew? I remember that some of our relatives strictly prohibited the use of the word "Jew," lest the servants hear. Instead of using the word "Jew," they said "Italian" or "our kind." In our house, the shame of Jewishness never reached this absurdity, but the same atmosphere prevailed. I myself, as a young child, was completely acclimated to it. My Jewish origin was a burden. It was a shame, a degradation, a sort of secret disease about which no one should know. And if people did know, then, if they were kind and friendly, they took no notice of it, just as one ignores the deformity of a hunchback so as not to hurt him.

This is why I used to become upset when my mother spoke Yiddish to old Leyke. Every word reminded me of the ugly disease: You are a Jew, a cripple. I did not want to be a Jew, I did not consider myself a Jew, and I used to prattle in imitation of the grown-ups: We are Russians.

This was the atmosphere of our circle and it led to conversion as the final and drastic cure for the secret disease. Actually, conversion was no more than a formality, the last rung of the ladder. My parents did not take this step until quite late. My father became converted at the age of fifty-six, a few months before his death. He was one of the most distinguished citizens of our city, a division doctor, a *statsky sovetnik*, a rank between colonel and general. He could not become a full general because he was a Jew. But that was not why be became converted. As I understood it (I was about thirteen years old then), new restrictions against Jewish officials had been introduced, and my father's position was endangered. Since he had no private practice, was old and sick, and could not possibly dream of beginning his career anew, he decided to join the Lutheran Church.

My mother became a Christian a short while later, soon after my father's death. She was very sick, and we children convinced her that her conversion had been our father's desire. She gave in unwillingly and with considerable distress. At that time, all the children were Christians. My sister had become converted together with my father in order to marry a Russian. My oldest brother had long been an army officer and, necessarily, a Christian. Two other brothers had been converted, but it was spoken of so little that I don't even remember when. Oddly enough, all became Lutherans, as did most Jews who joined the Christian church. I believe it was because conversion to Protestantism involved less ceremonial and fewer technical difficulties than Orthodoxy. Thus, our whole family gradually became Lutherans. Only I was an exception—I belonged to the Greek Orthodox church.

I was the first Christian in our family, even though I was the youngest. When I was born (July, 1879), my parents decided: We have suffered enough because of our Jewishness; let our youngest not know such sufferings. And I was baptized in a Greek Orthodox church just as if I had been born into an Orthodox family, while they themselves remained Jews for a long time.

The Child and the Church

Thus, I was a Greek Orthodox child, reared in a Jewish, later a half-Lutheran, and finally a wholly Lutheran family. I never felt any inconsistency between my Orthodoxy and the Jewishness around me. Actually, I was for a long time convinced that my father had become converted much earlier than he had in fact. In our home all the Russian church holidays were observed. On official festivals my father even used to go to church, so that I never felt any barrier to the full and free development of my religious feeling.

I was about five when I first went to church. It made a great impression on me: the dark gold, holy pictures, the glowing lights and candles, the somber mien of the priests in their extraordinarily beautiful vestments, the mysterious ceremonies, the vibrant bass of the proto-deacon, the singing of the choir. It is indeed hard to describe the full beauty of Russian church music with its earnest and sublime harmony.

My Jewish Friends

But as I grew older, my religious emotions, based on externals rather than conscious religious awareness, began to dissipate, and when I reached my second year in gymnasium, I began to develop critical attitudes. During my last years in gymnasium, my circle gradually and imperceptibly turned Jewish. The adults who visited us were still mostly Russian, but the friends with whom I associated were almost exclusively Jews. One was Alexander Eliasberg, the son of well-to-do Jews, who himself had already traveled, read much, and who influenced my taste in art and literature. Another was Yasha Kaplan. I used to visit him quite often, and there I found an unmistakably lower-middle-class Jewish house. Eliasberg's home was Jewish too; his family observed Jewish customs, so much so that he was afraid even to ride on the Sabbath lest they find out. But I hardly ever saw his family. With Kaplan's family, it was different: the home was more sociable, more familiar. A portrait of Baron de Hirsch adorned a wall; Yiddish was heard frequently. Once, I remember, some people came and sang Yiddish songs, some by Goldfaden, I think. By that time the sound of Yiddish no longer pained my ears.

There were other Jewish boys with whom I was friendly and who visited me. At home, my Jewish acquaintanceships did not pass without comment. My older brother used to joke good-naturedly about it. He would say, "Go on, one of your Ginsbergs has come; I don't know whether Kaplan or Eliasberg." But it was no more than a joke; no one disturbed my friendships.

At this time, I had two other Jewish friends of a different sort, not fellow students. They were sons of a Jewish storekeeper who had his shop in the yard of our house. All day the boys played in the yard until their mother drove them inside. When I outgrew the games, I turned to "education." I decided to teach them Russian, hygiene, and gentility.

Yet even though I made friends with more and more Jews, I cannot definitely say that I began to consider myself a Jew. The question of my own Jewishness was not yet posed.

In 1897, I enrolled in the University of Kiev. During this year, I learned about Karl Marx and his *Capital* from Yasha Kaplan. I used to consider socialists a group of dreamers who with fantastic plans and bombs and riots sought to change the order of the world. Now I learned there was another kind of socialism, not a fantasy nor a dream, but a logical and necessary product of human development. The next year I began to study political economy, and a little later I met real live Marxists and learned the name of the Bund.

Studying Hebrew

Besides studying Marx, I decided to learn Hebrew. But my interest in Hebrew was literary rather than Jewish. I wanted to read the Bible in the original. I did not consider the Bible a Jewish book, for, after all, it had been part of the Christian religious teaching I had had as a child. At home during the summer vacation, I did not have to search far for a teacher. Mitche, the older of the two boys who lived in our yard, agreed to teach me in exchange for Russian lessons. We began with Genesis. He taught me the alphabet and pronunciation. He did not have to translate because the Bible we used, one that my father had cherished, had a French translation. We used to sit in the yard and read aloud. But I wanted to study with system and I asked Mitche to teach me grammar. He began to tell me about dikduk, but I suspect that Mitche himself didn't understand very well what it was. His reputation as a Hebraist fell in my eyes. I never did learn Hebrew, but I did accomplish something: I learned the alphabet, gaining the key to the Yiddish language. I read very poorly at that time, but the first step had been made.

When I returned to the university, I became active in the student movement. My political work increased my homesickness for Jewishness. Even though no distinction as to Jew or Christian was made among the students, there was one specifically Jewish institution among them—the Jewish student kitchen. Actually, I don't recall that I had ever been there. It was not merely an eating place; it was an intellectual gathering place, a kind of club for the Jewish students. At first I had paid no attention to it, but getting back from a visit home, I felt something akin to envy. I saw that my Jewish friends had their own group from which I was excluded. It was as though I stood before a closed door that shut me out from warmth and hominess. I felt homeless, and longed for a home. This home was Jewish life. This feeling of envy was a sign that I was still on the wrong side of the door, that I still did not consider myself Jewish. But also it was an expression of an awakening desire to become one of those to whom I was drawn.

Turning to Jewishness

In various ways and for various reasons, I began to turn to Jewishness. Here I should mention my friendship with Isaac Tumin, a man considerably older than I, who had read and seen much, been to America, Switzerland, seen the world, been imprisoned, and was associated with the Jewish labor movement. Tumin was a person with strong Jewish feeling. He came from a traditional Jewish family, knew Jewish life intimately, and loved it. This love communicated itself to me.

Visiting a Synagogue

I was in Minsk during the summer and early fall of 1899. On Yom Kippur, Tumin took me to the synagogue. I remember that evening well. Earlier, I had wandered through the streets. Minsk is a Jewish city and the stores were closed, the streets empty and desolate. I recall the figure of a Russian hussar, in a light green coat and raspberry trousers with silver band, and a long sword. His strange figure in the empty streets enhanced the extraordinarily solemn appearance of the city. A gray dusk hung over a gray quiet. You could feel that the day was different from other days.

Later, Tumin and I went to the synagogue. I had been to a synagogue before, but that had been the large, new-style synagogue in Kiev, with its Western architectural style, its choir, and its rich Jews in top hats. Now for the first time I entered an old-fashioned synagogue.

First we went to the large synagogue and immediately I felt the presence of a new, hitherto-unknown atmosphere in all its uniqueness and magic. It was different from the Russian church. There, the large mass of people stood quiet, grave, and silent, and only the priest and the choir spoke and sang on behalf of the congregation, spoke and sang in lovely, carefully harmonic and measured tones. But here, it was as though I had fallen among torrential waves. Hundreds upon hundreds of worshippers—each one taking his own case to God, each in a loud voice with passionate eagerness. Hundreds of voices ascended to the heavens, each for himself, without concord, without harmony, yet all joining together in one tremendous clamorous sound. No matter how strange to the Western ear, it makes a deep impression and has a great beauty derived from the passion of mass feeling.

Afterward, we went to a small synagogue; it may have been a hasidic prayer room. There too, I was carried away by the passionate stream of hundreds of voices. Above the vast mass rumbling there rose a sharp and high-pitched voice, the voice of the old graybearded ba'al-tefilah [the cantor]. This was no singing or preaching. It was a lament, a true lament in which you could feel the scorching tears of an anguished heart. There was none of the solemnity or measured harmony of a Christian prayer. It was the true Oriental passion of a suffering soul, a voice from the gray past which wept and beseeched its old age-gray God. In it lay a great beauty.

Member of Bund

In the fall of 1899, Yasha Kaplan and I were expelled from the University of Kiev for our political activity among the student body and ordered by the police to return to Minsk. It was a foregone conclusion that we would sooner or later join the "movement," the Bund. We had enjoyed the taste of political work and it was clear that our place was in the local movement in Minsk. Even though I had some doubts as to whether the Russian workers were at a stage of readiness to accept socialist doctrines, I was well enough acquainted with the Jewish labor movement to know that its existence was an accomplished fact, and there could be no doubt about its survival. In the winter of 1899–1900, I became a member of the Bund.

At that time, I don't believe I understood the concept of the Bund as a Jewish organization, and its proper role in Jewish life. But, looking back, I realize that Bundist thought on this subject had not yet been clarified; Bundism as an ideology with its own concept of Jewish life and of the Jewish labor movement was still in the process of crystallization. The first formulation of the Bund's Jewish national program was made at the Bund convention of April, 1901, when I was in prison. At the time I began working for the party in Minsk, we were still in a period of searching, groping in the dark. The national question was hardly ever discussed in Bundist literature, and what there was of such discussion was inaccessible to me, for I still could not read Yiddish.

Jewishness of Bund

I remember once Yasha's coming to ask: "What do you think—are the Jews a nation?" I didn't know what to answer; I had never thought about it. But so far as the Jewish labor movement was concerned, we all recognized it then as a unique and independent movement. I remember a conversation concerning the uniqueness of the Jewish labor movement some time later, in 1901. We were in prison, together in one cell, and behind bars we held a discussion about the quality of our movement. I tried to summarize. Our movement, I said, has two major characteristics. Most of our people are employed in small or very tiny workshops belonging to artisans who themselves work. The second characteristic of our movement is that it consists of Jews, children of the Jewish people. Thus, there are two forces impelling the Jewish worker into our movement: his class feeling, the consciousness that he is a worker who is being exploited, that he wants to fight together with his brothers for a better life; and his Jewish feeling, the consciousness that he is a Jew.

What was my personal Jewishness at that time? My new friends, Jewish workers, used to call me the goy, and in externals I was really quite goyish.

I still had lots of trouble with Yiddish. I could understand it (I had heard it around so much), and my knowledge of German came to my aid. But the Hebrew elements used in Yiddish were strange and presented many difficulties. Nevertheless, I was able to follow the general content of a Yiddish speech. In fact I even remember that when I heard someone read Peretz's *Dos Kranke yingl* [The sick boy], I understood it very well. But I still could not speak Yiddish. Once I went to visit a worker who happened to be out. I asked his wife in Yiddish when he would come. They were just four simple words, but immediately she had the feeling that a *goy* was speaking and answered me in Russian.

Becoming Judaized

The articles I then wrote in the *Minsker arbayter* were written in Russian and then translated into Yiddish. I had already developed some feeling for the Yiddish language, and though I wrote in Russian, I used such expressions as readily lent themselves to Yiddish translation. I could not read Yiddish either at the time, but I was learning. Certainly the Jewish labor milieu influenced me greatly. I cannot say exactly how this influence expressed itself, but the constant association with Jews and Jewish life Judaized me. An especially strong influence was my friendship with Tumin.

I remember one evening when we went walking together through the Jewish quarter, in the outlying poor little streets with their poor little houses. It was Friday night; the streets were quiet and empty; the Sabbath candles burned in the little houses. We were talking about Jewish things. I don't remember the subject, but I do recall that I was strongly impressed by that unique charm of the peaceful Friday nights and felt a romantic association with the Jewish past, a warm, intimate closeness that one has with one's own past. And this feeling for the past has always remained associated with the small houses and quiet streets of a Lithuanian Jewish town. My sentiment for Jewry was always, as a Zionist might express it, a *galut* feeling. The palm trees and the vineyards of Palestine were alien to me. I think this is an indication that my Jewishness was really an ingrained living Jewishness, not a literary fancy.

As I have said, I cannot exactly determine how this "nationalizing" influence of the Jewish labor circles expressed itself. It was the quiet effect of day-to-day living. This life became dear and important to me. It was Jewish and it drew me into its environs. When did I clearly and definitely feel myself to be a Jew? I cannot say, but at the beginning of 1901, when I was arrested for clandestine political activity, the police gave me a form to fill in. In the column "Nationality," I wrote "Jew."

37. BECOMING A ZIONIST LEADER

CHAIM WEIZMANN

Chaim Weizmann (1874–1952) became the first president of the State of Israel. He was born in Russia, studied in Germany and Switzerland, and in 1907 settled in England to teach chemistry at a university. He early joined the Zionist movement and became one of its prominent leaders. His scientific discoveries helped the war effort of the Allies in the First World War. He was a key figure in the negotiations leading to the Balfour Declaration of 1917 (no. 86) and presented the case for Jewish rights in Palestine before British and international committees. He played an important role in the recognition of Israel by President Truman in 1948.

The selection is taken from Weizmann's autobiography, *Trial and Error*.

My Hometown in the Pale

The townlet of my birth, Motol, stood—and perhaps still stands—on the banks of a little river in the great marsh area which occupies much of the province of Minsk and adjacent provinces in White Russia; flat, open country, mournful and monotonous but, with its rivers, forests and lakes, not wholly unpicturesque. Between the rivers the soil was sandy, covered with pine and furze; closer to the banks the soil was black, the trees were leaf bearing. In the spring and autumn, the area was a sea of mud, in the winter a world of snow and ice; in the summer, it was covered with a haze of dust. All about, in hundreds of towns and villages, Jews lived, as they had lived for many generations, scattered islands in a Gentile ocean; and among them my own people, on my father's and mother's side, made up a not inconsiderable proportion.

Just outside Motol the river flowed into a large lake and emerged again at the other end on its way to join the Pina; that in turn was a tributary of the Pripet, itself a tributary of the Dnieper, which fell into the Black Sea many hundreds of miles away. On the further banks of the lake were some villages, mysterious to my childhood by virtue of their general name—"the Beyond-the-River." For them, Motol (or Motelle, as we affectionately Yiddishized the name) was a sort of metropolis.

A very tiny and isolated metropolis it was, with some four or five hundred families of White Russians and less than two hundred Jewish families. Communication with the outside world was precarious and intermittent. No railway, no metaled road, passed within twenty miles of us. There was no post office. Mail was brought in by anyone from the townlet who happened to pass by the nearest railway station on his own business. Sometimes these chance messengers would hold on to the mail for days, or for weeks, distributing it when the spirit moved them. But letters played no very important part in our lives; there were few in the outside world who had reason to communicate with us. . . .

Motol was situated in one of the darkest and most forlorn corners of the Pale of Settlement, that prison house created by Tsarist Russia for the largest part of its Jewish population. Throughout the centuries, alternations of bitter oppression and comparative freedom—how comparative a free people would hardly understand—had deepened the consciousness of exile in these scattered communities, which were held together by a common destiny and common dreams. Motol was typical Pale, typical countryside. Here, in this half-townlet, half-village, I lived from the time of my birth, in 1874, till the age of eleven; and here I wove my first pictures of the Jewish and Gentile worlds. . . .

Entering a Russian School

The first fundamental change in my life took place when, at the age of eleven, I left the townlet of my birth and went out "into the world"—that is, to Pinsk—to enter a Russian school: which was something not done until that time by any Motolite. From Motol to Pinsk was a matter of six Russian miles, or twenty-five English miles; but in terms of intellectual displacement the distance was astronomical. For Pinsk was a real provincial metropolis, with thirty thousand inhabitants, of whom the great majority were Jews. Pinsk had a name and a tradition as "a city and mother in Israel." It could not pretend to the cultural standing of great centers like Warsaw, Vilna, Odessa, and Moscow; but neither was it a nameless village. The new Hibbat Zion movement, the forerunner of Modern Zionism, had taken deep root in Pinsk. There were Jewish scholars and Jewish public leaders in Pinsk. There was a high school—the one I was going to attend—there were libraries, hospitals, factories, and paved streets.

A False Dawn

The years of my childhood in Motol and of my schooling in Pinsk coincided with the onset of the "dark years" for Russian Jewry; or perhaps I should say with their return. The reign of Alexander II had been a false dawn. For a generation, the ancient Russian policy of repression of the Jews had been mitigated by the liberalism of the monarch who had set the serfs free; and therefore many Jews believed that the walls of the ghetto were about to fall. Jews were beginning to attend Russian schools and universities, and to enter into the life of the country. Then, in 1881, came the assassination of Alexander, and on its heels the tide of reaction, which was not to ebb again until the overthrow of the Romanovs thirty-six years later. The new repression began with the famous "Temporary Legislation Affecting the Jews" enacted in 1882, and known as the May Laws. Nothing in czarist Russia was as enduring as "Temporary Legislation." This particular set of enactments, at any rate, was prolonged and broadened and extended until it came to cover every aspect of Jewish life; and as one read, year after year, the complicated ukases which poured from St. Petersburg, one obtained the impression that the whole cumbersome machinery of the vast Russian Empire was created for the sole purpose of inventing and amplifying rules and regulations for the hedging in of the existence of its Jewish subjects until it became something that was neither life nor death.

Jewish self-liberation

Parallel with these repressions, and with the general setback to Russian liberalism, there was a deep stirring of the masses, Russian and Jewish. Among the Jews, this first folk awakening had two facets, the revolutionary, mingling with the general Russian revolt, and the Zionist nationalist. The latter, however, was also revolutionary and democratic. The Jewish masses were rising against the paternalism of their "notables," their shtadlanim, the men of wealth and influence who had always taken it on themselves to represent the needs of the Jews vis-à-vis governmental authority. Theirs was, even in the best cases, a class view, characterized by a natural fear of disturbing the status quo or imperiling such privileges as they enjoyed by virtue of their economic standing. In the depths of the masses an impulse awoke, vague, groping, unformulated, for Jewish self-liberation. It was genuinely of the folk; it was saturated with Jewish tradition; and it was connected with the most ancient memories of the land where Jewish life had first expressed itself in freedom. It was, in short, the birth of modern Zionism.

Flight from Russia

By 1886, when I entered high school in Pinsk, the atmosphere of Jewish life was heavy with disaster. There had been the ghastly pogroms of 1881. These had not reached us in Motol, but they had shaken the whole Jewish world to its foundations. I was a child, and I had lived in the separateness of the Jewish life of our townlet. Non-Jews were for me something peripheral. But even I did not escape a consciousness of the general gloom. Almost as far as my memory goes back, I can remember the stampede—the frantic rush from the Russian prison house, the tremendous tide of migration which carried hundreds of thousands of Jews from their ancient homes to far-off lands across the seas. I was a witness in boyhood and early manhood of the emptying of whole villages and towns. My own family was once caught up in the fever—this was about the time of the Kishenev pogrom of 1903—and though we finally decided against flight, there were cousins and uncles and more distant relatives by the score who took the westward path . . .

School Life

The school regime in Pinsk, and for that matter, I suppose, in all other Russian cities at that time, was very different from that of the Western world. There was no contact between teachers and pupils, and little intercourse among the pupils themselves. As far as the Jewish boys were concerned, the teachers were looked upon as the representatives of an alien and hostile power; they were more *tchinovniks* [officials] than pedagogues, and in them human emotions and relationships were replaced by formalism and by the instinct for climbing inherent in the Russian official. With few exceptions—and there were some—the teacher had his eye not so much on the pupils as on the head of the school; the road to the good opinion of his chief, and therefore of promotion, was not the road of pedagogics, but of strict adherence to the decrees and ukases issued by the higher authorities. . . .

There was one outstanding exception among my teachers, a man by the name of Kornienko, to whom, very possibly, I owe whatever I have been able to achieve in the way of science. He was a chemist, with a genuine love of his subject and a considerable reputation in the world at large. He was, in fact, the glory of our school, and this perhaps explains why he was able to do as much as he did without falling foul of the authorities. He had managed to assemble a little laboratory, a luxury which was then almost unknown in Russian high schools. His attitude toward his pupils was in wholesome contrast with that of the other members of the staff. He was a decent, liberal-minded fellow, and treated us like human beings. He entered into conversation with us, and did his best to interest us in the wider aspects of natural science. I need hardly say that most of us responded warmly, and there grew up a kind of friendship between pupils and teacher—a state of affairs unimaginably rare in the Russian schools of that day . . .

First Experience in Zionism

Jewish Pinsk was divided into two communities, Pinsk proper and Karlin, each with its own set of synagogues, rabbis, hospitals, and schools. Karlin, where I lived, was considered, as they say in America, the right side of the tracks. It was here that I grew from boyhood into early manhood, here that I had my social and intellectual contacts, and here that I was inducted into the Zionist movement. Pinsk, then, set the double pattern of my life; it gave me my first bent toward science, and it provided me with my first experiences in Zionism . . .

We must not think of Zionism in Pinsk fifty-odd years ago, long before the coming of Theodor Herzl, in terms of the modern movement. Organized activity in the present-day sense simply did not exist. A youth organization was undreamed of. There were casual meetings of the older people, at which the youngsters sneaked in, to sit in a corner. On rare occasions when a circular was sent out, we were permitted to address the envelopes. Our financial resources were comically primitive; we dealt in rubles and kopecks. One of the main sources of income was the collection made on the Feast of Purim. Youngsters were enlisted to distribute leaflets and circulars from house to house, and modest contributions would be made by most of the householders. Not all, by any means. Not the very rich ones, for instance, like the Lurias, the great clan of industrialists with branches in Warsaw, Libau, and Danzig, who owned the match factory in Pinsk. For already, in those early days, the classic divisions in Zionism, which have endured till very recent days, manifested themselves. The Jewish magnates were, with very few exceptions, bitterly anti-Zionist. Our supporters were the middle class and the poor. An opposition—in the shape of a labor movement—did not exist yet, for the Bund, the Jewish revolutionary labor organization, was not founded until 1897—the year of the first Zionist Congress.

Jewishness and Zionism

The obstinacy and persistence of the movement cannot be understood except in terms of faith. This faith was part of our make-up; our Jewishness and our Zionism were interchangeable; you could not destroy the second without destroying the first. We did not need propagandizing . . . These, then, were the beginnings of Zionism, in the midst of which I lived my boyhood. They came from deep sources; and if the practical manifestations were rather pitiful at first, if a whole generation had to pass away and another take its place before action became planned and impressive, the significance of those who nurtured and transmitted the impulse must not be forgotten. It was because of them that Herzl found a movement ready for him. . . .

During my student years in Berlin and Freiburg, as well as later on, when I was teaching at the University of Geneva, I invariably went back to Russia for my holidays. Nine months of the year I spent in the free Western world; but every June I returned to the East, and until the autumn I was the militant Zionist in the land where Zionism was illegal. In the East our opponents were the Okhrana, the Russian secret police. In the West it was an open fight, in the East a conspiracy. The West preached liberty, the East practiced repression; but East and West alike were the enemies of the Zionist ideology.

My Missionary Work

It was in the fen and the forest area about Pinsk that I did my first missionary work, confining myself to the villages and townlets. In these forlorn Jewish communities it was not a question of preaching Zionism as much as of awakening them to action. I went about urging the Jews of places like Motol to enroll in the Hoveve Zion; to send delegates to the first Zionist Congress, when that was called in 1897; to buy shares in the first Zionist bank, the Jewish Colonial Trust, when that was founded in 1898. Most of the meetings were held in the synagogues, where, in case of a police raid I would be "attending services" or "preaching." My dreams were opulent, my demands modest. It was a gala day for me when I managed to raise twenty or thirty rubles for the cause. . . .

With the years, the areas assigned to me by the local committee widened out. Mozyr was the first fair-sized town to which I was sent as an apostle. Mozyr had a large synagogue; it also boasted an intelligentsia. So, from the tiny communities of the marshlands I graduated to Vilna in the north, to Kiev and even Kharkov, with their large student bodies, in the south.

Here the missionary work was of a very different order. I no longer had just the folk to deal with. Among the Russian-Jewish assimilating intelligentsia, and among many of the students, there was an ideological opposition to Zionism which had to be countered on another level. These were not the rich, orthodox Jewish families of Pinsk, obscurantist, reactionary. They were not, either, the shtadlanim, the notables, with their vested interests, their lickspittle attitude toward the Russian Government, their vanity, and their ancient prestige. Nor were they like the German assimilating Jews, bourgeois, or Philistine. For these last strove, in their assimilationist philosophy, to approximate to the type of the German Spiessbürger, the comfortable merchant, the Geheimrat, the professor, the sated, respectable classes. Most of the Russian-Jewish intelligentsia, and above all the students, assimilated toward the spirit of a Tolstoy or Korolenko, toward the creative and revolutionary classes. It was, I think, a tragically erroneous assimilation even so, but it was not base or repulsive. In Germany we were losing, through assimilation, the least attractive Jewish groups. The opposite was the case in Russia.

For me, then, it was a time of threefold growth. I was pursuing my scientific studies systematically, and to that extent resisting the pressure of bohemianism in my surroundings. At the same time, within the Russian Jewish Society, I was working out, in discussion and debate, my political philosophy, and beginning to shed the vague and sentimental Zionism of my boyhood. Third, I was learning, one might say from the ground up, the technique of propaganda and the approach to the masses. I was also weaving the web of my life's personal relationships. . . .

At the Universities

If Russian Jewry was the cradle of my Zionism, the Western universities were my finishing schools. The first of these schools was Berlin, with its Russian-Jewish Society; the second was Berne, the third Geneva, both in Switzerland. . . .

I finished my third year in Berlin; for the fourth—in 1898—I went to Freiburg to take my doctorate. My favorite professor, Bistrzycki, a distinguished German chemist, of Polish origin, had moved from Berlin to Freiburg, and I followed him. There were very few Jewish students at Freiburg; but in the neighboring university town of Berne—three-quarters of an hour away—there was a very large Russian-Jewish student colony, and here conditions were not at all like those which I had left behind me. Switzerland—and this meant chiefly Berne and Geneva—was, at the turn of the century, the crossroads of Europe's revolutionary forces. Lenin and Plekhanov made it their center. Trotsky, who was some years younger than I, was often there. The Jewish students were swayed—it might be better to say overawed—by the intellectual and moral authority of the older revolutionaries, with whose names was already associated the glamor of Siberian records. Against them the tiny handful of Zionist students could make no headway, having no authority of comparable standing to oppose them.

Lenin and Trotsky

Actually the fight was not of our choosing; it was thrust upon us. Our sympathies were with the revolutionaries; they, however, would not tolerate in the Jewish youth any expression of separate attachment to the Jewish people, or even special awareness of the Jewish problem. Yet the Jewish youth was not essentially assimilationist; its bonds with its people were genuine and strong; it was only by doing violence to their inclinations and upbringing that these young men and women had turned their backs, at the bidding of the revolutionary leaders, on the peculiar bitterness of the Jewish lot. My resentment of Lenin and Plekhanov and the arrogant Trotsky was provoked by the contempt with which they treated any Jew who was moved by the fate of his people and animated by a love of its history and its tradition. They could not understand why a Russian Jew should want to be anything but a Russian. They stamped as unworthy, as intellectually backward, as chauvinistic and immoral, the desire of any Jew to occupy himself with the sufferings and destiny of Jewry. A man like Chaim Zhitlowsky, who was both a revolutionary and a Jewish nationalist, was looked upon with extreme suspicion. And when the Bund was created—the Jewish branch of the revolutionary movement, national as well as revolutionary in character—Plekhanov sneered that a Bundist was a Zionist who was afraid of seasickness. Thus the mass of Russian-Jewish students in Switzerland had been bullied into an artificial denial of their own personality; and they did not recover a sense of balance until the authority of the "old men" was boldly challenged and in part overthrown by the dissidents—that is, by us. . . . We held our first organizational meeting in the back room of the Russian colony library; and we held it standing, for "the others" had got wind of our projected meeting and had removed the furniture. But we founded, on our feet, a Zionist society, the first in Switzerland, under the name of *Ha-Shahar*, the Dawn; and we resolved to carry the fight into the open.

The mere proclamation of our existence created a scandal. The "reactionary bourgeoisie" was on the march! The colony was in a turmoil, and attempts were made to browbeat us into submission. We refused to be browbeaten. Instead, we called a mass meeting of the Jewish student body for the purpose of increasing our membership, and the notices proclaimed that I was to read a paper and submit a resolution in favor of the Zionist program.

I cannot help saying that this step called for a certain degree of moral courage. Lenin was not the world figure which he became later; but he already had a name. Plekhanov, an older man, was widely known. We, on the other hand, were nobodies. So if the founding of Ha-Shahar was a scandal, this step was revolution. The other side mobilized all its forces; we, for our part, invited down from Berlin two gifted young Zionist speakers, Berthold Feivel and Martin Buber. The meeting, which was held in a *Bierhalle*, expanded into a sort of congress, and lasted three nights and two days! It was before the dawn of the third day, at four o'clock, that the resolution was put to a vote, and we scored a tremendous triumph. A hundred and eighty students enrolled in the Zionist Society—a striking revelation of the true inclinations and convictions of a large part of the Jewish student body.

This was the first real breach in the ranks of the assimilatory revolutionists in Switzerland. I recall that Plekhanov was particularly outraged by our success. He came up to me after the close of the meeting and asked me furiously: "What do you mean by bringing discord into our ranks?" I answered: "But Monsieur Plekhanov, you are not the Tzar!" There was already, in those days, something significant in the autocratic spiritual attitude of the revolutionaries.

Winning Over the Academic Youth

Seen from this distance, and across a turbulent period of human history, that incident in a Swiss university may seem to be rather unimportant. It had, however, serious repercussions in our young world. The shock of the

Berne rebellion was felt throughout the student body of the West, and Zionism was strengthened at a dozen different points. The struggle was on for the possession of the soul of that generation of young Russian Jews in the West. It must not be forgotten that of the thousands who were then preparing for a career in the West, a large proportion returned to Russia. The students who had been won for Zionism became influential cells in their hometowns. I found them there later, carriers of the movement in the Jewish communities.

38. RISE OF MODERN HEBREW LITERATURE

SIMON HALKIN

Simon Halkin was born in Russia in 1898, migrated with his parents to the United States in 1914, and finally settled in Israel, where he became professor of modern Hebrew literature at the Hebrew University in Jerusalem. He is well known as a poet, novelist, historian of Hebrew literature, and translator of American and English poets into Hebrew.
The selection is taken from his book *Modern Hebrew Literature*.

Life and Literature

Modern Hebrew literature is the product of the last two hundred years of Jewish life; and two hundred years are a relatively brief span in a history that encompasses three thousand years of growth and development, of inner and outer struggle. Yet, the changes produced in Jewish life the world over by the revolutionary trends of this period have proved so overwhelming that modern Hebrew writing, which has striven to comprehend these changes, to interpret them, if not to determine their directions and ultimate goals, has resulted in a body of letters that is quantitatively richer and qualitatively more complex than is generally known.

During many centuries the Jewish tradition, while at times absorbing certain alien cultural influences—Hellenistic, Islamic, occidental—remained fundamentally exclusive. Self-sufficiency was the keynote. However much they took over from other sources, or contributed to them, the Jews always felt themselves justified in their self-segregation from the rest of the world.

End of Self-Sufficiency

But two hundred years ago this self-sufficiency began to be shaken. With the advent of the modern world Jewish life began to undergo a series of vicissitudes, unprecedented in all its history. It came out of its seclusion and began to reach out for Western culture, extending, broadening, and complicating its own vision and its relations with the modern world, sometimes gradually, sometimes with an almost shattering impact to its own deepest essence. In seeking to possess itself of the fruits of modern thought and experiences, and fit itself into the new social-economic life which the French Revolution and the period of industrialization had initiated, it enlarged its horizon and increased its possibilities of development and influence; but it also found itself faced with a complex of new and disturbing problems, while many of its old tensions intensified in new forms.

A Revolutionary Change

During these two hundred years the Jewish people has striven to break away from the traditional patterns of its self-contained existence, to normalize and humanize its life materially and spiritually, to achieve greater happiness in all aspects of worldly existence: political and economic, social and cultural. And one of the most remarkable phenomena of this revolutionary change was the Hebrew literature that sprang into being with it, kept pace with it and reflected faithfully its innumerable facets, its strivings, victories and defeats, its sorrows and rejoicings. In poetry and prose, modern Hebrew literature has interpreted and evaluted the historic drama of the emergence of the modern Jew from the state of ghetto-Judaism. It has recorded the process of modernization which has fashioned the new Jew.

39. RISE OF YIDDISH LITERATURE

SOL LIPTZIN

Sol Liptzin, born in 1901, was professor of German at the City College of New York and settled in Israel in 1962. The selection is taken from his book *The Maturing of Yiddish Literature.*

Yiddish literature arose when the Yiddish language was formed, in the late Middle Ages in Ashkenazic territory, out of Hebrew, Romance, Slavic and Germanic components. It flourished during the centuries of minstrelsy and attained a peak of artistry in the sixteenth and early seventeenth centuries in verse epics and prose narratives. It declined following the destruction of hundreds of Yiddish-speaking communities in the mid-seventeenth century. Its decline was accelerated in the eighteenth century by the spirit of Enlightenment. Jewish reformers and rationalists ultimately succeeded in supplanting Yiddish with German in Central Europe, except for a few pockets of resistance in the Rhineland and Switzerland. They degraded this tongue by labeling it Jargon.

By the mid-nineteenth century, its survival as a vehicle for literary creativity in Eastern Europe also appeared to be unlikely, even though Yiddish folksongs continued to be sung by the Jewish masses, women continued to pour out their hearts in Yiddish devotional prayers, and Hassidim retold in ever new variations Yiddish tales of their saintly rabbis.

When the first periodical in Yiddish, Kol Mevasser [Voice of the Annoucer] was launched in 1862 by the Hebrew publicist Alexander Zederbaum, it was justified to the Russian authorities as an organ that would educate the unenlightened Jewish masses and prepare them for Russification. Yet, it was in this very periodical that Mendele Mocher Sforim, the Grandfather of Modern Yiddish literature, began two years later the publication of his Yiddish stories and helped to develop an audience for sophisticated belles-lettres.

In the following decade, Abraham Goldfaden replaced the dramatic improvisations of the Purim players and of Yiddish bards such as Berl Broder, Velvel Zbarzher and Eliakum Zunser with theatrical performances based on texts through which flowed artistry of a high order. In the 1880's the Russian poet S. S. Frug turned to Yiddish in order to weep with the victims of Czarist pogroms and to bring them comfort and new hope. A still higher level of creativity was reached by the end of this decade when Sholom Aleichem and Y. L. Peretz appeared upon the Yiddish scene.

The Classical Age of Yiddish literature was the quarter of a century between 1889 and 1914. From its base in Russia and Poland, Yiddish literature spread in all directions as mass migrations brought pogrom-fleeing, Yiddish-speaking Jews to distant lands. New York then became an ever more important center for Yiddish books, the Yiddish theater and the Yiddish press.

When writers from many countries gathered at the Czernovitz Yiddish Conference of 1908, they could proclaim Yiddish as a Jewish national language alongside of the older and more sacred Hebrew. Abraham Reisen, Sholem Asch and David Pinski opened wider horizons in various literary genres. Jacob Gordin ushered in the golden era of the Yiddish theater and was followed by Peretz Hirshbein, Leon Kobrin and Z. Libin. Ideological battles between original thinkers at the turn of the century, such as Chaim Zhitlowsky, Ahad-Haam and Shimon Dubnow, found repercussions in Yiddish prose and verse. Yehoash supplied readers inadequately versed in Hebrew with a Yiddish translation of the Bible comparable in quality to Martin Luther's German version or the King

James English rendering. Along with Joseph Rolnick and H. Rosenblatt, he paved the way on American soil for the first indigenous lyric movement in the New World, that of "Die Yunge," (The Young) out of whose midst arose on the eve of the First World War, H. Leivick, the finest Yiddish poet and dramatist of the post-classical generation.

Until 1914, Jewish life was comparatively stable in Eastern Europe. Despite the stirring of new forces, the Jewish personality was still intact in the Yiddish-speaking areas. There was a complex of characteristics which defined the Jew of the era of Mendele, Peretz and Sholom Aleichem, even though the process of dissolution had already set in. Against this stable traditional Jew, the Yiddish writers, pre-classical Maskilim as well as their successors of the generation of Mendele, Goldfaden and Linetzky, leveled effective satiric barbs. These Yiddish writers saw in the somnolent communities, symbolized as Kasrilevke and Yehupetz, medieval nests of unenlightenment and obscurantism.

After 1914, however, the tradition-encrusted, Yiddish-speaking townlets were no longer viable. War, revolution, pogroms, emigration decimated the Jewish Pale. Faith in the power of pure reason proved to be a false faith and yet could not be rejected. Gradually, as doubts concerning the vaunted Western progress increased, Jewish cultural tradition began to assume a romantic, nostalgic attractiveness in all the centers of Jewish concentration outside the Soviet realm. Attacks upon Hassidism as a diseased fanaticism yielded to admiration for its colorful, cheer-inducing practices.

The alliance of Socialism and anti-nationalism was weakened as Yiddish writers fought for Jewish minority rights in the Diaspora and a national base in the Jewish historic homeland. Though the enthusiasm which accompanied the Russian Revolution waned, though the hopes set upon the rise of an independent Poland, Lithuania and Greater Rumania were not fulfilled, though the longed-for Jewish commonwealth to which Zionists aspired ran into unforeseen difficulties soon after the Balfour Declaration of 1917, nevertheless the Jewish masses were saved from despondency and were repeatedly buoyed up by Yiddish poets and thinkers who kept them aware of the richness of the Jewish heritage, the unity of the Jewish people, the Messianic visions embedded in Jewish folklore.

As darkening clouds hovered over Europe's Jews, America became increasingly the center of Jewish creativity. Yiddish writers streamed to its shores in ever greater numbers and paved the way for the replacement of Warsaw, Vilna and Kiev by New York, Montreal and Buenos Aires. When the Eastern European cycle of Jewish history came to a tragic end, the regeneration of the Jewish people in other areas of the globe, above all in the United States and Israel, was in full swing.

Yiddish literature accompanied the Jewish people throughout the decades of vigorous growth, unprecedented horrors and glorious rebirth.

40. OUR HISTORICAL DEBT TO RUSSIAN JEWRY

GERSHOM SCHOLEM

Gershom Scholem was born in Berlin in 1897, became a Zionist in his youth, and settled in Palestine in 1923. He is a retired professor at the Hebrew University in Jerusalem and is recognized as the leading authority on Jewish mysticism and the Kabbalah.

The article is based on his speech at the World Conference of Jewish Communities on Soviet Jewry in Brussels, 1971.

Russian Jewry, of course, is only one of the tribes constituting the Jewish people. Each one of them has had its place and contributed to what we are, for better or worse. But few, if any, can compete with the depth, the intensity and vitality that Russian Jewry has brought to all dimensions of Jewish life, Jewish society and spirituality.

A Distinctive Jewish Life

What we call "Russian Jewry" was not that part of our people within the present boundaries of the Soviet Union alone. During the period when it became most important in Jewish history, there was little if any difference between Polish and Russian Jewry which, seen in a wider perspective, formed one large unit—not only because they were included for many generations within the boundaries of the Russian Empire and shared a common fate, but also because they led a distinctive Jewish life of their own, quite unlike the Jewish community in Central and Western Europe.

To a far greater extent than in those parts, the non-Jewish society among which they lived was unwilling to accept Russian Jews into its ranks, even those prepared to pay the price of assimilation. The "enlightened" and the Orthodox (the so-called "obscurantist" Jews) were all in the same boat and were never allowed to forget it. Thus, both the inner resources of this community and the tremendous pressure from outside contributed to the specific vitality and dynamism which characterized Russian Jewry through all its vicissitudes. Russia also meant the Baltic Provinces and States, Poland, Lithuania, Volhynia, Ukraine and Bessarabia. Even leaving aside Poland proper, places such as Riga, Minsk, Vilna, Kovno, Grodno, Bialystok, Lubavitch, Mohilev, Berditchev, Medzibozh, Odessa and

Kishinev—these and 100 others are unforgettable names reverberating through the spiritual world of Judaism.

Of course, these and innumerable larger and lesser towns and villages had their common share of material hardship and persecution, of suffering and bitter internal social conflict. Despite all these and perhaps because of all these, there arose an infinite fertility of mind, a boundless idealistic enthusiasm, an imagination and sensitivity. The figure of the Russian Jew as it is impressed on our mind is, at the same time, characterized by traits possibly reflecting some general influences from the surrounding Russian atmosphere, though transformed by the particular Jewish situation. I have in mind a certain generosity and spontaneity, a bent to disregard bourgeois considerations, a capacity for endless discussion and, last but not least, a Jewish variant of the Russian "Nitchevo."

The Jews of Russia have produced many of the decisive phenomena of later and modern Jewish life in widely different spheres. All these phenomena bear the unmistakable mark of the group that created them. Let me mention some of the outstanding ones.

Talmudic Tradition

Within the framework of traditional Talmudic culture Russian Jewry not only produced a long chain of great rabbis, scholars and protagonists of rabbinic tradition but in the archetypal figure of Rabbi Eliyahu, the Gaon of Vilna, gave to large parts of the world Jewish community the ideal image of what Jewish learning and devotion should represent. For 200 years his name has been a household word throughout Ashkenazic Jewry. An ascetic recluse who spent most of his years in a little room immersed in all branches of Jewish tradition and only once, when he set out to fight Hassidism, descended into the public arena, he captured the imagination of the Jewish people. His pupils, who founded the great Yeshivoth in Russia—Volozhin, Mir and all their successors—forged an instrument of Jewish education for which the Vilner Gaon became the guiding star. One can hardly overrate the importance of this institution, which provided Russian Jewry for more than 100 years not only with a rabbinical elite but also with many great minds who broke away and found their own path to Jewish activism.

Hassidism

In marked contrast to this contribution, Hassidism is essentially a creation of Russian Jewry in the sphere of intimate religious and emotional life, starting with the mystical experiences of Israel Baal Shem and the revivalist and inspired preaching of his pupils, and then branching out into ever wider circles. It presented the masses of Polish-Russian Jewry with an unprecedented galaxy of saints who became the living heart of Judaism for their thousands of followers. An emotional upheaval of tremendous power found its expression in a new way of life and, after violent clashes with unreconstructed Orthodoxy, managed to reach an uneasy compromise which left Hassidism as a dominant factor in large areas of Russia such as the Ukraine, Podolia, Volhynia and Russian Poland.

Mussar Movement

In Lithuania originated, on the other hand, the *Mussar* movement, which stressed another radical way of life formed of strong ethical inspiration and equally strong anti-bourgeois tendencies. The *Yeshivoth* of this movement—Novogrodek, Slobodka and others—became the center of what could be called a radical youth movement within the confines of Talmudic culture. Like Hassidism, it had wide repercussions beyond the Russian Pale. Its uncompromising attitude to standards of personal life and behavior formed a new ideal type of the unconventional Jew that impressed and attracted many of the most remarkable minds at the end of the nineteenth and the beginning of the twentieth centuries. Both Hassidism and Mussar have cultivated, each in its own way, the ideal of the strong religious and ethical personality.

Haskalah

But all this was only one side of the picture. There was also the deep unrest connected with the crisis in Jewish tradition in the wake of its encounter with the modern world. The Haskalah movement, the Jewish "Enlightenment" that became a strong factor in Russian Jewish life, sprang from dissatisfaction and criticism of tradition, from the feeling that a new era had set in that demanded new answers. True, the spokesmen of the Haskalah deluded themselves, like so many others, about the march of progress, about the chances of integration into Russian society, and their rosy visions were shattered when they came face to face with the bitter reality of the Russian pogroms and the intensification of persecution. But their unrelenting criticism of Jewish society and its depressing realities, often to the point of despair, did much to instill life into stagnation, to ask questions which those other movements had tried to evade. Rational analysis and romantic longings blended in their activities. They were the first who, however dimly, faced the problem of secularization in Jewish life that is still with us. It was from their radical wing that, with Morris Vinchevsky and Aron Liebermann, the first stirrings of Jewish socialism arose.

Yiddish and Hebrew Literature

The Haskalah was unsure of its steps, but its two great offsprings (although only in a dialectical sense) took a firm stand vis-a-vis their Jewish identification. I am speaking of Yiddish and modern Hebrew literature and of the national and social movements that carried them, nursed them and were in return immensely enriched by them. The creation of Yiddish and Hebrew prose and poetry is still another of those major contributions which we owe to Russian Jewry. Through these two media of expression, two mainsprings of Jewish vitality opened up. We all remember Khrushchev's saying some years ago that there were too many Abramowitches and Rabinowitches around in Russia. We have every good reason to affirm our debt of gratitude to them, symbolized by the great names of Sholem Jakob Abramowitch—known throughout the Jewish world as Mendele Mocher Seforim, the *zaide* or grandfather of both modern Yiddish and Hebrew prose—and Shlomo Rabinowitz, known as Sholem Aleichem. These two names stand for an unending line of great masters and gifted and industrious writers. For two generations before 1920, the life of Russian Jewry was both expressed and fructified by these literatures, by Ahad Ha'am and Bialik, by Berdyczewski and Brenner, by Peretz and Asch. They radiated far beyond Russia, and their struggles, discussions and achievements are enduring testimony to the prodigious creative power of Russian Jewry when it became aware of its national identity, whether of traditional or of secular coloring.

National Movements

True, the different branches of the Jewish national movement that sprang up after 1880 fought each other vehemently. There was Galut nationalism, represented in different shades by Dubnov or the socialist "bund" and the Yiddishists. There was Zionism in all its factions, from Pinsker to Syrkin and Borochov. But these and all the others were united in one basic proposition: that the Jews had a natural right to live the life of a national minority, to choose for themselves how to live their Judaism or Jewishness and to convey their national culture and tradition through education. They fought for full rights as citizens—not only as individuals, like in the West, but as a national group.

Jewish National Rights

When the Russian Revolution came in 1917, almost every Jewish party had included the demand for national autonomy for Russian Jewry in its program. Jews had become conscious of their national existence; they paid no heed to those isolated figures who demanded that they give up their national rights. An immense upsurge of great expectations for a Jewish future in a progressive and socialist Russia followed the Revolution; much of that energy and inspiration flowed over into the upbuilding of the new life in Israel, to which Russian Jewry has made such an outstanding contribution.

Foundations for the State of Israel

Much of the foundation of what is now the State of Israel was laid by the selfless pioneering and sacrifices of Russian Jews, from the Bilus on. The idea of self-defense, first advanced by Jews in Russia after the Kishinev pogrom in 1903, gave birth to the concept and practice of the Haganah, to the recognition that if necessary Jews must stand up and fight for themselves. On another plane, the idea of the Kibbutz was first conceived and realized by Russian Jews; A. D. Gordon from a village in Podolia became the prophet of the moral rebirth of the Jewish people through work. Nor can there be a place outside Russia where the ideas of Tolstoy have had a more profound impact than in Israel. Jabotinsky, Rabbi Kook, Chaim Weizmann, Berl Katzenelson and, to name only one among the living, David Ben-Gurion—these have been among the great figures in the social and political development of Israel. All are Russian Jews.

It is hardly an accident that the three Presidents of the State of Israel who have served until now, the four Prime Ministers and the first four Speakers of the Knesset—all have been Russian Jews. They symbolize our debt to Russian Jewry, and our continuing obligation to them.

QUESTIONS FOR THOUGHT AND DISCUSSION

1. What is the "Pale of Settlement"?

2. In his autobiography, Shmarya Levin, a Russian Jew, points out that, in its eager pursuit of civic rights, West European Jewry was not faithful to its origin and abandoned its right to a group existence. The Russian Jews, in contrast, were not prepared to deny their history and to destroy their culture for the sake of civic rights. Can you find examples to support Levin's contention? You may draw on the first chapter of this book, dealing with the emancipation in Western Europe.

3. What were the reasons for the resistance of the Russian Jews to Lilienthal's proposals about government schools, and why did Lilienthal's efforts fail?

4. What influence did the liberal reforms of Tsar Alexander II have on the Jews?

5. Some Russian Jews, especially among the youth, eagerly participated in revolutionary movements. Give an explanation for this attitude.

6. What were the particular concerns of the Jewish workers organized in the Bund?

7. How does Weizmann (no. 36) explain the stirring of the Jewish masses, the "first folk awakening" of the Jews in Russia in the last decades of the nineteenth century?

8. In his anguish resulting from the pogroms, Bialik wrote two poems, a short one, "On the Slaughter," reprinted here (no. 31), and a longer one, "In the City of Slaughter." You will find the text of the second poem in any English selection of Bialik's poems available in your local library. Read "In the City of Slaughter" and compare both poems. Is there a difference between them? Whom does Bialik accuse in the second poem?

9. The famous painter Marc Chagall, born in Russia in 1887 and living in France, has used the little Russian towns populated by Jews, the "shtetl," as a creative element in his paintings. You will find reproductions of his paintings in books on Chagall and in art books dealing with modern painting.

10. The first three presidents of the State of Israel were Russian Jews. Did it just happen this way, or are there reasons which help to explain it?

11. What have been the contributions of East European Jewry to Jewish life? Which of these contributions are reflected in (a) Jewish life in the United States and (b) the upbuilding of the State of Israel?

SUGGESTED READING

Note: Books suggested in more than one chapter are here listed by the
name of the author only. A key to such listings will be found at the
end of the book.
A paperback edition is indicated by the letters PB.

Books for the Student

Charry-Segal, chap. 19.
Chesler, pp. 1–44, PB.
Elbogen, pp. 41–66, 103–13, 200–223, 371–407, 453–65.
Grayzel, pp. 600–614, 637–39, 657–59, 661–62, 708–11, 713–15.
Margolis-Marx, chaps. 82, 90–93, 95, 98. PB.
Porath, pp. 26–67. PB.

Books for the Teacher

Baron, chaps. 1–10.
Dawidowicz, Lucy, S., ed. *The Golden Tradition: Jewish Life and Thought
in Eastern Europe.* New York, 1967.
Dubnow, S. M. *History of the Jews in Russia and Poland from the Earliest
Times to the Present Day.* New ed. New York, 1975.
Frumkin, J., et al. *Russian Jewry, 1860–1917.* New York, 1966.
Halkin, chaps. 1–5, PB.
Heschel, Abraham J. *The Earth Is the Lord's.* New York, 1968. PB.
Howe, Irving, and Eliezer Greenberg, eds. *Voices from the Yiddish: Essays,
Memoirs, Diaries.* New York, 1975. PB.
Liptzin, Solomon. *The Flowering of Yiddish Literature* and *The Maturing
of Yiddish Literature.* New York, 1963 and 1970.
Mahler, Raphael. *A History of Modern Jewry, 1780–1815*, chaps. 9–11, 13.
New York, 1971.
Sachar, chaps. 5, 9, 10, 12, 14, 17. PB.
Samuel, Maurice. *In Praise of Yiddish.* New York, 1971.
———. *Blood Accusation: The Strange History of the Beilis Case.* New
York, 1966.
Zborowski, Mark, and Elizabeth Herzog. *Life Is with People: The Culture of
the Shtetl.* New York, 1962. PB.

Autobiographies*

Chagall, Bella, and Marc. *Burning Lights.* Illustrated by Marc
Chagall. New York, 1963. PB.
Levin, Shmarya. *Childhood in Exile* and *The Arena.* New York, 1975.
Weizmann, Chaim. *Trial and Error.* New York, 1967. PB.

Fiction *

Einhorn, David, ed. *Seventh Candle and Other Folk Tales of Eastern Europe*. New York, 1968.

Howe, Irving, and Eliezer Greenberg, eds. *A Treasury of Yiddish Stories*. New York, 1973. PB.

————, eds. *I. L. Perez: Selected Stories*. New York, 1975. PB.

Malamud, Bernard. *The Fixer*. New York, 1967. PB.

Samuel, Maurice. *The World of Sholem Aleichem*. New York, 1943. PB.

Sholom Aleichem. *Selected Stories*. New York, 1956.

Steinberg, Jehuda. *In Those Days*. New York 1967. PB.

Pictorial Books

Schulman, Abraham, ed. *The Old Country: The Lost World of East European Jews*. New York, 1974.

Vishniak, Roman. *Polish Jews: A Pictorial Record*. New York, 1965. PB.

---

*Much of the material listed here for teachers can be read with benefit by students, too.

IV. THE JEWS OF SOVIET RUSSIA

Introduction

World War I and Civil War

The outbreak of World War I in 1914 found the Jews of Russia living in the Pale of Settlement right at the very heart of the Eastern Front. This area was one of the most active theaters of the war, in which Germans and Russians were for a long period engaged in furious and deadly combat. The retreat of the Russian army was marked by horrible brutalities against the Jewish population. Tsarist discrimination against the Jews that existed prior to the war continued after hostilities erupted. No change of policy occurred even though an estimated 600,000 Jews, more than their fair proportion in the Russian Empire's population, served in the Russian army.

During the years of the Civil War which followed (1918–22), Jews were exposed to attacks by both armies, the Red and the White forces, but particularly by the White armies in the Ukraine, which engaged in widespread and merciless pogroms. Estimates of the number of Jews killed in these pogroms vary from 60,000 to 200,000.

Equal Citizens

The fall of the oppressive tsarist government in February 1917 was welcomed by the Jews as it was by many Russians. The Provisional Government which replaced the tsars decreed the removal of all disabilities stemming from differences of race or religion and, at last, the Jews were declared equal citizens.

Nationality Rights

All the organized Jewish parties in Russia decided on an all-Russian, democratically elected, Jewish Congress. What was new and quite different from the struggle for emancipation in Western and Central Europe during the nineteenth century (see chapter 1), was that in Russia all parties were united in asking to be considered as a national minority with legally secured national rights. Elections were held in the fall of 1917. But due to the continuing war, the unstable conditions, and the final successful Communist revolution in October 1917, the congress never met.

In Russia the demand for Jewish national rights and national autonomy did not seem strange. Even Russian Jews who were not Zionists considered

Jews a nationality. They did not think of themselves as "Russians of Mosaic faith" but as Russian Jews. In the words of a prominent non-Zionist leader, Henry Sliosberg, (1867–1937): "We were not a foreign element, for Russia had many nationalities all of which were part of the Russian nation, and no one dominant nationality tried to absorb them. . . . It was not difficult for us to reconcile Jewish nationality with Russian citizenship and to make Russian culture our own as our own Jewish culture."*

The Bolshevik Revolution

The question was whether the Bolsheviks who, as a result of their successful revolution in October 1917, replaced Kerensky's liberal government, would agree to what the Jews of Russia were asking for. Lenin, the leader of the Bolsheviks, had as early as 1903 demanded that the Bund, the party of Jewish workers, give up its "separatism" and join the ranks of the Russian Socialist Party. Lenin had written that the idea of a Jewish "nationality" was "definitely reactionary" not only when expressed by the Zionists but likewise by those "who try to combine it with the ideas of Social Democracy" like the Bundists. He explained that to be regarded as a nation, a people must have "a territory on which to develop and . . . a nation must have a common language."†

Nevertheless, Lenin reversed his earlier stand upon coming to power in 1917, as there was almost complete unanimity among the Russian Jews that they be treated as a national minority. The Jews were, therefore, included in the new Declaration of the Rights of Nationalities, issued by the Council of Peoples' Commissars a few days after the Bolsheviks took over. The declaration guaranteed "the free development of the national minorities and ethnographic groups living within the confines of Russia." The Jews were elated and hoped that they would be finally free to control their own religious and cultural affairs. But events took a different course.

Fight Against Religion

In line with the Communist anti-religious stand, a government decree of June 1918 separated "Church from State and School from Church." All religious property and funds were confiscated, churches and church organizations were deprived of their previously recognized legal status, and religious instruction in the schools was prohibited.

Yevsektsia

Acts against the Jewish religion had reflected the anti-Semitic sentiments

---

*Quoted in Dawidowicz, *The Golden Tradition*, p. 473.
†Quoted in Baron, *The Russian Jew under Tsars and Soviets*, p. 205.

of the tsarist government. Only a few years previously a notorious ritual-murder trial had attracted worldwide attention. The Soviet government left it to the *Yevsektsia*, the Jewish sections of the Communist Party, entrusted with Jewish affairs, to carry on the fight against the Jewish religion. The government took it for granted that Jews would not be suspected of anti-Semitism and disregarded the fact that these Jewish Communists had no attachment to Judaism whatsoever. Instead, from their Marxist teachings they looked forward to the time when the Jewish people would disappear in the ultimate complete merging of all peoples in the common world nation. Jewish members of the Communist Party rarely considered themselves Jews but "internationalists" who "do not pursue special national tasks but only proletarian programs."

The *Yevsektsia* began a relentless fight against the Jewish religion, its traditional institutions, the synagogues, and the schools. In the course of time synagogues and schools were closed. The Jewish communal councils were abolished and there was now no longer a local or national Jewish organization to represent genuine Jewish interests. Before Jewish holidays the anti-religious campaigns carried on at all times were intensified. All Jewish practices were discouraged to the point that Jews unwilling to work on the Sabbath or the High Holidays were harassed.

Hebrew Instruction Prohibited

The teaching of Hebrew, the language of religious "reaction" and of the "counter-revolutionary" Zionists, was prohibited. For a time Hebrew survived in the works of some writers and in the Hebrew theater "Habimah," which enjoyed the protection of some non-Jews like Maxim Gorky. But a group of Hebrew writers, Bialik among them, left Russia in 1921, and the Habimah left in 1926. The few who remained felt that they were fighting a losing battle.

Zionism Outlawed

Zionism became a special target of the Jewish Communists. They passed resolutions against the Zionists as a "counter-revolutionary" group and persuaded the government to suppress all Zionist activities. In 1918 the Zionist organization had counted 1,200 local chapters and 300,000 members. But during the next few years the Zionist movement was outlawed, and thousands of Zionist leaders were arrested and deported to Sibera's political labor camps. A similar fate befell other Jewish groups, including the Bund. A totalitarian state had no room for a variety of political parties.

Yiddish

While Hebrew and Jewish religious life were suppressed, Yiddish and "secular" Yiddish culture were free to develop. In the first years of the Soviet government 75 percent of the Jewish population declared Yiddish to be their native tongue and their language for everyday purposes. Yiddish schools, newspapers, theaters, and research departments at institutions of higher learning were established. However, the Communist goal remained the eventual elimination of Jewish culture and the total assimilation of the Jews. A leading spokesman of the Communist Party declared at a conference of the Jewish sections in Moscow in 1926: "Considering the probability of . . . assimilation, we must . . . indoctrinate the Jewish workers and leaders not to judge each particular activity from the standpoint of national self-preservation, but rather from that of its usefulness to socialist reconstruction."*

Economic Position

The new Communist order had disastrous economic effects on the Jewish population. The dislocation caused by the years of the First World War and the destruction of homes and property which followed during the Civil War left many Jews pauperized. In the prewar period (before 1914) Jews had been merchants, petty shopkeepers, commercial agents, artisans, and home and factory workers. A small percentage were farmers and professionals. Under the Communist regime many of these classes were declared undesirable and unwanted. Even artisans who employed a single worker were similarly classified. Only peasants and workers were declared acceptable. Private trade was banned, and even small workshops were "nationalized." Jewish traders and craftsmen were left destitute. It became practically impossible to earn a living by the traditional means in the towns of the old Pale of Settlement. At a convention of Jewish farmers in Minsk in 1928, it was pointed out that the population in the small Jewish communities was dying of hunger.

A New Economic Structure

It speaks well for the vitality of Soviet Jewry that, instead of throwing up its hands in despair, it set about energetically to reconstruct its battered economic position. There was a vast migration of Jews to the big cities, where progressing industrialization offered new opportunities. During the decades which followed the outbreak of the revolution, Jews became workers, technicians, managers, and government administrative officials. They also found their way into the professions as doctors, engineers, architects, journalists, librarians, teachers, agronomists, and in the arts and the theater. They became well represented in research

---

*Quoted in Baron, op. cit., p. 213.

institutes as "scientific workers," such as physicists, economists, and many others. Some became prominent even in the army although Jews had no military tradition for many centuries. Trotsky built up the Red Army and became its first commander, and many officers of high rank, including generals in the army, navy, and air force, distinguished themselves during the Second World War, for example.

Agriculture

Starvation in the cities in the 1920s was so acute that Jewish families turned to agriculture. Jewish agricultural colonies had already existed under the tsarist regime. But now new Jewish agricultural colonies were founded in the Ukraine and the Crimea. Their efforts were helped by Jewish funds from abroad. The colonies were successful and attracted 6 percent of the Jewish population. They were, however, destroyed by the Nazi invasion during the Second World War and not rebuilt.

Biro-Bidzhan

During the transitional years of the 1920s, however, Jewish poverty, remained a problem. Hence in 1928 Biro-Bidzhan, a section of Russia in the Far East, was designated as an area for Jewish settlement, and in 1934 it was given the status of a Jewish autonomous region. Various reasons have been assigned for the adoption of this project. One was to create a Jewish territorial unit, a Jewish state in a sparsely populated, undeveloped area with a very harsh climate. The Soviet "Jewish state," it was hoped, would turn the attention of Russian and foreign Jews away from Zionism and stimulate the moral and financial support of Jews, mainly from America. Finally, the Soviet government seems to have been prompted by strategic considerations as well, namely, to safeguard its Far Eastern frontier with Japan by recruiting settlers for this exposed border area. The number of Jews who settled in the area was small; hence the project can for all practical purposes be considered a failure.

Trotsky Expelled

After the death of Lenin in 1924, an internal struggle within the Soviet leadership took place. In the final outcome Stalin prevailed against Trotsky, who was expelled from the party, exiled in 1928, and ultimately murdered in Mexico in 1940 by a Soviet agent. In the struggle against Trotsky, and in the subsequent years when Stalin eliminated other leading contenders like Kamenev and Zinoviev, attention was called to the Jewish origin of these men by mentioning their original names as, for example, Bronstein for Trotsky, Rosenfeld for Kamenev, and the like. In the "purges" of the 1930s, initiated by Stalin, practically all the old

Bolsheviks, among them many Jews, were tried and executed. It is true that during these purges many non-Jews were also put to death. But the fact remains that among Stalin's new appointees to high positions, there were no longer any Jews.

Russian Nationalism

The latter part of the 1930s saw a change in Soviet policies. Russian nationalism and patriotism were suddenly stressed as opposed to the previous emphasis on Marxian internationalism. The Russian nationality became preponderant, and Russification was intensified and took its toll from the smaller nationalities of the Soviet Union.

World War II

In line with these tendencies, Jewish (usually Yiddish) schools and newspapers were shut down and Jewish cultural and religious life was severely curtailed. The *Yevsektsia* had been abolished in 1930 and its functions were taken over by government agencies. The Stalin-Hitler pact of 1939 intensified anti-Semitic trends. But during the war years of 1941 to 1945, in order to help in enlisting support for the Soviet war effort and encourage the financial assistance of Jews in the Allied countries, Stalin found it expedient to create a Jewish Anti-Fascist Committee of prominent writers and artists.

Although Russian Jews fought with devotion and distinguished themselves in the army and among the partisans in the Nazi-occupied territories, neither their sacrifices nor their losses were identified and recognized in the years following the war. Everything was done by the regime to suppress any evidences of Jewish consciousness or existence. Even information about Hitler's war against the Jews and the Holocaust was toned down or suppressed.

The Black Years

A glimmer of hope was kindled among Jews when Russia in the United Nations supported the Partition Plan for Palestine in 1947 and the State of Israel in 1948. Russian policy was dictated by strictly tactical reasons to eliminate Great Britain from the Middle East and had no favorable influence on the treatment of the Jewish nationality within Russia. On the contrary, with the year 1948 began the "Black Years" of Russian Jewry, years of unmitigated terror directed against Jews by Stalin. The leaders of the Jewish Anti-Fascist Committee were murdered; all prominent Yiddish writers executed; and the remaining Jewish cultural institutions, the Yiddish theater, the publishing house, the only Yiddish newspaper, and the libraries were liquidated. Jews were accused of being "rootless cosmopolitans," and the anti-Jewish terror culminated in the notorious "Doctors' Plot" in 1953, linking Jewish doctors in a plot to murder Soviet leaders at the behest of American intelligence and the international Jewish bourgeoisie. Only Stalin's death during the same year put an end to the orgy of arrests and staged trials. However, the inevitable result of the actions and accusations during the Stalin years was a wave of popular anti-Semitism, unprecedented in its open and bold expression.

Against Israel

Although some of Stalin's terror, like the imaginary "Doctors' Plot," was belatedly admitted by his successors, they had succeeded in instilling fear and anxiety toward the regime. The anxiety of Russian Jews was reinforced when the Soviet Union, after its brief support of Israel, began to court the Arabs in order to realize Russia's age-old dream of gaining a foothold in the Mediterranean. The Soviets began to attack Israel as a Western "imperialist" pawn and to equate Zionism with Fascism. In the 1960s the attacks were extended to include Judaism as a religion. Contrary to the treatment accorded other nationalities, Jews were no longer permitted to have Yiddish schools, newspapers, books, theater, etc. As before, rights granted to other religions, such as providing religious education, maintaining national religious bodies, and obtaining ritual articles, were consistently denied to the Jews.

It is true that because of the heavy emphasis on technological progress and the need for educated people, Jews have found opportunities in state industries, in research laboratories, and in the professions. By virtue of their special ability, many Jews received individual recognition, especially in the sciences and the arts. But as a group Jews were denied national expression, with very limited opportunity for religious expression, and thus became the victims of discrimination by the state.

Silencing to Death

The Soviet government had hoped that Soviet conditions of life and government pressures would lead to the dissolution of the Jewish religion and nationality. It has been pointed out that the root cause of Soviet policy is distrust and suspicion of the Jew as Jew, of the Jewish people as such, and of Soviet Jewry insofar as it identifies with Jewry at large, with its history and destiny. Consequently, the aim of Soviet policy is to eradicate every trace of an identifiable and proudly self-aware Jewish group. Beginning in the 1950s the government tried every means to eliminate references to Jews as a group from textbooks and similar publications. Even the atrocities committed by the Nazis against Jews were expunged from public mention. Several monuments erected at the site of mass executions of Jews were removed, and other memorials, with no reference to Jews, were erected in their place. "The intention was to 'silence to death' a living organism by *creating the illusion that it did not exist—until such time as it would in fact cease to exist.*"*

National Jewish Loyalties

The Holocaust, the increased anti-Semitism under Soviet rule, and the establishment of the State of Israel have contributed to the strengthening of Jewish consciousness and loyalties among many Russian Jews. This has been especially true of the Jews in the territories acquired by Russia in 1939 and at the end of World War II, namely, the Baltic states (Lithuania, Latvia, Estonia), parts of Poland and Rumania, as well of the Jews of Georgia, all of whom could draw on strong Jewish religious and national traditions. At the end of the 1960s Jews in Russia began to speak up as Jews and even to apply for emigration to Israel, with a majority of the applicants from the territories mentioned above. To apply for emigration to Israel is considered a betrayal and almost like a crime in Soviet eyes. The harassment and persecution of Jews who dare to apply are indescribable. Yet the movement of Jewish reawakening could not be completely suppressed. Groups in various cities have begun to study Hebrew and Jewish history clandestinely, published and circulated material of their own as "underground" publications, and organized petitions and protests. One cannot but feel humble admiration in the face of the bravery of these people, who live in a country where any utterance of unacceptable ideas results in confinement in a prison camp or worse. "Considering the overwhelming obstacles, the defiance of the monolithic police power of the Soviet regime by a small, disdained minority must be recorded as one of the most stirring freedom stories of our time."*

Sources

Our selection of sources begins with an appeal of a representative committee of Russian Jews preparing for the election of a Jewish Congress in 1917 (no. 41), a resolution against Zionism by the Jewish Communist sections (no. 42), and a poem by Elisha Rodin bemoaning the death of Hebrew in Soviet Russia (no. 43).

A fact sheet describes the anti-Jewish discrimination practiced in Soviet Russia (nos 44 and 45). Anti-Semitism as a policy under Communist rule is discussed by Trotsky (no. 46).

---

*Kochan, *The Jews in Soviet Russia*, p. 175.
*Schroeter, *The Last Exodus*, p. 36.

The fight which was finally begun by Russian Jews against the anti-Jewish discrimination of their government, the struggle for permission to emigrate to Israel, and the reasons for leaving are documented in letters of Russian Jews (nos. 47, 49, 50, and 51).

The world protest against the anti-Jewish policy of the Soviet government is expressed in an address by former Supreme Court Justice Arthur Goldberg (no. 48) and letters of outstanding Russian physicists (no. 52).

The chapter concludes with the speech of a Ukrainian writer at a Babi Yar commemoration (no. 53) and the story of "Samizdat," the Jewish clandestine publications (no. 54).

41. FOR NATIONAL RIGHTS

A COMMITTEE OF RUSSIAN JEWS

After the February Revolution of 1917, the Provisional Government removed all previous disabilities and declared Jews equal citizens of Russia. A committee representing all organized Jewish parties, and charged with the preparations for the election of a democratically elected Jewish Congress, issued the following appeal to the Jewish communities.

Citizens, Jews! The Jewish people in Russia now faces an event which has no parallel in Jewish history for two thousand years. Not only has the Jew as an individual, as a citizen, acquired equality of rights—which has also happened in other countries—but the Jewish nation looks forward to the possibility of securing national rights. Never and nowhere have the Jews lived through such a serious, responsible moment as the present— responsible to the present and the future generations.

42. ZIONISM IS COUNTER-REVOLUTIONARY

THE JEWISH COMMUNIST SECTIONS

The Zionist organization had become the most potent force in Jewish political life, although it had to work underground in tsarist Russia. But a conference of the Jewish sections of the Communist Party adopted the following resolution in June 1919 in Moscow.

The Zionist party plays a counter-revolutionary role. It is responsible for strengthening, among the backward Jewish masses, the influence of clericalism and nationalist attitudes. In this way the class self-determination of the Jewish toiling masses is undermined and the penetration of communist ideas in their midst seriously hindered. Owing to its Palestine policy, the Zionist Party serves as an instrument of united imperialism which combats the proletarian revolution. In consideration of all these circumstances, the Conference requests the Central Bureau to propose to the pertinent authorities the promulgation of a decree suspending all activities of the Zionist Party in the economic, political and cultural spheres. The communal organs, which are the mainstay of all reactionary forces within the Jewish people, must be suppressed.

43. AN ELEGY FOR HEBREW

ELISHA RODIN

Elisha Rodin (1888–1946) was one of the last poets in the Soviet Union to write in Hebrew. He also wrote Yiddish poems which were published in Russia, but the Hebrew poems appeared in the 1930s in Palestine. This fact led to his imprisonment by the Soviet authorities.

On rivers of sorrow they stifled our song
The song of Zion, crystalline and bright,
Made old and young alike forget our tongue,
Snuffed out its sparkles of splendor and light.

On rivers of sorrow our tongue was slain,
How can I ever forget my shame?
The cup of our sufferings, the honor's stain,
All that I swallowed in the sorrow's name.

44. FACT SHEET ON ANTI-JEWISH DISCRIMINATION IN THE SOVIET UNION

These facts and figures were compiled in 1971 by the Bibliotheque Juive Contemporaine of Paris, an authoritative source of information concerning the status of Jews in Soviet Russia, under the direction of Joseph Fuks.

Discrimination in Education

. . . Although each nationality group in the USSR has the right to its own school system to teach its language and culture, there are no Jewish schools at any level in the USSR.

. . . The number of Jewish students in secondary schools remained constant at 47,000 from 1962–63 to 1967, compared to an increase in the total number of students of all nationalities during this period of 155 per cent. As a result, the number of Jewish students fell from fourth place to tenth place among all nationality groups.

. . . In higher education, Jews represented 14.5 per cent of all university students in 1886 under the Czar; 13 per cent in 1935; 3.2 percent in 1960; and 2.5 per cent in 1970. This is the result both of a sharp decline in the number of Jewish students and a parallel increase in the number of university students of other nationalities. The decline in university enrollment among young Jews is underscored by the fact that the great majority of university students in the USSR come from cities. With approximately 95 per cent of all Jews living in cities, Jews should represent a far higher percentage of the USSR's total university enrollment.

. . . Jews are totally excluded from Soviet military academies and training schools for diplomats.

. . . Annual quotas for preferential admission to colleges and universities are granted each republic in the USSR. Since the Jews do not have a republic of their own, they enjoy no college admission quota.

Discrimination in Public Life and the Professions

. . . Jews constitute a little over 1.5 per cent of the total population of the USSR. However, only 0.004 per cent of all members of local Soviets (councils) in the USSR are Jews.

. . . In 1937, 10.8 per cent of the Communist Party Central Committee were Jews. Today there is only one Jewish member out of a total of 241.

. . . Although Jews continue to play an important role in Soviet science, the percentage of Jewish scientific research personnel has dropped steadily from 16.8 per cent in 1947 to 11 per cent in 1955 to 7.7 per cent in 1967. It is believed the percentage is still lower today. A comparison with other nationality groups indicates that fewer and fewer young Jews are given the opportunity to follow scientific careers. Most Jewish scientists today are of the older generation.

Discrimination in Cultural Life

. . . Until the "purge" of 1936–38, some 160,000 Jewish students attended an estimated 11,000 classes in Jewish schools. Thousands of Jewish teachers taught there, having received their training in teachers' seminaries especially created for this purpose in various universities— among them, the University of Moscow and the University of Minsk. Today there is not a single school or classroom in the Soviet Union where Jewish culture and history are taught, either in Yiddish, Hebrew or

Russian. This is so even though 380,000 Jews declared Yiddish to be their mother tongue in the 1970 census and the Soviet Constitution grants every group of 20 parents the right to have their children educated in their mother tongue.

... In Birobidjan, the so-called "Jewish Autonomous Region" on the Sino-Soviet frontier, there are no Jewish schools either. Today Jews constitute less than 10 per cent of the estimated 170,000 inhabitants of Birobidjan.

... In 1953 the USSR had 16 Jewish theaters and two academies of Jewish dramatic art. Today there is not one full-time Jewish theatrical group. Instead, there are local part-time traveling theatrical companies in Vilna, Birobidjan and Kishinev whose success before Jewish audiences (an estimated 500,000 spectators per year) testifies to the yearning for Jewish culture and art among the Jews of the USSR.

... In 1947 there were 57 books published in Yiddish in the USSR. In 1948 there were 60. During the eight-year period from 1960 to 1968, however, there were only eight. Although the number of books published in Yiddish in the USSR has increased in the past two years—largely as a result of the pressure of world opinion—not one book has been published in Yiddish on the Holocaust.

... Those books that have been published since 1968 have been almost exclusively reprints of earlier volumes rather than original works. Moreover, they have been distributed in large part abroad—to serve Soviet propaganda purposes rather than Yiddish readers in the Soviet Union.

Discrimination in Religion

... There is no central Jewish institution or communal body, such as other religious groups in the USSR enjoy, nor is there the opportunity for Jews to take part in international conferences of their coreligionists, a right afforded the central bodies of other faiths in the USSR.

... In 1926—after almost a decade of Soviet rule and harassment of religion—there were 1,103 synagogues in the USSR. Thirty years later there were 450. In 1969 this figure had been reduced to 59—this despite the Soviet law that grants believers the right to form religious societies and to have religious buildings constructed for the purpose of prayer and worship. As of 1971 there were no more than 40 synagogues in the USSR still open for prayer. Of these, half are located in the non-European parts of the Soviet Union, in an area inhabited by less than 10 per cent of the total Jewish population of the country.

... There are only three functioning rabbis in the USSR today, two of them more than 75 years old.

. . . There is no Yeshiva or rabbinical training seminary in the Soviet Union—although in 1957 Rabbi Schlieffer announced at the inauguration of the first higher institute of Jewish religious learning that he had enough students to fill three large schools. A war of attrition followed. Students from outside Moscow were refused the right to return to Moscow after their summer vacations. Today the Yeshiva is no longer in operation. Nor has any Jewish rabbinical student ever been sent abroad for study—in sharp contrast to the treatment accorded to other religious cults in the country.

. . . The last Hebrew Bible was printed in the Soviet Union in 1917. Since then two prayer books were published, one in an edition of 3,000 in 1958, the other of 10,000 in 1968. The latter edition is generally regarded as having been published in response to complaints of tourists shocked at the continuing use of 50-year-old prayer books by worshipers in the Moscow Synagogue. More recently, tourists visiting Russian synagogues have reported that the new prayer books are locked away on shelves; the regular worshipers are apparently required to use the old ones.

. . . While crucifixes, candles and other Christian religious articles are manufactured in large quantities in the USSR, Jews are prohibited from manufacturing or from importing phylacteries, prayer shawls and other articles required for Jewish worship. Not until 1968 was the ban against accepting gifts or shipments of religious articles from abroad partially lifted. In that year a shipment of seven boxes of religious articles was permitted to enter the USSR—the first time in the 51-year history of the Soviet regime. There has been nothing since.

. . . No answer has been given to repeated requests by Jews for a new central Jewish burial ground in Moscow.

. . . Since 1966, the baking of *matzoth* for Passover has been again permitted in the USSR. This was a reversal of Soviet policy, beginning in 1957, to discourage the production of *matzoth*. Kharkov was the first city where *matzoth* could not be manufactured. By 1962 the prohibition was general. In 1965, however—largely as a result of world-wide protests—*matzoth* production was permitted in Moscow, Leningrad and Odessa, and since 1966 most cities with Jewish communities have been producing *matzoth* for Passover without interference.

. . . Circumcision, not prohibited by Soviet law, is practiced without hindrance by most of the USSR's 25 million Moslems. But the same practice when performed by Jews is scorned and subjected to harassment. It is impossible to ascertain the proportion of Jewish male infants who undergo the operation of circumcision, since most are performed in secret. We do know that very few *mohalim* are now functioning legally in the Soviet Union. Thus a basic Jewish ritual, observed almost universally by Jews for countless generations, is now a rarity in the USSR.

45. SOME UNANSWERED QUESTIONS

INFORMATION DIVISION, MINISTRY OF FOREIGN AFFAIRS, JERUSALEM

If Jewishness is a nationality recorded in identity cards yet Jews are denied the "national" life which is enjoyed by other nationalities in the USSR—what can be the object of this form of registration, if not to make things easier for the authorities in discriminating against Jews?

Is there any other minority in the world which is barred from studying its own history, literature and ancient tongue; from celebrating its festivals as tradition bids; from writing about its experiences; from keeping in touch with its fellow-nationals in other lands?

For years, anti-Semitism, implanted so long and so deeply among the peoples of Eastern Europe, has been officially encouraged and propagated by the Soviet authorities. We may well ask, on the basis of our historical experience, what might happen to the flesh and blood objects of this sponsored hatred if Soviet society were to undergo a calamitous upheaval or a desperate crisis?

If a State robs a minority of its right to uphold a national and cultural identity, can that minority be prevented from fighting to regain its identity and the right of repatriation to its free, historic, Homeland?

Is not Soviet Jewry's struggle for its identity and for the right to go to Israel evidence that Zionism is a national liberation movement?

Are not the Jews of the Soviet Union, as Jews, entitled to the right of self-determination, exactly as are Ukrainians and Uzbeks, or even the Germans dispersed in the several Soviet Republics, who enjoy cultural and educational rights and exercise them in their native language? If so, why do the Soviet authorities withhold these prerogatives from the Jews alone?

If the Soviet Union will not grant the Jews parity with the Russians, the Ukrainians, the Uzbeks and the Germans, does that not signify that it is seeking to coerce them into what is, from the cultural and the human point of view, a status of inferiority?

If the citizens of a State must live with feelings of deprivation and discrimination, are they not at least entitled to the human right that is enshrined in the Universal Declaration on Human Rights—the right to depart?

46. ANTI-SEMITISM IN SOVIET RUSSIA

LEON TROTSKY

Leon Trotsky (Bronstein, 1879–1940) was a Russian revolutionary and Soviet and Communist leader. He became commissar for foreign affairs in 1917 and leader of the Red Army in 1918. His position declined after the death of Lenin in 1924. Stalin had him expelled from the Communist Party in 1927 and exiled in 1928. In 1940 he was murdered in Mexico, probably by a Soviet agent. In his years of exile he wrote brilliant articles analyzing the totalitarian regime in Russia. He never identified with the Jewish people and considered himself "just a Socialist."

The selection is taken from Trotsky's article "Thermidor and Antisemitism," written in 1937.

At the time of the last Moscow trial I remarked in one of my statements that Stalin, in the struggle with the Opposition, exploited the anti-Semitic tendencies in the country. On this subject I received a series of letters and questions which were, by and large—there is no reason to hide the truth—very naïve. "How can one accuse the Soviet Union of anti-Semitism?" "If the USSR is an anti-Semitic country, is there anything left at all?" . . .

. . . It has not yet been forgotten, I trust, that anti-Semitism was quite widespread in Czarist Russia among the peasants, the petty bourgeoisie of the city, the intelligentsia and the more backward strata of the working class. "Mother" Russia was renowned not only for her periodic Jewish pogroms but also for the existence of a considerable number of anti-Semitic publications which, in that day, enjoyed a wide circulation. The October revolution abolished the outlawed status against the Jews. That, however, does not at all mean that with one blow it swept out anti-Semitism. A long and persistent struggle against religion has failed to prevent suppliants even today from crowding thousands and thousands of churches, mosques and synagogues. The same situation prevails in the sphere of national prejudices. Legislation alone does not change people. Their thoughts, emotions, outlook depend upon tradition, material conditions of life, cultural level, etc. The Soviet regime is not yet twenty years old. The older half of the population was educated under Czarism. The younger half has inherited a great deal from the older. These general historical conditions in themselves should make any thinking person realize that, despite the model legislation of the October revolution, it is impossible that national and chauvinist prejudices, particularly anti-Semitism, should not have persisted strongly among the backward layers of the population.

But this is by no means all. The Soviet regime, in actuality, initiated a series of new phenomena which, because of the poverty and low cultural level of the population, were capable of generating anew, and did in fact generate, anti-Semitic moods. The Jews are a typical city population. They comprise a considerable percentage of the city population in the Ukraine, in White Russia and even in Great Russia. The Soviet, more than any other regime in the world, needs a very great number of civil servants. Civil servants are recruited from the more cultured city population. Naturally the Jews occupied a disproportionately large place among the bureaucracy and particularly so in its lower and middle levels. Of course we can close our eyes to that fact and limit ourselves to vague generalities about the equality and brotherhood of all races. But an ostrich policy will not advance us a single step. *The hatred of the peasants and the workers for the bureaucracy is a fundamental fact in Soviet life.* The despotism of the regime, the persecution of every critic, the stifling of every living thought, finally, the judicial frame-ups are merely the reflection of this basic fact. Even by *a priori* reasoning it is impossible not to conclude that the hatred for the bureaucracy would assume an anti-Semitic color, at least in those places where the Jewish functionaries compose a significant percentage of the population and are thrown into relief against the broad background of the peasant masses. . . . The antagonism between the population and the bureaucracy has grown monstrously during the past ten to twelve years. All serious and honest observers, especially those who have lived among the toiling masses for a long time, bear witness to the existence of anti-Semitism, not only of the old and hereditary, but also of the new, "Soviet" variety. . . .

The Ukrainian bureaucrat, if he himself is an indigenous Ukrainian, will, at the critical moment, inevitably try to emphasize that he is a brother to the *muzhik* and the peasant—not some sort of foreigner and under no circumstances a Jew. Of course there is not—alas!—a grain of "socialism" or even of elementary democracy in such an attitude. But that's precisely the nub of the question. The privileged bureaucracy, fearful of its privileges, and consequently completely demoralized, represents at present *the most anti-socialist and most anti-democratic stratum of Soviet society.* In the struggle for its self-preservation it exploits the most ingrained prejudices and the most benighted instincts. If in Moscow, Stalin stages trials which accuse the Trotskyites of plotting to poison the workers, then it is not difficult to imagine to what foul depths the bureaucracy can resort in some Ukrainian or central Asiatic hovel!

He who attentively observes Soviet life, even if only through official publications, will from time to time see bared in various parts of the country hideous bureaucratic abscesses: bribery, corruption, embezzlement, murder of persons whose existence is embarrassing to the bureaucracy, violation of women and the like. Were we to slash vertically through, we would see that every such abscess resulted from the bureaucratic stratum. Sometimes Moscow is constrained to resort to demonstration trials. In all such trials the Jews inevitably comprise a significant percentage, in part because, as was already stated, they make up a great part of the bureaucracy and are branded with its odium, partly because, impelled by the instinct for self-preservation, the leading cadre of the bureaucracy at the center and in the provinces strives to divert the indignation of the working masses from itself to the Jews. . . .

The struggle against the Opposition* was for the ruling clique a question of life and death. The program, principles, ties with the masses, everything was rooted out and cast aside because of the anxiety of the new ruling clique for its self-preservation. These people stop at nothing in order to guard their privileges and power. . . .

Between 1923 and 1926, when Stalin, with Zinoviev and Kamenev, was still a member of the "Troika," the play on the strings of anti-Semitism bore a very cautious and masked character. . . .

After Zinoviev and Kamenev joined the Opposition the situation changed radically for the worse. At this point there opened wide a perfect chance to say to the workers that at the head of the Opposition stand three "dissatisfied Jewish intellectuals." Under the direction of Stalin, Uglanov in Moscow and Kirov in Leningrad carried through this line systematically and almost fully in the open. In order the more sharply to demonstrate to the workers the differences between the "old" course and the "new," the Jews, even when unreservedly devoted to the general line, were removed from responsible party and Soviet posts. . . . In the months of preparations for the expulsions of the Opposition from the party, the arrests, the exiles (in the second half of 1927), the anti-Semitic agitation assumed a thoroughly unbridled character. The slogan, "Beat the Opposition," often took on the complexion of the old slogan "Beat the Jews and save Russia." The matter went so far that Stalin was constrained to come out with a printed statement which declared: "We fight against Trotsky, Zinoviev and Kamenev not because they are Jews but because they are Oppositionists," etc. To every politically thinking person it was completely clear that this consciously equivocal declaration, directed against "excesses" of anti-Semitism, did at the same time with complete premeditation nourish it. "Do not forget that the leaders of the Opposition are—Jews." That was the *meaning* of the statement of Stalin, published in all Soviet journals. . . .

---

*See the introduction to this chapter.

Again: if such methods are practiced at the very top where the personal responsibility of Stalin is absolutely unquestionable, then it is not hard to imagine what transpires in the ranks, at the factories, and especially at the *kolkhozes.* . . .

. . . I have lived my whole life outside of Jewish circles. I have always worked in the Russian workers' movement. My native tongue is Russian. Unfortunately, I have not even learned to read Jewish. The Jewish question therefore has never occupied the center of my attention. But that does not mean that I have the right to be blind to the Jewish problem which exists and demands solution. . . .

47. JEWISH FREEDOM LETTERS FROM RUSSIA

MOSHE DECTER (ed.)

The State of Israel has become a source of pride and a fundamental issue for masses of Russian Jews, and has converted their feeling of oppression, resentment, and frustration into positive striving. This new conviction has encouraged Jews to speak up for their rights. The "Jews of silence," as they were called, have become the "Jews of audacity." The following letters bear ample witness to this change. They have been brought to the attention of the outside world by travelers, journalists, and others who have been in Russia, and in some cases they have come by regular mail.

See also the introduction to this chapter on the rise of Jewish self-awareness among Russian Jews.

a. Letter from Yakov Karakov—May 20, 1968

Yakov Kazakov was exactly twenty-one years old when, on June 13, 1967, he renounced his Soviet citizenship, in reaction against Soviet enmity to the State of Israel and the virulent propaganda campaign waged against it as a result of the Six-Day War. Nearly a year later, he wrote the following letter to the Supreme Soviet, reiterating his renunciation and demanding an exit permit for Israel. On December 19, 1968, the Washington Post published a lengthy report on this letter. Within a few weeks, he was given his exit permit, and he arrived in Israel in February 1969.

Comrade Deputies!

I am again applying to you, and I shall continue to apply until my request is granted. I demand what is mine by right, and any negative reply, no matter in what form it is given, is unlawful and contrary both to the Constitution of the USSR and to the Declaration of the Rights of Man, which the Soviet Union has undertaken to observe and to respect.

I, Yakov Yosifovich Kazakov, a Jew, born in 1947, residing at No. 6 Third

Institutskaya St., apt. 42, Moscow 2R-389, renounce Soviet citizenship, and, from the moment that I first announced my renunciation of USSR citizenship, that is, from June 13, 1967, I do not consider myself a citizen of the USSR.

Whether to be, or not to be, a citizen of this or of another country, is the private affair of every person.

By not agreeing to accept my renunciation of Soviet citizenship, you cannot force me to become a loyal citizen of the USSR. Independently of your decision, I am not a citizen of the USSR, and I act, and shall act, as one who does not have USSR citizenship.

I am a Jew, I was born a Jew, and I want to live out my life as a Jew. With all my respect for the Russian people, I do not consider my people in any way inferior to the Russian, or to any other, people, and I do not want to be assimilated by any people.

As in the Soviet Union there are no conditions for the existence of the Jewish nation, Jews who wish to leave the USSR should be given the possibility to do so (just as this is done in other countries: Rumania and Poland, for example).

I am a Jew, and, as a Jew, I consider the State of Israel my Fatherland, the Fatherland of my people, the only place on earth where there exists an independent Jewish State, and I, like any other Jew, have the indubitable right to live in that state.

The Jewish people has a right to its own, independent State and every Jew, no matter where he lives and no matter where he was born, has the right to live in the Jewish State.

This right has been confirmed in the corresponding UN resolution of November 29, 1947, for which the Soviet representative also voted.

It does not matter what the political regime in Israel is, what is the internal or the foreign policy of Israel. It is our country. Israel is a Jewish State, and only we, the Jews, have the right to change anything in that country, if we consider it necessary. This depends upon us, and only upon us.

I do not wish to be a citizen of the USSR, of a country that refuses to the Jews (and to other nations, too,) the right of self-determination.

I do not wish to be a citizen of a country where Jews are subjected to forced assimilation, where my people is deprived of its national image and of its cultural treasures, of a country where, under the pretext of a struggle against Zionism, all the cultural life of the Jewish people has been eradicated, where the dissemination of any literature on the history of the Jewish people or on the cultural life of Jews abroad in our times is persecuted.

I do not wish to be a citizen of a country that conducts a policy of genocide toward the Jewish people. If the fascists exterminated us physically, you are exterminating Jews as a nation. I do not wish to collaborate in this additional crime of yours against the Jewish people.

I know that the Soviet Union suffered great losses in its fight against fascism, but I also know that it was the Soviet Union that had closed its borders before the refugees from the fascist plague and thus doomed thousands of Jews to death in the Nazi camps.

I also know about the clearly anti-Semitic policy waged in 1948-53, when the best representatives of Russia's Jewry were annihilated, and I also know that this anti-Semitic policy is being carried out at present, even though in a somewhat changed form and by less barbaric methods.

I do not want to live in a country whose government has spilled so much Jewish blood. I do not want to participate with you in the extermination of the Jewish nation in the Soviet Union. I do not wish to live in a country in which have been re-established (even though in secret) limitations concerning Jews (concerning admittance to a number of educational institutions, establishments, enterprises, etc.). I shall not enumerate it all: you know this better than I do.

I do not wish to be a citizen of a country that arms and supports the remaining fascists and the Arab chauvinists who desire to wipe Israel off the face of the earth and to add another two and a half million of killed to the six million who have perished. I do not want to be a collaborator of yours in the destruction of the State of Israel because, even though this has not been done officially, I consider myself to be a citizen of the State of Israel (the more so as I possess an invitation for permanent residence in the State of Israel).

On the basis of the above, I renounce Soviet citizenship, and I demand to be freed from the humiliation of being considered a citizen of the Union of Soviet Socialist Republics.

I demand to be given a possibility of leaving the Soviet Union.

Kazakov

b. Letter of Eighteen Families of Georgia to the Secretary General of the United Nations, August 6, 1969

Mr. Secretary-General of the UN:

We, the eighteen religious Jewish families of Georgia, wish to remind you that we are alive and pray for our return to Israel.

A hundred days ago we applied to the UN with the request that we be helped to emigrate. We wrote that each of us, after being sent for by a relative in Israel, received the necessary questionnaires and oral promises not to impede his departure, from the USSR organs that are empowered to do so. Each of us, awaiting departure from day to day, had sold his property, including his house, and resigned from his job. We filled the questionnaires and remembered the promises. A year has passed (for many of us more than one) and nothing has changed.

As before, our bread is bitter, our tears are salty and the conditions in which we live are difficult. Here is an example: one of the families is huddled together in one room—small children, their parents and old people; at night there are rats.

We understand: our sad faces may dampen somewhat the holiday mood of the Soviet people who are preparing to celebrate the 100th anniversary of the birth of V. I. Lenin, who laid the foundations of the nationality policy of the USSR. But we have no way out: we applied a long time ago and the choice has been made—we wait, because we believe.

Who will help us?

The history of the Jews is the road of sufferings, on which each step is marked with blood. The Jews did not abandon their Fatherland of their own free will—they were expelled.

We are the descendants of those exiles.

It is doubtful whether there can be found another nation that had to defend so long and so stubbornly, with tears and blood, the right before the entire world to its own State. This tragedy began before our era; in 1948 the curtain started to come down on it, when the UN confirmed the right of the Jews to re-establish their national State on the land of their ancestors. But Israel is still calling on its sons and daughters to come.

As long as the curtain has not yet come down, it is possible to see millions of corpses on the stage, and we want you to know what it means to be a Jew: six million Jews were killed in the last World War—this means that each of us has been six million times shot, hanged, asphyxiated in gas chambers; and before this our children were murdered, taken by their feet and their heads crushed against the walls of houses; our mothers, wives and daughters were raped before our eyes.

We want you to know what it means to be a Jew: our hearts are cemeteries, where a few are buried individually, those that we know, such as Anne Frank and Hannah Senesh, and the other graves are fraternal graves. . . .

Who then will help us?

We have still not received the permit to emigrate; one might think that our case is the first one of its kind and that the competent organs are deliberating how they should act in this very case. However, there are known precedents.

There is much in common between the fate of the Armenians and the

Jews: both nations had for centuries been the victims of oppression. Both had been scattered all over the earth; in both cases the majority of the nation for many generations lived outside the boundaries of their historical Fatherland. The USSR has done everything to realize the centuries-old dreams of the Armenians; today hundreds of thousands of them have been repatriated to Armenia.

They can say: the Armenians left the capitalist hell into the country of victorious socialism, and that no comparison can be made here. Let it be so. But then, let us remember something else: the Spaniards who emigrated to the USSR at the end of the Thirties returned at the end of the Fifties, together with grown-up children who were born in the USSR, to their Fatherland—to Franco Spain; at that time the Spanish Republicans were not called betrayers and traitors by anyone.

Why is it that what has been permitted to the Armenians and the Spaniards is forbidden to the Jews?

We know that the famous internationalist and Leninist, W. Gomulka, has widely opened the gates for all the Jews who desire to go out of Poland; in this he is fulfilling his duty as a communist.

And so, there are precedents. What, then, is the matter?

In our first letter we wrote that it is not racial discrimination in the USSR that makes us want to return to Israel, but religious reasons, the desire to reunify the families that have been torn apart by the war. We are not coming out in the name of ALL the Jews of the USSR, we are not demanding the return to Israel of ALL the Jews of the USSR.

We apply only in the name of those 18 whose signatures were under the first letter and are under the present letter. We speak in the name of those who WISH to go. After all, everyone makes a choice for himself and only our God is one for all. Therefore, whoever wants to, should return, and whoever does not want to—let him go his own way.

In the 100 days that have passed none of us and none of the members of our families has changed his mind, we all want to return to Israel, and there is no power that can stop us.

We believe that we shall return. We are convinced of this on the basis of the Leninist doctrine on the right of nations to self-determination, which lies at the foundation of the national policy of the USSR, and on the statements of official persons, in particular of A. N. Kosygin (Paris, December 3, 1966).

There are also other documents, well known to you: "THE UNIVERSAL DECLARATION OF THE RIGHTS OF MAN" and the "INTERNATIONAL CONVENTION ON THE ELIMINATION OF ALL FORMS OF RACIAL DISCRIMINATION," signed by the USSR as well; in these international agreements is confirmed the right of everyone "to leave any country, including his own," and this is precisely what we ask. Since the UN Human Rights Commission, to which we first wrote, was unable to help us, we turn to you with the same request.

We state once again that we shall never give up our right to live on the land of Israel, because we are an integral part of the Jewish people, which has kept its faith and traditions.

May our prayers penetrate your mind and your conscience, Mr. Secretary General. We are expecting help from you, because time is short.

We are not afraid of anything, because, dead or alive—we are children of Israel.

Who will help us?

Signatures:
   Elashvili, Shabata Milhailovich, Kutaisi, Dzhaparidze 53
   Elashvili, Mikhail Shabatovich, Kutaisi, Dzhaparidze 33
   Elashvili, Izrail Mikhailovich, Kutaisi, Kirova 31
   Eluashivili, Yakov Aronovich, Kutaisi, Mayakovskoyo 5
   Khikhinashvili, Mordekh Isakovich, Kutaisi, Makharadze 19
   Chikvashvili, Mikhail Samuilovich, Kutaisi, Khakhanashvili 38
   Chikvashvili, Moshe Samuilovich, Kutaisi, Tsereteli 82
   Beberashvili, Mikhail Rubernovich, Kutaisi, Klara-Tsetkin 9
   Elashvili, Yakov Izrailovich, Kutaisi, Tsereteli 54
   Mikhelashvili, Khaim Aronovich, Poti, Tskhakaya 57
   Mikhailashvili, Albert Khaimovich, Poti, Tskhakaya 57
   Mikhelashvili, Aron Khaimovich, Poti, Dzhaparidze 18
   and six more signatures.

48. UNTIL JUSTICE IS DONE

ARTHUR GOLDBERG

Arthur Goldberg, born 1908, is a former Supreme Court justice who also served as secretary of labor under President Kennedy and as ambassador to the United Nations under President Johnson.
   This article is taken from his address at the World Conference of Jewish Communities on Soviet Jewry, held in Brussels in February 1971.

We meet out of a common concern for human rights and dignity, and not out of animosity toward any country or people.

We are citizens of many nations and deeply attached and loyal to our respective countries. And we are Jews proud of our spiritual heritage. We feel a common and uniting bond with our fellow Jews who have settled in the ancestral home, Israel, and a similar bond with our fellow Jews in the Soviet Union and elsewhere throughout the world. We believe that these attachments and loyalties are completely consonant and compatible.

I do not claim that my country has a perfect record of safeguarding basic human rights. But there is a governmental commitment to the still unrealized goal of equal rights for all our citizens, and our independent judiciary is vigorously seeking to enforce this great constitutional guaranty.

On a matter of particular relevance to this Conference, I recall a decision which I wrote on behalf of the Supreme Court during my service as Justice. In it, we upheld the right of two leading Communists to hold passports, to travel from the United States to countries of their choice, including the Soviet Union, and to return without penalty. The two individuals involved were Elizabeth Gurley Flynn, chairman of the American Communist Party, and Professor Herbert Aptheker, its leading theoretician. I do not have to say that my colleagues and I shared none of their ideology. But we did understand that, under our Constitution, basic rights of liberty include the freedom to travel. We quoted the principles of an earlier Court decision that:

> The right to travel is a part of the "Liberty" of which the citizen cannot be deprived without due process of law under the Fifth Amendment. . . . Freedom of movement across frontiers in either direction, and inside frontiers as well, was a part of our heritage. Travel abroad, like travel within the country, may be as close to the heart of the individual as the choice of what he eats, or wears, or reads. Freedom of movement is basic in our scheme of values.

In reaching this decision, I will add, we were faithful not only to our Constitution but also to the Universal Declaration of Human Rights, which clearly states: "Everyone has a right to leave any country, including his own, and to return to his country."

We are aware of the unwarranted attacks against us in the Soviet government-controlled press. But the concerns we express here today are of the deepest and noblest sentiments of our common humanity. They occur in the spirit of the most fundamental of the commands of moral and international law. They express our duty not to condone by silence further assaults of basic human rights. We have learned the price of silence in the face of oppression from the bitterly tragic experience of the Holocaust. And we are determined that we now will not be silent.

In exercise of this sacred duty, we meet not to malign the Soviet Union but rather in sorrow and concern to speak the truth about the repression of

Soviet Jews. The Soviet Union is a great power and a proud nation, and it is precisely because of this that we appeal to her today, in the interests of humanity and in her own self-interest, to grant to her Jewish citizens their human rights.

I do not believe that the Soviet Union can, in good conscience, deny the existence of widespread discrimination against her Jewish citizens. The testimony is in from too many sources, too many journalists, too many Soviet publications, too many emigrés to permit serious dispute over the nature and magnitude of this discrimination.

Just a year and a half ago I visited the Soviet Union, where I was warmly and hospitably received. While traveling to the birthplace of my parents in the Ukraine, I visited the capital of this great Soviet Republic. Ukrainian is freely spoken and taught, there are numerous books and publications and television broadcasts in Ukrainian. But the synagogue in Kiev, this city of more than 150,000 Jews, was "closed down for repair."

It is true that the Soviet Union is a materialistic country which does not believe in religion. Its repression of all religious groups is to be condemned. But it is also true that no other religious groups are treated as harshly as Jews.

The Soviet Union is a land of many nationalities. With one exception, each is permitted its own schools, books, language and culture. The one exception: Russia's Jews. Yet they are required always to have on their person the internal passport that gives their nationality: Ivrei—Jew. Thus the Jews of the Soviet Union are set apart but not allowed to live as Jews. This is indeed a cruel dilemma.

Soviet authorities contend there is no substantial demand for Jewish religious and cultural facilities. But if this is true, there would be no need for the barriers to free religious and cultural expression. If there is really no demand, then let it be tested through free and unpenalized opportunities for religious worship and cultural expression. By refusing to grant this opportunity, the Soviet Union is violating its very own Constitution which guarantees the free exercise of religion.

The Jews of the Soviet Union since Stalin's death do not face physical annihilation. But it cannot be seriously denied that they face the reality of spiritual annihilation. Nor, sadly, is the religious and cultural repression the whole of the matter. There is more. Official reprisals against individual Jews have increased, and Jews with a "Jewish consciousness" today risk loss of jobs and sometimes arrest. They, and even Jews who are so fully assimilated that no Jewish self-consciousness remains, endure a hate campaign under the cloak of anti-Zionism. Cartoons depict Jews in an unsavory light. Israel is infamously compared with Nazi Germany. Pseudo-scientific studies and even "literary works" published with government sanction portray Jews as swindlers, usurers, corrupters of Soviet morals and base agents of "foreign capitalists." Anti-religious tracts condemn Judaism as preaching "the bloody extermination of people of other faiths."

There is also increasing evidence of discrimination against Jews in employment and areas of public service. Of course there are Jews who are permitted to rise in the Soviet hierarchy. But the prerequisite for their doing so is abandonment of their Jewish religion and culture. And not so long ago an undue proportion of Jews were being prosecuted for alleged economic crimes.

Even more ominously, Pravda recently warned Soviet Jews that anyone espousing Zionist beliefs would "automatically become an agent of international Zionism and an enemy of the Soviet people." What a hideous and fantastical libel this is! How reminiscent of the frightening anti-Semitic Stalinist attacks! Not all Jews are Zionists, but Zionism is the supreme expression of the Messianic expectation—the belief in the old Testament prophecy that God selected Eretz Israel to be the Holy Land and set it aside for the people of Israel.

Indeed, the Pravda article highlights what is perhaps the essence of Soviet disregard for the rights of its Jewish citizens—its callous refusal to permit all Soviet Jews who wish to leave to depart and seek a life of dignity elsewhere. To be sure, there has been a trickle of emigration, authorized professedly to unite families. But for the many who might wish to leave—and the estimates suggest that hundreds of thousands would depart if permitted—there is truly no escape. A request for permission entails long delays, harassment, personal abuse, loss of jobs and property, and great expense. And even then permission is granted or denied on a completely arbitrary basis, often fragmenting families.

The requirements of the Universal Declaration of Human Rights, to which the Soviet Union is a signatory, are in the process ignored. We are told by Soviet authorities and apologists that all Jews are happy and few wish to go. Again, I say if this is true, let its truth be tested by opening the doors.

Discrimination against Russian Jews is best grasped from the perspective of history. I will not belabor this Conference with a history of Czarist repression and pogroms. Nor will I repeat the infamous details of the "Doctors' Plot" and of Stalin's anti-Semitism. Instead, I wish to advert briefly to the lessons of these and other events. Can it be denied that Czarist repression of Jews was part and parcel of the very reaction Soviet Communism professed to end? Can it be ignored that Stalin's anti-Semitism was part and parcel of his arbitrary and dictatorial rule? Can it be denied that some of the victims of anti-Semitism, be they the physicians of the "Doctors' Plot" or the defendants in the Slansky trial, have been exonerated and rehabilitated? Can it be refuted that the lesson of history is that anti-Semitism may begin by claiming Jews as its victims, but ends in a wave of repression of all enlightened opinion?

Yes, it is clear that repression of Jews is incendiary stuff. It burns all, Jew and non-Jew alike. It may start as an exercise in narrow and controlled discrimination. But it invariably ends by reviving the rule of terror, recrimination and mistrust. Nor is this really a mystery to the Communist world. It is why many Western Communist parties have objected to anti-Jewish policies by the Soviet Union and why they have understood that anti-Zionism can readily be a spark for the illimitable ravages of anti-Semitism.

It is a profound anomaly that the Soviet Union, which in 1948 was prominent in supporting the establishment of Israel, now launches a campaign of hatred and vituperation against this democratic state. The explanation can only be in terms of Russia's Middle East political objectives, but repression of Soviet Jewry cannot be condoned on this basis. Whatever one's views about the Middle East, Soviet Jewry has not affected the course of events in this area.

But there is even more to it than this. There is also the fact that we live in a world where all of us dedicated to peace wish to lessen international tensions and achieve détente among the superpowers. Speaking for myself, I am not a cold warrior. I have worked earnestly, officially and privately to improve relations between my country and the Soviet Union. I labored hard and successfully for the treaties controlling weapons in space, and I hope that we may soon achieve agreements on East-West trade and on strategic arms limitation. I know what is at stake here in terms of human survival.

But I would be less than candid if I did not say that these tentative steps toward détente may all too easily become steps of retreat if Soviet repression of Jews persists. For repression of any group is an expression of disregard for the opinion of mankind and there is nothing so quick to erode mutual trust on which international understanding depends.

And so I say to the Soviet leaders: Do not turn your back on the civilized world. Pay a decent respect to the opinions of mankind. Do not jeopardize the cause of peace and the progress of your land for so unfounded and inexcusable a prejudice. Understand that today all of us are in truth our brother's keeper, with a duty to speak out and act against the denial of human rights whenever and wherever they occur, in the Soviet Union or in our own lands.

In matters of conscience, there can be no missing voices. This is why we raise our voices here today. This is why we shall persevere in this cause until justice is done.

49. THE SUFFERINGS OF A SOVIET DANCER

VALERY S. PANOV

This letter of April 15, 1973, by the Soviet ballet dancer Valery S. Panov, was addressed to Senator Jackson, who led the congresstional fight for freedom of emigration for Soviet citizens as a condition for the extension of trade concessions to the Soviet Union by the United States.
One June 14, 1974 the Panovs were finally permitted to leave Russia to go to Israel.

Dear Mr. Jackson:

To give you an idea of my life and its present atmosphere I will tell you a short chronicle of my "departure case."

April 23, 1972: I and my wife, Galina Rogozina, a ballet soloist, declare our intention to leave for Israel, at the Kirov Theater.

April 27: My last performance. It is prohibited to me to greet and thank the public. Flowers presented to me are not given me on the stage. My wife is pushed aside from a tour abroad. She is advised to find another husband. Having firmly opposed the pressure, she is transferred to the *corps de ballet*.

April 29: Our "social trial" at the theater. Here are some quotations from our colleagues' speeches:

Kolpakova, prime ballerina, party member: "Out of the theater, you traitors, Fascists, Zionists!"

Vikulov, premier of ballet, party organizer: "It is a treason at the temple of the love, purity and friendship. Get out of here!"

Kaplan, my choreographer and teacher: "We gave birth to Panov. Now we must kill him."

Rassadin, premier of ballet: "Panov is leaving us, betraying the great art, the best in the world, in the name of petty profits in the decaying Western world."

Pavlovsky, dancer: "For Panov, we must contrive a punishment which is nonexistent in the human Soviet law—not to let him out and to exile him into Siberia. He and Rogozina are selling themselves to an imperialist service."

April 30; K.G.B.*officials intimidate my relatives, forbidding them to

*KGB: Committee on State Security. (Ed.)

give me their consent for leaving Russia. (Having given in, my father, though a pensioner, will be later rewarded with a title of Economist Emeritus). Same "work" with my mother-in-law.

May 1: Asked by my wife for her consent, her mother replies: "It is a pity there is no Stalin now. Had he been alive, he would have shot you down, you fascists-Zionists. And I, as the mother, would have been happy." Then she tried to beat her daughter, my wife. (Later, she was thanked with a good pension and an accommodation card in a sanatorium).

May 3 to 10: A process is being framed up against me for "having beaten my mother-in-law." After scandalous exposures by Western media, the "trial" is closed. I am expelled from the theater on the ground of a "staff reduction." Visas Dept. (Ovir) does not accept my papers under every pretext; they are accepted only on the eve of President Nixon's visit.

May 26: I am summoned to my local police station to explain why I am not working, being a jobless only during two weeks! On my way back, a man makes me a row, accusing me of having spit on him. A police car comes in that moment; I am arrested and given 10 days of imprisonment for hooliganism.

June 4: President Nixon left U.S.S.R.: Ovir gives me back all my papers as being wrong in form: An invitation from my relatives is requested instead of one from the Israeli Government. But my inquiries sent to Israel are left without a reply, all mail not reaching me.

June-August: We are trying to find work but are refused everywhere. To get money for life, we sell our belongings. Batsheva de Rothschild saves us from hunger.

September: We take part in a Minute of Sorrow over the Munich murders, in Moscow. Police are cruelly dispersing our gathering.

September 10: Jewish New Year, at the Moscow synagogue. Police and K.G.B. men are dispersing Jews, many are arrested. It seems to be a scene from some film about a ghetto under the Nazi regime.

October: We have, via some friends, a "correct" invitation from Israel. Now Ovir does not accept our papers without a consent from my mother-in-law who categorically refuses to give my wife any document.

November: K.G.B. men shadow us everywhere. We are forbidden to leave Leningrad till the holiday ends. K.G.B. begin to inquest my friends in order to frame me up. Such interrogatories are continuing up to March 1973.

December: Two weeks of shadowing by K.G.B., this time for fifty years of U.S.S.R. celebrations. I am summoned by Pavlov, vice chief of the Leningrad K.G.B. office. He threatens me with severe punishment for slandering the "Soviet reality" (letters, in which I thanked my friends abroad for their support and asked them to appeal to Soviet top instances, were given by me to an American friend but were later discovered at the Customs and taken away). Pavlov also made a menace to imprison me if I go on giving information about my life to Western people. Then he added: "Presidents will not ask for you nor stand up for you. As for other appeals, we are spitting upon them."

January 30, 1973: I told my friends abroad, over the telephone, about K.G.B.'s threats. My telephone is cut off since then.

February: I have several diseases discovered by doctors and caused by nervous exhaustion. With such illness almost impossible to make performance again. We feel being killed as artists.

February 15: My mother, resident in Vilnius, died, having learned, from my letters to my brother, that my situation was hopeless and I risked an imprisonment.

February 20: Ovir gives me back my documents for emigration, which I sent directly to President Podgorny. Once again Ovir refused to consider my papers because of a missing consent from my mother-in-law.

March-April 1: My appeals to Moscow and protests from my colleagues in the West are completely ignored.

Almost a year of fight and misery went by. It took away our physical form, we have been destroyed slowly and ruthlessly. We shall not survive such a year again. If possible, Dear Sir, help us to leave.

Wishing you good health and all the very best.

Yours sincerely
With high regards
V. S. Panov

50. THE RIGHT TO BE JEWISH

YEFIM DAVIDOVICH

Yefim Davidovich was born in Minsk in 1924 and joined the Red Army when the Nazis attacked Russia in June of 1941. His parents, younger brothers, and relatives were murdered by the Nazis. Davidovich fought throughout the war, was wounded five times, and was decorated on fifteen occasions. At war's end he was a twenty-one-year old major. After the war he graduated from the Frunze Military Academy, the Soviet West Point, and became a career officer. Because of serious heart attacks he retired as a colonel from military service in 1969. Davidovich was a loyal Communist and remained a member of the Central Committee of the Byelorussian Communist Party until October 1972. He was the most articulate of the Jewish dissidents and activitists in Minsk.

The following letter was addressed on December 19, 1972 to Party Chief Leonid Brezhnev.

On December 1, 1972, the workers of the KGB made a search of my house. I was held in the KGB prison for twenty-four hours. During the search, they took away copies of letters sent by me in the spring of 1971 to various Soviet bodies and to the organs of the Soviet press. These letters had been provoked by the unrestrained anti-Semitic orgy in the press which led to bloody crimes in Minsk: the murders of Professor Mikhelson, of the brother and sister Kantor (students), and of the 16-year-old schoolboy Grisha Tunik. The anti-Jewish atmosphere was later inflamed even more after an explosion in a radio plant. Only the urgent measures taken by the Commission of the Central Committee of the CPSU headed by Commissar Ustinov prevented worse happenings.

In my letters, I called upon the Soviet mass communications media to refrain from publishing anti-Jewish and anti-Israeli material of local and foreign origin, and called upon the Soviet press to join actively in the struggle against anti-Semitism. I received no reply to my letters. In addition to the copies of the letters, the confiscated documents included a short resumé of my two-and-a-half-year campaign in connection with these letters, as well as many other documents concerning Jews, Jewish history, and anti-Semitism. Some tapes of Jewish songs and melodies were also taken.

On December 8, 1972, the senior investigator of the KGB, I. I. Nikiforov, presented me with a formal charge sheet which stated: "The documents sufficiently established Davidovich's activity with the intent of undermining the Soviet regime by having spread, for many years, slanderous fabrications vilifying the Soviet government and society, as well as the production and distribution of literature of this nature, and the illegal possession of firearms.". . .

All my life, with all my strength, and with my blood, I always defended and strenghened the Soviet regime. All my letters and personal notes contain the truth and only the truth. Is telling the truth an anti-Soviet act? . . .

There is no memorial at Babi Yar or at the Minsk ghetto where 200,000 Jews were murdered. For many of us, their blood is not cheaper than that of the 200 Frenchmen from Oradour, the 160 Czechs from Lidice, and the 149 Byelorussians from Katyn, where great memorials have been erected.

My serious illness forced the KGB to release me from prison under a signed obligation not to leave the city. Detectives have surrounded my house and follow me step by step whenever I am able to leave for a walk. They follow the members of my family, my friends, and my acquaintances. In the sick minds of the organizers of this "operation," the impression was evidently created that I had been preparing terrorist acts of major proportions: the murder of all the sportsmen of the USSR, setting fire to all the homes for the aged in Byelorussia, placing hydrogen bombs in the Komarovsk market, the murder of the chairman of the Municipal Council and replacing him with Ben-Gurion. And with the TT 1941 model pistol with eight rusted bullets found in my possession I was supposed to be preparing to expand the Israeli borders from the Nile to the Euphrates, the annexation of Byelorussia to Israel, as well as effectuating all the designs of the Elders of Zion contained in the Protocols—the establishment of Jewish mastery over the entire world. All of this is not so funny as it is sad. The anti-Jewish hysteria under the slogan of anti-Zionism continues.

Neither the twenty-four hours spent in the KGB prison nor the interminable interrogations are helpful to my physical condition. After interrogations of this type, my wife brings me home only half alive. Her selflessness and extensive medical experience enable me to function, but with great difficulty. My wife, incidentally, is not Jewish. . . .

You understand that during one of the KGB interrogations, or after one, I shall die. My death will not bring laurels to anyone. Willingly or unwillingly I shall become a martyr, a victim of anti-Semitism. . .

I have committed no crimes and I had no intention of committing them. To write or even to say the truth is not a crime.

My experience of life brought me to the conclusion that my family and I can live a life worthy of a human being and a citizen only in the Jewish national State. Help us to go to our historical Homeland, to Israel. And, anyhow, I would not deny the truth, deny my words, even if I had to suffer everything from the beginning. . .

On January 7, 1973 Colonel Davidovich* issued the following appeal to veterans' groups and the Jewish people throughout the world:

The threat of judicial reprisal looms over me—reprisal for telling the truth, for struggling against anti-Semitism.

My complaints to the higher bodies of the Soviet Union have remained unanswered. . . .

The "investigation" is continuing and a court trial is being prepared. For forty days, scores of KGB agents have kept my house under siege, have dogged the footsteps of members of my family, my friends and acquaintances. Day and night they do not take their eyes off me, as if I were

---

*On April 24, 1976 Yefim Davidovich died of a heart attack. Despite his deteriorating condition, the Soviets refused to allow him to leave for Israel. The campaign of harassment, interrogations, and searches of his home continued to the last minute. (Ed.)

a dangerous criminal. . . . But the "criminal" is bedridden . . . and is kept alive only by injections.

I have committed no crimes nor had I any intention of committing any. . . .

The material confiscated from me by the KGB . . . contains only facts of anti-Semitism known to the entire world. . . . I have also cited scores of examples of unpunished anti-Semitism . . . committed not only by members of the Black Hundreds but also by officials.

The passing over in silence and the distortion of the truth about the Jewish people, its great history and its contribution to world civilization, is also a direct act of anti-Semitism.

When I . . . spoke about the great sons of the Jewish people, I was told that this was Zionist propaganda. My "crime"—not a feeling of national exclusivity, but elementary human dignity . . .

I am tied to my people by the trenches in which the Hitlerites buried old women and babies. In the past—rivers of blood; in the present—the malignant weeds grown from racist seeds, the hardiness of prejudices and superstitions. The struggle against these carriers of prejudices and superstitions, whether they are "individual" anti-Semites and hooligans or highly placed officials, is the duty of every honest person. I wrote and spoke the truth and there is an attempt to present it as "slanderous fabrications."

51. "I HAVE NO FUTURE IN THE COUNTRY IN WHICH I WAS BORN"

RAIZA PALATNIK

On October 14, 1970, police officers searched the apartment of Raiza Palatnik, a young Jewish woman born in 1936 in Odessa, and found there "slanderous, anti-Soviet, Zionist literature." After several interrogations by the police, she wrote the open letter reprinted below. In June 1971, she went on trial in the Odessa provincial court and was sentenced to two years in a detention camp, reportedly on charges of "planning to slander the Soviet Union."

Her sister Katya contacted foreign newsmen, joined Raiza in a hunger strike, and after many protests was allowed to leave Russia for Israel in January 1972. She quickly arranged a trip to various European countries and to the United States to plead for her sister's freedom. On December 1, 1972 Raiza was freed and with her elderly parents joined Katya in Israel.

I was born in a small town of a Jewish family. Yiddish and Jewish traditions were taught me at home. There was no Jewish school and therefore I attended a Russian one, In childhood I felt myself Jewish and consciously sought for ways to express a personal, national identification.

In the eighth grade my refusal to learn Ukrainian and insistence that my mother tongue was Yiddish confounded the school authorities. I was 14 when the unbridled anti-Semitic campaign known as the struggle against cosmopolitanism—bezrodny cosmopolity—began. I remember the atmosphere of fear and trepidation in the family, awaiting something terrible, frightful and unavoidable. During that period I kept a diary. Now that I reread it before destroying it so that it will not fall into the hands of the KGB, I again relive the pain and bitterness, anger and resentment of those days. Even then I could not understand why it was enough to be a Jew in order to be ostracized and persecuted.

Then Stalin died. The doctors were rehabilitated. Beria and his henchmen were executed. With childish naivete I exulted and believed that justice had triumphed. I enrolled in the Institute for Librarians in Moscow. I remember the enthusiasm with which I learned of the condemnation of the personality cult of Stalin by the 20th Congress of the Communist Party. But why did they not give so much as a hint of the physical destruction of the finest representatives of the Jewish intelligentsia from 1949 to 1952? Why did they not condemn anti-Semitism, which had been raised to the status of national policy? Why did they not open Jewish schools, theaters, newspapers, magazines? These questions and others like them puzzled me.

That my belief in the liquidation of anti-Semitism was only an illusion I began to understand when I finished at the Institute and began to look for work. No one was interested in my knowledge and capabilities. The fact that I belonged to the Jewish nationality shut out all opportunities for work in a major library. With difficulty I managed to find a job in Odessa in a small library, where I work to this day.

With renewed intensity dozens of questions came to me to which I found no answers in official literature. I began to read Samizdat.* The sentencing of Joseph Brodsky I perceived as part of a new stage of Soviet anti-Semitism. The poet was condemned on the evidence of patent anti-Semites who did not even know him personally, while the efforts of Marshak, Tshukovski, Paustovski and others who cried out in his defense were of no avail. After this came the trial of Daniel and Siniavsky. . . .

In search of a solution I began to think more and more of Israel. The

---

*Literally "self-publish," Samizdat refers to underground literature published clandestinely in the USSR. See no. 54. (Ed.)

prelude to the Six Day War shocked me to my very roots. It seemed to me that the whole world looked on apathetically while well-equipped armies prepared to finish Hitler's work, to annihilate the small Jewish nation of 2,500,000, to erase from the face of the earth the State of Israel reborn after 2,000 years. On the eve of the war, when the Strait of Tiran was closed, the UN forces were expelled and the Arab armies approached the borders of Israel; while Fedorenko was cynically declaring in the UN, "Don't over-dramatize events," I was close to nervous exhaustion. I wanted to shout to humanity, "Help!"

Then I understood that I could have no future in the country in which I was born, and that I had no alternative save reunion with my people who had suffered so much, in my ancestral homeland.

I remember the unbounded pride and happiness when the reborn David again conquered Goliath. The flood of anti-Semitic curses and hysteria from the Soviet press, radio and television forced me to feel even more strongly my unbroken bond to Israel and my personal responsibility for her. I began actively to interest myself in everything connected with Israel. Friends who felt as I did discussed the possibility of leaving for Israel.

The press conference [March 1970]* organized by the authorities in which the "loyal" Jews slandered Israel in the name of all Soviet Jews, meaning also in my name, aroused a deep bitterness. How to shout out that they are just a tiny group and that the majority thinks otherwise? And then I heard over the radio the letter of the 39. How sorry I was that I could not also sign that letter! I typed this letter so that my friends could also read it.

I applied to P.O.B. 92 with a request to locate my relatives in Israel. And then the KGB began to show an interest in me. They searched my apartment and that of my parents. I am constantly summoned for questioning. My friends and relatives, the people I work with, are interrogated and pressured to give witness to my anti-Soviet activity. I understand that arrest and maybe years of imprisonment await me. But I know one thing positively: my fate is tied irrevocably to Israel. No imprisonments in Leningrad, Riga and Kishinev can halt the struggle for repatriation to Israel.

To my regret I do not know my people's tongue, Hebrew, but in my trial I will cry out against all anti-Semites in the Yiddish I was taught by my mother and father.

---

*At this conference a number of Jews prominent in the arts, sciences, etc., affirmed their Russian loyalties and denounced Zionism and Israel. (Ed.)

52. TO THE PRESIDENT OF THE U.S.S.R. SUPREME SOVIET: ON THE PERSECUTION OF REPATRIATE JEWS.

VALERY N. CHALIDZE

The letters of May 20, 1971, printed below, by three famous Russian physicists are a public statement of leading citizens against authoritarian government policies. On November 4, 1970 these physicists took the courageous step of creating a Committee on Human Rights. Their letters may well be among the very first human-rights acts undertaken by the Soviet group. They question the spate of trials in the Soviet Union of Jews "whose only aim was to protest against the unlawful refusals to issue them visas for repatriation."

Sakharov was recently awarded the Nobel Prize but was not allowed to go to Stockholm to attend the ceremony at which the prizes are awarded.

The authorities' illegitimate actions in hindering the free departure of people from the Soviet Union, specifically, the free repatriation of Jews to Israel, have in recent years produced active protests by Jews who seek repatriation. They have protested against the arbitrary and unexplained refusals to issue visas; against red tape, which has no basis in law, in dealing with applications; against the excessively cumbersome procedure for submission of applications.

Illegitimate actions of one kind lead to others: The authorities have to take illegal measures to counter the protests. At the same time, official propaganda disseminates unfriendly and unsubstantiated reports about repatriation and Zionism. The press portrays Zionism as a reactionary (practically fascist) political trend; yet Zionism is no more than the idea of Jewish statehood, and one can only admire the persistence of an ancient and persecuted people, who in very difficult conditions have resurrected a long-vanished state. It is precisely such rebirth and elimination of the tragic consequences of dispersion for the Jewish people that constitute the goal of Zionism.

Zionism is portrayed in the press as an anti-Communist and anti-Soviet trend, yet the concerns of Zionism are entirely national.

Even more ridiculous is the statement that those Soviet citizens who wish to be repatriated are deliberately unfriendly toward the Soviet system. Some authorities try to prove this by holding trials—for example, in Leningrad and in Riga—bringing charges of anti-Soviet activities against Jews whose only aim was to protest against the unlawful refusals to issue them visas for repatriation.

In my efforts to study human rights in the Soviet Union, I have long considered it my duty to give intellectual assistance to Jews who desire repatriation. I am familiar with their problems and principles. Their main principle is non-interference in affairs here. They have one aim—to go to Israel—and they observe the non-interference principle so painstakingly that they are sometimes reproached for egoism by those who are concerned with the defense of human rights in our country. I am convinced that the charge of anti-Soviet activity against those seeking repatriation is ridiculous.

Whatever the authorities' displeasure with Jews' desire for repatriation, there have nevertheless been welcome signs of progress, and in recent months—speaking now of the departure of Jews, not of freedom of departure from the U.S.S.R. in general—the problem may be considered near solution in the sense that those Jews who wish to leave may have hopes of obtaining permission to do so.

It was difficult a year ago, when those who are now being tried in the above-mentioned cases were arrested. In the large cities permission to leave was hardly ever granted, and it is evident from the institution of criminal proceedings that protests against forcible detention were interpreted by the authorities as anti-Soviet activity. But now such protests bring results and help gain repatriation.

I hope that the Presidium, using its constitutional right of pardon, will take the change in the situation into account and recognize the legitimacy of the Jews' desire for repatriation and dismiss the criminal cases.

I call for an end to all persecution of Jews seeking repatriation, and I urge that there be no more violations of the obvious right of man to leave any country.

May 20, 1971   —V. Chalidze.

We agree with the arguments in V. Chalidze's letter and join in the appeals to end the persecution of repatriates and to stop violating the right to leave the country. We join in the appeal for dismissal of the criminal cases.

A. Sakharov,
A. Tverdokhlebov.

53. A SPEECH AT A BABI YAR COMMEMORATION

IVAN DZYUBA

Babi Yar is a ravine on the outskirts of Kiev where 50,000 Jews were murdered by the Germans in 1941. Soviet authorities tried to eliminate all references to Babi Yar. Their failure to erect a suitable memorial is considered a symbol of Soviet anti-Semitism.

The Ukraine calls to mind memories of the pogroms in the seventeenth century by Chmielnitzky, and during the Civil War, 1918–22, by the White armies. Jews also remember the Ukrainians as pogromists and collaborators of the Nazis. Hence the more noteworthy is the following speech delivered at a Babi Yar commemoration on September 29, 1966 by Ivan Dzyuba, an author and literary critic from Kiev and leader of the Ukrainian national movement.

Babi Yar is a tragedy of the whole of mankind, but it happened on Ukrainian soil. And therefore a Ukrainian must not forget it any more than a Jew. Babi Yar is our common tragedy, a tragedy for the Jewish and the Ukrainian nations. . . . Today in Babi Yar we commemorate not only those who died here. We commemorate millions of Soviet warriors—our parents—who gave their lives in the battle against fascism. . . .

Are we worthy of this memory? It seems not, if even now various forms of hatred of mankind are found among us, and one of them that form which we call by a weak, banal, yet terrible word, anti-Semitism. Anti-Semitism is an international phenomenon; it has existed and still exists in all societies. Sadly enough, our society is also not free of it. There might be nothing strange about this—after all, anti-Semitism is the fruit and companion of age-old barbarism and slavery, the foremost and inevitable result of political despotism. To conquer it in entire societies is not an easy task nor can it be done quickly. But what is strange is the fact that no battle has been waged against it during the postwar decades, and what is even stranger, it has often been artificially nourished. . . .

As a Ukrainian, I am ashamed that, as in other nations, there is anti-Semitism here, that these shameful phenomena, unworthy of mankind—phenomena which we call anti-Semitism—exist here.

We Ukrainians must fight in our midst against all forms of expression of anti-Semitism, disrespect toward the Jews, and misunderstanding of the Jewish problem.

You, Jews, must fight in your midst against those among you who do not respect the Ukrainian people, Ukrainian culture, the Ukrainian language, those who unjustly see a potential anti-Semite in every Ukrainian.

We must oust all forms of hatred of mankind, overcome all misunderstanding, and achieve a true brotherhood within our lives. . . .

The road to a true and honest brotherhood lies not in self-oblivion, but in self-knowledge; not in rejection of ourselves and adaptation to others, but in being ourselves and respecting others. The Jews have a right to be Jews and the Ukrainians have a right to be Ukrainians in the full and profound, not only the formal, meaning of the word. Let the Jews know Jewish history, Jewish culture and language, and be proud of them. Let them also know each other's history and culture and the history and culture of other nations, and let them know how to value themselves and others as their brothers. . . .

This is our duty to millions of victims of despotism. This is our duty to the better men of the Ukrainian and Jewish nations who urged us to mutual understanding and friendship. This is our duty to our Ukrainian land in which we live together. This is our duty to humanity.

54. THE SAGA OF SAMIZDAT

EZRA RUSINEK

How does one go about reading books on Jewish history or Israel in a country where such books may not be available or may be on a forbidden list? How does a Jew living in Soviet Russia read news about Jewish events not published in Russia? How does one organize study circles for Hebrew or Jewish history—all activities which are not allowed in Soviet Russia? The story of "how" is told by Ezra Rusinek, a Russian immigrant to Israel.

Samizdat, literally "self-published," refers to all materials published clandestinely by dissident groups in the Soviet Union.

In 1955 we lived in deep Russia in the town of Taganrog after having escaped from exile. Sarah, our old friend from Riga, came to visit us.

"I have a book for you to read from Yasha. Read it quickly."

Yasha was a friend of mine in my youth, a true Zionist, who had barely escaped persecution but managed to live on in Riga under a constant threat.

To read quickly meant to read it in one night. The book contained articles and speeches by Jabotinsky,* published in 1912.

That pamphlet of Jabotinsky was the beginning of *Samizdat*—self-publishing—in our family, though the Jewish spirit had always existed there. Quietly and cautiously we celebrated all Jewish holidays. Little silver stars of David were favorite precious things for our children. The words "shabbas," "barmitzvah," and "talis" were familiar to them. But Samizdat had to put into their minds and hearts something new and more important.

My daughter, Ilana, copied the text of the pamphlet and became interested. The manuscript was passed from one person to another among the few Jewish families in Taganrog. Some of them returned the pamphlet in an hour or two; others read and reread it several times and then came for a talk. And how long were those talks! There were a lot of things to discuss

---

*A Zionist leader. (Ed.)

in those years: the Sinai campaign of 1956, the Youth Festival in Moscow in 1957 and the Israeli delegation which took part in it, and, of course, rare broadcasts in Russian and in Yiddish by "Kol Israel."

And again Yasha sent a book to read. This time it was *Exodus* by Leon Uris in German translation. And again—sleepless nights. What an explosive! But why don't they have this book in Russian? Why do they have it in English, German, Hebrew, French, and God knows what other languages, but no one has thought of publishing it in Russian for us here?

1963. We were able to move back at last to Riga. After settling down we immediately plunged into a Jewish atmosphere and became acquainted with the families that wanted to emigrate to Israel. Soon after that Yasha, my old dear friend, got permission to leave for Israel. Before his departure he begged that *Exodus* be translated into Russian and typed. "Do whatever you can," he said, and with these words he handed me the beginning of his translation.

But the book was so long. To abridge it would be to lose a great deal of the impact. What could be done? To whom could I speak? Who would translate? From what language? Where should we get a typewriter? Who would type?

One thing was clear: we must hurry. But equally clear was something else. If the KGB learned about it, prison awaited those who would be caught. Even if I could find someone among my acquaintances who could translate, he might become frightened or even report me to the KGB. And if someone did agree to do it, how could we pay for his work? My own salary was just enough to make ends meet. How could we buy a typewriter in a shop? The KGB registers all typewriters in shops as well as in offices and repair shops. There seemed no answers to all the questions. But we decided to try.

Cautiously, step by step, we looked for someone who might help. Finally we found a typewriter that had always been privately owned. The owner had left for Israel. I took the typewriter, changed the type a little, lubricated it, and headed for Sarah. "No one can do it but you. You also promised Yasha you'd do something. You can type, even if only with two fingers. Okay? Get on with it."

We asked Boris, one of our old Riga acquaintances, an expert in the history of Israel, a man with several languages at his fingertips, to translate the book. We didn't have to ask him twice.

And Sarah, after a long working day—living in one room with two daughters—typed evening after evening, two pages in two hours. The typewriter stood on a blanket to lessen the noise, so that neighbors passing her door would not hear her. Sarah chain-smoked and cursed indecently every time she heard a ring at her door. An acquaintance had dropped in for a chat and a cup of tea—these good-for-nothing people. Immediately the typewriter and the typed pages were covered with the blanket.

And what a typewriter it was! All my life I shall remember it. There was an "e" that would constantly stick, and after "n" the carriage would move twice. It was an ordeal, but what could we do? We didn't have our own typewriter repairman and taking it to a shop would be dangerous. There was nothing to do but bear it.

Every week the diligent Boris would call Sarah, "Come for a cup of tea, Sarochka," which meant that the next portion of the translation was ready.

Then there were problems with the paper. What kind should we use? If we used thin paper, we could make eight copies, if we used thick, only five copies. We decided "better fewer but better." These books would have to live and work among Soviet Jews for years, so the paper had to be good and thick. But good paper is not always in the stores and if we bought more than two packages at one time it would seem strange. So we waited for the paper to appear in the shops and then bought two packages in each of the shops, being careful that no acquaintances see us doing it.

The most difficult problem was with carbon paper. Soviet carbon paper is not good. The fifth copy is hardly readable. And good Polish carbon paper is on the market only once in an eternity. When it appeared, we declared a celebration, for the acquisition of a package of it meant that work could continue.

As each page was typed, the carbon paper was burned and the pages were taken to "the refrigerator," an incurious and true friend. And then I would be able to go home with a feeling of deep satisfaction at having done something useful that day.

Sometimes I committed the crime of stealing "state property" at my place of work. I took several sheets of carbon paper. But I did not feel guilty. The law that prohibits my people from learning their own language and history made this "crime" necessary. Nor were we concerned that we had violated Leon Uris's copyright by translating his work without his permission. We were sure he would not be bothered by it.

It took a whole exhausting year to translate and type the six hundred pages of the book. How many days of rest, movies, or theater performances were missed. Sarah sat at her work every evening and didn't leave the typewriter until two pages were ready. It was really the work of a "chalutz," a pioneer. Jabotinsky quotes Trumpeldor's explanation of the meaning of "chaltutz": "Ground must be dug? I dig. To shoot, to be a soldier? I go. Police? Doctors? Lawyers? Teachers? Water-carriers? Here you are, I do everything."

What a triumphant moment it was when on the last page Sarah could type "The End" in big letters. A great burden had been taken off our minds.

The promise which we had given to Yasha and whose fulfillment had become our obligation toward the growing generation of proud Soviet Jews had been fulfilled.

But there were still problems. How should we bind our books? Giving them to a binding shop was out of the question. Again a friend helped. This time it was our pet crank; Tsipa. Few people knew his full name and it was hardly necessary. This middle-aged short man with the heart of a school-boy and the mind of a sage brought fun and laughter into every house. His asymmetrical eyes, like those of a kind Mephistopheles, twinkled with an always appropriate joke. But behind all this, his friends knew a devoted, selfless comrade who was to play an important role in the work.

This time Tsipa answered in his usual manner: "For a bottle of vodka? Okay." I promised to provide the bottle, and in a week the books were ready.

But the problems were not yet finished. Should the books remain in Riga or be sent to Russia? Who should read them first, young people or adults? How could we make certain that the KGB didn't find the books? And on and on.

After long discussions it was decided to keep two copies in Riga and to send the other three to true friends in Russia. The books should first of all be given to young people for reading. After each person read one, it had to be returned to the hands of the giver; there must be no passing from hand to hand. Every book must be kept under control.

A month passed. We were deluged by pleas from those who wanted to read the books. People came and begged: "For God's sake, put me on the list. My children must read it." Once in talking to a tourist from Israel I learned that many young tourists from the U.S.A. had begun to arrive in Israel and when they were asked why they chose to visit Israel rather than France, Italy, Sapin, they answered that they had read *Exodus* by Uris.

But can this be compared with the book's effect on the Soviet Jews? The influence of *Exodus* on the national rebirth of Jewish youth in the Soviet Union can hardly be overestimated. May God give many years of happiness to Leon Uris!

The diligent Boris had received for his work a precious present—a book on the War of Liberation in 1948, and Sarah—a cigarette lighter which played incorrectly the melody of Hatikvah, the Israeli anthem. She was very proud of this little thing until the musical mechanism ceased to work.

The main thing was that nobody in the city knew who had made the books. The book began its life and successful work among hundreds of people, but the few who knew about its source never mentioned it, and it remained a secret for years.

One day suddenly Tsipa ran in very excited: "Congratulations! We are not alone! I have just seen an abridged *Exodus* in Russian—one hundred fifty pages." It had been made by another group. We were hiding from them and they from us. "Well," I said then, happy and proud. "Let them be fruitful and multiply."

* * *

One thing must be understood. This is a story of one little group in Riga, their rebirth and the beginning of their Samizdat. But there were scores of such small groups and individuals who were seeking their own ways, found them, and also began to be active. Some of them began earlier, some later. In different parts of the huge Soviet Empire Jewish eyes began to open, Jewish hearts began to beat. Only several years later were we to learn that in 1957, forgetting their fears, Jews in Moscow came in contact with the Israeli delegation to the Youth Festival.

The Sinai War and the Festival lit a tiny fire which was to flame into this big movement for liberation. The Festival brought to Moscow the children of those whom we had seen off to Palestine in the thirties. These youths came, and their Jewish brothers and sisters in Russia met them, youths whose parents could not leave for Palestine on time and had gone through Hitler's and Stalin's concentration camps. The Soviet Jews could not forget the young Israelis—their suntanned faces, their happy smiles, the songs and dances of a free people.

In 1958 small crowds of not more than two hundred people for the first time gathered in front of the Moscow synagogue to celebrate the holiday of Simhat Torah. In a few years this small crowd had turned into a sea of people, many thousands, a phenomenon that sends waves of emotion throughout the Jewish world now and rivets its attention to this small street in Moscow every year.

Who knows what has been going on in other cities: Vilna, Leningrad, Kiev, Odessa, Sverdlovsk. Their stories will also be told sometime. Gathered all together they will add one more page to the heroic history of our people. I am a bad teller of tales. This story deserves beautiful words, songs of praise and honor; it deserves its own Leon Uris.

Why is Jewish Samizdat necessary in Russia? Is it worth running such a risk? Aren't talks and "Kol Israel" broadcasts enough? Isn't the awkward Soviet anti-Israel and anti-Zionist propaganda enough in itself to arouse national self-consciousness in Russian Jews? What is the purpose of this Samizdat? Is it directed against the present social order in the country?

I think Jewish Samizdat is necessary so long as Soviet Jews are deprived of objective information about Israel and about their own past and present. The most important task of Samizdat until 1970 was to create a reserve of

Jews interested in Israel and ready to come to it—in other words, the task of all Zionism.

One might ask the question: Weren't there in Riga and Vilna many people who were already potential emigrants? Yes, there were—several families—but the majority was completely ignorant about Jewish affairs. The younger generation was almost completely assimilated, dying in the national sense. Except for a narrow circle of intelligentsia in Moscow and Leningrad, the whole of Jewish Russia was sleeping. And in the Ukraine the Jews didn't even dare to dream about Israel. If asked about it, they waved their hands in fear and looked around to see who was watching.

No, talk alone couldn't help in this situation. Only written information could be decisive. . . .

. . . The interest of Jews, as well as the number of interested Jews, grew in geometric progression. The young demanded information.

Therefore it became necessary that different groups existing in different cities should come together and unite their efforts in Samizdat work. The first meeting was held in Moscow, on the sixteenth of August. People from Moscow, Leningrad, Riga, Kiev, Tbilisi, Kharkov, Orel attended. There were hours of discussion in an apartment, a park, in the street, arguments and decisions, and the main principles of future activities were defined: unity, co-ordination, and co-operation in Samizdat work; exchange of all items both new and old; mutual help in the means of publishing. The idea of publishing a periodical collection of works was also discussed. This has been done under the name of "Iton."* There was also a discussion about exchanging information about emigration and the signing of collective letters.

The meeting proved very fruitful, and other meetings were later held in Riga and Leningrad. Delegates informed each other of activities in their cities and discussed their plans. At the Riga meeting it was decided to fix definite telephone numbers and addresses for contacts between different cities. For this purpose the names of the towns were put into codes: Riga became Roman, Moscow, Misha, Leningrad, Lyonia. The same meeting decided also on the creation of the editorial board for publishing "Iton."

We in Riga, in our turn, gathered and discussed local activities. Until that time every group had worked separately; now united activities began in full swing. Almost all of us agreed with the opinion expressed by the majority of the participants in the Moscow meeting that we should refrain from forming an organization. The Soviet Criminal Code has a special statute about participation in an anti-Soviet organization, and any kind of

---

*The Hebrew word for "newspaper." (Ed.)

an organization can easily be labelled anti-Soviet. An organization would not have helped us in any way, but would have helped the KGB watch us. We could organize our work by just defining our main tasks. Those who took part in the activities were divided into two groups for the sake of more effective work. One group took part in an active open struggle, such as signing collective letters to the Government and to be sent abroad and demanding the right to leave for Israel. This group was usually called "Alef." The second group, "Beth," was engaged in preparing, duplicating, and distributing the materials of Samizdat.

The Moscow meeting had also discussed the problem of collective letters demanding the right to leave the country. We in Riga, in the summer of 1969, agreed that the time was not yet ripe to come out with such petitions. Georgian Jews were the first to begin this heroic campaign in August 1969. With their "Letter of 18" addressed to the U.N. Committee for Human Rights.*

A list of subjects about which information was needed was compiled and divided according to degree of importance. Then the information was typed, one subject after another. A number of old typewriters were acquired especially for Samizdat. But what monsters they were! Old-fashioned, terribly heavy. One of them weighed more than thirty kilograms and taking it from one house to another was an ordeal. Only one man was strong enough to do it. He walked with that monster on his back, sweating and stopping every twenty meters.

All the typewriters had to be coded. Could we say over the telephone "Bring me the Mercedes?" So this typewriter was christened "Crocodile." I wonder what the KGB thought listening to our telephone conversations about a crocodile. But the fact is that during the catastrophe of June 1970 and in later searches they didn't find the "Crocodile."

Every apartment where the materials were typed was thoroughly checked from the point of view of the neighbors: the noise of the typewriter could always betray us. The problem of typists was also a difficult one. Professional typists could work very quickly, but had little time for Samizdat. They had to earn their living. More than that they would never be willing to type on such typewriters as "Crocodile." But there were girls who could type with one or two fingers who agreed to work in any place and on any typewriter. Special attention was paid to secrecy. It was decided that each of us must know only his own typist and take the work to and from her only by himself.

In spite of numerous problems and obstacles, Samizdat materials came and went in a flood. Everyone had his own circle of readers among whom

---

*See selection no. 47b. (Ed.)

he worked. But it should be pointed out that we always thought it most important to send literature to Russia, to Jews who hadn't had it for fifty-two years, not just for twenty-five years like us Jews of Latvia. For this purpose young people would suddenly become very affectionate toward their relatives in other cities and would want to visit them. These trips were extremely dangerous and the boys and girls would spend sleepless nights on trains, keeping their eyes on their valises containing the literature. In return we received paper, carbon, tape, photo-paper, and so on.

• Circles for studying Hebrew had existed in Riga for many years but had been of an individual character. In 1969 they began to be organized and by 1970 a whole network of these groups existed in the city. But the shortage of books prevented people from intensive studying. There were only a few copies of the primer *Elef Milim* (one thousand words) in the city, and teachers had to use old newspapers, calendars, and the Bible for lessons. Either new books had to be obtained or copies made. But then our inter-city ties helped. Our Moscow friends informed us that they had managed to make a large number of copies of *Elef Milim*, and we soon received two suitcases of wonderfully photographed copies of the book. . . .

After we had acquired the textbooks, we began to seek among older Jews those who knew Hebrew and were ready to run the risk of teaching a group. The groups were formed of people of approximately the same age, knowledge, and activity. The places where the lessons were to be given were also thoroughly checked. It was necessary that the neighbors not be too curious. All these arrangements took much time and effort, but we had enough purpose and energy because we could see the results. Masses of new young people joined in the groups studying Hebrew. The interest in Israel grew and grew, and the youth began to get together in parties, learn Israeli songs, listen to records, show each other Israeli souvenirs; and they talked and talked.

QUESTIONS FOR THOUGHT AND DISCUSSION

1. What is the difference between the emancipation of the Jews in Western and Central Europe and the type of emancipation demanded by Russian Jews after the Revolution in February 1917?

2. The Soviet Jews are considered a nationality and the letter J is stamped in their passports attesting to this fact. Are the Jews in the same category as the other nationalities of the Soviet Union? What is the difference, if any?

3. What prompted the Jewish Communists in Russia to fight against Zionism and Hebrew? Why did the Soviets, who supported the establishment of the State of Israel in 1947–48, turn against Israel in subsequent years?

4. Describe the economic transformation which the Jews had to undergo under the Soviets.

5. Find out the main centers where Jews reside today in Russia. Which are the major cities with a large Jewish population?

6. What do you assume to be the reasons for the failure of Biro-Bidzhan, which was contemplated as a Jewish autonomous region to which a large Jewish population would be attracted?

7. What do you consider the positive and the negative aspects of Jewish life in Soviet Russia?

8. What are the reasons for the prominence of Jews in the Soviet government during the first years of its existence?

9. Why does Elie Wiesel, in one of his books, call the Russian Jews the "Jews of Silence"?

10. Read about Jewish activists in Russia and their tribulations in The Last Exodus by Leonard Schroeter.

11. Find out how many parents or grandparents of your classmates or of all the students in your school emigrated from Russia to the United States.

12. What can Jews in America and other free countries do to help their fellow-Jews in Russia?

SUGGESTED READING

Note: Books suggested in more than one chapter are here listed by the name of the author only. A key to such listings will be found at the end of the book.

A paperback edition is indicated by the letters PB.

Books for the Student

Chesler, pp. 45–133. PB.

Elbogen, pp. 469–73, 492–509, 574–56.

Cohen, Richard, ed. *Let My People Go: Today's Documentary Story of Soviet Jewry's Struggle to Be Free.* New York, 1971. PB.

Decter, Moshe, ed. *Redemption: Jewish Freedom Letters from Russia.* New York, 1970. PB.

Porath, pp. 70–197. PB.

Schroeter, Leonard. *The Last Exodus.* New York, 1974.

Wiesel, Elie. *The Jews of Silence.* New York, 1966. PB.

Autobiographies

Rusinek, Alla. *Like a Song, Like a Dream.* New York, 1973.

Books for the Teacher

Aronson, Gregor, ed. *Russian Jewry, 1917–1967.* New York, 1969.

Baron, chaps. 11–18.

Carr, Edward, *The Bolshevik Revolution. Vol. 1. New York, 1968.*

Eliav, Arie. *Between Hammer and Sickle.* New York, 1969.

Gilboa, Yehoshua A. *The Black Years of Soviet Jewry, 1939–1953.* Boston, 1971.

Goldberg, B. Z. *The Jewish Problem in the Soviet Union.* New York, 1961.

Kochan, Lionel, ed. *The Jews of Soviet Russia Since 1917.* 2d ed. London 1972.

Korey, William. *The Soviet Cage: Antisemitism in Russia.* New York, 1973.

Schaffer, Harry G. *The Soviet Treatment of Jews.* New York, 1974.

Schechtman, Joseph. *Star in Eclipse.* New York, 1961.

Smolar, Boris. *Soviet Jewry Today and Tomorrow.* New York, 1971.

Pamphlet material, films, etc., can be gotten from:

American Jewish Committee, 165 East 56th Street, New York, N.Y. 10022.

American Jewish Congress, 15 East 84th Street, New York, N.Y. 10028.

National Conference on Soviet Jewry, 11 East West 42nd Street, New York, N.Y. 10036.

V. THE HOLOCAUST

Introduction

The Holocaust was a shattering experience in the history of the Jewish people and resulted in the destruction of the European centers which had been the mainstay of world Jewry for a thousand years.

Germany

We start with events in Germany.

Although the Jews had achieved legal emancipation in Germany during the nineteenth century, certain trends developed which were exceedingly detrimental to Jewish hopes for attaining the full measure of civil rights. These trends should not be disregarded in a study of the Holocaust.

Anti-Semitic agitation, differing from mere anti-Jewish prejudice, appeared in the German Empire in the mid-seventies. This agitation was largely a by-product of the economic depression which prevailed between 1873 and 1896 and affected the lower middle class in particular. The artisans, the small shopkeepers, and the peasants came to be vulnerable to the arguments of the anti-Semitic agitators that their plight was largely the fault of the Jews. The propaganda of hate did not remain confined to this group. The historian Heinrich von Treitschke, in his university lectures and articles, made anti-Semitism respectable among the young generation of Germany's educated middle class.

Racial Anti-Semitism

Since the creation of the empire in 1871, the Jewish community in Germany had become increasingly urbanized. Their rising standards of living, their influx into the free professions, into commerce and banking, into the press and the arts, aroused mounting resentment. Charges were made that the Jews were exerting a growing stranglehold over the economic and cultural life of Germany and that they were a threat to the moral fiber of the German nation. Advocates of racial anti-Semitism thus became vocal, and their arguments were fused with the traditional forms of social and religious anti-Jewish prejudice. It was not only the Prussian aristocracy, the officer corps, the bureaucracy, the Conservative Party which were affected by the new anti-Semitism. The same was true also of the propertied and educated middle class, the liberals to whom the Jews owed whatever progress their struggle for emancipation had made during the nineteenth

185

century. Liberalism gave way to national chauvinism, with the help of professors like Treitschke, and anti-Semitism made inroads into the universities, the training ground for future officials, judges, and army reserve officers.

The defeat of Germany in the First World War, the years of inflation, the general weakness of the Weimar Republic, the agressive anti-republican agitation of the parties on the right, the economic crisis beginning in 1929, all these factors contributed to the rise of new waves of political, social, and racial anti-Semitism and helped pave the way for Hitler's rule.

Hitler Comes to Power

By 1932, aided by worldwide economic depression, the Nazi movement had grown from a relatively minor group to become Germany's dominant political party. Hitler took over the government in January 1933, and within a few months succeeded, by varied and devious means, in dismantling German democracy, replacing it with a dictatorial regime.

The New Government Policy

The Nazi program of racial anti-Semitism became the basis for official government policy. Beginning with a one-day economic boycott against the Jews in April 1933, the anti-Jewish policy gained momentum day by day. Within a period of two years, Jewish public servants, teachers, and other professionals were deprived of their livelihood.

Disfranchisement

In 1935, special legislation was introduced, known as the Nuremberg laws, which disfranchised the Jews and demoted them to vastly inferior status. Harassment of the Jews became more common from month to month. During the next few years, Jewish businesses and property were expropriated under various pretexts. In November 1938, a terror action which came to be known as Crystal Night (because of the many windows broken) was carefully staged; synagogues were burned, and some 35,000 Jews were thrown into concentration camps. By 1939, a year after the annexation of Austria, which inaugurated the planned conquest of Europe, Jews had been completely eliminated from the economic life of Germany and Austria.

Emigration

Suffering from discrimination and deprived of the possibility of earning a living, Jews tried to emigrate from the countries now under Nazi domination. Because of the worldwide economic depression, entry to other countries was exceedingly difficult. Yet, by September 1939, when the Germans began the Second World War, about 400,000 Jews, out of a total of 800,000 in Germany and Austria, had succeeded in emigrating. Another 50,000 managed to flee before the end of 1941 when no more escape routes were available.

Nazi Conquests

With the conquest of Poland by the German armies in 1939, of Belgium, the Netherlands, France, Denmark, and Norway in 1940, and of large parts of Soviet Russia after Germany attacked it in June 1941, millions of additional Jews came under Nazi rule. In Poland the Jews were forced into ghettos and were cut off from the rest of the world. The initial policy of the Nazis was to let the Jews die of starvation and disease and to use them as slave labor.

Policy of Murder

When, in March 1941, Hitler planned to attack Russia, a new policy, termed by the Nazis the "final solution of the Jewish problem," was decided upon: the systematic murder of all Jews in Nazi-occupied Europe. At first, special commandos following the troops advancing in Russia rounded up the Jews of a city and shot them. Later, death factories were set up, supplied with gas chambers for killing and furnaces for disposing of the bodies. Such death camps were established in various places, mainly in Poland, among them the ill-famed Auschwitz, Treblinka, and Maidanek. Jews from Nazi-held Europe were transported in cattle cars to these death camps. It is estimated that close to six million Jews perished in the Holocaust, most by murder in the death camps, others through planned starvation and disease purposely promoted by the Nazis. The victims who thus perished amounted to more than one-third of all the Jews in the world.

Was Resistance Possible?

The question has often been asked whether Jews allowed themselves to be led "like sheep to slaughter" without offering resistance, passively or actively. A number of facts will have to be considered when discussing this question.

In the first place, active resistance required a stock of arms and the backing of the non-Jewish population in which Jews found themselves. Arms were not to be had, and besides, what might be expected of people having to contend with the mighty war machine of the Germans? Even the non-Jewish people of European countries offered little or no resistance to the German conquerors, although they did not suffer to nearly the same extent the deprivations to which the Jews were subjected.

Another decisive element was that in the period of thirty months between the occupation of Poland and the time when the mass killings reached their peak, the Jews had experienced untold suffering which weakened and almost annihilated their powers of physical and mental resistance. They had been systematically starved. As an example, the amounts of food distributed in the Warsaw ghetto in 1941 came to a mere 229 calories a person, while the non-Jewish Poles lived on 1,790 calories a day. As a result, one-tenth of the Warsaw ghetto population died of starvation. There is good reason to believe that had the German occupation lasted a few more years, all the Jews might have perished even without the annihilation camps.

Nonviolent Resistance

The fact of the existence of the death camps was kept secret by the Nazis. With the manifold security restrictions that existed in wartime, such secrecy was not difficult to maintain. Death factories were disguised as labor camps. Jews were deceived by being told that they were transported to resettle in other territories. Nothing like the Holocaust had ever happened before, and nobody, either Jew or Gentile, could imagine that a country considered as civilized as Germany would pursue the systematic, mechanized mass murder of European Jewry, a crime without precedent in history.

Until the truth about the annihilation camps gradually emerged, Jewish resistance was nonviolent. Jewish underground papers appeared; underground schools were organized; religious services were held; and lectures, concerts, and plays were presented—all of these activities prohibited by the Nazis. The goal of the victims was to keep body and soul together, to survive and to hope for the defeat of the inhuman conqueror. The resistance was nonviolent, yet brave and heroic, and it defies imagination as to how the Jews were able to maintain any semblance of community life in the face of the unremitting threat of death.

Active Resistance

Once the truth about the death camps began to emerge, many Jews decided to offer resistance and fight. A few weapons had been smuggled into the ghettos, but always in very insufficient quantities. Young people, naturally, were more ready and able to fight than their elders. The most widely known of the revolts is the death struggle that took place in the Warsaw ghetto in April and May 1943. But there were uprisings in a number of other cities and even in concentration and death camps. By contrast, no uprisings are reported among the more than five million Soviet war prisoners, of whom four million perished in the prison camps. It is true, however, that there were a limited number of escapes of such war prisoners.

Some Jews took to the woods and became partisan fighters. Their existence was all the more precarious due to the anti-Semitic sentiments of the surrounding Polish and Ukrainian population, who often tried to kill them outright or to hand them over to the enemy.

In the West, too, Jews began to be active. In France, for example, the proportion of the Jews in the resistance movement reached the unusually high level of 20 percent of the total resistance fighters, whereas the total Jewish percentage of the general population was vastly smaller.

The Jews in Eastern Europe who took up arms suffered from all possible disadvantages. They knew in advance that they could not prevail. But "while they lived, they fought back, and what they did stands as one of the most stirring examples of the indomitable human spirit in all history."*

Sources

Our selections of sources begin with the words of Heinrich von Treitschke (no. 55), who helped to make anti-Semitism respectable in the universities and among the educated middle class during the last decades of the nineteenth century. In the climate thus created and aggravated by the defeat in the First World War, a dilemma was faced by the Jew who tried to live as both a German and a Jew. Such a dilemma was most acutely felt and expressed by Jacob Wassermann, the celebrated novelist (no. 56). With the rise of the Nazis to power, their anti-Jewish policy was legalized by the Aryan paragraph and the Nuremberg laws (no. 57). Harassed and humiliated, the Jews of Germany found a courageous and dignified representative and spokesman in Rabbi Leo Baeck (no. 58).

The Nazi aim of destroying the Jewish population systematically was realized during the war years (1939–45) by setting up ghettos and concentration and extermination camps in the occupied territories. The report of a German military officer after a visit to a ghetto in Poland provides involuntary testimony to the Nazi policy (no. 60).

To "be brave" and full of hope for the future was the decision of Anne Frank, an adolescent girl who confided to her diary, which she kept while hiding with her family in Nazi-occupied Holland. (no. 59).

The will to survive and even to maintain a cultural life in the Warsaw ghetto in spite of threatening death is recounted by the historian Emanuel Ringelblum (no. 61). A foreboding of the catastrophe which was to engulf

---

*Bauer, *They Chose Life*, p. 54.

Polish Jewry is found in a song of a folk balladist, Mordecai Gebirtig (no. 62).

The helplessness and the utter despair resulting from the indifference of the world to the fate of the Jews in Nazi-occupied Poland caused a leader of Polish Jewry to address a letter of protest to the Polish government-in-exile and to commit suicide (no. 63).

There were non-Jews, especially in northern, western, and southern Europe, who risked their lives in trying to help and save Jews. Even among the Poles, many of whom cooperated with the Germans in the policy of destruction of the Jews, there were found such selfless helpers, as attested by a member of the Jewish underground (no. 64).

Although powerless against the overwhelming might of the Nazi war machine, the Jews created a resistance movement, which led to uprisings in Warsaw, Vilna, and other places (nos. 65–67). An unforgettable account of the last days of the Warsaw ghetto has been preserved by a survivor, Ziviah Lubetkin (no. 68).

A chapter not well understood in the history of the Holocaust is the role of the Jewish Councils, the Nazi-sponsored Jewish ghetto governments in the cities of occupied Europe (no. 69). A wider meaning of resistance as practiced by Jews under Nazi rule is clarified in two selections (nos. 70 and 71). This wider meaning of resistance and the belief in a Jewish future found expression in the song of the Jewish partisans (no. 72) and in an inscription found in a cellar (no. 73).

What went on in the period of the liberation of the concentration camps is told by an inmate, Simon Wiesenthal, who later became a well-known hunter of Nazi criminals (no. 74).

The Nazi crime against the Jewish people is eloquently and comprehensively presented by Gideon Hausner, the attorney-general of the government of Israel, in his indictment of Eichmann, who played a leading role in the perpetration of this crime (no. 75).

The chapter concludes with expressions by a historian and a poet. H. H. Ben-Sasson, historian at the Hebrew University in Jerusalem, discusses the "shock of the Holocaust" and the new meaning of martyrology in the history of the Jewish people (no. 76). The Hebrew poet Abraham Shlonsky speaks of the obligation to remember the Holocaust (no. 77).

55. THE JEWS ARE OUR MISFORTUNE

HEINRICH VON TREITSCHKE

Henrich von Treitschke (1836–96) was a professor of history at the University of Berlin. He exerted a great influence on the academic youth and did much to promote the growing chauvinistic trend in Germany in the years following the establishment of the Grman Empire in 1871. The excerpt is taken from one of his articles, published in 1879, dealing with the Jews.

The present loud agitation appears as a brutal and hateful, yet natural reaction of the German national feeling against a foreign element which has appropriated too much space in our life. . . . Let us not deceive ourselves, the movement has become very far-reaching. . . . Everywhere, including men of education who would reject any thought of religious intolerance or national arrogance with disgust, one hears the unanimous call, "the Jews are our misfortune."

56. MY LIFE AS GERMAN AND JEW

JACOB WASSERMANN

Jacob Wassermann (1873–1934) was a well-known novelist whose books have been translated into many languages. All his life he considered himself to be both German and Jew, yet he felt that the Germans looked upon him as an alien. Such experiences caused him to raise questions and to discuss the relationship of Jew and German in a book, entitled *My Life as German and Jew*, published in 1921. The following excerpt sums up some of his sad conclusions.

An aristocratic Dane once asked me: What is the reason for the German hatred of Jews? In my country the Jews are universally loved. They are known as the most reliable of patriots; they are known to lead honorable private lives; they are respected as a sort of nobility. What do the Germans want?

I should have answered: Hate.

I should have answered: They want a scapegoat. Whenever they are badly off, after every defeat, in every difficulty, in every trying situation they shift the responsibility for their distress upon the Jews. So it has been for centuries. . . .

But what I did say was: A non-German cannot possibly imagine the heartbreaking position of the German Jew. German Jew—you must place full emphasis on both words. You must understand them as the final product of a lengthy evolutionary process. His twofold love and his struggle on two fronts drive him close to the brink of despair. . . .

With the realization of the hopelessness of all efforts the bitterness in one's breast becomes a mortal agony. . . .

Vain to adjure the nation of poets and thinkers in the name of poets and thinkers. Every prejudice one thinks disposed of breeds a thousand others, as carrion breeds maggots.

Vain to present the right cheek after the left has been struck. It does not move them to the slightest thoughtfulness; it neither touches nor disarms them. They strike the right cheek too.

Vain to interject words of reason into their crazy shrieking. They say: He dares to open his mouth? Gag him.

Vain to act in exemplary fashion. They say: We know nothing, we have seen nothing, we have heard nothing.

Vain to seek obscurity. They say: The coward! He is creeping into hiding, driven by his evil conscience.

Vain to go among them and offer them one's hand. They say: Why does he take such liberties, with his Jewish obtrusiveness?

Vain to keep faith with them, as a comrade-in-arms or a fellow citizen. They say: He is Proteus, he can assume any shape or form.

Vain to help them strip off the chains of slavery. They say: No doubt he found it profitable.

Vain to counteract the poison. They brew fresh venom.

Vain to live for them and die for them. They say: He is a Jew.

57. THE END OF EMANCIPATION

NAZI LEGISLATION

The "Aryan Paragraph," April 7, 1933. Civil servants of non-Aryan descent must retire.

From the "Nuremberg Laws," 1935. Only a Reich citizen as bearer of complete political rights may exercise the right to vote in political affairs or hold public office.

A Jew cannot be a Reich citizen. He is not allowed the right to vote in political affairs, he cannot hold public office.

Jew is he who is descended from at least three grandparents who are fully Jewish by race. (Among other restrictive regulations Jews were required to establish separate schools for their children. They were forbidden to employ female domestic help of "German blood" under forty-five years of age.)

58. A PRAYER BEFORE KOL NIDRE

LEO BAECK

Leo Baeck (1873–1956) was a leading rabbi and scholar in Germany and became president of the *Reichsvertretung der Juden in Deutschland*, the official representative organization of the Jews in Germany, established in 1933. In 1935, when the anti-Jewish legislation was well advanced (see no. 57) and the Jewish community harassed and humiliated, Rabbi Baeck wrote the prayer that follows. It was sent to all rabbis in Germany to be read from the pulpit as part of the service. The Nazi police discovered the text and apprehended its author. The prayer was not recited at the time; it was, however, read into the record of the Eichmann trial in Jerusalem.

In this hour all Israel stands before God, the judge and the forgiver.

In His presence let us all examine our ways, our deeds, and what we have failed to do.

Where we transgressed, let us openly confess: "We have sinned!" and, determined to return to God, let us pray: "Forgive us."

We stand before our God.

With the same fervor with which we confess our sins, the sins of the individual and the sins of the community, do we, in indignation and abhorrence, express our contempt for the lies concerning us and the defamation of our religion and its testimonies.

We have trust in our faith and in our future.

Who made known to the world the mystery of the Eternal, the One God?

Who imparted to the world the comprehension of purity of conduct and purity of family life?

Who taught the world respect for man, created in the image of God?

Who spoke of the commandment of righteousness, of social justice?

In all this we see manifest the spirit of the prophets, the divine revelation to the Jewish people. It grew out of Judaism and is still growing. By these facts we repel the insults flung at us.

We stand before our God. On Him we rely. From Him issues the truth and the glory of our history, our fortitude amidst all change of fortune, our endurance in distress.

Our history is a history of nobility of soul, of human dignity. It is history we have recourse to when attack and grievous wrong are directed against us, when affliction and calamity befall us.

God has led our fathers from generation to generation. He will guide us and our children through these days.

We stand before our God, strengthened by His commandment that we fulfill. We bow to Him and stand erect before men. We worship Him and remain firm in all vicissitudes. Humbly we trust in Him and our path lies clear before us; we see our future.

All Israel stands before its God in this hour. In our prayers, in our hope, in our confession, we are one with all Jews on earth. We look upon each other and know who we are; we look up to our God and know what shall abide.

"Behold, He that keepeth Israel does neither slumber nor sleep" (Psalm 121:4).

"May He who maketh peace in His heights bring peace upon us and all Israel" (From the prayerbook).

59. I SHALL REQUIRE COURAGE

ANNE FRANK

Anne Frank was born in Germany in 1929 and emigrated with her family to Holland in 1933. During the Nazi occupation of Holland the Frank family hid in an attic, and there Anne wrote her diary between 1942 and 1944. They were discovered by the German police in 1944 and taken away. Anne died in the Bergen-Belsen concentration camp in March 1945. The following excerpt is taken from her diary, which was discovered in the attic after the war.

We have been pointedly reminded that we are in hiding, that we are Jews in chains, chained to one spot, without any rights, but with a thousand duties. We Jews mustn't show our feelings, must be brave and strong, must accept all inconveniences and not grumble, must do what is within our power and trust in God. Sometime this terrible war will be over. Surely, the time will come when we are people again, and not just Jews.

Who has inflicted this upon us? Who has made us Jews different from all other people? Who has allowed us to suffer so terribly up till now? It is God that has made us as we are, but it will be God, too, who will raise us up again. If we bear all this suffering and if there are still Jews left, when it is over, then Jews, instead of being doomed, will be held up as an example. Who knows, it might be even our religion from which the world and all peoples learn good, and for that reason and that reason only do we have to suffer now. We can never become just Netherlanders, or just English, or representatives of any country for that matter; we will always remain Jews, but we want to, too.

Be brave! Let us remain aware of our task and not grumble, solution will come. God has never deserted our people. Right through the ages there have been Jews, through all the ages they have had to suffer, but it has made them strong too; the weak fall, but the strong will remain and never go under!

During the night I really felt that I had to die. I waited for the police, I was prepared, as the soldier is on the battlefield. I was eager to lay down my life for the country, but now, now I've been saved again, now my first wish after the war is that I may become Dutch! I love the Dutch, I love this country, I love the language and want to work here. And even if I have to write to the Queen myself, I will not give up until I have reached my goal.

I am becoming still more independent of my parents; young as I am, I face life with more courage than Mummy; my feeling for justice is immovable, and truer than hers. I know what I want, I have a goal, an opinion. I have a religion and love. Let me be myself and then I am satisfied. I know that I'm a woman, a woman with inward strength and plenty of courage.

If God lets me live, I shall attain more than Mummy has ever done, I shall not remain insignificant, I shall work in the world and for mankind!

And now I know that first and foremost I shall require courage and cheerfulness!

60. A GHETTO IN OCCUPIED POLAND

The following excerpt is from an official monthly report for April 16–May 15, 1941 by a German military officer (signed von Unruh) in the district of Warsaw. In setting up the ghettos in occupied Poland, it was the aim of the Nazi government by starvation and disease to destroy the Jewish population systematically.

The situation in the Jewish quarter is catastrophic. Dead bodies of those who collapsed from lack of strength are lying in the streets. Mortality, 80% undernourishment, has tripled since February. The only thing allotted to the Jews is 1½ pounds of bread a week. Potatoes, for which the Jewish council has paid in advance several million, have not been delivered. The large number of welfare agencies created by the Jewish council are in no position to arrest the frightful misery. The ghetto is growing into a social scandal, a breeder of illnesses and of the worst subhumanity. The treatment of the Jews in labor camps, where they are guarded solely by Poles, can be described as bestial.

61. JEWISH CULTURAL LIFE IN THE GHETTOS OF POLAND

EMANUEL RINGELBLUM

The eminent historian Emanuel Ringelblum, who lived in Warsaw, kept a diary which has been published. In 1944, a year after the uprising of the Warsaw ghetto, Ringelblum, who was in hiding with his family and other Jews in the cellar of a Polish worker in Warsaw, was arrested by the Germans and subsequently executed.

The excerpt which follows is from a letter which Ringelblum wrote to some

Jewish institutions and writers. The translation from the Yiddish is by Moshe
Spiegel. Besides systematically starving the Jews in the ghettos, the Nazis
tried to cut off most normal community functions. No social services or
medical care were provided; religious services and study were forbidden and
synagogues shut; schools were closed down; political parties and activities
outlawed. Yet the ghetto dwellers struggled to maintain a semblance of normal
life. Most Jewish activities were maintained underground.

Dear Friends:

We write at a time when 95 per cent of Polish Jewry has been wiped out,
wiped out under savage torture, in the gas chambers and charnel houses of
Treblinka, Sobibor, Chelmno and Oshpitzin or in the countless liquidations in the camps and ghettos. The fate of our people now painfully
rotting in the concentration camps is similarly predetermined.

Perhaps a handful of Jews will survive to live a precarious existence in
the Aryan sections of the cities or in the forest, hunted like beasts. It is
gravely doubtful that any of us, the communal leaders, will survive the
war, working under extremely hazardous conditions as we do.

When Polish Jews fell under the cruel yoke of the Nazis, the independent
Jewish communal leadership began its widespread, far-reaching work,
dedicated to self-help and resistance. With the active assistance of the
"Joint," a colossal network of social welfare agencies arose in Warsaw and
the hinterlands under the leadership of Z.H.T.O.S. [Society for Jewish
Social Welfare], Centos [Central Shelter for Children and Orphans], and
T.O.Z. [Society to Guard the Health of the Jewish Population]. O.R.T., too,
was active. With the help of these organizations and their committees tens
of thousands were able to prolong their lives. The work was kept up to the
last, as long as the Jewish community showed a spark of life. Political
parties and ideological groups were enabled to conduct their conspirato-
rial work in secrecy, and cultural activities were shielded.

The watchword of the Jewish social worker was, "Live and die with
honor," a motto we endeavored to keep in the ghettos. It found its
expression in the multi-faceted cultural program that grew in spite of the
terror, hunger and deprivation. It grew until the very moment of the
martyrdom of Polish Jewry.

As soon as the Warsaw Ghetto was sealed off, a subterranean
organization, Yikor [Yiddish Cultural Organization] was established to
conduct a wide program in Jewish culture. The program included
scientific lectures, celebrations to honor Peretz, Sholom Aleichem,
Mendele, Borochov and others, and projects in art and literature. The
prime mover of Yikor was the young economist Menachem Linder, who
was killed in 1942.

Under the mantle of Centos kitchens and children's homes there sprang up a network of underground schools representing varying shades of opinion: *Cisho, Tarbuth, Schulkult, Yavneh, Chorev, Beth Yaakov* and others. The secular schools were taught in Yiddish. These schools were established through the work of Shachna Zagan and Sonia Novogrudski, both of whom died at Treblinka.

A furtive central Jewish archive was formed under the deceptive title, "Society for Enjoyment of the Sabbath," by Dr. Emmanuel Ringelblum, who, in collaboration with [six names are mentioned here] gathered material and documents concerning the martyrdom of the Polish Jews. Thanks to the efforts of a large staff, about twenty trunkfuls of documents, diaries, photographs, remembrances and reports were collected. The material was buried in . . . , which even we could not enter. Most of the material sent abroad comes from the archive. We gave the world the most accurate information about the greatest crime in history. We are continuing our work on the archive, regardless of circumstances.

In 1941 and 1942 we were in contact with . . . in Vilna, who, under German control, managed to coordinate and conceal a good portion of the Y.I.V.O. documents. Today there are no Jews in Vilna. This once great center of Jewish culture and modern scientific research is in shambles.

But throughout almost the entire existence of the ghetto practically every Jewish organization participated in underground work, especially youth groups. We put out newspapers, magazines and anthologies. The most active groups in this work were the Bund, which published the "Bulletin," "Current Events," "Voice of Youth," "*Nowa Mlodziez,*" "*Za Nasza i wasza Wolnosc*"; *Hashomer Hatzair*, which published "*Jutrznia Przewiosnie,*" "Upsurge," and a series of anthologies; Left *Poale Zion*, "*Nasze Haslo,*" "Proletarian Thought," "Call of Youth," "Vanguard"; Right *Poale Zion*, "Liberation"; *Dror, "Dror Yedios," "Hamadrich,"* "*G'vura,*" "*Pine*"; the anti-Fascist bloc, "The Call"; the Communists, "Morning *Freiheit,*" and others. Some publications reached almost all other ghettos despite extreme difficulty in communications with Warsaw.

Centos, the central child care organization, led much activity among the children. Led by . . . and the unforgettable Rosa Simchovich (who died of typhoid contracted from street waifs), teachers, educators and artists, *Centos* founded a central children's library, a theater and classes in Yiddish language and literature. Thousands of adults joined in for "Children's Month," a program of cultural and artistic projects which provided a little happiness far from the hideous realism of their existence. Today there are no more Jewish children in Poland. Some 99 per cent were murdered by the Nazis.

The ghetto even had a symphonic orchestra, under Shimon Pullman. Its concerts and chamber music afforded us moments of relaxation and forgetfulness. Pullman and most of the other musicians perished at Treblinka along with violinist Ludwig Holzman. The young conductor Marion Noitich died at the Travniki camp.

A great deal of young talent was found in the ghetto. The daughter of a director of the Warsaw Synagogue, Marisha Eisenstadt, was called the "Nightingale of the Ghetto." She was killed during the liquidations. There were many choral groups, notably the children's chorus directed by Feivishes, who died at the Poniatow camp. Other choirmasters were Gladstein and Sax, among those who died at Treblinka. Jewish painters and sculptors, living in frightful poverty, organized occasional exhibits. Felix Friedman was one of the best; but they all died at Treblinka.

Our activities continued in the concentration camps. In Ponyatow, Treblinka and other camps we formed secret social societies and even arranged secret celebrations during holidays. Activity continued as long as there was life, in desperate struggling against the barbarism that imprisoned us.

When the deportations began our organizations turned to battle. The youths showed the way in Zionist organizations and all branches of the labor movement. Armed resistance began in Poland. We defended the Warsaw Ghetto and fought at Bialystock. We destroyed parts of Treblinka and Sobibor. We fought at Torne, Bendim and Czestochowa. We proved to the world that we could fight back, and we died with dignity.

That's what we wanted to tell you, dear friends. There are not many of us left. There are ten writers [names follow] we would like you to attempt to contact through the Red Cross; we don't know if they are still alive. Enclosed is a list of the dead who have helped in our work.

We doubt if we will see you again. Give our best to the builders of our culture, and to all who fight for human redemption.

Dr. E. Ringelblum

62. OUR TOWN IS BURNING

MORDECAI GEBIRTIG

The author of the poem which follows worked all his life as a carpenter in his native town, Cracow, and became a very popular folk balladist in prewar Poland. Gebirtig was killed in 1942 in the Cracow ghetto. His poem "Our Town Is Burning," written in 1938, became one of the most popular songs in the ghettos, the concentration camps, and among the survivors in the D.P. camps.

> Our town is burning, brothers, burning,
> Our poor little town is burning.

Angry winds are fanning higher
The leaping tongues of flame and fire,
The evil winds are roaring!
Our whole town burns!

And you stand looking on with folded arms,
And shake your heads.
You stand looking on, with folded arms
While the fire spreads!

Our town is burning, brothers, burning,
Our poor little town is burning.
Tongues of flame are leaping,
The fire through our town goes sweeping,
Through roofs and windows pouring.
All around us burns.

And you stand looking on with folded arms,
And shake your heads.
You stand looking on with folded arms
While the fire spreads!

Our town is burning, brothers, burning.
Any moment the fire may
Sweep the whole of our town away,
And leave only ashes, black and gray,

Like after a battle, where dead walls stand,
Broken and ruined in a desolate land.

And you stand looking on with folded arms,
And shake your heads.
You stand looking on with folded arms
While the fire spreads!

Our town is burning, brothers, burning.
All now depends on you.
Our only help is what you do.
You can still put out the fire
With your blood, if you desire.

Don't look on with folded arms,

And shake your heads.
Don't look on with folded arms
While the fire spreads!

63. A PROTEST AGAINST THE INDIFFERENCE OF THE WORLD

SAMUEL ZYGELBOJM

Samuel Zygelbojm was one of the leaders of the Bund, the Jewish Socialist Party in Poland. In 1940 he managed to flee from Poland. When he reached London in 1942, he, as representative of the Polish Jews, joined the National Polish Committee, which became the Polish Government-in-Exile. Zygelbojm and others tried desperately to draw the attention of the Allied governments to the fate of the Jews in Poland. When the news of the revolt in the Warsaw Ghetto came, and with it the final phase of the extermination, Zygelbojm committed suicide as an act of protest against the indifference of the Allied governments to the fate of his people. Before his death he addressed to the Polish government the following letter, which was transmitted to the British and American governments.

With these, my last words, I address myself to you, the Polish Government, the Polish people, the Allied Governments and their peoples, and the conscience of the world.

News recently received from Poland informs us that the Germans are exterminating with unheard-of savagery the remaining Jews in that country. Behind the walls of the ghetto is taking place today the last act of a tragedy which has no parallel in the history of the human race. The responsibility for this crime—the assassination of the Jewish population in Poland—rests above all on the murderers themselves, but falls indirectly upon the whole human race, on the Allies and their governments, who so far have taken no firm steps to put a stop to these crimes. By their indifference to the killing of millions of hapless men, to the massacre of women and children, these countries have become accomplices of the assassins.

Furthermore, I must state that the Polish Government, although it has done a great deal to influence world public opinion, has not taken adequate measures to counter this atrocity which is taking place today in Poland.

Of the three and a half million Polish Jews (to whom must be added the 700,000 deported from the other countries) in April, 1943, there remained alive not more than 300,000 Jews according to news received from the head of the Bund organization and supplied by government representatives. And the extermination continues.

I cannot remain silent. I cannot live while the rest of the Jewish people in Poland, whom I represent, continue to be liquidated.

My companions of the Warsaw Ghetto fell in a last heroic battle with their weapons in their hands. I did not have the honor to die with them but I belong to them and to their common grave.

Let my death be an energetic cry of protest against the indifference of the world which witnesses the extermination of the Jewish people without taking any steps to prevent it. In our day and age human life is of little value; having failed to achieve success in my life, I hope that my death may jolt the indifference of those who, perhaps even in this extreme moment, could save the Jews who are still alive in Poland.

My life belongs to my people in Poland and that is why I am sacrificing it for them. May the handful of people who will survive out of the millions of Polish Jews achieve liberation in a world of liberty and socialist justice together with the Polish people.

I think that there will be a free Poland and that it is possible to achieve a world of justice. I am certain that the President of the Republic and the head of the government will pass on my words to all concerned. I am sure that the Polish Government will hasten to adopt the necessary political measures and will come to the aid of those who are still alive.

I take my leave of all those who have been dear to me and whom I have loved.

Samuel Zygelbojm

64. POLISH FRIENDS

"WLADKA"

Among the non-Jewish people in the countries occupied by the Germans, the Poles had the worst record when help for the Jews was needed. They eagerly cooperated with the German administration in carrying out the anti-Jewish decrees. The record would not, however, be complete without a report like the following by "Wladka" (Feigl Peltl-Miedzyrzecki), who, born in Poland, was seventeen years old when the Nazis occupied Warsaw. She was assigned the dangerous task of serving as a courier on the Aryan side as an agent of the underground Bund. She came to America in 1946.

It would not be right to suppose that all the gentile Poles with whom we were in contact were unreliable people, provocateurs, or mere mercenaries at best. True, most of the gentiles with whom we dealt accepted money for the least service rendered. But not a few of them were kindhearted, with much sympathy for our tribulations. There were even some who risked their lives to rescue Jews from danger.

Even though their number was few, it must be acknowledged that without the cooperation of this handful of friendly gentiles, we, the members of the Jewish underground who carried out our work outside of the ghetto, could not have accomplished much. At crucial moments, in times of great risk, these friends enabled us to carry out our important missions.

I have previously mentioned the part played in our misfortune by Polish villains, informers, and provocateurs, as well as by the indifferent majority of the Polish population. Therefore, I am duty-bound to refer as well to those who stretched forth a helping hand to us then. I shall mention only a few of these, with whom I was in close contact.

Wanda Wnorowska was one of the first gentiles with whom I had anything to do after I left the ghetto. The widow of a Polish officer, she was in her forties, a gentle aristocrat, and a member of the so-called better Polish society. She ran a ladies' tailoring establishment, and I found employment with her as soon as I crossed to the Aryan side. To have a job and warm quarters during the winter was good in itself and an important camouflage for my underground work.

When I was called upon to devote all my time to illegal activities, and therefore had to give up my job as a seamstress, the gentile Wanda gladly accepted in my place friends of mine who had just succeeded in getting out of the ghetto: Khautche Werktzeig-Elenbogen, Rivka Rosenshtein, Zoshka Kersh, Helenka and Bronka of Piotrkov. She welcomed them all warmly, paid them relatively good wages, and made every effort to ease their lot. Wanda soon made friends with her Jewish girl employees, took an interest in their hardships, and endeavored not only to give advice but to help them through her contacts with gentiles. She was gradually drawn into our little world, and became one of our confidantes.

The new quarters at 39 Vspulne to which Wanda had had to move had already become a clandestine rallying point for the Jews, frequented primarily by those who came from Piotrkov in various sorts of disguise. Wanda had an open hand as well as an open heart for everyone. The downtrodden and desperate came to seek her counsel and help. Whether it was living quarters, documents, or anything else that was needed, Wanda could usually find the right connection to solve the problem.

Whenever I appeared, Wanda would take me aside to discuss "her" poor Jews. This gentile woman would confer with me, insisting that more help must somehow be obtained for "her people." She could not comprehend the difficulties which limited the scope of action possible by us. One thing was uppermost in her mind: to render help to the needy.

I was the one who managed to transfer considerable sums of money from the underground organization to Wanda, and she, in turn, distributed these funds in accordance with our instructions. She never wanted anything for herself. When we offered her money to ease her own strained circumstances, she felt offended and refused to accept the offer.

"You are in more trouble than I am," she would answer modestly.

She was most happy on her birthday, when her house overflowed with flowers from her Jewish friends. Proudly she pointed to the various bouquets and showed the notes attached to them. That was the only compensation this splendid woman would take from us.

Juliana Larish, a young gentile girl who before the war had worked as a bookkeeper for the Jewish family of Zilberberg in Prague, was another Polish "woman of righteousness."

When the deportations to concentration camps began in the ghetto, some Jews turned for help to their gentile friends of former days. And the kindhearted Miss Larish responded. Moving with caution, she succeeded in enabling twenty-one of her Jewish friends to escape from the ghetto. She concealed ten Jews in her own house at 7 Bzeske; she sent a three-year-old little girl named Iza Blokhowitz to a friendly Polish family in Radzimin; and one Jewish woman with Aryan features was put up in a newly bought house.

Juliana had a thriving meat supply business, and most of its profits went to Jews in hiding. She provided them not only with a refuge but also with such things as clothes and books. This gracious woman was constantly preoccupied with Jewish affairs, running from one secret hiding place to another as she endeavored to lighten the burden of the unfortunate. She helped them observe the Jewish holy days, and even lent a hand in baking the *matzoth* for Passover!

To distract the attention of her neighbors from the huge baskets of provisions she provided for those in hiding, Juliana began frequently to invite her Polish and German customers in for a snack. This brought the respect of the neighbors who observed her from the courtyard.

Through the thin walls of their hideouts, the Jews used to eavesdrop on German conversations, occasionally overhearing venomous anti-Semitic remarks.

In this way weeks and months went by, and everything seemed to be going smoothly. Then, one early morning, the German police knocked on Juliana Larish's door at 7 Bzeske. Fortunately the Jews in hiding managed to conceal themselves in time.

Juliana's courage and presence of mind were admirable. She slipped away from the gendarmes on some pretext, and contrived to telephone her friend of the imminent danger. Thus no incriminating evidence was found there when the police burst in. Later, Juliana learned that her own employees had denounced her to the authorities. Undismayed by the police raid, she continued her work of mercy until the end of the war, sheltering the refugees until new places of concealment could be found for them.

I used to make the rounds of all of Juliana's hideouts, supplying the Jews there with forged documents. Of the hidden Jews, twenty-one survived: three of the Blokhowitz family, three of the Zifferman family, four of the Zilberbergs, four of the Miendzizhetski, three of the Goldsteins, and four of the "hotel Polski" group.

The gentile Pero, a middle-aged clerk in a Polish hotel on Marskalovska Street, was another hero. Through a Jewish woman named Malie Piotrkovska and her thirteen-year-old daughter, Bronka, he became our ally.

The extent of his generosity is attested by the harrowing story related to me by Mrs. Piotrkovska, who came from Lodz. Compelled to leave her hideout at 36 Krochmalnia in broad daylight, Mrs. Piotrkovska, who could not pass for an Aryan, wandered about with her daughter in search of lodging for the night.

At one point a group of gentile youngsters had recognized poor Mrs. Piotrkovska as a Jewess, for they pursued her with shouts of "*Zhidowa, Zhidowa!*" (Jewess).

When they tried to snatch her pocketbook, she started to run. The Polish police then took the woman and her daughter into custody and brought them to the German authorities.

It now seemed clear to the mother and the daughter that their doom was sealed. The fate of every Jew who fell into the clutches of the Germans was well known. But since the Piotrkovskas possessed false documents attesting to their antecedents, they decided to play the role of gentiles, even if their cause was a lost one anyhow. They were interrogated about their origin and about their knowledge of Christian prayers, customs, and so on. The daughter replied accurately, but the mother fumbled. The German examiners were at a loss, but they suspected the two of being Jewish. The accused were jailed overnight, and were told that they must produce a Pole who would vouch for having known them as Christians before the war—or else they would be liquidated.

Pero was the only Polish friend the Piotrkovskas had who might be able to save them. It was evening. There was no telephone in Pero's home. He had to be reached by phone at the place where he worked. And there was no guarantee that he would care to risk his life on their behalf. He could be put to death if he perjured himself for them. However, to reach him was their last chance—their only hope!

They racked their brains for the telephone number of Pero's employer, and at last they remembered it. Now everything depended on whether Pero would stand by them. The authorities of the German headquarters telephoned Pero to learn whether he knew Frau Piotrkovska and her daughter. They were suspected of being Jewish—an accusation which they denied. Could he vouch for them? If so, he was to report in the morning for questioning.

Mother and daughter await Pero with shuddering hearts. Will he dare come? He arrives at last, and is subjected to interrogation. Pero sticks to his guns, maintaining that he has known the Piotrkovskas as Christians since some time before the war began. The Germans remind him that perjury is punishable by death. In his flawless German Pero assures them he would take no such risk, again asserts that the Piotrkovskas are good Christians, and at last convinces the dubious officials. The accused women are cleared, and the authorities actually apologize to them for the trumped-up charge. The interrogators urge Frau Piotrkovska, in the event of future inconvenience, to report to the German authorities, since the accusation of being Jewish is no trifling matter!

Though his own home was under surveillance, Pero then let the Piotrkovskas stay with him. Later we even persuaded him to give shelter to still other Jews. He cooperated with us until the very end.

All the Jews who found asylum with Pero have survived. Ironically enough, as a Polish officer he himself died in the Warsaw uprising in 1944.

Helena Schiborowska of 36 Krochmalnia was another dedicated worker for us. She was a small, dark-skinned widow with children who hardly took time to bother with her own household chores because she was so busy helping persecuted, browbeaten Jews. When a hideout became unsafe, its occupant would call upon Helena for help. Her house had been raided as a result of tips supplied by informers, yet on occasion she would shelter a desperate Jew. She also tried to persuade her gentile neighbors to accommodate Jews, refusing to be daunted by their coolness toward the suggestion. When she did manage to enlist the cooperation of some neighbors, she would come to our secret meetings to tell us joyfully of her new achievement.

Helena Schiborowska did accept money for her efforts; however, she would then spend it on the unfortunate Jews under her care. All of us admired her generosity.

She herself lived in poverty. She sold her jewelry and donated the money to needy Jews. Not a few Jews owe their survival to the efforts of this benevolent little woman, who rendered help in so straight-forward a manner, and with such understanding. She is still alive, and now lives in Warsaw.

These are a few of the "good Poles," with whom I chanced to come into contact during the Nazi regime. Unfortunately, the number of such commendable and kindhearted gentiles was rather small. Our relief and rescue mission would have been greater, and more Jews would have survived, if in their midst, the Polish people had had more individuals with such heart and conscience.

65. MORDECAI ANILEWICZ: COMMANDER OF THE WARSAW GHETTO UPRISING

EMANUAL RINGELBLUM

While hiding with his family and other Jews in the cellar of a Polish worker in Warsaw (see no. 61), Ringelblum wrote a number of biographical sketches of the leading personalities of the Warsaw ghetto, including the following.

He was a young fellow, about twenty-five, of medium height, with a narrow, pale, pointed face and a pleasant appearance. I met him for the first time at the beginning of the war, when he came to me, dressed casually, and asked me to lend him a book. From that day on he came to me frequently to borrow books on Jewish history, especially on economics, in which Comrade Mordecai was greatly interested.

Who could have known that this quiet, modest, and sympathetic fellow would emerge as the man who, three years later, would be mentioned with awe by some, with fear by others.

Conducting Seminars

Soon after the outbreak of the war the Hashomer Hatzair,* under the leadership of Comrade Mordecai, began to conduct educational and cultural circles embracing hundreds of young people of both sexes. This work was conducted in the refugee area at 23 Nelewki Street, where members from the outlying areas had found a haven. The Hashomer strove not only to provide their people with cultural nourishment but simultaneously with guidance for their spiritual development.

Circles and seminars were created where young students received both a general and Jewish education. In the seminars for older comrades, leaders were prepared for the Hashomer circles. The Hashomer embraced with its activity not only Warsaw but the outlying areas as well. Hashomer

---

*Hashomer Hatzair: Zionist-socialist youth movement educating its members for kibbutz life in Israel. It was founded in Poland before World War I as a scouting movement. (Ed.)

instructors risked their lives traveling around the country on "left" (false) permits as Jews, and more frequently as Aryans, distributing the illegal publications of the movement and revitalizing legal organizations.

Seminars were set up in Warsaw to develop leaders for the groups in the outlying areas. These seminars were attended not only by the boys and girls from the *General Gubernie* (General Government—region administered by the Nazis in Poland) but by would-be students smuggled into Warsaw from the "Reich" (part of Poland incorporated directly into Hitler's Reich—Bendin, Sosnowice), some walking several weeks until they reached Warsaw. Only one who knew the dangers involved in moving about on trains in those days could appreciate the heroism of these young people thirsting for knowledge.

It so happened that several times I was a lecturer at the Hashomer seminars. When I peered into the glowing faces of the eager youth, I forgot that there was a war on in the world.

The seminars took place right opposite the German watch that guarded the ghetto gates. The Shomer bunch felt so at home in its own headquarters that more than once they would forget there was a war on. Now and then they would dance a hora, accompanied by Eretz Yisroel and revolutionary songs. Once the singing attracted a German guard, who came to ask what was going on. Upon learning that this was a gathering point for young scouts, the guard sat down to have a chat with the youngsters. At dawn he bade the Shomrim a hearty farewell and returned to his post.

Devotion to Comrades

Mordecai was exceptionally devoted to the people in Hashomer. Day and night they were the objects of his thoughts and concern. From various sources he procured provisions for the kitchen of the Shomer kibbutz—the main source of Hashomer's subsistence, however, was the earnings of its members, who worked at various slave labor jobs outside the ghetto and contributed their wages to the membership treasury.

One seldom finds in an organization or party Comrade Mordecai's exceptional devotion to his fellows. For a fellow member he was ready to leap into fire. As an illustration I should like to cite the following incident, which I witnessed myself. This happened to a member of Hashomer, Zandman, in Halman's shop on Nowolipki, where I lived after the first "resettlement action." This was in January, 1943. The Fighters' Organization had, at that time, carried out a number of reprisals against individuals guilty of crimes against the Jewish community of Warsaw. As punishment they were splashed with vitriol. At Halman's a former policeman was splashed. Fortunately the perpetrators escaped. But Zandman, who was connected with the carrying out of the verdict, was detained by the

Werkschutz [factory guards] and splashed with vitriol. The German administration was also notified by the Werkschutz about Zandman's detention.

When Mordecai learned about this he came that very day to Halman's shop and, together with the leadership of the Fighters' Organization and myself, worked out the plan to rescue Zandman. Four o'clock at dawn, five masked strong men entered the Werkschutz headquarters and freed Zandman, taking with them at the same time all the Werkschutz papers and charts. This happened several hours before the beginning of the January action. Zandman was hauled off for the second time to the *Umschlagplatz,* where his comrades freed him.

The Zandman incident was not unique. Mordecai was ready to sacrifice himself for the comrades just as they were ready to risk their lives for him. Such an attachment of a leader to his comrades was rare even in the ghetto.

This was the kind of loyalty found in underground organizations where all thought of themselves as true brothers. Such mutual aid and devotion were then found only in workers' organizations, which organized mutual aid groups not only in the shops but even in the work camps of the SS. . . .

Relationship with the Polish Scouts

Even before the war Comrade Mordecai had established good relationships with the Polish scout movement, the Polish Harcesz. This was perhaps one of the rare instances in which a Jewish organization worked together with a Polish one, and the Hashomer benefited greatly from those contacts. In Vilna these contacts with the Polish Harcesz opened the way for the Shomrim to the Polish clergy, which assisted in the illegal activities of Hashomer. Thanks to this some individuals from Hashomer were quartered with Polish families in the region of Vilna. Comrade Mordecai related to me an interesting fact about the friendly relationships between the Polish scouts and the Shomrim. One of the leaders of the Polish Harcesz was, because of his German origin, mobilized as a doctor for the eastern front. From Leningrad he sent greetings by field post to the illegal gathering of Hashomer in Warsaw. Later this same doctor, while on furlough in Warsaw, smuggled himself into the ghetto and spent several days with the comrades of Hashomer. He recounted some interesting details of the severe catastrophe that the German army suffered in the winter of 1941–1942.

A Secret Evening Meeting

Once I saw the modest and quiet Mordecai in the role of Hashomer commander. That was in the winter of 1941–1942. Mordecai one day wanted to gather all the members of the movement together to strengthen their consciousness of collectivism and demonstrate what a force this represented for the Shomer movement. Despite the danger that this meeting entailed, I made available for Shomer gathering the second floor of the Judaic Institute at Tlomacki 5, headquarters of the communal department in charge of the House Committees. The evening was camouflaged as a legal literary affair.

In the hall they gathered together the desks, arranged the chairs in rows, and set up a real stage. There came to the hall an audience of about 500 Shomrim and Shomrot, the latter dressed in white blouses. The culture program of the evening was carried through by their own members, young men and women. The caliber of the evening was high. After the program the entire *gan* (garden-youth group) marched around the room.

Simultaneously the graduation from one group into another took place, accompanied by a solemn declaration of dedication to the movement. A comrade of the Polish scout movement witnessed the ceremony.

This affair demonstrated to me with how much love, respect, and devotion the members of Hashomer surrounded the person of Comrade Mordecai. This same loyalty later was shown him when he was commander of the Fighters' Organization. This power, however, did not go to his head—he remained as modest as ever.

Creating a Fighters' Organization

Once during an intermission between one lecture and the next at the seminar of Hashomer (I lectured there on the history of the Jewish resistance movement), the comrades Mordecai and Yosef Kaplan called me down to the courtyard of Nalewki 23, took me into a private room, and showed me two revolvers. These revolvers, the comrades of the top leadership explained, would be used to train the youth in the use of weapons. That was the first step taken by Hashomer, even before the creation of the Fighters' Organization.

Bad times were approaching. From all over the country awful reports came streaming in, first about the terrible slaughter in Vilna and in other Lithuanian cities, brought by the Comrades Vilner of the Vilna Hashomer and Solomon of the Hanoar Hatzioni (Zionist Youth). Then came the accounts of the slaughter in Slonim and other cities in the east. Mordecai realized that the fate of the Polish Jews was sealed and that the Jews of all of Poland were doomed to destruction.

The young but quickly maturing Mordecai understood that at present there was but one question: What kind of death will the Polish Jews select for themselves? Will it be the death of sheep led to the slaughter without resistance, or of people with honor who want the enemy to pay for their death with his own blood? Mordecai wanted the slaughter of the Polish

Jews not to come easy for the enemy; he must be made to bleed for it.

The moment Mordecai decided on struggle, no other questions existed for him. The scientific circles and the seminars came to an end; the manifold cultural and education work was interrupted. Now he and his comrades concentrated only on the area of struggle. . .

Mordecai threw himself into the defense activity with all his zeal. Together with other groups and parties the Fighters' Organization was created, at whose head the coordinating commission of the political organizations placed Comrade Mordecai. This is not the place to describe the history of the Fighters' Organization. Comrade Mordecai was the soul of the organization, one of its most devoted workers. He was not one of those leaders who sent others into the line of fire and themselves remained at a distance. In January, 1943, he participated actively in the fighting action. His revolver claimed German sacrifices.

Once he pressed his revolver to the head of a German guard. The revolver jammed and Comrade Mordecai was only saved from counterfire thanks to a comrade who rescued him from the danger. He was active in the April action. (The Warsaw Ghetto uprising began April 19, 1943.) Death found him several weeks after the beginning of the action, together with the best fighting comrades. He was in a hideout in the ghetto that had five entrances. Someone most likely betrayed the bunker of the valiant fighters who ordinarily went out from this place to attack the SS and Ukrainians. The "Juden-Sieger" (Jew conquerors)—as the SS were called by the Wehrmacht—entered through five sides of the hideout, but first they filled it with gas. Comrade Mordecai fell together with the best comrades of the Fighters' Organization.

66. THE LAST WISH OF MY LIFE

MORDECAI ANILEWICZ

See the preceding selection and the introduction to this chapter about Jewish resistance to the Nazis.

It is now clear to me that what took place exceeded all expectations. In our opposition to the Germans we did more than our strength allowed—but now our forces are waning. We are on the brink of extinction. We forced the Germans to retreat twice—but they returned stronger than before.

One of our groups held out for forty minutes; and another fought for about six hours. The mine which was laid in the area of the brush factory exploded as planned. Then we attacked the Germans and they suffered heavy casualties. Our losses were generally low. That is an accomplishment too. Z. fell, next to his machine-gun.

I feel that great things are happening and that this action which we have dared to take is of enormous value.

We have no choice but to go over to partisan methods of fighting as of today. Tonight, six fighting-groups are going out. They have two tasks—to reconnoitre the area and to capture weapons. Remember, "short-range weapons" are of no use to us. We employ them very rarely. We need many rifles, hand-grenades, machine-guns and explosives.

I cannot describe the conditions in which the Jews of the ghetto are now "living." Only a few exceptional individuals will be able to survive such suffering. The others will sooner or later die. Their fate is certain, even though thousands are trying to hide in cracks and rat holes. It is impossible to light a candle, for lack of air. Greetings to you who are outside. Perhaps a miracle will occur and we shall see each other again one of these days. It is extremely doubtful.

The last wish of my life has been fulfilled. Jewish self-defense has become a fact. Jewish resistance and revenge have become actualities. I am happy to have been one of the first Jewish fighters in the ghetto.

Where will rescue come from?

MORDECAI ANILEWICZ
During the Revolt, 1943
Warsaw

67. A MANIFESTO OF THE JEWISH RESISTANCE IN VILNA

Offer armed resistance! Jews, defend yourselves with arms!

The German and Lithuanian executioners are at the gates of the ghetto. They have come to murder us! Soon they will lead you forth in groups through the ghetto door.

In the same way they carried away hundreds of us on the day of Yom Kippur. In the same way those with white, yellow and pink *Schein** were deported during the night. In this way our brothers, sisters, mothers, fathers and sons were taken away.

Tens of thousands of us were despatched. But we shall not go! We will not offer our heads to the butcher like sheep.

---

*Safe conduct passes. To deceive and bewilder the Jews, the Germans constantly changed the colors of the passes which were to have safeguarded them against deportation, always further limiting the number of persons entitled to them.

Jews, defend yourselves with arms!

Do not believe the false promises of the assassins or believe the words of the traitors.

Anyone who passes through the ghetto gate will go to Ponar!

And Ponar means death!

Jews, we have nothing to lose. Death will overtake us in any event. And who can still believe in survival when the murderer exterminates us with so much determination? The hand of the executioner will reach each man and woman. Flight and acts of cowardice will not save our lives.

Active resistance alone can save our lives and our honor.

Brothers! It is better to die in battle in the ghetto than to be carried away to Ponar like sheep. And know this: Within the walls of the ghetto there are organized Jewish forces who will resist with weapons.

Support the revolt!

Do not take refuge or hide in the bunkers, for then you will fall into the hands of the murderers like rats.

Jewish people, go out into the squares. Anyone who has no weapons should take an ax, and he who has no ax should take a crowbar or a bludgeon!

For our ancestors!

For our murdered children!

Avenge Ponar!

Attack the murderers!

In every street, in every courtyard, in every house within and without the ghetto, attack these dogs!

Jews, we have nothing to lose! We shall save our lives only if we exterminate our assassins.

Long live liberty! Long live armed resistance! Death to the assassins!

The Commander of the F.P.A.

Vilna, the Ghetto, September 1, 1943.

68. THE LAST DAYS OF THE WARSAW GHETTO: A SURVIVOR'S ACCOUNT OF A HEROIC CHAPTER IN JEWISH HISTORY

ZIVIAH LUBETKIN

The uprising in the ghetto of Warsaw, which began on April 19, 1943, and was finally crushed in the closing days of May, was Europe's first major act of anti-Nazi defiance. By the time the resistance movements in France and elsewhere became active, the great bulk of the millions of Jews in the ghettos had already been murdered.

Ziviah Lubetkin's may be the first account by a participant and witness of the actual events of the uprising and the aftermath. Thirty to fifty thousand, it has been estimated, were in the ghetto at the time the uprising began; perhaps a few hundred escaped.

Ziviah Lubetkin, a girl in her twenties, was one of the prominent leaders of the struggle and belonged at that time to the Hechalutz organization in Poland. She subsequently settled in a kibbutz in Palestine. Her story, as printed here, is a condensation of a talk she gave in Palestine in 1947.

The Ghetto was burning. For days and nights it flamed, and the fire consumed house after house, entire streets. Columns of smoke rose, sparks flew, and the sky reflected a red, frightening glow. Nearby, on the other side of the wall, citizens of the capital strolled, played, and enjoyed themselves. They knew that "the Jews were burning." The wind blew smoke and soot from the burning ruins in their direction. Sparks scattered and now and then a house outside the Ghetto would catch fire. But these fires were immediately extinguished. Only in the Ghetto no one hastened to put out the flames, to come to the rescue. Everything was burning and there was no one to halt the blaze.

Beginning to Fight

This was the Ghetto of the largest Jewish community that had ever existed in Europe. Within its walls the last remaining Jews, still numbering tens of thousands, were trapped. Some days before, in April 1943, the Germans had planned to kill this remnant, to send it in death cars to Oswiecim and Belsitz, as they had previously sent hundreds of thousands without opposition. But this time they met with an unexpected situation. Units of the "Fighting Jewish Organization" manned the street corners and the ruins, planting land mines and hurling grenades into the files of German troops. Taken by surprise, the Germans retreated. They attacked the next day and the next, but each time they met with resistance. After ten days of battle, the Germans did not dare to enter the Ghetto.

Setting Fire to the Ghetto

Then the Germans set fire to the Ghetto, first from airplanes and then on the ground, at the four corners. They celebrated their victory from afar—certain that the fire would complete the extermination which they could not inflict in open warfare.

It was not the triumph they had planned. With their last vital energy the Jews found shelter behind every wall, among ruins that could no longer burn. The inhabitants of entire bunkers—men, women, and children— crawled out from their underground hiding places and wandered about,

loaded with their last bits of food, blankets, pots. Babies were carried in
their mothers' arms, older children trailed after their parents, in their eyes
an abyss of suffering and a plea for help. . . .

On the night the great fire started, I ran from my hiding place. The
blazing light stunned me. All around I heard the roar of the fire, the noise of
falling walls. Outside the Ghetto it was spring, but here a holocaust
reigned. The smoke forced us above ground. We threaded our way through
the ruins, circling the flames, traveling from attic to attic through the
breaks in the walls, and, when they had burned to the ground, from one
basement to another. The Germans were firing at anything that moved.

The flames had not yet penetrated the great yard in front of a block of
buildings at Milah No. 7. And here, on the first night of the fire, swarmed
hundreds of the fighters who had taken refuge after a day's wandering
through the Ghetto. Tired, tense, dazed, we lay on the ground, and the
question to which there was no answer hung in the air: What now?
Thousands of fleeing Jews were massed around us, resting on their pitiful
bundles, waiting for our answer.

Nazis Avoid Battle

We were the fighters, the leaders of the rebellion, but all our old plans
were now useless. We had dreamed of a battle face to face with the enemy,
like our first intoxicating victory from which the Germans had fled.
Patiently we had organized our ambushes and waited for the enemy to
return. But the Nazis had avoided open battle, sending fire instead to
destroy us. We had never expected this.

It was the first of May, which seemed to make our responsibility all the
heavier. But there we sat, our useless weapons beside us, surrounded by
the thousands straining to hear some word of hope from us, the last,
desperate Jewish fighters. It was clear we could not hold out for long
among the raging flames, without food or water or equipment.

Some way of escape had to be found, but where, how? One young fellow
told us that he knew a passage that led from the Ghetto to the Aryan part of
the city through the sewers. For a moment, his confidence was infectious.
But what would be the use of this? With no one there to shelter us, death
was certain. . . . It was simply exchanging one fire for another. After much
discussion we decided, however, to experiment. Five young people of
Aryan appearance were chosen to go with the guide to reconnoiter the
escape route. If any of them returned, we should make a decision. They left
. . . and the tortured waiting began.

Children wept, the weak moaned, and the flames could be seen drawing
closer. A sound of low singing came from a group of fighters. Some lucky

person came in with a piece of bread and hundreds besieged him to get the taste of a crumb. Hours passed. At one in the morning, two of the scouts returned, the guide and Tovyah Buzhikovski, who was wounded and bloody. They told us that the sewer had been safely traversed. When they reached the exit they had raised the manhole cover and the two girls and two young men had tiptoed across the silent street. A few minutes later, while Tovyah was still standing in the opening, the Germans opened fire. Two bullets struck Tovyah. The fate of the others who had made their getaway was unknown.

Refuge in a Bunker

The mass exodus had to be abandoned. For the present, our only hope lay within the burning Ghetto. . . . A roll-call of fighters was held. Instructions were issued to fortify ourselves in bunkers protected from the fire and in ruins not yet consumed by the flames. We told the waiting Jews who were huddled around us to find temporary shelter, but they stayed by our side. They felt more secure near the fighters, and as groups of us departed, we were followed by these clusters of unarmed Jews. Finally, all had dispersed in search of hiding places for the night. Many who could find no other shelter went down into the sewers to wait through the next day. For the time being, deep underground in bunkers and sewers, the pulse of Jewish life still beat on.

Below the smoldering ruins, far from the spring day, at a depth of five meters, hundreds of us lay in absolute darkness on the floor of a bunker. Not a ray of daylight could penetrate—only the clock told us that outside the sun was setting. Here, on Milah No. 18, was the headquarters of the Fighting Jewish Organization. When night fell and in the city beyond the Ghetto walls there was silence, the streets of the Ghetto would awake. Those who had been lying in the bunkers got up and crawled out from the depths. The yearning for daylight could not be satisfied, but one could move about in the open air.

The fighters, too, arose to action. There was much to be done. The ration of thin soup had to be doled out, orders to scouting, patrol, and combat units issued. Sometimes we would discover a telephone that still worked; then we would try to contact our comrades on the Aryan side. Deserted bunkers were ransacked for food.

Only a few days before we were still sending out combat units to ambush the Germans who entered the Ghetto during the day. Our young men would take up positions in the ruins, look through the cracks of some destroyed house, and wait. For hours they would lie there; silence all around, and the May sun caressing after the chill of winter. Many were eager to go to these battle positions, if only to avoid lying in the bunkers all day.

The Nights

Each night, freed from the dark and suffocating shelters, Jews would roam the streets, searching for their families and friends. And each night we saw how much smaller our numbers grew. We were gradually vanishing, and the terror of inactivity gnawed at our spirit with a strange insistence.

The Jewish combat units were not the only occupants of the bunker at Milah No. 18. Our real landlords were called the "Chumps." They had been part of the Warsaw underworld—thieves and even murderers—and had originally built the bunker for themselves, a spacious and astonishingly well-equipped underground dugout. Electric light had been installed and a well had been dug. To top it off, there were luxuries here; a reading room and a game room.

The leader of the gang was Shmuel Asher, a broad and fleshy Jew who ruled his henchmen with an iron hand. But he did not hesitate to share his supplies with us and was especially tender with the children. By accident we had stumbled into his bunker, and now the place was densely crowded with three hundred persons. He had treated our fighters with cordial respect and put everything he had at our disposal. "Our strength is still with us," he told us, "and the hands of my men are trained to open locks. At night we can walk quietly without being observed. We can climb fences and walls and all the paths and holes of the Ghetto are well known to us. . . ."

The Chumps proved very useful. They guided us at night to spy out the German positions. And when the Ghetto was nearly all burned, and it was hard to distinguish the location of the streets, one of the thieves would lead us confidently, climbing like a cat through the wreckage. Every day at sundown, Shmuel Asher would put on his shining boots, hang two pistols in his belt, and crawl out to forage for food. The hole he squeezed through just fitted his mighty torso. Later on, it became much too wide for his wasted body.

One hundred and twenty Jewish fighters, including the command, lived in this bunker.

The Ghetto swiftly crumbled away. Starvation and the discovery of bunker after bunker by the patrolling Germans took their toll. At night, German soldiers would hide in a corner of the ruins and listen for voices and signs of activity. In that way they smelled out our bunkers. Then they would come and force their way in. But more often they captured some starved Jew whose strength and courage were gone and would promise him immunity if he led them to the hiding places. Corpses of our comrades lay strewn everywhere. I dreaded walking at night for fear of stepping on them. Flocks of crows descended on the decaying bodies in the streets.

Sometimes, while walking through the ruins, silence all about, suddenly one heard a low, despairing moan. We would search the rubble. To call aloud was dangerous and when we approached the wounded person, he would fall silent, afraid we might be Germans. Once I found a woman and her child. They had been without food and water for days . . . more dead than alive. More than once, the wounded begged us: Kill me! Although we knew there was reason in their pleas, we lacked the heart to shoot. Many others had gone insane from the horrors and agonies of our life and now wandered aimlessly about the Ghetto.

During one of these days I visited Geffner's bunker and was confronted with a deep silence. It was a great shock. No one was in it, all had been captured by the Germans. Geffner was one of the most compassionate men I had ever known. One of the wealthiest and most respected members of the Jewish community, he alone of the rich class had understood the Jewish youth when they called for resistance. After the Germans established the Ghetto, he had been put in charge of the supplies provided by the Germans. Smuggling of food began from the Aryan side, food prices were enormous, and much money could be made by speculators. Geffner refused to speculate. Instead, he founded children's and orphans' homes and public kitchens. Even our movement, the Hechalutz Organization, esteemed him. When the rebellion broke out, he and his employees went underground, and this old man lived side by side with all the others and was always ready to help us.

At first this bunker had housed the fighting units of Shlamek Schuster and Henich Guttman. One day the bunker was suddenly attacked by the Germans. They shouted an order to surrender. Guttman acted quickly. He assumed the Nazis would not fire at a girl, so he sent Dvorah Barn out first. For a split second, the Germans were immobilized, amazed at her beauty and daring. She used this moment to throw a hand grenade and they scattered in fright. Our fighters then came out and attacked. Guttman was wounded and Eiger died, but many Germans paid with their lives. As he lay dying, Eiger shouted to his comrades. "It's a shame to waste pistols. Take my pistol!"

Unfortunately, after this attack, we others took too long to find a new place of refuge for our comrades and, in the meantime, the Germans returned to the bunker, threw in grenades, and ten of the fighters, among them Dvorah Barn, were killed. Guttman was carried to Zechariah's bunker; when that was attacked too, he died with the others. He was one of the best men in our movement and a leader from the start of the rebellion. His men all loved and obeyed him with a steadfast devotion.

Without Food

It was now three weeks since the beginning of the rebellion. We were hungry and no supplies could reach us. Time passed in endless talk—talk about hunger, the retelling of heroic deeds, the exultant tale of battle with the Germans, and always talk of the Palestine none of us had been able to attain. We tried to keep our voices low, but inevitably a debate would burst out—about Hebrew versus Yiddish or Zionism versus Communism. Forgetting ourselves, we shouted until our "leader" would rush in and silence us, smiling, with the promise that we should have an early opportunity to end the debate—in the next world.

Behind such wry jokes lay the reality. We were trapped and the only prospect was a slow death from hunger. What could we do? Contact with the city was completely cut off. Some days before we had sent groups of comrades through the sewers and a secret tunnel, but no word had come from them. Any mission to the Aryan side was terribly risky. With great luck a messenger might succeed in getting through, but if he did, who would give sanctuary to a hunted Jew? All doors were locked in his face. And our friends among the Gentiles had not yet found hiding places for us.

The hopeless debate flowed on. Berl Broide suggested that we stage a daylight surprise attack on the German patrols, overcome them, and flee to the forests. Someone argued against him: "Fine, let's say we overcome the Nazi patrol. But how will we get to the forests through the Warsaw streets?" Finally, Aryeh Wilner summed up the argument—it was clear we had no choice but to continue sending groups of comrades through the sewers to the city. It was better than remaining here to die of hunger and suffocation. If only a few of us got through, it would still be worth while.

Tovyah Buzhikovski again spoke of the direct route to the sewers which he had been told about in the Franciskanska No. 20 bunker. By this approach it was possible to get to the sewers entirely through underground passages. Many objected. Suppose we did reach the sewers? We all knew how large and complicated they were, how easy it was to enter them but how difficult to find an exit. How many had sought escape through them, had wandered fruitlessly for days and perished at last from hunger, thirst, and terror?

Tovyah answered our doubts. There was a guide in the other bunker who could lead us safely through the labyrinth. Even so, others argued, there was still the old question of shelter on the Aryan side. A despairing silence fell. We knew all these arguments by heart. In desperation we brushed aside all fears and made a plan. A group of ten would be sent into the sewers. They would leave at night and hide in the ruins of abandoned houses on the Aryan side. Once there, comrades with a Gentile appearance would try to find the ones who had gone before and together work out an escape. I was directed to accompany the group, to negotiate with the guide and to send our scouts on their way.

Searching for an Escape

Final preparations were made. We dressed, took our weapons, and parted from our friends. Would we ever see each other again? Outwardly we were calm; we smiled and even joked. Handshakes were exchanged. We grasped our pistols and left.

One by one, we crawled on our bellies out of the bunker. The passage was narrow and covered with stones. We had been so engrossed in the debate that we had forgotten it was night. For some reason, we expected daylight. After weeks of darkness there was a great yearning for light. Above ground, we drank in the fresh air with open mouths. In a whisper the guard posted outside told us: "There is firing from the left; on the right it is quiet and you can go that way." We moved ahead quietly, our feet bound in rags to deaden our footsteps.

Wreckage, skeletons of burned buildings, ruins. Occasionally a smoldering house flared up in flames. It was strange; each time we came above ground it was more difficult to recognize the Ghetto, things changed so rapidly. . . . Silence. . . . From time to time the quiet was broken by a window swinging on its hinges in the charred remains of a wall, or by the iron bars of a ruined shop screeching and beating. . . .

Tensely and cautiously, our fingers on the triggers of our pistols, we proceeded along hidden paths. Here and there on our way we met survivors, who were encouraged to see armed Jews still active. They regarded us with envy, having no idea that we were as helpless as they. "What is to be done?" they asked. "There is no more food. Everything is burned." Oppressed by a feeling of futility, we nevertheless said some heartening words. We left them behind and crawled on our bellies across the dark street. Again we were enveloped by the ruins.

On our way we stopped in at various bunkers to relay instructions from the command post. At Zechariah Erdstein's bunker we were reminded of the early days of the fighting. The chief of this bunker was a Communist whom we had met during the first part of the battle. We had been tired and shaken and this young man had taken us into his bunker, revived our spirits, and given us food and drink. We had been moved by this display of solidarity after so many disappointments with the masses of Jews.

We also visited the bunker of the Pinkert family. They had been the heads of "Chevra Kadisha," the burial society. The Nazis had spared the gravediggers of the Ghetto because they needed them to bury the dead. The Jewish cemetery lay outside the Ghetto, so, with the gravediggers' assistance, we had been able to maintain contact with the Aryan side. But it was three days now since they had gone outside our walls. They were supposed to bring us back twenty rifles and news of help from the capital. The bunker was still empty. The Pinkerts had not come back.

At Franciskanska No. 20, where we were to find our guide, there was an emotional reunion with our friends. It was some time since we had heard from them. There was much to tell them, for they had no radio and could get no news. This bunker had once been surrounded by the Germans and nearly wiped out, but the survivors, 160 out of the 300, had escaped into the sewers. Unable to find a new shelter, they had returned and continued to live on in the old bunker, hoping the enemy would think they had killed everyone and not bother to attack again.

We found the guide and arranged for him to accompany the group that was to go out that night. After leading them to the exit from the sewers, he was to return so as to teach the way to one of our young men, then the next night he would escape to the Aryan side with the second group. To prepare for the trip each person was given a bag with a piece of sugar and a few dried crusts.

Their instructions were to emerge from the manhole on Belinska Street and take cover in a group of houses which we knew had been blasted by the 1939 bombardments. Once there, Pavel and Helen Shipper, whose appearance was Aryan, were to wait until dawn and then try to contact our comrades outside the Ghetto. Carefully we taught them the addresses and telephone numbers. The others were to wait in the bombed buildings until they returned. In a day or two another group would leave. These would be at the exit at nine in the evening and there wait for the signal—three consecutive raps—which would tell them that the first group had got to safety and that they could come out. The exit was in the middle of the street, in full view—a dangerous spot.

Murmurs of farewell, handshakes. Then, one after another, the comrades jumped from the floor of the bunker into the tunnel, which was about one meter deep. We could hear the water splash with every jump. Each had a candle to light his way. They disappeared and their splashing footsteps were soon no longer audible.

Two and a half hours later, two of them returned; one was the guide. They told us how they had reached the street. It was silent. But as soon as they had closed the manhole and started to return, they heard shots fired on the street above. Had the shots been fired at our comrades? They couldn't be sure.

Unable to throw off our weariness, we spent the whole day in the bunker. Once during the day the guard passed in a panicky message. The Germans were coming! There was great disorder and it became necessary for us to stop the hysteria among the people in the bunker by threatening to shoot. Nerves were taut and the fear of the Germans had become greater than the fear of death. But the Germans did not come.

That night, Chaim P., Marek Edelstein, and I started back to our bunker. Marek, a daredevil, took a candle to light our way. This was forbidden, but it was hard to do without it. We walked calmly through the debris.

Suddenly the candle was put out by the wind. We were in a dark ruin and had no idea how to find our way. We began to climb over the wreckage. I slipped and fell into an opening in the rubble. I knew I must not cry out. They found me in the dark and with difficulty pulled me from the hole. Limping, and with bruised hands, I went on. As we neared our bunker, we joked and even made some silly plans to scare our comrades.

Surrender of a Bunker

When we reached our bunker, I hardly recognized the place. I thought we'd made a mistake. There was no guard and the entrance was closed up. We dashed to all six entrances but they were unrecognizable and there were no guards. We screamed the password but there was no answer. Then in a nearby yard, among the shadows, we found some of our comrades, smeared with mud, weak and trembling. We were surrounded by wrecked people. The Germans had descended upon them and only a few had escaped.

At noon the previous day the guards had warned them—Germans were in the neighborhood. In such emergencies we usually had two plans of defense. The first was for a group of fighters to respond to the call of the enemy, stun them with a sudden burst of fire, and then try to scatter among the ruins. Our second scheme was not to respond at all: the Germans never tried to enter a bunker during the day, and at night there would be a better chance to escape. Our comrades had decided on the second plan.

When the Germans called out, the Chumps and the civilians surrendered, but none of our fighters. The call was repeated. The Germans announced that everyone who came out would be taken to work; all the others would be shot at once. Our comrades entrenched themselves near the entrance and waited with their weapons ready for the Germans. Finally the Germans began to send gas into the bunker. They let in a small quantity of gas, then stopped, trying to break their spirit with a prolonged suffocation. A terrible death faced the 120 fighters.

Aryeh Wilner was the first to cry out: "Come, let us destroy ourselves. Let's not fall into their hands alive!" The suicides began. Pistols jammed and the owners begged their friends to kill them. But no one dared take the life of a comrade. Lutek Rotblatt fired four shots at his mother but, wounded and bleeding, she still moved. Then someone discovered a hidden exit, but only a few succeeded in getting out this way. The others slowly suffocated in the gas. Thus the best of the Jewish fighters met death, one hundred in all; among them was Mordecai Anilewicz, our handsome commander whom we all had loved.

Twenty-one had escaped; of these eighteen were fighters. Some of them were wounded as a result of their suicide attempts. Others were suffering from the gas. We felt now that death was certain for all of us. But though we longed for the end, we still tried to remove the heaped-up stones blocking the entrance to our bunker. Perhaps we could reach the bodies, rescue the weapons. It was impossible; everything had been blasted with dynamite.

Here was buried our last hope; we moved away, a file of spiritless bodies, to find a place for the handful of wounded and weakened comrades.

On our way, we stopped at Zechariah's unit to tell what had happened and to announce that our command post would now be at Franciskanska No. 20. Zechariah flared out: "Then what are we waiting for? Let us all go out against them, in the middle of the streets, in the light of day. Let's fire at them and fall ourselves and let the end come!"

This was my last meeting with Zechariash—as everyone called him. There was not a Jew in the Ghetto who did now know, love, admire him. He was the one who had brought us, at the time of the January uprising, the first German rifle. At that time a German had caught him; he pretended to surrender and raised his hands. Then he pulled out his pistol, shot his captor, took the rifle, and brought it to us. How happy we had been with that first rifle!

New Headquarters

When we reached our new headquarters we slumped to the floor and lay as if paralyzed. We didn't bandage the wounded, nor did we touch the soup. We had promised to wait at the exit from the sewers for the signal of three raps, but no one was sent.

Responsibility for the survivors stirred us into action. Another group must be sent through the sewers. No one wanted to go. In our despair we wanted to stay right there and end our lives together. All signs indicated that the Germans would soon find us. At last ten comrades were ordered to go, and with them went the two who had returned the night before.

We wept at their leaving. And each of us thought: what testament shall I send to dear ones, to the world, to coming generations, to comrades in the longed-for land? One after another we murmured: "Tell about our fight; tell of our loneliness; tell about our last stand. Tell! Tell!"

I lay on my pallet, exhausted and unable to sleep after the terrible day. Only chance had saved me. I couldn't understand it, couldn't accept it. Then I saw the two guides. I was dazed. What were they doing here? Some new calamity must have befallen the others. Breathing excitedly, they told us that in the sewers they had found Simcha Rithauser, whom we knew as Kazhik, and that he was waiting for us.

It was a week since we had sent Kazhik, together with Sigmund Friedlich, through a tunnel to the Aryan side to meet our comrades there. It opened on Moranovska near the Ghetto wall. Every day we went to the opening of the tunnel in the hope of getting some message from them. The Germans on the other side of the wall often saw us and fired at us. Luckily, we suffered no casualties. Each evening we expected to get some word, but when none came we were sure they were dead. We learned only later that this particular area was surrounded by German patrols and even Poles were not permitted to enter it. Our comrades got out at dawn while the neighborhood was quiet. A German patrol was near but they reached the gate of a yard across the way and persuaded the Polish gatekeeper to help them. They told him they were Poles who had been stranded in the Ghetto when the rebellion had broken out and had been unable to leave. They begged his help in getting away from the patrol. The gatekeeper hid them in his house. Later he guided them out through secret passageways, and they found a refuge; but they could get no word to us.

Practically no help came from the Polish underground. Kazhik and Friedlich searched for someone familiar with the intricate sewage system, but inquiries after former workers in the sewage system aroused suspicion that they were Jews or that they had been hired to help the Jews. With great difficulty they contacted a Pole who consented, for a large sum, to go with Kazhik through the sewers to the Ghetto and back. More than once the Pole tried to turn back. Kazhik kept him going, sometimes with whiskey, sometimes by threatening him with his pistol. When they came close to the Ghetto, the Pole remained underground and Kazhik ventured out at night to look for us. But everything had changed so much, our hiding places were not where they used to be. Kazhik ran about in frenzy, even shouting loudly amid the ruins, but no one answered. At last, by accident, he met the group we had sent out along the sewer.

Now, said our guides, the others were waiting in the sewer; they had returned to lead us to them, and we must all come immediately. We felt no joy. Just the day before, death had seized a hundred who might have come with us now and been saved. We sat stunned, unable to rise. But the two comrades urged us. The Pole would not wait and, if we wasted time, we should all be lost.

It was hard to leave the Ghetto, the dead. The thought of forsaking

Zechariash's and Josef Farber's units tormented us. We had arranged to meet them the following day. Now at dawn there was no opportunity to contact them . . . if we emerged in the light we would only give them away to the enemy. Logic told us that nothing could be done now, that we had to go. Still, some comrades refused: "We will not stir from here. So long as even one of us stays in the Ghetto, all of us will stay."

In the Sewers

But we knew we must go. With heavy hearts we descended into the sewer. The guides were in front, Marek and I in the rear. The sewer was an abyss of darkness. I felt the water splash around me as I jumped and then resume its flow. I was overcome by a dreadful nausea there in the cold, filthy water. I felt that nothing—not even freedom—was worth this.

Very few could come with us. The aged and the children would only die on such a trip. They did not even ask to go along. Sixty people crawled through the narrow sewer, bent almost in half, the filthy water reaching up to their knees. Each held a candle. We half-walked, half-crawled like this for twenty hours, one behind the other, without stopping, without food or drink, in that terrible cavern. Hunger and thirst weakened us. Part of our group were the eighteen who had survived the catastrophe at Milah No. 18 and who had not yet recovered from the effects of the gas. Some of them were unable to walk and we dragged them through the water by their hands and feet.

One crawls through the sewer, and always there is the agonizing thought: how shall we explain, when we meet our comrades again, why we did not remain, why we are alive at all? All of us were poisoned by the thought of those we had left behind, and this robbed us of all possible joy in our good fortune. More than once, one of us would fall, and beg to be left lying there. But no one in all that journey was abandoned.

Early the following morning we reached a spot under Frosta Street on the Aryan side. There we stopped to rest. Kazhik and his Polish companion lifted the sewer lid and vanished. We sat in the water and waited. That day we had no word from them. Impatient, Marek and I, who were at the end of the column, decided to go up front and discuss what should be done. Pressing flat against the walls, we squeezed behind the file of seated comrades until we reached those near the exit. They too knew nothing.

The idea of returning to the Ghetto and leading out the others seized us. Many volunteered for the mission. But only two were assigned. One was Shlamek Schuster, a youth of about seventeen. Everybody knew there was no one better suited for the daring job. We all remembered how he had saved his unit from a burning house surrounded by Nazis in the

Brushmakers Quarter. He had broken through a wall of Germans by flinging hand grenades, and when they recovered he had already cut a path for himself and his comrades. He was now to be joined by Yorek Blons, an older comrade whom we valued for his intelligence and courage. They left before evening.

It was not until midnight that the comrades from the Aryan side contacted us. The lid over the sewer was lifted and some soup and loaves of bread were handed down. We could scarcely touch the food; only thirst troubled us. Yehuda Vengrover, still weak from gas, could not bear his thirst. He had bent down in the sewer and drunk from it. Who knows whether this was not the cause of his death? When we reached the forest the following day, he fell to the ground and died within a few minutes.

The comrades on the outside—among them a Pole whom the P.P.R. [Polish Labor party] had appointed to assist the Jewish Fighting Organization—told us that they could come for us in the morning. We told them that two of our comrades had gone back to fetch the others; there was no telling when they would return, and we would not stir till they came. We were worried lest it should be impossible to take others out of here after we left, because the Germans would surely discover the exit and watch it carefully.

Above us the life of the street went on as usual. We listened to street noises, heard the gay sounds of Polish children playing in the street. One of the children in the game was called Monik, a derogatory equivalent of Moishe. We felt the world nearby. Underneath it, we lay in the filthy water.

In the morning our messengers, Shlamek and Yorek, returned, their faces distorted with suffering. All the sewer passages to the Ghetto had been blocked. Shlamek acted like a man insane with grief.

The Escape

In our sorrow we prayed that everything would come to an end. Physical and spiritual strength were ebbing. Then at ten o'clock we heard a noise and soon the tunnel was flooded with such bright light as we had not seen for many days. All of us were sure the Germans had discovered our hiding place and we rushed further into the depths of the sewer. But it was our comrades, who had come to take us out. They called to us excitedly and began to help us climb the ladder. Near the exit stood a truck. In a few minutes, after forty persons got on the truck, it moved away and another one pulled up.

Now when we saw each other by daylight—dirty, wrapped in rags, smeared with the filth of the sewers, faces thin and drawn, knees shaking with weariness—we were overcome with horror. Only our feverish eyes showed that we were still living human beings. All of us stretched out on the floor of the truck in order to be invisible from the street, each with his weapon beside him. In this manner the truckload of armed Jewish fighters proceeded through the very heart of Nazi-occupied Warsaw on May 12, 1943. The Pole Kasczek, who was our ally, sat near the driver and directed him, while in the truck Kazhik stood upright, visible to all. We who lay below were calmed by the expression on his face. We did not know where we were going nor through what streets we were passing. We did not speak. All about us was the noise of the life of Warsaw, sounds of passing automobiles and crowds of people.

We traveled for only one hour, but the minutes dragged. Several times a whispered command was given—"Weapons ready! We see Germans!" Yet things did not come to a clash. The most difficult minutes came while trying to cross the bridge which leaves the city. There were German sentries near each bridge who examined and searched every auto. Our truck wandered from one street to another, and when the driver noticed that careful examination was being made at a bridge, he would turn back to look for another exit. At the fourth bridge, we succeeded in crossing safely in the confusion of heavy traffic. Thus we reached the Mlochini forest, seven kilometers from Warsaw.

Our escape had been organized by our comrades on the Aryan side. Had the Polish underground attempted an action of this kind in the capital during the daytime, it would have had to activate large combat units. In our case the action was carried out by only three Jews and one Pole. Two of them stood at either end of the street, and with the aid of weapons prevented anyone from entering it. A Polish policeman accidentally appeared on the scene and one of our comrades shouted to him: "Get out of here or I'll shoot!" He fled for his life.

In the morning one of our comrades had phoned a transport company to send two trucks to Frosta Street to transport some wooden shoes. When the trucks arrived everything was ready for the rescue. Our comrades, armed, came up to the drivers and said: "There are no wooden shoes here. We have a group of Jewish fighters. You must take them to the forests outside Warsaw. Otherwise we shall kill you." They obeyed, and the first of the trucks took us outside the city.

Throughout the trip we were worried about the others who had remained in the sewer. They had been some distance away from the exit and by the time they reached it the comrades outside could no longer hold back the traffic in the street. The driver of the second truck became frightened and left his cab. There was only time to tell them: "Follow the sewer to the exit in the nearest street. We will come to get you later." But they had apparently tired of waiting and came up out of the sewer. Immediately the entire neighborhood was surrounded by large numbers of Germans, who had in the meantime learned of our escape. They threw grenades into the sewer. When the twenty had come into the street there was a terrible and prolonged hand-to-hand battle between our handful of hungry and weakened people and the German troops. Amazed admiration was expressed by the Poles for this handful of Jewish boys and girls who dared break out into the city to fight the Germans. Legends were woven about this encounter, in which all the young Jews met their death.

The Last Survivors

We did not know where we were being taken, but when we approached the forest we suddenly found ourselves among friends. A group of fighters who had left the small Ghetto, Tebens-Schultz, ran out to greet us. They too had escaped like us, coming here about ten days before. They had already mourned us, believing that we were lost, and that they were the last survivors. In the Ghetto, we had been cut off from each other; several empty streets had separated us. The walls between these streets had been carefully guarded by German sentries. At the beginning of the rebellion we had tried to establish contact with them but had failed.

We were so dehumanized in our rags and filth, our dirty faces still unwashed, that we were hardly recognizable. They at once brought us warm milk, the first we had had in many days. Everything was strange. About us was the green forest and a beautiful spring day. It had been a long time since we had known a forest, spring, and the sun. All that had been buried and restrained in our frozen hearts for years now stirred. I burst into tears.

Soon there was a new sorrow. Even as we were excitedly talking with one another, Yehuda Vengrover lay down on the ground. Still weak from the gas, Yehuda was now dying, and in a few minutes his eyes closed forever.

For hours we sat silent, till one comrade arose and began to dig a grave. That night we all sat about a campfire that was burning in a hole in the ground and in our hearts we felt that we were the last survivors of a people that had been exterminated. We did not know what was happening throughout Poland, but we felt that the end had come for all our people and that we were the last to remain, the smoking and dying embers. . . . Our future was veiled in darkness and we who had been rescued felt superfluous and alone, abandoned by God and man. What more could be done that we had not done?

We lay down on the ground, but we could not fall asleep. We thought of the mystery of the world and man, we remembered the murder of our people, the beloved dead comrades who were part of the ashes of our burned souls. The heart wondered and asked, wondered and asked—but there was no answer.

69. THE JEWISH COUNCILS

YEHUDA BAUER

Professor Yehuda Bauer is head of the Institute of Contemporary Jewry at the Hebrew University in Jerusalem, and in charge of its Department of Holocaust Studies.

One of the strangest and least understood chapters in the history of the Holocaust is the role of the Jewish Councils, the Nazi-sponsored Jewish ghetto governments in each city or town. When these bodies were first established, the Jews who served on them were led to believe that their function would be to represent the Jewish population before the occupying Germans and to run the ghetto's internal affairs, albeit in line with the occupiers' orders. Actually, the Nazis intended them merely as an apparatus for forcing the Jewish communities to cooperate in their own destruction.

For example, when the Germans in a given city wanted roundups of Jews for deportation, they ordered the local council (the "Judenrat," as it was called in German) to compile lists or to assemble so and so many persons by a given deadline. Collecting tribute or confiscating property from individuals was also usually left to the Councils. A Jewish police force was organized to help them carry out orders and keep the Jewish population in line. It was made clear to Council members that failure to carry out the Nazis' instructions might cost them their own lives.

The Jewish Councils have often been condemned wholesale for willingly playing the role assigned to them by the enemy. But the truth is not that simple. Different Councils wrote different records for themselves. Some were corrupt, oppressive bureaucracies, and their police forces, who were often unpaid, lived on bribes and knuckled under to the Germans in every way. Others acted in ways that can only be called heroic.

In a study of 73 Jewish Councils in southeastern Poland, 45 were found to have resisted even before the ghetto residents knew that their lives were forfeit in any case. In all 45 towns, the Councils refused to hand over either lists of people or the people themselves; some also refused to collect the clothing or money the Nazis demanded.

In the town of Ludmir, for example, a Council chairman, named Weiler, when ordered to hand over a list of people to be deported, replied: "I am not God, and I will not decide who will live or die." In Borszczow, the Council chairman, Dr. Wolf Chess, refused to turn over money "contributions" to the Germans and was deported to the Belzec death camp, where he was murdered.

In two of the places studied, Council chairmen worked with the underground; in two others, they actually headed armed revolts.

This defiance had a price. Of the 45 defiant Council chairmen, 16 were eventually executed for refusing to hand over people or property, or for some other act of resistance. Five committed suicide as an act of protest. Four refused to go on serving on the Councils and survived. Three others hid so they would not have to go on serving; two of these were caught, but the third escaped. The ultimate fate of the rest is not known, but according to survivors, nearly all acquitted themselves well.

In Western Europe, too, there were compliant Jewish Councils and defiant ones. The countrywide Council in the Netherlands, for example, was a group of frightened men who obeyed the Germans' orders without question.

In France it was a wholly different story. The Jewish Council there was divided into two sections: one for northern France, where the Germans took over in 1940, and one for the south, which was not occupied until 1942. The heads of both sections belonged to the underground and were in constant touch with the resisters. Both Councils steadfastly refused to hand over lists of Jews and contributed significantly to the saving of most of the Jews in the country.

Thus, to claim that the Jewish Councils uniformly functioned as instruments of self-destruction, the way the Nazis meant them to, is untrue. If it is true that there were cowards and opportunists on the Councils, it is equally true that there were heroes and men of principle.

In this respect, Jews did not differ from the many others who suffered under Nazi rule. The people of Denmark carried out an epic rescue operation for their Jewish fellow citizens, while in other nations the people did little or nothing when their Jewish neighbors were taken away.

If anything, the record of the Jewish Councils compares favorably with that of non-Jewish officialdom—, not, of course, because Jews are intrisically any braver than others, but perhaps because they were much more severely oppressed and in greater danger. Not many non-Jewish government officials anywhere stepped down when legitimate governments were toppled by the German occupiers; nearly all stayed on and by their routine labors helped the Germans run their countries. Few refused to collect levies or arbitrary fines, to confiscate and turn over private property, or even to hand over people for forced labor far from home.

70. THE MEANING OF RESISTANCE

ABRAHAM FOXMAN

Abraham Foxman was born in Poland in 1910. During the Nazi occupation he was on the Aryan side of Vilna. He arrived in 1950 in the United States and has written in English and Hebrew about the Holocaust.

The word *resistance* usually signifies an organized, armed collective action prepared and carried out according to the rules and regulations of military strategy. This, however, is not the only means of resistance. Resistance does not necessarily have to be armed, organized, collective, or active.

The Jewish resistance was a varied one. It was armed and unarmed, organized and unorganized, planned and spontaneous, collective and individual, passive and active, offensive and defensive, moral, spiritual and psychological. Each one of these types of resistance involved the risk of life.

The greater part of resistance was of a passive nature. Attempting to stay alive was passive resistance. Escaping, hiding, or giving birth to a child in the ghetto was resistance. Praying in a congregation, singing, or studying the Bible was resistance.

71. THE SANCTIFICATION OF LIFE

YEHUDA BAUER*

In the earlier years of the war, the Jews did not take up arms against their oppressors. They knew that armed resistance could succeed only if at least a modest stock of arms was available, and if the non-Jewish population backed the attempt. But arms were not to be had, and the Poles, Czechs and others, themselves often hostile to Jews, could not be counted on to help. Taking a stand against the German tanks thus would have meant certain death—and at this time the Jews did not yet know that death awaited them in any case. . .

The absence of armed revolt during the early war years does not mean that the Jews everywhere unquestioningly accepted the fate decreed for them by the Nazis. It means that until the truth about the death camps leaked out in 1942, resistance was nonviolent, designed to conserve lives and make them as meaningful as possible.

---

*See no. 69. (Ed.)

"This is a time for *kiddush ha-hayyim*, the sanctification of life, and not *kiddush ha-shem*, the holiness of martyrdom," wrote a Warsaw rabbi, Isaac Nissenbaum. "Previously the Jew's enemy sought his soul and the Jew sacrificed his body in martyrdom; now the oppressor demands the Jew's body and the Jew is obliged therefore to defend it, to preserve his life."

Thus, when rabbis and other leaders in those days counseled against taking up arms, they did not advocate giving in to the forces of evil; they meant that the struggle should be carried on, as long as possible, by other, life-affirming means. It was a strategy that seemed well suited to the circumstances in 1940 and 1941, when no one could know how totally different Nazi persecution would be from any sufferings experienced before.

72. NEVER SAY THAT THERE IS ONLY DEATH FOR YOU

HIRSH GLICK

Hirsh Glick was born in Vilna in 1920. He was sent to a concentration camp in Estonia when the ghetto was liquidated by the Germans. He escaped, joined the partisans, and died while fighting as a partisan. His song became the hymn of the Jewish partisan organizations.

Never say that there is only death for you
Though leaden skies may be concealing days of blue—
Because the hour we have hungered for is near;
Beneath our tread the earth shall tremble: We are here!

From land of palm-tree to the far-off land of snow
We shall be coming with our torment and our woe,
And everywhere our blood has sunk into the earth
Shall our bravery, our vigor blossom forth!

We'll have the morning sun to set our day aglow,
And all our yesterdays shall vanish with the foe,
And if the time is long before the sun appears,
Then let this song go like a signal through the years.

This song was written with our blood and not with lead;
It's not a song that birds sing overhead,
It was a people, among toppling barricades,
That sang this song of ours with pistols and grenades.

So never say that there is only death for you.
Leaden skies may be concealing days of blue—
Yet the hour we have hungered for is near;
Beneath our tread the earth shall tremble: We are here!

73. I BELIEVE

Inscription on the walls of a cellar in Cologne, Germany, where Jews hid from Nazis.

I believe in the sun even when it is not shining.
I believe in love even when feeling it not.
I believe in God even when He is silent.

74. LIBERATED—AT LAST

SIMON WIESENTHAL

The following selection from the author's memoirs describes the feelings and condition of an inmate when liberated from a concentration camp at the end of the war and the downfall of the Nazi tyrrany. Though concerned with the fate of an individual, the story has historical value as a document of the times which it describes.

In the years following the war Simon Wiesenthal has become known as a hunter of German war criminals, a task to which he has devoted his life.

The Americans Arrive

It was ten o'clock on the morning of May 5, 1945, when I saw a big gray tank with a white star on its side and the American flag waving from the turret. It stood on the windswept square that had been, until an hour earlier, the courtyard of the Mauthausen concentration camp. The day was sunny, with a scent of spring in the air. Gone was the sweetish smell of burned flesh that had always hovered over the yard.

The night before, the last SS men had run away. The machinery of death had come to a stop. In my room a few dead people were lying on their bunks. They hadn't been taken away this morning. The crematorium no longer operated.

I do not remember how I'd got from my room into the courtyard. I was hardly able to walk. I was wearing my faded striped uniform with a yellow J in a yellow-red double triangle. Around me I saw other men in striped dungarees. Some were holding small flags, waving at the Americans.

Where had they gotten the flags from? Did the Americans bring them? I shall never know.

The tank with the white star was about a hundred yards in front of me. I wanted to touch the star, but I was too weak. I had survived to see this day, but I couldn't make the last hundred yards. I remember taking a few steps, and then my knees gave way and I fell on my face.

Somebody lifted me up. I felt the rough texture of an olive-drab American uniform brush against my bare arms. I couldn't speak; I couldn't even open my mouth. I pointed toward the white star, I touched the cold, dusty armor with my hands, and then I fainted.

When I opened my eyes after what seemed a long time, I was back on my bunk. The room changed. There was only one man on each bunk, no longer three or four, and the dead had been taken away. There was an unfamiliar smell in the air. It was DDT. They brought in big kettles with soup. This was *real* soup, and it tasted delicious. I took too much of it—my stomach wasn't used to such nourishing fare—and I got violently sick.

Medical Help

The next days went by in a pleasant apathy. Most of the time I dozed on my bunk. American doctors in white coats came to look at us. We were given pills and more food—soup, vegetables, meat. I still was so weak that a friend had to help me when I wanted to go out. I had survived, I didn't have to force myself to be strong any longer; I had seen the day I'd prayed for all these years, but now I was weaker than ever. "A natural reaction," said the doctors.

I made an effort to get up and walk out alone. As I shuffled through a dark corridor, a man jumped at me and knocked me down. I collapsed and lost consciousness. I came to on my bunk, and an American doctor gave me something. Two friends sat next to me. They had picked me up in the corridor and carried me to my bunk. They said that a Polish trusty had beaten me. Perhaps he was angry because I was still alive.

People in room A said I must report the trusty to the American authorities. We were free men now, no longer *Untermenschen*. The next day my friends accompanied me to an office in the building that had formerly been the camp headquarters. A handwritten sign WAR CRIMES was on the door. We were told to wait in a small anteroom. Somebody brought me a chair, and I sat down.

Frightened Nazis

Through the open doors, I saw American officers behind desks who interrogated SS men who stood at attention in front of them. Several former prisoners worked as typists. An SS man was brought into the room.

Instinctively I turned my head sideward so he wouldn't see me. He had been a brutal guard; when he walked through the corridor and a prisoner did not step aside quickly and snap to attention, the SS man would whip the prisoner's face with the riding crop he always carried. The sight of this man had always brought cold sweat to the back of my neck.

Now I stared; I couldn't believe it. The SS man was trembling, just as we had trembled before him. His shoulders were hunched, and I noticed that he wiped the palms of his hands. He was no longer a superman; he made me think of a trapped animal. He was escorted by a Jewish prisoner—a former prisoner.

I kept staring, fascinated. I didn't hear what was said as the SS man stood before the American interrogator. He could hardly stand at attention, and there was sweat on his forehead. The American officer motioned with his hand and an American soldier took the SS man away. My friends said that all SS men were being taken to a big concrete pillbox, where they were to be kept under guard until they were tried. I made my report on the Polish trusty. My friends testified that they had found me lying unconscious in the corridor. One of the American doctors also testified. Then we went back to our room. That night the trusty apologized to me in front of our comrades, and extended his hand. I accepted his apology but did not give him my hand.

The trusty wasn't important. He was already part of the past. I kept thinking of the scene at the office. Lying on my bunk with my eyes closed, I saw the trembling SS man—a contemptible, frightened coward in his black uniform. For years that uniform had been the symbol of terror. I had seen apprehensive German soldiers during the war (the soldiers too, were afraid of the SS men), but never a frightened SS man. I had always thought of them as the strong men, the elite, of a perverted regime. It took me a long time to understand what I had seen: the supermen became cowards the moment they were no longer protected by their guns. They were through.

I got up from my bunk and walked out of the room. Behind the crematorium, SS men were digging graves for our 300 comrades who had died of starvation and exhaustion after the arrival of the Americans. I sat down, looking at the SS men. Two weeks ago they would have beaten me half-dead if I dared look at them. Now they seemed to be afraid to walk past me. An SS man begged an American soldier for a cigarette. The soldier threw away the cigarette that he'd been smoking. The SS man bent down, but another SS man was faster and got hold of the butt, and the two SS men began to scuffle until the soldier told them to get away.

Only two weeks had gone by, and the elite of the Thousand Year Reich were fighting for a cigarette butt. How many years had it been since we had been given a cigarette? I walked back to my room and looked around. Most of my comrades were lying apathetically on their bunks. After the moment of exhilaration many of them suffered attacks of depression. Now that they knew they were going to live, they were aware of the senselessness of their lives. They had been spared—but they had no one to live for, no place they could go back to, no pieces they could pick up. . . .

I had to do something so I wouldn't succumb to such apathy. Something had to keep me from having nightmares when it got dark, and daydreams in the daytime. I knew exactly what I could do, and what I *had* to do.

War Crime Office

I went to the War Crimes office and offered my services. I hoped they wouldn't notice my appearance. The American lieutenant listened to me and shook his head. What could they do with me? He said I had neither training nor experience.

"And, incidentally, how much do you weigh?" he asked.

I lied. "Fifty-six kilos [123 pounds]."

The lieutenant laughed. "Wiesenthal, go and take it easy for a while, and come to see me when you really weigh fifty-six kilos."

Ten days later I'd gained some weight . . . The lieutenant must have sensed how much the job meant to me, for he said I could start at once, and assigned me to a Captain Tarracusio, a former Russian aristocrat who had emigrated to the United States in 1918 from the province of Georgia. He had taught international law at Harvard University.

After the establishment of the four military zones of Austria in 1945, Mauthausen [the former concentration camp] became part of the Soviet zone. Our War Crimes group moved to Linz, in the U.S. Zone. Many of the former inmates of Mauthausen were brought to a Displaced Persons camp that had been set up in the public school in Leonding, a small town near Linz.

Looking for Survivors

I spent the mornings at the War Crimes office and the afternoons at the newly established Jewish Committee in Linz (later expanded into the Jewish Central Committee of the U.S. Zone in Austria), of which I became vice-chairman. The Committee set up a makeshift office in two small rooms.

The rooms were always crowded. In the months after the war our visitors were human wrecks who always seemed to be wearing somebody else's clothes. They had sunken cheeks and bloodless lips. Many said they had been at Mauthausen. We recognized each other by stories of SS men we all knew or by memories of friends who had died. Some of them acted like people who had just survived an earthquake or a hurricane and cannot understand why they have been saved while everybody else has died in the disaster. They would ask each other: "Who else is alive?" one couldn't understand that one had survived, and it was beyond comprehension that others should still be alive. They would sit on the steps of the office and talk to one another. "Can it be that my wife, my mother, my child is alive? Some of my friends, some of the people in the town where we lived?"

There was no mail service. The few available telephone lines were restricted to military use. The only way to find out whether someone was alive was to go and look. Across Europe a wild tide of frantic survivors was flowing. People were hitchhiking, getting short jeep rides, or hanging onto dilapidated railway coaches without windows or doors. They sat in huddled groups on haycarts, and some just walked. They would use any means to get a few miles closer to their destination. To get from Linz to Munich, normally a three-hour railroad trip, might take five days. Many of them didn't really know where to go. To the place where one had been with his family before the war? To the concentration camp where the family had last been heard of? Families had been torn apart too suddenly to make arrangements for the day when it would be all over.

... And yet the survivors continued their pilgrimage of despair, sleeping on highways or in railroad stations, waiting for another train, another horse-drawn cart to come along, always driven by hope. "Perhaps someone is still alive. . . ." Someone might tell where to find a wife, a mother, children, a brother—or whether they were dead. Better to know the truth than to know nothing. The desire to find one's people was stronger than hunger, thirst, fatigue. Stronger even than the fear of border patrols, of the CIC and NKVD, of men saying "Let's see your papers."

The first thing we did at the Committee in Linz was to make up lists of known survivors. People who came in to ask for someone were asked where they were from. They were nomads, vagabonds, beggars. But once upon a time they had had a home, a job, savings. Their names were put on the list of some town or village. Slowly the lists grew. People from Poland, Czechoslovakia, or Germany brought us lists. We gave them copies of our lists. We worked long into the night to copy these lists. Early in the morning, the first people would arrive to look up names. Some waited all night to get in. Behind a man another waited for a glance that might mean hope or despair. Some people were impatient and there were brawls. Once two men began to scuffle because each wanted the same list. In the end they tore up the precious piece of paper. Another time two men started to argue, their eyes glued to the list in the hands of a third man. Each wanted it next. Suddenly they looked at each other and gasped, and the next moment they were in each others' arms. They were brothers and each had been trying to find the other for weeks.

And there were moments of silent despair when someone discovered that the person he was looking for had been there only a few days before, looking for him. They had missed each other. Where should one look now? Other people scanned the lists of survivors, hoping against hope to find the names of people they had seen killed before their very eyes. Everybody had heard of some miracle.

I hardly ever looked at the lists. I didn't believe in miracles. I knew that all my people were dead. After the Pole from Warsaw had told me what happened in Topiel Street, I had no hope that my wife was alive. When I thought of her, I thought of her body lying under a heap of rubble, and I wondered whether they had found the bodies and buried her. In a moment of illogical hope I wrote to the International Committee of the Red Cross in Geneva. They promptly answered that my wife was dead. I knew that my mother did not have a grave; she had died in the death camp of Belzec. I hoped that at least my wife might have a grave.

One night, when I had nothing else to do, I looked at a list of survivors from the Polish city of Cracow and found the name of an old friend from Buczacz, Dr. Biener. I wrote him a letter. I told him that my wife's body might still be lying under the ruins of the house of Topiel Street. I asked him to go to Warsaw and look at what was left of the house. There was no mail service to Poland, so I gave the letter to a man who specialized in getting things through Czechoslovakia to Poland.

I didn't know that a miracle had indeed happened. My wife told me all about it later. When the German flame-thrower squads had closed in on Topiel Street, in the darkness and confusion my wife and a few other people had managed to get away. For a while they hid. After the battle of Warsaw, the few survivors were driven together by the Germans and assigned to forced-labor transports for Germany. My wife was sent to a factory in Heiligenhaus, near Gelsenkirchen in the Rhineland, where they made machine guns for the Wehrmacht. The Polish laborers were decently housed and fed, and the Gestapo left them alone. The Germans knew that the war was lost.

Liberated by the British

My wife was liberated by the British, who marched into Gelsenkirchen on April 11, 1945. (That day I was lying on my bunk in the death block of Mauthausen.) My wife went to the British authorities and reported that she was Cyla Wiesenthal, a Jewish woman from Poland. Six women in her

group turned out to be Jewish, but they had not known of each other. One
of them told my wife that she was going home.

"Home?" asked my wife. "Where is home?"

"To Poland, of course. Why don't you come with me?"

"What for? My husband was killed by the Gestapo in Lwow last year.
Poland has become a large cemetery to me."

"Have you proof that he's dead?"

"No," said my wife, "but . . ."

"Don't believe it. Now, suppose he were alive: where is he likely to be?"

Cyla thought it over. "In Lwow, I would think. We spent the years before
the war there."

"Lwow is now in the Soviet Union," said her friend. "Let's go there."

Traveling after the War

The two women left Gelsenkirchen in June 1945. (At one point on her
journey, we later discovered, my wife had been less than thirty miles from
Linz.) After an arduous trip, they reached the Czechoslovak-Polish border
at Bohumin. They were told that a train left that night for Lwow. They got
on the overcrowded cars and arrived in Cracow, Poland, in the morning. It
was announced that there would be a four-hour stop.

At the Cracow railroad station somebody stole my wife's suitcase with
everything she owned. That was her homecoming. To cheer her up, her
friend suggested that they walk into town. Perhaps they would meet
someone they had once known. The beautiful old city of the Polish kings
looked deserted and ghostlike that morning. Suddenly my wife heard her
name called out, and recognized a man named Landek, who had been a
dentist in Lwow. (Landek now lives in America.) For a while they
exchanged hectic questions and unfinished sentences, as always happened when survivors met. Landek had heard that Simon Wiesenthal was
dead. He told my wife to talk to Dr. Biener. He might know more.

"Dr. Biener from Buczacz?" asked my wife. "Is he in Cracow?

"He lives five minutes from here." Landek gave her the address and
hurried away.

When they came to Dr. Biener's house, my wife asked her friend to wait
downstairs. She walked up the stairway with a heavy heart. On the third
floor she saw a sign reading Biener and rang the bell. The door was
opened. For a moment she saw Dr. Biener's face and heard a muffled cry.
Then the door was quickly shut again.

"Dr. Biener!" my wife shouted, banging her fists against the door. "Open
up! It's Cyla. Cyla Wiesenthal from Buczacz!"

The door was opened. Dr. Biener was pale, as if he were seeing a ghost.

"But—you are dead," he said, "I just got a letter. . . ."

"I'm very much alive," my wife said angrily. "Of course I look half-dead, after spending the night on the train."

"Come in," Dr. Biener said hastily, and closed the door. "You don't understand. Yesterday I had a letter from your husband. Simon writes that you died under the ruins of a house in Warsaw."

Now my wife got pale. "Simon? But he's dead. He's been dead for over a year."

Dr. Biener shook his head. "No, no, Cyla. Simon is alive, in Linz, Austria. Here, read the letter."

They called my wife's friend from downstairs. She was not at all surprised. Hadn't she told Cyla that her husband might be alive? They sat down and talked, and when they remembered the train it was much too late. If my letter hadn't reached Dr. Biener the day before, if my wife hadn't met Landek, if Dr. Biener hadn't been at home, the two women would have gone back to the station and continued their journey to the Soviet Union. My wife might have been sent into the interior of the USSR, and it would have taken years to find her again.

My wife stayed in Cracow, and tried to get in touch with me. Dr. Biener knew several illegal couriers who would carry letters for a fee, with no guarantee of delivery. She wrote three letters and gave them to three men working different routes. I received one of them, from a man who had come to Linz by way of Budapest—which is quite a detour.

Getting Travel Documents

I'll never forget the moment when I saw Cyla's handwriting on the envelope. I read the letter so many times that I knew it by heart. I went to see the OSS captain for whom I was then working and asked him to give me travel orders to Cracow. He didn't like the idea of my going to Poland. He said I might never be able to come back. He suggested we think it over until next morning.

I didn't go to the Jewish Committee that afternoon. I was happy and perhaps feeling a little guilty at being a happy man among so many unhappy people. I wanted to be alone. I knew a peasant not far from where I lived who had a few horses. I thought of my summer vacations in Dolina, where I loved to ride horses. I asked the peasant to let me have a horse for an hour. I forgot that I was a little older and not yet in good physical condition. I mounted the horse. Something went wrong. I suppose the horse sensed at once that I was still weak. I was thrown and landed in a potato field with a broken ankle.

I had to stay in bed. That settled the matter of my projected journey to Poland. I asked a Jewish friend, Dr. Felix Weisberg, to go to Cracow and gave him a letter for my wife. He promised to bring her back to Linz. My

OSS friends made out the necessary travel documents for her, so she would have no difficulty in getting into the U.S. Zone of Austria.

They were fine travel documents, but unfortunately my wife never received them. Crossing Czechoslovakia on his way to Poland, Dr. Weisberg was warned that there was an NKVD road-block ahead, with "very strict controls." He got nervous; if the Soviet secret police found any American dokumenty on him, they might arrest him as a spy. He destroyed the documents. Too late he realized that he had also destroyed my wife's address in Cracow. As it turned out, NKVD didn't even search him. In Cracow, he went to the local Jewish Committee and put a notice on the bulletin board. Mrs. Cyla Wiesenthal, the wife of Simon Wiesenthal, was asked to get in touch with Dr. Felix Weisberg, who would take her to her husband in Linz.

My wife saw the notice the next morning and went to see Dr. Weisberg. She was not the first visitor. Two other women were already there, each claiming to be the one and only Cyla Wiesenthal. A lot of people in Poland were trying to get to Austria, hoping they might later try to get to America. Poor Felix Weisberg had a trickier problem than the mythological Paris. Weisberg didn't know my wife. In all the excitement preceding his sudden departure, I had foolishly forgotten to give him her exact description. He faced the unpleasant possibility of bringing back the wrong Mrs. Wiesenthal. Weisberg told me later that he'd asked each of the three women to describe how I looked. Two seemed rather vague, but one knew a lot of details, naturally. Also, Weisberg admitted to me, he'd liked her best. He decided to take a chance and bought false traval papers for her in the black market.

Finally United

One evening, late in 1945, I was early in bed as usual. My broken ankle still gave me a lot of trouble. There was a knock at the door. Felix Weisberg came in, confused and embarrassed. It took him quite a while to explain how he'd foolishly thrown away the American documents, and his dilemma over three women each claiming to be Mrs. Cyla Wiesenthal.

"I brought one of them with me. She's waiting downstairs. Now, don't get excited, Simon. If she isn't your wife, I'm going to marry her myself."

"You?"

"Yes, my word of honor. You're under no obligation whatsoever. To tell the truth, I thought it safest to bring the one I liked best. That way. I knew even if she was not your wife I would——"

But then she came into the room, and Felix Weisberg, God bless him, knew that he could not marry her.

75. THE INDICTMENT OF ADOLF EICHMANN

GIDEON HAUSNER

From the opening speech of Gideon Hausner, the attorney-general of the government of Israel, at the trial of Adolf Eichmann in Jerusalem on February 21, 1961. Eichmann was accused of "crimes against the Jewish people" and "crimes against humanity." The accused, "together with others, during the period 1939 to 1945, caused the killing of millions of Jews, in his capacity as the person responsible for the execution of the Nazi plan for the physical extermination of the Jews, known as 'the final solution of the Jewish problem.' "

Eichmann was found guilty by the court and the verdict was confirmed by the Supreme Court of Israel. He was executed in prison on May 31, 1962; his body was cremated and the ashes cast into the Mediterranean.

The indictment which follows has been abbreviated.

Six Million Accusers

When I stand before you here, Judges of Israel, to lead the Prosecution of Adolf Eichmann, I am not standing alone. With me are six million accusers. But they cannot rise to their feet and point an accusing finger towards him who sits in the dock and cry: "I accuse." For their ashes are piled up on the hills of Auschwitz and the fields of Treblinka, and are strewn in the forests of Poland. Their graves are scattered throughout the length and breadth of Europe. Their blood cries out, but their voice is not heard. Therefore I will be their spokesman and in their name I will unfold the awesome indictment.

A New Kind of Murder

The history of the Jewish people is steeped in suffering and tears. . . . Yet never, down the entire blood-stained road travelled by this people, never since the first days of its nationhood, has any man arisen who succeeded in dealing it such grievous blows as did Hitler's iniquitous regime, and Adolf Eichmann as its executive arm for the extermination of the Jewish people. In all human history there is no other example of a man against whom it would be possible to draw up such a bill of indictment as has been read here. . . .

At the dawn of history, there were examples of wars of extermination, when one tribe assaulted another with intent to destroy, when, in the heat and passion of battle, peoples were slaughtered, massacred or exiled. But only in our generation has an organized State set upon an entire defenceless and peaceful population, men and women, grey-beards, children and infants, incarcerated them behind electrified fences, imprisoned them in concentration camps, and resolved to destroy them utterly.

Murder has been with the human race since the days when Cain killed Abel; it is no novel phenomenon. But we have had to wait till this twentieth century to witness with our own eyes a new kind of murder: not the result of the momentary surge of passion or mental black-out, but of a calculated decision and painstaking planning; not through the evil design of an individual, but through a mighty criminal conspiracy involving thousands; not against one victim whom an assassin may have decided to destroy, but against an entire people.

A New Kind of Killer

In this trial, we shall also encounter a new kind of killer, the kind that exercises his bloody craft behind a desk, and only occasionally does the deed with his own hands. Indeed, we know of only one incident in which Adolf Eichmann actually beat to death a Jewish boy, who had dared to steal fruit from a peach tree in the yard of his Budapest home. But it was his word that put gas chambers into action; he lifted the telephone, and railway trains left for the extermination centres; his signature it was that sealed the doom of thousands and tens of thousands. He had but to give the order, and at his command the troopers took to the field to rout Jews out of their homes, to beat and torture them and chase them into ghettoes, to pin the badge of shame on their breasts, to steal their property—till finally, after torture and pillage, after everything had been wrung out of them, when even their hair had been taken, they were transported en masse to the slaughter. Even the corpses were still of value: the gold teeth were extracted and the wedding rings removed.

We shall find Eichmann describing himself as a fastidious person, a "white-collar" worker. To him, the decree of extermination was just another written order to be executed; yet he was the one who planned, initiated and organized, who instructed others to spill this ocean of blood, and to use all the means of murder, theft, and torture. He is responsible, therefore, as though he with his own hands had knotted the hangman's noose, had lashed the victims into the gas-chambers, had shot in the back and pushed into the open pit every single one of the millions who were slaughtered. Such is his responsibility in the eyes of the law, and such is his responsibility by every standard of conscience and morality. His accomplices in the crime were neither gangsters nor men of the underworld, but the leaders of a nation—including professors and scholars, robed dignitaries with academic degrees, linguists, educated persons, the "intelligentsia." We shall encounter them—the doctors and lawyers, scholars, bankers and economists, in those councils which resolved to exterminate the Jews, and among the officers and directors of the work of murder in all its terrible phases.

The Crime of Genocide

This murderous decision, taken deliberately and in cold blood, to annihilate a nation and blot it out from the face of the earth, is so shocking that one is at a loss for words to describe it. Words exist to express what man's reason can conceive and his heart contain, and here we are dealing with actions that transcend our human grasp. Yet this is what did happen: millions were condemned to death, not for any crime, not for anything they had done, but only because they belonged to the Jewish people. The development of technology placed at the disposal of the destroyers efficient equipment for the execution of their appalling designs.

This unprecedented crime, carried out by Europeans in the twentieth century, led to the definition of a criminal concept unknown to human annals even during the darkest ages—the crime of Genocide.

The calamity of the Jewish people in this generation was considered at a number of the trials conducted in the wake of Germany's defeat in the Second World War, when mankind resolved to set up instruments of defence, through the establishment of courts and execution of judgments, to ensure that the horrors of war which our generation has witnessed shall not recur. But in none of those trials was the tragedy of Jewry as a whole the central concern. It was among the subjects treated; sometimes it was given great weight, always it evoked sentiments of horror; but it was never at the centre, since the accused at these trials were indicted for crimes against members of many and various nations. There was only one man who had been concerned almost entirely with the Jews, whose business had been their destruction, whose role in the establishment of the iniquitous regime had been limited to them. That was Adolf Eichmann. If we charge him also with crimes against non-Jews, committed as it were by the way, this is because we make no ethnic distinction. But we should remember that the mission of the accused, in which for years he saw his destiny and calling, and to which he devoted himself with enthusiasm and endless zeal, was the extermination of the Jews.

How Could It Have Happened?

Men still ask themselves, and they will certainly continue to ask in days to come: How could it have happened: How was it possible in the middle of the twentieth century? The judges at the Nuremberg trials also asked themselves this question, examined its various aspects, and arrived at interesting formulations; yet it would be difficult to claim that a full or satisfactory answer was given. I doubt whether in this trial we on our part will succeed in laying bare the roots of the evil. This task must remain the concern of historians, sociologists, authors and psychologists, who will try to explain to the world what happened to it. But we shall nevertheless endeavor, however briefly, to describe the background, in an attempt to explain what is perhaps altogether inexplicable by the standards of ordinary reason.

Hitler, his regime and crimes, were no accidental or transient phenomenon. He did not come to power as a result merely of a unique combination of circumstances. Historical processes are usually the product of many developments, like many streams flowing each in its own channel until they combine into a mighty river. They will come together only if their flow is in the same general direction.

The Rise of Nazism

No doubt various events contributed to the rise of Nazism: the defeat of Germany in the First World War; the subsequent economic difficulties; lack of leadership and futile party divisions; fratricidal strife and disunion—all these impelled the German people, disoriented and groping, to turn its eyes towards the false prophet. But Hitler would not have been able to remain in power, and to consolidate in his support all the strata of the German people, including most of the intellectuals—to win the support of so many university professors and professional men, the civil service and the whole army—if the road to his leadership had not already been paved. Not even the oppressive regime of the concentration camps, and the atmosphere created by the terror so rapidly activated against all opposition by the hooligans of the S.S. and the S.A., are adequate alone to explain the enthusiastic and devoted support he received from the majority of the nation, unless it had been preceded by an extensive spiritual preparation. When we read today the declarations of the scientists, authors, and journalists—including many who had not been among his adherents before—who chanted his praises and willingly gave him their support and backing, how they willingly and joyfully accepted his yoke, we must reach the conclusion, however reluctantly, that the people were ready and prepared to crown him as their leader. . . .

Hitler denied the existence of a common basis for all humanity. According to his doctrine, there is no mutual responsibility between men. In place of the injunction "And thou shalt love thy neighbor as thyself" (Leviticus 19:18), we find "Crush him that is unlike thyself!" Instead of the ideal of human brotherhood, we have the principle of race superiority.

The Nuremberg Laws

Only those whose blood was Aryan were worthy of citizenship. This was established by the Nuremberg laws. . . .

Institutes were established in Nazi Germany, devoted to racial research and the determination of the hierarchical pyramid of racial superiorities. The Jews found themselves at the bottom of the list, followed only by the Gipsies and the Negroes.

And Hitler did free the hatred of the Jew which was latent in the hearts of large sections of the German people, intensify it and stimulate it into greater activity. The germ of anti-Semitism was already there; he stimulated it and transformed it into the source of an epidemic. For the purposes of Nazi Germany's internal policy, the Jew was a convenient object of hatred; he was weak and defenceless. The world outside remained silent when he was persecuted, and contented itself with verbal reactions that did little harm. The Jew was pilloried as a supporter of Communism—and therefore an enemy of the German people. In the same breath he was accused of being a capitalist—and therefore an enemy of the workers. National-Socialism had found in the Jew an object of hostility appropriate to both halves of its name, and it set him up as a target for both national enmity and class hatred. The Jew was also a ready target through which the attention of the public could be diverted from other problems. This too was an age old weapon, which had been used by many anti-Semites down the ages. On this point we shall find the accused himself saying:

"The Jewish Question was a welcome tactic to divert attention from other reverses. . . . Whenever any difficulties of another sort arose, they took refuge, at least at this time, in the Jewish Question, and immediately the diversion was created. This was done not only by Himmler* himself, not only by the Gauleiters; this was the practice of every one among the so-called high leadership."

Denial of Human Rights

A confused and blinded world was not alarmed by this campaign of hatred and the denial of human rights. It did not understand that the persecution of the Jews was only the beginning of an onslaught on the entire world. The man whose henchmen howled the infamous words:

> "When Jewish blood spurts from the knife,
> Then all goes doubly well!"
> (Wenn Judenblut vom Messer spritzt—
> Dann geht's nochmal so gut!)

—the same man would soon, by a natural development and led by the same

---

*Heinrich Himmler (1900–45), a Nazi Leader and chief of the secret police (Gestapo). He was captured by the British and committed suicide. (Ed.)

master-feeling of hate, proclaim that all the cities of England would be
subjected to the same fate as bombed Coventry.

A German Minority

In order to complete the picture, we should point out that there were in
Germany tens of thousands of scientists and ecclesiastics, statesmen and
authors and ordinary people, who dared to help the Jews, to raise their
heads in opposition to the iniquitous regime, and even to rebel against it,
and among these were men whose names were famous in German science
and culture. Thousands of opponents of the bloody regime were imprisoned and were later destined to suffer greatly in concentration camps
before the Nazi monster was brought low. Thousands of these died without
seeing the day of liberation. Hundreds of ecclesiastics were arrested and
imprisoned. There were also examples of personal bravery—like that of
the priest who was sent by Eichmann to a concentration camp for
intervening openly on behalf of the Jews. There were Germans who hid
Jews and shared their rations with them and who at the risk of their lives
helped them to hide or obtain "Aryan" papers, and there were others who
maintained an anti-Hitler underground. During the War there were
Germans who even protested to Hitler at the disgrace the Gestapo was
bringing on the German people by acting like beasts of prey, as they
described the extermination of the Jews. There were also soldiers who
tried to frustrate the killings by direct intervention.

But after all is said and done, these were a very small minority. The
decisive majority of the German people made peace with the new regime;
and were phlegmatic witnesses of the most terrible crime ever perpetrated
in human history. And when Goebbels, the Nazi Propaganda Minister,
made a public bonfire of the creations of men of the spirit, Jewish and
non-Jewish—the works of such men as Heinrich Heine, Thomas Mann,
[Jakob] Wassermann, [Albert] Einstein, [Sigmund] Freud, Upton Sinclair,
H. G. Wells, [Emile] Zola, Havelock Ellis, and scores of others, because
they were "in opposition to the German spirit," he proclaimed:

> "The soul of the German people can again express itself. These
> flames not only illuminate the final end of an old era; they also light up
> the new."

The Passion of Hate

The majority of German intellectuals were ready to warm themselves at
those bonfires, and to accept as their spiritual guide the false glitter of their
flames.

Nazi Germany became the scene of an anti-Jewish campaign directed and spurred on by brutish passions of hate. The slogan, "Germany awaken—Jewry die!" (*Deutschland erwache—Juda verrecke!*) appeared on the walls. The Jews were accused of every fault and defect in existence. A poisonous diet of bestial incitement was published weekly in *Der Stuermer*, that odious newspaper edited by Julius Streicher, who was eventually executed by sentence of the International Military Tribunal.

In order to denigrate the Jew, all his works had to be denounced. For this purpose, the Nazis defiled the greatest Jewish creation of all the ages—the Bible. Alfred Rosenberg, one of the "thinkers" of the Movement, demanded that the Holy Scriptures be removed from any sphere where they could be a spiritual influence or source of religious faith. He considered it a prime defect of the Protestant faith that it sanctifies the Old Testament. There was talk of "the redemption of Jesus" from his connections with Judaism, in order to make it possible to degrade the people into which he was born. . . .

The Yellow Badge

Even before the power was firmly in their hands, the Nazis initiated official measures of persecution against the Jews. On April 1, 1933, only two months after they obtained power, they organized the "Day of Boycott," to give symbolic form to the goal of uprooting the Jews and driving them out of the German Reich. Jews were beaten and imprisoned in concentration camps; Aryan customers were forbidden to enter Jewish places of business. It was then that Robert Weltsch wrote his unforgettable article in the *Jüdische Rundschau*, the organ of German Zionism: "Wear the Yellow Badge with Pride!" But even Weltsch could not foresee that the yellow badge could become the distinctive sign which, a few years later, would be forced upon all the Jews in countries ruled by the Nazis, so that they might be more easily identified for the purpose of the blood-bath. . . .

Anti-Semitism Exploited

After the Nazis had succeeded in using anti-Semitism as an important instrument for securing their power in Germany itself, they planned to use the same poison of hate to bind together the enemies of the Jews throughout the world, in order, by this means, to undermine opposition to the hegemony of Nazi Germany. And while German military might cast its shadow of terror on peoples and lands, silencing the voice of reason, anti-Semitism was exploited as a deliberate expedient to undermine the conscience of the nations, to excite the basest of passions, and to encourage

Quisling* and other collaborators. The Jew was described, in the official publications of the Party and the German Reich, as an enemy to the peace of the world, and there was a proposal for a league of nations against Jewry, ein *Völkerbund gegen Juda.*

Wherever the Nazi conqueror set foot, there awaited him a prepared group of adventurers, traitors to their country, underworld characters—sometimes plain assassins, who cast lustful eyes on Jewish property and lent their unclean hands to the task of destruction. Wherever the German legions trod, they introduced the suppression of human freedom and whipped up Jew hatred. . . .

There is a Hebrew saying: "The wicked, even at the gate of Hell, do not repent." In April 1945, at the moment of his death agonies, when the Soviet cannon were thundering in the streets of Berlin, when Hitler sat imprisoned in the cellar of the Reichskanzlei, his entire world in ruins and his country stricken, over the corpses of six million Jews—at that moment, the Führer wrote his political last will and testament. He bequeathed to his people the injunction of eternal hatred for the Jews, and he concluded:

> "Above all, I enjoin the government and the people to uphold the racial laws to the limit and to resist mercilessly the poisoner of all nations, international Jewry."

Even from beyond the grave, Hitler was still trying to sow the seeds of hatred and destruction for the Jewish people.

Eichmann's Guilt

Adolf Eichmann's guilt lies in the planning, initiation, organization and execution of the crimes specified in the indictment. We shall prove his guilt as planner, initiator, organizer and executor of the crime known as "the final solution of the Jewish problem," his direct part in the implementation of this criminal program, his role as administrator, director and commander of the operation, as well as the part he played as partner and accomplice in the implementation of the program by others. He was the pivot of the criminal conspiracy to exterminate the Jewish people, wholly or in part, and he was partner in the crimes committed by the S.S., the S.D., the Gestapo, including the members of the Einsatzgruppen, the Security Police commanders, senior S.S. and police officers, their emissaries and branch offices, and all those who were under their command and carried out their instructions in respect of all the acts of murder, plunder, torture and persecution specified in the indictment.

---

*Vidkun Quisling, Norwegian politician who collaborated in the German conquest of Norway in 1940. (Ed.)

We shall prove that Eichmann performed all these deeds with the intention of destroying the Jewish people.

We shall prove that his deeds were crimes against the Jewish people, crimes against humanity, and war crimes, as specified in the indictment.

We shall also prove the offences he committed against persons of other nationalities.

We shall call witnesses who met Eichmann at the time of these acts and others who will describe his actions and crimes as they experienced them in their own persons and will give evidence of what they saw and heard during the period of the Holocaust. The extermination of millions of Jews means the extermination of millions of witnesses, but witnesses still survive who can report what they saw with their own eyes, heard with their own ears and suffered in their own persons.

To the best of our ability, we shall try to demonstrate to this Court in full what Adolf Eichmann did to the Jewish people, but we shall not be able to bring proof as to the fate of each community or the destruction of each Jewish group. This will remain the task of the historian. Accordingly, we shall bring before the Court all the evidence at our disposal on the decisions made to carry out the extermination program, the methods by which these decisions were carried out, and evidence as to the role and responsibility of the accused therein. . . . It is beyond our power to give a complete description of this terrible disaster in all its depth.

I am afraid that even after submitting all the evidence and material which is in our possession, we shall not be able to do more than give a pale reflection of the enormous human and national tragedy which beset Jewry in this generation.

Adolf Eichmann will enjoy a privilege which he did not accord to even a single one of his victims. He will be able to defend himself before the Court. His fate will be decided according to law and according to the evidence, with the burden of proof resting upon the prosecution.

And the judges of Israel will pronounce true and righteous judgment.

76. THE SHOCK OF THE HOLOCAUST

H. H. BEN-SASSON

The writer is professor of Jewish history at the Hebrew University in Jerusalem.

Avoiding a Moral Crisis

In recent times the thought and the whole being of the Jews has been shocked by the forcible confrontation with bestial human cruelty—with the crimes of the Nazis. The terror of the deeds committed by one of the world's most cultured peoples, the atrocity of silence on the part of many bodies that the Jews assumed might react to the most systematic and complete murder of non-combatants in history, murder in the name of Race theory, which utterly denies humanity and God's image in man,—all these might have been thought to constitute a spiritual danger to the Jews. The attack on them from the forces of moral anarchy was a feat of the highest organizing technique using all the accepted instruments and terms of state and society. It might have been thought that the Jews would respond with a moral anarchy of their own, by a declaration of no confidence in man and disbelief in humanitarianism as a real possibility. But the immense inner force of the Jewish heritage, of a people long schooled in suffering inflicted from outside, saved them from a moral crisis. The appalling shock brought them together—those who survived—and fertilised their thought.

Drawing People into Judaism

The shock drew these people into Judaism: individuals and groups of Jews who had fought with messianic fervour for social revolution, for the freeing of oppressed classes and peoples, now saw their own people humiliated and ground into the dust in the name of racial hatred, inescapably. Moreover, the national and social upheaval in the world after the Second World War showed many of them that classes and societies today prefer their own leaders, from their own ranks; and that it matters little to them whether the Jew identifies himself with their interests and will work for them wholeheartedly in a cause he has made his own; it became clear that the virus of Nazism had not left the body politic unaffected. At the same time the distress of their own people demanded relief from them as a matter of common humanity, while the great constructive work begun by the Jews in the State of Israel demanded more concretely that they should do their share in realizing the messianic dream by building Israel in its land.

Aid and Rehabilitation for the Survivors

The shock also found relief in extensive works of aid and rehabilitation for the survivors of the holocaust. Yet all the while, within the people, moral tension continued to grow, as they took a new look at reality. The Polish writer Czeslaw Milosz has suggested to westerners the essential difference in the feel of life between those who underwent the horrors of Nazi occupation and those who did not: "A man is lying under machine-gun fire on a street in an embattled city. He looks at the pavement and sees a very amusing sight: the cobblestones are standing upright like the quills of a porcupine. The bullets hitting their edges displace and tilt them. Such moments in the consciousness of man *judge* all poets and philosophers. . . In the intellectuals who lived through the atrocities of war in Eastern Europe there took place what one might call the *elimination of emotional luxuries.*" (*The Captive Mind* [New York, 1955], p. 39).

As far as the Jew was concerned, such "elimination of emotional luxuries" was far sharper and more drastic—for even if he himself had not lain in the body at the edge of the pavement, he knew well that the brothers with whom he felt inward and outward solidarity—for they were spiritually himself and physically the same in the eyes of the oppressor— his brothers were thrown daily into the gutter; self-respect must be taken from the Jew because he is a Jew, before you take his life. Today the Jew knows that to stand upright facing the enemy and to look straight into the eyes of the aggressor means the salvation not only of the body but of the soul.

The Tradition of Martyrdom

So it was that the holocaust engendered a willingness for supreme sacrifice. The seed of courage, which has flowered among the youth of Israel in heroic deeds, was watered by the blood of the martyrs. We have heard Buber* speak of the ancient tradition of martyrdom from a human and religious standpoint. In the Middle Ages, from the first Crusade onwards, the Jews clave to traditions of enduring torture and facing death that reached back to the days of Antiochus Epiphanes and the first revolt against the Romans; they laid down a way to die for their faith, and more than that, to kill themselves and their dear ones when they saw that active resistance was no longer possible, and they feared that not all of them would face enemy weapons bravely. The techniques of deluding the victim and breaking him down psychologically prevented most of the Nazis' victims from taking this way out. Yet the heroic and doomed rising of the Warsaw ghetto and the deeds of Jewish partisans, dogged by quislings in the forests and underground, are a mass martyrdom in different circumstances. Now a change has come over this ancient value; it seems to have become merged in the consciousness of the Jewish fighting youth with the active heroism they so boundlessly display.

Moral Unity and Human Courage

This short survey of modern Jewish thought, thought bubbling with life

---

*Martin Buber (1878–1965), philosopher, theologian, Zionist thinker worked in Germany until 1938 when he settled in Jerusalem. (Ed.)

in different channels, takes as the crux of the social and mental situation in
the Jewish people the question of endurance, of autonomy, the question
how free man should meet God and man face to face. It emerges that even
in old patterns of thought and expression the question still most actual is
that of the sovereignty of individual freedom and the need to limit it
voluntarily, in order to live with other free men, equal "in image of God",
that is in freedom. The results of the holocaust too, the miraculous moral
unity and human courage it begot among the Jews, seem central to the
Jews, and they are of value to all humanity. The individual, freedom, open
dialogue, the ability to endure humiliation and to come out of it with a
straight back—by these things not the Jews alone will be tested.

77. THE VOW

ABRAHAM SHLONSKY

Abraham Shlonsky (1900–1973) was born in Russia and came to Palestine in
1913 to pursue his studies. During World War I he lived in Russia and returned
to Palestine in 1921, working as a road laborer and simultaneously writing
poetry and literary articles. Collections of his poems and translations have
been published in numerous volumes. Shlonsky's work is thought to have
created a new Hebrew poetic language. His influence on a whole generation of
Israelis and the development of the Hebrew language has been epoch
making. Shlonsky, regarded as one of the finest translators in modern Hebrew
literature, rendered classics from several languages into Hebrew, among
them works by Shakespeare, Molière, Pushkin, Brecht, and others.
    Shlonsky's lament entitled Neder ("The Vow") is carved into the wall of
Yad Vashem, the Jerusalem shrine for the martyrs of the Holocaust.
    The obligation to remember was similarly expressed by Professor Gershom
Scholem of the Hebrew University of Jerusalem in the closing words of his
speech "Jews and Germans" in 1966: "However sublime it might be to
forget, we cannot. Only by remembering a past that we will never completely
master can we generate new hope in the resumption of communication
between Germans and Jews, and in the reconciliation of those who have been
separated."

> My eyes have seen desolation and grief
> And heaped anguish upon my heart;
> My goodness begged and urged to forgive
> But the infinite horror forbade a new start.
> I vow to remember as long as I live;
> Forgiveness to me is lost as an art.
> To the tenth generation not to forget,
> Until the offence has abated and also the vow,

And my wrath has faded and finally set.
I promise to carry in me all I know.
I promise not to unlearn and later regret
But to inscribe and remember all that I saw.

QUESTIONS FOR THOUGHT AND DISCUSSION

1. How was the formerly liberal middle class of Germany drawn into the anti-Semitic movement during the latter part of the nineteenth century?

2. What problems developed for the Jews of Germany as a result of the anti-Semitic movement?

3. In recent decades the term "alienation" has been used in literature and philosophy. Find out the meaning of this term. Can it be applied to the situation in which, for example, a writer like Jacob Wassermann found himself?

4. What legal basis did the Nazi government choose for its anti-Jewish policy in Germany? Do you find any such precedent in Jewish history?

5. In what way does the legal basis of anti-Jewish legislation of previous centuries differ from that of the Nazis?

6. How did the Jews of Germany react to the policy of the Nazi government?

7. What was the actual aim of the Nazi government toward the Jews of Europe as documented in the indictment of Eichmann? Has international legislation dealt with this question in the years after the Second World War?

8. How did Eichmann defend and justify his role? Was this line of defense accepted by the judges of the Nuremberg war criminals? If not, why not?

9. Explain why you think the song "Our Town Is Burning" became popular among the population of the ghettos and the survivors of the concentration camps?

10. Describe the cultural life which the Jews of the ghettos created.

11. What was the purpose of the Nazi-sponsored Jewish Council, or ghetto governments? Should the councils be condemned or defended?

12. Did the suicide of Zygelbojm, the representative of the Polish Jews in London, influence the Allied governments during the war in ways which Zygelbojm had hoped for?

13. In some of the Nazi-occupied territories of Europe, the Jews found Christians who helped and saved them. Find out about the heroic role of the Danish people.

14. What was the final motivation which led to the uprisings in the ghettos?

15. What thought do you find expressed in the song of the Jewish partisans? In the diary of Anne Frank?

16. What is understood by the wider meaning of the term "resistance"?

17. The idea of *Kiddush Hashem* has a special meaning in Jewish history. Can this idea or term be applied to the Nazi victims or does it have to be modified? In what way?

18. How can we, living today, honor the memory of the victims of tho Holocaust?

SUGGESTED READING

Note: Books suggested in more than one chapter are here listed by the
name of the author only. A key to such listings will be found at the
end of the book.
A paperback edition is indicated by the letters PB.

The literature on the Holocaust is voluminous. The following biblio-
graphic guides will be found helpful:
Robinson, Jacob, and Philip Friedman. *Guide to Jewish History Under
Nazi Impact*, New York: Ktav, 1974.
Robinson, Jacob, assisted by Mrs. Philip Friedman. *The Holocaust and
After: Sources and Literature in English.* Jerusalem: Israel Universities
Press, 1973.

Books for the Student

Bauer, Yehuda. *They Chose Life: Jewish Resistance in the Holocaust.* New
York, 1973. PB.
Charry-Segal, chap. 23.
Elbogen, bk. 5, chap. 6.
Friedlander, Albert H. *Out of the Whirlwind: A Reader of Holocaust
Literature.* New York, 1968.
Grayzel, pp. 640–44, 771–74, 782–93.
Pilch, Judah, ed. *The Jewish Catastrophe in Europe.* New York, 1965.
Suhl, Yuri, ed. *They Fought Back: The Story of the Jewish Resistance in
Nazi Europe.* New York, 1975. PB.
Schwarz, Leo W. *The Redeemers: The Saga of the Years 1945–1952.* New
York, 1953.

Diaries, Memoirs

Flinker, Moshe. *The Young Boy Moshe.* Jerusalem, 1965. PB.
Frank, Anne. *The Diary of a Young Girl.* New York, 1953. PB.
Wiesenthal, Simon. *The Murderers Among Us.* New York, 1967.

Fiction

Hersey, John. *The Wall.* New York, 1951.
Wiesel, Elie. *Night. Dawn. The Gates of the Forest.* New York, 1960, 1961,
1967. PB.

Books for the Teacher

Dawidowicz, Lucy S. *The War against the Jews, 1933–1945.* New York and
Philadelphia, 1975.

Glatstein, Jacob, Israel Knox, and Samuel Margoshes, eds. *Anthology of Holocaust Literature*. Philadelphia, 1969. PB.

Hausner, Gideon. *Justice in Jerusalem*. New York, 1966.

Hilberg, Raul. *Documents of Destruction: Germany and Jewry, 1933–1945*. Chicago, 1971.

Korman, Gerd, ed. *Hunter and Hunted: Human History of the Holocaust*. New York, 1973.

Levin. Nora. *The Holocaust: The Destruction of European Jewry, 1933–1945*. New York, 1973. PB.

Liptzin, Solomon. *Germany's Stepchildren*. Philadelphia, 1944.

Marcus, Jacob R. *The Rise and Destiny of the German Jew*. Cincinnati, 1936.

Mark, Ber. *Uprising in the Warsaw Ghetto*. New York, 1976. PB.

Pinson, Koppel S. *Modern Germany: Its History and Civilization*. New York, 1966.

Sachar, chap. 20. PB.

Wiesel, Elie. *One Generation After*. New York, 1970.

Diaries, Memoirs

Kaplan, Chaim. *The Warsaw Diary*. New York, 1974. PB.

Ringelblum, Emanuel. *Notes from the Warsaw Ghetto*. New York, 1974. PB.

Shapell, Nathan. *Witness to the Truth*. New York, 1974.

VI. A STATE IS BORN: THE RETURN TO ZION

Introduction

During the thirties and forties of the twentieth century, the Jewish people experienced a great tragedy and a miraculous rebirth: the ruin and destruction of most of European Jewry, and the founding of the State of Israel. "In the long history of the Jews, few milestones can compare with these two" (Yehudah Bauer).

The Jews, living in dispersion over a period of almost nineteen centuries, never abandoned the hope of a return to Palestine, the land of Israel as it was called in Hebrew, conquered by the Romans in the year 70. Even as early as the first exile in Babylonia in the sixth century B.C.E. they mourned: "By the rivers of Babylon,/there we sat,/sat and wept,/as we thought of Zion" (Psalm 137). And they vowed then that they would never forget the land from which they had come: "If I forget you, Jerusalem,/let my right hand wither." On the holiest day of the year, Yom Kippur, and on other sacred occasions they repeated the expression of this sentiment with the words "Next year in Jerusalem." Prayers for the restoration of Zion were also incorporated into every Jewish service.

Long before modern times the belief developed that there would be a miraculous return to the land of Israel and the restoration of political independence under the leadership of the Messiah, the "anointed one" of God. Centuries of oppression and persecution did not diminish this religious and political attachment of the Jews to the Holy Land. It was only for a short period, in the time of the enlightenment and emancipation in Western Europe (see chapter 1), that this attachment weakened and almost disappeared.

Political Zionism, however, as it developed in the nineteenth century, although intimately related to the earlier yearning for Zion and the belief in the coming of the Messiah, in a sense represented a break with Jewish tradition. The establishment of the Jewish state is the most profound change that has taken place in the life of the Jews in the last two thousand years.

Not unlike the new religious movements discussed in chapter 2 of this book, political Zionism can be considered as another of the constructive attempts to meet the problem of the Jew in the modern world and to arrive at a new definition of what is meant by Jewishness in the present day.

What were the ideas and forces which brought this change about and ultimately led to the establishment of the State of Israel? What are some of

261

the telling statements of its builders? What problems has the state had to face in the international community, and how has Jewry been affected by the change of its position in the contemporary world? How does the state view itself as it confronts its Arab neighbors, the Jewish people, and the world at large? The answers to these questions will be considered and then developed by the source materials in this chapter.*

Sources

Our first selections are excerpts from *Rome and Jerusalem* by Moses Hess (no. 78), a forerunner of modern Zionism, who in his book foreshadowed and stated its main ideas. Then follow passages from Leo Pinsker's *Auto-Emancipation* (no. 79), an analysis of the Jewish situation and a call to action. The new aspirations are further reflected in a manifesto of a group of young students, the "lovers of Zion" (no. 80).

With the publication of *The Jewish State* by Theodor Herzl (no. 81), one may date the birth of modern Zionism. The Zionist Congress which Herzl assembled in Basel, Switzerland, formulated the program and the aims of the movement (no. 82). An American interpretation of these aims is presented by an American Zionist, Richard Gottheil (no. 83), while the Hebrew thinker Ahad Ha-Am places his emphasis on a "spiritual center" (no. 84).

Chaim Weizmann recalls his first meeting with Lord Balfour, the British statesman, in the years before the First World War (no. 85). Balfour, strongly impressed by Weizmann, appreciated and supported Zionist aspirations. The Balfour Declaration (no. 86), issued by the British government during the First World War, held out hope for a Jewish National Home in Palestine. What Weizmann, the eminent Zionist leader, expected from this statement of government policy is revealed in quotations from his speeches (no. 87).

The ideal of labor as one of the main emphases of the Kibbutz movement in the upbuilding of the land is presented by an outstanding thinker, A. D. Gordon (no. 88).

The difficulties involved in trying to carry out the Palestine mandate and the failure to achieve an agreement between the Arabs and the Jews brought the question to the United Nations, which in 1947 decided on the partition of Palestine (nos. 89 and 90). The Provisional Government of

---

*It would go beyond the limits set by the purpose of this source book to discuss in this chapter all topics about Israel, its history, its geography and climate, its population, its political parties, its economic and social structure, its kibbutzim, its schools and universities, etc. There is an abundance of books available on these topics, and they are listed as "Suggested Reading" at the end of this chapter.

Israel issued its Proclamation of Independence (no. 91) and Israel's parliament passed the "Law of Return," which defined the immigration policy of the newly established Israeli government (no. 92).

Hebrew, miraculously revived, became the official language of the new state (no. 93).

The Six-Day War of 1967, which brought occupied territories under Israeli administration and added new phases to the Israel-Arab conflict, is documented by a speech of General Yitzhak Rabin, later Israel's prime minister, by some quoted reflections of Israeli soldiers about the war, and by the Security Council's resolution of November 1967 on the Middle East (nos. 94–96).

The attitude of the Arabs, always extreme in its opposition, became even more so with the rise of the Al Fatah movement, as indicated in the statement of its goals (no. 97).

The fourth Arab-Israeli war of 1973, known as the Yom Kippur War, and some of its effects on Israel are discussed by Hanoch Bartov, an Israeli writer, and several members of kibbutzim (nos. 98–99).

The chapter concludes with an expression of two viewpoints on the Israel-Arab conflict by Albert Hourani, an Arab historian, and J. L. Talmon, a historian at the Hebrew University in Jerusalem (no. 100).

78. THE REAWAKENING

MOSES HESS

Moses Hess (1812–75) was born in Germany but spent most of his life in France. He belonged to the first generation of German Jews who grew up in Western civilization. He received a good Jewish education by studying with his grandfather. As an adult he became active in socialist circles, but later withdrew from the leadership of Marx and Engels, as he no longer shared their views on socialism. He turned once more to Jewish interests and in 1862 published *Rome and Jerusalem*, a classic of Jewish literature and Jewish nationalism. The book was properly appreciated only with the birth of the Zionist movement. The selection which follows is taken from this source.

My Way of Return

After twenty years of estrangement I have returned to my people. Once again I am sharing in its festivals of joy and days of sorrow, in its hopes and memories. I am taking part in the spiritual and intellectual struggles of our day, both within the House of Israel and between our people and the gentile world. The Jews have lived and labored among the nations for almost two thousand years, but nonetheless they cannot become rooted organically within them.

A sentiment which I believed I had suppressed beyond recall is alive once again. It is the thought of my nationality, which is inseparably connected with my ancestral heritage, with the Holy Land and the Eternal City, the birthplace of the belief in the divine unity of life and the hope for the ultimate brotherhood of all men.

For years this half-strangled emotion has been stirring in my breast and clamoring for expression, but I had not the strength to swerve from my own path, which seemed so far from the road of Judaism, to a new one which I could envisage only vaguely in the hazy distance.

As long as the Jew denies his nationality, as long as he lacks the character to acknowledge that he belongs to that unfortunate, persecuted, and maligned people, his false position must become ever more intolerable. What purpose does this deception serve? The nations of Europe have always regarded the existence of the Jews in their midst as an anomaly. We shall always remain strangers among the nations. They may even be moved by a sense of humanity and justice to emancipate us, but they will never respect us as long as we make *ubi bene ibi patria* * our guiding principle, indeed almost a religion, and place it above our own great national memories. Religious fanaticism may cease to cause hatred of the Jews in the more culturally advanced countries; but despite enlightenment and emancipation, the Jew in exile who denies his nationality will never earn the respect of the nations among whom he dwells. He may become a naturalized citizen, but he will never be able to convince the gentiles of his total separation from his own nationality.

The really dishonorable Jew is not the old-type, pious one, who would rather have his tongue cut out than utter a word in denial of his nationality, but the modern kind, who, like the German outcasts in foreign countries, is ashamed of his nationality because the hand of fate is pressing heavily upon his people. The beautiful phrases about humanity and enlighten-ment which he uses so freely to cloak his treason, his fear of being identified with his unfortunate brethren, will ultimately not protect him from the judgment of public opinion. These modern Jews hide in vain behind their geographical and philosophical alibis. You may ask yourself a thousand times over; you may change your name, religion, and character; you may travel through the world incognito, so that people may not recognize the Jew in you; yet every insult to the Jewish name will strike you even more than the honest man who admits his Jewish loyalties and who fights for the honor of the Jewish name.

Ubi bene ibi patria: where things go well for me, there is my fatherland. (Ed.)

The Nation as Part of Humanity

I believe that the national character of Judaism does not exclude universalism and modern civilization; on the contrary, these values are the logical effect of our national character. If I nonetheless emphasize the national root of Judaism rather than its universalist blooms, that is because in our time people are all too prone to gather and deck themselves out with the pretty flowers of the cultural heritage rather than to cultivate them in the soil in which they can grow. Judaism is the root of our whole contemporary universalist view of life. . . . Until the French Revolution, the Jewish people was the only people in the world whose religion was at once nationalist and universalist. It is through Judaism that the history of humanity became a sacred history, by which I mean that history became a unified, organic development which has its origin in the love of the family. The process will not be completed until the whole of humanity becomes one family . . .

The life of man in society begins with a primal differentiation of folk types, which at first, plantlike, existed side by side; then, animal-like, fought each other and destroyed or absorbed one another; but which will finally, in order to attain absolute freedom, live together in friendship and *each for the other*, without surrendering their particular and typical identities . . .

Jewish Restoration

Have you never read the words of the prophet Isaiah?* "Comfort ye, comfort ye My people, saith your God. Bid Jerusalem take heart, and proclaim unto her, that her time of service is accomplished, that her guilt is paid off; that she hath received of the Lord's hand double for all her sins. . . . Clear ye in the wilderness the way of the Lord, make plain in the desert a highway for our God. Every valley shall be lifted up, and every mountain and hill shall be made low; and the rugged shall be made level, and the rough places a plain. And the glory of the Lord shall be revealed, and all flesh shall see it together; for the mouth of the Lord hath spoken it." Do you not believe that in these opening words of the prophecies of Second Isaiah, as well as in the closing verse of the book of Obadiah (I:21), the conditions of our day are depicted? Is not everything being made even and prepared; is not the road of civilization being laid in the desert by the digging of the Suez Canal, and by the work on a railroad which will connect Europe and Asia? To be sure, none of this reflects any intention to re-establish our nation, but you know the proverb: Man proposes and God disposes.

---

*Chapter 40. (Ed.)

What we have to do at present for the regeneration of the Jewish nation is, first, to keep alive the hope of the political rebirth of our people, and, next, to reawaken that hope where it slumbers. When political conditions in the Orient shape themselves so as to permit the organization of a beginning of the restoration of a Jewish state, this beginning will express itself in the founding of Jewish colonies in the land of their ancestors.

Jewish Creativity

. . . The holy spirit, the creative genius of the people, out of which Jewish life and teaching arose, deserted Israel when its children began to feel ashamed of their nationality. But this spirit will again animate our people when it awakens to a new life; it will create new things which we cannot at present even imagine. No one can foretell what form and shape the newborn life and spirit of the regenerated nation will assume. . . .

79. AUTO-EMANCIPATION

LEO PINSKER

Leo Pinsker (1821–91), a successful physician, was born in Poland. In his earlier years he favored assimilation in a liberal Russia. The pogroms of 1881 (see chapter 2), not only the work of an illiterate mob but supported by the press and men of education, shook Pinsker's faith in assimilation as that of many of his contemporaries.

Under the impact of the pogroms, Pinsker wrote in German the pamphlet *Auto-Emancipation: An Appeal to His People by a Russian Jew*. He analyzed the situation of the Jews living in various countries as aliens without a fatherland and exposed to anti-Semitism. The only solution to the Jewish problem, as he saw it, was for the Jews to live concentrated in a country of their own. Although originally not arguing for Palestine, he became a leader of the *Hibbat Zion* (Love of Zion) movement, which came into being in Russia in 1882 and which stimulated groups to begin to settle and to undertake agricultural work in the Holy Land (see no. 80).

"*Auto-Emancipation* is the first great statement of the torment of the Jew driven to assert his own nationalism because the wider world had rejected him. The theme was to recur in Theodor Herzl" (Arthur Hertzberg).

The Jewish Question

The eternal problem presented by the Jewish question stirs men today as it did ages ago. It remains unsolved, like the squaring of the circle, but unlike it, it is still a burning question. This is due to the fact it is not merely a problem of theoretic interest, but one of practical interest, which renews its youth from day to day, as it were, and presses more and more urgently for a solution.

The essence of the problem, as we see it, lies in the fact that, in the midst of the nations among whom the Jews reside, they form a distinctive element which cannot be assimilated, which cannot be readily digested by any nation. Hence the problem is to find means of so adjusting the relations of this exclusive element to the whole body of the nations that there shall never be any further basis for the Jewish question.

We cannot, of course, think of establishing perfect harmony. Such harmony has probably never existed, even among other nations. The millennium in which national differences will disappear, and the nations will merge into humanity, is still invisible in the distance. Until it is realized, the desires and ideals of the nations must be limited to establishing a tolerable modus vivendi. . . .

Without a Center

. . . The Jewish people has no fatherland of its own, though many motherlands; it has no rallying point, no center of gravity, no government of its own, no accredited representatives. It is everywhere a guest, and nowhere *at home*.

The nations *never* have to deal with a Jewish *nation* but always with mere *Jews*. . . .

In seeking to fuse with other peoples, they [the Jews] deliberately renounced, to a certain extent, their own nationality. Nowhere, however, did they succeed in obtaining recognition from their neighbors as native-born citizens of equal rank.

No Desire for National Independence

The strongest factor, however, operating to prevent the Jews from striving after an independent national existence is the fact that they do not feel the need for such an existence. Not only do they feel no need for it, but they go so far as to deny the reasonableness of such a need.

In a sick man, the absence of desire for food and drink is a very serious symptom. It is not always possible to cure him of this ominous loss of appetite. And even if his appetite can be restored, it is still a question whether he will be able to digest food, even though he desires it.

The Jews are in the unhappy condition of such a patient. We must discuss this most important point with all possible precision. We must prove that the misfortunes of the Jews are due, above all, to their lack of desire for national independence; and that this desire must be aroused and maintained in them if they do not wish to exist forever in a disgraceful state—in a word, we must prove that *they must become a nation* . . .

Fear of Jews

Among the living nations of the earth the Jews occupy the position of a nation long since dead. . . .

This ghostlike apparition of a people without unity or organization, without land or other bond of union, no longer alive, and yet moving about among the living—this eerie form scarcely paralleled in history, unlike anything that preceded or followed it, could not fail to make a strange and peculiar impression upon the imagination of the nations. . . .

Fear of the Jewish ghost has been handed down and strengthened for generations and centuries. It led to a prejudice which, in its turn, in connection with other forces to be discussed later, paved the way for Judeophobia [=Fear of Jews].

. . . No matter how much the nations are at variance with one another, no matter how diverse in their instincts and aims, they join hands in their hatred of the Jews; on this one matter all are agreed. The extent and manner in which this antipathy is shown depends, of course, upon the cultural level of each people. The antipathy as such, however, exists in all places and at all times, no matter whether it appears in the form of deeds of violence, as envious jealousy, or under the guise of tolerance and protection. To be robbed as a Jew or to require protection as a Jew is equally humiliating, equally hurtful to the self-respect of the Jews. . . .

Considered an Alien

Since the Jew is nowhere at home, nowhere regarded as a native, he remains an alien everywhere. That he himself and his forefathers as well were born in the country does not alter this fact in the least. Generally, he is treated as an adopted child whose rights may be questioned; never is he considered a legitimate child of the fatherland. The German, proud of his Teutonic character, the Slav, the Celt—not one of them admits that the Semitic Jew is his equal by birth; and even if he be ready, as a man of culture, to admit him to all civil rights; he will never go as far as to forget the Jew in this, his fellow citizen. The *legal emancipation* of the Jews is the crowning achievement of our century. But *legal emancipation* is not *social* emancipation, and with the proclamation of the former the Jews are still far from being emancipated from their exceptional *social position*. . . .

If all the peoples of the earth were not able to blot out our existence, they were nevertheless able to destroy in us the feeling of our national independence. And as for ourselves, we look on with fatalistic indifference when in many a land we are refused a recognition which would not lightly be denied to Zulus. In the dispersion we have maintained our individual life, and proved our power of resistance, but we have lost the common bond of our national consciousness. Seeking to maintain our material existence, we were constrained only too often to forget out moral dignity. We did not see that on account of tactics unworthy of us, which we were forced to adopt, we sank still lower in the eyes of our opponents, that we were only the more exposed to humiliating contempt and outlawry, which have finally become our baleful heritage. In the wide, wide world there was no place for us. We prayed only for a little place anywhere to lay our weary heads to rest; and so, by lessening our claims, we gradually lessened our dignity as well, which was diminished in our own and others' eyes until it became unrecognizable. We were the ball which the peoples tossed in turn to one another. The cruel game was equally amusing whether we were caught or thrown, and was enjoyed all the more, the more elastic and yielding our national respect became in the hands of the peoples. Under such circumstances, how could there be any question of national self-determination, of a free, active development of our national force or of our native genius?

Regaining Independence

. . . Nowadays, when in a small part of the earth our brethren have caught their breath and can feel more deeply for the sufferings of their brothers; nowadays, when a number of other dependent and oppressed nationalities have been allowed to regain their independence—we, too, must not sit even one moment longer with folded hands; we must not admit that we are doomed to play on in the future the hopeless role of the "Wandering Jew." This role is truly hopeless; it is enough to drive one to despair.

If an individual is unfortunate enough to see himself despised and rejected by society, no one wonders if he commits suicide. But where is the deadly weapon to give the *coup de grâce* to all the Jews scattered over the face of the earth, and what hand would offer itself for the work? Such destruction is neither possible nor desirable. Consequently, it is our bounden duty to devote all our remaining moral force to re-establishing ourselves as a living nation, so that we may finally assume a more fitting and dignified role.

We are no more justified in leaving our national fortune entirely in the hands of the other peoples than we are in making them responsible for our national misfortune. The human race, and we as well, have scarcely traversed the first stage of the practice of perfect humanitarianism—if that goal is ever to be reached. Therefore we must abandon the delusive idea that we are fulfilling by our dispersion a Providential mission, a mission in which no one believes, an honorable station which we, to speak frankly, would gladly resign, if the odious epithet "Jew" could only be blotted out of the memory of man.

Restoring National Bond

We must seek our honor and our salvation not in illusory self-deceptions, but in the restoration of a national bond of union. Hitherto the world has not considered us as an enterprise of standing, and consequently, we have enjoyed no decent credit.

If the nationalistic endeavors of the various peoples who have risen to life before our eyes bore their own justification, can it still be questioned whether similar aspirations on the part of the Jews would not be justified? They play a more important part than those peoples in the life of the civilized nations, and they have deserved more from humanity; they have a past, a history, a common, unmixed descent, and an indestructible vigor, an unshakable faith, and an unexampled history of suffering to show; the peoples have sinned against them more grievously than against any other nation. Is not that enough to make them capable and worthy of possessing a fatherland?

One Single Refuge

. . . Of course, the establishment of a Jewish refuge cannot come about without the support of the governments. In order to attain such support and to insure the perpetual existence of a refuge, the creators of our national regeneration will have to proceed with patience and care. What we seek is at bottom neither new nor dangerous to anyone. Instead of the *many refuges* which we have always been accustomed to seek, we would fain have *one single refuge*, the existence of which, however, would have to be politically assured.

Let "Now or never!" be our watchword. Woe to our descendants, woe to the memory of our Jewish contemporaries, if we let this moment pass by!

SUMMARY

The Jews are not a living nation; they are everywhere aliens; therefore they are despised.

The civil and political emancipation of the Jews is not sufficient to raise them in the estimation of the peoples.

The proper and the only remedy would be the creation of a Jewish nationality, of a people living upon its own soil, the auto-emancipation of the Jews; their emancipation as a nation among nations by the acquisition of a home of their own.

We should not persuade ourselves that humanity and enlightenment will ever be radical remedies for the malady of our people.

The lack of national self-respect and self-confidence, of political initiative and of unity, are the enemies of our national renaissance.

In order that we may not be constrained to wander from one exile to another, we must have an extensive and productive place of refuge, a gathering place which is our own.

The present moment is more favorable than any other for realizing the plan here unfolded.

The international Jewish question must receive a national solution. Of course, our national regeneration can only proceed slowly. We must take the first step. Our *descendants* must follow us with a measured and unhurried pace.

A way must be opened for the national regeneration of the Jews by a congress of Jewish notables.

No sacrifice would be too great in order to reach the goal which will assure our people's future, everywhere endangered.

The financial accomplishment of the undertaking can, in the nature of the situation, encounter no insuperable difficulties.

Help yourselves, and God will help you!

80. THE MANIFESTO OF THE BILU

Bilu are the first Hebrew letters in the words of a passage in Isaiah (2:5): "House of Jacob, come let us go." The Biluim, about 500 young people, mainly from the Kharkov region in Russia, were part of a wider movement of "Love of Zion" (*Hibbat Zion*) which had developed in Russia in the early 1880s, mainly under the impact of the pogroms of 1881 (see no. 79). This manifesto was issued by a Bilu group in Constantinople in 1882.

To our brothers and sisters in Exile!

'If I help not myself, who will help me?'

Nearly two thousand years have elapsed since, in an evil hour, after a heroic struggle, the glory of our Temple vanished in fire and our kings and chieftains changed their crowns and diadems for the chains of exile. We lost our country where dwelt our beloved sires. Into the Exile we took with us, of all our glories, only a spark of the fire by which our Temple, the abode of our Great One, was engirdled, and this little spark kept us alive while the towers of our enemies crumbled into dust, and this spark leapt into celestial flame and shed light on the heroes of our race and inspired them to endure the horrors of the dance of death and the tortures of the *autos-da-fé*. And this spark is again kindling and will shine for us, a true pillar of fire going before us on the road to Zion, while behind us is a pillar of cloud, the pillar of oppression threatening to destroy us. Sleepest thou, O our nation? What hast thou been doing until 1882? Sleeping, and dreaming the false dream of Assimilation. Now, thank God, thou art awakened from thy slothful slumber. The Pogroms have awakened thee from thy charmed sleep. Thine eyes are open to recognize the cloudy delusive hopes. Canst thou listen silent to the taunts and mockeries of thine enemies? . . . Where is thy ancient pride, thine olden spirit? Remember that thou wast a nation possessing a wise religion, a law, a constitution, a celestial Temple whose wall is still a silent witness to the glories of the past; that thy sons dwelt in palaces and towers, and thy cities flourished in the splendour of civilization, while these enemies of thine dwelt like beasts in the muddy marshes of their dark woods. While thy children were clad in purple and fine linen, they wore the rough skins of the wolf and the bear. Art thou not ashamed?

Hopeless is your state in the West; the star of your future is gleaming in the East. Deeply conscious of all this, and inspired by the true teaching of our great master, Hillel, 'If I help not myself, who will help me?' we propose to form the following society for national ends.

1. The Society will be named 'Bilu', according to the motto 'House of Jacob, come, let us go'. It will be divided into local branches according to the numbers of its members.

2. The seat of the Committee shall be Jerusalem.

3. Donations and contributions shall be unfixed and unlimited.

We Want:

1. A home in our country. It was given us by the mercy of God; it is ours as registered in the archives of history.

2. To beg it of the Sultan himself, and if it be impossible to obtain this, to beg that we may at least possess it as a state within a larger state; the internal administration to be ours, to have our civil and political rights, and to act with the Turkish Empire only in foreign affairs, so as to help our brother Ishmael in the time of his need.

We hope that the interests of our glorious nation will rouse the national spirit in rich and powerful men, and that everyone, rich or poor, will give his best labours to the holy cause.

Greetings, dear brothers and sisters!

Hear, O Israel! The Lord our God, the Lord is one, and our land Zion is our one hope.

God be with us! THE PIONEERS OF BILU.

81. THE JEWISH STATE

THEODOR HERZL

Theodor Herzl (1860–1904) was born in Budapest, Hungary, studied law in Vienna, and became a successful journalist and writer of feuilletons (short essays), plays, etc. As Paris correspondent of the Vienna newspaper *Neue Freie Presse*, he witnessed the Dreyfus affair and had to report on the trial to his newspaper. In 1894, Alfred Dreyfus, a captain in the French army, was accused of spying for Germany. Herzl was present when Dreyfus was condemned, stripped of his epaulettes, drummed out in disgrace with the shouts of the mob, "Down with the Jews." This event was the turning point in Herzl's life and resulted in his becoming a Zionist.

Herzl wrote the booklet *The Jewish State*, which was published in 1896 and contained what became the Zionist program. His Jewish knowledge at the time was scant, and when he wrote the booklet he did not know of people like Hess and Pinsker, who had preceded him, nor of the *Hibbat Zion* movement which had developed in Russia (see nos. 78–80). In answer to his call, close to two hundred delegates from all over the world assembled in 1897 in Basel, Switzerland to found the World Zionist Organization. This congress, as it was called, formulated the aims of the organization (no. 81).

During the few remaining years of his life—he died young and exhausted at the age of forty-four—Herzl devoted all of his strength to the Zionist Movement. In contrast to the Hibbat Zion movement, he emphasized political action and diplomatic negotiations. Thus he met with the leaders of nations like the sultan of Turkey, the German emperor, the king of Italy, and Pope Pius X. He wrote for *Die Welt* (The World), the official organ of the World Zionist Organization, extensive diaries and a novel, *The Old-New World*.

In his diary Herzl entered the notation: "In Basel I created the Jewish State. Were I to say this aloud I would be greeted by universal laughter. But five years hence, certainly fifty years hence, everyone will perceive it." In 1949 his remains were flown from Vienna to the Jewish country which his dream helped to create.

The following selection is taken from his book *The Jewish State*.

Introduction

The idea which I have developed in this pamphlet is an ancient one: it is the restoration of the Jewish State.

The world resounds with clamor against the Jews, and this has revived the dormant idea. . . .

The Jewish question still exists. It would be foolish to deny it. It is a misplaced piece of medievalism, which civilized nations do not even yet seem able to shake off, try as they will. They proved they had this high-minded desire when they emancipated us. The Jewish question persists wherever Jews live in appreciable numbers . . .

Anti-Semitism is a highly complex movement, which I think I understand. I approach this movement as a Jew, yet without fear or hatred. I believe that I can see in it the elements of cruel sport, of common commercial rivalry, of inherited prejudice, of religious intolerance—but also of a supposed need for self-defense.

I consider the Jewish question neither a social nor a religious one, even though it sometimes takes these and other forms. It is a national question, and to solve it we must first of all establish it as an international political problem to be discussed and settled by the civilized nations of the world in council.

We are a people—one people.

We have sincerely tried everywhere to merge with the national communities in which we live, seeking only to preserve the faith of our fathers. It is not permitted us. In vain are we loyal patriots, sometimes superloyal; in vain do we make the same sacrifices of life and property as our fellow citizens; in vain do we strive to enhance the fame of our native lands in the arts and sciences, or her wealth by trade and commerce. In our native lands where we have lived for centuries we are still decried as aliens, often by men whose ancestors had not yet come at a time when Jewish sighs had long been heard in the country. The majority decide who the "alien" is; this, and all else in the relations between peoples, is a matter of power. I do not surrender any part of our prescriptive right when I make this statement merely in my own name, as an individual. In the world as it now is and will probably remain, for an indefinite period, might takes precedence over right. It is without avail, therefore, for us to be loyal patriots, as were the Huguenots, who were forced to emigrate. If we were left in peace . . .

But I think we shall not be left in peace.

Oppression and persecution cannot exterminate us. No nation on earth has endured such struggles and sufferings as we have. Jew-baiting has merely winnowed out our weaklings; the strong among us defiantly return to their own whenever persecution breaks out. This was most clearly apparent in the period immediately following the emancipation of the Jews. Those Jews who rose highest intellectually and materially entirely lost the sense of unity with their people. Wherever we remain politically secure for any length of time, we assimilate. I think this is not unpraiseworthy. . . .

Although I speak here in terms of reason, I am well aware that reason alone will not suffice. Long-term prisoners do not willingly quit their cells. We shall see whether the youth, whom we must have, is ripe; the youth—which irresistibly draws along the aged, bears them up on powerful arms, and transforms rationality into enthusiasm . . .

The Plan

The whole plan is essentially quite simple, as it must necessarily be if it is to be comprehensible to all. Let sovereignty be granted us over a portion of the globe adequate to meet our rightful national requirements; we will attend to the rest.

To create a new State is neither ridiculous nor impossible. Haven't we witnessed the process in our own day, among nations which were not largely middle class as we are, but poorer, less educated, and consequently weaker than ourselves? The governments of all countries scourged by anti-Semitism will be keenly interested in obtaining sovereignty for us.

The plan, simple in design but complicated in execution, will be executed by two agencies: the Society of Jews and the Jewish Company.

The scientific plan and political policies which the Society of Jews will establish will be carried out by the Jewish Company.

The Jewish Company will be the liquidating agent for the business interests of departing Jews, and will organize trade and commerce in the new country.

We must not visualize the exodus of the Jews as a sudden one. It will be gradual, proceeding over a period of decades. The poorest will go first and cultivate the soil. They will construct roads, bridges, railways, and telegraph installations, regulate rivers, and provide themselves with homesteads, all according to predetermined plans. Their labor will create trade, trade will create markets, and markets will attract new settlers—for every man will go voluntarily, at his own expense and his own risk. The labor invested in the soil will enhance its value. The Jews will soon perceive that a new and permanent frontier has been opened up for that spirit of enterprise which has heretofore brought them only hatred and obloquy. . . .

If we planned to erect buildings, we should not drive a few shaky piles in a marsh like the lake dwellers, but should build as men build now. Indeed, we shall build in bolder and more stately style than has ever been done before; for we now possess means which heretofore did not exist.

The emigrants standing lowest in the economic scale will be gradually followed by those of the next grade. Those now in desperate straits will go first. They will be led by the intellectual mediocrities whom we produce so abundantly and who are oppressed everywhere.

Let this pamphlet serve as the beginning of a general discussion on the question of Jewish emigration. That does not mean to suggest, however, that the question should be called to a vote. Such an approach would ruin the cause from the outset. Whoever wishes may stay behind. The opposition of a few individuals is quite immaterial.

Who would go with us, let him fall in behind our banner and fight for the cause with word and pen and deed.

Those Jews who agree with our State idea will rally around the Society. Thereby they will give it the authority in the eyes of governments to confer and treat on behalf of our people. The Society will be recognized as, to put it in terminology of international law, a State-creating power. And this recognition will, in effect, mean the creation of the State.

Should the powers show themselves willing to grant us sovereignty over a neutral land, then the Society will enter into negotiations for the possession of this land. Here two regions come to mind: Palestine and Argentina. . . .

Palestine or Argentina?

Is Palestine or Argentina preferable? The Society will take whatever it is given and whatever Jewish public opinion favors. The Society will determine both these points.

Argentina is one of the most fertile countries in the world, extends over a vast area, is sparsely populated, and has a temperate climate. It would be in its own highest interest for the Republic of Argentina to cede us a portion of its territory. The present *infiltration* of Jews has certainly produced some discontent, and it would be necessary to enlighten the Republic on the intrinsic difference of the new *immigration* of Jews.

Palestine is our unforgettable historic homeland. The very name would be a marvelously effective rallying cry. If His Majesty the Sultan were to give us Palestine, we could in return undertake the complete management of the finances of Turkey. We should there form a part of a wall of defense for Europe in Asia, an outpost of civilization against barbarism. We should as a neutral state remain in contact with all Europe, which would have to guarantee our existence. The holy places of Christendom could be placed under some form of international exterritoriality. We should form a guard of honor about these holy places, answering for the fulfillment of this duty with our existence. The guard of honor would be the great symbol of the solution of the Jewish question after what were for us eighteen centuries of affliction.

82. THE ZIONIST PROGRAM

The official statement of Zionist purpose was adopted by the First Zionist Congress in Basel in 1897.

Zionism strives to create for the Jewish people a home in Palestine secured by public law.

For the attainment of this aim the Congress contemplates the following means:

1. The promotion, on suitable lines, of the settlement of Palestine by Jewish agricultural and industrial workers.

2. The organization and unification of the whole of Jewry by means of appropriate local and general institutions in accordance with the laws of each country.

3. The strengthening of Jewish national sentiment and consciousness.

4. Preparatory steps toward securing the consent of governments necessary for the attainment of the aim of Zionism.

83. THE AIMS OF ZIONISM

RICHARD J. H. GOTTHEIL

In contrast to many of his fellow workers in Zionism, Chaim Arlosoroff (1899–1933), a Zionist labor leader, who became head of the Jewish Agency's Political Department, believed that American Jewry represented something new in Jewish history and different from any of the Jewries of modern Europe: "One must judge the new Jewry in America as a different kind of historical phenomenon, a unicum, which has no precedent in the history of our people . . . for it lives and is developing under unique conditions which have never existed before and which cannot recur. Consequently, new forces and forms of life are arising, the likes of which have never existed and will never again exist, and which are, therefore, not to be compared with any others. These are forces and forms in which a new Jewish life is coming to bloom."*

This observation may be helpful in understanding the philosophy of American Zionism and the ensuing debates whether Zionism means total abandonment by Jews of the countries of the Western world and whether as a Zionist one was unpatriotic to the country of which he was a citizen.

The "reworking" of Herzl's Zionism in the light of the American experience is apparent in the selection which follows taken from the pamphlet *The Aims of Zionism* published in 1898 by Richard J. H. Gottheil (1862–1936), the first president of the Federation of American Zionists. Richard Gottheil was a distinguished scholar, professor at Columbia University, and director of the Oriental Department of the New York Public Library. Like his father, Gustav Gottheil, rabbi of the Reform Temple Emanu-El in New York, he belonged to the small group of intellectual "westerners" who had joined Zionism.

A professor at the University of Vienna has recently said: "The best way to protect ourselves from the Jews is to shoot them off." I admit, this is a practical solution; I will even say, a magnanimous one in very many cases. But such stoic magnanimity is not for us who are of their flesh and of their blood. If we are to save these Jews—and mind you we are here speaking of fully three-quarters of the Jewish people—we must take them out of the places in which it has become impossible for them to live. Whatever our own personal consideration may be, whether we like it or not, we dare not leave these unfortunates to their fate. Every fiber in our body cries "shame" to the very suggestion that we adopt such a course as that. What then? . . . The history of the Jews is but the log of a storm-tossed ship which can find no rest until it gets back again into the haven from which it started.

That haven from which it started was Palestine; and to that haven it must again come; to that haven, protected by the international guarantees which will keep the waves from once more touching our ship. And all through the

---

*Quoted in Hertzberg, *The Zionist Idea*, p. 87.

Jewish Middle Ages, though the ship has been forced westward, the hearts of those who were in it have turned in secret longing and in public prayer to this place of rest. Though the Jew clothed this hope in his Messianic Prophetism, it was no less of a real hope. . . .

. . . Zionism . . . wishes to give back to the Jew that nobleness of spirit, that confidence in himself, that belief in his own powers which only perfect freedom can give. With a home of his own, he will no longer feel himself a pariah among the nations, he will nowhere hide his own peculiarities—peculiarities to which he has a right as much as any one—but will see that those peculiarities carry with them a message which will force for them the admiration of the world. He will feel that he belongs somewhere and not everywhere. He will try to be something and not everything. The great word which Zionism preaches is conciliation of conflicting aims, of conflicting lines of action; conciliation of Jew to Jew. It means conciliation of the non-Jewish world to the Jew as well. It wishes to heal old wounds; and by frankly confessing differences which do exist, however much we try to explain them away, to work out its own salvation upon its own ground, and from these to send forth its spiritual message to a conciliated world.

But, you will ask, if Zionism is able to find a permanent home in Palestine for those Jews who are forced to go there as well as those who wish to go, what is to become of us who have entered, to such a degree, into the life around us and who feel able to continue as we have begun? What is to be our relation to the new Jewish polity? I can only answer, exactly the same as is the relation of people of other nationalities all the world over to their parent home. What becomes of the Englishman in every corner of the globe; what becomes of the German? Does the fact that the great mass of their people live in their own land prevent them from doing their whole duty toward the land in which they happen to live? Is the German-American considered less of an American because he cultivates the German language and is interested in the fate of his fellow Germans at home? Is the Irish-American less of an American because he gathers money to help his struggling brethren in the Green Isle? Or are the Scandinavian-Americans less worthy of the title Americans because they consider precious the bonds which bind them to the land of their birth, as well as those which bind them to the land of their adoption?

Nay! it would seem to me that just those who are so afraid that our action will be misinterpreted should be among the greatest helpers in the Zionist cause. For those who feel no racial and national communion with the life from which they have sprung should greet with joy the turning of Jewish immigration to some place other than the land in which they dwell. They must feel, e.g., that a continual influx of Jews who are not Americans is a continual menace to the more or less complete absorption for which they are striving.

But I must not detain you much longer. Will you permit me to sum up for you the position which we Zionists take in the following statements:

We believe that the Jews are something more than a purely religious body; that they are not only a race, but also a nation; though a nation without as yet two important requisites—a common home and a common language.

We believe that if an end is to be made to Jewish misery and to the exceptional position which the Jews occupy—which is the primary cause of Jewish misery—the Jewish nation must be placed once again in a home of its own.

We believe that such a national regeneration is the fulfillment of the hope which has been present to the Jew throughout his long and painful history.

We believe that only by means of such a national regeneration can the religious regeneration of the Jews take place, and they be put in a position to do that work in the religious world which Providence has appointed for them.

We believe that such a home can only naturally, and without violence to their whole past, be found in the land of their fathers—in Palestine.

We believe that such a return must have the guarantee of the great powers of the world, in order to secure for the Jews a stable future.

And we hold that this does not mean that all Jews must return to Palestine.

This, ladies and gentlemen, is the Zionist program.

We take hope, for has not that Jewish Zionist said, "We belong to a race that can do everything but fail."

84. A SPIRITUAL CENTER

AHAD HA-AM

Ahad Ha-Am (Asher Ginsberg, 1856–1927), Hebrew essayist, thinker, and leader of the *Hibbat Zion* movement (see nos. 79 and 80), emphasized "cultural" rather than "political" Zionism. He wrote many essays on Judaism, its thought and philosophy. He was very influential, and was considered by Bialik and other eminent Jewish writers and leaders as their "teacher." The selection is taken from an essay written in 1907.

"A *centre* of our nationality" implies that there is a national *circumference*, which, like every circumference, is much larger than the centre. That is to say, the speaker sees the majority of his people, in the future as in the past, scattered all over the world, but no longer broken up into a number of disconnected parts, because one part—the one in Palestine—will be a centre for them all and make them all into a single, complete circumference. When all the scattered limbs of the national body feel the beating of the national heart, restored to life in its native home, they too will once again draw near to one another and welcome the inrush of living blood that flows from the heart.

"Spiritual" means that this relation of centre and circumference between Palestine and the lands of the diaspora will of necessity be limited to the spiritual side of life. The influence of the centre will strengthen the Jewish national consciousness in the diaspora; it will restore our independence of mind and self-respect; it will give to our Judaism a national content which will be genuine and natural, unlike the substitutes with which we now try to fill the void.

85. MY FIRST MEETING WITH LORD BALFOUR

CHAIM WEIZMANN

In 1903 the British government proposed to the Zionist Organization to establish an autonomous Jewish colony in British East Africa. The proposal became known as the "Uganda scheme." To relieve the pressure on Russian Jewry, especially after the Kishinev pogrom in 1903, a temporary asylum was by some Zionists felt to be necessary. The Zionist Congress opposed the plan and ultimately rejected it in 1905.

In the selection which follows, taken from his autobiography, Weizmann tells how he met Lord Balfour, the British statesman, for the first time and explained to him the meaning of Zionism and the reason for the rejection of a refuge in Africa. On Weizmann see the prefatory note to no. 37.

I was brought in to Balfour in a room in the old-fashioned Queen's Hotel, on Piccadilly, which served as his headquarters. The corridors were crowded with people waiting for a word with the candidate. I surmised that Mr. Balfour had consented to see me for a few minutes—'a quarter of an hour,' Dreyfus warned me—simply to break the monotony of his routine. He kept me for well over an hour. . . .

I had been less than two years in the country, and my English was still not easy to listen to. I remember how Balfour sat in his usual pose, his legs stretched out in front of him, an imperturbable expression on his face. We plunged at once into the subject of our interview. He asked me why some Jews, Zionists, were so bitterly opposed to the Uganda offer. The British Government was really anxious to do something to relieve the misery of the Jews; and the problem was a practical one, calling for a practical approach. In reply I plunged into what I recall as a long harangue on the meaning of the Zionist movement. I dwelt on the spiritual side of Zionism, I pointed out that nothing but a deep religious conviction expressed in modern political terms could keep the movement alive, and that this conviction had to be based on Palestine and on Palestine alone. . . .

. . . "I looked at my listener, and suddenly became afraid that this apparent interest and courtesy might be nothing more than a mask. I remember that I was sweating blood and I tried to find some less ponderous way of expressing myself. I was ready to bow myself out of the room, but Balfour held me back, and put some questions to me regarding the growth of the movement. He had heard of 'Dr. Herzl'—a very distinguished leader, who had founded and organized it. I ventured to correct him, pointing out that Herzl had indeed placed the movement on a new footing, and had given the tradition a modern political setting; but Herzl had died young; and he had left us this legacy of Uganda, which we were trying to liquidate.

Then suddenly I said: "Mr. Balfour, supposing I were to offer you Paris instead of London, would you take it?"

He sat up, looked at me, and answered: "But, Dr. Weizmann, we have London."

"That is true," I said. "But we had Jerusalem when London was a marsh."

He leaned back, continued to stare at me, and said two things which I remember vividly. The first was: "Are there many Jews who think like you?"

I answered: "I believe I speak the mind of millions of Jews whom you will never see and who cannot speak for themselves, but with whom I could pave the streets of the country I come from."

To this he said: "If that is so, you will one day be a force."

Shortly before I withdrew, Balfour said: "It is curious. The Jews I meet are quite different."

I answered: "Mr. Balfour, you meet the wrong kind of Jews."

86. THE BALFOUR DECLARATION

ARTHUR JAMES BALFOUR

Arthur James Balfour (1848–1930), British statesman and philosopher, began to take an interest in the Jewish question in 1902–03, when Herzl conducted negotiations with the British government on possible settlement in British East Africa (see no. 85). When he met Weizmann in later years, he was strongly impressed by him and developed sympathy for Zionist aspirations. The British

statement, known as the Balfour Declaration, was the result of long
negotiations initiated by Weizmann and others at the end of 1914 during World
War I. In 1917 President Wilson, influenced by the thinking and persuasion of
Brandeis, agreed to the proposed declaration, which hastened its approval by
the British government.

The Balfour Declaration was made known in the form of a letter by Balfour to
Lord Lionel Walter Rothschild.

Foreign Office
November 2nd, 1917.

Dear Lord Rothschild,

I have much pleasure in conveying to you, on behalf of His Majesty's
Government, the following declaration of sympathy with Jewish Zionist
aspirations which has been submitted to, and approved by, the Cabinet.

"His Majesty's Government view with favour the establishment in
Palestine of a national home for the Jewish people, and will use their best
endeavours to facilitate the achievement of this object, it being clearly
understood that nothing shall be done which may prejudice the civil and
religious rights of existing non-Jewish communities in Palestine, or the
rights and political status enjoyed by Jews in any other country."

I should be grateful if you would bring this declaration to the knowledge
of the Zionist Federation.

Yours sincerely,
ARTHUR JAMES BALFOUR.

87. DEFINITIONS AND STATEMENTS

CHAIM WEIZMANN

On Weizmann see no. 37.

A Jewish State

I trust to God that a Jewish state will come about; but it will come about not
through political declarations, but by the sweat and blood of the Jewish
people. That is the only way of building up a state. No other way is known
to me in all the history of the world. What I say is that it is the golden key
which unlocks the doors of Palestine and gives you the possibility to put
all your effort into that country. . . . (1919)

Foundation of Zionism

We have never based the Zionist movement on Jewish suffering in
Russia or in any other land. These sufferings have never been the

mainspring of Zionism. The foundation of Zionism was, and continues to be to this day, the yearning of the Jewish people for its homeland, for a national center and a national life. (1917)

The Joy of Creation

All over the world we Jews have shown a wonderful capacity for adaptation. We have come to the United States, we have adapted ourselves to this civilization, to this organism, and we have performed wonderful work. We have come to other countries, good and bad, and we have adapted ourselves to their respective organisms. But wherever we came we found the organism ready, we found the laws, the language, the civilization. What we had to do was adapt ourselves, and adapt ourselves well.

There is a difference in Palestine. There, nothing is ready. Everything is yet to be done, and we are at present building a country from its very rock elements, from the field to the orchard, from the village to the town, from the kindergarten to the university. From these new elements a new life is being built up, and it is this great joy of creation which today pulsates through world Jewry. And this is why a little house in Palestine, a book published in Palestine, makes this peculiar appeal to you. This is the fundamental difference between what is happening in Palestine and what is happening to us all over the world, and this difference is a challenge and a call. (1923)

88. PEOPLE AND LABOR

AARON DAVID GORDON

Aaron David Gordon (1856–1922), Hebrew writer and thinker, guided the wing of the Zionist labor movement which emphasized self-realization through settlement on the land and thus engaging in farming. Although he had never done physical work, he settled in Palestine in 1904, at the age of forty-eight, and insisted on doing the regular work of a farmer, which meant tilling the soil. He wrote numerous articles in which he expressed his outlook on labor and Zionism, which came to be known as the "religion of labor."
The selection is taken from an article written in 1911.

The Jewish people has been completely cut off from nature and imprisoned within city walls these two thousand years. We have become accustomed to every form of life, except to a life of labor—labor done at our own behest and for its own sake. It will require the greatest effort of will for such a people to become normal again. We lack the principal ingredient for national life. We lack the habit of labor—not labor performed out of external compulsion, but labor to which one is attached in a natural and organic way. This kind of labor binds a people to its soil and to its national culture, which in turn is an outgrowth of the people's soil and the people's labor.

Now it is true that every people has many individuals who shun physical labor and try to live off the work of others. But a normal people is like a living organism which performs its various functions naturally, and labor is one of its basic and organic functions. A normal people invariably contains a large majority of individuals for whom labor is second nature. But we Jews are different. We have developed an attitude of looking down on manual labor, so that even those who are engaged in it work of mere compulsion and always with the hope of eventually escaping to "a better life." . . .

What are we seeking in Palestine? Is it not that which we can never find elsewhere—the fresh milk of a healthy people's culture? What we are come to create at present is not the culture of the academy, before we have anything else, but a culture of life, of which the culture of the academy is only one element. We seek to create a vital culture out of which the cream of a higher culture can easily be evolved. We intend to create creeds and ideologies, art and poetry, and ethics and religion, all growing out of a healthy life and intimately related to it: we shall therefore have created healthy human relationships and living links that bind the present to the past. What we seek to create here is life—our own life—in our own spirit and in our own way. Let me put it more bluntly: In Palestine we must do with our own hands all the things that make up the sum total of life. We must ourselves do all the work, from the least strenuous, cleanest and most sophisticated, to the dirtiest and most difficult. In our own way, we must feel what a worker feels and think what a worker thinks—then, and only then, shall we have a culture of our own, for then we shall have a life of our own.

It all seems very clear: From now on our principal ideal must be Labor. Through no fault of our own we have been deprived of this element and we must seek a remedy. Labor is our cure. The ideal of Labor must become the pivot of all our aspirations. It is the foundation upon which our national structure is to be erected. Only by making Labor, for its own sake, our national ideal shall we be able to cure ourselves of the plague that has affected us for many generations and mend the rent between ourselves and nature. Labor is a great human ideal. It is the ideal of the future, and a great ideal can be a healing sun. Though the purpose of history is not, to be sure, to act the teacher, still the wise can and must learn from it. We can learn from our condition in the past and in the present, for we must now set the example for the future. We must all work with our hands.

We need a new spirit for our national renaissance. That new spirit must be created here in Palestine and must be nourished by our life in Palestine. It must be vital in all its aspects, and it must be all our own.

What we need is zealots of Labor—zealots in the finest sense of the word.

Any man who devotes his life to this ideal will not need to be told how difficult it is, but he will also know that it is of immense importance.

89. THE UNITED NATIONS DECIDES ON A JEWISH STATE

CHAIM WEIZMANN

In 1922, after World War I, the League of Nations assigned to Britain the mandate to administer the territory of Palestine, formerly a part of the Turkish Empire. The mandate reaffirmed the Balfour Declaration (no. 86). As a result of the new possibilities that Palestine offered, Jewish immigration to Palestine increased. At the same time Arab opposition to Jewish immigration became stronger and there were frequent riots (in 1920–21, 1929, 1933, 1936–39). The British began to curtail Jewish immigration and in 1939 decided that Palestine was to have a permanent Arab majority. This policy led to strong opposition by Jews and active organized resistance after World War II. The British referred the future of the country to the United Nations, which on November 29, 1947 decided to partition it into separate Arab and Jewish states. Although the decision was violently opposed by the Arabs in Palestine and their supporters in the neighboring Arab countries, the State of Israel, as it was called, was established by the Jews in Palestine on May 14, 1948.

The selection as well as the following, no. 90, are taken from Weizmann's autobiography, *Trial and Error*. On Weizmann see no. 37.

The official pleading of our cause before the United Nations was conducted with great skill and energy by Mr. Moshe Shertok, the head of the Political Department of the Jewish Agency for Palestine, and Dr. Abba Hillel Silver, the head of the American Section of the Jewish Agency, but many American Jews who until recently were remote from the Zionist movement took a keen interest in the United Nations discussion and helped us in the work. Foremost among the organizations not affiliated with the Zionist Movement, whose help was generous and constant, was the B'nai B'rith, first under the leadership of the late Henry Monsky, and later, his successor, Frank Goldman. There was a welcome and striking change in the attitude of the American Jewish Committee, under the leadership of Judge Joseph M. Proskauer. Mr. Bernard Baruch and Mr. Herbert Bayard Swope, particularly the latter, who visited me frequently, were helpful among the various delegations. Among the younger men there were George Backer and Edward M. Warburg, of whom the latter had inherited from his father a deep interest in Jewish affairs, and has come very close to the Zionist ideology. Of particular assistance was Mr. Henry Morgenthau, Jr., with whom I had been privileged to come in contact some years before, when he was a member of the Roosevelt administration. This contact continued after he left the Cabinet and was strengthened when he became chairman of the United Jewish Appeal—a responsibility which he took very seriously, like everything else to which he devotes his attention. All these names, and many others which could be added, especially my good friend, Edward Jacobson, of Kansas City, make up an astonishing demonstration of the unity of American Jewry with regard to the Jewish National Home; it is in reality a fulfilment of what I had striven for in my old plans for the Jewish Agency.

There were many tense moments preceding the final decision on November 29, and these had to do not only with the probable votes of the delegates. There was, for instance, the actual territorial division. When this was discussed some of the American delegates felt that the Jews were getting too large a slice of Palestine, and that the Arabs might legitimately raise objections. It was proposed to cut out from the proposed Jewish State a considerable part of the Negev, taking Akaba away from us. Ever since the time of the Balfour Declaration I had attached great value to Akaba and the region about it. I had circumnavigated the gulf of Akaba as far back as 1918, when I went to see the Emir Feisal, and I had a notion of the character of the country. At present it looks a forbidding desert, and the scene of desolation masks the importance of the region. But with a little imagination it becomes quite clear that Akaba is the gate to the Indian Ocean, and constitutes a much shorter route from Palestine to the Far East than via Port Said and the Suez Canal.

I was somewhat alarmed when I learned, in the second week of November, that the American delegation, in its desire to find a compromise which would be more acceptable to the Arabs, advocated the excision of the southern part of the Negev, including Akaba. After consultation with members of the Jewish Agency Executive, I decided to go to Washington to see President Truman and to put the whole case before him.

On the morning of Wednesday, November 19, I was received by the President with the utmost cordiality. I spoke first of the Negev as a whole, which I believe is destined to become an important part of the Jewish State. The northern part, running from Gaza to Asluj or Beersheba, is beautiful country. It needs water, of course, which can either be brought from the North, as projected in the Lowdermilk scheme, or provided locally by desalting the brackish water which is found in abundance in these parts. We are, in fact, busily engaged in our Rehovoth Institute in experiments on the second alternative, and have succeeded in producing drinking water at an economic price; the question of larger quantities for irrigation still needs study. The settlements which are already receiving water from a pipe line are showing remarkable results. Mr. Henry A. Wallace, who had recently returned from a visit to the Negev, was struck by a great plantation of carrots, which had been preceded on the same soil by a good crop of potatoes, while near by there was a plantation of bananas. All this seems fantastic when one takes into account that there has not been a blade of grass in this part of the world for thousands of years. But it is, as I told the President, in line with what the Jews have done in many other parts of Palestine.

I then spoke of Akaba. I pleaded that if there was to be a division of the Negev, it ought to be vertical and not horizontal; this would be eminently fair, giving both sides part of the fertile soil and part of the desert. But for us it was imperative that in this division Akaba should go to the Jewish State. Akaba is at present a useless bay; it needs to be dredged, deepened and made into a waterway capable of accommodating ships of sizeable dimensions. If Akaba were taken away from us, it would always remain a desert, or at any rate for a very long time to come. As part of the Jewish State it will very quickly become an object of development, and would make a real contribution to trade and commerce by opening up a new route. One can foresee the day when a canal will be cut from some part of the eastern Mediterranean coast to Akaba. It is not an easy undertaking, but it has already been adumbrated by American and Swedish engineers. This would become a parallel highway to the Suez Canal, and could shorten the routes from Europe to India by a day or more.

I pleaded further with the President that if the Egyptians choose to be hostile to the Jewish State, which I hope will not be the case, they can close navigation to us through the Suez Canal when this becomes their property, as it will in a few years. The Iraqis, too, can make it difficult for us to pass through the Persian Gulf. Thus we might be cut off entirely from the Orient. We could meet such an eventuality by building our own canal from Haifa or Tel Aviv to Akaba. The project has a great many attractive possibilities; and the mere fact that such a thing could be done would probably serve as a deterrent against closing the road to India for the Jews. I was extremely happy to find that the President read the map very quickly and very clearly. He promised me that he would communicate at once with the American delegation at Lake Success.

At about three o'clock in the afternoon of the same day, Ambassador Herschel Johnson, head of the American delegation, called in Mr. Shertock of the Jewish Agency in order to advise him of the decision on the Negev, which by all indications excluded Akaba from the Jewish State. Shortly after Mr. Shertock entered, but before the subject was broached, the American delegates were called to the telephone. At the other end of the

wire was the President of the United States, telling them that he
considered the proposal to keep Akaba within the Jewish State a
reasonable one, and that they should go forward with it. When Mr. Johnson
and General Hilldring emerged from the telephone booth after a half-hour
conversation, they returned to Mr. Shertok, who was waiting for them,
tense with anxiety. All they had for him was the casual remark: "Oh, Mr.
Shertok, we really haven't anything important to tell you." Obviously the
President had been as good as his word, and a few short hours after I had
seen him had given the necessary instructions to the American delegation.

This decision opened the way to the vote of the General Assembly on
November 29, when, by a majority of thirty-three to thirteen, the United
Nations declared: "The Mandate for Palestine shall terminate as soon as
possible, but in any case not later than August first, 1948. . . . Independent
Arab and Jewish States, and the specific international regime for the City of
Jerusalem . . . shall come into existence in Palestine two months after the
evacuation of the armed forces of the Mandatory Power has been
completed, but in any case no later than October first, 1948."

90. THE UNITED STATES RECOGNIZES THE STATE OF ISRAEL

CHAIM WEIZMANN

The United Nations resumed the debate on Palestine in the months following
its vote for the termination of the British mandate and for partitioning the
country into separate Arab and Jewish states. Because of the violence of Arab
resistance and the threat of the invasion of Palestine by the neighboring Arab
countries, plans were advanced for an international "trusteeship" of Palestine
which would nullify the U.N. decision of November 29. 1947. Dr. Weizmann
was urged to refrain from proclaiming Jewish independence and statehood,
but he stood firm. As American support, previously assured, seemed to waver,
Weizmann undertook the steps described in the following selection.

Many friends and colleagues thought I was being somewhat less than
realistic, and tried to dissuade me from encouraging a step which in their
opinion could only end in retreat and disaster. They expressed astonishment at what they called my unwonted intransigence. In Palestine, where
the doubts and hesitations which reigned at Lake Success found no echo,
there was no thought of relinquishing the rights conferred on us, and by a
suicidal act of self-denial refusing statehood; or, if there was any doubt, it
was connected with our intentions in America rather than with those of the
Palestinian Jews. In the general breakdown of British administration, there
was a period when communications between America and Palestine were

irregular and unreliable. Our views at the American end were not at all clear to the *Yishuv*. Mr. Ben-Gurion, the chairman of the Jewish Agency Executive, was trying, without success, to ascertain exactly where I stood. In the early part of May, Mr. Shertok left for Palestine to clear matters up, and in the second week of that month I strengthened our contacts with our friends in Washington, and affirmed my intention of going ahead with a bid for recognition of the Jewish State as soon as it was proclaimed. On May 13 I addressed the following letter to the President of the United States:

Dear Mr. President:

The unhappy events of the last few months will not, I hope, obscure the very great contributions which you, Mr. President, have made toward a definitive and just settlement of the long and troublesome Palestine question. The leadership which the American Government took under your inspiration made possible the establishment of a Jewish State, which I am convinced will contribute markedly toward a solution of the world Jewish problem, and which I am equally convinced is a necessary preliminary to the development of lasting peace among the peoples of the Near East.

So far as practical conditions in Palestine would permit, the Jewish people there have proceeded along the lines laid down in the United Nations Resolution of November 29, 1947. Tomorrow midnight, May 15, the British Mandate will be terminated, and the Provisional Government of the Jewish State, embodying the best endeavors of the Jewish people and arising from the Resolution of the United Nations, will assume full responsibility for preserving law and order within the boundaries of the Jewish State, for defending that area against external aggression, and for discharging the obligations of the Jewish State to the other nations of the world in accordance with international law.

Considering all the difficulties, the chances for an equitable adjustment of Arab and Jewish relationship are not unfavorable. What is required now is an end to the seeking of new solutions which invariably have retarded rather than encouraged a final settlement.

It is for these reasons that I deeply hope that the United States, which under your leadership has done so much to find a just solution, will promptly recognize the Provisional Government of the new Jewish State. The world, I think, will regard it as especially appropriate that the greatest living democracy should be the first to welcome the newest into the family of nations.

Respectfully yours,

CHAIM WEIZMANN

On the fourteenth of May the President and his advisers were in constant consultation on the Palestine issue. The Assembly of the United Nations had neither revoked nor reaffirmed its resolution of November 29. In Palestine the British Mandate had only a few more hours to run.* On the same day a historic assembly of the representatives of the *Yishuv* was convoked in Tel Aviv, and proclaimed to the world the rightful independence of the Jewish State, to take effect as of the hour of the termination of the British Mandate.

At a few minutes past six o'clock, American time, unofficial news reached Lake Success that the Jewish State had been recognized by the Government of the United States. The delegates were incredulous, which perhaps was natural at a time when many wild rumors were running through the corridors of the United Nations building. The United States delegation was unaware of any such decision. Finally, after much confusion, Professor Jessup rose to read the following statement issued from the White House:

> This Government has been informed that a Jewish State has been proclaimed in Palestine, and recognition has been requested by the Provisional Government itself. The United States recognizes the Provisional Government as the *de facto* authority of the new State of Israel.

This historic statement must be regarded not only as an act of high statesmanship; it had a peculiar and significant fitness, for it set the seal on America's long and generous record of support of Zionist aspirations.

On May 15 a great wave of rejoicing spread throughout the Jewish world. We were not unmindful of the dangers which hung over the new-born State. Five Arab armies were at its frontiers, threatening invasion; our forces were not yet properly organized; we were cut off from international support. But the die was cast. The demoralizing illusions of trusteeship and truce were behind us. We were now face to face with the basic realities, and this was what we had asked for. If the State of Israel could defend itself, survive and remain effective, it would do so largely on its own; and the issue would be decided, as we were willing it should be, by the basic strength and solidity of the organism which we had created in the last fifty years.

May 15 was a very full day. Recognition was extended to the State of Israel by the Soviet Union and Poland, to be followed shortly by several

---

*It should be borne in mind that Palestine time is seven hours in advance of Washington time.

countries of Eastern Europe and South America. Great Britain remained silent, and I received reports that Mr. Bevin was bringing pressure to bear on the British Dominions and Western Europe to withhold recognition. However, I bethought myself of one surviving author of the Balfour Declaration and addressed a cablegram to General Smuts. This was closely followed by South African recognition.

On this same day, amidst the avalanche of messages reaching me from Tel Aviv, there was one signed by the five Labor Party leaders in the Provisional Government, David Ben-Gurion, Eliezer Kaplan, Golda Myerson, David Remez and Moshe Shertok.

> On the occasion of the establishment of the Jewish State we send our greetings to you, who have done more than any other living man toward its creation. Your stand and help have strengthened all of us. We look forward to the day when we shall see you at the head of the State established in peace.

91. STATE OF ISRAEL PROCLAMATION OF INDEPENDENCE

The Proclamation of Independence was issued by the Provisional State Council in Tel Aviv on May 14, 1948. The Provisional State Council was the forerunner of the Knesset, the Israeli parliament. The British mandate was terminated the following day, and regular armed forces of Transjordan, Egypt, Syria, and other Arab countries invaded Palestine to destroy the new state.

The Land of Israel was the birthplace of the Jewish people. Here their spiritual, religious and national identity was formed. Here they achieved independence and created a culture of national and universal significance. Here they wrote and gave the Bible to the world.

Exiled from the Land of Israel the Jewish people remained faithful to it in all the countries of their dispersion, never ceasing to pray and hope for their return and the restoration of their national freedom.

Impelled by this historic association, Jews strove throughout the centuries to go back to the land of their fathers and regain their statehood. In recent decades they returned in their masses. They reclaimed the wilderness, revived their language, built cities and villages, and established a vigorous and ever-growing community, with its own economic and cultural life. They sought peace, yet were prepared to defend themselves. They brought the blessings of progress to all inhabitants of the country and looked forward to sovereign independence.

In the year 1897 the First Zionist Congress, inspired by Theodor Herzl's vision of the Jewish State, proclaimed the right of the Jewish people to national revival in their own country.

This right was acknowledged by the Balfour Declaration of November 2, 1917, and re-affirmed by the Mandate of the League of Nations, which gave explicit international recognition to the historic connection of the Jewish people with Palestine and their right to reconstitute their National Home.

The recent holocaust, which engulfed millions of Jews in Europe, proved anew the need to solve the problem of the homelessness and lack of independence of the Jewish people by means of the re-establishment of the Jewish State, which would open the gates to all Jews and endow the Jewish people with equality of status among the family of nations.

The survivors of the disastrous slaughter in Europe, and also Jews from other lands, have not desisted from their efforts to reach Eretz-Yisrael, in face of difficulties, obstacles and perils; and have not ceased to urge their right to a life of dignity, freedom and honest toil in their ancestral land.

In the second World War the Jewish people in Palestine made their full contribution to the struggle of the freedom-loving nations against the Nazi evil. The sacrifices of their soldiers and their war effort gained them the right to rank with the nations which founded the United Nations.

On November 29, 1947, the General Assembly of the United Nations adopted a Resolution requiring the establishment of a Jewish State in Palestine. The General Assembly called upon the inhabitants of the country to take all the necessary steps on their part to put the plan into effect. This recognition by the United Nations of the right of the Jewish people to establish their independent State is unassailable.

It is the natural right of the Jewish people to lead, as do all other nations, an independent existence in its sovereign State.

Accordingly we, the members of the National Council, representing the Jewish people in Palestine and the World Zionist Movement, are met together in solemn assembly today, the day of termination of the British Mandate for Palestine; and by virtue of the natural and historic right of the Jewish people and of the Resolution of the General Assembly of the United Nations.

We hereby proclaim the establishment of the Jewish State in Palestine, to be called Medinath Yisrael (The State of Israel).

We hereby declare that, as from the termination of the Mandate at midnight, the 14th-15th May, 1948, and pending the setting up of the duly elected bodies of the State in accordance with a Constitution, to be drawn up by the Constituent Assembly not later than the 1st October, 1948, the National Council shall act as the Provisional State Council, and that the National Administration shall constitute the Provisional Government of the Jewish State, which shall be known as Israel.

The State of Israel will be open to the immigration of Jews from all countries of their dispersion; will promote the development of the country

for the benefit of all its inhabitants; will be based on the principles of
liberty, justice and peace as conceived by the Prophets of Israel; will
uphold the full social and political equality of all its citizens, without
distinction of religion, race or sex; will guarantee freedom of religion,
conscience, education and culture; will safeguard the Holy Places of all
religions; and will loyally uphold the principles of the United Nations
Charter.

The State of Israel will be ready to co-operate with the organs and
representatives of the United Nations in the implementation of the
Resolution of the Assembly of November 29, 1947, and will take steps to
bring about the Economic Union over the whole of Palestine.

We appeal to the United Nations to assist the Jewish people in the
building of its State and to admit Israel into the family of nations.

In the midst of wanton aggression, we yet call upon the Arab inhabitants
of the State of Israel to preserve the ways of peace and play their part in the
development of the State, on the basis of full and equal citizenship and due
representation in all its bodies and institutions—provisional and permanent.

We extend our hand in peace and neighbourliness to all the
neighbouring states and their peoples, and invite them to co-operate with
the independent Jewish nation for the common good of all. The State of
Israel is prepared to make its contribution to the progress of the Middle
East as a whole.

Our call goes out to the Jewish people all over the world to rally to our
side in the task of immigration and development, and to stand by us in the
great struggle for the fulfillment of the dream of generations for the
redemption of Israel.

With trust in the Rock of Israel, we set our hand to this Declaration, at
this Session of the Provisional State Council, on the soil of the Homeland,
in the city of Tel-Aviv, on this Sabbath eve, the fifth of Iyar, 5708, the
fourteenth of May, 1948.

92. THE LAW OF RETURN

The Law of Return was passed unanimously by the Knesset, the Israeli
parliament, on July 5, 1950 and written into the law of the country.

The Law of Return states:
1. Every Jew has the right to immigrate to the country.
2. (a) Immigration shall be on the basis of immigration visas.
   (b) Immigrant visas shall be issued to any Jew expressing a desire to

settle in Israel, except if the Minister of Immigration is satisfied that the applicant:

   (i) acts against the Jewish nation; or

   (ii) may threaten the public health or State security.

3. (a) A Jew who comes to Israel and after his arrival expresses a desire to settle there may, while in Israel, obtain an immigrant certificate.

  (b) The exceptions listed in Article 2 (b) shall apply also with respect to the issue of an immigrant certificate, but a person shall not be regarded as a threat to public health as a result of an illness that he contracts after his arrival in Israel.

4. Every Jew who migrated to the country before this law goes into effect, and every Jew who was born in the country either before or after the law is effective enjoys the same status as any person who migrated on the basis of this law.

5. The Minister of Immigration is delegated to enforce this law and he may enact regulations in connection with its implementation and for the issue of immigrant visas and immigrant certificates.

93. HEBREW, THE NATIONAL LANGUAGE OF THE STATE: THE MIRACLE OF REVIVAL

CHAIM RABIN

How an ancient language has become the language of a modern nation and the vehicle of expression in all the areas of the life of its citizens is considered a historical miracle. There is no similar successful effort in all of recorded history. The following selection is taken from an article by a professor of Hebrew at the Hebrew University of Jerusalem.

The Revival of the National Spirit

In an age when the best spirits amongst Jewry saw full citizenship of the Jews in their respective countries as the ultimate ideal, the cultivation of a separate literary language seemed indeed a luxury. It was only when the Russian pogroms of the 1880's brought it home to all that the solution of the Jewish problem must come from within, through the rebuilding of Jewish nationhood, that the importance of the national language in this reconstruction was instinctively recognized. Hebrew became the language of *Hibbat Zion*, a forerunner of Zionism. The immediate result was a spectacular development of Hebrew literature in all branches between 1880 and 1914. This period, which included such writers as Ahad Ha'am, Bialik and Tchernichowsky, is generally considered the classical age of Hebrew literature. It also saw, from 1886 onwards, the rise of a Hebrew daily press, and the penetration of Hebrew into the United States. Mendele Mocher Seforim (1835–1917) created a synthesis between the Biblical Hebrew of the *Haskalah* writers and the Rabbinic Hebrew, which had been used during the latter Middle Ages. He thus gave Modern Hebrew the character it has retained ever since.

The connection between the language and national revival was seen most clearly, even before the pogroms, by Eliezer Ben-Yehuda (born near Vilna, 1858; died Jerusalem, 1922). In the spring of 1879 he published an article in which he proposed the foundation of a Jewish State in Palestine as a national centre. The literary language of that State would be Hebrew, and thus Hebrew literature would find a natural soil for its growth. In 1880 he wrote on his way to Palestine: "Today we are speaking foreign languages, tomorrow we shall speak Hebrew."

A Spoken Language Again

Ben-Yehuda immediately put his new idea into practice: on the boat from Marseilles to Jaffa he spoke to his wife in Hebrew. His son, born in 1882, was the first child in our time to be brought up with Hebrew as his mother-tongue; he afterwards became an author under the name of Itamar Ben-Avi. Ben-Yehuda found kindred spirits amongst the educated families in Jerusalem, especially those of Sephardi (Spanish) origin who had been accustomed to speaking Hebrew, as in the Middle Ages, as a means of communication with Jews ignorant of Ladino or Arabic (the discussions about the foundation of the first secular school in Jerusalem, in 1855, were conducted in Hebrew). Ben-Yehuda clearly saw that the way to full revival lay by way of making Hebrew the sole medium of school teaching, so as to produce a generation which carried on its entire life in the Hebrew language. Immediately after his arrival in Jerusalem, at the end of 1880, he published in the Hebrew periodical *Ha-Havatzelet* an impassioned call to make Hebrew the language of the country's schools. He himself took a post as teacher in 1883, but soon had to give up because of his chronic ill-health. In 1888, however, the local school in Rishon le-Zion taught all subjects in Hebrew, and in 1892 teachers from all over Palestine decided for the exclusive use of Hebrew in schools. The Hebrew *Gymnasia* of Jaffa, founded in 1906, and of Jerusalem, founded in 1908, carried this policy over into secondary-school teaching. The German-Jewish *Hilfsverein* also founded a number of schools in which Hebrew was the main teaching language. When, in 1913, that organization planned a technical high-school (the present *Technion*) in Haifa, they considered it advisable to teach technical subjects in German, in view of the still undeveloped state of Hebrew. The reaction of the *Yishuv* was unexpectedly violent: thousands of children and teachers left the schools, holding lessons in the open air. In the end the *Yishuv* won this "Language Struggle", the first of many fights for the full recognition of Hebrew. The results of Ben-Yehuda's struggle are clearly shown by a census undertaken in 1916–18, which showed that amongst the whole Jewish population of Palestine outside Jerusalem, some 40% (34,000) were Hebrew-speakers. Amongst children the percentage was 54, and in Tel Aviv and the villages as high as 77.

International Recognition

The Palestine Mandate of 1921 recognized Hebrew as one of the official languages of the country, with English and Arabic as the other two. It was henceforth used in the administration, in postal services, etc., and especially in the ever-extending field of autonomous Jewish institutions. Numerous daily and weekly papers, a network of schools catering to almost 100% of the Jewish children, the Hebrew University founded in 1925, and a vigorous literature saw to it that the 576,000 Jews added to the population (by immigration and natural increase) during the Mandatory period became effectively "hebraized". The means adopted were sometimes drastic: the kindergarten and the elementary school implanted in the children the idea that it was wrong to speak other languages, and thus turned them into a pro-Hebrew influence in their homes. . . .

Hebrew Lives on in Writing

Although between the years 200 and 1880 Hebrew was not spoken in everyday life, the ability to speak it was not lost. It was used as a means of communication between Jews of different countries who could not understand each other's native languages; some of the pious spoke Hebrew on the Sabbath. But while such activities were exceptional, the use of Hebrew in writing was widespread through that entire period. . . .

Language of a State

When, in May 1948, the State of Israel was founded, Hebrew regained a position which it had lost 1985 years earlier, when the Hasmonean dynasty fell. It became the official language of the State. Arabic is used only in matters concerning the Arab minority, although it appears on coins, stamps and street signs in some towns; in fact, most Arabs in Israel nowadays can speak Hebrew. The revival of Hebrew has thus ceased to be an ideal for the future and has become an established fact, since every citizen of Israel is at least a potential Hebrew-speaker. During the period of mass immigration there were times when Hebrew-speakers seemed likely to be engulfed by a sea of foreign languages, but every time the immigrants (except for older people) rapidly acquired a smattering of Hebrew, which to them was a necessity in work, social life and official contacts, . . . though many still speak other languages at home and may read daily papers in languages other than Hebrew. Some of these will no doubt be completely "hebraized" in the course of time; at any rate the existence of the State means that their children will be Hebrew-speakers. The Hebrew language is thus spoken by more people than Albanian, Latvian or Welsh. In it are published eleven daily papers, innumerable periodicals and over 1,000 books a year, and there are five academic institutions using it as their sole language of instruction. A number of countries (amongst them several Arab States) broadcast daily programmes in Hebrew.

The revival of Hebrew is thus completed, not quite eighty years after the idea was first mooted, and in spite of the scepticism which was often expressed as to its chances of success.

Why Hebrew Succeeded

Even when the revival of Hebrew had gone a long way, many people objected to the whole undertaking on the ground that never had a dead language come to life again. Events have proved them wrong, but we may well ask what were the causes which enabled Hebrew to regain a full life while attempts to revive other languages, which had not even died completely, were less successful.

One reason is that for the Jewish people Hebrew never was a dead language. They always felt that the languages they spoke in the Diaspora were only temporary expedients, and that at some time they would return to Zion and speak Hebrew. Ben-Yehuda only demonstrated that the time for doing so was now, not in some distant future. This is why the early Halutzim were willing, on top of a hard life of physical labour, to take upon themselves the arduous task of conversing in a language they knew but imperfectly, and young people were prepared to jeopardize their education so as to have it in Hebrew only.

Moreover, to the immigrant from Eastern Europe and from Asia and North Africa, Hebrew was familiar as the language in which he read many or all his books, in which he often wrote letters and even kept his business accounts, and above all as the language of his religious life. The literature of the Haskalah, which preceded the revival, had introduced Hebrew to many other fields of life. Even before the revival, the newspapers which (since 1863) appeared in Palestine—and most of those published by Jews in Eastern Europe—were in Hebrew.

Its extensive use in writing throughout the ages had largely prepared Hebrew for the refitting it needed to express all the needs of modern life. Many words used today were invented in the Middle Ages by philosophers, Kabbalists (students of Jewish mysticism), or rabbis; but what is more important, they established the methods by which the Language Academy and other bodies and individuals enriched the language in our time.

Given the rebuilding of the Jewish National Home in Israel, there was in fact no alternative to the revival of Hebrew. It was the only language all Jews had in common. Yiddish and Ladino were each spoken only by a part of the Jewish people, and those who did not speak them could not have been expected to accept a language which was not connected with their own Jewish past. Nor, of course, was it possible to impose any other language, such as English, on those returning to the National Home, for they returned in order to be Jews, not to exchange one assimilation for another. The reintroduction of Hebrew was thus an essential part of the Jewish renaissance.

The dominance of Hebrew in daily life was assured by the rhythm of immigration, which was such that no single Jewish group ever held considerable numerical superiority in the *Yishuv,* which superiority might have caused its daily language to spread to other groups. Hebrew was the natural medium for all contacts between people from different countries, and the natural language for those homes where the partners came from different communities. As such unions increase in number, and the old *Landsmannschaften* (close-knit groups of people from the same region of origin) give way to a unified Israel society, the other languages spoken in private life gradually disappear. . . .

94. A GENERAL SPEAKS AFTER THE SIX-DAY WAR

YITZHAK RABIN

By force of arms the Arabs had tried to prevent the establishment of the State of Israel. This attempt failed, and Israel in the war that followed seized areas beyond those defined in the U.N. resolution of partition. The armistice of 1949 did not restore peace. An Arab refugee problem also came into being, and guerilla attacks, Israeli retaliation, and Arab blockage of the Suez Canal and the Straits of Tiran led to the second and third Arab-Israel wars in 1956 and 1967. The Six-Day War in June 1967 ended with a brilliant victory by the outnumbered Israeli army.

On June 28, 1967 the title of honorary doctor of philosophy was conferred by the Hebrew University of Jerusalem on Major General Yitzhak Rabin, then chief of staff of the Israel Defense Forces, who later became Israel's prime minister. He delivered the following address at a ceremony held in the amphitheater of the University on Mount Scopus.

Mr. President, Mr. Prime Minister, the President of the Hebrew University, the Rector of the Hebrew University, members of the Board of Governors of the Hebrew University, Ladies and Gentlemen:

I stand in awe before you, leaders of this generation, here in this ancient and magnificent spot overlooking Israel's eternal capital and the birthplace of our nation's earliest history.

Together with several distinguished persons who are without doubt worthy of this honour, you have chosen to do me great honour by conferring upon me the title of Doctor of Philosophy. Permit me to express my feelings on this occasion.

I regard myself here as the representative of the entire Israel Defence Forces, of the thousands of officers and tens of thousands of soldiers who brought victory to the State of Israel in the Six-Day War.

It may be asked why the University saw fit to award the title of Honorary Doctor of Philosophy to a soldier in recognition of his military activities. What do soldiers have in common with the academic world, which stands for civilisation and culture? What is there in common between those whose profession is violence and those who are concerned with spiritual values? I am, however, honoured that you have chosen through me to express your deep appreciation of my comrades-in-arms and of the uniqueness of the Israel Defence Forces, which is no more than an extension of the uniqueness of the Jewish people as a whole.

The world has recognised that the Israel Army is different from other armies. Although its first task is the military one of maintaining security, it has numerous peace-time roles, not of destruction but of construction and of strengthening the nation's cultural and moral resources.

Our educational work has been widely praised, and it received national recognition in 1966 when the Israel Prize for Education was awarded to the Israel Defence Forces. The Nahal, which combines military training and agricultural settlement, also provides teachers for border villages who contribute to their social and cultural development. These are only some examples of the Israel Defence Forces' uniqueness in this sphere.

Today, however, the University is conferring on us an honorary degree in recognition of our Army's spiritual and moral superiority, as revealed precisely in the heat of war. For we are all here in this place only by virtue of the war which, though forced upon us, was forged into a victory which has astounded the world. War is intrinsically harsh and cruel, and blood and tears are its companions. But this war which we have just waged brought forth rare and magnificent instances of courage and heroism, and at the same time humane expressions of brotherhood, comradeship and even of spiritual greatness.

Anyone who has not seen a tank crew continue its attack though its commander has been killed and its track badly damaged, who has not watched sappers risking their lives to extricate wounded comrades from a minefield, who has not witnessed the concern and the extraordinary efforts made by the entire Air Force to rescue a pilot who has fallen in enemy territory, cannot know the meaning of devotion among comrades-in-arms.

The entire nation was exalted and many wept when they heard of the capture of the Old City. Our *sabra* youth, and most certainly our soldiers, do not tend to be sentimental and they shrink from any public show of feeling. But the strain of battle, the anxiety which preceded it, and the sense of salvation and of direct confrontation with Jewish history itself cracked the shell of hardness and shyness and released well-springs of emotion and stirrings of the spirit. The paratroopers who conquered the Wailing Wall leaned on its stones and wept—in its symbolism an act so rare as to be almost unparalleled in human history. Rhetorical phrases and cliches are not common in our Army, but this scene on the Temple Mount, beyond the power of words to describe, revealed as though by a flash of lightning truths that were deeply hidden.

And there is more to be told. The joy of triumph had seized the entire nation. Nevertheless, a strange phenomenon can be observed among our soldiers. Their joy is incomplete, and their celebrations are marred by sorrow and shock. There are even some who abstain from celebrations entirely. The men in the front lines saw with their own eyes not only the glory of victory, but also the price of victory—their comrades fallen beside them soaked in blood. I know too that the terrible price paid by our enemies also touched the hearts of many of our men. It may be that the Jewish people has never learned and never accustomed itself to feel the triumph of conquest and victory, with the result that these are accepted with mixed feelings. The Six-Day War brought to the fore numerous instances of heroism far beyond the kind manifested in the daring, one-time assault in which the attacker goes unthinkingly forward. In many places there were desperate and lengthy battles. In Rafia, in El-Arish, in Um Katak, in Jerusalem, on the Golan Heights and elsewhere, our soldiers displayed spiritual courage as well as bravery and tenacity in a degree to which no-one who has witnessed this great and inspiring human phenomenon can remain indifferent. We speak a great deal of the few against the many. In this war, perhaps for the first time since the Arab invasions of the spring of 1948 and the battles of Negba and Degania, units of the Israel Defence Forces stood few against the many in every sector. In other words, relatively small units often entered seemingly endless networks of fortifications, surrounded by hundreds and thousands of enemy troops, and had to force their way, hour after hour, in this veritable sea of dangers. Even after the momentum of the first attack had passed and all that remained was the overwhelming necessity of believing in our own strength and in the goal for which the battle was being fought, since there was no alternative, we summoned up every spiritual resource in order to continue the fight to the end.

Thus our armoured forces broke through on all fronts, our paratroopers fought their way into Rafia and Jerusalem, and our sappers cleared minefields under enemy fire. The units which penetrated the enemy lines and reached their objectives after hours of struggle, continuing on and on while their comrades fell to the right and left of them, were carried forward by great moral force and by deep spiritual resources far more than by their weapons or the techniques of warfare. We have always demanded the cream of our youth for the Israel Defence Forces. We coined the slogan *Hatovim l'Tayis*—The Best for the Air Force—and this became a meaningful phrase. It referred not only to technical and manual skills. What it meant was that if our airmen were to be capable of defeating the forces of four enemy countries within a few short hours, they had to be imbued with moral values and human values.

Our airmen who struck the enemies' planes so accurately that no-one understands how it was done and the world seeks technological explanations in secret weapons; our armoured troops who stood their ground and defeated the enemy even when their equipment was inferior to his; our soldiers in all the various branches of the Israel Defence Forces who overcame our enemies everywhere, despite their superior numbers and fortifications—all of them revealed not only coolness and courage in battle but a burning faith in the justice of their cause, and sure knowledge that only their personal stand against the greatest of dangers could bring victory to their country and to their families, and that if the victory were not achieved the alternative was annihilation. Furthermore, in every sector our commanders, of all ranks, far outshone those of the enemy. Their insight, their understanding, their preparedness, their ability to improvise, their care for their men and, above all, the fact that they went at the head of their troops into battle—all these are not matters of equipment or technique. They have no rational explanation, except in terms of a deep consciousness of the moral justice of their fight. All this springs from the spirit and leads back to the spirit. Our warriors prevailed not by their weapons but by their sense of mission, by the consciousness of the rightness of their cause, by a deep love for their country and an understanding of the difficult task laid upon them: to ensure the existence of our people in its homeland, to protect, even at the price of their lives, the right of the Jewish people to live in its own state, free, independent and in peace.

This Army, which I had the privilege of commanding through these battles, came from the people and returns to the people—to a people which rises to great heights in times of crisis and prevails over all enemies by virtue of its moral and spiritual strength. As the representative of the Israel Defence Forces, and on behalf of every one of its soldiers, I accept with pride this token of your appreciation.

95. SOLDIERS TALK ABOUT THE SIX-DAY WAR

In the days following the war in 1967, some of the soldiers, especially the youth from the kibbutzim, sat with their friends to ponder the whys and wherefores of the war and its outcome in victory. It was a searching and frank conversation. Similarly, during the summer of the following year, a dozen young and active members of an equal number of kibbutzim used tape-recorders to sample the thinking current at the time among their peers. These recordings were undertaken in an effort to understand the individual and the collective and national experience of that crucial week during the previous June. The excerpts which follow are taken from the collection of these discussions, published in English under the title of *The Seventh Day;* they present an extraordinary Jewish and human document.

Mobilization

I was leaning on a newspaper stall at the time. The newspaper seller was in the very act of stretching out his hand towards the paper I wanted when suddenly the voice caught his attention. His eyes widened, he looked through me rather than at me, and said, as if in surprise, 'Oh! They've called me up too.' He rolled up his papers and went. The salesgirl came out of the shop opposite, stopped jerkily at the door, adjusted her blouse, a little nervously, snapped her handbag shut, and walked off. The butcher took off his apron, pulled down his shutters, and left. A group of men stood huddled round a transistor in the middle of a patch of lawn. Whenever one of them heard his code-word read out by the announcer, he detached himself from the group and left. Without a word, another left. Then a third. Silently the group broke up. Each went his own way. A girl came towards me, clicking along on high heels. She too was struck by the voice, and stopped. She listened, turned around, and left. A unique silence descended on the town.

I have seen cities on mobilization day. I have seen nations go to war. I have seen them marching off to the blare of raucous loudspeakers. I have seen them in the railway stations clasped in the arms of their weeping wives, their despairing mothers. I have watched them pass through the cheering crowds, receiving the embraces of foolish women. I have watched them go off, their bayonets wreathed in gay flowers, their hobnailed boots crashing out the rhythm of the marching songs that swell from their throats. I have seen them smiling, and proud. Always surrounded by crowds waving them on with shouts of 'Hurrah! 'Vivat!' 'Hoch Hoch!' 'Nych Dzhiah!' But never before have I seen a city rise so silently to answer the call of duty. This nation went to war filled with a sense of destiny, gravely and quietly prepared, in a way that cannot be surpassed.

(Abba, Kibbutz Ein Hachoresh)

The Will to Fight

We know the meaning of genocide, both those of us who saw the holocaust and those who were born later. Perhaps this is why the world will never understand us, will never understand our courage or comprehend the doubts and the qualms of conscience we knew during and after the war. Those who survived the holocaust, those who see pictures of a father and a mother, who hear the cries that disturb the dreams of those close to them, those who have listened to stories—know that no other people carries with it such haunting visions. And it is these visions which compel us to fight and yet make us ashamed of our fighting. The saying, 'Pardon us for winning' is no irony—it is the truth.

(Muki, Kibbutz Ein Gev)

Hate of Arab?

Right through the war when boys from your own unit had fallen alongside you—people you'd known for years, whose families and children you knew—even when they'd fallen and been killed and burned, even after all this, there still wasn't any hatred. It simply didn't exist. It was a professional encounter—if you can use a term like that—a question of who could fire first.

(Hillel, Kibbutz Giv'at Hashlosha)

When the fighting began, and the mountains around Ein Gev began to spit fire, a group of our reconnaissance troops on one of the hills next to the Syrian border was busy—putting out a fire in a little field belonging to an Arab peasant. 'A field is a field,' said one of the boys. Could anything be more paradoxical? And yet it seems to me that behavior like this really symbolizes the situation we are caught up in. Our feelings are mixed. We carry in our hearts an oath which binds us never to return to the Europe of the holocaust; but at the same time we do not wish to lose that Jewish sense of identity with the victims.

Muki, Kibbutz Ein Gev)

Respect for Human Life

The big problem is one of education. How—despite the fact that from our point of view this was a just war—are we going to avoid turning into militarists? How are we going to retain respect for human life? This is the contradiction, this is the paradox within the whole business. What we've got to avoid is cheapening life and becoming conquerors. We mustn't become expansionists at the expense of other people.

(Nachman, Kibbutz Geva)

96. RESOLUTION ON THE MIDDLE EAST

SECURITY COUNCIL OF THE UNITED NATIONS

Israel's swift victory in 1967 led not only to the defeat of the Arab armies but left Israel in possession of the West Bank (country west of the Jordan river), the Gaza Strip, the Sinai Peninsula, and the Golan Heights. In the aftermath of the war the following resolution was adopted by the Security Council of the United Nations on November 22, 1967.

The Security Council,

Expressing its continuing concern with the grave situation in the Middle East,

Emphasizing the inadmissibility of the acquisition of territory by war and the need to work for a just and lasting peace in which every state in the area can live in security,

Emphasizing further that all member states in their acceptance of the Charter of the United Nations have undertaken a commitment to act in accordance with Article 2 of the Charter,

1. Affirms that the fulfillment of Charter principles requires the establishment of a just and lasting peace in the Middle East which should include the application of both the following principles:

(i) Withdrawal of Israeli armed forces from territories of recent conflict;

(ii) Termination of all claims or states of belligerency and respect for and acknowledgment of the sovereignty, territorial integrity and political independence of every state in the area and their right to live in peace within secure and recognized boundaries free from threats or acts of force;

2. Affirms further the necessity

(a) For guaranteeing freedom of navigation through international waterways in the area;

(b) For achieving a just settlement of the refugee problem;

(c) For guaranteeing the territorial inviolability and political independence of every state in the area, through measures including the establishment of demilitarized zones;

3. *Requests* the Secretary General to designate a special representative to proceed to the Middle East to establish and maintain contacts with the states concerned in order to promote agreement and assist efforts to achieve a peaceful and accepted settlement in accordance with the provision and principles in this resolution.

4. *Requests* the Secretary General to report to the Security Council on the progress of the efforts of the special representative as soon as possible.

97. THE SEVEN POINTS

AL FATAH

Al Fatah is the name of the Palestine Liberation Movement, founded in 1955 by Yassir Arafat. The aim of this organization of Palestinian Arabs is the "liberation of the homeland" (Palestine) and the destruction of the State of Israel. It is supported by Arab governments and has concentrated its forces in Syria and Lebanon while conducting terrorist activities against Israel, especially after the war of 1967. The seven "points" of their program were passed by the Central Committee of Al Fatah in January 1969.

1. *Al Fatah*, the Palestine National Liberation Movement, is the expression of the Palestinian people and of its will to free its land from Zionist colonisation in order to recover its national identity.

2. *Al Fatah*, the Palestine National Liberation Movement, is not struggling against the Jews as an ethnic and religious community. It is struggling against Israel as the expression of colonisation based on a theocratic, racist and expansionist system and of Zionism and colonialism.

3. *Al Fatah*, the Palestine National Liberation Movement, rejects any solution that does not take account of the existence of the Palestinian people and its right to dispose of itself.

4. *Al Fatah*, the Palestine National Liberation Movement, categorically rejects the Security Council Resolution of 22 November 1967 and the Jarring Mission to which it gave rise.

This resolution ignores the national rights of the Palestinian people—failing to mention its existence. Any solution claiming to be peaceful which ignores this basic factor, will thereby be doomed to failure.

In any event, the acceptance of the resolution of 22 November 1967, or any pseudo-political solution, by whatsoever party, is in no way binding upon the Palestinian people, which is determined to pursue mercilessly its struggle against foreign occupation and Zionist colonisation.

5. *Al Fatah*, the Palestine National Liberation Movement, solemnly proclaims that the final objective of its struggle is the restoration of the independent, democratic State of Palestine, all of whose citizens will enjoy equal rights irrespective of their religion.

6. Since Palestine forms part of the Arab fatherland, *Al Fatah*, the Palestine National Liberation Movement, will work for the State of Palestine to contribute actively towards the establishment of a progressive and united Arab society.

7. The struggle of the Palestinian People, like that of the Vietnamese people and other peoples of Asia, Africa and Latin America, is part of the historic process of the liberation of the oppressed peoples from colonialism and imperialism.

98. ISRAEL AFTER THE YOM KIPPUR WAR: BACK TO ABNORMAL

HANOCH BARTOV

On Yom Kippur, the Day of Atonement, October 6, 1973, Egypt and Syria attacked Israel. The Syrian forces, after achieving initial successes, were driven back despite reinforcements of Iraqi, Jordanian, and other Arab troops. The Egyptians maintained a hold on the east bank of the Suez Canal, but the Israeli army succeeded in crossing the western bank of the canal and encircling the Egyptian Third Army. With the Arabs threatened by defeat, the Soviet Union hastened to arrange a cease-fire with the help of the United States. The cease-fire called for future peace negotiations.

In this war Israel suffered heavy casualties in proportion to the size of its population. Although the Israeli army was undefeated, the suffering and the losses left their mark on Israeli society as reflected in our selection as well as the following one, no. 100.

Hanoch Bartov is an Israeli novelist whose works include *The Brigade*.

Yom Kippur in Israel will never be the same again, at least not for my generation, whose sense of the world came from two decisive experiences: first the Holocaust, then the establishment of the Jewish state. And not for our children either, the eighteen-, and twenty, and twenty-five-year-olds to whom those experiences had always seemed irrelevant, part of a past which scarcely touched on their own situation in a thriving, self-confident society—the only Israel they had ever known. Suddenly on the afternoon of Yom Kippur 1973, that situation changed drastically, as they found themselves not only fighting for their lives, but almost breaking under a burden they had been asked to carry virtually alone—that of the very survival of the State of Israel.

The memory of this past Yom Kippur will be with us for a long time, and not just as another scar from a battle bitterly fought and gallantly won. As I write this, many weeks have elapsed since the initial shock of the war, yet things show no sign of returning to the way they were before October 6. Rather, I have the impression that the experience was a kind of national trauma, that the Yom Kippur War may well become a turning-point in the formation of Israel's identity; or, to put it more precisely, in the formation of Israel's *Jewish* identity. Whether such a change is dream or nightmare depends on one's point of view, but in any case the trip to "normalcy" is over, for the time being at least. We are back to abnormal.

The invasion launched simultaneously on the 6th of October from both Egypt and Syria was meticulously planned—there are indications that even the assaults on individual outposts of the Suez Canal had been rehearsed dozens of times. Exactly which elements in that rather complex operation were devised by the Egyptian and Syrian general staffs, and which should be credited to their Soviet mentors, will take a while to sort out—in the meantime we can ponder the remark of the Soviet ambassador to Egypt, as quoted by the editor of *al-Ahram*: the Yom Kippur assault, said Ambassador Vinogradov with tears in his eyes, was the happiest day of his three years in Cairo, and the culmination of his efforts there. Some journalists have even speculated that the very decision to attack on Yom Kippur was a Soviet contribution. If so, it was the wrong decision—laden with symbolism though it was. Indeed, of all the days of the calendar, Yom Kippur was possibly the worst of all for achieving the grim objectives of that onslaught—though our enemies, misunderstanding the nature of Israeli society, could not have known that.

Of all the Jewish holidays, Yom Kippur is the one that has been least affected by its encounter with Zionism. Passover, Shavuot, Hanukkah, as well as a host of other occasions and customs, have all been changed in one way or another by the effort—going all the way back to the first settlement in Palestine almost a hundred years ago—to reinterpret Jewish traditions both in terms of the biblical past (the "return to our sources," as the old phrase had it), and the new society being forged in Palestine. Only Yom Kippur resisted all attempts at change. It remained the one purely religious holiday—the Day of Atonement, the Day of Judgment, the one day of the year set aside for the encounter between man and God. One could either accept it as such, or not accept it at all.

In the early radical days of the frontier generation, the tendency was to forego Yom Kippur altogether; indeed, the supreme test of one's "liberation" at that time was how far one could go in ostentatiously ignoring the day. But this particular brand of militant secularism has long since vanished from the Israeli scene. I cannot date its disappearance exactly, but in my mind it is linked to the terrible Yom Kippur eve in the autumn of 1939, when the approaching doom of Europe's Jews could no longer be denied. That year, the makeshift synagogue in my boyhood town of Petach Tikvah—hastily improvised out of two classrooms in the local girls' school—was overflowing with people who had never been seen there before: young, sunburned kibbutzniks from various settlements in the vicinity, resolutely secularist, whose fears for their families in Eastern Europe proved weightier than ideology. That day we had heard the news that Poland was all but occupied, that Warsaw was burning, and that final capitulation to the Germans was a matter of hours. It was not only my father, wrapped in his prayer shawl, who wept during the service that night in Petach Tikvah; so did the kibbutzniks, in their white shirts, all of them sensing that the fathers, mothers, brothers, and sisters they had left behind were lost to them forever.

I have never forgotten that Yom Kippur of 1939 when the Yishuv first mourned its European brethren, and perhaps it left its mark too on the collective memory of Israel—or at least on that part of it which came of age when I did. From then on, Yom Kippur and the Holocaust were in some way linked inextricably in our minds, whether or not we had—as I had—long since given up going to the synagogue.

Be that as it may, the nearly full Yom Kippur moon of October 1973 shone over a muted country, its radio and television stations already off the air, its restaurants, theaters, and cafés already shut down. Here and there, a lone car was still to be seen, hurrying to its destination, but in a few minutes the streets would be empty, and the country at a standstill. On any other holiday, the whole population would have been on the move—hiking in the woods, climbing Mt. Hermon, swimming in the Gulf of Eilat; on this particular day people were either at the synagogue or in their own homes, observing a kind of voluntary curfew appropriate to the spirit of the day. This factor was to prove of enormous importance in the emergency mobilization that would begin in the morning hours of October 6. With the benefit of hindsight, we can see now that only on Yom Kippur, on no other day but Yom Kippur in fact, contravening the murderous intentions of our enemies, could tens of thousands of Israeli civilians have been transformed so quickly into an army. Only on that day could the reservists have been located so quickly in one of two places; only on that day could they have been sped with so few delays over highways that were virtually empty, to the assistance of that besieged handful of men who were attempting to hold back the invaders against overwhelming odds.

At Suez, along the eastern shore of the Canal, a few hundred reservists from Jerusalem and an even smaller number of conscripts had been under massive artillery fire since 1:50 that afternoon, trying in vain to hold the Bar-Lev line against wave after wave of Egypt's best-trained commando and infantry soldiers. Before twenty-four hours had passed, about a thousand Egyptian tanks would have succeeded in crossing the Canal. In the Golan Heights, enemy penetration would be even swifter, threatening the heavily populated settlements throughout the Upper Galilee. Some 1,400 tanks, it has since been estimated, launched the offensive there along a line only a few dozen miles long, with odds of more than ten to one against the Israelis.

The devout spend the eve of Yom Kippur in the study of holy texts; my wife and I spent it, as usual, talking politics with friends late into the night. The elections were just around the corner, and we all agreed that there were only two real issues in the campaign, and both of them were internal. First, there was the "social issue," as it had come to be known: could measures be found to redress that growing sense of social inequality—itself, ironically, a product of unprecedented economic success—which was threatening to tear Israeli society apart? A special committee appointed by the Prime Minister two years earlier in the wake of the "Black Panther" demonstrations had just issued its report, and it seemed to bear out the general sense that the material prosperity which the country had been enjoying since the Six-Day War carried with it a burden of dangerous social tension. There seemed to be a growing gap between the haves and have-nots. It was not that the poor had grown poorer; rather, that the sudden emergence of a conspicuously affluent "new class" was generating increasing resentment in Israeli society. Old-timers were openly envious of new settlers; young couples begrudged the help being given to immigrants from the Soviet Union. And nowhere was this resentment more keenly felt than in the lower third or quarter of the population, those low-income families with many children, originating mainly from the Jewish communities in the Arab countries of Asia and North Africa, who were still poorly housed and deprived of educational opportunities.

The second issue before the electorate was the question of the territories held by Israel since 1967 and what was to be done with them, a question which, it was growing clearer by the day, could not be avoided for very much longer. It was over this issue that the National Coalition broke apart in 1970, as Likud took the view that the Land of Israel could never again be divided up, and this break was to cast a long shadow over all subsequent political developments. Some six months before the scheduled election, the Labor party had been dragged into a public debate on policy in the territories, a debate which was intensified by the reiterated demands of Defense Minister Moshe Dayan, within whose province the territories fell, for an ultimate policy statement on the question. Dayan's own proposals for developing the territories, coupled with the prospect that he might even test these proposals by running for office on a separate ticket, and on top of other pressures both internal and external, had finally culminated in the government's first official policy statement on the territories since the Six-Day War. Known as the Galili Document, it provided for development and some purchase of the Arab territories within the next four years. Nothing perhaps so well symbolizes the state of Israel's unawareness of its own situation in the fall of 1973 as the preoccupation with this document, imbued as it was with the confident assumption that the status quo could continue long into the foreseeable future.

When my wife's mother telephoned the next morning, it was shortly before noon, and we were still asleep. Did I know anything about what was going on? For the past two hours people had been leaving the synagogue in the middle of the service. Some had simply taken off their prayer shawls then and there, jumped into cars that were waiting outside, and driven off. Could fighting have broken out somewhere? It seemed unlikely. The only possibility that came to mind—some sort of military operation in response to the terrorist hijacking of the Moscow-Vienna train—was ruled out by the fact that it was Yom Kippur. Surely no reprisals would be undertaken on that particular day. As we talked, I opened the shutters and looked out the window. For the first time in memory, the Yom Kippur streets were heavy with traffic—and traffic of every conceivable kind: army trucks, buses, commercial vans, everything on wheels had been pressed into service. From the small airfield that was within sight of our windows I could also see planes taking off every few seconds. Something was indeed going on, but I was still more puzzled than alarmed, unable to imagine anything like the cataclysm that was to begin in less than two hours—one which, as we now know, had been in preparation for a long time, possibly years. I turned to the radio, but there was still nothing being broadcast.

Even when the radio finally came alive and we heard the official announcement that heavy fighting had broken out along the Syrian and Egyptian fronts, we were not unduly alarmed; surely the tide would turn in a few hours. I went over to my office at Ma'ariv,* where a bit more

---

*An Israeli newspaper. (Ed.)

information was by this time available, and where a similar mood prevailed. Dayan, on television, seemed rather tense, to be sure, but no less confident than usual. Even the fact that nothing was being said about actual battlefield positions seemed, at the time, encouraging. It called to mind those first hours of the Six-Day War, when the extravagant propaganda claims of the Arabs were deliberately left unchallenged.

Like almost everyone else during those first few hours, I tried to figure out a way of getting to where the action was, but my laughable military record did not help much—after long years as a sergeant, possibly the oldest living sergeant in the Israeli army, I had finally been transferred two years ago to a sedate "educational" unit. Finally, on Sunday night, after a day of pulling strings, I was able to get myself assigned to the Sinai front as a military correspondent. The next morning, I took off in my own car for Beersheva, from which point I eventually managed to reach the Northern Command Post of the Canal front, arriving there late Monday night. The full moon had turned the desert into a surrealistic dreamland: mute, flashing lights on the horizon, endless convoys, tanks galloping madly across the dunes, and from a distance the muffled roar of guns. Was I too late? Was the war already over? Had I missed out on the last phase of yet another victory against our would-be destroyers?

By now we all know how wrong I was. The situation that Monday night two-and-a-half days after the outbreak of the war was worlds away from what it looked like to me at the time—the tide was still very far from turning. Yet I do not altogether blame my own faulty powers of observation for the error. I had more or less discharged my duties as a journalist, running here and there to gather impressions, talking to officers and men in an effort to size up the situation. Rather, there was simply no way at that point to assess the full magnitude of what had happened—how grave the danger to Israel had actually been, and still was; how high a price had already been paid in the lives of those who absorbed the first shock of the attack and how high a price was still to be paid, before the tide did eventually turn in our favor.

Much has already been written about this war, and much more is still to come. In terms of tanks, guns, fire-power, and the numbers of soldiers thrown into battle, it was a far fiercer and bloodier encounter than any we had known in the past. Israel's spectacular victory in the Six-Day War, for example, was child's play compared to the stunning reversal she was able to achieve in those eighteen days—with a force arrayed against her that staggers the imagination. The number of tanks alone deployed against Israel in this war (2,700 by the Syrians and 2,600 by the Egyptians) was twice that used by Montgomery in the battle of El Alamein. When one considers, in addition, the use of missiles on a scale hitherto unprecedented, the factor of total surprise, the vast initial superiority of the attackers in sheer numbers, and their continued advantage in both amounts and kinds of weaponry, the fact that the Arab armies were close to total collapse by the time the ceasefire went into effect seems nothing short of stupefying.

When the full story of this war is written, we will be in a better position to see what went into the making of those eighteen days: the myriad small encounters whose outcome was determined by the bravery and tenacity of a handful of soldiers in an encircled outpost; the many instances in which a single tank succeeded in destroying dozens; the innumerable examples of brilliant tactical ingenuity in the face of sudden reverses on the battlefield; the total, unquestioning involvement of Israel's civilian army. Only then will we be able to appreciate the astonishing fact that an undertaking so carefully and secretly prepared, and so brutally launched, achieved—militarily—almost nothing.

But my purpose here is less to talk about the war itself, than about the changes it has wrought in the inner life of Israel. Not for nothing have the events of October 6 been dubbed, in popular parlance, the "Earthquake."

Scarcely had the cease-fire been accepted when a great public debate was under way in Israel over the causes of that inexplicable failure of vigilance—the "Breakdown" as it has come to be known—which provided the enemy with its long-awaited chance to strike at an unguarded Israel. The "hawks," under Menahem Begin's leadership, charged gross negligence by the government in failing to alert the political leadership to warning signals of an Arab buildup during the pre-war period. The "doves," in turn, countered with the charge that the negligence was of prior origin—a failure to realize long ago that neither strategic depth nor military deterrence capacity could substitute for a peace settlement, however tentative. Yet a third faction pointed out that intelligence reports may themselves have been influenced by previous expectations and preconceptions, and may have been rejected by the political leadership when they failed to conform with them. This has happened before in history—for instance when Stalin failed to heed repeated warnings of a coming invasion of Russia in 1941—and it was no doubt the case also when the government of Israel made what the Prime Minister herself called "the fatal error" of misinterpreting intelligence reports that war was imminent.

Oceans of ink have already been spilled in this debate, which will no doubt be going on long into the future. What started out as a political argument, however, and an attempt to assign immediate blame for the war, has since deepened into a discussion that goes far beyond the question of technical responsibility for the surprise attack, or the question of whether the hawks or the doves were proved right by the events of last Yom Kippur. On those questions, nothing like a consensus has as yet emerged, and even the recent election results are difficult to read clearly in this regard. What more and more people do seem to be saying, however, is that the causes of the recent cataclysm precede by far those "ten days between Rosh Hashana and Yom Kippur"—as the Likud campaign slogan put it. They go back at least to July 1972 when, following the expulsion of the Russians from Egypt, it became possible to believe that a kind of de facto peace—a period that might last as long as ten years, Dayan had said—was about to settle on the Middle East during which Israel could set about consolidating her gains.

Whether Dayan and other military leaders actually believed their own reassurances there is no way of knowing, but in any case their views had a great impact on a nation which was steadily growing more complacent. The constant prophecies of how devastatingly the Arab armies would be defeated if they ventured to attack Israel seem now like a tragically perverse case of a self-fulfilling prophecy. And to say this is not necessarily to take a "dovish" view—in the sense of posing imaginary alternatives of "peace" and "territories"—but only to cry out against that state of euphoria which had existed for too long in Israel, causing even seasoned veterans of the labor movement to lose their sense of reality. The main distinction, after all, between Zionism and the false Messianic movements had always lain in Zionism's refusal—even when stretching possibility to its utmost boundaries—to cross the line into the illusory realm of the impossible.

I represent the middle-aged Israeli, a generation—many of whose members are now in uniform for the *fifth* time—that still remembers when there was no Israel. Those of us who were born in the country grew up with the vision of Jewish statehood as something to be achieved at the end of a very long and arduous road. It happened much sooner than we had expected, though only after bitter fighting which, quite literally, decimated our generation—more than 6,000 fell, out of a Jewish population of 650,000. We were sure we would never forget the magnitude of the achievement, and indeed, it took years for the members of my generation—especially those who had come to Israel as refugees—to get used to the sheer matter-of-factness of Israel, which our children took so for granted. But if one never really gets used to privation, nothing is easier to get used to than success. After a while, it begins to seem natural.

What finally did us in, I'm afraid, was the Six-Day War, in whose glowing aftermath we lost all sense of reality, all sense of what it still means to be Jewish in a hostile world. That "normalization of the Jewish

people" for which we had so long yearned, that Zionist promise which had
for so long eluded us, seemed finally within our grasp. Insecurity gave way
to ease, a feeling that the sky was the limit. A nation which had always
taken pride in achievements of the spirit felt entitled, for the first time in its
history, to a share in the good things which come with material and
military success.

As in Joseph's dream of the fat and lean cows, we had our seven good
years, shadowed though they were by the war of attrition, and the birth of
guerrilla terrorism. New immigrants were arriving by the hundreds and
thousands, there was an economic boom, the continued Arab refusal to
settle for nothing less than total capitulation left us, or so we let ourselves
believe, no choice but to enjoy the present to the fullest.

In the meantime, a new generation was growing up whose sense of the
world had been formed almost entirely by the heady climate of the
post-1967 period. To them the early struggles for statehood, and all that
they entailed, seemed as remote a part of the past as the story of King
David, or the legend of the Maccabees. When they pictured the future they
could see it only as a continuation of the glistening present. And an older
generation failed in its duty to remind them of the lessons of Jewish
history.

Now we are all on the other side of Yom Kippur, and the important
questions being asked today have little to do with party politics, or the
issue of whether the country has grown more "hawkish" or "dovish" in
the aftermath of its recent experience. Even while the political pundits
have been busy proving how right they had been all along, the country
itself has been engaged in a far deeper kind of self-examination. A clue to
its nature may be found in the curious fact, noticeable from the very first
days of the war, that the popular hit songs of the 70's—so beloved of the
younger generation—seemed all at once to have faded from earshot.
Instead, the army was suddenly singing the old tunes from the War of
Independence that had not been heard in Israel since the late 40's and early
50's—the songs of their parents' generation. Even before these young
soldiers told us—as they would again and again—that the life-and-death
struggle of the Yom Kippur War had made the War of Independence real to
them in a way that it had never been before, we got the message from the
songs they sang.

Many other things have changed since last October. Suddenly, the style
of life that came into being with the new affluence of the late 60's and early
70's seems to be on the wane. The new bars, coffee shops, and boutiques, so
much in vogue only a short time ago, are half deserted these days. People
stay at home more, and spend more time with friends. A new mood of

introspection has taken hold. Over and over again, in one way or another, one hears the same sentiment expressed: something has gone wrong, we must return to ourselves.

How long this new mood will last, or how deep it goes, it is impossible to say—prophecy is always hazardous, especially where such intangible questions are concerned. For the moment however, the evidence seems unarguable that a genuine inner change has taken place in Israel as a result of the war. One sees it in the way this war has come to be identified with the ordinary soldiers of Israel's army, rather than with the generals. One sees it in the absence of the kind of self-glorifying souvenir books and albums that flooded the market after the Six-Day War. One sees it in the quiet dignity and determination with which the populace reacted to the heavy casualties. One sees it in the uncomplaining acceptance of heavier taxes, and the willing submission to extended military service by many who had been called up on Yom Kippur morning and were still—as of this writing—on active duty for an indefinite period.

This side of Yom Kippur is an Israeli who seems quite different from the jaunty prototype of recent years, closer in spirit to the Israeli of an earlier day when the state first came into being. This side of Yom Kippur is an Israeli who awoke from a pipedream, only to find himself trapped in a nightmare. Perhaps the shock will yet prove to have been salutary. The new Israeli may be more willing than before—acknowledging the realities of his situation—to strike some sort of bargain with his adversary. But whatever he does his eyes are open at last, and he will not soon be caught dreaming again. I am reminded of an exchange which took place in what seems now like the far distant past—it must have been about two years ago or so—between a young, aggressively dovish writer, and Prime Minister Golda Meir. "Do you ever have a dream?" the writer asked Mrs. Meir. The question seemed apt at the time, but now her answer seems more so. "I have hardly a moment for dreams," she replied. "They wake me up nights."

99. INVITATION TO WEEPING

ARNON LAPID

Shortly after the Yom Kippur War, *Iggeret,* weekly organ of the Mapai kibbutz movement, published a moving article by a veteran of that war—Arnon Lapid, of Kibbutz Givat Haim. Lapid's essay was entitled "Invitation to Weeping." It was a disturbing summons that evoked responses as moving as Lapid's own outcry. Some of the replies to the "invitation" were published in *Shdemot,* the youth division quarterly of the Mapai kibbutz movement.

The following are excerpts from the "Invitation" and the replies, selected and translated from the Hebrew by Moshe Kohn, literary editor of the *Jerusalem Post*.

We lay curled up in a shallow foxhole in the soft sand, Uriel and I. It was an ugly dawn hour, sky and earth were aflame. Uriel, a boy slim and beautiful as a girl, talked about Milan, from whence he had landed the day before yesterday, and I told him about New York which I had left four days before.

Uriel was saying he just had to fix me up with this gorgeous girl, Iris, because it wasn't possible that we shouldn't meet—we were simply made for each other.

He was inserting sparkling new bullets into his clip, and I was sucking a mint to freshen my mouth after the night's sleep. Before the order came to leave the foxholes, we made a quick decision to have a big party at his house after the war.

Uriel promised to send me a gilded invitation.

At noon, his body was lying under a blanket in the field hospital.

Funny that we had thought of a party.

I want to send you an invitation to weeping.

The date and the hour don't matter, but the program, I guarantee you, will be a rich one: weeping. We'll cry for hours, and together—because I just can't do it alone. All through the war I wanted to cry but couldn't. This time it will work; it must. Nothing can stop us.

I'll cry for my dead: Avremele, Ilan, Amitai, Dudu, Uzi, Yair, Uriel—and you'll cry for yours.

And we'll cry together for the dreams out of which we've been shaken, for the grand things turned trivial, for the gods that failed, for the meaninglessness, the lack of will, the impotence, the present devoid of even a single ray of light. . . .

We'll cry for the fast friendships that have been cut off, the pricked illusions . . . the plans that will never be carried out, the dark cloud that will now hang forever over every celebration.

And we'll feel sorry for ourselves, because we deserve pity—a lost generation of a tormented people in "a land that consumes its inhabitants."

The big deciders, the oh-so-sober ones, won't be allowed in. This isn't for them.

Oh, will we cry. Bitterly we'll cry. Heartrendingly. Hugely.

We'll cry cupfuls. Kettlefuls. Rivers.

Anyone feeling that he's had it, that he's all dried up, that he hasn't a tear left in him—will sneak out. On tiptoe, so as not to spoil the evening.

Most likely, I'll be the last one left.

But, anytime at all—next month, in two months, next year—you can come again. The door's open. It's a standing invitation: from now on, my place is always open for crying. . . .

REPLIES AND COMMENTS

From Lotte Aharon, member of the same kibbutz as Arnon Lapid and mother of two boys who fell in the Yom Kippur War—Yehuda (the Dudu mentioned in the "invitation") and Hanokh:

No, Arnon, I don't agree with you. I'm the mother of Dudu and Hanokh, and they wouldn't have agreed with you either. They wouldn't want to see us cry. . . .

Not cry. Let's all sit down together—you and those who loved them: Amitai and Avremele and Yair and Hanokh and all the rest of them—and think! Think hard, and not about "failures" or "wars of the generals" or political parties. Think about how to go on, how to build a society that really knows what's special about itself. They didn't come here to get killed or to kill. They came because this is where their roots are. Here is where they were shaped. Let's sit together and think about how to build a society, a nation, a homeland.

And let's help the widows, the orphans, the brothers and sisters, the friends . . . till we hear them laugh again. Let's feel the confidence they felt. No, Arnon—when Yisrael fell, Dudu shouted at me: "Mama, you mustn't cry! Paratroopers don't cry." (I know he cried—but out of sight, alone; and we also cry—but alone, each one of us separately, and then smoothen ourselves out for each other.)

In his last postcard, Dudu wrote me to "keep up the company's good name." No, Dudu, we'll be worthy of you. We'll sit and plan.

Be strong, Arnon. That's the way they would have wanted us.

From Yehoshua, a soldier then stationed on the western shore of the Suez Canal:

Such sensitivity and courage. What bravado and cheek it takes to write so sincerely and intimately on weeping and pain without paying lip service to "strength" and "valor" and "manliness," to "happy end" and "glimmering hope," the way everybody is doing with nauseating banality. How wise of you to forego politics and "constructive suggestions." I hate, I hate (maybe because I fail to understand) those who don't allow themselves to bow thier heads, to weep absolutely, cathartically, pessimistically.

I know, Arnon: tomorrow or the next day, in a month or two, you'll get over it, and then you'll be the same optimistic, hedonistic, cynical Arnon I've known for years. But promise you'll never be ashamed of having written what you did. . . .

From Alex Barzel, of Kibbutz Kfar Hahoresh:

My door has also been open, for years, for people to come and weep with me. But I'll come, Arnon, I'll come to you. Now I must stand weeping alongside you so that you may be able to help me carry my burden.

. . . I have wept for the shadowy column of women being led off to slave labor and worse, for the children and old people—of my own family as well—being tormented, and all the rest of that suffering throng, of all nations and languages, around me. I was shaken, and I wept in Rome's gloomy railway station when I faced that 30-foot wall on which hung pictures of my dear ones with all the details written underneath. . . .

Afterwards, I wept for a blue-eyed boy with whom I had plowed in Galilee, a boy who was the personification of love, of life, of tomorrow—and who now lies buried at Huleikat. I wept for the husky boy in the next bunker after a shell tore a hole in his chest.

And I wept for the driver of the armored vehicle with whom I traveled to the Negev one pitchblack, menacing night, and who two days later was one of the shattered monuments in Shaar Hagai.

And I wept for the father of five who was still alive as we carried him under a rain of mortar shells at Sharm el-Sheikh. Then, in the years that followed, as Welfare Sergeant of the brigade that never forgot, I wept with his widow and orphans.

In the Six-Day War, my heart went out to the fallen sons of my friends, to my fallen pupils.

Today, too.

You see, Arnon, I'm carrying a frightful burden. I came into the world two decades before you, and in so short a time this world has become filled with so much hate, so much bereavement—but also, always, so much hope. . . .

I'll come to weep with you. But not over ourselves. I've never wept over myself as though I were a "lost generation." There have been, and there are today, people who are far more lost than I.

No Arnon, there is no time now to cry over myself, because in an hour, tomorrow, I have to get on with building a world which may somehow be better. . . . We will bring to that world a burden of never-ceasing weeping, but also renewed vitality. I will not "sneak out on tiptoe." I will stay so that, between cries, we will be able, together, to look the future in the face.

From Nira, of Kibbutz Hulda:

This winter, Arnon, we will join you for the big weeping party. But after the winter comes the spring, and then we'll have to put an end to the weeping. . . .

It will be necessary to harvest the winter crops. And others will be sitting on the tractors in place of those who are gone. They will be young and beautiful, and we shall not wish to weep with them—we will want to live with them.

You've invited us to come and weep with you always. But we are a people that cannot weep endlessly. We've had enough weeping since the days of the "Waters of Babylon," through the pogroms and expulsions, to the European Holocaust. . . . This coming summer many babies will be born, children of those who are gone and those still with us, a new generation recalling those left on the battlefield. These babies will grow up and laugh, and we will smile along with them, knowing that *this* is the way, the only way.

So forgive me, Arnon, if, come spring, I don't show up at the weeping party. I hereby invite you to the living party, the living that thrusts forward toward hope.

100. THE ISRAEL-ARAB CONFLICT: TWO VIEWPOINTS

ALBERT HOURANI and J. L. TALMON

The following two articles, "Palestine and Israel" by Albert Hourani and "Israel and the Arabs" by J. L. Talmon, were published in September 1967 in the *London Observer*. Hourani, an Arab, is director of the Middle Eastern Center and fellow of St. Antony's College in Oxford. Talmon is professor of modern history at the Hebrew University of Jerusalem.

A. Palestine and Israel

Albert Hourani

At the heart of the Middle Eastern problem lies the problem of Palestine: the struggle of Palestinian Arabs and Jewish settlers for possession and mastery of the land. Now that the Powers have been drawn in and a local crisis has become a world-wide one, it is easy to forget the local causes of it; but it is dangerous, for unless they are treated the crisis may return.

The struggle of Arabs and Jews for Palestine cannot be explained by ancient religious hostility. Jews (and Christians) had always lived among the mainly Arab Muslim population of Palestine, and relations between them had usually been correct. But in the 1880s a new type of Jewish immigration began, mainly from Eastern Europe, inspired by the Zionist idea of a Jewish national home: this soon aroused the hostility of Ottoman officials and part of the population.

During its 30 years of rule, 1917-47, Britain bound itself by the Balfour Declaration and the Mandate to encourage the Jewish national home, subject to the rights of the existing population; immigration increased, particularly after the rise of Hitler, and Arab opposition became almost universal and drew in the surrounding Arab States.

This hostility sprang from the attempt to implant a new society in a land already occupied by an old one. When the settlers came they found a complete society already there: farmers, craftsmen and merchants, ancient towns and villages, religious institutions, a culture expressed in Arabic, a leadership which formed part of the Arab Ottoman *élite*. The aim of the newcomers was not to be absorbed into it but to create their own society with its farms and cities, institutions, Hebrew culture and political leaders.

In the age of European expansion, other such attempts were made to plant new societies amidst old ones. They always caused strain, but Zionist settlement in Palestine had special features. The new Jewish society, by the nature of the Zionist idea, was to be a complete and exclusive one. Its aim was to create a wholly Jewish economy: land bought by the Jewish National Fund became the inalienable property of the Jewish people and no non-Jew could ever be employed on it.

Zionist Idea

It is true, the Zionists bought their land. But in the Middle East political power and ownership of land have always gone together, and the Arabs were convinced that if the Jews had power they would seize the greater part of the land. That the Jews *would* take power became first a danger, then a certainty, as the Jewish population grew. Because of the nature of the Zionist idea, the new Jewish society was an expanding society, open to all who wished to come in. In 1922 Jews formed 13 per cent of the population of Palestine; in 1935, 28 per cent; in 1947, 33 per cent.

As numbers grew, the idea of a Jewish national home turned into that of a Jewish State, and this was unacceptable to the Arabs, not only because by the 1930s most of them were moved by the idea of an Arab State of which Palestine would be part, but because in a Jewish State they would have no choice (whatever guarantee the Mandate might contain) except between being a powerless minority and leaving their country.

Some Zionist leaders did indeed talk of a 'bi-national State,' but attempts at political agreement broke on the question of immigration. The Arabs wanted to preserve the Arab character of Palestine, and so wanted little or no Jewish immigration. The Zionists wanted to keep the doors of Palestine open, no matter what the form of government.

Here lay the dilemma of their policy: they wanted agreement with the Arabs and they wanted unlimited immigration, but they could not have both, and if forced to choose most of them would choose immigration.

The British, who were politically responsible, had no clear or stable policy on this matter. They had obligations to the Arabs and so opposed the idea of a Jewish State: they had obligations to the Zionists and so permitted immigration, not as much as the Jews wanted but enough to make a Jewish State possible. In 1948, unable to reach agreement with the two parties, they withdrew in circumstances which made fighting inevitable, and there happened what the Arabs had feared for so long.

The dynamic, exclusive, alien society which had grown up among them seized power in the greater part of Palestine, with encouragement and help from some Western States, secured control of the land and brought in immigrants on a large scale; and two-thirds of the Arab inhabitants lost their lands and homes.

All wars create refugees, and after the armies have departed the peasants and merchants return to take up their lives again. Civilised Governments accept that they have a responsibility for those who live in the land they rule. But after the armistice agreements of 1949 Israel refused—with limited exceptions—to allow the Arab refugees to return. In a situation like this everything becomes political, and the Israelis made political use of the refugees.

Conquered Land

By refusing to consider the refugee problem except in the framework of a peace settlement with the surrounding Arab States, they linked together two matters which had no moral connection; for the return of the refugees was an obligation which they owed not to the surrounding Arab States but to the Palestinian Arabs themselves, as inhabitants of the land they had conquered. To make such a connection was the more tempting because Israel did not really wish the refugees to return. Even at a peace settlement it would only have offered to take back a small number; for what it wanted was to have the land without its inhabitants, so as to settle its own immigrants.

(This policy was made morally acceptable to Israelis and the outside world by the 'myth' that the Arabs left willingly under orders from their leaders. No more than the most tenuous evidence was produced for this, and, in fact, the flight of the Arabs presents no mystery. Some left for reasons of prudence, some from panic during the fighting, some were forced to go by the Israeli Army. What has happened this year throws some light on this. It is clear that no Arab Government ordered the Palestinians to leave this year, but a quarter of the inhabitants of the West Bank left in two months—and for the same reasons.)

Nothing could show more clearly that the basic dilemma of Zionist policy was still there. If it wanted land for immigrants, it was sensible to stop the return of the refugees. But if it wanted peace with the Arabs, then it was fatal.

After 1948, the first step to peace was that Israel should recognise its responsibility to the Arabs who lived in its territory but had been displaced by the fighting. Only this could have set in motion a train of events leading towards peace; and only Israel, as victor and beneficiary of the war, could have taken the step. Israel never did so, and its attitude was accepted by the Western Powers. Every year the United Nations passed a resolution calling for the return or compensation of the refugees, but no one tried seriously to carry it out.

Shock of Exile

The assumption which underlay the attitude of Israel and the Western Powers was that sooner or later the refugees would melt away, absorbed into the surrounding Arab peoples, and then the problem of Palestine would cease to exist. But this was a false assumption. It was not a mass of individuals who fled in 1948, it was the greater part of a society. A common land and language, a common political fate, and the shock of exile created a Palestine Arab nation. After 1948 it lived scattered.

Allowing for natural increase, by the beginning of this year there must have been rather more than two million Palestinian Arabs: almost 400,000 in the Gaza Strip, 300,000 in Israel, 1,300,000 in Jordan, 150,000 each in Lebanon and Syria. About two-thirds of them were still registered refugees. Many of these had become wholly or partly self-supporting; if more had not, it was not (as was often said) because the host-countries did not wish them to be settled, but because the absorption of refugees depended on the pace of economic development, and this was bound to be slow in the early stages. In no country was their position satisfactory.

In Jordan they had full citizenship, but Palestinians and Transjordanians had not yet been welded into a complete unity, and positions of real power remained in Transjordanian hands; an intelligent policy of development created an economy into which some of them were absorbed, but the refugees formed a third of the whole population, and a country with such limited resources could not absorb so large a number in 20 years.

In Israel, their position was tolerable: they had civil and political rights, but fewer opportunities of higher education and skilled employment than Jews, they lived under a strict military control (until a relaxation in recent months), and were virtually shut out of the political community.

Thus the Palestinian Arabs remained in being as a nation which had lost almost everything but was determined to continue to exist: that is to say, to live with one another, and to live in Palestine. After 1948 this was the heart of the 'Palestine problem'; the *de facto* existence of Israel was not in serious danger, but what remained to be assured was the existence of the Palestinian nation. Its attitude to Israel was shared by the other Arab nations, for many reasons. The individual losses of the refugees were felt throughout Jordan, Syria and Lebanon, which belonged to the same geographical and historical unit as Palestine, and where almost every family had Palestinian connections.

More widespread still was a sense of human indignity, a feeling that in the eyes of Israel and the West the Arabs were surplus human beings, to be removed and dumped elsewhere to redress a wrong not they but Europe had done to the Jews. It seemed to most Arabs that Western Governments talked in one way about the rights of the Jews and in another about those of the Arabs. They often said that Israel was here to stay; they never said that the Palestinian Arab nation was here to stay. They talked in language of high principles and threats about Israel's right to free navigation; they used a milder language about the right of the refugees to return or compensation. Unwise statements by Arab spokesmen about throwing Israel into the sea were widely quoted and condemned; no one seemed to care that Israel had, in fact, thrown a large number of Arabs into the desert.

Together with this went an almost universal fear. So long as Israel remained open to all Jews who wished to immigrate, so long as it could maintain Western standards of technology and hope for wide support in Europe and America, there would be a danger of its expanding into the territory of the surrounding States. Sooner or later, most Arabs believed, Israel would absorb the rest of Palestine, and perhaps parts of southern Syria and Lebanon as well; for a second time the Palestinians would have to move out, and would find themselves walking down the road to Jericho or scrambling across the Jordan bridges.

Self-defeating

Whatever their differences on other matters, the Arab States were united in their attitude to Israel, and attracted the support—within limits—of most Afro-Asian and communist States. But coalitions are fragile, in particular if they include States of unequal strength. The common object which brings them together becomes entangled with the separate interests and claims of each, and it was this which led the Arabs into statements and acts which were self-defeating. The essential point of their progaganda was justice for the Palestinian Arabs.

Before 1948 it had been possible to argue that a Jewish State should not be set up because this would be unjust to the Arabs; but once Israel had become a member of the UN, to talk in terms of its disappearance as a State was to embarrass allies and touch a sensitive spot in the European conscience. The official policy of the Arab States was not to destroy Israel but to return to the settlement of 1947-48 and a fulfilment of all the UN resolutions; but at the same time they insisted they were still in a state of active belligerence.

Extreme Terms

This was a dangerous policy for a weaker party to adopt towards a stronger: it gave Israel a license to attack whenever it could claim that its interests were in danger. Israel indeed always remained balanced between two policies: it wanted peace with the Arabs if it could obtain it on its own terms; but war with the Arabs might give it better frontiers.

An Arab policy based on inferior power but expressed in extreme terms played into Israel's hands. This was shown clearly in the events of May and June. For 10 years Egypt and Jordan had kept their frontiers with Israel quiet, and there is no reason to think they wanted a change. But the Syrian frontier was disturbed because of the difficult problem of the demilitarised zone.

Syria began supporting Palestinian activist groups; Israel replied, first by an unprovoked attack on Jordan, not Syria, then by threats which constituted a challenge to Egypt. Egypt replied by sending its Army to the frontier. In so doing Egypt acted as prisoner of the hopes it had aroused, but clearly it did not expect to fight. Egypt's acts were directed towards a political settlement, and its mistake was to think not that the Russians would support it more than they did, but that the Americans would restrain Israel more than they did—that the United States could or would force Israel to give Egypt a victory which might lead to further demands.

Israel called the Egyptian bluff in circumstances which brought it the greatest possible support in the Western world, not only because of Egypt's bad relations with the US and Britain but because of foolish statements by Arab leaders skilfully used by Zionist propaganda.

The frightening wave of anti-Arab feeling which swept Europe and America in June is not the subject of this article. Ordinary people, Jews and non-Jews, certainly felt that Israel was threatened with destruction. It is more difficult to believe that the Israel Government thought so, knowing its own military strength and that it had a guarantee (implicit or formal) from the strongest Power in the world. However that may be, the defensive

war soon became a 'defensive-offensive' one, and once more what the
Palestinians had feared came true.

More Refugees

The Israeli victory has changed many things in the Middle East, but it
has not changed the problem of Palestine. The Palestinian Arab people are
still there, still in ruin and exile, still determined to exist. Perhaps
two-thirds of them are now under Israeli rule; many more refugees have
been created, and it is not certain that Israel will allow most of them to
return; many who are not refugees have been ruined by the occupation of
half Jordan; every individual Palestinian had now suffered or lost
something because of Israel.

The attitude of the Palestinians towards Jordan may well have changed,
and if the West Bank is returned Jordan may become a more solid and
united State. But in spite of Israeli hopes and efforts, there is no reason to
believe that the attitude of Palestinian Arabs towards Israel has changed,
except to be hardened by new losses. The Arab States have more and not
less reason to think of Israel as an expansionist State which, with the help
or acquiescence of the US, may dominate politically and economically the
region lying between Nile and Euphrates.

It seems not impossible that the Arab States will be persuaded to make a
declaration of non-belligerence and the Israelis to withdraw from the
conquered lands. Even so, the basic dilemma of Israeli policy remains. The
Palestinian Arabs are the estranged neighbours with whom Israel must be
reconciled if it is to become 'like all nations'; and it remains true, as it has
been since 1948, that the first step towards a stable *modus vivendi* is one
which only Israel can take—to accept its responsibility towards the
indigenous people of the land it controls, and to grant the refugees the
right of return or compensation.

In the long run it may be in Israel's interest to do this: only as a mixed
State has it a chance of being accepted by its neighbours. But in the short
run, the desire for security and for further immigration works against it. It
seems more likely than not that Israel will do nothing. If so, it may stay in
Gaza and the West Bank; part of the Arab population may be squeezed out;
the rump of Jordan may be absorbed into some other State; and in a few
more years the Palestinian Arab nation may rise once more to haunt Israel,
this time inside as well as outside its frontiers.

B. Israel and the Arabs

J. L. Talmon

The Arab-Israeli dispute has become a world issue. This time the world
has had a lucky escape, possibly thanks to the swiftness and completeness

of the Israeli victory. No one can be sure of such good luck in the case of another round.

Who are the parties to the Israel-Arab conflict? Clearly not only the Jews of Israel on the one side, and the Palestine Arabs on the other. They are Israel—representing in some way world Jewry—and the Arab world acting on behalf of the Palestine Arabs.

To me, after reading Dr. Hourani's article 'Palestine and Israel' in the *Observer* last week, the conflict illustrates that the view one takes on the particular rights and wrongs is determined by one's disposition towards the general case—recognition or non-recognition of an overriding right, a will to war or a will to peace.

But no one who believes and claims for his own people the right of national liberation and self-determination may decry Zionist settlement as 'imperialist invasion.' Nor must its significance be reduced to the dimensions of an asylum for a mob of refugees driven out by Hitler and then thrown upon the Arabs, who had no share in the persecution. It was only natural, once the urge for corporate self-expression in conditions of sovereign mastery over their own fate—the most potent and universal impulse in modern times—had seized the heirs of one of the most ancient peoples on earth, that the aspiration should rivet itself to their ancient home, where their identity was first evolved and where their distinct and so significant contribution to mankind's heritage was shaped.

Persecution

Millions of Europe's Jews were then overtaken by a wave of murderous persecutions without precedent. Literally hunted for their lives, they had no Government to appeal to for protection, no tribunal to turn to for redress—delivered into the hands of assassins on the sole condition that they would be put to death. This traumatic experience fired the Israelis with the desperate resolve to gain, in one place in the world, political sovereignty, without having to rely on the protection or help of others, and to fight for it to death.

On the plane of lesser urgency, the annihilation of that compact and vital Jewish civilisation in central and eastern Europe, coupled with the loss of cohesion in Jewish life in the remaining Diaspora, has left Israel as sole guarantor of the survival of the corporate identity of the Jews as a people. This explains the recent upsurge of first anguished and then proud solidarity with Israel in all parts of Jewry.

But what about the Arab rights and claims? I would classify myself as one of those Zionists who, though passionately convinced of the rightness of the Jewish case, are nevertheless made acutely uneasy by the thought of the Arabs. They can find no sustenance in ascribing to the Arabs some special dose of original sin and selfish greed, let alone inferiority. Dr. Weizmann aptly described our position when he spoke of the Jewish-Arab conflict as a clash of rights, for which a solution could be found only on the lines of least injustice, and where no perfect justice was possible.

Dr. Hourani seems to make the distinction between the Palestine Arabs as a mass of human beings and Palestinian Arab nationhood. On the sufferings of the former, I must confess I have no answer, no more than to the bafflingly cruel mystery why innocent people suffer and die when States engage in wars, nor to the chilling fact that there has not been a nation in history, including the mightiest Powers and richest civilisations on earth, which has not established itself through invading, subjugating, expelling, or indeed annihilating vast native populations. Dr. Hourani himself admits that the situation of the Arabs under Israeli jurisdiction has been tolerable.

Identity

Just as there is no justification for the claim that Israel is in any way an obstacle to the flowering of an Arab renaissance in the vast territories around Palestine, there is no ground for maintaining that Palestinian Arab national identity and culture have suffered mortal injury from the encroachment of the Jews. The Arabs themselves had until recently been vehemently denying the existence of such an entity as Palestine, insisting that the Holy Land was nothing but southern Syria, as administratively it was under the Turks. There has never been a distinct Arab-Palestinian culture, literature, dialect or national consciousness. Although it is one of the holy Muslim cities, Jerusalem has never played any role comparable to Cairo, Damascus or Baghdad in Arab history. And so, while the obliteration of Jewish Israel would make the survival of the Jewish entity very problematic, even a complete de-Arabisation of Palestine—which is hardly at stake—would have no vital effect on the Arab totality nor, in the last analysis, on even the aspiration towards permanent Arab unity.

Admittedly, not much thought was given to the Palestine Arabs before or at the end of the First World War. Britain, which issued the Balfour Declaration of 1917, and the countries which endorsed the Mandate on Palestine in 1921, had all been nurtured on biblical reminiscences of the eternal bond between the children of Israel and their promised land. They knew next to nothing of the Arabs, nor were they particularly worried about the rights of the native populations of the partitioned Ottoman Empire—especially since the Arabs had emerged after the First World War from centuries of Turkish bondage with large self-governing territories, in comparison with which what was promised to the Jews seemed so little.

For a fleeting moment it seemed also as if the Weizmann-Faisal agreement might ensure a *modus vivendi* between the diverse aspirations of the two races. Addicted to their idealistic endeavour, so pathetically eager to turn the desert into garden, the Jews would at first meet any argument about the Arabs with vague expressions of benevolence, quite sincerely disclaiming any wish to hurt them. They were passionately anxious to build up a normal integrated Jewish society and to disprove the slander of their detractors that they were made only for usury and commerce and not for labour and toil. They were also afraid of being put in the position of European planters in Asia and Africa, and so they insisted on employing only Jewish labour on the Jewish national land.

Then, in 1937, when the clash between Arabs and Jews became too acute, the Jews accepted the Royal (or Peel) Commission plan for partition, although by then the need for a refuge from antisemitic persecution was already desperately urgent. It was rejected uncompromisingly by the Arabs. The same happened in 1947—when the United Nations, with the United States and Russia acting as sponsors, resolved upon partition. The Arabs have never since tired of proclaiming a state of war against Israel. In violent and blood-curdling language they continued to voice their intention to wipe out Israel, and indeed its inhabitants. Survivors of Auschwitz could not be expected to treat such threats as mere rhetoric or figures of speech. Nor could they be blamed if they resolved to acts of war, when day in and day out it was not only dinned into their ears that a state of siege was on, but demonstrated to them in the form of infiltration, sabotage, murder and arson.

Intransigent

It was as if God had hardened the heart of Pharaoh: the more intransigent the form of Arab enmity toward Israel, the worse were the consequences for the Arabs themselves. The armed resistance of the Arab States to the UN plan created the refugee problem; the resumption of fighting after the first cease-fire resulted in the loss of more Arab territory; Arab sabotage on the one hand and alliance with Russia on the other only led to a strengthening of Israel's might; finally, this year, the attempt to strangle Israel brought the Arabs a most humiliating *débâcle*.

The armistice agreements concluded in 1949 between the new State of Israel and the Arab countries contained *prima facie* all the guarantees for peace, if not in form, at least in substance. They forbade hostile propaganda, acts of sabotage, operations by military or paramilitary formations, above all armed intrusions or incursions by Army detachments.

In a state of war no points of contact are possible. Hence the irrelevance of the empirical approach, so dear to Anglo-Saxon statesmanship, which sets its hopes on gradual, imperceptible sliding from a state of half-war, half-peace into a state of full peace, from contact and cooperation in small things—such as sharing the waters of the Jordan—to sustained neighbourly give-and-take in all spheres.

This is the context of the question of refugees. Acute as the problem is in terms of human suffering, and few Jews, sons of a nation of exiles and refugees, can be callously indifferent to this aspect of the problem, the state of war makes its solution quite impossible. The world is understandably deeply exercised by the plight of hundreds of thousands of refugees wasting away their lives in camps in pitiable conditions.

One often hears the well-intentioned opinion that this is the most serious obstacle to peace, and that if this tragedy were to be put out of the way, peace could easily be established. The Arabs themselves have never said that the return of the Arab refugees to Palestine was their condition for peace; quite the reverse. In October 1949 the Egyptian Foreign Minister said: 'It should be known and well understood that in demanding the return of the refugees to Palestine the Arabs mean their return as masters of their country and not as slaves. More clearly, they envisage the liquidation of Israel.' In a speech in 1964 President Nasser stated: 'There have been attempts to separate the issues and present them in an imaginary way, as if the question of Israel is just the problem of refugees, and that once this problem is solved the Palestine question would be solved and no trace would be left of it. The Israeli danger lies in the very existence of Israel and in what this State represents.'

If war was the objective, no one could blame the Israelis for believing that the demand for the readmission of refugees, or compensation for them, was motivated not just by the wish to see them restored to their homes, but by the desire to use them as an instrument, a Trojan horse, to disrupt Israel. Besides, the way to solve the refugee problem is surely not by revanchism. What Pandora's boxes would be opened if all nations whose members had been driven from their homes by armed hostilities were to resort to war to right the wrong or merely to wreak vengeance.

Immigrants

Israel has already absorbed in the last 20 years about 600,000 Jewish immigrants from the Arab countries. The Arab refugee problem is intractable, not because no solution can be found through their resettlement and absorption elsewhere in the Arab countries, but because of the implacable Arab refusal even to consider such a possibility lest this blunt the edge of the refugee issue as a political weapon. In fact, the refugee problem is not the sole or even the main obstacle to peace: it is the state of war that is the chief obstacle to the solution of the refugee problem. But

Arabs would not, and perhaps could not, see that, because Israel has become to them an obsession, indeed a neurosis.

The Arabs are a proud race emamoured of the memories of their past glories. When they woke up so late from their long lethargy, they were, like all late-comers, in a great haste to recover their place in the sun. They were then faced by the inexorable facts of actual weakness, underdevelopment and vast misery. The combination of resentment towards the West and the envious desire to appropriate and utilise its achievements and levers of power, plus the frustrations encountered in the attempt to skip centuries of social and economic development, led Arabs to put all the blame on imperialism—although in comparative terms the brunt of imperialism was felt much more heavily by other races.

World support for Zionist settlement, for which Arab consent was neither sought nor obtained, and then the establishment of Israel, assumed in the eyes of Arab nationalism the dimensions of a mortal injury, especially as it came from the hands of the Jews, whom they had been accustomed to despise as second-class citizens and a non-martial race of infidels.

The Palestine issue has become the symbol and focus of all Arab frustrations. Their sense of grievance blinds them to the historic rights, the background of tragedy behind the Jewish aspirations, the ardour and high idealism motivating them and the genuine interest of the civilised world in the restoration of Jewish statehood.

The student of Arab opinion and Arab thought is often horrified to watch the growth of the anti-Israel obsession to the point of it having become the cornerstone of a kind of systematic Manichean* metaphysic, with the Jew as devil incarnate.

The paramount task at present is to put an end to the general atmosphere of 'kill him before he kills you.' The Arabs threaten to kill the Jews; the Jews then feel they must forestall the Arabs; the Arabs are convinced the Jews are out to kill them off, and so when an armed clash occurs they start running; the Arabs swear bloody vengeance; the Jews insist on maximum guarantees. Any historian knows what a corroding effect this sense of a state of mortal emergency has on peace, morality and freedom. The Arabs are now, understandably, in a state of shock. But one believes one perceives wiser and more prudent counsels stirring among some of them, although for the time being these are too inhibited to come out into the open.

Israel is still more deeply divided. There are those who anxiously 'await

---

*Manichean: a religious system in ancient Persia which assumed the rule of two equal principles, good and evil, God and Satan. (Ed.)

a telephone call from King Hussein,' hoping for an arrangement with him whereby Jordan would receive back most of the West Bank, except some strategic points and of course, excepting Jerusalem, plus access to and possibly control over the Muslim holy places. These hopes also assume that world-wide financial support, combined with a substantial Israeli contribution—by way of compensation—would not only make the resettlement of refugees possible, but also put Hussein back on his feet, and create a network of joint, international sponsored ventures in the form of vast works for desalination, irrigation, and so on, for the benefit of all concerned.

There are the others who, pointing to Arab intransigence, claim to see in the triumph of Israel arms the hand of God. Such a chance occurs only once in history, they say. The present generation of Israelis has no right to barter away the promised inheritance, which belongs to all generations. There can be no retreat from the strategic frontiers, particularly on the Jordan, the heights of Golan, and the Suez Canal. (Others would be content with the demilitarisation of Sinai.) They insist on the sacrosanct character of the geopolitical entity that is Palestine.

Romantics

While the mystics and romantics are obsessed with the danger from outside, the moderate realists fear the enormous difficulties inside, arising out of the presence of a large compact territorial Arab minority. They are also beset by grave moral scruples and are apprehensive of world public opinion. To this the former, among them a surprising number of declared leftists, retort by condemning their adversaries as men of small Zionist faith, who also lack confidence in the ability of Israel to treat an Arab minority humanely and well and to solve all the social and economic problems involved.

In the hopeless view they take of the Arab readiness to recognise the existence of Israel, the hawks of Israel are most likely to add fuel to the hawks in the Arab world. This paradoxical 'alliance' can be countered, and the vicious circle broken, only by an 'alliance' of the moderate realists on both sides. And I can only hope that my friend Hourani and men like him will heed this appeal to their moral obligation towards their own people and mankind in general.

QUESTIONS FOR THOUGHT AND DISCUSSION

1. What are the reasons which prompted Moses Hess to suggest the restoration of the Jewish state?

2. Why does Leo Pinsker plead for the establishment of a Jewish state? Does his reasoning differ from that of Moses Hess? If yes, in what way?

3. The restoration of Zion is an ancient Jewish hope. What is the difference between this hope and modern political Zionism?

4. What ideas are common to Hess, Pinsker, and Herzl?

5. Richard Gottheil was the first American Zionist leader to explain the aims of Zionism in behalf of the American Zionist Federation, founded shortly after the First Zionist Congress in 1897. Does Gottheil's article contain any basic difference that would be characteristic of American Zionism?

6. Explain the attitudes of various Jewish groups that opposed Herzl's Zionism.

7. Explain the "Uganda scheme."

8. What are the new emphases that Herzl's Zionism brought into Jewish life?

9. In what way can Zionism be considered an answer to the "Jewish question" that arose in the nineteenth century as a result of the emancipation?

10. What has made possible the revival of Hebrew as a modern language?

11. What is the basic cause of the Israel-Arab conflict?

12. A modern nation usually exercises independent sovereignty and possesses a land of its own as well as a language of its own. In modern times nationalities which lack one or the other of the above features, or possess them only in part, have developed national movements that aim to acquire the missing elements and thus become a nation in the full sense of the word. What tasks common to all national movements did Zionism have to undertake, and which are additional ones characteristic only of the Jewish situation?

13. Which Zionist hopes have been realized by the establishment of the State of Israel? Which have not?

SUGGESTED READING

Note: Books suggested in more than one chapter are here listed by the name of the author only. A key to such listings will be found at the end of the book.

A paperback edition is indicated by the letters PB.

Books for the Student

Textbooks

Charry-Segal, chap. 22.
Elbogen, pp. 245–308, 473–84, 589–635.
Grayzel, pp. 664–84, 722–25, 759–66, 793–800.
Grayzel II, pp. 21–23, 61–67, 79–82, 127–43. PB.

Israel

Essrig, Harry, and Alfred Segal. *Israel Today.* New York, 1968.
Levin, Meyer. *Story of Israel.* Berkeley, Calif., 1972, PB.

Zionism

Heller, Joseph. *The Zionist Idea.* New York, 1949.
Parzen, Herbert. *A Short History of Zionism.* New York, 1962.

Biographies

Bein, Alex. *Theodor Herzl: A Biography.* Philadelphia, 1956. PB.
Omer, Dvorah. *Rebirth: The story of Eliezer ben Yehudah and the Modern Hebrew Language.* Philadelphia, 1972.
St. John, Robert. *Ben Gurion: A Biography.* Garden City, N.Y., 1971.
———. *The Tongue of the Prophets: The Life Story of Eliezer ben Yehudah.* North Hollywood, Calif., 1972. PB.
Zeitlin, Rose. *Henrietta Szold: Record of a Life.* New York, 1952.

Anthologies

Blocker, Joel, ed. *Israeli Stories.* New York, 1968. PB.
Katzenelson Shazar, Rachel. *The Plough Woman: Memoirs of the Pioneer Women in Palestine.* New York, 1975. PB.
Yaari, Avraham. *The Goodly Heritage: Memoirs Describing the Life of the Jewish Community of Eretz Israel from the Seventeenth to the Twentieth Centuries.* Jerusalem, 1958.

Books for the Teacher

Zionism

Buber, Martin. On Zion. New York, 1973.
Halpern, Ben. The Idea of the Jewish State. Cambridge, Mass., 1969.
Hertzberg, Arthur, ed. The Zionist Idea. New York, 1959. PB.
Laqueur, Walter. A History of Zionism. New York, 1972.

Israel

Ben-Gurion, David. Israel: Years of Challenge. New York, 1963.
Eban, Abba. My Country: The Story of Modern Israel. New York, 1972.
Elon, Amos. The Israelis: Founders and Sons. New York, 1972. PB.
Sachar, Howard M. The Peoples of Israel: From the Ends of the Earth. New York, 1970. PB.
Schwarz, chap. 17.

Arabs

Hottinger, Arnold. The Arabs: Their History, Culture and Place in the Modern World. Berkeley, Calif., 1963.

Arabs and Jews

Goitein, S. D. Jews and Arabs: Their Contacts Through the Ages. Rev. ed. New York, 1974. PB.
Memmi, Albert. Jews and Arabs. Chicago, 1975. PB.

Israel-Arab Conflict

AlRoy, Gil Carl. Behind the Middle East Conflict: The Real Impasse Between Arabs and Jews. New York, 1975.
Collins, Larry, and Dominique Lapierre. O Jerusalem. New York, 1972.
Davis, Moshe, ed. The Yom Kippur War: Israel and the Jewish People. New York, 1974.
Gilbert, Martin. Atlas of the Arab-Israeli Conflict. London, 1974.
Hart, Harold H., ed. Yom Kippur Plus 100 Days: The Human Side of the War and Its Aftermath, as Shown Through the Columns of "The Jerusalem Post." New York, 1974.
Herzog, Chaim. The War of Atonement. Boston, 1975.
Laqueur, Walter, ed. The Israel-Arab Reader: A Documentary History of the Middle East Conflict. New York, 1970. PB.
Near, Henry, ed. The Seventh Day. London. 1970

Autobiographies

Meir, Golda. *My Life*. New York, 1975.
Ruppin, Arthur. *Memoirs, Diaries, Letters*. New York, 1972.
Weizmann, Chaim. *Trial and Error*. New York, 1967. PB.

Biographies

Avi-Hai, Avraham. *Ben Gurion: State Builder*. New York, 1974.
Baker, Rachel. *Chaim Weizmann: Builder of a Nation*. New York, 1950.

Special Topics

Bentwich, Joseph. *Education in Israel*. Philadelphia, 1965.
Chomsky, William. *Hebrew: The Eternal Language*. Philadelphia, 1957.
  PB.
Halkin, PB.

VII. In the Land of the Free—The Jews in the United States

Introduction

The Jewish community in the United States began its history in 1654 with twenty-three families and has grown to nearly six million people. As an essentially white-collar group of city dwellers it is involved in every aspect of American life.

During the period discussed in this source book, the Sephardic influence with which American Jewish history began was already coming to an end. In fact by 1720 the Sephardim no longer constituted a majority among American Jews. The Ashkenazim, who were Central and East European Jews, began to be in the ascendancy. The tightly governed Sephardic synagogue-community lost its power with the rise of independent synagogues which developed mainly in the eastern part of the country but which spread as far west as St. Louis. In the synagogues the Ashkenazic ritual was almost universally adopted. The period of 1840–1920 is considered the age of the rise and dominance of the German Jew, whose leadership, however, would soon be challenged by the Jews from Eastern Europe. In the period after the Civil War, Reform Judaism, to which most of the German Jewish immigrants adhered, set the tone in American Jewish religious and social life, though it never became a majority movement.

The ancient Jewish tradition of social welfare—providing for the poor, advancing free loans, aiding the aged, nursing the sick, providing for the widowed and the orphaned—had been practiced by the Orthodox Sephardic and early German synagogue. But from the 1820s on, the Ashkenazic immigrants preferred to create their own mutual-aid and welfare institutions. As a result, most of the new organizations removed themselves from synagogue control and thereby initiated the "secularization of American Jewish charities."*

By the middle of the nineteenth century, some of the new immigrants, following in the wake of those who settled in the West, became peddlers who, with packs on their backs, provided for the needs of people now living in more isolated communities. In time these peddlers set up permanent businesses and became storekeepers. If successful they became merchants on a large scale: department-store owners, bankers, and early

---

*Marcus, *Studies in American Jewish History*, p. 200. Much of the information supplied in this introduction has the Marcus volume as its source.

investors. As the industrial age advanced in the post–Civil War era, Jews in increasing numbers turned to manufacturing, and many Jews helped to develop the clothing industry. The children of some of these German immigrants went to college and entered the professions. As the immigrants and their children adjusted to American life, and as state after state removed its disabilities against non-Christians, some even went into politics and sought public office.

Overlapping the years of German dominance, there began the third period in American Jewish life, the age of the coming and the rise to independence and power of the East European Jew (1852–1920). "Thus, there were two disparate, yet parallel, Jewish cultures in the country from 1852 on, when the first Russian Orthodox synagogue was established."*

When the large immigration of masses of East European Jews began in the decades after the Russian pogroms of 1881, the economic scene had undergone a transformation. The period of the peddler and the horse-drawn vehicle was now at an end. By the 1890s the last western frontier had been breached. With the rapidly developing industrialization of the country, the future now belonged in large measure to the factory, and with the factory came the rise and development of cities.

The rich Jews of the East, the "Germans," made efforts to disperse into the interior the masses of immigrants arriving from Eastern Europe. But the immigrants appeared to have a better grasp of the economic realities. They settled in the eastern metropolitan centers and became workers in the clothing industry. After decades of hardship in sweatshops and seeking ways to improve their lot, they created labor unions like the Amalgamated Clothing Workers of America and the International Ladies Garment Workers Union. In time these unions developed new ways in labor relations and served a model to other industries in promoting wholesome relations between capital and labor. "For the first time in its history, America sheltered a substantial body of Jewish proletarians" (Marcus). Most of them, however, climbed up the economic ladder and their sons did not succeed them as laborers.

After the First World War immigration to this country was no longer as free as it had been previously. The quota laws of the 1920s restricted Jewish immigration to the United States and as a result most Jews would be natives within a few decades. The old labels "Spanish," "German," and "Russian" lost their meaning, and with continuing unification, the age of the American Jew began. This epoch may be considered a fourth period in American Jewish history.

---

*Ibid., p. 10.

The most recent decades witnessed pronounced economic changes as far as American Jewry is concerned. The children of the East European immigrant have moved upwards on the economic ladder and have become members of the white-collar class, largely concentrated in commerce and trade. A substantial percentage are college graduates and are today heavily represented in the professions.

The Jews have without reservation become involved in all phases of American life. Although they constitute less than 3 percent of the population, their achievements in the sciences, in medicine, law, music, and literature, and their participation in the economic life of the nation have led them to play important roles greatly out of proportion to their numbers in the total population.

The Second World War, during which European Jewry was essentially destroyed, left American Jewry the greatest Jewish community both in numbers and resources. The Holocaust and the establishment of the State of Israel have led to an intensification of Jewish loyalties. Today American Jews have a stronger sense of kinship with other Jews, resulting in an increased concern and responsibility for the welfare of Jews in other countries. At the present time the American Jewish community consists mainly of third- and fourth-generation Jews whose main concern is not one of seeking to adjust to American ways. Having entered the mainstream of American life, the American Jew faces new problems involving continuity and survival and also improving the quality of Jewish life.

Sources

The selection of sources for this chapter reflects some of the way stations in the development of the American Jewish community, sometimes highlighted by events, sometimes by personalities.* Our selections begin with an exchange of letters between the Newport Congregation and George Washington in which the first president of the United States reaffirms the rights of free citizens, among whom the Jews are obviously included (nos. 101–102).

The relationship between the state and religion during the first half of the nineteenth century is touched upon in the controversial questions of state aid to parochial schools and the observance of Sunday laws (nos. 103, 106).

---

*It should be kept in mind that some related topics have been previously discussed and documented in the earlier chapters of this book as, for example, the enfranchisement of American Jews in chapter 1; the new religious movements necessitated by the Jews emerging into the modern world in chapter 2; the rise of Yiddish literature in chapter 4; the American interpretation of Zionism in chapter 6. These topics will, therefore, not be repeated here.

The traditional effort to aid the needy, initiated by early Jewish settlers on this continent, is documented by an appeal of New York Jews in 1837 (no. 104). The will to make room for additional immigrants and even establish a special territory for them is expressed by Mordecai M. Noah (no. 105).

There was no period in American Jewish history which was completely free of anti-Jewish prejudice. An example from the first half of the nineteenth century was the difficulty experienced in obtaining land to be used as a Jewish cemetery (no. 107), a need which every Jewish settlement in the dispersion tried to meet.

Economic and political events obviously affected the Jews as they did all Americans, as, for example, the westward movement to California and the Civil War (nos. 108, 109).

The life of a peddler and storekeeper, a German-Jewish immigrant, and his family in the South, is told in the autobiography of his son, Oscar Straus, who became the first Jewish cabinet member and ambassador to Turkey (no. 110).

The vast immigration of Jews from Eastern Europe beginning in the 1880s, the first impressions of the immigrants, their homes in tenements and crowded streets, their work, and their family life are described in memoirs and reports of contemporary observers (nos. 111–15).

Selections nos. 116–20 deal with the Jews in the clothing industry, the sweatshops, the factory system, employer-employee relations, the unions, and the contributions made by employers and employees to this sector of American industry.

The public schools, the libraries, and the settlement houses played an important role in the Americanization of the immigrants (no. 122). In this process the Yiddish press took an active part (nos. 123–25).

Four men with careers of distinction, a labor lawyer, a sculptor, a philosopher, and a writer, all children of East European immigrants, tell in their autobiographies of the problems which they faced and of the ways they chose (nos. 121, 126–28). These life stories are somewhat typical and might be multiplied many times over.

The vigilance against violations of Jewish rights could never be relaxed even in this land of the free, as documented in Louis Marshall's fight against Henry Ford's malicious anti-Semitic propaganda (no. 129).

The Jewish problem as seen by a Supreme Court justice and the task facing Jews, especially those in the United States, is discussed in a speech by Louis D. Brandeis (no. 130).

The chapter closes with a summary of the findings of a survey undertaken among Jews of a metropolitan suburb and how they view their Jewishness as Americans of today (no. 131).

101. TO BIGOTRY NO SANCTION

HEBREW CONGREGATION OF NEWPORT, RHODE ISLAND

The following letter, was addressed by the Hebrew Congregation of Newport, Rhode Island, to George Washington on the occasion of his visit to the city in 1790. It reflects the concern of the Jews for perpetuating the freedom which they had found in America and which they did not enjoy abroad.

August 17

Sir:

Permit the Children of the Stock of Abraham to approach you with the most cordial affection and esteem for your person and merits—and to join with our fellow-citizens in welcoming you to New Port.

With pleasure we reflect on those days—those days of difficulty and danger, when the God of Israel, who delivered David from the Peril of the sword—shielded your head in the day of battle—and we rejoice to think that the same Spirit, who rested in the bosom of the greatly beloved Daniel, enabling him to preside over the Provinces of the Babylonish Empire, rests, and ever will rest upon you, enabling you to discharge the arduous duties of Chief Magistrate in these States.

Deprived as we have hitherto been of the invaluable rights of free citizens, we now, (with a deep sense of gratitude to the Almighty Disposer of all events) behold a Government erected by the Majesty of the People, which to bigotry gives no sanction, to persecution no assistance—but generously affording to all liberty of conscience, and immunities of citizenship—deeming everyone, of whatever nation, tongue, or language equal parts of the great governmental machine. This so ample and extensive federal union whose basis is Philanthropy, mutual confidence, and great public virtue, we cannot but acknowledge to be the work of the Great God, who ruleth in the armies of Heaven, and among the inhabitants of the Earth, doing whatsoever seemeth him good.

For all the blessings of civil and religious liberty which we enjoy under an equal and benign administration we desire to send up our thanks to the Ancient of Days, the great Preserver of Men—beseeching him that the Angel who conducted our forefathers through the wilderness into the promised land, may graciously conduct you through all the dangers and difficulties of this mortal life—and when like Joshua full of days and full of honor, you are gathered to your Fathers, may you be admitted into the heavenly Paradise to partake of the water of life and the tree of immortality.

Done and signed by order of the Hebrew Congregation in New Port, Rhode Island, August 17, 1790.

Moses Seixas, Warden

102. INHERENT NATURAL RIGHTS

GEORGE WASHINGTON

In this letter Washington answers the Hebrew Congregation.

Gentlemen,

While I receive with much satisfaction your address replete with expressions of affection and esteem; I rejoice in the opportunity of assuring you that I shall always retain a grateful remembrance of the cordial welcome I experienced in my visit to New Port from all classes of Citizens.

The reflection on the days of difficulty and danger which are past is rendered the more sweet from a consciousness that they are succeeded by days of uncommon prosperity and security. If we have wisdom to make the best use of the advantages with which we are now favored, we cannot fail, under the just administration of a good government to become a great and a happy people.

The Citizens of the United States of America have a right to applaud themselves for having given to mankind examples of an enlarged and liberal policy, a policy worthy of imitation.

All possess alike liberty of conscience and immunities of citizenship. It is now no more that toleration is spoken of, as if it was by the indulgence of one class of people, that another enjoyed the exercise of their inherent natural rights. For happily the government of the United States, which gives to bigotry no sanction, to persecution no assistance, requires only that they who live under its protection should demean themselves as good citizens, in giving it on all occasions their effectual support.

It would be inconsistent with the frankness of my character not to avow that I am pleased with your favorable opinion of my administration, and fervent wishes for my felicity.

May the children of the Stock of Abraham, who dwell in this land, continue to merit and enjoy the good will of the other inhabitants, while every one shall sit in safety under his own vine and fig-tree, and there shall be none to make him afraid.

May the Father of all mercies scatter light and not darkness in our paths, and make us all in our several vocations useful here, and in his own due time and way everlastingly happy.

G Washington.

103. STATE AID TO PAROCHIAL SCHOOLS

CONGREGATION SHEARITH ISRAEL

The petition which follows dates from January 1811. At a time when the enforcement of the separation of church and state had not yet led to the withdrawal of financial support from parochial schools, the congregation sought for its school equality of treatment. The request was finally granted. In 1842 free public education solved the problem, at least for that period.

To the Honorable the Legislature of the State of New York.

The petition of the trustees of the Congregation of Shearith Israel in the City of New York most respectfully represent:

That from the year 1793 a school has been supported from the funds of the said Congregation for the education of their indigent children. That on the 8th of April, 1801, certain school monies were distributed among seven charity schools of the said city, supported by religious societies. That the free school of the Roman Catholic church and that of your memorialists were overlooked in this benevolent distribution. That on the 21st of March, 1806, a law was passed placing the school of the former on the same footing as the others. That your memorialists also made application to the legislature, but did not succeed owing as they presume to the pressure of business. Your memorialists fully persuaded that the Legislature will look with an equal eye upon all occupations of people who conduct themselves as good and faithful citizens, and conscious that nothing has been omitted on their part to deserve the same countenance and encouragement which has been exhibited to others, do most respectfully pray your Honorable body to extend the same relief to their charity school which has been granted to all others in this city.

104. AID TO NEEDY IMMIGRANTS

CIRCULAR ADDRESSED TO JEWS IN NEW YORK

It is estimated that in 1836 there were about 2,000 Jews affiliated with synagogues in New York City. In 1840 the number increased to 7,000, which indicates a high rate of immigration. The following excerpts from the circular of September 3, 1837, are typical of a traditional Jewish attitude concerning aiding the poor.

The undersigned have been appointed an Executive Committee, for the purpose of raising funds to aid and assist persons, recently arrived from foreign countries, and who may be in a destitute situation.

In addressing you, it is proper to state that a meeting was convened, of a number of the House of Israel, at the suggestion of the officers of the several Hebrew Benevolent Societies, to take into consideration the distressed situation, of a great number of Israelites, lately arrived in this city from foreign countries. The funds of the different Societies having been nearly exhausted.

The gentlemen composing the meeting, having interchanged opinions, adopted the following Preamble, preceeding certain resolutions, one of which was as follows:—

"Resolved, that the Executive Committee be, and they are hereby impowered, under their hands and seals, to authorize such persons as they may think proper, to solicit Subscriptions in money, fuel, clothing, or such articles of food as the charitable and humane may be disposed to contribute."

. . . In addition to the duties of the Executive Committee, they will, as far as the funds admit, assist such persons as may be disposed to leave the city, and also endeavour to procure work for those who have trades.

An account of all donations will be duly entered on the minutes of the Committee, and a full and correct Journal kept of all proceedings, and which will always be open to the inspection of the contributors.

Relief in fuel, &c. will be delivered in preference to money, which will only be given under special circumstances of the applicant. The Committee, deem it quite unnecessary to make any appeal to the feelings of their brethren: satisfied as they are that they have never failed to answer the call of the distressed. . . .

We are respectfully

Your humble Servants,
Moses L. Moses, Abraham Mitchell, Solomon J. Joseph, Morland Micholl, Israel B. Kursheedt, T. I. Tobias, Eleazer S. Lazarus, Myer Naphtali Phillips.

105. ARARAT: A CITY OF REFUGE

MORDECAI MANUEL NOAH

Mordecai M. Noah (1785–1851) was a Jew of many talents: journalist, dramatist, American consul in Tunis, politician, sheriff of New York, and active in Jewish affairs. Brought face to face with Jewish deprivation of civic rights in most countries of the Old World, he developed the plan of establishing, under the flag of the United States, a territorial home for the Jews on Grand Island at the western terminus of the Erie Canal, soon to become the most popular highway to the interior of the continent. He bought a tract of land and called the refuge Ararat (suggested by the biblical story of Noah). The cornerstone of the new city was laid with great pomp and ceremony in 1825, but the scheme fell through. In attempting to establish this planned refuge, Noah at no time relinquished the hope of the restoration of Palestine. In a "Discourse on the Restoration of the Jews," delivered in 1844, he called on the free people of America to aid the Jews in their effort to regain Palestine.

The following selection is taken from Noah's proclamation to the Jews of the world.

. . . *Therefore*, I, Mordecai Manuel Noah, citizen of the United States of America, late Consul of the said States to the City and Kingdom of Tunis, High Sheriff of New York, Counsellor at Law, and by the grace of God, Governor and Judge of Israel, have issued this my Proclamation, announcing to the Jews throughout the world, that an asylum is prepared and hereby offered to them, where they can enjoy that peace, comfort and happiness which have been denied them through the intolerance and misgovernment of former ages; an asylum in a free and powerful country remarkable for its vast resources, the richness of its soil, and the salubrity of its climate; where industry is encouraged, education promoted, and good faith rewarded, "a land of milk and honey," where Israel may repose in peace, under his "vine and fig tree," and where our people may so familiarize themselves with the science of government and the lights of learning and civilization, as may qualify them for that great and final restoration to their ancient heritage, which the times so powerfully indicate.

The asylum referred to is in the State of New York, the greatest State in the American confederacy. . . .

The desired spot in the State of New York, to which I hereby invite my beloved people throughout the world, in common with those of every religious denomination, is called Grand Island, and on which I shall lay the foundation of a City of Refuge, to be called Ararat.

Grand Island in the Niagara river is bounded by Ontario on the north, and Erie on the south, and within a few miles of each of these great commercial lakes.

. . . Deprived, as our people have been for centuries of a right in the soil, they will learn, with peculiar satisfaction, that here they can till the soil, reap the harvest, and raise the flocks which are unquestionably their own; and, in the full and unmolested enjoyment of their religious rights, and of every civil immunity, together with peace and plenty, they can lift up their voice in gratitude to Him who sustained our fathers in the wilderness, and brought us in triumph out of the land of Egypt. . . .

In His name do I revive, renew and *reestablish* the government of the

Jewish Nation, under the auspices and protection of the constitution and laws of the United States of America; confirming and perpetuating all our rights and privileges, our name, our rank, and our power among the nations of the earth, as they existed and were recognized under the government of the Judges. And I hereby enjoin it upon all our pious and venerable Rabbis, our Presidents and Elders of Synagogues, Chiefs of Colleges and brethren in authority throughout the world, to circulate and make known this, my Proclamation, and give it full publicity, credence and effect. . . .

106. THE JEWS AND SUNDAY LAWS

SUNDAY TIMES

Should the Jews, observers of Saturday as a day of rest, be compelled to observe Sunday laws (closing of stores, etc.) in a country which has proclaimed the separation of church and state? The following editorial which appeared in the *Sunday Times* and Noah's *Weekly Messenger* on February 13, 1848 dealt with this question which came before the courts in Charleston, South Carolina.

A very interesting case, involving the constitutionality of Sunday Laws, was argued before the Court of Errors in Charleston, South Carolina, on an appeal from the decision of the recorder of the city, who decided that it was not unlawful for an Israelite to vend goods on the first day of the week called the Lord's day, and that the ordinence [sic] against it was in violation of the constitution of the United States and that of the state. The case was argued with great ability on both sides, and, as a question of religious liberty, created great interest and attracted a crowded court. It was contended by the learned counsel for the city and the commonwealth, that this was not a constitutional question, or a question of conscience at all; that the state had conferred the power on the city council to pass such laws for order and good government as that body might see fit, and the proper observence [sic] of Sunday as a day of rest was supposed to be included in that power. The learned counsel maintained that Christianity was part and parcel of the common law—that the common law was the law in South Carolina, and had made the first day of the week a day of religious observence [sic] and rest from labor, as was equally binding on Jews as well as Christians. Col Phillips for the respondents, made a very able and powerful argument, contending that the law was not binding on the Jews, and was in itself a violation of their rights under the constitution. He cited, in particular, that law which made it obligatory for the Jews to labor six days and rest on the seventh day, which was the Sabbath of the Lord; and that the Sunday law, compelling them to rest on two days, in effect violated the divine commmandment to labor every day in the week excepting the seventh. He contended that the law of Sinai was equally binding on Christians as well as Jews; and that that law, so impressive and so holy, had been set aside by an ordinance of the city council. The learned counsel also contended that it violated the constitution of the state, which had secured liberty of conscience to all religious denominations. The argument on both sides was learned, luminous and interesting; but Judge O'Neal, in a very able opinion, concurred in by the whole court, reversed the decision of the court below, sustaining the Sunday laws.

We entirely agree with the court in this opinion. The question has nothing to do with liberty of conscience at all: it is a mere local or police regulation, which should be carried into effect by all religious denominations living in the city and protected by its government. The free exercise and enjoyment of religious opinions and worship secured by the constitution, is not molested by an ordinance requiring shops to be closed on Sunday: hence Sunday is recognized as a day set apart and devoted to rest and religious observence [sic]. Freedom of religion means a mere abolition of all religious disabilities. You are free to worship God in any manner you please; and this liberty of conscience cannot be violated. An ordinance for the better observance of Sunday is a mere prohibition of public employment in the way of labor, trade, and business. We cannot in this perceive how liberty of conscience is to be invaded. It does not say to the Hebrew, 'You shall not keep holy the seventh day;' but merely declares that you shall not disturb the Christian by business or labor on his Sabbath. We can see nothing wrong in this. If the Israelites possessed a government of their own, they would assuredly prohibit labor on the Sabbath day. It would be their duty to do so, enjoined by their own law. Why prohibit the Christians from enforcing the same regulations? The question ought not to have been raised. Respect to the laws of the land we live in, is the first duty of good citizens of all denominations.

107. ESTABLISHING JEWISH CEMETERIES

Anti-Jewish sentiments did not disappear in the New World and could be the result of prejudices "imported" from Europe, as evidenced by the following account in a New York newspaper, August 12, 1849.

There are some 12 or 14,000 persons of the Jewish persuasion in this city, and finding it difficult to obtain burial grounds within the city limits, they have purchased land on Long Island and in other places. A German congregation purchased a burying ground near East New York, and one day last week, having occasion to bury an aged member, the German population of that place, with stones, gun, and clubs, dispersed the members, ordered them off, wounded several persons severely, and compelled them to deposit the body in the Cypress Hills Cemetery. Complaint was made of the outrage to the authorities of Brooklyn, and we presume the parties will be arrested and made to answer for their conduct. These German emigrants imagine that a free country means the privilege of doing what they please, and violating law and order whenever it suits their purpose. A lesson or two will let them understand in what their rights consist.

108. SETTLING IN CALIFORNIA

HENRY J. LABATT

The general migration westwards stimulated by the gold rush of the 1850s included Jews. They were found in mining camps and in cities. Jewish communities were developed in San Diego, Sacramento, Stockton, and San Francisco. In an article, written in 1861, Henry J. Labatt, a lawyer who had migrated to San Francisco from New Orleans, describes the economic activities of the Jews in San Francisco, the largest Jewish community of his time.

On a first arrival in our city, it becomes a matter of astonishment to all who see the large number of mercantile houses conducted by Israelites, being much greater, in proportion to the commerce, than in any other city in America. Every line of business is engaged in by them, with credit to themselves and honor to the community.

Among the largest importers, rank foremost many Jewish firms, the prosperity of whose engagements is evident in the large returns which are made on every steamer day.

The influence they command upon the trade in the State, the weight of their transactions, and the generality of their mercantile callings, may well class them among the most useful, beneficial, and respectable merchants.

Each mining town and city has a large representation, and everywhere you hear of their success and prosperity, which in turn they devote to the improvement of the place, by erecting substantial buildings and warehouses for the increase of their business, caused by industry, economy, and attention.

In all the great fires which have devastated the settlements of California, they have been great sufferers. Year after year, have they seen the hard earnings of their labor swept away by the ruthless conflagration, and yet, with the indomitable energy of their race, have they toiled on to regain what they thus were deprived of by misfortune. Often, indeed, would they not lose what they had accumulated, but become reduced by being brought into debt by the destruction of their stock. Even this would not deter them.—The previous character which prudence and honesty had stamped upon them, created unmistakable confidence and sympathy, and they soon rose above these accidents.

Everywhere they seemed anxious to guard against this great affliction of our country and, by erecting substantial tenements, avoid another calamity.

In all commercial enterprises they keep pace with the marked improvements of the day, and, as merchants, are courted, admired—nay, even sometimes envied.

The almost universal success of the Jews, as merchants; in California, must be attributed to some peculiar reasons; for while many of all nations have succeeded in this State, yet, as a general thing, no class of people who began with so small a capital, have accumulated the same amount of fortune. Any close observer will find that their individual industry dispenses with the necessity for extra clerks, who, at the exorbitant rates necessary for their support, soon make sad inroads upon the monthly profit. They seldom pay unwarrantable rents, being willing to submit to many inconveniences rather than indulge in extravagance. They eschew all display of brilliant fixtures, or other unnecessary expenses, but study economy in every department of their business. Yet, after years of success, when they are conscious of their ability to display their wares and merchandise, then you may find a few who indulge in such outlays.

Their method of conducting business is also worthy of consideration. They seem anxious to dispose of their stock in a short time, and at little profit, and you will generally find throughout the country, that their stores are known as the "cheap stores." This is a great secret of trade; and when once that reputation is acquired, the customer will seek that store. For the most part, they first seek this enviable notoriety for their establishment, and then, by courtesy and a determination to give satisfaction, success seems inevitable; and what is thereby gained, economy secures.

Their quick perception gives them an insight into the requirements of every branch of trade, and when they once embark in it they are determined to call to their assistance every available faculty; and the natural sympathy of, and connection with, the other members of their faith, incite them to an emulation, the result of which is a high commercial position in the community. . . .

109. FROM A RESOLUTION DURING THE CIVIL WAR

Like the rest of the country the Jews, too, were divided in the conflict between the North and the South. The selection which follows is from a resolution of the Hebrew Congregation of Shreveport, Louisiana, in 1861. It reflects the conflict and indicates that there was no unanimous Jewish position on this question. The resolution was in response to an editorial in a magazine, the *Jewish Messenger*, which appealed for support of the Union cause.

Whereas, we received the "Jewish Messenger" on the 26th of April, a paper published in New York, in which an appeal has been made to all, whether native or foreign born, Christian or Israelite. An article headed "stand by the Flag!" in which the editor makes an appeal to support the stars and stripes, and to rally as one man for the Union and the Constitution. Therefore be it.

Resolved, That we, the Hebrew congregation of Shreveport, scorn and repel your advice, although we might be called Southern rebels; still, as law-abiding citizens, we solemnly pledge ourselves to stand by, protect, and honor the flag, with its stars and stripes, the Union and Constitution of the Southern Confederacy with our lives, liberty, and all that is dear to us.

Resolved, That we, the members of said congregation, bind ourselves to discontinue the subscription of the "Jewish Messenger," and all Northern papers opposed to our holy cause, and also to use all honorable means in having said paper banished from our beloved country.

Resolved, That while we mistook your paper for a religious one, which ought to be strictly neutral in politics, we shall from this hour treat it with scorn, as a black republican paper, and not worthy of Southern patronage; and that, according to our understanding, church and politics ought never to be mingled, as it has been the ruination of any country captivated by the enticing words of preachers.

Resolved, That we, the members of said congregation, have lost all confidence and regard to the Rev. S. M. Isaacs, Editor and Proprietor of the "Jewish Messenger," and see in him an enemy to our interest and welfare, and believe it to be more unjust for one who preaches the Word of God, and to advise us to act as traitors and renegades to our adopted country, and raise hatred and dissatisfaction in our midst, and assisting to start a bloody civil war amongst us. . . .

Resolved, That papers friendly to the southern cause, are politely requested to publish the foregoing resolution.

110. A GERMAN IMMIGRANT IN THE SOUTH

OSCAR SOLOMON STRAUS

Oscar Straus (1850–1926) was not born a Southerner. As a four-year-old child he landed in New York in 1854, where his father was waiting for him and the rest of the family, who had arrived from their native Germany. After the Civil War the family moved to New York City.

Oscar Straus attended Columbia College, went into business with his family, but leaned toward a government career. He became U.S. minister to the Ottoman Empire and was on President Wilson's staff in Paris at the Peace Conference in 1918–19. President Theodore Roosevelt appointed him secretary of commerce and labor, the first Jew to occupy a post in a presidential cabinet.

Oscar Straus took an active part in many Jewish affairs and differed in this respect from men like Judah P. Benjamin, Philip Phillips, and Lewis Charles Levin, who either avoided their fellow-Jews or had little contact with them.

The selection is taken from Oscar Straus's autobiography.

The Family and Its Name

My ancestors, on both my father's and my mother's side, were natives of the Palatinate of Bavaria, of the town of Otterberg and immediate vicinity. Up to the time [1802] of Napoleon's taking possession of that part of the country, the Jews of the Palatinate had not adopted family names. This they did later, beginning in 1808, when, under Napoleon, the Palatinate became the Department of Mont Tennérre [Tonnerre] and part of France. My great-grandfather, for instance, before adopting the family name of Straus, was known as Jacob Lazar, from Jacob ben Lazarus, or Jacob son of Lazarus, as in biblical times. . .

Revolution and Emigration

My father . . . was active in the revolutionary movement in 1848 . . . Having been active only locally in the revolutionary movement, my father was not prosecuted. He was made aware, however, of the suspicions of the authorities and was subjected to all those petty annoyances and discriminations which a reactionary government never fails to lay upon people who have revolted, and revolted in vain. My father decided, in consequence, to emigrate. . . .

Becoming a Peddler

He landed at Philadelphia, where he met a number of former acquaintances who had preceded him to America, some of whom were already established in business. They advised him to go south. Acting on this suggestion, he went on to Oglethorpe, Georgia, where he met some more acquaintances from the old country. Through them he made a connection with two brothers Kaufman, who plied the peddler's trade. They owned a peddler's wagon with which they dispensed, through the several counties of the state, an assortment of dry goods and what was known as "Yankee notions."

For my father this [peddling] was indeed a pioneer business in a pioneer country, yet it was not like the peddling of today. In the fifties the population of the whole state of Georgia was only about 90,000. Because of the existence of slavery, there were on the large plantations often more colored people than there were whites living in the nearby villages. The itinerant merchant, therefore, filled a real want, and his vocation was looked upon as quite dignified. Indeed, he was treated by the owners of the plantations with a spirit of equality that it is hard to appreciate today. Then, too, the existence of slavery drew a distinct line of demarcation between the white and black races. This gave to the white visitor a status of equality that probably otherwise he could not have enjoyed to such a degree.

Southern Hospitality

Provided only, therefore, that the peddler proved himself an honorable, upright man, who conscientiously treated his customers with fairness and made no misrepresentations regarding his wares, he was treated as an honored guest by the plantation owners—certainly a spirit of true democracy. The visits were made periodically and were quite looked forward to by the plantation owners. The peddler usually stayed one night at the house of his customer and took his meals with the family. Another ideally democratic feature about these sojourns was that spirit of Southern hospitality which, even in the relationship between the wealthiest, most aristocratic family and the humble peddler, permitted no pay for board and lodging, and only a small charge for feed for the horses. The peddler in turn usually made a gift to either the lady or her daughter. Often he provided himself with articles for this purpose, but usually on one visit he would find out what might be welcome and on the next visit bring it. The bonds of friendship thus made are, I venture to say, hardly understandable in our day.

Choosing a Town to Settle

In the course of these wanderings my father came to Talbotton, a town of some 800 or 900 inhabitants, the county seat of Talbot County, and about forty miles east of the Alabama boundary. Talbotton immediately impressed him so favorably that he selected it as the next home for his family. It had an air of refinement that pleased him; there were gardens with nicely cultivated flowers and shrubbery, and houses that were neat, well kept, and properly painted. Upon inquiry he found further that there were splendid schools for both boys and girls.

There was another factor which doubtless caused father to be favorably impressed with Talbotton; it was court week when he arrived, at which time a town has a more or less festive appearance and is at its best so far as activity is concerned. Then there was a third factor that influenced him to settle there. Before doing business in any county, peddlers were required to go to the county seat to buy a license. At Talbotton this license was very high, and my father doubted that his business in Talbot County would warrant the expense. The idea occurred to him to utilize the presence of the many strangers in town to test the possibilities of the place by unpacking and displaying his goods in a store. An interview with Captain Curley, the only tailor in the town, developed the fact that the store he occupied was too large for his needs and he would be willing to share it with my father. So this arrangement was promptly made, and at a cost less than the expense of the county license for itinerant merchandising.

Opening a Store

The experiment proved most satisfactory. In a few weeks the stock was so depleted that my father proposed to his partner [Kaufman] that they rent a store and settle in Talbotton. This they did. My father then prepared to go to Philadelphia to get a stock of goods. His partner counseled against this. There was a merchant in Oglethorpe who, up to this point, had supplied them with all their merchandise; they would need to refer to him for credit, and they were still indebted to him for the stock in hand; also, he would probably not approve of their settling down in a store instead of peddling. The new store offered large display space in comparison with the wagon, and the partner doubted my father's ability to get enough credit in Philadelphia to make a proper display. Still another obstacle: the line of merchandise that was to constitute most of their stock was what was then known as dry goods and domestics. This business was entirely in the hands of the Yankees and the most difficult one in which to gain a foothold, especially for a German immigrant without capital.

However, in the end my father did go to Philadelphia. He had found several acquaintances in that city, as I have already said, who had been resident in his neighborhood in the old country. These people were established in several of the wholesale houses in the different lines of merchandise he required, except the dry goods. And, solely on the strength of his character and the reputation he had had in Europe, he was able to establish with them the necessary credit, which neither his capital nor his business experience in a new field and a strange country warranted. In fact, their faith in him was so strong that one of them gladly introduced him to the wholesale dry-goods merchants, and he was able to accomplish the full purpose of his mission, to the great amazement of his partner.

Migration

That was in 1853, and marked the beginning of my family's history in this country. This bit of success encouraged my father to write home that he might be able to have us join him the following year. Accordingly, on August 24, 1854, our little party left Otterberg. It was a journey that required no little courage and resourcefulness. My mother had three years before suffered a paralytic stroke, and of her four children the eldest, my brother Isidor, was only nine years old. My sister Hermina was a year and a half younger; Nathan was six, and I was only three and a half. My mother's father accompanied us from Otterberg to Kaiserslautern, he on horseback, and the rest of us with our nursemaid in a carriage. We then took the train to Forbach, a French frontier town, where we remained overnight. The next morning we left for Paris. There we stayed until August 29th, when we started for Havre to board the steamer "St. Louis" on her maiden voyage. As our boat was being docked in New York on September 12th, my mother recognized my father energetically pacing the wharf. Minutes seemed like hours.

We did not go directly to Talbotton. Yellow fever was raging in Savannah, and, as we had to go through that port en route to Talbotton, we waited in Philadelphia for a few weeks, until the danger was considered over. Even then we avoided entering the city (Savannah) until it was time to board the train for Geneva, where we were to take the stagecoach for the remaining seven miles to Talbotton. The boat docked at Savannah in the morning, and we spent the day until evening in the small shanty that was called the station. When finally we reached Talbotton we found a very comfortable home ready for us. My precocious brother Isidor immediately inspected the whole and thought it odd to be in a house built on stilts, as he called it. The house, typical of that locality, had no cellar, but was supported by an open foundation of wooden pillars about twenty-five feet apart.

The Family Reunited

Our family was received with kindness and hospitality, so that in a very few years our parents were made to feel much at home. My mother, who had considerable experience in the cultivation of flowers and vegetables, soon had a garden which was very helpful and instructive to her circle of neighbors and friends. My father, always a student and well-versed in biblical literature and the Bible, which he read in the original, was much sought by the ministers of the various denominations, several of whom habitually dined at our house when in Talbotton on their circuit. At such times the discussion usually ran along theological lines. One of my earliest recollections is hearing my father take passages from the Old Testament and translate them literally for the information of these ministers.

We were the only Jewish family in the town. This at first aroused some curiosity among those who had never met persons of our race or religion before. I remember hearing someone doubt that we were Jews and remarking to my father, who had very blond hair and blue eyes, that he thought all Jews had black hair and dark complexion.

Schooling and Religious Education

My brother Isidor and my sister were immediately sent to school, and my second brother and I were sent as soon as we arrived at school age. I was seven years old when I began learning my letters.

My main religious instruction came from conversations with my father and from the discussions the ministers of various denominations had with him, which I always followed with great interest. When my brother Nathan and I were respectively about eleven and eight and a half years old, we were sent to the Baptist Sunday school upon the persuasion of the Baptist minister, who had become an intimate friend of my father's. There we heard the Bible read and were taught principally from the Old Testament. Our teacher was a gunsmith who had more piety than knowledge, and what he lacked in erudition he made up by good intentions which, after all, had a cultural value. We continued our attendance some two years. . . .

Slavery

As a boy brought up in the South, I never questioned the rights or wrongs of slavery. Its existence I regarded as [a] matter of course, as most other customs or institutions. The grown people of the South, whatever they thought about it, would not, except in rare instances, speak against it, and even then in the most private and guarded manner. To do otherwise would subject one to social ostracism. We heard it defended in the pulpit and justified on biblical grounds by leading ministers. With my father it was different. I frequently heard him discuss the subject with the ministers who came to our house, and he would point out to them that the Bible must be read with discrimination and in relation to the period to which the chapters refer; and it must not be forgotten that it is the history of a people covering more than a thousand years, and that even then there had been no such thing as perpetual bondage, as all slaves were declared free in the year of jubilee.

Looking backward and making comparisons between my observations as a boy in the South and later in the North, I find there was much more freedom of expression in the North than in the South. Few people in the South would venture to express themselves against the current of dominant opinion upon matters of sectional importance. The institution of slavery with all that it implied seemed to have had the effect of enslaving, or, to use a milder term, checking freedom of expression on the part of the master class only in lesser degree than among the slaves themselves.

Frugal Living

The people throughout the South, with the exception of the richer plantation owners, lived simply. In our household, for instance, we always lived well, but economically. My mother was very systematic and frugal. She had an allowance of $20 a month, and my brother Isidor has well said that she would have managed to save something even if it had been smaller. It was her pleasure to be her own financier, and small as her allowance sounds now, she was able in the course of two or three years to save enough to buy a piano for my sister. This she felt to be an expense with which my father's exchequer should not be taxed.

We raised our own vegetables and chickens. Fresh meat. except pork, might have been termed a luxury. Many of the families had their own smokehouses, as we did, which were filled once a year, at the hog-killing season. There was no such thing as a butcher in our little town. When a farmer in the country round wanted to slaughter an ox or a sheep, he would do so and bring it to town, exhibit it in the public square in a shanty called the market (used for that particular occasion and at other times empty), toll the bell that was there, and in that way announce that some fresh meat was on sale. This procedure never occurred oftener than once in two or three weeks during the cold weather.

Ice was another luxury in that community. It had to be shipped many miles and was therefore brought in only occasionally, mainly for a confectioner who at times offered ice cream to the people.

There was no gas lighting. Oil lamps were used, but to a larger extent candles, which were manufactured in each household, of fat and bees' wax. In that process we children all helped.

No Public Schools or Libraries

Indeed, with a small business in a small town in those days, it was possible for a man to accumulate a surplus only through the practice of the strictest economy by his family as well as by himself, an economy almost bordering parsimony. There were no public or free schools in that part of the South; every textbook had to be bought and tuition paid for, and there were four of us. . . .

In 1863 our family moved to Columbus, Georgia. It was a much larger place than Talbotton, having a population of about 12,000, offered more opportunities, and, too, my brother Isidor had already found employment there. With its broad main street and brick residences it looked like a great city to me. . . .

Outdoor Life

There were no public libraries; and few families, other than those of professional men, had many books. The standard assortment consisted of the Bible, Josephus, Burns; some had Shakespeare's works. I do not recall at this period reading any book outside of those we had for study at school. Boys of my age led an outdoor life, indulging in seasonable sports which rotated from top-spinning to marbles, to ball-playing, principally a game called town ball. We all had shotguns, so that in season and out we went bird hunting and rabbit hunting.

We went barefooted nine months of the year, both for comfort and economy. As in Talbotton, we lived most economically. We were not poor in the sense of being needy; we never felt in any way dependent. Our home was comfortable, wholesome, full of sunshine and good cheer, and always hospitable to friends. Our wants were few and simple, so we had plenty, and I felt as independent as any child of the rich. . .

111. I DISCOVER AMERICA

ABRAHAM CAHAN

With the mass immigration of Jews from Eastern Europe to America during the last decades of the nineteenth century, we encounter a new type of Jewish immigrant. The following selection is taken from a chapter of the novel *The Rise of David Levinsky* by Abraham Cahan, writer and famous editor of the popular Yiddish newspaper *Jewish Daily Forward (Forverts)* in New York. There is more about him in the prefatory note to no. 125.

I was one of a multitude of steerage passengers on a Bremen steamship on my way to New York. Who can depict the feeling of desolation, homesickness, uncertainty, and anxiety with which an emigrant makes his first voyage across the ocean? I proved to be a good sailor, but the sea frightened me. The thumping of the engines was drumming a ghastly accompaniment to the awesome whisper of the waves. I felt in the embrace of a vast, uncanny force. . . .

When Columbus was crossing the Atlantic, on his first great voyage, his men doubted whether they would ever reach land. So does many an

America-bound emigrant to this day. Such, at least, was the feeling that
was lurking in my heart while the Bremen steamer was carrying me to New
York. Day after day passes, and all you see about you is an unbroken waste
of water, an unrelieved, a hopeless monotony of water. You know that a
change will come, but this knowledge is confined to your brain. Your
senses are skeptical.

In my devotions, which I performed three times a day, without counting
a benediction before every meal and every drink of water, grace after every
meal and a prayer before going to sleep, I would mentally plead for the
safety of the ship and for a speedy sight of land. My scanty luggage
included a pair of phylacteries and a plump little prayer book, with the
Book of Psalms at the end. The prayers I knew by heart, but I now often said
psalms, in addition, particularly when the sea looked angry and the
pitching or rolling was unusually violent. I would read all kinds of psalms,
but my favorite among them was the 104th, generally referred to by our
people as "Bless the Lord, O my soul," its opening words in the original
Hebrew. It is a poem on the power and wisdom of God as manifested in the
wonders of nature, some of its verses dealing with the sea. It is said by the
faithful every Saturday afternoon during the fall and winter; so I could
have recited it from memory; but I preferred to read it in my prayer book.
For it seemed as though the familiar words had changed their identity and
meaning, especially those concerned with the sea. Their divine inspiration was now something visible and audible. It was not I who was reading
them. It was as though the waves and the clouds, the whole farflung scene
of restlessness and mystery, were whispering to me:

"Thou who coverest thyself with light as with a garment, who stretchest
out the heavens like a curtain: who layeth the beams of his chambers in the
waters: who maketh the clouds his chariot: who walketh upon the wings of
the wind . . . So is this great and wide sea wherein are things creeping
innumerable, both small and great beasts. There go the ships: there is that
leviathan whom thou hast made to play therein . . ."

When the discoverers of America saw land at last they fell on their knees
and a hymn of thanksgiving burst from their souls. The scene, which is one
of the most thrilling in history, repeats itself in the heart of every
immigrant as he comes in sight of the American shores. I am at a loss to
convey the peculiar state of mind that the experience created in me.

When the ship reached Sandy Hook I was literally overcome with the
beauty of the landscape.

The immigrant's arrival in his new home is like a second birth to him.
Imagine a new-born babe in possession of a fully developed intellect.
Would it ever forget its entry into the world? Neither does the immigrant
ever forget his entry into a country which is, to him, a new world in the

profoundest sense of the term and in which he expects to pass the rest of his life. I conjure up the gorgeousness of the spectacle as it appeared to me on that clear June morning: the magnificent verdure of Staten Island, the tender blue of sea and sky, the dignified bustle of passing craft—above all, those floating, squatting, multitudinously windowed palaces which I subsequently learned to call ferries. It was all so utterly unlike anything I had ever seen or dreamed of before. It unfolded itself like a divine revelation. I was in a trance or in something closely resembling one.

"This, then, is America!" I exclaimed, mutely. The notion of something enchanted which the name had always evoked in me now seemed fully borne out.

In my ecstacy I could not help thinking of Psalm 104, and, opening my little prayer book, I glanced over those of its verses that speak of hills and rocks, of grass and trees and birds.

My transport of admiration, however, only added to my sense of helplessness and awe. Here, on shipboard, I was sure of my shelter and food, at least. How was I going to procure my sustenance on those magic shores? I wished the remaining hour could be prolonged indefinitely.

Psalm 104 spoke reassuringly to me. It reminded me of the way God took care of man and beast: "Thou openest thine hand and they are filled with good." But then the very next verse warned me that "Thou hidest thy face, they are troubled: thou takest away their breath, they die." So I was praying God not to hide His face from me, but to open His hand to me; to remember that my mother had been murdered by Gentiles and that I was going to a strange land. When I reached the words, "I will sing unto the Lord as long as I live: I will sing praise to my God while I have my being," I uttered them in a fervent whisper. . . .

One of my fellow passengers was a young Yiddish-speaking tailor named Gitelson. He was about twenty-four years old, yet his forelock was gray, just his forelock, the rest of his hair being a fine, glossy brown. His own cap had been blown into the sea, and the one he had obtained from the steerage steward was too small for him, so that gray tuft of his was always out like a plume. We had not been acquainted more than a few hours, in fact, for he had been seasick throughout the voyage and this was the first day he had been up and about. But then I had seen him on the day of our sailing and subsequently, many times, as he wretchedly lay in his berth. He was literally in tatters. He clung to me like a lover, but we spoke very little. Our hearts were too full for words.

As I thus stood at the railing, prayer book in hand, he took a look at the page. The most ignorant "man of the earth" among our people can read holy tongue (Hebrew), though he may not understand the meaning of the words. This was the case with Gitelson.

"Saying, 'Bless the Lord, O my soul'?" he asked, reverently. "Why this chapter of all others?"

"Because—Why, just listen." With which I took to translating the Hebrew text into Yiddish for him.

He listened with devout mien. I was not sure that he understood it even in his native tongue, but, whether he did or not, his beaming, wistful look and the deep sigh he emitted indicated that he was in a state similar to mine.

When I say that my first view of New York bay struck me as something not of this earth, it is not a mere figure of speech. I vividly recall the feeling, for example, with which I greeted the first cat I saw on American soil. It was on the Hoboken pier, while the steerage passengers were being marched to the ferry. A large, black, well-fed feline stood in a corner, eyeing the crowd of newcomers. The sight of it gave me a thrill of joy. "Look! there is a cat!" I said to Gitelson. And in my heart I added, "Just like those at home!" For the moment the little animal made America real to me. At the same time it seemed unreal itself. I was tempted to feel its fur to ascertain whether it was actually the kind of creature I took it for.

We were ferried over to Castle Garden. One of the things that caught my eye as I entered the vast rotunda was an iron staircase rising diagonally against one of the inner walls. A uniformed man, with some papers in his hands, ascended it with brisk, resounding steps till he disappeared through a door not many inches from the ceiling. It may seem odd, but I can never think of my arrival in this country without hearing the ringing footfalls of this official and beholding the yellow eyes of the black cat which stared at us at the Hoboken pier.

The harsh manner of the immigration officers was a grievous surprise to me. As contrasted with the officials of my despotic country, those of a republic had been portrayed in my mind as paragons of refinement and cordiality. My anticipations were rudely belied. "They are not a bit better than Cossacks," I remarked to Gitelson. But they neither looked nor spoke like Cossacks; so their gruff voices were part of the uncanny scheme of things that surrounded me. These unfriendly voices flavored all America with a spirit of icy inhospitality that sent a chill through my very soul.

The stringent immigration laws that were passed some years later had not yet come into existence. We had no difficulty in being admitted to the United States, and when I was, I was loath to leave the Garden.

Many of the other immigrants were met by relatives, friends. There were cries of joy, tears, embraces, kisses. All of which intensified my sense of loneliness and dread of the New World. The agencies which two Jewish charity organizations now maintain at the Immigrant Station had not yet been established. Gitelson, who like myself had no friends in New York, never left my side. He was even more timid than I. It seemed as though he were holding on to me for dear life. This had the effect of putting me on my mettle.

"Cheer up, old man!" I said, with bravado. "America is not the place to be a ninny in. Come, pull yourself together."

In truth, I addressed these exhortations as much to myself as to him; and so far, at least, as I was concerned, my words had the desired effect.

I led the way out of the big Immigrant Station. As we reached the park outside we were pounced down upon by two evil-looking men, representatives of boarding houses for immigrants. They pulled us so roughly and their general appearance and manner were so uninviting that we struggled and protested until they let us go—not without some parting curses. Then I led the way across Battery Park and under the elevated railway to State Street. A train hurtling and panting along overhead produced a bewildering, a daunting effect on me. The active life of the great strange city made me feel like one abandoned in the midst of a jungle. Where were we to go? What were we to do? But the presence of Gitelson continued to act as a spur on me. I mustered courage to approach a policeman, something I should never have been bold enough to do at home. As a matter of fact, I scarcely had an idea what his function was. To me he looked like some uniformed nobleman—an impression that in itself was enough to intimidate me. With his coat of blue cloth, starched linen collar, and white gloves, he reminded me of anything but the policemen of my town. I addressed him in Yiddish, making it as near an approach to German as I knew how, but my efforts were lost on him. He shook his head. With a witheringly dignified grimace he then pointed his club in the direction of Broadway and strutted off majestically.

"He's not better than a Cossack, either," was my verdict.

At this moment a voice hailed us in Yiddish. Facing about, we beheld a middle-aged man with huge, round, perpendicular nostrils and a huge, round, deep dimple in his chin that looked like a third nostril. Prosperity was written all over his smooth-shaven face and broad-shouldered, stocky figure. He was literally aglow with diamonds and self-satisfaction. But he was unmistakably one of our people. It was like coming across a human being in the jungle. Moreover, his very diamonds somehow told a tale of former want, of a time when he had landed, an impecunious immigrant like myself; and this made him a living source of encouragement to me.

"God Himself has sent you to us," I began acting as the spokesman; but he gave no heed to me. His eyes were eagerly fixed on Gitelson and his tatters.

"You're a tailor, aren't you?" he questioned him.

My steerage companion nodded. "I'm a ladies' tailor, but I have worked on men's clothing, too," he said.

"A ladies' tailor?" the well-dressed stranger echoed, with ill-concealed delight. "Very well; come along. I have work for you."

That he should have been able to read Gitelson's trade in his face and figure scarcely surprised me. In my native place it seemed to be a matter of course that one could tell a tailor by his general appearance and walk. Besides, had I not divined the occupation of my fellow passenger the moment I saw him on deck?

As I learned subsequently, the man who accosted us on State Street was a cloak contractor, and his presence in the neighborhood of Castle Garden was anything but a matter of chance. He came there quite often, in fact, his purpose being to angle for cheap labor among the newly arrived immigrants.

We paused near Bowling Green. The contractor and my fellow passenger were absorbed in a conversation full of sartorial technicalities which were Greek to me but which brought a gleam of joy into Gitelson's eye. My former companion seemed to have become oblivious of my existence.

As we resumed our walk up Broadway the bejeweled man turned to me.

"And what was your occupation? You have no trade, have you?"

"I read Talmud," I said, confusedly.

"I see, but that's no business in America," he declared. "Any relatives here?"

"No."

"Well, don't worry. You will be all right. If a fellow isn't lazy nor a fool he has no reason to be sorry he came to America. It'll be all right."

"All right" he said in English, and I conjectured what it meant from the context. In the course of the minute or two which he bestowed upon me he uttered it so many times that the phrase engraved itself upon my memory. It was the first bit of English I ever acquired.

The well-dressed, trim-looking crowds of lower Broadway impressed me as a multitude of counts, barons, princes. I was puzzled by their preoccupied faces and hurried step. It seemed to comport ill with their baronial dress and general high-born appearance.

In a vague way all this helped to confirm my conception of America as a unique country, unlike the rest of the world.

When we reached the General Post Office, at the end of the Third Avenue surface line, our guide bade us stop.

"Walk straight ahead," he said to me, waving his hand toward Park Row. "Just keep walking until you see a lot of Jewish people. It isn't far from here." With which he slipped a silver quarter into my hand and made Gitelson bid me good-by.

The two then boarded a big red horse-car.

I was left with a sickening sense of having been tricked, cast off, and abandoned. I stood watching the receding public vehicle, as though its scarlet hue were my last gleam of hope in the world. When it finally disappeared from view my heart sank within me. I may safely say that the half-hour that followed is one of the worst I experienced in all the thirty-odd years of my life in this country.

The big, round nostrils of the contractor and the gray forelock of my young steerage-fellow haunted my brain as hideous symbols of treachery.

With twenty-nine cents in my pocket I set forth in the direction of East Broadway.

112. THE STREET OF PEDDLERS AND PUSHCARTS

NEW YORK TRIBUNE, SEPTEMBER 15, 1898

The new East European immigrants tried to gain an economic foothold in the metropolis in which many of them remained. A newspaperman describes one example of their economic activities.

The neighborhood of Hester, Norfolk and Essex Streets presents a quaint scene. The streets are black with purchasers, and bright with the glare of hundreds of torches from the pushcarts. The faces are markedly of a Oriental type; and the voices of the peddlers crying their wares, the expostulations of the purchasers, the mingling of the "Yiddish" of the elders with the English of the young people, make a strange medley of sounds.

Great is the variety of wares to be seen on the carts. Dr. Wolborst, who is much interested in the peddlers, has stated that what cannot be bought in the pushcart market cannot easily be bought in New York. A friend of his wanted to match some draperies. After visiting the best stores uptown she inspected the wares of some Hester Street peddlers and found what she required. The dry goods peddlers buy remnants, odd pieces and samples from wholesale houses at low prices. A woman bought a remnant of valuable lace from the peddler. A pair of curtains of similar lace would have cost $75. She paid 50 cents. A friend of hers begged her to sell the piece for $20. She did so, returned to the peddler and invested in a sufficient number of similar remnants to make vestibule curtains and other lace furnishings for all the rooms in her house. From bits of lace, bought for a trifle from the peddlers, other women have made fichus, capes, overskirts, etc. Pieces of fine cloth in sizes from half a yard to several yards are often sold at low rates. Squares of carpets such as the sales-men take out on the road as samples have been bought from the peddlers for a trifle and converted into handsome rugs. One ingenious woman carpeted a large room by joining a number of squares of harmonious pattern and color. She called it a "harlequin carpet" and it was much admired.

But the peddlers who vend such materials are not numerous. Most of the goods are of ordinary quality. Stockings may be bought for 6 cents a pair, children's undergarments for 5 cents apiece. Many of the carts are filled with rolls of oilcloth or wallpapers. The smaller articles of household furniture—crockery, glassware, tins, etc.—are displayed. Readymade clothing is cheap. Each cart has its specialty, but in the line of carts there is a strange medley. Dried fruits, fresh fruit, pickles, preserves, vegetables, meat and fish alternate with household utensils, boots and shoes, jewelry and clothing, books and stationery.

The fish carts are largely in the majority. The wholesale merchants sell the fish at auction to the peddlers who go in crowds to the stores of the dealers and have a lively but anxious time in trying to outbid one another. Sometimes the fish is condemned by the Health Department, to the great loss of the peddlers. As many as fifty tons of fish are sometimes seized from them in a day. Charles B. Stover and other members of the Social Reform Club have taken up the cause of the fish peddlers and are trying to remedy some of the ills from which they suffer. It is proposed to utilize a part of the Hester Street Park for a fish market in the mornings, the building to be used for other purposes later in the day. In this way the peddlers would be relieved from paying tribute to the police which they do in order to avoid arrests for obstructing the streets. Those who pay regularly are not molested.

It is estimated that there are 1,500 peddlers of various wares in that vicinity. The regular peddler pays $25 a year for his license with the additional fees to the police. He can hardly earn more than $5 a week so he often hires a pushcart for his wife, and sometimes the children too are brought into the service. The rent of a pushcart is 10 cents a day. Many of the peddlers are only temporarily in the trade. Tailors or mechanics who are out of work hire a pushcart until they find a position. Recently landed immigrants are advised by their friends to take a pushcart until they can establish themselves in some business.

113. BEGINNINGS: LIFE IN THE NEW COUNTRY

JACOB RIIS

The poor immigrant was constantly engaged in an economic struggle. The following excerpts are taken from the book *How the Other Half Lives* (1886) by Jacob Riis (1849–1914). Himself an immigrant from Denmark, Riis was a newspaperman, photographer, reformer, and a keen observer of the new environment and its people. He described what he saw realistically and sympathetically.

The Home—a Workshop

. . . The homes of the Hebrew quarter are its workshops also. Reference will be made to the economic conditions under which they work in a succeeding chapter. Here we are concerned simply with the fact. You are made fully aware of it before you have travelled the length of a single block in any of these East Side streets, by the whir of a thousand sewing-machines, worked at high pressure from earliest dawn till mind and muscle give out together. Every member of the family, from the youngest to the oldest, bears a hand, shut in the qualmy rooms, where meals are cooked and clothing washed and dried besides, the live-long day. It is not unusual to find a dozen persons—men, women, and children—at work in a single small room.

Health in the Crowded Tenements

. . . When, in the midnight hour, the noise of the sewing-machine was stilled at last, I have gone the rounds of Ludlow and Hester and Essex streets among the poorest of the Russian Jews, with the sanitary police, and counted often four, five, and even six of the little ones in a single bed, sometimes a shake-down on the hard floor, often a pile of half-finished clothing brought home from the sweater, in the stuffy rooms of their tenements. In one I visited very lately, the only bed was occupied by the entire family lying lengthwise and crosswise, literally in layers, three children at the feet, all except a boy of ten or twelve, for whom there was no room. He slept with his clothes on to keep him warm, in a pile of rags just inside the door. It seemed to me impossible that families of children could be raised at all in such dens as I had my daily and nightly walks in. And yet the vital statistics and all close observation agree in allotting to these Jews even an unusual degree of good health. The records of the Sanitary Bureau show that while the Italians have the highest death-rate, the mortality in the lower part of the Tenth Ward, of which Ludlow Street is the heart and type, is the lowest in the city. Even the baby death-rate is very low. But for the fact that the ravages of diphtheria, croup, and measles run up the record in the houses occupied entirely by tailors—in other words, in the sweater district, where contagion always runs riot—the Tenth Ward would seem to be the healthiest spot in the city, as well as the dirtiest and the most crowded. The temperate habits of the Jew and his freedom from enfeebling vices generally must account for this, along with his marvellous vitality. I cannot now recall ever having known a Jewish drunkard. On the other hand, I have never come across a Prohibitionist among them. The absence of the one renders the other superfluous.

Morals and Family Life

. . . Whatever the effect upon the physical health of the children, it cannot be otherwise, of course, than that such conditions should corrupt their morals. I have the authority of a distinguished rabbi, whose field and daily walk are among the poorest of his people, to support me in the statement that the moral tone of the young girls is distinctly lower than it was. The entire absence of privacy in their homes and the foul contact of the sweaters' shops, where men and women work side by side from morning till night, scarcely half clad in the hot summer weather, does for the girls what the street completes in the boy. But for the patriarchal family life of the Jew that is his strongest virtue, their ruin would long since have been complete. It is that which pilots him safely through shoals upon which the Gentile would have been inevitably wrecked. It is that which keeps the almshouse from casting its shadow over Ludlow Street to add to its gloom. It is the one quality which redeems, and on the Sabbath eve when he gathers his household about his board, scant though the fare be, dignifies the darkest slum of Jewtown.

How strong is this attachment to home and kindred that makes the Jew cling to the humblest hearth and gather his children and his children's children about it, though grinding poverty leave them only a bare crust to share, I saw in the case of little Jette Brodsky, who strayed away from her own door, looking for her papa. They were strangers and ignorant and poor, so that weeks went by before they could make their loss known and get a hearing, and meanwhile Jette, who had been picked up and taken to Police Headquarters, had been hidden away in an asylum, given another name when nobody came to claim her, and had been quite forgotten. But in the two years that passed before she was found at last, her empty chair stood ever by her father's, at the family board, and no Sabbath eve but heard his prayer for the restoration of their lost one. It happened once that I came in on a Friday evening at the breaking of bread, just as the four candles upon the table had been lit with the Sabbath blessing upon the home and all it sheltered. Their light fell on little else than empty plates and anxious faces; but in the patriarchal host who arose and bade the guest welcome with a dignity a king might have envied I recognized with difficulty the humble pedlar I had known only from the street and from the police office, where he hardly ventured beyond the door.

114. ADJUSTING TO THE NEW WORLD

NEW YORK TRIBUNE, AUGUST 16, 1903

One of the important settlement houses (in some ways comparable to a Jewish center of today) in New York City, which was of considerable help to the immigrant and his children, was the Educational Alliance, headed in those years by Dr. David Blaustein. The statement which follows was given to a newspaper.

"It is impossible to understand the Lower East Side," said Dr. David Blaustein, head of the Educational Alliance, speaking apropos of his recent statistical investigations of conditions in that section, "or the attitude of the people there toward American institutions without knowing the conditions from which these people came in Eastern Europe. . . .

Religious Life

"You can imagine the confusion in the immigrant's mind when he reaches America. He finds his church of no account whatever. No one cares what church he belongs to or whether he belongs to any church or not. The state delegates no rights or powers to the church. All that is asked is whether he is an American or not and whether he is loyal to his adopted country. No one cares anything about his loyalty to his church or regards his religious belief as a matter of any importance to anyone but himself. In place of finding the congregation all powerful and all embracing, he finds when he joins a congregation that he has simply joined a liberal society.

Social Life

"The change in social life is as peculiar and puzzling to the immigrant as that in the religious life. In Eastern Europe the social life centers in the church and the home, and is pervaded by a devotional atmosphere. It is spontaneous. It flows from natural occasions. The social life to which we are accustomed—balls, receptions, banquets, class reunions—is not spontaneous; it is organized. All these affairs are arranged.

"For instance, it is the custom in the Jewish church to celebrate the eighth day after the birth of a son. This festival in Europe is always an occasion of much rejoicing. Suppose the day falls on a weekday, when there is work in the shop. The man goes to the shop, and the celebration is postponed until the following Sunday. Then the host knows and his guests know that it is not the right day. Their consciences smile then, and the occasion is one of secret sadness rather than rejoicing. They fall to mourning over the economic conditions which will not permit them to observe the old customs, rather than enjoying themselves.

"Always, before, the immigrant had room in which to entertain his friends. In the crowded condition of the quarter where he now lives, he cannot do this. The wedding is the pinnacle of Jewish social life. But on the Lower East Side the wedding must take place in a hall. The guest must pay at the door for his hat and coat check, and this at the very start takes away all the old feeling of openhanded hospitality. The hall wedding is a cold and comfortless function.

"So economic conditions prevent him from enjoying himself in his home with his family and his religion in the old way. If he seeks social enjoyment, he finds he must accommodate his time to that of others. A ball is to be held at a certain time. There is no special reason for it at that time, but the date has been fixed by a committee of arrangements, and he is asked to purchase a ticket. Remembering his good times in the old country, he goes, hoping to enjoy himself once more. He finds himself in a sea of strangers, with nothing as he has been used to it. He goes away weary and disheartened. It is the same in summer when he buys a ticket for one of the mammoth picnics. When he compares such a picnic with the harvest festival at home, a thing as happy and spontaneous as the play of children, his heart is sick. Often he says that America is no good and he would rather be back in the old country.

Position of the Woman

"As the woman in Eastern Europe has no religious life, so she has no social life. If you call at a house, you are received by the man of the house, not the woman. There are certain social feasts and celebrations of the church, but the men participate in them, not the women. If invitations are sent out to a wedding they are sent to the males of a family, not to the women. At the wedding, the highest social function of Judaism, there are five men present to one woman.

"The woman is also a minor. She belongs to her father before her marriage, to her husband after. She cannot own property in her own name. Her testimony is not received in the ecclesiastical courts, although in the civil courts it has recently been admitted.

"Can you imagine what all this means to the immigrant? He goes to church here and finds women in the majority. He goes to the schools and finds women teaching most of them. He finds them behind every counter, beside him in every shop. What is the result? The result is that he loses all his respect for women."

Dr. Blaustein paused to let this declaration sink in and then went on to explain: "You may think," he said, "that from what I have said of the position of women among the Jews of Eastern Europe that she is despised. On the contrary, she is an idolized being. She is adored. She is the queen of the home. The theory upon which she is excluded from all the things I have mentioned is not that she is not entitled to them, but that being busy with her household duties she is excused from them. She is excused from religious duties because something at home may require her attention. She is excused from education because more important duties await her. She is excused from looking after her own property. The men of her family will do that for her and protect all her rights. She is even excused from social duties," concluded Dr. Blaustein gravely.

"The immigrant sees woman in America excused from nothing. She bears the heat and burden of the day at his side. She has become his equal, and he supposes she is to be treated as an equal. He loses all respect for women and acts accordingly. Then he goes out into the American world and finds to his astonishment that women have privileges in America. He finds that there is a rule, 'ladies first.' It surprises him very much. He can't understand the apparent contradiction of things. It requires another mental readjustment.

Athletics

"There is nothing that disturbs the Jew so much as to see his boy, and still more his girl, taking part in the athletics of the schools. The rage is something incomprehensible to him. He has cultivated his mind so long at the expense of his body that the American maxim 'a sound mind in a sound body' is something he cannot understand.

"All these things may explain to a slight degree the puzzled condition of the immigrant's mind, the difficulty he has in assimilating and adjusting himself to new conditions, his heavyheartedness, oftentimes, and his frequent estrangement from his own children."

115. PHILANTHROPISTS AND IMMIGRANTS

BORIS D. BOGEN

As revealed in Boris Bogen's autobiography, *Born a Jew*, relations between the philanthropists, the rich German-Jewish Americans, and the East European immigrants, about whose welfare they were deeply concerned, were not without conflicts. The philanthropists had as the goal uppermost in

their minds to Americanize the immigrant as fast as possible. They were not
sufficiently sensitive to the immigrant's having a cultural tradition which could
serve as a source of strength in the hour of his need. Then there were also the
Jewish socialists, who presented a problem not only to the philanthropists but
to the Orthodox immigrants as well.

   Boris Bogen (1869–1930), from whose autobiography the excerpt which
follows is taken, was born in Russia and came to the United States in the early
1890s. After the usual economic struggle of an immigrant, he turned to Jewish
social work, in which he carved out a distinguished career for himself. He was
director of the United Jewish Charities in Cincinnati, became director-general
of the Joint Distribution Committee during the First World War, and was
prominent in B'nai B'rith.

The Reading Room of a Settlement House

At the university I came to know well and to love Professor Dubs Shimer
who was humanitarian as well as teacher, a double identity that should be,
but is not always, found in all teachers. From him shone the first genuine
sympathy I was to see in America. Another like him was Dr. Saul Badanes
who was a teacher at the Hebrew Technical School and who led my feet to a
social-service career; for it was he who obtained for me the position of
custodian of the reading room of the Hebrew Institute.*

But an adventuring young man needs stern masters as well as kind
friends and it fell to me to have as master, in the Hebrew Institute, a
benevolent tyrant, Dr. Henry M. Leipziger. He was like those good fathers
who know how to use the rod judiciously and who, if they are not loved,
are vastly respected, and thanked in later years.

If the ways of Dr. Leipziger were almost cruel at times, one came to
understand afterward that his harsh discipline had the kindliest of
purposes. Roughly enough, he kept pushing his subordinates toward
higher endeavors.

"How long do you intend to remain on this job?" he would say to us.
"Why don't you try for a higher position? This place is not a lifetime berth.
There are other deserving young men who need a start. Why don't you
vacate it?"

He understood immigrants and treated them as individuals and not as a
crowd. The rich benefactors of the immigrants thought of them as a mass to
be thrown into a melting pot and made over into Americans.

These philanthropists were of German immigration and in them was all
the wealth of Jewry. They were proud Americans who thought the way to
assimilate Europeans was to strip them of their inheritance of language
and custom and bedeck them in a ready-made suit of Americanism.

---

*Hebrew Institute: later called "Educational Alliance." (Ed.)

Yiddish must be stricken from the tongues of Jewish immigrants, though these protested, saying, "Is this America, where we may not speak our mother tongue? Even in Russia they permitted us to speak Yiddish."

Upon non-Jews who had immigrated to America, there was no such high-pressure Americanism inflicted by their countrymen who were already here, and even in the second generation German-Americans were speaking German in their homes, and they were proud of their *Männerchor* which sang German songs with resounding voices in public places, while in the Civil War there had been several regiments of German immigrants to whom commands were given in the German language.

Americanization Policy

I looked about the queer reading room, thrilled to feel that I, but recently an immigrant, was already part of the great force for the Americanization of my people. Here, in the Hebrew Institute, one spoke English if one could—and if not, there were English classes available. American flags, American pictures, adorned the walls. American holidays were celebrated with a fervent gesture. American ladies and gentlemen, zealous in behalf of the newcomer, exhorted the children to love this new land of theirs, and to join the classes and clubs at the Institute. This great, stately building seemed of another world than that of the seething, clamoring, steaming street. I was impressed by the order, the beauty, the quiet of it all.

Then, suddenly, the quiet struck me as strange. The reading room was almost deserted, its well-stacked shelves undisturbed. Where were the eager immigrants, yearning for knowledge? Now and then some one drifted in, gazed about—and drifted out again. A member of the Board of Directors passed through and stopped to inquire about my work; in so crowded a neighborhood, and with people in the building at the time, there seemed no reason why the library should not be crowded; I looked at him helplessly. The well-bred voice, the faultless American attire, the cool, appraising glance, made me feel uncouth, barbaric. A queer loneliness oppressed me; I almost wished that I, too, could tiptoe from the room with the other immigrants.

To-day I can smile at the furious mixture of emotions aroused in me at that early encounter with a director. Humility, distrust, resentment—a faint glimmer of understanding. Here was an American gentleman whose forbears perhaps hailed not from the misery of the Pale, but from urbane West Europe. And he was established here, an American. He wanted to help us, to make us like himself, to have us shed our foreign speech, our old customs, our dark memories, as one might shed an outworn coat. And I, who had so longed to forsake that past, who had dreamed only of becoming part and parcel of this new world, somehow resented that proffered help. I wanted to voice my resentment. I wanted to tell this fine gentleman that I, too, did not come bare and empty-handed.

But instead I decided to wait for an opportune moment to suggest the addition of Yiddish and Russian newspapers and periodicals to the reading room; I was thrilled when, shortly thereafter, this suggestion was put into effect and workingmen and students began to come in, to study and to read. This was not Americanization, perhaps, but it was bringing the people into the building and must not this, after all, be the first step?

I found a friend and kindred spirit in Isaac Spectorsky, who was superintendent of the Institute. He disagreed thoroughly with the inflexible Americanization policy laid down by the Board. I was won over completely by his disarming sincerity and earnestness. Within the narrow latitude permitted him, he was attempting to draw the immigrants into the Institute through interests and activities of their own choice. It could not compel the neighborhood to reflect its American spirit and culture; it must itself reflect the life and interests of the ghetto. And here, in this palace of the immigrants, they would come to know the real America, the America of freedom, of tolerance, of justice. So, while the directorate attempted to emphasize the pure Americanism of the Institute by eliminating the religious implication in its name, transforming it into the "Educational Alliance," it grudgingly consented to the use of Yiddish in its adults' groups.

Mr. Spectorsky was respected and loved in the neighborhood. His office was a small room under a stairway, his records were not tabulated with that perfection that social workers to-day consider so vital, and he was perhaps lacking in modern technique.

My work at the university taxed my energies. I was doing rather well, not setting the world on fire—struggling to grasp the often rapidly spoken classroom lectures, wondering, the while, how we could make ends meet. I tried to eke out my salary from the reading room by giving private lessons in English. I scanned the newspapers, burrowed deep into my encyclopedia, and dogged the footsteps of notables to secure material for my Russian press correspondence. Somehow we must struggle along until I could qualify as an educator. I was no longer fearful of such a career, for I now realized that my future would lie among my own people.

The Jewish Socialists

The rich, older Jews were quite upset by the strange mixture that was pouring in upon them from Eastern Europe and which by a generous giving of money they were trying to make American. There were Socialists of several varieties who, far from consenting to be made over, were resolved to help make America over. When one Sunday I offered to a group of them a lecture on the need of Jewish education, terrible was the reproach that fell upon my head. I was denounced by various members of my audience. I was only an echo from a dead past. I was seeking to revive an institution which their superior minds had long ago rejected. I should not have been permitted to speak, they said.

These Socialists were most embarrassing to the bountiful German Jews who believed that the best interest of Jewry demanded that these new Jews be brought up to cherish the regular parties instead of bringing heterodox political doctrine to the new land. What would the neighbors say?

The shades of Jewish radicalism tapered to the deepest red of the Anarchists who were fond of scandalizing Orthodox Jews on the Day of Atonement. If for the Orthodox this was a day for fasting, for the Anarchists it was a day for feasting and dancing. They made their rendezvous in a restaurant on Division Street and on the day before a certain Yom Kippur they advertised that the restaurant would be open for the feeding of all freethinkers on the holy day.

And though there is no day in the Jewish calendar holier than Yom Kippur and though the time of pious Jews should be spent altogether in the synagogue on that day, many of the Orthodox Jews went to serve Jehovah as pickets before the Division Street restaurant. And whatever Jew attempted to enter was severely beaten, and the police sent reserves to quell the tumult of outraged Jewry.

Hearing of this, I hastened to the restaurant and persuaded the proprietor to close it; but mine was the unhappy lot of the peacemaker, for when I emerged from the restaurant, there were shouts of "Anarchist! Anarchist!" and the mob fell upon me and belabored me and it was only with the aid of the police that I escaped with my life.

The New York ghetto was a comparatively new thing then and the hundreds of thousands were yet to be put into it, and the problem of what to do for the inhabitants had become a vitalizing factor in American Judaism. The American Jews of Reform persuasion made contributions of money for the welfare of these immigrants and the immigrants in turn made contributions of new Jewish life and provided their benefactors with causes for new Jewish devotions.

The Yiddish Theater

While the rich patrons of Jewish charity were trying to make them over into Americans, these perverse immigrants insisted on living their own lives in their own way. Every night they were filling their theaters to see the plays of Jacob Gordin who was turning out new dramas at high speed. He had brought new ideals to the Jewish stage, which had fallen to a low estate in the United States. Gordin, tall, imposing, austere, was more

Russian than Jew and loomed in the streets of the East Side above the heads of the multitude of undersized men.

It was disgust with the Jewish stage he found in America that prompted him to write plays of his own, and his success was almost instantaneous. He wrote in three days plays that live and are revived from time to time even to this day, and in a few years he had produced sixty of them. He was no steady worker, but in a few hours of inspiration his genius conceived and wrote a play for which a less gifted mind would have consumed months.

More amazing is the fact that Yiddish was not a familiar language on his tongue when he came here, for his speech was Russian; he mastered Yiddish and in his plays polished it to the elegance of a classic tongue.

Israel Zangwill came to the United States and there was an occasion when he and Gordin were thrown together in a certain place of Jewish resort. Being told that Gordin was in the room, Zangwill desired to meet him.

"Gordin," I said, "Zangwill wants to meet you."

"I, the father of eleven children, should go to meet him!" exclaimed the whimsical Gordin. "It is he who should come to meet me—the father of eleven children."

Upon receiving this message, Zangwill straightway went to Gordin.

"You should have come to me," Zangwill said reproachfully. "You have only eleven children? Well, I have 'The Children of the Ghetto.' "

Never before had I seen the nimble-witted Gordin caught without a ready retort. He could only laugh.

Gordin gave release to Jewish life wretched in foul tenements. But with all its miseries, Jewish life in New York slums was more endurable than the life of the non-Jewish neighbors in the same environment. Jewish life had, at least, the comfort of Jewish tradition which was the only riches it had brought from Europe; it established Hebrew schools for the children and in the basements of synagogues old men studied the Talmud the livelong day. Saturday was still honored as the day of rest, and Zionists were in force, dreaming the timeless dream.

116. SWEATSHOPS: WHAT IS THE SWEATING SYSTEM?

JOHN R. COMMONS, *U.S. Industrial Commission Reports,* 1901

Jews were heavily represented in the clothing industry as tailors, manufacturers, and merchants. The Jewish share in the industry was at its peak in the 1920s. Both employers and employees, German and East European immigrants, made significant contributions to this industry by providing the masses with ready-made apparel of good quality at prices which they could afford. Another contribution was the creation of labor unions whose social and economic policies are considered the most enlightened and exemplary of the organized crafts. Selections 116–22 describe some of the stages in this development.

The term "sweating," or "sweating system," originally denoted a system of subcontract, wherein the work is let out to contractors to be done in small shops or homes. "In practice," says the report of the Illinois Bureau of Labor Statistics, "sweating consists of the farming out by competing manufacturers to competing contractors of the material for garments, which in turn is distributed among competing men and women to be made up." The system to be contrasted with the sweating system is the "factory system," wherein the manufacturer employs his own workmen, under the management of his own foreman or superintendent, in his own building, with steam, electric, or water power. In the sweating system the foreman becomes a contractor, with his own small shop and foot-power machine. In the factory system the workmen are congregated where they can be seen by the factory inspectors and where they can organize or develop a common understanding. In the sweating system they are isolated and unknown.

The position of the contractor or sweater now in the business in American cities is peculiarly that of an organizer and employer of immigrants. The man best fitted to be a contractor is the man who is well-acquainted with his neighbors, who is able to speak the languages of several classes of immigrants, who can easily persuade his neighbors or their wives and children to work for him, and who in this way can obtain the cheapest help. During the busy season, when the work doubles, the number of people employed increases in the same proportion. All the contractors are agents and go around among the people. Housewives, who formerly worked at the trade and abandoned it after marriage, are called into service for an increased price of a dollar or two a week. Men who have engaged in other occupations, such as small business and peddling, but who are out of business most of the year, are marshaled into service by the contractor, who knows all of them and can easily look them up and put them in as competitors by offering them a dollar or two a week more than they are getting elsewhere. Usually when work comes to the contractor from the manufacturer and is offered to his employees for a smaller price than has previously been paid, the help will remonstrate and ask to be paid the full price. Then the contractor tells them, "I have nothing to do with the price. The price is made for me by the manufacturer. I have very little to say about the price." That is, he cuts himself completely loose from any responsibility to his employees as to how much they are to get for their labor. The help do not know the manufacturer. They cannot register their complaint with the man who made the price for their labor. The contractor, who did not make the price for their labor, claims that it is of no use to complain to him. So that however much the price for labor goes down, there is no one responsible for it.

There is always cutthroat competition among contractors. A contractor feels more dependent than any of his employees. He is always speculating on the idea of making a fortune by getting more work from the manufacturer than his neighbor and by having it made cheaper. Usually when he applies for work in the inside shop he comes in, hat in hand, very much like a beggar. He seems to feel the utter uselessness of his calling. Oftentimes the contractor is forced to send work back because he cannot make it under the conditions on which he took it; yet he does not dare to refuse an offer for fear the manufacturer will not give him more of his work. So he tries to figure it down by every device, and yet, perhaps, in the end is forced to send it back.

117. CHILDREN IN SWEATSHOPS

EDWIN MARKHAM, *Cosmopolitan Magazine*, January 1907

Long before Hannah made a coat for little Samuel, women sat in the home at garmentmaking. The sweated sewing in the tenement home today is only a belated following of this custom of the ages. But the leisurely sewing of the old times was far away from the nerve-racking work of our hurried age. The slow ways are gone. In unaired rooms, mothers and fathers sew by day and by night. Those in the home sweatshop must work cheaper than those in the factory sweatshops if they would drain work from the factory, which has already skinned the wage down to a miserable pittance. And the children are called in from play to drive and drudge beside their elders. The load falls upon the ones least able to bear it—upon the backs of the little children at the base of the labor pyramid.

All the year in New York and in other cities you may watch children radiating to and from such pitiful homes. Nearly any hour on the East Side of New York City you can see them—pallid boy or spindling girl—their faces dulled, their backs bent under a heavy load of garments piled on head and shoulders, the muscles of the whole frame in a long strain. The boy always has bowlegs and walks with feet wide apart and wobbling. Here, obviously, is a hoe man in the making. Once at home with the sewing, the little worker sits close to the inadequate window, struggling with the snarls of thread or shoving the needle through unwielding cloth. Even if by happy chance the small worker goes to school, the sewing which he puts down at the last moment in the morning waits for his return.

Never again should one complain of buttons hanging by a thread, for tiny, tortured fingers have doubtless done their little ineffectual best. And for his lifting of burdens, this giving of youth and strength, this sacrifice of all that should make childhood radiant, a child may add to the family purse from 50 cents to $1.50 a week. In the rush times of the year, preparing for the changes of seasons or for the great "white sales," there are no idle fingers in the sweatshops. A little child of "seven times one" can be very useful in threading needles, in cutting the loose threads at the ends of seams, and in pulling out bastings. To be sure, the sewer is docked for any threads left on or for any stitch broken by the little bungling fingers. The light is not good, but baby eyes must "look sharp."

Besides work at sewing, there is another industry for little girls in the grim tenements. The mother must be busy at her sewing, or, perhaps, she is away from dark to dark at office cleaning. A little daughter, therefore, must assume the work and care of the family. She becomes the "little mother," washing, scrubbing, cooking. In New York City alone, 60,000 children are shut up in the home sweatshops. This is a conservative estimate, based upon a recent investigation of the Lower East Side of Manhattan Island, south of 14th Street and east of the Bowery. Many of this immense host will never sit on a school bench. Is it not a cruel civilization that allows little hearts and little shoulders to strain under these grown-up responsibilities, while in the same city a pet cur is jeweled and pampered and aired on a fine lady's velvet lap on the beautiful boulevards?

118. FACTORY SYSTEM INSTEAD OF TASK WORK

ERNEST POOLE,
The Outlook, November 21, 1903

Go tonight at nine or even ten o'clock down through the ghetto. You will find scores of small coat shops still lighted. These are nonunion shops, and a glimpse into one of them reveals the task system running at full speed. The room is low and crowded. The air is close, impure, and alive with the ceaseless whir of machines. The operator bends close over his machine— his foot on the treadle in swift, ceaseless motion; the baster stands just behind, at the table; the finisher works close between them. On the table is a pile of twenty coats. This is their "task"—the day's work, which most teams never accomplish. Of the three teams here, the swiftest can finish their task in fourteen hours' labor. The other two seem forever behind and striving to catch up. Five tasks a week is their average. They need no overseer, no rules, no regular hours. They drive themselves. This is the secret of the system, for three men seldom feel sick or dull or exhausted at the same moment. If the operator slackens his pace, the baster calls for more coats. If at six o'clock the baster gives out, the finisher spurs him on through the evening.

The positions are tense, their eyes strained, their movements quick and nervous. Most of them smoke cigarettes while they work; beer and cheap whisky are brought in several times a day by a peddler. Some sing Yiddish songs—while they race. The women chat and laugh sometimes—while they race. For these are not yet dumb slaves, but intensely human beings—young, and straining every ounce of youth's vitality. Among operators twenty years is an active lifetime. Forty-five is old age. They make but half a living.

This is but the rough underside of the system. Widen the focus, include employers, then employers of employers, and the whole is a live human picture of cutthroat competition. At the top the great New York manufacturers of clothing compete fiercely for half the country's trade—a trade of sudden changes, new styles, rush seasons. When, three years back, the raglan overcoat came suddenly into favor, at once this chance was seized by a score of rivals, each striving to make the coat cheapest and place it first on the market. Each summoned his contractors and set them in turn competing for orders. He knew them all and knew how desperately dependent they were upon his trade. Slowly the prices were hammered down and down until the lowest possible bids had been forced. Then enormous rush orders were given.

This system is now hard pushed by a swifter rival, and is falling behind in the race. In these days of machine invention, a process to live must not only be swift and cheap; it must be able, by saving labor, to grow forever swifter and cheaper. This the task system can no longer do. The factory system, so long delayed by the desperate driving of the task, began in 1896. In New York today, 70 per cent of the coats are made by the factory. The small shops—on task or week wages—are mere survivals of the past.

Endless saving, dividing, narrowing labor—this is the factory. Down either side of the long factory table forty operators bend over machines, and each one sews the twentieth part of a coat. One man makes hundreds of pockets. On sewing pockets his whole working life is narrowed. To this intensity he is helped and forced and stimulated at every possible point. His strength is no longer wasted on pushing a treadle; the machine is run by other power. The coat passes down the long bench, then through the hands of a dozen pressers and basters and finishers—each doing one

minute part swiftly, with exact precision. Through thirty hands it comes
out at last fourteen minutes quicker, four cents cheaper; the factory has
beaten the task shop.

And the human cost—is it, too, reduced? Is the worker better off here
than he was in the sweatshop? To consider this fairly we must compare the
nonunion factory with the nonunion sweatshop. Wages by the week for the
most skilled workers are slightly higher in the factory than they were in the
sweatshop. They are lower for the unskilled majority. This majority must
slowly increase, for the factory system progresses by transferring skill to
machinery. Hours are shorter; work is less irregular; the shop is sanitary;
the air is more wholesome—but the pocketmaker is often as exhausted at
6:00 P.M. as the coatmaker was at 10:00 P.M., for his work is more minute,
more intense, more monotonous. This concentration, too, is growing.

Still, the workers have gained most decidedly. The factory is a help to
the union. Through the past twenty years labor unions were formed again
and again, only to be broken by new waves of ignorant immigrants. In the
system of small scattered shops the unions had no chance. The free
American workman bargained alone, with a contractor who said, "I have
no power," and a manufacturer who said, "I have no workmen." All this is
ended. Contractor and manufacturer are slowly becoming one. The
bargain is direct, and the workmen are learning to strike it together.

119. ACHIEVEMENTS

ABRAHAM CAHAN

The selection is taken from Cahan's novel *The Rise of David Levinsky*. See
nos. 111 and 125.

. . . The old cloak-manufacturers, the German Jews, were merely
merchants. Our people, on the other hand, were mostly tailors or cloak
operators who had learned the mechanical part of the industry, and they
were introducing a thousand innovations into it, perfecting, revolutioniz-
ing it. We brought to our work a knowledge, a taste, and an ardor which the
men of the old firms did not possess. And we were shedding our
uncouthness, too. In proportion as we grew we adapted American
business ways. . . .

Our rush season had passed, but we were busy preparing for our removal
to new quarters, on Fifth Avenue near Twenty-third Street. That locality
had already become the center of the cloak-and-suit trade, being built up
with new sky-scrapers, full of up-to-date cloak-factories, dress-factories,

and ladies'-waist-factories. The sight of the celebrated Avenue swarming with Jewish mechanics out for their lunch hour or going home after a day's work was already a daily spectacle.

The new aspect of that section of the proud thoroughfare marked the advent of the Russian Jew as the head of one of the largest industries in the United States. Also, it meant that as master of that industry he had made good, for in his hands it had increased a hundredfold, garments that had formerly reached only the few having been placed within the reach of the masses. Foreigners ourselves, and mostly unable to speak English, we had Americanized the system of providing clothes for the American woman of moderate or humble means. The ingenuity and unyielding tenacity of our managers, foremen, and operatives had introduced a thousand and one devices for making by machine garments that used to be considered possible only as the product of handwork. This—added to a vastly increased division of labor, the invention, at our instance, of all sorts of machinery for the manufacture of trimmings, and the enormous scale upon which production was carried on by us—had the effect of cheapening the better class of garments prodigiously. We had done away with prohibitive prices and greatly improved the popular taste. . . .

The average American woman is the best-dressed average woman in the world, and the Russian Jew has had a good deal to do with making her one.

120. THE BIRTH OF THE JEWISH UNIONS

MORRIS HILLQUIT

Morris Hillquit (1870–1933) was born in Latvia and came to the United States at the age of seventeen. He worked as a laborer in the garment industry and was greatly depressed by the poverty which he observed on the East Side of New York. He studied English and Yiddish, became a union organizer, and founder in 1890 of the first Yiddish-language socialist newspaper, the *Arbeiterzeitung.*

Hillquit studied law, became a distinguished lawyer, and ran for Congress on the Socialist Party ticket. Although he did not gain public office, he was widely respected as a lawyer and as a spokesman for the working man. He represented many unions before arbitration boards and helped frame for the garment industry a labor code which was a model for later codes in the trade union movement.

The following selection is taken from his autobiography.

East Side Tea Shops

Aside from the roofs on Cherry Street our favorite gathering places were the East Side tea shops. There, particularly during the long winter nights, we would pass many hours talking and occasionally sipping weak tea served in tumblers, Russian style. A glass of tea and a "coffee twist" of ample proportions were, as a rule, the limit of a guest's consumption. The price of each was five cents.

I often wondered how the owners of the establishments could keep going on such meager income, and I suppose the owners were kept wondering harder than I. But they somehow managed. In some cases, they were of the same kind and type as their guests, and they took it for granted that the tea shop was there not so much for drinking or eating as for discussions.

Of discussion there was plenty, but the purely vocal exercise did not long satisfy the enthusiastic young Socialists' yearning for action. They cast about for a promising field of practical work and inevitably discovered it among their own countrymen. The anti-Jewish riots or "pogroms" of 1881 and 1882 had set in motion a powerful stream of Jewish emigration from Russia and Poland. Thousands of immigrants arrived on the shores of this country every week seeking shelter and bread. By 1890 their number was estimated at no less than half a million. In New York they formed the largest Jewish settlement of the world, the largest, most congested, and poorest.

In two thousand years of homeless wandering among the nations of Africa, Europe, and Asia, in centuries of outlawry and persecution, the Jewish people had been largely excluded from productive work and had become a race of traders and money lenders. In the new world they evolved for the first time a solid proletarian block.

A Jewish Proletariat

In the early days of immigration, many of them turned to the lowest form of trade—peddling; but that occupation proved utterly inadequate when their numbers rose to hundreds of thousands. They were compelled to seek employment at manual labor. The great majority of the new arrivals found work in the different branches of the clothing industry. Others tried to eke out a precarious existence as bakers, cigar makers, house painters, and factory workers. Their conditions of life and labor were pitiful. Ignorant of the language and ways of the country of their adoption, mostly without technical training of any kind, penniless and helpless, they were left at the mercy of their employers, mostly men of their own race. Many of these "employers" were mere middlemen or contractors acting as intermediaries between manufacturers and workers.

There were hundreds of these middlemen in the clothing industry, and they operated in fierce competition with one another. A number of hired sewing machines set up in a tenement-house room, often connected with

their own living quarters, constituted their whole capital and establishment. In these close, dark, ill-ventilated and unsanitary shops a welter of
working and perspiring humanity, men and women, from three to twenty
or thirty in number, were crowded together. Their pay was almost
nominal, their work hours were unlimited. As a rule they were employed
"by the piece," and as their work was seasonal and irregular, they were
spurred to inhuman exertions in the rare and short busy periods.

Mercilessly exploited by their employers and despised by their
American fellow-workers as wage cutters, they completely lacked
self-assertiveness and the power of resistance. They were weak from
overwork and malnutrition, tired and listless, meek and submissive.
Tuberculosis, the dread white plague of the tenements, was rife among
them.

Here was a situation that fairly cried out for sympathy and help. Our
group was quick to heed the summons. We resolved to undertake the task
of bettering the lives of our laboring countrymen, of educating them to a
realization of their human rights, of organizing them for resistance to their
exploiters, and of securing for them tolerable conditions of labor and life.

Organizing the Workers

It was a task beset with baffling difficulties. Several attempts to organize
the Jewish workers of New York had been made before and had failed. A
few spontaneous strikes had been quickly quelled. A few nuclei of labor
unions had been stillborn. The Jewish workers seemed to be unorganiz-
able. They had not been trained in any form of collective action in the
countries of their birth. They were dull, apathetic, and unintelligent. And
worst of all, we did not speak their language, both figuratively and
literally. Our language was Russian. The workers spoke Yiddish, a
corrupted German dialect with several provincial variations. Few of us
knew Yiddish well enough to embark on a campaign of propaganda. The
only one among us who could speak Yiddish and did it fluently, lovingly,
and artistically was Abraham Cahan, who subsequently made equally
enviable places for himself in the English and Yiddish worlds of letters.*
Cahan was somewhat older than the rest of us. He was nearly thirty at that
time, and we looked up to him with envy and respect, not only on account
of his venerable age but also because of his incomparable knowledge of the
language of the people.

We all began perfecting our Yiddish. Those of us who happened to know

---

*About Cahan see selection no. 125. (Ed.)

German had a somewhat easier task than those who spoke only Russian and had to labor at it word by word and idiom by idiom.

The next problem was to make contacts with the workers. This also proved a highly elusive undertaking. There were so many of them, and they were hopelessly scattered.

It would have taken decades to build a Jewish labor movement from the bottom up, educating individual workers, forming them into organized trade groups and finally uniting them into one cooperating body. We were forced to reverse the logical process and to attempt to build from the top down.

United Hebrew Trades

Taking the bull by the horns, we founded the United Hebrew Trades in October, 1888. It was a central labor body without affiliated labor unions, a mere shell within which we hoped in time to develop a solid kernel. The idea originated among the Jewish members of the Socialist Labor Party, the political organization of American Socialism at that time.

The party had two Jewish branch organizations or "sections" in New York, one composed of Yiddish-speaking members, known as Section 8, and the other, Section 17, whose members spoke Russian. The task of setting the contemplated organization in motion was entrusted to a joint committee of the two sections, each electing two members. The Yiddish-speaking section was represented on the committee by I. Magidoff and Bernard Weinstein.

Magidoff, who may be termed the father of the idea, was very active in the initial stages of the Jewish labor movement, but later dropped out of it and devoted himself entirely to newspaper work. Bernard Weinstein was and remained one of the best types produced by the Jewish labor movement in the United States. A native of Odessa, in the southern part of Russia, he came here as a boy with the first wave of Russian emigration in 1882, and found employment in a cigar factory alongside Samuel Gompers, then also an obscure cigar maker.

He associated himself with the early Socialist and labor movements immediately upon his arrival, and has remained wholeheartedly devoted to their cause for fifty years. Handicapped by a slight facial deformity, devoid of the gift of popular oratory and modest to the point of shyness, Bernard Weinstein was never very prominent in the leadership of the movement. But he did not seek prominence or even recognition. He served the cause for the sake of the cause, served it with simple and unwavering faith, steadily, unostentatiously, and with utter self-abnegation.

The "Russian section" was represented on the committee by Leo Bandes and by myself. Bandes was a somewhat maturer man than most of us. He had won his revolutionary spurs as a member of the redoubtable "Will of the People," and had served time in Russian prisons for his Socialist activities. He was a person of kind disposition and rare idealism and occupied a leading and authoritative position in our councils. But we were not long permitted to enjoy his companionship. He had contracted a tubercular infection of the lungs during his prison life, and the tenement air of New York was not at all conducive to recovery. He languished before our eyes and died in less than two years.

The organization meeting of the United Hebrew Trades took place at 25 East Fourth Street, the headquarters of the Socialist Labor Party, and the meeting place of the United German Trades (Vereinigte Deutsche Gewerkschaften). It was the latter organization that inspired the name of the newcomer in the field of organized labor.

The United German Trades was a powerful body in those days. It was a federation of labor unions composed of German workers, who practically controlled several important industries in New York. Originally called into being for the sole purpose of supporting the German labor press, it soon broadened its functions to include those usually exercised by central labor bodies in cities. It was a progressive organization and worked in close cooperation with the Socialist movement.

The United German Trades assisted in the formation of its younger Jewish brother by practical advice and made a generous contribution of ten dollars to its war chest.

Before we called the organization meeting, Bernard Weinstein and I made a minute and painstaking search of all nuclei or remnants of Jewish labor unions in New York. There had been, we knew, unions of shirt makers, cloak operators, and bakery workers at one time or another. We thought them dormant. We found them dead.

The only Jewish unions that could lay any claim to existence were two in number, the Hebrew Typographical Union and the union of chorus singers. The typesetters' union was only a few months old. It was made up of employees of the struggling newspapers and job printing shops on the lower East Side.

The Chorus Singers' Union was somewhat of an anomaly in the labor movement. It was composed of members of the chorus of the two Yiddish theaters then operating in New York. In the daytime they were employed at other trades, the men mostly as cigar makers and the women as garment finishers. The work at rehearsals and in the nightly performances was strenuous, and the pay ranged from three to four dollars a week. But it was not so much the hard work and low wages that drove them to seek protection in organization, as the brutal treatment to which they were subjected by the theater managers.

In membership the two "unions" together represented a grand total of forty. This was the modest beginning of the organization that in later years boasted of an affiliated membership of a quarter of a million workers.

Aims

Undaunted by the slim foundation, we proceeded to the formal organization of the United Hebrew Trades, with Bernard Weinstein as recording secretary and myself in the somewhat vague post of "corresponding secretary." The triple aim of the new organization was declared to be: (1) mutual aid and cooperation among the Jewish trade unions of New York; (2) organization of new unions; (3) the propaganda of Socialism among the Jewish workers.

An Actors' Union

A somewhat humorous sample of the work ahead of us presented itself at the very first meeting of our newly formed body. Just before adjournment a delegation from an actors' union appeared and applied for affiliation.

The Jewish theaters of New York were in their infancy and had a hard struggle for existence. The members of the troupes were not paid fixed salaries but worked on shares. The lion's share of these "shares," however, went to the numerous stars, while the lesser lights of the stage were left with little more than the gratification of their artistic aspirations. The class struggle in this instance was between the minor parts and the headliners, and the former had just formed a union against the latter. The definite organization meeting of the new union was to be held in a few days, and we were asked to send a speaker to initiate the neophytes in the principles and practices of trade unionism.

Of course, we were eager to serve, but the spokesman for the theatrical proletariat was careful to attach proper conditions to his request. Actors are artists after all, he explained, and cannot be expected to receive instruction in coarse and common Yiddish. Our speaker would have to address them in German, the language of the poets and thinkers. All eyes turned on me. I nodded assent, and this part of the problem seemed to be solved. But not so with the next condition of our theatrical comrade. "To have the attention and respect of the audience," he calmly proceeded, "the speaker will have to appear in proper attire, i.e., dressed in frock coat and silk hat."

Again all eyes turned on me, but this time not with confidence but with consternation succeeded by irrepressible mirth. I was nineteen and looked younger. Frock coats and silk hats were not among the customary articles of my wardrobe and were generally not sported at our meetings.

This was our first taste of some of the difficulties of practical trade-union politics, and we just gave it up. The organization meeting of the actors' union was held without a representative of our group and seems to have gotten along quite well, for the Jewish Actors' Union was definitely and firmly organized and has remained in continued and effective existence ever since. For years one of the favorite and exciting subjects of our debates was, whether actors were wage workers and had a legitimate place in the labor movement. The final decision was in the affirmative.

Our work among the genuine and simon-pure proletariat began very soon. Our first effort was to reorganize the defunct shirt makers' union. This was accomplished within a few weeks after the foundation of the United Hebrew Trades. It was a comparatively easy task because this particular trade happened to employ large numbers of Socialist intellectuals.

The problem was infinitely more difficult in the other branches of the needle industry, but gradually a technique of organization was developed.

I remember most vividly the origin and early history of the Knee Pants Makers' Union, and shall rapidly sketch them because they were typical of all tailoring trades.

Sweatshops

In 1890 there were about one thousand knee pants makers employed in New York, all "green" and most of them illiterate. It was a sweat-shop industry *par excellence*. The work was done entirely on the contracting system. A contractor employed about ten workers on the average and usually operated his shop in his living-rooms. His sole function consisted of procuring bundles of cut garments from the manufacturer and having them made up by the workers. He did not even furnish the sewing machines. The operator provided his own machine as well as the needles and thread. The work day was endless, and the average earnings of experienced operators ran from six to seven dollars per week. Often the contractor would abscond with a week's pay; often the worker would be discharged because he was not fast enough to suit the contractor, and often he would be compelled to quit his job because of maltreatment or intolerable working conditions. Every time a knee pants maker changed contractors, he was compelled to put his sewing machine on his back and carry it through the streets to his new place of employment. It was at this point that their patience finally gave out. In the early part of 1890, they struck. The movement was spontaneous, without program, leadership, or organization. It was a blind outbreak of revolt and was destined to collapse if left to itself, sharing the fate of many similar outbursts in the past.

Strikes and Victory

In this case the United Hebrew Trades stepped in during the very first hours of the strike. Through a committee of five, of whom I was one, it took complete charge of the situation.

Our first step was to hire a meeting hall large enough to accommodate all the strikers. There were about nine hundred, and we gathered them in from all shops and street corners. In the hall we held them in practically continuous session, day and night, allowing them only the necessary time to go home to sleep. We feared to let them go, lest they be tempted to return to work, and we entertained them all the time with speeches and such other forms of instruction and amusement as we could devise.

While the continuous performance was going on in the main hall, we tried to bring order and system into the strike and to organize the strikers into a solid and permanent union.

In consultation with the most intelligent men and women from the ranks of the strikers, we worked out a list of demands centering upon the employer's obligation to furnish sewing machines and other work tools at his own expense. Then we chose pickets, relief committees, and settlement committees, all operating under our direct supervision and guidance.

The men did not know how to conduct meetings or transact business of any kind. They had never acted in concert. Our discourses on the principles of trade unionism and the philosophy of Socialism were interspersed with elementary lessons in parliamentary procedure and practical methods of organization. We tried to pick out the most promising among them and train them for leadership of their fellows. The strike was a course of intensive training and education, but it was of short duration. After one week without a break in the ranks of the workers, the contractors weakened; one Saturday night they became panicky and stormed the meeting hall of the strikers in a body, demanding an immediate and collective settlement on the workers' terms.

The United Hebrew Trades had scored a great victory and was encouraged to new efforts in other fields.

The Bakery Workers

One of the most difficult tasks the pioneering group was called upon to tackle was the organization of the Jewish bakery workers. In the early days of Jewish immigration a limited number of bakeshops had sprung up on the lower East Side. They specialized in "Jewish" rye bread and other bakery products to which the Jewish consumers had been accustomed in the countries of their origin. These bakeries were in deep and dark subcellars, without ventilation or any hygienic accommodations. The walls and ceilings were moist and moldy. The shops were infested with rats and reeked with dirt. The air was pestilential. The bake ovens were primitive. No machinery was used. The work was all done by hand.

The new industry employed a total of a few hundred workers, mostly immigrants from Galicia, Hungary, and Poland. They were different from the bulk of the Russian Jewish workers, more stolid, unemotional, and irresponsive. They worked seventeen to eighteen hours a day except on Thursday, when their "work day" began early in the morning and lasted until noon on Friday. As a rule they boarded and lodged with their employers. They worked at the ovens naked from the waist up and slept in the bakery cellars. When they did not receive board and lodging, their wages averaged six to seven dollars a week.

Their only leisure time was between making the dough and its rising, and these hours they spent in their favorite saloons, drinking beer and playing cards.

The beer saloons, particularly one on the corner of Ludlow and Hester streets, provided the only romance in their drab lives. Here were their social clubs and also their labor bureaus. Here they would exchange information about jobs and here also employers would come in quest of "hands."

Pale-faced, hollow-chested, listless, and brutified, they seemed to be hopeless material for organization and struggle. In 1887 the newly organized Bakery and Confectionery Workers International Union of America had succeeded in enlisting a number of them into a Jewish local union, but the organization collapsed within a year, for a reason very characteristic of the workers' mentality.

Anxious to remove them from the demoralizing atmosphere of the Ludlow Street saloon, the secretary of the national organization of bakery workers had secured new headquarters for them. It was a room back of a beer saloon on Orchard Street. Meeting halls connected with saloons were the customary thing for labor unions in New York in those days. The saloon keeper would make no charge for the use of the room, expecting to be compensated in trade. In the case of the German and Irish unions the scheme worked well, but with the Jewish unions it mostly proved unprofitable from the saloon keeper's point of view.

The attempted removal of the organized Jewish bakers from the Ludlow Street saloon met with considerable opposition. They were used to their old gathering place and its ways, and many of them were suspicious of the proposed change. A severe factional fight broke out between the conservative adherents of Ludlow Street and the radical supporters of Orchard Street. To the Jewish bakery workers of that period the class struggle assumed the form of a fight between two rival beer saloons. With the help of the proprietor and the support of the employers, the anti-union Ludlow Street saloon won out. The union disbanded.

Undeterred by this miscarried attempt, the United Hebrew Trades launched a new campaign to organize the bakers in 1889. After some preparatory propaganda, a strike was called. The principal demand of the workers was for the six-day week with one day of rest, on Saturdays, a radical demand in those days.

The strike call met with general response. The Jewish bakeshops were tied up, and within a few days their proprietors surrendered to the union.

As in the case of the knee pants makers, the strike was organized and conducted by a group of young Socialists acting in behalf of the United Hebrew Trades; and as in that case we tried to take advantage of the situation to give the workers an intensive course of instruction in the principles and methods of trade unionism. Our efforts seemed to be successful beyond our most optimistic expectations. Within a few months the organization numbered about four hundred members, constituting practically the whole body of Jewish bakery workers. The Union became their religion, and they zealously adhered to its tenets as they understood them.

Inhuman Labor Conditions

A tragic incident which occurred shortly after the organization of the Jewish bakers' union served to call general public attention to the revolting conditions in the bakeshops of New York's East Side and led to important consequences in the field of labor legislation.

One early morning the secretary of the newly organized union reported to Bernard Weinstein at the office of the United Hebrew Trades that a baker had collapsed while working at night and was still in the bakeshop, critically ill. The secretary, as well as the employer, were at a loss as to what to do. When Weinstein reached the bakery cellar, he found a most appalling condition of filth, with three emaciated and exhausted bakers continuing to work at the side of their agonizing comrade. He made arrangements to have the sick man taken to a hospital and reported the case to the Labor Department.

An investigation of the bakeshops on the East Side followed and resulted in a sensational report condemning the inhuman labor conditions in these shops and branding them as a standing menace to public health.

Hours of Labor

As a consequence of this investigation and report the New York State Legislature shortly thereafter enacted a law, limiting work in bakeries to ten hours a day. The law had an interesting career in the courts and largely served to determine the limit of protective labor legislation.

Contesting the constitutionality of the law, the employers fought it in all courts of the state and in the Supreme Court of the United States. It was upheld by the trial judge, whose decision was affirmed in the Appellate Division by the narrow margin of three to two votes and in the Court of Appeals by a vote of four to three. In the United States Supreme Court it was reversed by a vote of five to four.

"There is no reasonable ground for interfering with the liberty of person or the right of free contract, by determining the hours of labor, in the occupation of a baker," declared Mr. Justice Peckham, who wrote the prevailing opinion in the case of Lochner against New York. "There is no contention that bakers as a class are not equal in intelligence and capacity to men in other trades and manual occupations, or that they are not able to assert their rights and care for themselves without the protesting arm of the state interfering with their independence of judgment and of action."

The learned court held that the law curtailed both "the right of the individual to labor for such time as he may choose" and the right of the employer "to purchase labor" in such quantities as he may choose.

I have often wondered whether Mr. Justice Peckham and his four concurring associates would have felt quite so certain about the capacity of the bakers to assert their rights and to exercise "their independence of judgment and of action," if they had met the Jewish bakers in their hang-out in the Ludlow Street corner saloon, or gone through the numerous strikes with them, or accompanied Bernard Weinstein in his mission of help to the sovereign and independent baker who fell in the midst of his free labor like an overburdened beast. And I am still wondering why a few theorists, ignorant of the daily struggles and sufferings of the toiling masses, should be allowed to determine industrial relations, social conflicts, and human rights, irrevocably and regardless of public sentiment and the enactments of popularly chosen legislative bodies.

The bakers' union subsequently became one of the strongest, most progressive, and best disciplined organizations among the Jewish workers of America. But that development took many years of patient and persistent struggle punctuated by recurring disappointments, failures, and defeats.

In spite of its promising beginning, the union founded by the United Hebrew Trades had a short life. With the immediate objects of their strike attained, the members lost interest in their organization and within a short time the union disbanded. The lack of organization led to a new deterioration of labor standards and to a new revolt, another strike, and a revival of the union, followed by an inevitable decline and eventual dissolution. The disheartening process was repeated at fairly regular intervals every two or three years, each new organization being a little stronger and lasting a little longer than its predecessor, until stability and permanence were at last achieved after a zigzagging course of fifteen to twenty years.

Such also was the history of the Knee Pants Makers' Union and of practically all other Jewish trade unions organized since the advent of the United Hebrew Trades.

Educating the Workers

I have dwelt at length on the organizations of the Jewish knee pants makers and bakers because they were typical instances of the accomplishments and problems of the United Hebrew Trades. But these organizations were by no means the only ones called into life by the United Hebrew Trades, nor the most important ones. In its early career the Jewish Hebrew Trades was incessantly busy organizing and reorganizing Jewish trade unions. During the first eighteen months of its existence it had increased the number of its affiliated bodies from two to thirty-two. These included practically all industries in which Jewish workers were engaged in substantial numbers. Heading the list were the different tailoring branches, such as the cloak makers, men's tailors, furriers, and cap makers, but included in it were also such occupations as musicians, retail store clerks, book-binders and soda-water workers. And in practically all cases the unions were short-lived. They came and went and had to be reorganized every few years. In the minds of the Jewish workers of that period unions were associated with strikes and were little more than instruments of strikes. They were mostly born in strikes and died with the end of the strikes. It took twenty years of patient and persistent work to educate the Jewish workers to a realization of the value of trade unions in peace as well as in war, and it was not until about 1910 that the Jewish labor movement was organized on a solid and stable basis.

One of the important factors that contributed to that result was the consolidation of the multifarious organizations of separate branches of the needle-trade crafts into large unions embracing all parts of a related industry, such as the International Ladies' Garment Workers Union, whose jurisdiction extends to all branches of the manufacture of women's apparel and the Amalgamated Clothing Workers Union, which is composed of all workers in the men's tailoring industry.

At this time several hundred thousand Jewish workers are normally organized in national and local trade unions. They have been fully accepted by their fellow workers as an organic part of the American labor movement, and have made a distinct contribution to the general progress of the movement.

During the half-century of their struggles, trials, errors, and experiences, the Jewish workers in America have been strikingly transformed, mentally, morally, and even physically. From a race of timid, submissive, cheerless, and hopeless drudges they have grown into a generation of self-reliant, self-respecting men and women, conscious of their social and industrial rights and ever ready to defend them.

Working in a Shirt Shop

I was seventeen when I came to America with my mother, a younger brother, and two sisters. My father and an older brother had preceded us by about two years and established a "home" for us in a two-room apartment in a tenement house on Clinton Street.

It was the unanimous decision of the family that I resume my interrupted studies and prepare myself for a professional career. My first step in that direction was to enroll in a public high school on Fourteenth Street.

I had come to New York with a smattering of school English, which served me very well in Russia, but proved utterly inadequate and largely incomprehensible in New York. My prime object in attending public school was to learn some real American English.

I liked the school, its friendly atmosphere and free and easy ways. Most of my fellow students were younger than I, and I must have appeared to them queer with my foreign ways and quaint English; but the boys were kind and helpful, and the teachers took a sympathetic interest in my progress.

After a short time, however, I was again compelled to interrupt my studies.

My parents were frightfully poor. My elder brother and the older of my sisters were working. I felt uncomfortable in the role of the drone of the family, and determined to go to work.

To decide to work was one thing, but to find work was, as I soon discovered, quite another thing. Because of my fragmentary knowledge of English and total lack of business connections I could not look for anything but manual labor. I was frail and untrained for any trade and almost inevitably gravitated into a shirt shop. For some fortuitous reason, shirt making had become the favorite occupation of the circle of young Russian intellectuals in which I moved. It was a trade easy to learn principally because of the minute division of labor that prevailed in it.

Nobody made a complete shirt. The task of each worker was confined to one small and uniform operation, such as making the front or the sleeve, the collar or cuff, hemming the bottom or sewing some parts together. The cuff was the simplest part and required least skill and training. The operation of the "cuff maker" consisted of stitching together two square pieces of cut material on three sides and attaching it to the sleeve. I started my career as a cuff maker and never advanced to a higher stage of the art.

The work was not exacting, and the surroundings were not uncongenial. The operators in the stuffy little workshop spent at least as much time in discussing social and literary topics as in turning out shirts, and the whir of the sewing machines was often accompanied by the loud and hearty sound of revolutionary songs.

But the monetary returns were distressingly slim. The "boss," i.e., the contractor who ran the shop, took no business chances. He practically paid no rent, since the work was done in one of the rooms of his living quarters. He had no outlay on machinery because every worker hired his own sewing machine, at a rental of two dollars per month. Wages were low and were paid "by the piece." Work was seasonal and irregular. The machine rent was the only constant element in the peculiar industrial scheme, so that a worker of my skill and productivity sometimes wound up the month with a deficit in earnings.

Disappointed with the financial aspect of the shirt industry, I turned my talents to waist making. For a short time I also held down a job in a picture frame factory. But in all of these occupations my earnings were highly precarious, to say the least. . . .

A Yiddish Labor Paper

From the very beginning of our efforts to organize and consolidate the Jewish trade unions we felt the crying need of a labor paper as an organ of the movement, as a medium of communication between the unions and their members, and, above all, as an instrument of propaganda and education.

There was at that time a well-edited German Socialist daily newspaper in New York, the New Yorker Volkszeitung; but the Jewish workers could not read German. Nor could they read English. They knew only Yiddish.

Plans for the publication of a Yiddish weekly labor paper were often discussed among the leaders of the movement and in the fall of 1889 several formal conferences were held on the subject . . .

Months of incessant and enthusiastic preparatory work ensued. Funds had to be raised, the paper planned, and its management organized. Among the most active promoters of the project were Abraham Cahan, one Louis E. Miller, and I.

Cahan's life always was an uninterrupted succession of enthusiasms. Whatever interest happened to take hold of him at the moment dominated his thoughts and actions to the exclusion of everything else. He now threw himself body and soul into the new enterprise and never tired of discussing the proposed paper and working for its realization. He had two advantages over the rest of us. He knew Yiddish well, and he had the instincts of a born journalist. . . .

Together we set out soliciting contributions for the projected paper. Almost every night we visited one or more Jewish trade unions and friendly German labor organizations, making our plea and receiving donations.

Within a few months we raised the enormous capital of $800.

On the 6th of March, 1890, the first number of our *Arbeiter-Zeitung* (Workers' Paper) appeared. It was an event of first magnitude in the Jewish Socialist and labor movements and an occasion for boundless rejoicing. For hours a throng of eager sympathizers stood in front of the printer's shop waiting for the first copies to come off the press. As fast as they did, they were handed out to the waiting crowds and snatched up by them with reverence and wonder. Here it was "in the flesh," a four-page paper neatly printed in the familiar Hebrew characters, all written for them and about them. Their hopes and dreams of many months were finally realized.

The paper was an instantaneous success. For weeks and weeks we had carefully planned every detail of its contents. It was our aim to conduct the paper along broad educational lines rather than to confine it to dry economic theories and Socialist propaganda. The Jewish masses were totally uncultured. They stood in need of elementary information about the important things in life outside of the direct concerns of the Socialist and labor movement. Without a certain minimum of general culture they could not be expected to develop an intelligent understanding of their own problems and interest in their own struggles.

Alongside a weekly chronicle of the Socialist and labor movements, the *Arbeiter-Zeitung* printed simple expositions of the philosophy of the movements in their different phases, articles on popular science, descriptions of travel, good fiction, and even poetry. Abraham Cahan largely supplied the "human interest" features. I contributed editorials, historical sketches, and articles on Socialist theory and a variety of other subjects. Other contributions came from the editor-in-chief and a number of volunteer writers who gradually augmented our forces.

The paper soon reached a circulation of about eight thousand copies, an almost fantastic figure in view of all our handicaps and modest expectation. Its size was increased from four pages to eight.

The *Arbeiter-Zeitung* exerted a powerful influence on the course of the

Jewish labor movement and contributed materially to the intellectual development of the Jewish laboring masses. It retained the field until it was succeeded by the Jewish *Daily Forward,* which, under the able editorship of Abraham Cahan, became one of the great Socialist newspapers of the world and probably the most prosperous.

121. BECOMING A LABOR LAWYER

LOUIS WALDMAN

Louis Waldman, born in Russia in 1892, migrated to the United States as a poor boy and became a famous labor lawyer. The selection which follows is taken from his autobiography and is typical of the experiences of many young intelligent young immigrants (see also nos. 126–28). It may also sum up the preceding selections dealing with the clothing industry in which Jewish immigrants played such a prominent role.

Among Immigrants

Without ever having seen a large city in Russia, although Kiev and Zhitomir were not far from Yancherudnia, I was now on my way across the world to America. I was young, I was hopeful, and for the first time in my life I had seventy-five dollars in ready cash in my pocket. My tickets were paid for in advance, my practical father having made all the arrangements through a travel agent.

The first detour I met on my highroad to adventure occurred at a frontier town in Germany where I discovered that, unaccountably, my railway ticket to Rotterdam had not yet arrived. But, refusing to let that little setback dampen my spirits, I settled down to wait and enjoy my new role as world traveler.

This way station was a clearing center for the hordes of emigrants pouring out of the Ukraine and Russia. While I waited for my tickets I wandered among them and was moved to pity when I found that hundreds were stranded there, defrauded by unscrupulous travel agents. Whole families were completely without funds and without means of continuing the journey. My heart went out to these poor unfortunates and, with a youngster's serene unconcern with money matters, I distributed my wealth lavishly among them.

The days stretched into weeks, until one day I realized that all my money was gone. It was only then that it finally dawned on me that I, the great benefactor, was in the same boat as the other stranded emigrants. My ticket never made its appearance, nor did the disreputable travel agent.

I rallied quickly from this blow, however. A mere lack of money was not

going to keep me from America, after I had got that far. Boldly I sought out
the head of a travelers' aid organization and told him of my plight. I must
have presented a heart-rending spectacle, for I walked out of his office
generously supplied with money for a ticket—which was all that I, with
characteristic improvidence, had asked for.

I had absolutely no money for food on the trip. Somehow I had managed
to obtain some bread before I left and this, with unlimited quantities of
water, served to keep me alive on the three day train journey from eastern
Germany to Holland. I saw absolutely nothing of the cities or countryside
through which we passed. I was chained to my seat in the train by
weakness and my complete lack of money. When I arrived at the steamship
office in Rotterdam I fell into a dead faint. By some miracle, I found the
steamship ticket waiting for me.

Steerage

I traveled steerage to America—and I marvel at the equanimity with
which I write these words. Crossing the Atlantic in steerage thirty-odd
years ago was a terrifying and nauseating experience. There were some
forty or fifty men, women, and children crowded into one room with
absolutely no ventilation other than that provided by the hatchway
through which we had entered. Cots were set up in tiers with just enough
space between the sets of bunks for one person to squeeze through with
difficulty. The odors were indescribable, and breathing was far from a
reflex activity; it required actual effort. Baggage had to be kept either on the
floor or beneath the cot or on the cot itself. People were constantly
stumbling over stray bags and packages.

We ate at long tables and from large bowls into which the entire meal,
except for liquids, was dumped. But the foul odors of the ship and of
unwashed bodies packed into close quarters were not conducive to hearty
eating. In a way this was fortunate because there was not enough food for
all. It was only after seasickness began to take its toll that those who could
eat had enough food. After starving my way across Europe, at first I
attacked the ship's victuals ravenously. But I could not stomach them for
long and spent the rest of the trip detesting food and longing for an end to
this tormenting journey.

Arrival

Wasted, unsteady on my feet, but still hopeful, I arrived at Battery Park,
New York, on September 17, 1909. Behind me was the bustling harbor
with its innumerable boats, the sight of which made me seasick all over
again. Facing me, beyond the open spaces of the park, were the tall
buildings of lower Manhattan, buildings which were more magnificent

and higher than any I had ever imagined, even in my wildest dreams of this metropolis of the new world.

No one had come to meet me, for no one knew precisely when I was to arrive. And there I stood in Battery Park in my tight pants and round hat, with my knowledge of the Talmud, Yiddish, and Ukrainian, but in abysmal ignorance of English. I wandered around the park for some time, trying to find someone who could understand my language and direct me to 118 Orchard Street, where my sister Cecilia lived. After enduring the blank stares of several park bench idlers I at last discovered someone who understood me, and I was off via horse-car in the direction of the lower East Side.

When I got to the Orchard Street address I had to climb five flights of rickety and malodorous stairs to my sister's tenement flat. It was the first day of Rosh Hashanah and all my four sisters were there, seated around a festive table. They were at the same time overjoyed and alarmed when I walked in, for I was pale and gaunt from hunger and from the days I had spent below decks. They had known, of course, that I was coming, but my difficulties with the fraudulent travel agent and the delay in Rotterdam had confused them as to the exact day and hour of my arrival.

New Clothes

First on the order of business for the new immigrant was a visit to a clothing store.

"You think you can walk around like that, looking as green as grass?" my sister Anna said. "Why, no one, not even a peddler, will give you a job!"

And so it was that I parted forever with my tight pants, my round hat, and my high, creaking Ukrainian boots.

My American store clothes became a sort of passport which gave me the right to walk the streets as an equal of anyone and to consider myself as belonging to this vast city. Ths cheap, ready-to-wear East Side suit bridged the first gap, a sartorial gap, to be sure, between my past and my present.

However, while my new suit put me more at ease in the streets, my ignorance of English made me envious of other immigrants who spoke even a few halting words of the new language. Above all, if I wanted to become a real American, I realized, it was necessary for me to speak the language of Americans. And so, within a week after my arrival I enrolled in an East Side night school and set about the task of learning to read and speak the language of my adopted land.

Soon the entire neighborhood in which I lived became a school room, so to speak. As I walked in the streets I would pronounce aloud the words I saw written on signs, on billboards, or street corners. "Butcher shop," I slowly spelled out. "Gayety Burlesque" (what a strange word!), "Shoes Repaired Here," "Uneeda Biscuit." Mumbling to myself I would stand before some store window struggling with a strange unintelligible word until an irate shopkeeper told me to move on. I did move on but only to take up my post at another establishment, for I was determined to learn to speak my adopted language fluently even if the entire East Side had to listen painfully to my lessons.

Finding a Job

One of the first things I learned was that if I were ultimately to study law I would first have to find a job. In the house in which I lived everyone worked, men, women, and even children, and before long I joined their ranks.

Getting a job in those days had a certain directness about it which is lacking in our larger American cities today. My sisters told me where the various factories were located and all I had to do was to go from door to door to find out whether anyone could use my services.

Finally I stumbled across a chandelier factory on Canal Street which proclaimed on a crudely painted sign—but in three languages—that a "hand" was wanted inside. I walked up several flights of stairs and finally spoke to the foreman. He looked me over, and made careful note of my husky appearance, and told me I could start working. My salary was to be two dollars a week, but he added: "Don't worry, there's room for advancement." Five months later when I quit I was still getting two dollars a week.

I was not asked whether I had done this type of work before or whether I had a union or apprenticeship card, nor was there any labor organization to represent my interests and to see that I received a fair wage for my work. I was hired, I was shown the machine I was expected to operate, and then, after a few brief instructions, I set to work.

Working in a Factory

I worked at a press which bent a strip of metal into a ring. My job was to keep feeding my hungry, clattering machine strip after strip of metal. The tempo of work was set with complete disregard to myself. I had no control over the speed with which the press came down. If I failed to feed it at the rate to which it was regulated, this fact immediately became known, for if the metal was not inserted in time the press descended with a loud, hollow telltale clang which could be heard throughout the shop. The foreman checked on our work by continually passing along the row of machines and closely watching the size and pile of rings which accumulated at the side of each press.

There were about one hundred men and women who worked in this hot, noisy loft. And we worked from seven in the morning until six at night with half an hour off for lunch. But this ten-and-a-half-hour day seemed much longer than it really was because of the monotonous clang of the machine and the unvarying routine of my work.

I paid my sister Cecilia one dollar a week for my room and board and I shared a narrow, almost cell-like room with another boarder. My lunches usually cost me two or three cents; one cent for a sizable hunk of rye bread and another cent for an apple or a half of a salt herring, and since I invariably walked to work I found myself with a small surplus at the end of the week.

Yet, despite the monotony of the work and the low pay and despite the fact that my fingers soon became sore, bruised, and swollen from the constant handling of the metal, I was reasonably happy. The working conditions, though onerous, were acceptable to me because I did not know that factory work might be easier or that my pay might be greater. It was all very different from the farm and outdoor work which I had hitherto known, but I assumed that the monotony, the heat, and the unpleasantness of it all were part of any city job.

At the machine next to me there was an Irish-American girl called Mary Bolan. Since I could not talk English and Mary could not talk Ukrainian or Yiddish, we smiled at each other above the clattering din of the chandelier factory. We smiled and smiled—and understood each other.

Months of work at the same task had given Mary Bolan speed and skill. Her nervous hands moved rapidly and deftly under the constant threat of mutilation by her machine. Unable to express myself to this delightful Irish-American girl other than through a wholly inadequate smile, I spent hours at my machine dreaming of the day when I would master both English and my natural timidity and summon courage to ask her to go for a walk with me some evening after work.

Fear of Accidents

Absorbed in this pleasant daydreaming late one afternoon, I was startled out of it by a girl's scream. At once, all machines in the shop came to a halt. Looking up in alarm, I saw Mary Bolan lying on the floor at the side of her machine, blood streaming from the fingers of her right hand. The hovering threat had become actual.

I leaped from my place and ran to her side. She was unconscious and was bleeding profusely. I tore a strip from my shirt and made vain efforts to staunch the flow of blood. Workers gathered around the prostrate girl, some frightened, some giving expression to anger.

"It's those God-damned machines."

"It's cut off two of her fingers."

"Why the hell haven't they got guards on these machines?"

The foreman pushed his way through the crowd angrily, shouting: "Come on! Back to your machines, get back to your machines!"

We went back to work but somehow there was some difficulty getting the power started again. We sat silently in that dark loft, each man holding his own fear.

A little later we heard the clang of an ambulance in the street outside. Two orderlies carried the unconscious girl out of the factory. Then, once again, the stamping machines began their incessant clatter.

That night and for many nights thereafter I kept thinking of Mary Bolan. Her right hand had been mutilated, made useless, gone forever. Who would take care of Mary Bolan now? Owners of factories wanted strong healthy workers, workers with ten, not eight, fingers.

The day after the accident a man with a black portfolio came into the shop and, together with the foreman, started to make the rounds of the workers. Those who had seen the accident were asked to sign a certain paper. The man with the portfolio came over to my machine and shoved the paper under my face and asked me to sign.

"What is it?" I asked.

"We simply want you to sign saying that it was her fault. It's just a formality."

The word was a strange one to me.

"What," I asked in my broken English, "is this formality?"

"Never mind," the man with the portfolio said abruptly, "just sign!"

I hesitated.

"Go ahead, sign the paper," the foreman ordered.

"But it wasn't her fault," I objected.

"Then say it was the fault of the boy who brings the metal to the machines. He must have pushed her accidentally."

"I don't know anything about that," I replied.

The foreman spoke up sharply: "Listen, you! Don't you want to work here?"

"No," I answered.

Discharged

Most of the workers, intimidated by the foreman and the man with the portfolio, signed. A few of us, however, refused and were discharged on the spot. I made fruitless inquiries about where Mary had been taken but no one seemed to know. I never saw her again.

I had received my first lesson in labor relations.

When I arrived home that evening, friends and neighbors gathered around to hear the story of my rebelliousness and to offer sage advice.

"You should have signed the paper, Louis."

"You will get nowhere in America by fighting the bosses."

"You see, there were some to be found who signed it anyway. And now you are without a job."

My sisters held solemn conclaves about my future and finally, after much discussion, they came to the conclusion that I should apply for work in the shop in which they worked and where one Benjamin Hirshorn was boss.

"When you apply for the job," one of my sisters said, "don't tell Hirshorn anything about refusing to sign any papers. Say that the work was too hard or that the pay was too low."

"If you don't get into fights with your employers and if you do as you're told, some day you will be a cutter."

While my sisters talked and argued, plotting the chart of my future, I sat by, silent and a little amused. For I had another plan which, for the time being, I kept secret. I still held fast to the ambition that one day I might become a lawyer.

Night School

Night after night I went to the neighborhood night school and hungrily devoured instruction. And because it was an utter impossibility to study in the wrangling, noisy intimacy of my family, I decided to perform a domestic surgical operation. Astonishingly enough, even on the two dollars a week I had been earning at the chandelier factory, I was able to save fifty or sixty cents a week, so that now, after several months of work, I had accumulated a nest egg of thirteen dollars. With this fortune I was determined to leave the noisy shelter of Cecilia's flat and move out into the world and find a room where I could have solitude and peace in which to continue my studies.

The immigrant's world in New York in those years was limited by the boundaries of the lower East Side. New York might be a vast sprawling city with several boroughs and wide spacious suburbs, but for those of us who were trapped by poverty, the East Side was all that we knew.

In a Tenement

I found a room on Allen Street which by comparison made the one on

Orchard Street seem a paradise. I lived in a six-story tenement where families were doubled up in small apartments and where each family kept its quota of boarders to help meet the monthly rent. Some slept by day and others by night and very frequently, except on Sunday, the beds never had an opportunity to be aired. Each floor had a community toilet and a water tap in the hall and in some of the houses on Allen Street sanitary facilities were located in the back yard.

At night, when the gas light consumed the little air that managed to come through the halls and narrow windows, my room was stifling, and I suffered from headaches, dizziness, and nervous irritation. But I was alone, my time in the evenings was my own and I could study whenever the spirit moved me, which was often. I still recall vividly that curious, congested, miserable, yet fascinating life. I see Allen Street with its elevated structure whose trains avalanched between rows of houses. I see the gloom of the street where the sunlight never penetrated. I see the small shops, shops which somehow never achieved the dignity of selling anything new, but specialized in old furniture, old clothes, old dishes. It was a street which dealt in castoff merchandise. Even the pale children who played on Allen Street seemed old, second hand, not wanted. This street I now called home.

My room looked out on a dark air shaft blackened by dirt and time. My studies were continually carried on to the accompaniment of bedlam: screams of babies, the ceaseless loud-voiced wrangling of neighbors, and occasionally a snatch of song. There I would sit of a night studying American history, reading of its great figures: Jefferson, Paine, Washington, reading of the great nation they had founded and wondering whether my lot in it would always be confined to a cell-like room on Allen Street.

It was at times such as these that I thought of the openness and freedom of my life in Yancherudnia, of the pond behind our house and the forest encircling our little Ukrainian village. On a hot summer's night when breathing was almost impossible, when all the East Side odors seemed to come down the air shaft and into my room, I lay on my bed and in my imagination breathed deep drafts of the sweet-smelling air of the forest where I had played and worked as a boy.

My rent was four dollars a month. As for food, there were weeks and even months when I somehow managed to live on three to four cents a day. A fifth of a sizable loaf of rye bread cost me one cent. The endless rows of pushcarts on Orchard, Delancey and Allen Streets offered a variety of fruits and vegetables all at astonishingly low prices. Sometimes when I felt in a particularly spendthrift mood, I would buy one or two cents' worth of *halvah*, an Eastern European confection which is made of crushed sesame seeds, honey, nuts and albumen. But of course I had *halvah* only on special festive occasions. For the rest, my fare was simple, usually monotonous, but nourishing.

Cutter of Ladies' Garments

Finally, through the efforts of my sisters, in March 1910, I was given an opportunity to become an apprentice to a cutter of ladies' garments. I worked six weeks without pay but this was considered a privilege, for cutters in the garment industry were the aristocrats of the needle trades. I learned my work quickly and on the whole rather enjoyed it; in addition, my prospects for increased pay were greatly enhanced.

On Strike

This routine of factory work from eight in the morning until six at night, followed by evenings in the classroom or study at home continued pleasantly until it was interrupted by the great cloakmakers' strike of 1910. Without hesitation I walked out with the rest of the workers, and, since I was now on strike, I joined the union. Our grievances were many and just and included an upward revision of the wage scale, the shortening of the work day, and improvement of sanitary conditions, and called for an investigation into possible fire hazards as well as demands for the abolition of the sweatshop system. More than fifty thousand cloakmakers answered the strike call.

I found the tense, exciting union meetings far more interesting than evenings spent at home studying, and I was soon drawn into the maelstrom of union activity. The cutters on the whole were an intelligent, literate group of men and our meetings were filled with lively discussion and debate. I enjoyed these debates both for the content and for the opportunities which they offered for putting my limited English to use.

It did not take very long, however, for me to become painfully aware that being on strike was more than a matter of picket-line heroics or thundering rhetoric. We received no strike benefits and this, quite, naturally, meant that we had to live on savings, friends, or, as was the case with many of us, on miracles. I could not turn to my sisters for help because they too were on strike. I had no savings. The few dollars I had accumulated as a result of my work in the chandelier factory had been used up during my six weeks' apprenticeship without pay. True, my activities in those days were largely confined to the picket-line and the picketing committee saw that all pickets were more or less adequately fed. But I did not picket continually, and on picketless days I went hungry.

Still, there was a certain compensation for not working. When I was through with my day's activity on the picket line, which was usually fairly early in the morning, I ran off to the library to lose myself in reading and studying.

Breaking the Strike

On the second day of the strike, as we approached our factory, we found several toughs strolling nonchalantly back and forth before the entrance. The older and more experienced workers looked at each other and whispered:"Shtarke!" I had heard the expression before. These"shtarke" were in reality strong-arm men, gangsters, hired by the employers to help break the strike. As we proceeded to march up and down before the building, not only peacefully but timidly as well, the strong-arm men soon began to walk at our sides pretending to be ordinary pedestrians. Now and then one would brutally push a picket off the sidewalk, sending him flying into the gutter, at the same time muttering to the stunned picket: "Quit pushing!" If the picket stood firm the gangster would then, in "self-defense," knock him down.

All day long this brutal game went on, but the pickets stuck it out. And the police, I observed, were nowhere to be seen while the thugs were at work. This state of affairs called for the special attention of the cutters. They were the most Americanized group in the union, while the tailors had the customary timidity of immigrants, fearful to strike out in defense of their rights. The cutters were thus obliged to act as an emergency squad, subject to the call of the tailors wherever the going was toughest. They pitted their courage and bare hands against the blackjacks and lead pipes of the gangsters.

Since the days of the great cloakmakers' strike, I have heard many fulminations against racketeering in the American labor movement. But I know today, on the basis of what I witnessed in 1910, that strike-breaking was the door through which gangsterism entered the American labor movement.

The "Protocol of Peace"

In the early days of the strike, several prominent and public-spirited citizens interested themselves in the plight of the workers. These included the late Justice Louis D. Brandeis and the late Louis Marshall,* who made efforts to bring about peace between the manufacturers and the workers. After the strike, the ladies' garment industry, then one of the most backward and disorganized in America, adopted what has since been

---

*About Brandeis and Marshall see nos. 129–30. (Ed.)

described as the most advanced and enlightened code of labor relations in the form of a collective agreement which was known as "the perpetual protocol of peace."

This document became famous in American labor history. Its findings and provisions were the basis of surveys and investigations by the departments of labor in many states and by the Federal Government. The protocol was, in fact, a remarkable instrument and went beyond the usual economic conditions in most labor agreements. As a means of eradicating the sweatshops a joint board was set up, composed of representatives of employers, workers and the public, with elaborate machinery for periodical inspection of factories and lofts and the abatement of unsanitary conditions. The protocol also made provision against harsh treatment of workers and their summary dismissal from employment.

Active in the Union

The strike had lasted eleven weeks and now I was back at work as a lining cutter. I also had special responsibilities toward the union which included "police" duties. There was a provision in the protocol which called for protection against chiseling, and so, on one occasion when I observed that the agreement was being violated, I promptly reported this to the union. And just as promptly my employer discharged me.

Officials of the union wanted to call a strike on my account but I insisted that I could take care of myself and get a job elsewhere. However, my optimism was short-lived. I soon discovered that I was on a black list. My employer had informed the industry that I was a troublemaker and there was no one in the industry, the protocol notwithstanding, who wanted to hire me.

This was my second lesson in labor relations, a process that was to continue for several years.

Peddling

And so once again I found myself without work and again I led a precarious existence. Unable to find work in the garment industry, I became a peddler, going from house to house with a basket of ribbons, but apparently I was unsuited for commerce even on this modest scale and I later took a job in a paper-box factory. After three months of this I found work as a cutter in a millinery factory. The work was hard, the pay was low, and, worst of all, the hours were long. But after two periods of unemployment, following each other in rapid succession, I clung desperately to the job because, while it offered me only the barest of livings, it enabled me to continue my studies.

Education for Freedom

When I was eighteen-and-a-half years old, that is to say, after I had been in the United States for nearly a year, I was graduated into high school. It is true that it was an evening high school, but it was high school nevertheless. We were an eager, intense lot to whom free education was more than something to be taken for granted. We worked assiduously, and among these immigrant high school students the cutting of classes and other student pranks were unknown things. Education represented to us the only avenue of freedom from long hours, hard work, poverty, and the thralldom of the East Side slums. Classes consisted of youngsters and middle-aged people of both sexes. A list of the graduates of my class, if it were compiled, would constitute a minor Who's Who in art, business, and the professions of New York today.

High School Graduation

I finished my course in the East Side Evening High School in 1911 and during the summer of that year, in order to make up for a few deficiencies in my curriculum and to prepare for the regents examinations, I took several courses in the Eron Preparatory School—the Groton of the East Side—then located on East Broadway. I was determined to pursue some professional study, preferably law, but here the problem of finances became paramount. To say that I had no money is a gross understatement. I was literally penniless, living from day to day on my meager, inadequate earnings.

It is true that there were colleges such as the College of the City of New York which required no tuition fee, but what I wanted was professional training, which City College did not then provide. I made inquiries at Columbia, New York University, and the New York Law School but found that the basic requisite of study was the payment of tuition fees and expenses which amounted to about $200 a year. My chances of earning $200 a year in those days, let alone saving that amount for tuition, were as remote from possibility as anything I could imagine. I talked this situation over with Dr. Shipley at the East Side Evening High School and he persuaded me to enter Cooper Union and take up engineering, for which no tuition fee was required. And so by force of circumstance and lack of funds, a boyhood ambition came to be realized in the fall of 1911 when I entered Cooper Union. Immigrant, semi-skilled worker, one-time aspirant for the law, I now bent all my energies toward becoming a civil engineer.

My life at this time was a continuous routine of factory during the day and school in the evening, and, because I had no money to spend on amusement and since my social life was virtually non-existent, all my free time was spent in a near-by library.

The Triangle Fire

One Saturday afternoon in March of that year—March 25, to be precise—I was sitting at one of the reading tables in the old Astor Library, now the building of the Hebrew Immigrant Aid Society on Lafayette Street. It was a raw, unpleasant day and the comfortable reading room seemed a delightful place to spend the remaining few hours until the library closed. I was deeply engrossed in my book when I became aware of the sounds of fire engines racing past the building. By this time I was sufficiently Americanized to be fascinated by the sound of fire engines. Along with several others in the library, I ran out to see what was happening, and followed crowds of people to the scene of the fire.

A few blocks away, the Asch Building at the corner of Washington Place and Greene Street was ablaze. When we arrived at the scene, the police had thrown a cordon around the area and the firemen were helplessly fighting the blaze. The eighth, ninth, and tenth stories of the building were now an enormous roaring cornice of flames.

Word had spread through the East Side, by some magic of terror, that the plant of the Triangle Waist Company was on fire and that several hundred workers were trapped. Horrified and helpless, the crowds—I among them—looked up at the burning building, saw girl after girl appear at the reddened windows, pause for a terrified moment, and then leap to the pavement below, to land as mangled, bloody pulp. This went on for what seemed a ghastly eternity. Occasionally a girl who had hesitated too long was licked by pursuing flames and, screaming with clothing and hair ablaze, plunged like a living torch to the street. Life nets held by the firemen were torn by the impact of the falling bodies.

The emotions of the crowd were indescribable. Women were hysterical, scores fainted; men wept as, in paroxysms of frenzy, they hurled themselves against the police lines. As darkness came on, the fire was brought under control and by word of mouth the details of the dreadful story spread through the East Side.

The Triangle Waist Company, owned by Max Blanck and Isaac Harris, was a non-union shop which the previous year had stubbornly held out against the equitable demands of the Waistmakers' Union. One of the conditions which the union had won during the strike called for a half-day's work on Saturdays. And so while all other waist factories in New York were closed that afternoon, the Triangle factory was open with a full shift of about 850 workers, most of them young girls.

The factory had woefully inadequate sanitary facilities, so that it was necessary for the workers to leave the plant in order to reach the toilets. As a precaution against what the employer called "interruption of work" the heavy steel door which led to the hall and stairway had been locked. Piles of oil-soaked waste lay under the sewing machines. A carelessly tossed cigarette or match had ignited these piles of waste material and the fires leaped from machine to machine, converting the overcrowded plant into a roaring holocaust. The girls, sitting at the machines, were packed in tightly, row upon row, chairs back to back. In the face of such crowding, escape was virtually impossible, and panic must have been instantaneous.

One of the owners of the Triangle Waist Company who was in the building at the outbreak of the fire left it hurriedly without unlocking the exits, thus dooming the girls inside. Nor had the girls ever been permitted to use the passenger elevators, due to the owners' fear that they might carry out stolen material.

When the fire was over the toll of the Triangle disaster was 147 killed and burned to death and several hundred suffering from serious burns. Police and firemen on entering the charred building discovered bodies literally burned to the bone. Blackened skeletons were found bending over machines. In one of the narrow elevator shafts of the building they found lifeless bodies piled six stories high.

A Mass Funeral

A few days later the Waistmakers' Union arranged for a mass funeral of the dead, since most of the victims had been burned or mangled beyond recognition. City officials prohibited any demonstration, but the plans for the funeral were carried out nevertheless. More than one hundred thousand workers marched in a silent cortege behind the flower-laden hearses. The streets through which the sad procession passed were draped in black and purple; East Side places of business were closed for the day.

Together with thousands of others I stood on the sidewalk and watched the funeral procession go by. A mass emotion of sorrow and despair was felt everywhere on the East Side that day. But in the weeks that followed these emotions gave way to angry questioning and a determination that a similar tragedy must never take place in New York again. We all felt that the workers who had died in the plant of the Triangle Waist Company were not so much the victims of a holocaust of flame as they were the victims of stupid greed and criminal exploitation.

Memorial Meeting

Shortly after the mass funeral, a crowded meeting was held at Cooper Union to consider the tragedy and its meaning for the working people of

New York. The historic basement auditorium of Cooper Union was jammed long before the meeting was scheduled to open. I have been to many a meeting in that auditorium since and I have addressed many meetings there myself, but never have I witnessed anything remotely comparable to that one. The audience was silent. There was none of the friendly chatter which is usually heard before a meeting starts. There were no greetings, no one smiled.

The families of the Triangle victims were there, reminding us, if any of us needed reminding, of the recent tragedy. The finest orators of the New York labor movement were there, among them, of course, Meyer London, later to become the first Socialist congressman from New York City. But more memorable, indeed unforgettable, was another speaker whose oratorical powers and great personal charm impressed me as perhaps no other man has impressed me since. He commanded the breathless attention of the audience with his first few words. His thought was clear, logical, and every sentence which he spoke was uttered with a purity of diction which transformed everything he said into literature.

Quietly, out of the memory of the days when he himself had been a factory worker, the speaker recounted life in the factories: the long hours, unsanitary conditions, fire hazards, unguarded and dangerous machines. And sitting there in that packed auditorium we all felt that this man was the spokesman of our unexpressed thoughts, a voice for the voiceless. It is thirty-two years since the night of that meeting and I still recall vividly every word he spoke, remembering it as though it were yesterday.

He spoke of the law of the sea by which the master of a vessel is always the last to leave a sinking ship. But the masters of industry, he said, were bound by no such honorable code. The masters of the Triangle Waist Company had locked the steel doors of the factory, had locked them and left the women and children, the crew of the factory, to their dreadful fate. The Triangle fire was simply a dramatic demonstration of what was constantly happening in the lives of workers, it was the epitome of a thousand similar, if smaller, tragedies which had occurred over a period of many years. The life of the worker was constantly attended by fire, disease, mutilation under machines without safety devices. And now, as a result of the Triangle tragedy we must make the cause of New York's workers known to everyone, to other workers, to city officials, to the legislators in Albany, to the country at large. . . .

America would listen to us if only we could find the voice with which to declare our wrongs and the will to declare them earnestly and constantly. Sympathetic editorials in the newspapers were good, but not enough. The governor must act, the legislature must live up to its reputed function of truly representing the people. The speaker ended with these words: "The greatest monument we can raise to the memory of our 147 dead is a system of legislation which will make such deaths hereafter impossible."

Never in all my life had I been held and fascinated as I was by this speaker. A few days before, we had stood sorrowful and helpless on the sidewalks of the East Side as the funeral cortege slowly passed by; but now there was a firm determination that the victims of the Triangle fire should not have died in vain. I felt that I was now ready to follow wherever this speaker led. The audience stood and cheered when he concluded, and since I had not caught his name when he was introduced I turned to my neighbor and asked who the orator might be.

Incredulously, the man replied: "Do you mean to tell me you've never heard Morris Hilquit* before?"

Humane Labor Legislation

Others at that meeting at Cooper Union might have stirred the audience with demagogic oratory into an angry destructive mob whose actions might have been spectacular but fleeting. Hillquit, however, galvanized us all into public energy ready to work. Committees were appointed to bring our problem before the public and before the proper officials. Everyone's service was enlisted in one way or another. Some of us were instructed to distribute leaflets, others to undertake the letter-writing campaign to the governor, still others to arrange for street corner meetings throughout the city. I, who had never taken part in any political activity, was placed on a local committee to assist in arranging meetings in the neighborhood in which I lived. The fight for more humane labor legislation was launched and in the weeks and years that followed I knew that the mutilation of Mary Bolan was not to be a forgotten individual tragedy or the deaths of the 147 girls in the Triangle fire an utterly meaningless catastrophe.

122. BECOMING AMERICANIZED

HUTCHINS HAPGOOD and HARRY GOLDEN

The process of Americanization was helped by the public schools, the libraries, and the settlement houses.
  Hutchins Hapgood (1869–1944) was a loving observer of the strange world of East European Jewish immigrants in New York City. He described his book

---

*See no. 120. (Ed.)

written about the East Side of New York as "an attempt made by a Gentile to report sympathetically on the lives of Jews with whom he maintained relations of considerable intimacy." His book, *The Spirit of the Ghetto,* from which the following selection is taken, has been recently reissued in a new edition with comments and notes by Harry Golden, indicated here by italics.

The Public Schools

No one knew in 1902 that the free public school would become the most important factor in the development of the Jewish community of America. But so it became probably because the free public school became as important a development to modern America itself. Not a day went by that we didn't see new immigrants walking down the middle of the street, each with a tag around the neck bearing a surname and with a piece of paper in hand, which was the address of a relative. And on the next Monday, the children of these immigrants enrolled in the public school. And it was the public school that proceeded to make citizens out of immigrants and do it within a single generation, surely the most successful endeavor in the history of personal relationships.

We learned history and English. When a new greenhorn came to the class, frightened and confused, unable to manage any English, all knew that within six months he would be able to stand before us and, heavy accent and all, recite:

> *I love the name of Washington,*
> *I love my country, too.*
> *I love the flag, the dear old flag,*
> *The red, the white, the blue.*

This public-school system also provided many of us with an understanding of the Christian world, which heretofore had been a strange and forbidding world. The first Christians the younger Jews knew were the public-school teachers, far different from those Christians our parents muttered about who had populated Europe. These public-school teachers were sexless saints to most of us, and we fully believed they were unencumbered by the usual physical apparatus that slowed everyone else down. We considered these teachers the most wonderful people in the world, and it is surprising to remember the awe in which the Jewish community held them. . . .

Libraries

The vast majority of the immigrants wanted their children to reflect the life and culture of America, and as quickly as possible.

There were mothers unable to speak a word of English who went to the branch library on Rivington Street and simply held up to the librarian a finger for each child. And the librarian issued cards, one for each finger. The mother went home and distributed the cards to her off-spring and instructed them: "Go. Go and learn. Go now."

I have insisted that the public school was the greatest influence on the immigrant Jews. Next in importance was the library, followed by the settlement house and the clubs they fostered.

Night Schools, Colleges, and Clubs

. . . The night schools of the East Side are used by practically no other race. City College, New York University, and Columbia University are graduating Russian Jews in numbers rapidly increasing. Many lawyers, indeed, children of patriarchal Jews, have very large practices already, and some of them belong to solid firms on Wall Street, although as to business and financial matters they have not yet attained to the most spectacular height. Then there are innumerable boys' debating clubs, ethical clubs, and literary clubs in the East Side. Altogether there is an excitement in ideas and an enthusiastic energy for acquiring knowledge which has interesting analogy to the hopefulness and acquisitive desire of the early Renaissance. It is a mistake to think that the young Hebrew turns naturally to trade. He turns his energy to whatever offers the best opportunities for broader life and success. Other things besides business are open to him in this country, and he is improving his chance for the higher education as devotedly as he has improved his opportunities for success in business.

Settlement Houses

. . . *Helping in the Americanization of the Jews was the Educational Alliance, opened in 1883 as the Y.M.H.A.'s downtown branch, then expanded by merging with the Hebrew Free School Association and the Hebrew Technical Institute. The Educational Alliance was the first settlement house in the United States. Its volunteer teachers included some of the city's most cultured Jews—among them Emma Lazarus, the poet; Oscar Straus, the diplomat; and Henry Leipziger, founder of the adult education system and first principal of the Alliance. Out of the Alliance's classes came a long line of eminent citizens. David Sarnoff, radio and TV tycoon, learned English there, and so did his British counterpart, Sir Louis Stirling. Eddie Cantor's career began as an amateur entertainer at the Alliance's summer camp, and at the Alliance hall, Arthur Murray learned to dance. Morris Raphael Cohen tested his ideas as a youthful Alliance orator. It was as a member of the Alliance that Sholom Aleichem wrote many of his works, lectured in the auditorium, and discussed literature and world Jewish themes with other members. Sir Jacob Epstein, Jo Davidson, Chaim Gross, William Auerbach-Levy, and Abraham Walkowitz paid three cents a lesson at the Alliance's art school. . . .*

The bad housing, health, and social conditions on the Lower East Side after 1880 impelled dedicated reformers to establish the Henry Street Settlement, the University Settlement, the College Settlement, the Clark House, the Christadora House, and the Madison House. In the settlement house on Henry Street, founded by Lillian Wald, and in other East Side settlements, uptown Jewish volunteers introduced practical social welfare and developed some of the liberal concepts that were later converted into legislation by Al Smith, F.D.R., Robert Wagner, and Herbert H. Lehman.

123. YIDDISH NEWSPAPERS

HUTCHINS HAPGOOD

About Hutchins Hapgood see the preceding selection. For the multitude of Yiddish-speaking immigrants, the Yiddish newspapers served an important function. They taught the immigrants about America, kept them in touch with the Old World, and promoted political understanding and social adjustment. See also the next two selections, nos. 124 and 125.

. . . Yiddish newspapers have, as compared with their contemporaries in the English language, the strong interest of great freedom of expression. They are controlled rather by passion than by capital. It is their joy to pounce on controlling wealth and to take the side of the laborer against the employer. A large proportion of the articles are signed, a custom in striking contrast with that of the American newspaper. The prevalence of the unsigned article in the latter is held by the Yiddish journals to illustrate the employer's tendency to arrogate everything to himself and to make the paper a mere organ of his own policy and opinions. The remark of one of the Jewish editors, that the "Yiddish newspaper's freedom of expression is limited by the penal code alone" has its relative truth. It is, of course, equally true that the new freedom of the Jews, who in Russia had no journal in the common Yiddish, runs in these New York papers into an emotional extreme, a license which is apt to distort the news and to give over the editorial pages to virulent party disputes.

Nevertheless, the Yiddish press, particularly the socialistic branch of it, is an educative element of great value in the ghetto. It has helped essentially to extend the intellectual horizon of the Jew beyond the boundaries of the Talmud, and has largely displaced the rabbi in the position of teacher of the people. Not only do these papers constitute a forum of discussion, but they publish frequent translations of the Russian, French, and German modern classics, and for the first time lay the news of the world before the poor Jewish people. An event of moment to the Jews, such as a riot in Russia, comes to New York in private letters and is printed in the papers here often before the version "prepared" by the Russian government appears in the Russian newspapers. Thus a Jew on the East Side received a letter from his father in Russia asking why the reserves there had been called out, and the son's reply gave him the first information about the war in China.

The make-up of the Yiddish newspaper is in a general way similar to that of its American contemporary. The former is much smaller, however, containing only about as much reading matter as would fill six or eight columns of a downtown newspaper. The sporting department is entirely lacking, the Jew being utterly indifferent to exercise of any kind. They are all afternoon newspapers and draw largely for the news upon the morning editions of the American papers. The staff is very limited, consisting of a few editors and, usually, only one reporter for the local news of the quarter. They give more space proportionately than any American paper to pure literature (chiefly translations, though there are some stories founded on the life of the East Side) and to scientific articles of popular character.

124. WHAT THE YIDDISH PRESS TAUGHT ME

MORRIS RAPHAEL COHEN

The excerpt is taken from Cohen's autobiography *A Dreamer's Journey*. About Cohen see the prefatory note to no. 127.

... What chiefly helped me in attaining an understanding of the ways of my adopted country was the Jewish press, principally the old *Arbeiter Zeitung*, which Abraham Cahan, Feigenbaun and Kranz edited and to which the old grandfather of the Jewish socialist movement, Winchevsky, frequently sent letters from England. I owe a good deal of my education to the Yiddish press. It taught me to look at world news from a cosmopolitan instead of a local or provincial point of view, and it taught me to interpret politics realistically, instead of being misled by empty phrases.

As I look back on the Yiddish and the English press in the last decade of the nineteenth century I cannot help feeling that the former did more for the education of its readers than the latter. Having no army of reporters to dig up sensational news, the Yiddish press necessarily paid more attention to things of permanent interest. It tried to give its readers something of enduring and substantial value.

125. FROM "BINTEL BRIEF"

JEWISH DAILY FORWARD

Abraham Cahan (1860–1951) was editor of the Yiddish newspaper *Jewish Daily Forward (Forverts)* from 1902 to 1951 and became the dominant figure of Jewish journalism in the United States (see no. 111). He was also a successful writer in English and the author of *The Rise of David Levinsky*. He built the *Forverts* from a circulation of 5,000 to a modern newspaper with a circulation of a quarter of a million at its peak in the 1920s.

Cahan wanted to incorporate the realities of Jewish life in America in his newspaper. In 1906 he established a special section in which the readers could write letters to the paper, express their sentiments and opinions and present their problems. This daily feature of the *Forverts,* called "A Bintel Brief" (= a bundle of letters) became very popular and is still, to this day, an important feature of the newspaper.

Abraham Cahan wrote in his memoirs (1929) the following about the "Bintel Brief":

"People often need the opportunity to be able to pour out their heavy-laden hearts. Among our immigrant masses this need was very marked. Hundreds of thousands of people, torn from their homes and their dear ones, were lonely souls who thirsted for expression, who wanted to hear an opinion, who wanted advice in solving their weighty problems. The 'Bintel Brief' created just this opportunity for them.

"Many of the letters we receive are poorly written and we must correct or rewrite them. Some of the letters are not written directly by the people who seek the advice, but by others who do it for them. It has even become a special occupation for certain people to write letters for those who cannot write. There also appeared small signs with the inscription 'Here letters are written to the "Bintel Brief." ' [The price for writing such a letter ranged from twenty-five to fifty cents. I.M.] Often the professional 'Bintel Brief' writer let himself go with his own eloquence, but this, naturally, was deleted. And from time to time men and women came to the editorial office to ask that someone write a letter for them about their problems.

"Through the 'Bintel Brief' mothers have found the children they had lost many years ago. One mother, who had lost her child when it was an infant, found it through the 'Bintel Brief' some twenty years later. Such cases occurred countless times in the twenty-three years since the feature was first established.

"The name of the feature, 'Bintel Brief,' became so popular that it is often used as a part of American Yiddish. When we speak of an interesting event in family life, you can hear a comment like 'A remarkable story—just for the "Bintel Brief." ' Other times you can hear, 'It's like a "Bintel Brief" story!' Many of the themes from the letters have been used by writers of dramas and sketches for their works, because a world of literary import can be found in them.

"The first few years I used to answer all the letters myself. I did it with the greatest pleasure, because in the letters one sees a rare panorama of human souls and because I also had a literary interest in the work."

Over the years thousands of letters were printed in the "Bintel Brief" of which a selection is reprinted here. The letters reflect the problems which the immigrants had to face. The themes change with the passage of time. Old problems vanish and new ones appear. It has been pointed out that all the letters, even the most commonplace and most sentimental, "can serve as a sociological study of the people, of their environment, and of the times in which they lived."

1907

Study or Work

Worthy Editor,

Allow me a little space in your newspaper and, I beg you, give me some advice as to what to do.

There are seven people in our family—parents and five children. I am the oldest child, a fourteen-year-old girl. We have been in the country two years and my father, who is a frail man, is the only one working to support the whole family.

I go to school, where I do very well. But since times are hard now and my father earned only five dollars this week, I began to talk about giving up my studies and going to work in order to help my father as much as possible. But my mother didn't even want to hear of it. She wants me to continue my education. She even went out and spent ten dollars on winter clothes for me. But I didn't enjoy the clothes, because I think I am doing the wrong thing. Instead of bringing something into the house, my parents have to spend money on me.

I have a lot of compassion for my parents. My mother is now pregnant, but she still has to take care of the three boarders we have in the house. Mother and Father work very hard and they want to keep me in school.

I am writing to you without their knowledge, and I beg you to tell me how to act. Hoping you can advise me, I remain,

Your reader,
S.

ANSWER:
The advice to the girl is that she should obey her parents and further her education, because in that way she will be able to give them greater satisfaction than if she went out to work.

1909

On Ellis Island

Dear Editor,

We, the unfortunates who are imprisoned on Ellis Island,* beg you to have pity on us and print our letter in your worthy newspaper, so that our brothers in America may know how we suffer here.

The people here are from various countries, most of them are Russian Jews, many of whom can never return to Russia. These Jews are deserters from the Russian army and political escapees, whom the Czar would like to have returned to Russia. Many of the families sold everything they owned to scrape together enough for passage to America. They haven't a cent but they figured that, with the help of their children, sisters, brothers and friends, they could find means of livelihood in America.

You know full well how much the Jewish immigrant suffers till he gets to America. First he has a hard enough time at the borders, then with the agents. After this he goes through a lot till they send him, like baggage, on the train to a port. There he lies around in the immigrant sheds till the ship finally leaves. Then follows the torment on the ship, where every sailor considers a steerage passenger a dog. And when, with God's help, he has endured all this, and he is at last in America, he is given for "dessert" an order that he must show that he possesses twenty-five dollars.

---

*The place of immigration inspection near the harbor of New York. Every immigrant had to pass this immigration inspection before being allowed to enter the country.

But where can we get it? Who ever heard of such an outrage, treating people so? If we had known before, we would have provided for it somehow back at home. What nonsense this is! We must have the money on arrival, yet a few hours later (when relatives come) it's too late. For this kind of nonsense they ruin so many people and send them back to the place they escaped from.

It is impossible to describe all that is taking place here, but we want to convey at least a little of it. We are packed into a room where there is space for two hundred people, but they have crammed in about a thousand. They don't let us out into the yard for a little fresh air. We lie about on the floor in the spittle and filth. We're wearing the same shirts for three or four weeks, because we don't have our baggage with us.

Everyone goes around dejected and cries and wails. Women with little babies, who have come to their husbands, are being detained. Who can stand this suffering? Men are separated from their wives and children and only when they take us out to eat can they see them. When a man wants to ask his wife something, or when a father wants to see his child, they don't let him. Children get sick, they are taken to a hospital, and it often happens that they never come back.

Because today is a holiday, the Fourth of July, they didn't send anyone back. But Tuesday, the fifth, they begin again to lead us to the "slaughter," that is, to the boat. And God knows how many Jewish lives this will cost, because more than one mind dwells on the thought of jumping into the water when they take him to the boat.

All our hope is that you, Mr. Editor, will not refuse us, and print our letter which is signed by many immigrants. The women have not signed, because they don't let us get to them.

This letter is written by one of the immigrants, a student from Petersburg University, at Castle Garden, July 4, 1909, on the eve of the fast day of *Shivah Asar B'Tamuz* [the seventeenth day of the month of *Tamuz*, when Jews fast in memory of Nebuchadnezzar's siege and destruction of Jerusalem].

Alexander Rudnev

One hundred immigrants, aged from eight to fifty-eight, had signed this letter (each one had included his age).

The *Forward* had previously printed many protests against the unjust treatment of the immigrants confined on Ellis Island, also against the fact that masses were being sent back, and the *Forward* was not silent on this letter.

1909

A Freethinker on Yom Kippur

Dear Mr. Editor,

I was born in a small town in Russia, and until I was sixteen I studied in *Talmud Torahs* and *yeshivas,* but when I came to America I changed quickly. I was influenced by the progressive newspapers, the literature, I developed spiritually and became a freethinker. I meet with free-thinking, progressive people, I feel comfortable in their company and agree with their convictions.

But the nature of my feelings is remarkable. Listen to me: Every year when the month of *Elul* rolls around, when the time of *Rosh Hashanah* and *Yom Kippur* approaches, my heart grows heavy and sad. A melancholy descends on me, a longing gnaws at my breast. At that time I cannot rest, I wander about through the streets, lost in thought, depressed.

When I go past a synagogue during these days and hear a cantor chanting the melodies of the prayers, I become very gloomy and my depression is so great that I cannot endure it. My memory goes back to my happy childhood years. I see clearly before me the small town, the fields, the little pond and the woods around it. I recall my childhood friends and our sweet childlike faith. My heart is constricted, and I begin to run like a madman till the tears stream from my eyes and then I become calmer.

These emotions and these moods have become stronger over the years and I decided to go to the synagogue. I went not in order to pray to God but to heal and refresh my aching soul with the cantor's sweet melodies, and this had an unusually good effect on me.

Sitting in the synagogue among *landsleit* and listening to the good cantor, I forgot my unhappy weekday life, the dirty shop, my boss, the bloodsucker, and my pale, sick wife and my children. All of my America with its hurry-up life was forgotten.

I am a member of a Progressive Society, and since I am known there as an outspoken freethinker, they began to criticize me for going to the synagogue. The members do not want to hear of my personal emotions and they won't understand that there are people whose natures are such that memories of their childhood are sometimes stronger than their convictions.

And where can one hide on *Yom Kippur?* There are many of us, like me. They don't go to work, so it would be good if there could be a meeting hall where they could gather to hear a concert, a lecture, or something else. What is your opinion of this? Awaiting your answer, I remain,

Your reader,
S.R.

ANSWER:

No one can tell another what to do with himself on *Yom Kippur*. If one is
drawn to the synagogue, that is his choice. Naturally, a genuinely sincere
freethinker is not drawn to the synagogue. The writer of this letter is full of
memories of his childhood days at home, and therefore the cantor's
melodies influence him so strongly. Who among us isn't moved by a
religious melody remembered from his youth? This, however, has no
bearing on loyalty to one's convictions. On *Yom Kippur*, a freethinker can
spend his time in a library or with friends. On this day he should not flaunt
himself in the eyes of the religious people. There is no sense in arousing
their feelings. Every man has a right to live according to his beliefs. The
pious man has as much right to his religion as the freethinker to his
atheism. To parade one's acts that insult the religious feeling of the pious,
especially on *Yom Kippur*, the day they hold most holy, is simply
inhuman.

1932

Searching for Roots

Dear Editor,

I am an immigrant from Russia, my wife is American-born, and we are
both freethinkers. We have two grown children, a son and a daughter, who
know they are Jews but never saw any signs of religion or holidays in our
home. Even *Yom Kippur* is just another day to us. For the last twenty years
we've lived among Christians and we socialize with them. Our children
also go around with Gentiles.

Some time ago a Christian girl began to come to our house, seemingly to
visit our daughter, but it was no secret to us that she was after our
twenty-three-year-old son, with whom she was friendly. We said nothing
about it, because we wouldn't have minded having her for a daughter-in-
law.

Once the girl invited our son to a party at her house where all the other
guests were Gentiles. They were all having a good time until one of the
guests, whether in jest or earnest, began to make fun of Jews. I don't know
what happened there, but I am sure they didn't mean to hurt my son,
because none of them, not even his girl friend, knew that he is Jewish. But
he was insulted and told the girl so. Then he told her that he is Jewish and
this was a surprise to her.

My son left the party immediately and from that day on he is changed.
He began to ask questions about religion, debated with me about things

that formerly hadn't interested him. He wanted to know where I was born, how many Jews there are in the world, why the religious don't eat pork, where the hatred of Jews came from, and on and on. He was not satisfied with my short answers but began to read books looking for more information. My son also berated me for not giving him a Jewish upbringing.

His Gentile girl friend came to beg him to forgive her. She cried and explained that it was not her fault, but he didn't want to have anything to do with her because, it seems, he was deeply insulted. His head was filled with one thought, Jewishness. He found Jewish friends, he was drawn into a Zionist club and they worked on him so that he has come to me with a suggestion that I give up the business and we all go to Palestine. And since he sees that I am not about to go, he's getting ready to go alone.

At first we took it as a joke, but we see now that he's taking it very seriously. Well, my going is out of the question, I am not that crazy. But what can be done about him? I'm willing to give in to his whim. I'm sure that in Palestine he'll sober up and realize that not everyone who is Jewish must live in Palestine. My wife is carrying on terribly; what do I mean, allowing my son to travel to a wild country where Arabs shoot Jews? She says we should not give him the money for the trip. But our son says he will find a way to reach the Jewish Homeland.

My wife and I are very anxious to hear your opinion.

Respectfully,
A Reader

ANSWER:
Your son is a very sensitive and thinking person. Since he is an adult you must let him go his way and do what he wants to do.

1932

Job Discrimination

Worthy Editor,

Though I am only a simple tailor, my mind is not occupied only with scissors and needle. I also like to read, to learn, and I have great respect for educated people. I am a man of middle age with grown children, and I have been a reader of your newspaper for the past twenty years.

All my life I strove to give my children a good upbringing because I wanted them to be serious, educated people. And I am appealing to you for advice about one son who will soon finish high school. My son distinguished himself in chemistry all through high school and got the highest marks in that subject. He is absorbed in it with all his heart and soul. He studies day and night, carries on experiments, and never gets tired.

This pleases me very much, because when someone studies a subject he loves, he can, in time, achieve something and maybe even become great in that field. Who knows? But in spite of this joy I'm unhappy. Why? Because I read in the Jewish newspapers that in this profession there is no future for Jewish graduates. I read that a graduate chemist cannot get a position in a large firm if he is a Jew.

I didn't want to believe that in America, in such a free land, it was really so. But recently I met a graduate, a Jewish chemist, and he confirmed that what I read was true.

As yet there are no large Jewish firms that hire chemists, and among the non-Jewish firms there is a sort of understanding to keep Jews out of this profession which has a great future.

I don't expect you to be able to help me but I think you might be better acquainted with the situation and you can advise me whether I should let my son continue his studies in this field. Maybe I should make my son a tailor.

I thank you in advance for printing my letter and for your answer.

Your reader,
S.G.

ANSWER:
We maintain that your son should study the profession in which he is so strongly interested. In spite of all difficulties, he will, in time, find his way in life.

1933

Yiddish or English?

Worthy Editor,
I am sure that the problem I'm writing about affects many Jewish homes. It deals with immigrant parents and their American-born children.

My parents, who have been readers of your paper for years, came from Europe. They have been here in this country over thirty years and were married twenty-eight years ago. They have five sons, and I am one of them. The oldest of us is twenty-seven and the youngest twenty-one.

We are all making a decent living. One of us works for the State Department. A second is a manager in a large store, two are in business, and the youngest is studying law. Our parents do not need our help because my father has a good job.

We, the five brothers, always speak English to each other. Our parents know English too, but they speak only Yiddish, not just among themselves but to us too, and even to our American friends who come to visit us. We beg them not to speak Yiddish in the presence of our friends, since they can speak English, but they don't want to. It's a sort of stubbornness on their part, and a great deal of quarreling goes on between our parents and ourselves because of it.

Their answer is: "Children, we ask you not to try to teach us how to talk to people. We are older than you."

Imagine, even when we go with our father to buy something in a store on Fifth Avenue, New York, he insists on speaking Yiddish. We are not ashamed of our parents, God forbid, but they ought to know where it's proper and where it's not. If they talk Yiddish among themselves at home, or to us, it's bad enough, but among strangers and Christians? Is that nice? It looks as if they're doing it to spite us. Petty spats grow out of it. They want to keep only to their old ways and don't want to take up our new ways.

We beg you, friend Editor, to express your opinion on this question, and if possible send us your answer in English, because we can't read Yiddish.

Accept our thanks for your answer, which we expect soon,

Respectfully,
I. and the Four Brothers

ANSWER:
We see absolutely no crime in the parents' speaking Yiddish to their sons. The Yiddish language is dear to them and they want to speak in that language to their children and all who understand it. It may also be that they are ashamed to speak their imperfect English among strangers so they prefer to use their mother tongue.

From the letter, we get the impression that the parents are not fanatics, and with their speaking Yiddish they are not out to spite the children. But it would certainly not be wrong if the parents were to speak English too, to the children. People should and must learn the language of their country.

1939

Reading a Yiddish Newspaper in the Subway

Dear Editor,

I haven't been in the country very long, and I ask you to clarify a certain matter for me. I was brought here by my brother-in-law, with whom I get along very well, but we have a difference of opinion on one thing. I think I'm right, my brother-in-law believes he's right, so I decided to ask you. This is the problem:

A short time ago I had occasion to ride on a train and I took along the *Forverts* to read on the way. My brother-in-law said it wasn't nice, that it wasn't fitting to read a Jewish newspaper on the train. Even though I'm still a "greenhorn" in America, my Americanized brother-in-law's statement didn't have any effect on me.

I know America is a free country and the Jew is not oppressed here as in other lands, so why should I have to be ashamed of my language here? I certainly would not read a Jewish paper in a train in Germany or Poland. And do you know why? Because there they would beat me up for such *chutzpa*. Here, in America, though, I don't have to be afraid of anyone.

A few days later I had to take the subway somewhere with a friend and I noticed that he wouldn't leave the house until he finished reading his Yiddish newspaper. I remarked that he could take the paper along and read it on the way. And listen to this answer: "I've been in this country seventeen years and never yet read a Jewish paper on the subway." When I asked him why, he avoided giving me a direct answer.

I would like to hear your opinion about this.

> With thanks,
> The "Greenhorn"

ANSWER:

No, people should not be ashamed to read a Yiddish newspaper in the train or subway. Many are not ashamed to do so. One should only be ashamed of something bad or not respectable. And something not respectable should not even be done in secret. The *Talmud* says, "That which should not be done hidden in a closed room is also not permitted in the open."

It is well known that our mother tongue has already gained an honorable position among the world languages. The writings of Yiddish authors and poets are being translated into various languages, including English, and have received their due recognition by literary critics. There is absolutely no reason to be ashamed of or to hide the Yiddish newspaper.

1941

Christmas Trees

Dear Editor,

My husband and I came from Galicia to America thirty-three years ago right after we were married. At home I had received a secular education, and my husband had been ordained as a rabbi. However, he did not want to be a rabbi here, and since we had brought along a little money from home, we bought a small business and made a good living. My husband is religious but not a fanatic. I am more liberal, but I go to *shul* with him on *Rosh Hashanah* and *Yom Kippur*.

We have five children—two boys and three girls. The boys went to a *Talmud Torah*, and the girls, too, received a Jewish education. We always kept a Jewish home and a *kosher* kitchen.

Our eldest son is now a college teacher, tutors students privately, and earns a good deal of money. He is married, has two children, four and seven years old. They live in a fine neighborhood, and we visit them often.

It happened that on Christmas Eve we were invited to have dinner with friends who live near our son and daughter-in-law, so we decided to drop in to see them after the meal. I called up, my daughter-in-law answered the telephone and warmly invited us to come over.

When we opened the door and went into the living room we saw a large Christmas tree which my son was busy trimming with the help of his two children. When my husband saw this he turned white. The two grandchildren greeted us with a "Merry Christmas" and were delighted to see us. I wanted to take off my coat, but my husband gave me a signal that we were leaving immediately.

Well, I had to leave at once. Our son's and daughter-in-law's pleading and talking didn't help, because my husband didn't want to stay there another minute. He is so angry at our son over the Christmas tree that he doesn't want to cross the threshold of their home again. My son justifies himself by saying he takes the tree in for the sake of his children, so they won't feel any different than their non-Jewish friends in the neighborhood. He assures us that it has nothing to do with religion. He doesn't consider it wrong, and he feels his father has no right to be angry over it.

My husband is a *kohen* and, besides having a temper, he is stubborn, too. But I don't want him to be angry at our son. Therefore I would like to hear your opinion on this matter.

With great respect,
A Reader from the Bronx

ANSWER:
The national American holidays are celebrated here with love and joy, by Jews and Gentiles alike. But Christmas is the most religious Christian holiday and Jews have nothing to do with it. Jews, religious or not, should respect the Christmas holiday, but to celebrate it would be like dancing at a stranger's wedding. It is natural that a Jew who observes all the Jewish

traditions should be opposed to seeing his son and grandchildren trimming a Christmas tree.

But he must not quarrel with his son. It is actually your husband's fault because he probably did not instill the Jewish traditions in his son. Instead of being angry with him, he should talk to his son and explain the meaning of Christmas to him.

1952

Eating Non-Kosher Meat

Dear Editor,

The question came up in our family as to how religious parents who keep strictly kosher should act when they come to visit their children who do not keep kosher homes. Should religious people eat non-kosher meat when they are at their children's homes in order not to insult them?

My opinion is that non-religious children respect their religious parents more when they live up to their beliefs and don't eat non-kosher foods. Others in the family do not agree with me.

I say that in America, where, thank God, there is enough food, everyone can indulge himself with whatever food he desires. And when children know that their parents keep a kosher home, they should not even think of serving them non-kosher meat.

The parents do not visit that often, and the children should not find it difficult to make a dinner that they know is kosher and can eat. They should do this out of respect for their parents. But not everybody in the family agrees with me. Therefore I decided to write to you for your opinion. The fact is that parents are concerned because they think their children will be insulted if they don't eat the food they prepare.

With respect and thanks,
M.A.

ANSWER:
We cannot imagine that children would demand of their religious parents that they eat their non-kosher food. In such a case, the parents do not have to adapt to the children's way, but just the opposite. Not the children but the parents should feel insulted when they come to visit and are served a non-kosher meal.

1956

The "Good Old Days"

Dear Friend Editor,

I was sitting with a group of old friends who were speaking nostalgically about the "good old days," and I interrupted with the question, Were the old days really that good? In connection with the discussion we had, we would like to hear your opinion.

I think that when older people long for the old days and say it was better then, it's only because they were young and still had their whole lives before them. But the truth is that those times were not so good.

I still remember my home town in Russia, our simple little house lighted at night by a small kerosene lamp, the door thatched with straw nailed down with sackcloth to keep it warm in winter. I still remember the mud in the streets of the town, so deep it was difficult to get around; our fear of the Gentiles; and who can forget the poverty—the times when there wasn't even a crust of bread?

When we came to New York, I thought we were entering heaven. But here in the new land, in those old days, we lived on the East Side in tenements and had to climb to the fourth and fifth floors to tiny rooms that were dark and airless. There were no bathrooms in the flats. A large bathtub stood in the kitchen near the old iron stove that was heated with coal in which mothers also did the laundry.

In those "good days" we worked in the shops fourteen and sixteen hours a day, six days a week, and the bosses treated the workers like slaves. Summertime, in the great heat, we couldn't breathe in the house at night and we slept on the roofs or on the sidewalks.

When I think of the modern conveniences we live with now, of the wonderful inventions, achievements in various fields, that we enjoy, and about the opportunities for everyone in this blessed country, I see there's nothing to be nostalgic about. I say we now have the good times and we do not have to long for the past.

Not all my friends agree with me, and it will be interesting for us to hear what you have to say about it.

With great respect,
K.S.

ANSWER:
Your conclusion is correct. The little town with its mud, the poor hut with the kerosene lamp, the bitter life in Czarist Russia and the old-time

sweatshops here, contrast dramatically with today's comfortable life in our country. It's like the difference between day and night.

But it is natural for the older immigrant to see that past in beautiful colors. His longing is actually not for that time but for his childhood, his youth, when he was happy with very little.

126. BECOMING A SCULPTOR

JACOB EPSTEIN

Jacob Epstein (1880–1959) was born on the Lower East Side of New York. He was the child of Russian-Polish Jews. His talent for art revealed itself early, and he pursued studies at the Art Students League in New York. The journalist Hutchins Hapgood commissioned him to do a series of drawings for his collection of articles about the Jewish East Side entitled *The Spirit of the Ghetto* (see nos. 122, 123). Epstein became a distinguished sculptor, settled in England, and was knighted. The following selection is taken from his autobiography.

Hester Street

My earliest recollections are of the teeming East Side where I was born.

This Hester Street and its surrounding streets were the most densely populated of any city on earth, and looking back at it, I realise what I owe to its unique and crowded humanity. Its swarms of Russians, Poles, Italians, Greeks, and Chinese lived as much in the streets as in the crowded tenements, and the sights, sounds, and smells had the vividness and sharp impact of an Oriental city.

Hester Street was from one end to the other an open-air market, and the streets were lined with push-carts and pedlars, and the crowd that packed the side-walk and roadway compelled one to move slowly.

Being Different

As a child I had a serious illness that lasted for two years or more. I have vague recollections of this illness and of my being carried about a great deal. I was known as the "sick one." Whether this illness gave me a twist away from ordinary paths, I don't know, but it is possible. Sometimes my parents wondered at my being different from the other children, and would twit me about my lack of interest in a great many matters that perhaps I should have been interested in, but just wasn't. I have never found out that there was in my family an artist or anyone interested in the arts or sciences, and I have never been sufficiently interested in my "family tree" to bother. My father and mother had come to America on one of those great waves of immigration that followed persecution and pogroms in Czarist Russia and Poland. They had prospered, and I can recall that we had Polish Christian servants who still retained peasant habits, speaking no English, wearing kerchiefs and going about on bare feet. These servants remained with us until my brother Louis, my older brother, began to grow up; and then with the sudden dismissal of the Polish girls, I began to have an inkling of sexual complications. My elder sister, Ida, was a handsome, full-bosomed girl, a brunette, and I can recall a constant coming and going of relatives and their numerous children. This family life I did not share. My reading and drawing drew me away from the ordinary interests, and I lived a great deal in the world of imagination, feeding upon any book that fell into my hands. When I had got hold of a really thick book like Hugo's *Les Misérables* I was happy, and would go off into a corner to devour it.

Interest in Drawing

I cannot recall a period when I did not draw, and at school the studies that were distasteful to me, Mathematics and Grammar, were retarded by the indulgence of teachers who were proud of my drawing faculties, and passed over my neglect of uncongenial subjects. Literature and History interested me immensely and whatever was graphic attracted my attention. Later, I went to the Art Students' League up town and drew from models and painted a little, but my main studies remained in this quarter where I was born and brought up. When my parents moved to a more respectable and duller part of the city, it held no interest for me whatever and I hired a room in Hester Street in a wooden, ramshackle building that seemed to date back at least a hundred years and, from my window overlooking the market, made drawings daily. I could look down upon the moving mass below and watch them making purchases, bartering, and gossiping. Opposite stood carpenters, washerwomen, and day-workers, gathered with their tools in readiness to be hired. Every type could be found here, and for the purpose of drawing, I would follow a character until his appearance was sufficiently impressed on my mind for me to make a drawing. . . .

The New York Ghetto was a city at that time transplanted from Poland. Parallel with all this was the world of the "intelligentsia," the students, journalists, scholars, advanced people, socialists, anarchists, free-thinkers, and even "free lovers." Newspapers in Yiddish, Yiddish theatres, literary societies, clubs of all kinds for educational purposes, night-classes abounded, and I helped to organize an exhibition of paintings and drawings by young men of the quarter. . . .

The many races in this quarter were prolific, children by hundreds played upon the hot pavements and in the alleys. Upon the fire-escapes

and the roofs the tenement dwellers slept for coolness in summer. I knew
well the roof life in New York, where all East Side boys flew kites; I knew
the dock life on the East and West Sides, and I swam in the East River and
the Hudson. To reach the river the boys from the Jewish quarter would
have to pass through the Irish quarter, and that meant danger and fights
with the gangs of that quarter: the children of Irish immigrants.

Chinatown

The Jewish quarter was on one side bounded by the Bowery, and this
street at that time was one long line of saloons, crowded at night by visitors
to the city, sailors, and prostitutes. As a boy I could watch through the
doors at night the strange garish performers, singers and dancers; and the
whole turbulent night-life was, to my growing and eager mind, of
never-ending interest. I recall Steve Brodie's saloon with its windows
filled with photographs of famous boxers, and the floor inlaid with silver
dollars. A tour along the Bowery, for a boy, was full of excitement, and
when you reached Chinatown, crooked Mott Street, leading to Pell Street,
you could buy a stick of sugarcane for one cent and, chewing it, look into
the Chinese shop windows, and even go into the temple, all scarlet and
gilding, with gilded images. The Chinamen had a curious way of slipping
into their houses, suddenly, as into holes, and I used to wonder at the
young men with smooth faces like girls. Chinese children were delightful
when you saw them, although no Chinese women were to be seen. Along
the West Front, on the Hudson side, you saw wagons being loaded with
large bunches of bananas, and great piles of melons. Bananas would drop
off the overloaded wagons; you picked them up, and continued until you
came to the open-air swimming baths with delightful sea water. I was a
great frequenter of these swimming places, and went there until they shut
down in November for the winter.

The City of Ships

New York was at this period the city of ships of which Whitman wrote. I
haunted the docks and watched the ships from all over the world being
loaded and unloaded. Sailors were aloft in the rigging, and along the docks
horses and mules drew heavy drays; oyster boats were bringing their loads
of oysters and clams, and the shrieks and yells of sirens and the loud cries
of overseers made a terrific din. At the Battery, newly arrived immigrants,
their shoulders laden with packs, hurried forward, and it must have been
with much misgiving that they found their first steps in the New World
greeted with the hoots and jeers of hooligans. I can still see them hurrying
to gain the Jewish quarter, and finding refuge amongst friends and

relatives. I often travelled the great stretch of Brooklyn Bridge, which I crossed hundreds of times on foot, and watched the wonderful bay with its steamers and ferry-boats. The New York of the pre-skyscraper period was my formation ground. I knew all its streets and the water-side, I made excursions into the suburbs; Harlem, Yonkers, Long Island, and Coney Island I knew well, and Rockaway where I bathed in the surf. I explored Staten Island, then unbuilt on, and the palisades with their wild rocks leading down to the Hudson river.

Negroes

Early on I saw the plastic quality in coloured people, and had friends amongst them, and later was to work from coloured models and friends, including Paul Robeson, whose splendid head I worked from in New York. I tried to draw Chinamen in their quarter, but the Chinese did not like being drawn and would immediately disappear when they spotted me. The Italian Mulberry Street was like Naples, concentrated in one swarming district. Within easy reach of each other, one could see the most diverse life from many lands, and I absorbed material which was invaluable.

A Voracious Reader

At this time I was a tremendous reader, and there were periods when I would go off to Central Park, find a secluded place far away from crowds and noise, and there give myself up to solitary reading for the day, coming back home burnt by the sun and filled with ideas from Dostoyevsky's *Brothers Karamazov*, or Tolstoy's novels. Also I absorbed the New Testament and Whitman's *Leaves of Grass*, all read out of doors, amongst the rocks and lakes of the Park. It was only later I read the English poets, Coleridge, Blake, and Shelley, and still later Shakespeare.

Studying Sculpture

I began to feel at this period that I could more profoundly express myself, and give greater reality to my drawings by studying sculpture. I had been drawing and reading to excess, sometimes in dim light, and my eyes had suffered from the strain, so that sculpture gave me relief, and the actual handling of clay was a pleasure.

Naturally my family did not approve of all that I did, although they saw that I had what might be called a special bent. My turning to sculpture was to them mysterious. Later they could not understand why I did certain things, any more than do the critics who profess to see in me a dual nature, one the man of talent, and the other the wayward eccentric, the artist who desires to *épater.* What chiefly concerned my family was why I did things which could not possibly bring me in any money, and they deplored this mad or foolish streak in me.

They put it down to the perversity that made me a lonely boy, going off on my own to the woods with a book, and not turning up to meals, and later making friends with Negroes and anarchists. . . .

The Passover Holidays always interested me for the picturesque meal ceremonies, and I remember my father, who was "somebody" in the synagogue, bringing home with him one of the poor men, who waited outside to be chosen to share the Passover meal. These patriarchal manners I remember well, although there was about them an air of bourgeois benevolence which was somewhat comic. The earnestness and simplicity of the old Polish Jewish manner of living has much beauty in it, and an artist could make it the theme of very fine works. This life is fast disappearing on contact with American habits, and it is a pity that there is no Rembrandt of to-day to draw his inspiration from it before it is too late.

Illustrating a Book

My parents did not discourage me, but could not understand how I could make a living by art. Their idea of an artist was that of a person who was condemned to starvation. Sculpture became to me an absorbing interest. When I started seriously to work I felt the inadequacies of the opportunity to study. For one thing, only a night class existed in New York, and also there was very little antique sculpture to be seen; modern sculpture hardly existed. I longed to go to Paris, and my opportunity came when I met Hutchins Hapgood, the writer, who was very interested in the East Side, and asked me to illustrate a book which he had written about it. I drew for him the poets, scholars, actors, and playwrights, and also made some drawings of the people.

Finding Models

I was known in the market, and wherever I took up a position to draw I was looked upon sympathetically, and had no difficulty in finding models. Jewish people look upon the work of an artist as something miraculous, and love watching him, even though they may be extremely critical. I sometimes think I should have remained in New York, the material was so abundant. Wherever one looked there was something interesting, a novel composition, wonderful effects of lighting at night, and picturesque and handsome people. Rembrandt would have delighted in the East Side, and I am surprised that nothing has come out of it, for there is material in New York far beyond anything that American painters hunt for abroad.

127. BECOMING A PHILOSOPHER

MORRIS RAPHAEL COHEN

Morris Raphael Cohen (1880–1947) was born in Minsk, Russia, and was brought to the United States at the age of twelve. After studies at the College of the City of New York and at Harvard, he taught philosophy at the City College of New York and later at the University of Chicago. He was highly respected in his field and was called by some "the most penetrating and creative United States philosopher since William James." His students regarded him with awe as a "modern Socrates."

Although not identified with any synagogue group, Cohen retained his sense of Jewish identity and a deep concern for the welfare of the Jewish people. In 1933 he helped to organize the Conference on Jewish Relations and became the editor of *Jewish Social Studies,* a magazine which he helped to found.

The selection which follows is taken from Cohen's autobiography, *A Dreamer's Journey,* one of the classics of immigrant narrative and of intellectual biography.

First Impressions

What I first saw of America did not come up to the high expectation which popular accounts of its unlimited wealth and radical difference from the Old World had led me to entertain. Almost all the people I met in the street and in the stores, with the exception of some children, spoke Yiddish; and though their dress had a somewhat different tone from the one to which I was accustomed, it did not seem much richer in quality. Grand Street, which at that time was the great business thoroughfare of the East Side, and still had department stores such as Ridley's and Lord and Taylor, did not seem so much grander than the great mercantile streets of Minsk, such as the Franciscaner.

The most marked outer difference was the uniformity of the many-storied houses and the absence of any wooden ones. Though in those days there were still some private residences on the East Side, the streets presented solid fronts, with no gardens or vacant spaces between the houses. I was also impressed with the fact that the roofs of houses were flat rather than slanted. But I soon found out the advantage of a roof on which one could sleep on hot summer nights . . .

On the inner side of life, the chief characteristic difference was the greater intensity and hurry. At six o'clock in the morning the alarm clock would wake us all up. My mother would prepare breakfast, my father would say his prayers and after a hurried meal my father and my brother Sam would leave the house so that they could begin their work at the moment when the clock struck seven.

My Father's Shop

I had occasion to visit my father's "shop" and I was impressed with the tremendous drive which infiltrated and animated the whole establishment—nothing like the leisurely air of the tailor shop in Minsk where my Uncle Abraham had worked and where the men would sing occasionally. Sometimes my father and another presser would start a competitive drive to see who could press the largest number of jackets during the day. We all knew by his appearance that this had happened when he came home at seven o'clock in the evening. It was hard to dissuade my father from engaging in such drives, for he was paid according to the number of jackets pressed.

I soon understood why the unions were fighting so hard for a weekly wage to take the place of payment for piece work. That experience made me realize what later my friends educated in economics could not see, namely, the wisdom as well as the humanity of some limitation of output. For, in the long run, excessive work diminishes the effective life span and thus reduces the chief productive power of the nation. Even a machine cannot be economically run if it functions always at maximum speed. What good is it to a nation to increase the number of its commodities if it exhausts and brutalizes its human beings?

When later I learned of the large profits that the manufacturers were making and how lavishly they spent their money, I could not dismiss as mere rhetoric the complaint against the harsh injustice of the distribution of wealth under capitalism. But at first I knew only that my father worked in a "shop" in the rear building of a yard on Ridge Street, and that his boss, a certain Mr. Riemer, received the cloth all properly cut, ready to be sewed up into garments, after which it was returned to the manufacturers, who were referred to as "the warehouse" and who sold the product to distributors. Mr. Riemer, as the boss, was an Olympian figure to us. He was the one who paid my father. But the Sampters, who paid Mr. Riemer, were dim figures whose magnitude I had no opportunity to measure. (Little did I dream that some years later the daughter of one of these would sit at my feet in a philosophy class at my home.)

... One of the great conveniences which made life simpler for my mother in this country was the availability of gas for lighting and especially for cooking purposes. No more need for chopping wood, for making a fire in the oven or sweeping out the ashes. Just by lighting a match the business of cooking could be quickly achieved ...

On the religious side there was at first much less difference than I had expected. All the people that I knew (with the exception of my brother Tom who was a clerk in a shoe store on the Bowery) refrained from working on Saturdays, and all the stores in our immediate neighborhood were closed on that day. On Friday nights, on Saturdays and on holidays I would accompany my father to a hall on Broome Street where the Neshwieser Verein held religious services in the regular Orthodox manner. . . .

Self-Help

The Neshwieser Verein was an important institution in the life of its members and typical of a class of organizations that helped the immigrant to overcome the difficulties of life in the new land and adjust himself to its demands. Some time at the end of the eighties a group of immigrants from Neshwies met in the store of one of their members and decided that it would be very helpful if they formed a society for mutual assistance. The initial dues were ten cents per month. The society grew and by 1892 it had several hundred members. It offered the latter the necessary opportunities for religious services. The majority of the members were workingmen who had to go to work early in the morning and came home so late that few could afford to come to daily prayers. Besides, it was doubtful whether the Verein could afford to pay rent for the whole week. The renting of a meeting hall for Friday night and Saturday of each week and for the traditional holidays met the most pressing needs of the group. The Verein owned a burial ground and had a special group to attend to funerals, as well as a committee to visit the sick and the needy. The hall on Broome Street not only served as a house of prayer, but was also a place where the business of the society was transacted on Saturday nights.

Though my father was a native of Kletsk and lived in Neshwies only a short time, he became, through my mother, associated with the Neshwieser Verein almost from its beginnings and was a faithful member of it for over forty-four years. Though there were times when there was no bread in his house, and there was no money for rent, he never applied for relief. My mother inherited her father's dignity and extraordinary capacity for good household management. Today the bodies of both of them lie in the Neshwieser Cemetery, after sixty-seven years of married life together. No one ever accused my father of a base deed or ever heard a foul word cross his lips. Nor did anyone ever hear my mother utter anything foolish. For all its poverty and lack of modernity Neshwies was a noble nursery of men and women.

The society, which later became known as the Progressive Brethren of Neshwies, grew and later it built a synagogue on Henry Street, acquired extensive plots in three cemeteries, and helped to start other societies of folk from Neshwies in the Bronx and Brownsville. Finally it contributed considerably to the welfare of the people in Neshwies itself—though it seemed to me that so many had come here that there could hardly be any left in the old town.

Loss of Religious Faith

I continued to attend religious services with my father up to 1899 although I had drifted away from my religious Orthodoxy long before that. In the first place there was no incentive and little opportunity for me to continue my Hebraic and Talmudic studies. There were no suitable books in our house and no one urged me to continue such study. It was taken for granted that in a few years I would join my father in some phase of tailoring, for I had no desire to become a rabbi. I did, indeed, once go to the synagogue on Norfolk Street where I found some tractates of the Talmud, but I lacked the ardor to engage in such study by myself long enough to surmount the difficult places . . .

A more important factor, however, in my drift from religious Orthodoxy, was provided by a conversation which I overheard between my father and a certain Mr. Tunick, in the fall of 1892. Mr. Tunick's brother had been a neighbor of ours in Minsk, and my father had helped him to come to this country. Our visitor challenged my father to prove that there was a personal God who could be influenced by human prayers or deeds, or that the Jewish religion had any more evidence in favor of its truth than other religions. To this challenge my father could only answer, "I am a believer." This did not satisfy my own mind. And after some reflection I concluded that in all my studies no such evidence was available. After that I saw no reason for prayer or the specifically Jewish religious observances. But there was no use arguing with my father. He insisted that so long as I was in his house I must say my prayers regularly whether I believed in them or not. Such is the Orthodox conception. I had to conform to it until I was in a position to refuse to obey and tell my father I would leave his house if he insisted. This occurred in the fall of 1899.

Though my father respected my independence it came as a heavy blow that I should desert the only intellectual life we had ever shared. To him the synagogue meant a great deal. He would go to services every morning and in addition would attend the class in Mishnah on Saturday afternoons. He was a devout believer in all the teachings of Orthodox Judaism and conformed to all its laws in most faithful fashion. In later years the synagogue at Bensonhurst became almost the center of his life. He had no doubt about a life after death but was not certain as to what punishment would be accorded to his son who was morally good (according to his view) but religiously an infidel.

My abandonment of Judaism as a religion was later reinforced in my mind by my scientific, historical and philosophical studies. Although I never abandoned my interest in the history and in the welfare of the Jewish people, I ceased to read Hebrew, so that after many years it became almost a foreign language to me. . . .

Public School

In September, 1892, my sister and I were sent to public school. In those days there were no special provisions for older and more advanced immigrant children unfamiliar with English; and so I was put into the beginners' or ABC class. I do not recall that I was particularly embarrassed by being placed among small children, but I was dazed because I understood little of what it was all about. Despite all that, in the course of a few weeks I was promoted several times from one class to another— probably to make room for new entrants. Thus I soon reached the third grade. (In those days the classes in public school were numbered not according to the progress of the pupil, but in the reverse order so that the final or graduating class was called the first.) The teacher of this grade seemed sympathetic and showed considerable patience at my inability to answer in English . . .

Reading Yiddish Books

My intellectual life before I could read English books with understanding would have tapered off to nothing, had it not been for the stimulus of the little Yiddish literature at home which I devoured as one famished for food. My brother Sam . . . had bought a series of paper-bound booklets which constituted a Yiddish translation of Gaboriau's *Monsieur Lecoq* ("For the Honor of a Name"). Another such series which I read with avidity told the story of Napoleon. For years I could not overcome the highly favorable attitude toward Napoleon which the author entertained. But even more thrilling, indeed possibly the most thrilling story that I ever read, was a Yiddish translation of the first part of Dumas' *Monte Cristo*, published as a serial in a journal called *The House Friend*, of which we had a bound volume. The story of the persecution of Edmond Dantés, his education by the Italina *abbé*, his marvelous escape, and finally his possession of the treasure, was a rare delight. The rest of the story was not printed and I did not miss it.

But for intellectual stimulus I turned every week to the *Arbeiter Zeitung*, the Jewish organ of the Socialist Labor Party.* In its columns I read translations of Flaubert's *Salammbô*, and of Smolenskin's *Kevuras Hamor* (disgraceful burial). The former stirred me by its military narratives, the latter by the revelations of the chicanery and corruption of the old fanatical leaders of Jewish communities. I was, moreover, seriously interested in the news of the week and in Abraham Cahan's articles on socialism, which were in the form of addresses like those of the old Hebrew preachers. The

---

*See no. 120. (Ed.)

early numbers of the Socialist monthly *Die Zukunft* also gave me much
mental nourishment. . . .

As soon as I learned to read English, I began to borrow books from the
Aguilar Free Library, which was located on the top floor of the Educational
Alliance (formerly the Hebrew Institute) building. . . .

College

Towards the end of the term we went up to the City College to take our
entrance examinations. I thought I did fairly well in arithmetic, history,
geography and drawing, but during the grammar examination I got into a
nervous stew. I wrote, not on both sides of the paper, but on what I
supposed to be the wrong side of the paper. When I discovered my mistake,
I hurriedly began to rewrite the whole thing. Naturally I could not finish
and I was certain that I had failed. During the two weeks or so before the
results of the examinations were announced, I was downcast and stayed
awake at night, forming all sorts of plans as to how I might continue my
education. I thought of taking the Regents' examinations to qualify for
some professional school. I was of the opinion that his work as a tailor had
suppressed my brother Sam's finer abilities and I was determined to
struggle against a similar fate. On the afternoon when Mr. Adams was to
inform us of the results of the examination, I came to school in a resigned
mood. To my utter amazement Mr. Adams announced that "the highest
mark was attained by Morris Cohen, who is thus entitled to the Adams gold
medal." He asked me to come up and be congratulated. I looked sheepish; I
could hardly believe that this was true. Even when I went home I could not
realize that I had actually passed. My mother at that time was bed-ridden,
and when I told her that I had passed the examination and was thus
admitted to college, a flood of tears came into her eyes. She was not at all
interested in the fact that I had received the gold medal. It was only later
that I appreciated her discriminating wisdom. The medal made little
subsequent difference, except that occasionally we were able to borrow a
few dollars on it. However, my admittance to college did make a
tremendous difference. When one of my aunts remonstrated with my
mother, "You cannot afford to send your boy to college," she replied, "If
need be I'll go out as a washerwoman and scrub floors so that my Morris
can have a college education." For people who had all their lives been
scrupulously careful not to incur any expense which could possibly be
avoided, this was a lavish luxury. But by a rare good fortune it proved the
best investment that my parents ever made. . . .

Conflict Between the Generations

The life of the East Side in the days of my adolescence was characterized by a feverish intensity of intellectual life and a peculiar restlessness. We had no patience with the prevailing evils and corruptions of the day. Our eagerness to help usher in a better social order was well-nigh desperate and our anxiety about our own achievements and shortcomings in this endeavor was almost morbid. In all this we reflected not only the traditional current of European Jewish life, with its emphasis upon intellectual values, but also the impact of the New World on eyes that could see its problems and potentialities with the fresh vision generally ascribed to foreign visitors or to the "man from Mars."

The eastern Jewish immigrants to this country in the 1890's had, for the most part, been subjected to a highly rigorous training along pietistic lines. Ten hours or more of study day after day took up the childhood of every self-respecting eastern Jewish boy. Fortunate were those who were permitted to continue this routine as students of the Talmud, as teachers or as rabbis for the rest of their lives. Those not so fortunate were expected to devote the same long hours and endless energies to the mastering of some trade or business. But even those who were not permitted to devote their adult years primarily to learning were expected to devote a considerable portion of their time to reading, prayer, and argument, carried on in a sacred language and dealing largely with a totally foreign environment.

The migration to the New World broke the old patterns. The old limitations on the proper subjects of intellectual inquiry and discussion were removed, but the intellectual passion, the tradition of study, the high value which the family circle put upon learning and skill continued. Parents continued to grind their own lives to the bone in order to make it possible for their children to achieve some intellectual distinction or skill that might be considered a New World substitute for the Talmudic learning which represented the highest achievement in the old environ- ment. So it was that many of the first generation and many more of the second, despite the difficulties of a new environment and a strange language, brought to the tasks which the New World presented a force that was more than the force of any single individual. It was as if a great dam had broken and the force of water accumulated over many years had been let loose. This mighty force permeated every nook and corner of human endeavor.

Opinions may differ as to the worth of many of the enterprises to which this force was directed. The second generation had its boxers, gamblers and shyster lawyers, as well as great judges, teachers and scientists. Doctors, movie magnates, writers, merchants, philanthropists, com- munists or defenders of corporate wealth all showed an intensity that must have seemed a bit outlandish to the more comfortable and easy-going segments of the American population. Perhaps something of the same

intensity characterized earlier American generations disciplined under
the hard patterns of Puritan, Quaker or Mormon protests against the life of
ease and comfort.

This intensity of life, this striving for perfection in diverse fields,
surrounded me and the men and women of my generation at the turn of the
century, in City College and in the various clubs, circles and societies that
dotted our intellectual horizons. . . .

This indestructible urge which . . . I and so many of our mutual friends
had, to possess for ourselves the fruits of the Age of Reason, dominated all
our activities. Even in the field of social reform our socialism was, above
all, not a seeking for better food or drink or clothing or even homes for
ourselves and our less fortunate fellows. It was a protest against economic
conditions which denied to so many of us, and to our less fortunate
brothers and sisters, access to the riches of the spirit. Those who toiled
twelve hours a day, month after month, from childhood to old age, were
deprived of all the things that made human life worth living. And so our
socialist activity, though often cast in Marx's materialistic terms, was
directed primarily to the conquest and democratization of the things of the
spirit.

The world that we faced on the East Side at the turn of the century
presented a series of heartbreaking dilemmas. To the extent that we made
the world of science and enlightenment a part of ourselves, we were
inevitably torn from the traditions of narrow Orthodoxy. For some two
thousand years our people had clung to their faith under the pressure of
continual persecution. But now, for us at least, the walls of the ghetto had
been removed. We learned that all non-Jews were not mere soulless
heathens. We found that the Jews had not been the only conservators of
wisdom and civilization. And having been immersed in the literature of
science we called upon the old religion to justify itself on the basis of
modern science and culture. But the old generation was not in a position to
say how this could be done. With all respect for our old Orthodoxy, it
would not be honest to deny that it harbored a great deal of superstition—
indeed, who is free from superstition? But because this superstition was
regarded as an integral part of Judaism, because no distinction was drawn
between ritual and religious convictions and feelings, the very word
"religion" came to be discredited by many liberal people—who, whatever
might be said about their errors, at least attempted to think for themselves.

What ensued was a struggle between the old and new ideals, resulting in
a conflict between the older and younger generations fraught with
heart-rending consequences. Homes ceased to be places of peace and in
the ensuing discord much of the proverbial strength of the Jewish family
was lost. As the home ceased to be the center of interest, the unity of life,

nurtured by pride in the achievements of one's forebears and by parental pride in the achievements of children, was broken. There was scarcely a Jewish home on the East Side that was free from this friction between parents and children. This explosive tension made it possible for the same family to produce saints and sinners, philosophers and gunmen.

Filling a Void

We might, if we could, mask our unorthodox ideas, and use the word "God," with Spinoza, to mean what scientists call the system of nature, or, by proper verbal camouflage, otherwise conceal our departures from the old, pious outlook upon the universe. Every impulse of filial piety, of gratitude to the parents who had made it possible for us to enjoy the fruits of the world of science, drove us to this hypocrisy. But to the extent that we succumbed, we could not preserve the integrity of the intellect and the spirit. And this meant that young men and women were forced to play the hypocrite at the very dawn of their moral sense. No wonder that the development of religious sentiment was stunted among us and that cynicism or pessimism came so often to displace the natural idealism of youth.

However we resolved this dilemma, and whatever concessions we made to the old ritual, the loss of the religious faith which had sustained our parents through so many generations of suffering left a void in our lives which we tried with every fiber of our beings to fill in one way or another. All our organizations and circles were attempts to fill this void. . . .

128. Becoming a Writer

MAURICE HINDUS

Maurice Hindus (1891–1969) was born in a peasant village in tsarist Russia and moved to the United States in 1905 while still a boy. He attended Colgate and Harvard and became a lecturer and author of novels and of many books on Soviet Russia.

Hindus first lived on New York's Lower East Side but at the age of seventeen he decided to move to upstate New York, where he became a farm worker. The years of work on "Yankee" farms had a decisive influence on his later life and made his experience unique and quite different from that of other Jewish immigrants. It gave him an opportunity to know intimately and to appreciate native America. It enabled him to compare American rural life with that of Russia and thus provided the basis for his future work as a writer on Soviet Russia. Above all, the years of work on American farms molded his outlook on life, inspired self-confidence, and nurtured "a sense of inner security." The selection is taken from his autobiography, A Traveler in Two Worlds.

Arriving in New York

I arrived in New York wearing my best clothes—my Russian school uniform, black belted tunic, long trousers, and military cap with a black shiny visor. I must have been an outlandish sight, especially to children. They stared and laughed at me, and overnight my oldest brother, who had come ahead of us and had paid for our ship tickets, changed me into an American outfit: knee pants, jacket, black stockings, and a soft cap. Proudly I walked the streets, but inwardly I felt bewilderingly alien, for no two worlds could have been more stupendously unlike than the mud-sodden village from which I had been uprooted and the towering New York into which I was flung.

Though my four years in a Russian school had enlarged and enriched my knowledge of the world, it had not prepared me for the overpowering surprises of New York—the tall buildings, incredibly tall, the gas and electric lights that banished night from the streets, the horsecars and trolleys that carried one wherever one chose to go and, marvel of marvels, the elevated trains thundering right over one's head. Least of all did rural or town Russia prepare me for the newsstands which sold enormous-sized dailies at a penny each—an unbelievably low price for so much paper. In any muzhik bazaar it would have been worth five times the price as cigarette paper. I marveled at the richness of America where people threw the precious newspapers into ash cans or gutters with no more concern than muzhiks spat out the shells of the pumpkin and sunflower seeds they loved to chew on Sundays and holidays.

Absence of Uniforms

Having always associated law with a uniformed official, my happiest impression of the new country, was the absence of uniforms in the streets of New York. It was reassuring to discover that government in the New World did not parade its power in the pomp of silver and golden braid, brass and silver buttons. True, the helmeted and uniformed policeman on the beat was in my early months in the big city a slightly sinister figure. I couldn't quite dissociate him from the overawing *uryadnik*, so whenever I saw him I hurried across the street or dodged around the corner. But in time I ceased associating him with the intimidating and bribe-grasping *uryadnik*.

An older brother and two sisters had preceded us in their migration to America, and when we arrived we settled in with them on the Lower East Side on the fourth floor of a walk-up apartment. We had gas lights, though only when a quarter was put into the slot of the meter. We had running water and even a bathtub. There were eight in our family and to help pay the rent we of course kept boarders, two of them. Soon another sister and her husband came from Russia, so the four rooms were shared by twelve people which caused no distress to anybody, least of all to me, for privacy was no part of my upbringing. Besides, I was so overpowered with curiosity about the big city that the streets lured me irresistibly. They were my first American school. It was in the streets that I saw for the first time Negroes, Chinese, Italians, Hungarians, Irish, others of the multitude of nationalities that made up New York. I had read of these people and now I saw them in the flesh. I yearned to speak to them, to learn all I could about them: how they lived, what foods they ate, what books they read, what they talked about when they were by themselves, what they thought of the peoples among whom they lived, and how they differed from the muzhiks, the Jews, the intellectuals I had known in the Old World. But language was a barrier I couldn't hurdle—not yet. I contented myself with watching and wondering about them—the Chinese in the laundries, the Negroes as day laborers, the Irish as truck drivers, policemen, and saloonkeepers, the Italians as shoe-shiners, ice and coal carriers, peanut venders, and organ-grinders.

My First Earnings

One day I passed a Chinese basement laundry. The door was open and I paused to watch a little man with a pigtail at his ironing. He came to the door, smiled, and beckoned me to come in. I smiled back and shook my head. He went back into the shop and returned with a handful of Chinese nuts. He appeared so amiable that I finally followed him into the basement. Smiling and chattering he led me to the rear of the shop, which was cluttered with bags and cases. In dumb show he indicated that he wanted me to help him clean up the place. I worked for about an hour and when we finished he gave me a nickel, the first money I earned in America. I was surprised and overjoyed. In the Russian town where I had gone to school I had helped people lift sacks of grain and load carts of stove wood and they never gave me a kopeck, though they usually rewarded me with a pear or an apple. In America the laborer was worthy of his hire: even a Chinese laundryman paid cash for a service rendered. The heartening realization broke on me that despite my knee pants, I could earn money. Soon I was working as errand boy for a manufacturer of boys' clothing for two and a half dollars a week.

The Italians

Of all the national groups I observed in the streets, the Italians attracted me the most. They were always friendly and cheerful, always ready to speak to you even if they knew you couldn't understand a word they said. Their hands were as eloquent as their tongues. No other people, it seemed to me, gesticulated as gracefully and as expressively. After I discovered Mott Street I often walked there for the pure pleasure of observing Italians. They were so vibrantly alive that they appeared never to be bored or to harbor grudges against other people. Their fruit and vegetable stands and pushcarts were an exciting and memorable sight; fruits and vegetables I had never seen before piled neatly tier on tier, color on color, not like produce offered for sale to immigrants but like works of art created to delight the passer-by.

Whenever an Italian organ-grinder appeared on the block he brought with him a holiday spirit. The moment he started grinding out a tune, little girls came tumbling out of doorways, shrieking and giggling with delight. Some of them had pennies for the wizened-faced little monkey who accepted the coins with a solemn doff of his tiny red cap. Forming circles, the little girls danced on the sidewalks and into the streets. To the fourteen-year-old immigrant boy they made a pretty scene—none of them ragged or barefooted like little girls in the old Russian village, all clean and neatly dressed, with bright bows on the end of their bobbing pigtails. Though they were children of the slums, tap water, cheap soap, low-priced dress goods which their immigrant mothers sewed into dresses or inexpensive store clothes made them look as attractive as the daughters of merchants and landlords in the Old Country.

Wonderful little girls! The immigrant boy in his American-style knee pants and long stockings was captivated with them. They were so pretty and so unconscious of the snobberies of the Old World. Wherever their parents came from, whatever their fathers did for a living—tailor, carpenter, plumber, ragpicker, pushcart peddler, storekeeper, or even owner of a tenement—gliding and hopping and circling to the mechanical tune of the hurdy-gurdy, they were equals together. No mother or nursemaid pulled any of them out of their charmed circle of innocence because others were born into the wrong families.

I loved to wander the streets of the Lower East Side and get lost in the adventure. The noisy bustling crowds fascinated me, everyone so feverishly busy. Immigrants mostly, they seemed like a new race in the world, different in manners and behavior from the people I had known on the other side of the ocean. Energetic and purposeful, they were astonishingly informal: well-to-do shopkeepers walked around without coats, sometimes with shirt sleeves rolled up as no member of their profession would deign to do in the scruffy little city where I had gone to school. Overalled janitors, icemen, peddlers tipped their caps to nobody—the very custom was unknown, and so was hand-kissing.

Hester Street

Several blocks away from where we lived was roaring, bustling Hester Street. The pavement was lined with stalls and pushcarts, and men with cribs or baskets suspended on leather straps from their necks pushed their way along, crying their wares—needles, thread, shoelaces, soap, socks—like hawkers in a Russian bazaar. The filthiest section of the neighborhood, it was also the busiest and most exciting. Customers haggled over prices as violently and abusively as muzhiks. Shopkeepers grabbed the arms of passers-by and with torrents of cajolery endeavored to pull them inside their stores, cursing those who escaped their clutching hands. Russian or Polish women, obviously peasants, struggled through the crowds calling for someone to rescue them from clinging Hungarian or Romanian peddlers or shopkeepers whose language they didn't understand. All was bedlam, a cacophony of voices, the Yiddish dialects of Eastern Europe rising above all others. Here the Old World strove loudly against the New with all its undisciplined brashness, a product of the ruthless century-old struggle for survival.

One day I bought a penny piece of chocolate from a Jewish peddler. His Yiddish like mine was corrupted with Russian, and recognizing our common origin he switched to that language. He cursed America for the wretched life he was living. In his native Odessa he had given private lessons in Russian to sons and daughters of the most respectable families in the city—Russians, Jews, Greeks, Georgians, Armenians. His pupils and their fathers bowed and raised their caps or hats when they passed him in the street. He had never wanted to come to America; it was all his wife's fault. She had grown so hysterically fearful of a possible pogrom that he had yielded to her pleas and emigrated. But in America nobody cared to learn Russian, so he was without a profession. Never before in his life had he done menial work, but now he was forced to peddle, to carry heavy baskets twelve hours a day, coming home tired and sweating and aching in every bone, and what was he now? A nobody, a frog in a mud pond, a door mat for others to wipe their feet. Cursed, ever cursed be America!

He was a tragic misfit in the new country. Having no respect for the sweating brow or the calloused hand, he felt lost and degraded. America has never been a land for the non-technical intelligentsia of Eastern Europe. The American rough-and-tumble scramble for survival and success wounds their inflated self-esteem.

Learning a New Language

The most vexing problem before me in those days was of course the English language. Uncomprehending and envious, I listened to the sounds of the new tongue all around me: children chattering, grownups gossiping, truck drivers swearing; even the Italian bootblack on the corner spouted English and laughed at my blank stare when, despite his supplementary gestures, I failed to understand him.

The street was my English classroom. When American-born boys accepted me as a playmate, I deliberately cultivated the high school students, certain that from them I should learn the language at its purest. Their lessons were not without cost to my self-esteem: once they sent me into a candy store to buy a penny's worth of "son-of-a-bitch"; another time, as we passed an ice cream parlor crowded with girls, they gave me a nickel and told me to go in and ask for five-cents' worth of an obscenity. The girls screamed with shock and the man at the fountain kicked me out onto the sidewalk. My playmates roared with amusement and I felt like crying. Though they never duped me again, they taught me a vocabularly of choice obscenity.

Yet just being with them tuned my ears to the new language. Every day more of the strange sounds took on meaning as words arranged themselves into sentences. During the day I worked as errand boy and evenings and Sundays I played with the boys and studied English. I sweated over a Russian-English dictionary and grammar, often discovering that the dictionary definitions and idiomatic usage were far apart. The new language was a perverse tongue twister, replete with expressions that meant the opposite of what they should. "He is going to die," you said. How absurd! To me it meant he chose to die and what sane person would make such a choice? "Chewing the rag." What a monstrosity! The hungriest muzhik would rather chew wild onions or even birch bark. English was a baffling and maddening tongue.

To hasten familiarity with it, I enrolled in a public night school. The other students were peddlers, shopkeepers, factory workers, who often fell asleep in class. Instruction was necessarily slow, too slow for me and I quit night school.

Then an extraordinary thing happened. One evening while wandering the streets of my neighborhood I passed a building where a sign announced a lecture on Herbert Spencer. Admission was free and I walked in. The lecturer was a Scotsman named Edward King, once a teacher of philosophy, as I subsequently learned, at Edinburgh University. As I understood only a part of his lecture, I did not learn much about the philosophy of evolution: still, I enjoyed being in the audience of a man who sounded so learned. After the lecture a small group gathered around him to ask questions and to argue and I hung about on the fringes. King was a short, paunchy man, broad-shouldered, with a massive head, iron-gray hair and thick walrus mustaches. Seeing me standing there, the only boy in the audience, he beckoned to me. With kindly interest he asked how I came to attend a lecture on Herbert Spencer. Hesitantly and awkwardly I replied that I had come out of curiosity and admitted that my knowledge of English was so poor I had understood little of what he had said. Forgetting Herbert Spencer, King proceeded to advise me on the best way to enlarge my vocabulary. Every day I was to read at least one page of a book, write down the words I didn't understand and their definitions from my English-Russian dictionary. Once I finished the page, I was to commit to memory all the definitions I had written down and read no further until I had mastered the page. He invited me to come back to his next lecture that following week when he would have a book for me he thought I should read. The book was George Eliot's *Adam Bede*, the first novel I ever read in English.

Thus I set out to acquire a vocabulary. Proudly I would recite my newly learned words to my playmates, and sometimes they found my accomplishments so amusing that they doubled up with laughter. They called me "professor" and teased me for using big words, which, when I strung them together, didn't mean what I thought they did. I still had to learn the difference between dictionary and spoken English. I have since studied a number of foreign languages and not one of them has proved such a puzzle and torment as the richly idiomatic English tongue . . .

An Unpleasant Experience

If my acquaintance with Edward King was one of the happiest experiences of my early immigrant days, my experience with social settlements was one of the most disheartening. Once a playmate took me to the Educational Alliance, and afternoons I often went there to browse through the books in the reading room. I loved to take an armful of books, sit at the table and just turn the pages and look at the illustrations. One evening a new librarian appeared—a slender, gray-haired woman with tight lips and a stern look in her eyes. When she saw me put an armful of books on the table she came over and asked why I took so many books at a time. In my halting English I explained that I loved to look at them, to study the illustrations and read isolated passages. After eyeing me with indecision for a moment, she went back to her desk. Soon she was at my side again.

"Sit up straight, please," she commanded.

Startled, I looked at her with protesting eyes. I had not been aware how I was sitting and now that she had made me conscious of it, I wondered what difference it made to her. But without a word of rejoinder I obeyed. She went away and soon I forgot myself and again propped my head on my hand. In an instant she was back at my side.

"I told you to sit up straight."

This time I ignored her.

Again she repeated her order in a louder voice and the boys and girls at my table looked up as though expecting trouble.

"I like it better this way," I growled.

"You've got to sit up straight," she ordered.

Was I tearing up the books? No. Was I calling her names? No. Why then did she insist that I sit in a position I disliked? Incensed at her arbitrariness I shoved the books off the table, darted out of the room and never again stepped inside the Educational Alliance.

At another time a playmate invited me to go with him to the Eldridge Street Settlement House. Presently I was surrounded by a group of smartly dressed girls older than myself. Smilingly and persistently they put me through an interrogation about myself and my home life. I could not quite make out why they were so set on discovering whether I slept alone or shared a bed with others or whether—as was the case in our family—some of us slept on the floor. They seemed to consider sleeping on the floor a hardship or degradation. In the Old Country I had slept in summer on grass on the ground, in a haymow or on straw on the barn floor and never minded it. The more the girls pried into my private life and the life of others in my family, the more incensed I grew. I felt as though I were in an inquisition chamber. Perhaps they were Junior Leaguers who descended on the slums to sweeten the life of immigrants. Perhaps they were college girls assigned to write a term paper on How the Other Half Lives. Their approach was so tactless that I finally sickened of their questioning and fled the house, never to return.

Years later I happened to be at a dinner party where I met the late Lillian Wald, founder of the Henry Street Settlement. I recounted to her my experience at the Eldridge Street Settlement House. She was quite amused and assured me that at her house blunderers like those girls, however well-intentioned, were quickly weeded out of social work. After an evening with that remarkable woman, I regretted that I had not found my way to her house in those days, when her influence would have been of enormous value to me.

Joining a Debating Club

When I had been in New York some six months a playmate called Bert, son of a butcher who lived in the next block and who was a student at the now defunct Townsend Harris High School, decided that my English was fluent enough for me to join his debating club. I had never heard of debating clubs in Russia and my curiosity was aroused. The club met evenings in a public school, and though the members were all high school students, the director, a tall, gray-haired men with a youthful pink face and an urbane manner, made an exception of me. The first time he called on me to speak, I was so frightened that I shook and stammered and the words stuck in my throat. My platform debut in America was a sorry failure. Embarrassed and humiliated I expected to be dropped from the club, but the director cheered me by saying that first failure in public speaking was not uncommon even to American-born boys. He himself had had a similar experience with his first extemporaneous address. So I stayed in the club and listened with envy to boys who strode confidently to the speaker's table and argued their points with a fluency that seemed forever beyond me. Yet debating excited me. It was an intellectual exercise that called for quickness of thought, fluency of speech, economy of words, and I was determined someday to master it. The debating clubs of boys in knee pants in the public schools of the East Side in my early immigrant days were to me a brilliant demonstration of intellectual freedom. Though the director was there to guide the boys in manner and procedure, he never attempted to get us to express any opinions other than our own.

The new language challenged me and I dreamed of the time when I too would stand at the speaker's table and surprise the director, the boys, and myself with my eloquence. At last one evening the director and the boys insisted that the time had come for me to try again. I froze with panic, but the insistence was so friendly and the director's suggestion that I take as my subject the emigration of my family to America appeared so easy to explain that I mustered the courage to rise and walk up to the speaker's table. I remember looking straight into the director's eyes and he nodded and smiled encouragement. Suddenly my tension left me. Words I had been garnering and hoarding through the months were ready for use. After a brief moment of uncertainty, they poured out of my lips in a steady stream. Laughter and applause acclaimed me, and I felt that at last I had broken through the barrier of language and that I was no longer an alien. Now I really belonged to the New World in mind and in spirit.

I envied the boys in my neighborhood who were in high school, and I yearned for the day when I too would be admitted to the school, which to me was the equivalent of the Russian gymnasium, the steppingstone to college. The craze of these boys for college had communicated itself to me, but I was baffled by their veneration of medicine as the choicest of all professions in the world. "To be a doctor" was the impassioned ambition of many of them, and I observed that high school girls viewed with special admiration a boy who had set his mind on being a doctor. They esteemed him as something of a hero and were transcendently happy when they had won his attention. The vicissitudes of life in the city, the overcrowding, the filth in the street, the utter absence of greenery except in one near-by park, were of no moment to these boys. Of course they were city born and city bred. They had never known the wild forests and fields, the swamps and streams, the vast array of birds from crows and blackbirds to storks and swallows, to nightingales and skylarks, that had been my unforgettable and ever-beloved heritage. They didn't have and could not have the feeling for nature that I had brought with me from the far away poverty-stricken Byelorussian village—a feeling that I had now come to regard as one of the most precious rewards Czarist Russia had accorded me. Never would I want to spend all the years of my life in so bleak and unnatural a part of the world as the Lower East Side was in those days. So to hell with being a doctor or a lawyer, the second most popular profession among my playmates, even if at the moment they did bring the pleasure of being a favorite with the most attractive girls in the neighborhood.

Entering High School

When my English was fluent enough for my high school friends to assure me that I would have no trouble in pursuing high school courses, I consulted with them as to which high school would be best for me. I finally decided on the Stuyvesant, and only because it was a manual training school. I loved the idea of acquainting myself with tools so that when the time came to devote myself to my chosen profession, which was agriculture, both my mind and hands would be attuned to mechanical contrivances.

At last the day came when I went to see the principal of the Stuyvesant High School. His name was Dr. Frank Rollins, and when I was ushered into his office, he greeted me with a friendly smile and a firm handshake. I can still see him in his black frock coat, winged collar, the formality of his dress contrasting with the ease of his manner. His eyes were understanding and humorous, and seated beside him I felt surprisingly at ease as I summarized my studies in the Russian school from which I had graduated. Dr. Rollins was astonished at the amount of studying I had crowded into four years. He was particularly impressed with my familiarity with the great Russian poets and novelists as well as with the translations of certain American authors and of Dickens, the only British author I had read in the Russian school.

Looking back to my Russian school years, I marvel at the extraordinarily high academic quality of those Czarist schools, scattered and few as they were in my native Byelorussia and for the most part beyond reach of the masses. The discipline was stern, but the teaching was excellent, inculcating from the very beginning the habits of concentration and intellectual earnestness. In the teaching of literature the Czarist schools had achieved their greatest glory, or maybe my old teachers had a special gift for making us, young as we were, see and feel the wonder and the beauty of great books, or were so fired by the warmth, the indignation, the humanity in them that the students quickly caught their enthusiasm.

Anyway, Dr. Rollins was satisfied that my Russian education more than qualified me for entry into his school. He filled in an admission card and told me to present myself for classes the following Monday morning. When he asked if I had yet decided on my future profession, I answered that I had set my heart on farming. He laughed, not with condescension but with surprise at an East Side immigrant boy's unusual ambition. As I left, Dr. Rollins shook my hand and asked me to drop in on him and let him know how I liked the school and how I was progressing in my studies.

The man's ease and kindliness, the lack of both uniform and pompousness in one so highly placed, buoyed my spirits more than any other experience in this exciting and confusing New World. I had been admitted to what was to me a Gymnasium and with no trouble at all. Nobody had asked a single question about my family's social standing, economic condition, or religion; tuition would be free, books, too, would be supplied. I strode down the street feeling as though I had suddenly entered into a new life and a new adventure. . . .

I suddenly realized that while I was in America, I was not of it, not really, not of the immense and alluring America that lay beyond Manhattan Island of which I had read in books and of which "Teddy" Roosevelt, as the boys in the neighborhood affectionately called him, wrote glowingly, but which the tall buildings shut out of my view.

I would explore this America, live in it, mingle with its people, learn to know them, discover how alike and how different they were from the people I had known. More than ever was I resolved to make farming my life work. I longed for trees and brooks, for wild flowers and open skies, for the peace and tranquility of the land, the real American land, far from the tumult and the filth, the frenzies and obsessions of New York.

At the age of seventeen I fled the city to a farm upstate.

I could not then have foreseen what a boon life and work on an American farm would prove to be in my future career—indeed, as priceless a boon as my childhood and boyhood in a muzhik village.

Working on a Farm

On a steep bank over a highway in upstate New York sprawls an old cemetery, very small, about a fifth of an acre in area. All around are hills and fields and in the rear the land slopes into a meadow that sinks down to a wooded swamp towered over by the loftiest hill in the neighborhood. Rusty barbed wire strung on high, wobbly cedar posts keeps pasturing cattle out of the graveyard. Tall maples shadow the grounds and in summer the grass grows lush and wild; dandelions, clover stalks, orchid daisies, now and then wild roses peep furtively out of the grass, and here and there a patch of myrtle, green as the sea, smothers all other growth.

The old cemetery dates back to a time after the War of Independence when pioneers from New England came in oxcarts to make new homes in the wilderness. Prominent on the headstones are the names of Faulkner and Moore, two families that had always been neighbors, if not always friends. The headstones of the Faulkners, fifteen of them, flank the front part of the cemetery and the Moores, five of them, are in the rear. The last Moore to be buried there was James, or Jim, as everybody called him. A slab of marble, square-cornered and about two feet high, rests over the graves of Jim, his father Alford, and his mother Sarah. No pious epitaph is carved into the headstone, only the names and the years of birth and death, Jim's being 1841 to 1926. Jim had hoped to live to a hundred, but nature had the last word. He died at eighty-five, and his proud boast had been that never in his life had he been so sick that he had to miss his "three squares" a day.

Early in March 1908 Jim had written to the Chelsea Employment Agency on the Bowery in New York asking for a young immigrant to work on his farm, offering fifteen dollars a month and keep. I was the applicant selected to be Jim Moore's hired hand. The agency manager was pleased to find a city boy willing to work in the country. He complained that few city boys cared for farm work and questioned me at length to make certain I wouldn't get homesick for dance halls, burlesque shows, Coney Island, and other city pleasures. I assured him he didn't have to have any misgivings. Then he asked whether I could plow land and milk cows. I never had done either, but I had seen my father plow and my mother milk our cow and I was certain that I could do as they did. I left the office of the employment agency with a railroad ticket in my pocket to a village upstate called North Brookfield in Madison County.

At the time I couldn't have known what a providential accident it was that I had applied for a farm job at this particular agency at the time I did. I shall always cherish the memory of Jim Moore. Long after I had left him and to the end of his life, we remained close friends and I often journeyed back to his farm to visit him. Poorly educated though he was, I always think of him as one of the most extraordinary characters I have known and his influence on my impressionable young mind has remained with me to this day. He flung open the doors of a new world for me, taught me a new way of farming, inculcated in me a set of priceless disciplines, introduced me to a new humanity, and gave me insight into an America I never should have discovered had I stayed in the city and even gone to college there. Working for him and living in his home was an education I never could have acquired from school teachers or textbooks, an education that in later years, when I began to write articles and books on Russia, proved a sounder guide to the understanding of some of the whys and wherefores of the Soviet Revolution than all the works of Marx and Engels or Lenin and Stalin.

Yet that spring day in 1908, while I was on the train heading upstate, I wondered about the life that lay ahead of me. What would I eat—would it be the thick soups with big lumps of bread, boiled potato, and porridge, with an occasional slice of raw pig fat, the usual fare of *batraky* (hired hands) on landed estates in the Old Country? And where would I sleep—would it be in a barn, a barracks, a shed, or at best in a kitchen? I kept wondering even more about James Moore, the man who had sent to New York for a farm hand. I could only picture him as a gentleman of leisure like the Russian landlords who wouldn't wear overalls, not even on weekdays.

But the moment I jumped off the milk wagon that had picked me up at the railroad station some two miles away from the farm and glimpsed the shabby house, I realized how far off the mark my speculations had been. It looked nothing like any landlord's mansion I had seen. The two-story clapboarded frame structure, set back from the road and shaded by stately maples, was utterly unimpressive. It had not even been painted. When I stepped inside the door and met my new employer, I was truly amazed. He wore faded and stained bib-overalls and a gray turtle-neck sweater with a big patch on the elbow. I knew at once that this was no gentleman of leisure but a farmer who worked with his hands. The discovery was comforting: it reduced Mr. James Moore to my own humble level of humanity.

All my other preconceptions fell like stalks of rye before a sickle. Instead of being separated from the family, I was made a part of it from the moment I stepped into the house. I shared a room with another hired man, and when he left I had it all to myself, the first time in my life that I had ever enjoyed the luxury of complete privacy. It was a large wallpapered room with three tall windows, one facing the road and looking out on a neighbor's house and land across the way, the other two offering a view of fields and hills and the wooded swamp whose wilderness brought to mind the age-old forests of my childhood.

The farmer's housekeeper (who, I learned later, was his mistress) was a short, slender, pale-faced woman with shining white hair and a pronounced limp. Every day she swept my room and made my bed. When my lamp chimney smoked she washed and polished it. She laundered my clothes, sewed on buttons, darned my socks, and mended barbed-wire tears in my shirts and overalls. When in line of duty I did chores for her—filled the wood box in the kitchen, fetched water from the pump in the woodshed, she would thank me as though I was conferring a special favor on her. The gentle, sweet-tempered though tight-lipped woman couldn't have looked after a son with greater solicitude.

Of course I sat at the same table with Jim and other members of his family. The cooking was new and exotic to me: the dishes quite unlike anything I had tasted in New York or in my old home in Russia. Soup, the stand-by of muzhiks and of immigrants from Russia, rarely appeared on Jim's board, and when it did, it was only a few spoonfulls of hot water in which floated particles of fat and sometimes a few crumbs of toasted bread, a few grains of rice, or bits of potato. A muzhik served such a watery concoction would have flung it, bowl and all, at his wife's head. The slices of bread were so small and thin, and Yankees* ate so little of it that I often wondered why they bothered to put it on the table. So soup and bread, the traditional belly-fillers of Russians, stout foods that often made a meal in themselves, were more shadow than substance, more token than satisfaction on a Yankee farm.

But there were so many other dishes on the table that I soon lost the craving for soup and bread. Meat and vegetables, potatoes and gravy, salads in season, honey from Jim's own hives and an endless variety of corn meal preparations that were new to me: johnnycake, muffins, mush, fritters, rusks, griddlecakes. And there was always a dessert for breakfast as well as dinner and supper, homemade pies, cakes, cookies, doughnuts, or "fried cakes," as we called them at Jim's. A meal without dessert was as unthinkable as potatoes without gravy, biscuits without honey, mush without milk. The astonishing variety of dishes at the farmer's table was a wonder and delight to me.

By prevailing American standards, Jim, who carried a mortgage on his farm, was what Russians would call a *bedniak*—poor man. Yet to a Russian *bedniak*, whose passion for land Lenin would exploit as a weapon of Bolshevik conquest, Jim's board would have been a landlord's luxury. And no Russian today, however high his salary and position, eats as great a variety of foods as we did at Jim's table some sixty years ago! Russia simply does not produce the vast variety of foods that America does, especially in fruits and vegetables, but remains principally a cereal and potato-cabbage-eating country. Khrushchev extolled corn as "the miracle plant," "queen of the field," "milk and meat on the stalk," and with enthusiasm had sought to promote corn and corn products as foods. But even he during his two journeys to America had never discovered the many corn delicacies that I learned to enjoy on a farm in Madison County, New York, a

---

*On the Lower East Side, Anglo-Americans were spoken of as "Yankees," and it is in this sense that I use the word throughout the book.

farm which by Soviet Russian standards would have invoked on its hard-working and always cash-poor owner the epithet of "kulak" and would have rendered him subject to liquidation.

What Working on a Farm Taught Me

All the uncertainty that had oppressed me during my journey from the city into the unknown, vanished overnight. Jim and his housekeeper took me into the family as though I were their son. They accepted me without reservations, with a courtesy and a kindness that touched me, though to Jim it was all as natural as washing his hands before a meal. But to the young immigrant who was still sensitive to the Old World distinctions between class and class and man and man, it was a heartening revelation of daily living in a democratic community. Jim of course was no exception. All the Yankee farmers in the countryside treated their immigrant help, principally newly arrived young peasants from Russia, Poland, the Ukraine, Hungary, with equal regard for their comfort and their persons. This was the custom, in fact the morality of the country, which of course negates the Soviet-Marxist doctrine of perpetual class struggle in the capitalist countryside. Even so brilliant a man as Nikolay Bukharin, one of Lenin's closest associates who on the eve of the Soviet Revolution had spent several months in the United States, was loath to believe me when I once told him of the way I was treated when I had been a *batrak* on an American farm.

I happen to belong to the college generation of Vincent Sheean, Malcolm Cowley, and Scott Fitzgerald with whom I was to have a memorable encounter years later.

In an interview with a reporter of the New York *Times* (March 14, 1969), Sheean said, "There is no place that I can call home. . . . I've always been rootless." In his *Exile's Return*, Cowley makes a similar statement: "Our whole training was involuntarily directed toward destroying whatever roots we had in the soil." Sheean and Cowley are of course native-born Americans, as I am not. Yet to this day I am baffled by the intellectuals of my college generation who speak of themselves as rootless, without a home, without a feeling for home. I had been uprooted once, when I left Russia, and had I remained in the slums of New York, I too would probably have remained rootless and might have become as fiercely rebellious as the rest, some of them journalists who went on assignments to Russia about the time I did. But the America in which I lived after my flight from New York—an America of hills and valleys, of woods and swamps, of fields and streams, and of people who lived on the land—had been so congenial to my taste and temperament that I could not help striking roots into it, roots that were growing deeper and stronger. Though over sixty years have passed since I first went to the small farming village of North Brookfield, I have come to regard it as home. The fact that I do not live there is of no consequence. I only know that socially and emotionally it is as indispensable to me as the bed in which I sleep and that whenever I go back there I feel refreshed and exhilarated. I can conceive of no greater misfortune than to find myself cut off from the farming community in which I spent some of the happiest and most fruitful years of my youth.

. . . I never qualified for membership in the so-called "lost generation." To me it was enough to be living in a society that knew no feudalism and nothing of the prerogatives that go with it that divide humanity into the privileged and the lowly. America had given me confidence in myself and a sense of inner security that I never lost.

129. A CHAMPION OF JEWISH RIGHTS

LOUIS MARSHALL

For seven years, 1920–27, Henry Ford, the automobile manufacturer, made anti-Semitic attacks through his company's publication, the *Dearborn Independent*. They were based on a forged document, the *Protocols of the Elders of Zion*, which charged that Jews plotted to establish a worldwide Jewish dictatorship. In 1927, following a libel suit, Ford published a retraction and apology with an accompanying letter to Earl J. Davis, a former assistant attorney general of the United States.

Louis Marshall (1856–1929) was a prominent lawyer and Jewish communal leader. He was a founder and president of the American Jewish Committee and a member of the Jewish delegation to the Paris Peace Conference in 1919. Although not a Zionist, he cooperated with Weizmann in establishing the Jewish Agency in 1929.

The statement by Henry Ford to Louis Marshall and Marshall's reply follow.

Ford's Statement

For sometime I have given consideration to the series of articles concerning Jews which since 1920 have appeared in the Dearborn *Independent*. Some of them have been reprinted in pamphlet form under the title *The International Jew*. Although both publications are my property, it goes without saying that in the multitude of activities it has been impossible for me to devote personal attention to their management or to keep informed as to the contents. It has therefore inevitably followed that the conduct and policies of these publications had to be delegated to men whom I placed in charge of them and upon whom I relied implicitly.

To my great regret I have learned that Jews generally and particularly those of this country not only resent these publications as promoting anti-Semitism, but regard me as their enemy. Trusted friends with whom I have conferred recently have assured me in all sincerity that in their opinion the character of the charges and insinuations made against the Jews, both individually and collectively, contained in many of the articles which have been circulated periodically in the Dearborn *Independent* and have been reprinted in the pamphlets mentioned, justifies the righteous indignation entertained by Jews everywhere toward me because of the mental anguish occasioned by the unprovoked reflections made upon them.

This has led me to direct my personal attention to this subject, in order to ascertain the exact nature of these articles. As a result of this survey I confess that I am deeply mortified that this journal, which is intended to be constructive and not destructive, has been made the medium for resurrecting exploded fictions, for giving currency to the so-called *Protocols of the Wise Men of Zion*, which have been demonstrated, as I learn, to be gross forgeries, and for contending that the Jews have been engaged in a conspiracy to control the capital and the industries of the world, besides laying at their door many offenses against decency, public order, and good morals.

Had I appreciated even the general nature, to say nothing of the details, of these utterances, I would have forbidden their circulation without a moment's hesitation, because I am fully aware of the virtues of the Jewish people as a whole, of what they and their ancestors have done for civilization and for mankind toward the development of commerce and industry, their sobriety and diligence, their benevolence, and their unselfish interest in the public welfare.

Of course there are black sheep in every flock, as there are among men of all races, creeds, and nationalities who are at times evildoers. It is wrong, however, to judge a people by a few individuals, and I therefore join in condemning unreservedly all wholesale denunciations and attacks.

Those who know me can bear witness that it is not in my nature to inflict insult upon and to occasion pain to anybody, and that it has been my effort to free myself from prejudice. Because of that I frankly confess that I have been greatly shocked as a result of my study and examination of the files of the Dearborn *Independent* and of the pamphlets entitled *The International Jew*.

I deem it my duty as an honorable man to make amends for the wrong done to the Jews as fellow men and brothers, by asking their forgiveness for the harm I have unintentionally committed, by retracting so far as lies

within my power the offensive charges laid at their door by these
publications, and by giving them the unqualified assurance that henceforth they may look to me for friendship and goodwill.

Finally, let me add that this statement is made on my own initiative and
wholly in the interest of right and justice and in accordance with what I
regard as my solemn duty as a man and as a citizen.

Marshall's Reply

July 5, 1927

I am in receipt of your letter to Mr. Earl J. Davis accompanied by your
statement regarding the long series of vituperative articles which since
May, 1920, has appeared in the Dearborn Independent and which contains
the most violent attacks upon the Jews. You now declare that after an
examination of those articles you feel shocked and mortified because of the
harm which they have done, and you ask our forgiveness.

For twenty centuries we Jews have been accustomed to forgive insults
and injuries, persecution and intolerance, hoping that we might behold
the day when brotherhood and good-will would be universal. We had
fondly hoped that in this blessed republic, with its glorious Constitutions
and its just laws, it would be impossible to encounter the hatred and rancor
to which our brethren have been and still are subjected in other lands. We
could not at first credit the information that the Dearborn Independent had
permitted itself to be made the vehicle for disseminating exploded
falsehoods and the vilest concoctions of vicious minds, invented by
adventurers who had barely found asylum here when they attempted to
introduce the exotic growths of anti-Semitism.

Happily such excrescences could not flourish on American soil. Happily
the enlightened press of this country treated them with contempt and as
unworthy of notice. But we Jews none the less suffered the anguish of
tortured memories, the nightmares of a horrible past, and the sorrow that,
in spite of the progress of civilization, there were those who stood ready to
misunderstand us. What seemed most mysterious was the fact that you
whom we had never wronged and whom we had looked upon as a kindly
man, should have lent yourself to such a campaign of vilification apparently carried on with your sanction.

The statement which you have sent me gives us assurance of your
retraction of the offensive charges, of your proposed change of policies in
the conduct of the Dearborn Independent, of your future friendship and
good-will, of your desire to make amends, and what is to be expected from
any man of honor, you couple these assurances with a request for pardon.
So far as my influence can further that end, it will be exerted, simply

because there flows in my veins the blood of ancestors who were inured to suffering and nevertheless remained steadfast in their trust in God. Referring to the teachings of the Sermon on the Mount, Israel Zangwill once said that we Jews are after all the only Christians. He might have added that it is because essentially the spirit of forgiveness is a Jewish trait.

It is my sincere hope that never again shall such a recrudescence of ancient superstition manifest itself upon our horizon.

130. THE JEWISH TASK

LOUIS DEMBITZ BRANDEIS

Louis Dembitz Brandeis (1856–1941) was born in Louisville, Kentucky, where his parents migrated from Prague after the failure of the 1848 revolution. He attended Harvard and became an outstanding lawyer and jurist. In 1916 he became the first Jew to be appointed to the Supreme Court. Brandeis was known as the "people's attorney." Through his opinions on the Supreme Court he was instrumental in sustaining such measures as minimum wage laws, and price control laws, and in protecting unions against injunctions in labor disputes.

Brandeis had been brought up without any formal religion and, until he was fifty-four, he had little contact with the Jewish community. In 1910 he was called in to help settle a strike in New York in the Jewish-dominated garment industry (see no. 121). He learned a good deal about the life of the Jewish immigrants on the East Side of New York and was moved by deep kinship with the workers whom he met at the arbitration table. He subsequently joined and became active in American Zionism. His greatest service to Zionism is probably his influence in obtaining the approval of President Wilson for the Balfour Declaration as proposed by the British Government (no. 86). He remained actively concerned with Zionism and granted his advice and support until the end of his life in 1941.

Brandeis addressed himself to the relationship between his Jewish loyalties as expressed through Zionism and his American patriotism. The selection which follows is taken from an address which he delivered at a conference of Reform rabbis in 1915.

Aim of Zionism

Zionism seeks to establish in Palestine, for such Jews as choose to go and remain there, and for their descendants, a legally secured home, where they may live together and lead a Jewish life, where they may expect ultimately to constitute a majority of the population, and may look forward to what we should call home rule. The Zionists seek to establish this home in Palestine because they are convinced that the undying longing of Jews for Palestine is a fact of deepest significance; that it is a manifestation in the struggle for existence by an ancient people which has established its right to live, a people whose three thousand years of civilization has produced a faith, culture, and individuality which will enable it to contribute largely in the future, as it has in the past, to the advance of civilization; and that it is not a right merely but a duty of the Jewish nationality to survive and develop. They believe that only in Palestine can Jewish life be fully protected from the forces of disintegration; that there alone can the Jewish spirit reach its full and natural development; and that by securing for those Jews who wish to settle there the opportunity to do so, not only those Jews, but all other Jews will be benefited, and that the long perplexing Jewish problem will, at last, find solution. . . .

Since the destruction of the Temple, nearly two thousand years ago, the longing for Palestine has been ever present with the Jew. It was the hope of a return to the land of his fathers that buoyed up the Jew amidst persecution, and for the realization of which the devout ever prayed. Until a generation ago this was a hope merely, a wish piously prayed for, but not worked for. The Zionist movement is idealistic, but it is also essentially practical. It seeks to realize that hope; to make the dream of a Jewish life in a Jewish land come true as other great dreams of the world have been realized, by men working with devotion, intelligence, and self-sacrifice. It was thus that the dream of Italian independence and unity, after centuries of vain hope, came true through the efforts of Mazzini, Garibaldi, and Cavour; that the dream of Greek, of Bulgarian, and of Serbian independence became facts.

Beginnings of Restoration

The rebirth of the Jewish nation is no longer a mere dream. It is in process of accomplishment in a most practical way, and the story is a wonderful one. . . .

This land, treeless a generation ago, supposed to be sterile and hopelessly arid, has been shown to have been treeless and sterile because of man's misrule. It has been shown to be capable of becoming again a land "flowing with milk and honey." Oranges and grapes, olives and almonds, wheat and other cereals are now growing there in profusion.

This material development has been attended by a spiritual and social development no less extraordinary; a development in education, in health, and in social order; and in the character and habits of the population. Perhaps the most extraordinary achievement of Jewish nationalism is the revival of the Hebrew language, which has again become a language of the common intercourse of men. The Hebrew tongue, called a dead language for nearly two thousand years, has, in the Jewish colonies and in Jerusalem, become again the living mother tongue. The effect of this common language in unifying the Jew is, of course, great; for the Jews of

Palestine came literally from all the lands of the earth, each speaking, excepting those who used Yiddish, the language of the country from which he came, and remaining, in the main, almost a stranger to the others. But the effect of the renaissance of the Hebrew tongue is far greater than that of unifying the Jews. It is a potent factor in reviving the essentially Jewish spirit.

Our Jewish Pilgrim Fathers have laid the foundation. It remains for us to build the superstructure.

Zionism and American Patriotism

Let no American imagine that Zionism is inconsistent with Patriotism. Multiple loyalties are objectionable only if they are inconsistent. A man is a better citizen of the United States for being also a loyal citizen of his state, and of his city; for being loyal to his family, and to his profession or trade; for being loyal to his college or his lodge. Every Irish American who contributed toward advancing home rule was a better man and a better American for the sacrifice he made. Every American Jew who aids in advancing the Jewish settlement in Palestine, though he feels that neither he nor his descendants will ever live there, will likewise be a better man and a better American for doing so.

Note what Seton-Watson* says:

"America is full of nationalities which, while accepting with enthusiasm their new American citizenship, nevertheless look to some centre in the old world as the source and inspiration of their national culture and traditions. The most typical instance is the feeling of the American Jew for Palestine, which may well become a focus for his déclassé kinsmen in other parts of the world."

There is no inconsistency between loyalty to America and loyalty to Jewry. The Jewish spirit, the product of our religion and experiences, is essentially modern and essentially American. Not since the destruction of the Temple have the Jews in spirit and in ideals been so fully in harmony with the noblest aspirations of the country in which they lived.

America's fundamental law seeks to make real the brotherhood of man. That brotherhood became the Jewish fundamental law more than twenty-five hundred years ago. America's insistent demand in the twentieth century is for social justice. That also has been the Jews' striving for ages. Their affliction, as well as their religion, has prepared the Jews for effective democracy. Persecution broadened their sympathies. It trained

---

*"Robert W. Seton-Watson (1879–1951), a British historian who specialized in the multinational regions of the Austro-Hungarian monarchy and the Balkans" (Hertzberg).

them in patient endurance, in self-control, and in sacrifice. It made them think as well as suffer. It deepened the passion for righteousness.

Indeed, loyalty to America demands rather that each American Jew become a Zionist. For only through the ennobling effect of its strivings can we develop the best that is in us and give to this country the full benefit of our great inheritance. The Jewish spirit, so long preserved, the character developed by so many centuries of sacrifice, should be preserved and developed further, so that in America as elsewhere the sons of the race may in the future live lives and do deeds worthy of their ancestors. . . .

Duty of American Jews

Since the Jewish problem is single and universal, the Jews of every country should strive for its solution. But the duty resting upon us of America is especially insistent. We number about 3,000,000, which is more than one-fifth of all the Jews in the world, a number larger than that comprised within any other country except the Russian Empire. We are representative of all the Jews in the world; for we are composed of immigrants, or descendants of immigrants, coming from every other country, or district. We include persons from every section of society, and of every shade of religious belief. We are ourselves free from civil or political disabilities, and are relatively prosperous. Our fellow Americans are infused with a high and generous spirit, which insures approval of our struggle to ennoble, liberate, and otherwise improve the condition of an important part of the human race; and their innate manliness makes them sympathize particularly with our efforts at self-help. America's detachment from the old world problem relieves us from suspicions and embarrassments frequently attending the activities of Jews of rival European countries. And a conflict between American interests or ambitions and Jewish aims is not conceivable. Our loyalty to America can never be questioned.

Let us therefore lead, earnestly, courageously, and joyously, in the struggle for liberation. Let us all recognize that we Jews are a distinctive nationality of which every Jew, whatever his country, his station, or shade of belief, is necessarily a member. Let us insist that the struggle for liberty shall not cease until equality of opportunity is accorded to nationalities as to individuals. Let us insist also that full equality of opportunity cannot be obtained by Jews until we, like members of other nationalities, shall have the option of living elsewhere or of returning to the land of our forefathers.

The fulfillment of these aspirations is clearly demanded in the interest of mankind, as well as in justice to the Jews. They cannot fail of attainment if we are united and true to ourselves. But we must be united not only in spirit but in action. To this end we must organize. Organize, in the first place, so that the world may have proof of the extent and the intensity of our desire for liberty. Organize, in the second place, so that our resources may become known and be made available. But in mobilizing our force it will not be for war. The whole world longs for the solution of the Jewish problem. We have but to lead the way, and we may be sure of ample co-operation from non-Jews. In order to lead the way, we need not arms, but men; men with those qualities for which Jews should be peculiarly fitted by reason of their religion and life; men of courage, of high intelligence, of faith and public spirit, of indomitable will and ready self-sacrifice; men who both think and do, who will devote high abilities to shaping our course, and to overcoming the many obstacles which must from time to time arise. And we need other, many, many other men, officers commissioned and noncommissioned, and common soldiers in the cause of liberty, who will give of their efforts and resources, as occasion may demand, in unfailing and ever-strengthening support of the measures which may be adopted. Organization thorough and complete can alone develop such leaders and the necessary support.

Organize, Organize, Organize, until every Jew in America must stand up and be counted, counted with us, or prove himself, wittingly or unwittingly, of the few who are against their own people.

131. THE SUBURBAN JEW

MARSHALL SKLARE AND OTHERS

In 1967 the Lakeville studies were published, a sociological survey undertaken by Marshall Sklare, Joseph Greenblum, and Benjamin J. Ringer with the purpose of determining with documented data "how an American Jewish community lives with itself and its neighbors." Although the suburb described is a very wealthy one (Lakeville is not its real name), the expressions of Jewishness and the relationship to non-Jewish neighbors are probably characteristic of many other Jewish communities.
The selection is taken from the summary of the survey.

In many important characteristics—education, occupation, income and percentage of native-born—the Jews of Lakeville, a suburb of a large Midwestern city, present a probable forecast of American Jewry as a whole in the not-too-distant future. How these second-and-third-generation American Jews view their Jewishness, which aspects of their faith they seem to be most attached to, and how they relate to their non-Jewish neighbors may well offer a reliable index to future developments in Jewish identity on the American scene.

The Jewish community of Lakeville consisted of a small, strongly acculturated, wealthy group of families with a German background, who had been residents of the town for as much as half a century, and a large number of middle to upper-middle class families of East European descent, who had arrived after the Second World War as part of a sudden, massive population influx which brought extensive community modernization in its wake.

The community was free from overt discrimination against Jews, and relatively free from gross bigotry, although incidents with an anti-Semitic aspect were not unknown. Large majorities of both gentiles and Jews thought relations between their groups were good, at least on the surface. This tranquility was sometimes attributed to cultural similarities of gentiles and Jews, sometimes to the social distance between them.

Generally speaking, the Jewish community—in which the newcomers had assumed a clear majority by the time of the survey—was more assertively Jewish than in earlier days. Membership in synagogues was widespread, and the community's five congregations (four Reform, one Conservative) provided a wide variety of viewpoints on Jewish religion and peoplehood, forms of worship, and educational and social activities. To some extent, particular congregations were associated with particular socio-economic or intellectual levels. Most were centers of sociability as well as of worship and study.

Nearly all parents sent their children to Sunday or Hebrew school, whether or not they themselves had received such schooling in their own childhood. The Bar Mitzvah ceremony was holding its own compared with former generations; Confirmation of both boys and girls was much more widely practiced than formerly; and Hanukkah, traditionally a minor festival in the Jewish year, had been elevated to an important and widely celebrated occasion.

The community's numerous Jewish organizations also contributed significantly to the individual's sense of Jewish identity. Involvement in such groups often functioned as a secular alternative to religion.

At the same time, traditional emphasis on ritual acts had become greatly weakened; synagogue attendance was irregular and desultory (though it still exceeded home observance); and religiousness was defined by many solely in terms of morality, or belief in God. However, the decline both in synagogue attendance and in observance of traditional rituals appeared to have been slowed since a generation earlier.

An individual's patterns of synagogue attendance and home observance were affected by the religious upbringing he had received, and by the needs of his children at various times of life. The need for religious training of children was the chief reason why families joined a congregation. Yet, once they were enrolled, the parents usually remained members even after the children were grown up.

Home rituals were most likely to be retained if they were capable of redefinition in modern terms, did not demand social isolation, provided a "Jewish alternative" to the customs of the larger community, appealed to children and were not too frequent.

Most individuals, both adults and children, felt their homes were Jewish enough, but actual Jewishness was often minimal. It was felt by many that families were more harmonious than in former generations, and that lessened insistence on tradition was the reason. The training of children in the fundamentals of their Jewish heritage had largely lost its traditional basis in the family, and religious education of the young had become primarily a synagogue function.

Some degree of sympathy or identification with Israel was felt by all except a small minority. Commitment to Israel was most developed among the more religious. A majority considered Israel's existence beneficial to Jews in the United States, largely because it had created a new, heroic image of the Jews; only a minority feared possible accusations of "double loyalty" against American Jews. The Six-Day War of 1967 set off intense anxiety and a highly successful fund-raising campaign, but did not appear to have altered attitudes toward Israel permanently.

Perhaps most revealing were the qualities which the Lakeville Jewish community considered essential in a good Jew. Specifically Jewish religious and cultural values, while thought to be desirable, were not deemed essential. Overwhelmingly, the emphasis was on humaneness, morality and citizenship—qualities which, though selected from Jewish precepts, added up to a model that was more American than Jewish.

Many parents thought their children might marry gentiles, and most were resigned or only moderately unhappy about this prospect. Love was widely felt to outweigh religion as a criterion for marriage, although religion in turn outweighed considerations of wealth and prestige. Opposition to intermarriage was usually attributed to concern over possible personal difficulties rather than over Jewish survival.

A number of significant contradictions marked the relationships between the Jews of Lakeville and their non-Jewish neighbors. Most Jews had no realistic notion of how gentiles felt about them and vice versa. How Jews estimated gentiles' attitudes often appeared to be determined by their own anxieties. The most realistic assessments came from those who thought gentile-Jewish relations were fairly but not very strained.

Many gentile old-timers were still critical of the population wave that had brought most of the Jewish residents to the community, while others, mostly younger residents, were willing to credit recent community improvements to the Jewish newcomers. The long-established Jewish residents were often preferred to the more recent ones, because of their conformity to gentile standards, customs and traditions. The newcomers were frequently criticized for supposed clannishness, status striving or overly permissive and materialistic ways of child-rearing.

The long-time Jewish residents, for their part, often echoed the criticisms of the Jewish newcomers voiced by gentile old-timers, expressing the fear that "undesirable" or nonconformist Jews might arouse anti-Semitism. The recent Jewish settlers were less concerned about potential anti-Semitism attendant on the Jewish population influx than about individual "problem Jews." They saw themselves as useful, responsible citizens, and resented what they felt was snobbery or self-hatred among Jewish old-timers.

Without exception, Jews felt they should be integrated into the larger society in at least some degree. They considered mixed gentile-Jewish neighborhoods preferable to solidly Jewish ones, if only to provide children with the experience of living in a mixed society; and they thought they ought to cultivate personal relationships with gentiles.

Principles like these were often at odds with emotions. Thus, half of those queried—including many who strongly favored integration in principle—admitted to being uncomfortable in the closer kinds of encounters with gentiles. A feeling of uneasiness, or of having to watch one's step, was reported by many. This feeling, however, seemed destined to wane in the next generation.

Gentiles were far less willing than Jews to live in mixed neighborhoods, particularly in evenly mixed ones. Those who preferred neighborhoods with no Jews, or with limited numbers of Jews, frequently gave concern with maintaining traditional gentile values and customs as their reason. Jews were usually considered more acceptable if they conformed to gentile norms; their distinctive qualities were far more often ignored or criticized than welcomed.

Both Jews and gentiles were most likely to have mixed social contacts if they lived in areas where the opposite faith predominated, and this was even more true for Jews living in largely gentile areas than for gentiles in Jewish areas. One reason was the greater interest of Jews in community organizations. The fact that Jews were generally overrepresented in groups like the PTA tended to make such groups more or less evenly mixed in mainly gentile areas, but almost solidly Jewish in mainly Jewish ones.

Gentiles were more likely than Jews actually to carry out any impulse for closer social relations with their opposite numbers. Both groups tended to assume that in such situations the role of the Jew was to seek acceptance, and that of the gentile to do the accepting. Hence Jews, more wary of possible rejection, were less likely to press for personal contacts, and often considered themselves sufficiently integrated into the larger community if they merely joined nondenominational organizations.

Semi-social encounters on the job, though superficial in themselves, often led to more personal relationships between gentile and Jewish men. Voluntary organizations were the chief bases for friendly relations between gentile and Jewish women. Usually, groups organized for communal or charitable purposes were most effective in fostering such relationships; groups devoted to hobbies or cultural interests were less effective in this respect.

Jews tended to belong to more nonsectarian groups than did gentiles. Leisure-time pursuits of Jews and gentiles also differed: The former, regardless of economic class, were more often culture-oriented and given to a diversity of sports and games, while the latter tended to cultural interests only among the rich, and concentrated on fewer interests with greater intensity. Country clubs—the leading leisure-time institutions—remained essentially segregated.

Jewish-gentile friendships usually required more intimacy to get started than did those within either religious group. They also took longer to mature and reached real closeness less often. Thus, even though at various times in their lives Lakeville Jews had experienced far more mixed friendships than earlier generations, their really close ties were still overwhelmingly with other Jews.

Both in their feelings about themselves and in their relationships with their gentile neighbors, the Jews of Lakeville illustrate a unique paradox of American society: The very freedom which permits groups to maintain their distinctive cultural traits also permits group identity to be washed out. Lakeville-style Jewishness differs in many ways from that of earlier generations; it is much poorer in tradition and ritual. Still, there is good evidence that the Jews of Lakeville want to, and mean to, remain Jews in some significant sense. Just what being Jewish will mean to the generation of Jewish Americans now coming to maturity—and whether their desire for a distinctive group identity will be understood and accepted by their neighbors without the present demand for conformity—only the future can tell.

QUESTIONS FOR THOUGHT AND DISCUSSION

1. Read some autobiographies of American Jews and report to your class or group. Good selections are found in Jacob R. Marcus, *Memoirs of American Jews, 1795–1865*, and Harold U. Ribalow, *Autobiographies of American Jews*.

2. Read the selections from "Bintel Brief" (no. 125) and list the problems which the writers of these letters encountered as Jewish immigrants.

3. Find out why the Amalgamated Clothing Workers and the International Ladies' Garment Workers are considered model unions in industrial relations. Consult encyclopedias and the literature listed there.

4. What functions did the Jewish peddler perform, driving with his wagon and visiting farms?

5. Find out about Jewish national organizations such as the American Jewish Committee, the American Jewish Congress, the B'nai B'rith and their programs. Again you may consult encyclopedias, the *American Jewish Year Book*, and write to the national offices for descriptive literature.

6. Do a similar study for the national religious organizations, Orthodox, Conservative, and Reform.

7. As you have read, German Jewish immigrants first became peddlers and storekeepers and later manufacturers and merchants. The East European Jewish immigrant turned to labor in factories. In what way do these differences in the choice of occupations relate to the economic development of the United States at various periods?

8. There are efforts today to fill positions in private industry and in government with people from ethnic minorities in accordance with their proportionate share in the American population. How do such efforts affect the Jews?

9. Many years have passed since Justice Brandeis explained that there is no conflict between Zionism and the patriotism of an American Jew. The State of Israel has been established in the meantime, and although America supports Israel, there may be occasions when the foreign policy interests of both countries do not agree or may even conflict. What do you think should be the position of an American Jewish citizen when such disagreements or conflicts arise?

10. Make a study of the students in your class or school to find out how many are first-, second-, third-, or fourth-generation Americans.

SUGGESTED READING

Note: Books suggested in more than one chapter are here listed by the name of the author only. A key to such listings will be found at the end of the book.
A paperback edition is indicated by the letters PB.

In 1975, the Jewish Book Council of America (15 East 26th Street, New York, N.Y. 10010) published annotated bibliographies on *American Jewish History* and *American Jewish Biography*. Both booklets will be found helpful. The *American Jewish Year Book* should be available as reference for the study of this chapter.

Books for the Student

Butwin, Frances. *The Jews in America: History and Sources*. New York, 1973. PB.
Charry-Segal, chaps. 21 and 24.
Eisenberg, Azriel, ed. *The Golden Land: A Literary Portrait of American Jewry, 1654 to the Present*. New York, 1965.
Elbogen, pp. 114–38, 224–41, 326–52, 427–49, 559–88.
Grayzel, pp. 615–32, 685–704, 774–81, 800–805.
Grayzel II, pp. 23–61, 67–73, 96–105, 147–51, 157–69. PB.
Learsi.
Wiernik, Peter. *History of the Jews of America*. 3rd ed. New York, 1972.

Books for the Teacher

General

Feingold, Henry L. *Zion in America: The Jewish Experience from Colonial Times to the Present*. New York, 1975. PB.
Fishman, Priscilla, ed. *The Jews of the United States*. New York, 1974.
Glazer, Nathan. *American Judaism*. 2d ed. Chicago, 1972. PB.
Handlin, Oscar, *The Uprooted: The Epic Story of the Great Migrations That Made the American People*. Boston, 1951.
Karp, Abraham J., ed. *The Jewish Experience in America; Selected Studies from the Publications of the American Jewish Historical Society*. 5 vols. Waltham, Mass., and New York, 1960.
Marcus, Jacob R. *Studies in American Jewish History: Studies and Addresses*. Cincinnati, 1969.
Sachar, chaps. 8, 15, 16, 24. PB.
Schwarz, chap. 18.

Documents and Sources

Blau, Joseph L., and Salo W. Baron, eds. *The Jews of the United States 1790–1840: A Documentary History*. 3 vols. New York, 1964.
Schappes, Morris U., ed. *A Documentary History of the Jews in the United States, 1654–1875*. 3d ed. New York, 1975. PB.
Sloan, Irving J., ed. *The Jews in America 1621–1970: A Chronology and Fact Book*. Dobbs Ferry. N.Y., 1971.

Autobiographies, Memoirs, Letters

Chyet, Stanley F., ed. *Lives and Voices: A Collection of American Jewish Memoirs*. Philadelphia, 1972.
Howe, Irving, ed. *World of Our Fathers: The Journey of the East European Jews to America and the Life They Found and Made*. New York, 1976.
Marcus, Jacob R., ed. *Memoirs of American Jews, 1775–1865*. 3 vols. Philadelphia, 1955.
Metzker, Isaac, ed. *A Bintel Brief: Sixty Years of Letters From the Lower East Side to the Jewish Daily Forward*. Garden City. N.Y., 1971. PB.
Ribalow, Harold U., ed. *Autobiographies of American Jews*. Philadelphia, 1973.

Sociology

Janowsky, Oscar I., ed. *The American Jew: A Reappraisal*. Philadelphia, 1964.
Sherman, Bezalel C. *The Jews within American Society: A Study in Ethnic Individuality*. Detroit, 1965. PB.
Sidorsky, David, ed. *The Future of the Jewish Community in America*. Philadelphia, 1973.
Sklare, Marshall, *America's Jews*. New York, 1971. PB.
————, ed. *The Jewish Community in America*. New York, 1974.

Yiddish

Doroshkin, Milton. *Yiddish in America: Social and Cultural Foundations*. Rutherford, 1969.
Madison, Charles A. *Yiddish Literature: Its Scope and Major Writers*. New York, 1971. PB.

Pictorial

Schappes, Morris U. *A Pictorial History of the Jews in the United States*. Rev. ed. New York, 1965.
Schoener, Allon, ed. *Portal to America: The Lower East Side, 1870–1925*. New York, 1967. PB.

Special Topics

Angoff, Charles, and Meyer Levin, eds. *The Rise of American Jewish Literature: An Anthology of Selections from the Major Novels.* New York, 1970.

Davis, Moshe. "Jewish Religious Life and Institutions in America." In Louis Finkelstein, ed., *The Jews* (New York, 1970), vol. 1, pp. 488–587. PB.

Epstein, Melech, *Jewish Labor in U.S.A., 1882–1914.* New York, 1950.

Gartner, Lloyd P. *Jewish Education in the United States: A Documentary History.* New York, 1969.

Gross, Theodore L., ed. *The Literature of American Jews.* New York, 1973.

Hapgood, Hutchins. *The Spirit of the Ghetto.* New York, 1966. PB.

Lifson, David S. *The Yiddish Theater in America.* New York, 1965.

Ribalow, Harold U. *The Jew in American Sports.* New York, 1973.

KEY: BOOKS LISTED WITH NAME OF AUTHOR ONLY

This is an alphabetical listing of books which have been quoted with the name of the author only in "Suggested Reading" supplied for each of the chapters.

Baron, Salo W. *The Russian Jew under Tsars and Soviets*. New York, 1964.

Charry, Elias, and Abraham Segal. *The Eternal People: The Story of Judaism and Jewish Thought Through the Ages*. New York, 1967.

Chesler, Evan R., ed. *The Russian Jewry Reader*. New York, 1974. PB.

Graetz, Heinrich. *History of the Jews*. 6 vols. Philadelphia, 1967.

Grayzel, Solomon. *A History of the Jews: From the Babylonian Exile to the End of World War II*. Philadelphia, 1968.

Grayzel II=Grayzel, Solomon. *A History of the Contemporary Jews: From 1900 to the Present*. Philadelphia, 1960. PB.

Halkin, Simon. *Modern Hebrew Literature: From the Enlightenment to the Birth of Israel, Trends and Values*. New York, 1970. PB.

Learsi, Rufus. *The Jews in America*. New York, 1972.

Margolis, Max L., and Alexander Marx. *A History of the Jewish People*. Philadelphia, 1927. PB.

Porath, Johnathan D. *Jews in Russia: The Last Four Centuries; A Documentary History*. New York, 1973. PB.

Sachar, Howard. *The Course of Modern Jewish History*. New York, 1963. PB.

Schwarz, Leo W., ed. *Great Ages and Ideas of the Jewish People*. New York, 1956.

SOURCES AND ACKNOWLEDGMENTS

Grateful acknowledgment is made to the following authors and publishers for permission to reprint materials:

1. THE VIRGINIA ACT: Memoirs, Correspondence and Printed Papers of Thomas Jefferson, ed. by Thomas Jefferson Randolph (London, 1829), vol. 2, p. 65.
2. RELIGIOUS FREEDOM: Constitution of the United States.
3. AN EXAMPLE WORTHY OF IMITATION: George Washington, in the Jewish Encyclopedia, vol. 9, pp. 294 f. By permission of KTAV Publishing House, Inc.
4. FRANCE: DEMAND FOR EQUAL RIGHTS: Isaiah Berr-Bing, in Heinrich Graetz, Geschichte der Juden (1900), vol. 11, p. 174. Trans. by the editor.
5. RIGHTS FOR INDIVIDUALS: Clermont-Tonnerre, in Arthur Hertzberg, The French Enlightenment and the Jews (New York, 1968), p. 360. Copyright © 1968 by Columbia University Press and used by its permission.
6. PROCLAMATION OF JEWISH EMANCIPATION: Julius Hoexter and Moses Jung, Source Book of Jewish History and Literature (London, 1938), p. 227. By permission of Mitchell, Vallentine & Co., London.
7. QUESTIONS SUBMITTED BY NAPOLEON TO THE ASSEMBLY OF JEWISH NOTABLES and 8. THE ANSWERS: Jewish Encyclopedia, vol. 11, p. 46. See item 3.
9. PRUSSIA: NEW LEGISLATION PROPOSED: Wilhelm von Humboldt, "Regarding a Draft of a New System of Legislation for the Jews, July 17, 1809," trans. by Max Kohler, in Publications of the American Jewish Historical Society (Waltham, Mass.), vol. 26 (1918), pp. 104 ff. (abridged). Reprinted by the society's permission.
10. CITIZENS OF PRUSSIA; 11. CONTINUING THE STRUGGLE FOR FULL EQUALITY; and 12. EQUAL STATUS IN GERMANY: quoted and trans. in Julius Hoexter and Moses Jung, op. cit., pp. 236–40. See item 6.
13. LET US FIGHT THE BATTLE OF TRUTH: From The Life and Works of Lord Macaulay (London, 1897), vol. 8, pp. 108 ff. (abridged).
14. SCHOLARSHIP AND EMANCIPATION: Leopold Zunz, Die gottesdienstlichen Vorträge der Juden (Berlin 1832), trans. by Harry Zohn, and quoted in Nahum N. Glatzer, ed., The Judaic Tradition (Boston, 1969), pp. 515–17 (abridged). By permission of Professor Glatzer and Beacon Press.
15. A CALL FOR REFORM: Berlin Reformers; and 16. INTELLIGENT

RELIGION: Isaac Mayer Wise. Quoted in David Philipson, *The Reform Movement in Judaism*, rev. ed. by Solomon B. Freehof, (New York, 1967), pp. 351 ff., 343 ff. Copyright © 1967 by KTAV Publishing House, Inc., and used by its permission.

17. FROM THE PITTSBURGH PLATFORM: Quoted in the *Jewish Encyclopedia*, vol. 4, p. 215 (abridged). See item 3.

18. FROM THE COLUMBUS PLATFORM: Quoted in W. Gunther W. Plaut, *The Growth of Reform Judaism* (New York, 1968), pp. 96 ff. (abridged). Copyright © 1968 by World Union for Progressive Judaism and used by its permission.

19. NEO-ORTHODOXY: Samson Raphael Hirsch, *The Nineteen Letters on Judaism*, prepared by Jacob Breuer (New York, 1960), pp. 160 ff. (abridged). Copyright © 1960 by Philipp Feldheim, Publishers, and used by their permission.

20. RABBINIC LAW-MAKING: Immanuel Jakobovits, "Jewish Law Faces Modern Problems," in Leon D. Stitskin, ed., *Studies in Torah Judaism* (New York: Ktav, 1969), pp. 325 ff. (abridged). Copyright © 1969 by Yeshiva University Press and used by its permission.

21. THE MIDDLE WAY: Alexander Kohut, *The Ethics of the Fathers* (New York, 1920), quoted in Moshe Davis, *The Emergence of Conservative Judaism* (Philadelphia, 1963), pp. 222 ff. (abridged). Copyright © 1963 by the Jewish Publication Society of America and used by permission of the society.

22. CONSERVATIVE JUDAISM: Solomon Schechter, quoted in Mordecai Waxman, ed., *Tradition and Change* (New York: Burning Bush Press, 1958), pp. 163 ff. (abridged). Copyright © 1958 by The Rabbinical Assembly of America and reprinted by its permission.

23. RECONSTRUCTIONISM: Ira Eisenstein, *Creative Judaism* (New York: Jewish Reconstructionist Foundation, 1953), pp. 175 ff. Copyright 1935 by Ira Eisenstein. Reprinted by permission of Rabbi Eisenstein.

24. THE JEWS UNDER THE TSARS; and 25. A STATEMENT OF THE GOVERNOR OF KIEV: Michael Davitt, *Within the Pale* (New York, 1903), pp. 68–71, 160–61; p. 20.

26. JEWISH CANTONISTS UNDER TSAR NICHOLAS I: Alexander Herzen, quoted in S. M. Dubnow, *History of the Jews in Russia and Poland* (Philadelphia, 1916), vol. 2, pp. 24–25. Copyright 1916 by the Jewish Publication Society of America and reprinted by the society's permission.

27. A FOLKSONG: Quoted in Isaac Levitats, *The Jewish Community in Russia, 1772–1844* (New York, 1943), p. 65. Copyright © 1943 by Columbia University Press and used by its permission.

28. MODERN SCHOOLS BY GOVERNMENT DECREE; and 29. A SABBATH IN VILNA: Max Lilienthal, "My Travels in Russia," in David Philipson, *Max Lilienthal, American Rabbi: Life and Writings* (New York, 1915), pp. 258, 261–66, 294–98; pp. 273–76. Copyright 1915 by Bloch Publishing Co. and reprinted by its permission.

30. ANTISEMITISM AND ASSIMILATION: Pauline Wengeroff, *Memoiren einer Grossmutter* (Berlin, 1908–10), trans. from the German and quoted by Lucy Dawidowicz, *The Golden Tradition: Jewish Life and Thought in Eastern Europe* (New York, 1967), pp. 166–68 (abridged). Copyright © 1967 by Lucy Dawidowicz. Reprinted by permission of Holt, Rinehart and Winston, Publishers.

31. POGROMS IN SOUTH RUSSIA: An Eyewitness, quoted in S. M. Dubnow, op. cit., pp. 252–54. See item 26.

32. ON THE SLAUGHTER: trans. from the Hebrew by Abraham Klein in *Selected Poems of Hayyim Nahman Bialik*, ed. by Israel Efros (New York: Bloch Publishing Co., 1964), pp. 112–13. Copyright 1948 by Histadrut Ivrit and reprinted by its permission.

33. BEGINNING OF SELF-DEFENSE: Zalman Shazar, *Shtern fartog* (1952), trans. from the Yiddish by Lucy Dawidowicz, op. cit., pp. 383–88. See item 30.

34. SHAME AND INDIGNATION: Maxim Gorky, letter quoted in Michael Davitt, op. cit., pp. 272 ff. (abridged). See item 24.

35. PORTRAIT OF A "SHTETL" IN RUSSIA: Abraham Ain, "Swislocz, Portrait of a Shtetl," in Irving Howe and Eliezer Greenberg, eds., *Voices from the Yiddish* (Ann Arbor, Mich., 1972), pp. 87 ff. (abridged). Copyright © 1972 by University of Michigan Press and reprinted by its permission.

36. BECOMING A LEADER OF JEWISH LABOR: Vladimir Medem, "The Youth of a Bundist," trans. from the Yiddish by Lucy Dawidowicz, op. cit., pp. 427–34. See item 30.

37. BECOMING A ZIONIST LEADER: *Trial and Error: The Autobiography of Chaim Weizmann* (New York, 1949), pp. 3–4, 16–17, 20–22, 24–28, 40–42, 49–51 (abridged). Copyright © 1949 by the Weizmann Foundation. Reprinted by permission of Harper & Row, Publishers.

38. RISE OF MODERN HEBREW LITERATURE: Simon Halkin, *Rise of Modern Hebrew Literature* (New York, 1950), pp. 15–16. Copyright © 1950, 1970 by Schocken Books, Inc., and reprinted by their permission.

39. RISE OF YIDDISH LITERATURE: Sol Liptzin, *The Maturing of Yiddish Literature* (New York, 1970), pp. ix–xii. Copyright © 1970 by Sol Liptzin. Reprinted by permission of Jonathan David Publishers, Inc.

40. OUR HISTORICAL DEBT TO RUSSIAN JEWRY: Gershom Scholem, in Richard Cohen, ed., *Let My People Go* (New York: American Conference on Soviet Jewry, 1971), pp. 273–78. Copyright 1971 by Richard Cohen and reprinted by his permission.

41. FOR NATIONAL RIGHTS; and 42. ZIONISM IS COUNTER-REVOLUTIONARY. Quoted in Salo W. Baron, *The Russian Jew under Tsars and Soviets* (New York, 1964), p. 201; p. 208. Copyright © 1964 by Salo W. Baron. Reprinted by permission of the Macmillan Publishing Co.

43. AN ELEGY FOR HEBREW: Elisha Rodin, trans. from the Hebrew by Salo W. Baron, op. cit., p. 213. See the preceding item.

44. FACT SHEET ON ANTI-JEWISH DISCRIMINATION IN THE SOVIET UNION: in Richard Cohen, op. cit., pp. 143–47. See item 40.

45. SOME UNANSWERED QUESTIONS: from "The Problem of Soviet Jewry," in *Answers and Questions*, Pamphlet no. 7 (Jerusalem: Information Division of the Ministry of Foreign Affairs, December 1972), pp. 3–4, 19–20. Reprinted by permission.

46. ANTISEMITISM IN SOVIET RUSSIA: Leon Trotsky, "Antisemitism and Thermidor," in *The Basic Writings of Trotsky*, ed. by Irving Howe (New York: Random House, 1963), pp. 206 ff. (abridged). Copyright © 1963 by Irving Howe. Reprinted by permission.

47. JEWISH FREEDOM LETTERS FROM RUSSIA: Moshe Decter, ed., *Redemption! Jewish Freedom Letters from Russia* (New York: American Jewish Conference on Soviet Jewry, 1971), pp. 14–17, 36–39. Reprinted by permission.

48. UNTIL JUSTICE IS DONE: Arthur Goldberg, in Richard Cohen, op. cit., pp. 175–81. See item 40.

49. THE SUFFERINGS OF A SOVIET DANCER: Valery S. Panov, in *New York Times*, February 17, 1974. Copyright © 1974 by the New York Times Company and reprinted by its permission.

50. THE RIGHT TO BE JEWISH: Yefim Davidovich, in Moshe Decter, ed., *Terror in Minsk, KGB Case Number 97: The Jewish Officers "Plot"* (New York: National Conference on Soviet Jewry, 1973), pp. 17–24 (abridged). Reprinted by permission.

51. "I HAVE NO FUTURE IN THE COUNTRY IN WHICH I WAS BORN": Raiza Palatnik, in Richard Cohen, op. cit., pp. 69–72. See item 40.

52. ON THE PERSECUTION OF REPATRIATE JEWS: Valery A. Chalidze, in *Saturday Review*, September 18, 1971. Copyright 1971 by Saturday Review and reprinted by its permission.

53. A SPEECH AT A BABI YAR COMMEMORATION: Ivan Dzyuba, in Leonard Schroeter, *The Last Exodus* (New York, 1974), pp. 379–80.

Copyright © 1974 by Universe Books and reprinted by their permission.

54. THE SAGA OF SAMIZDAT: Ezra Rusinek, in *Hadassah Magazine*, December 1972. By permission of Ezra Rusinek and Hadassah Magazine.

55. THE JEWS ARE OUR MISFORTUNE: Heinrich von Treitschke, *Ein Wort über unser Judentum* (Berlin, 1881) (abridged). Trans. by the editor.

56. MY LIFE AS GERMAN AND JEW: Jacob Wassermann, *My Life as German and Jew*, trans. by S. N. Brainin (New York, 1933), pp. 219–27 (abridged). Copyright 1933 by Jacob Wassermann. By permission of Coward, McCann & Geognegan.

57. THE END OF EMANCIPATION: Nazi Legislation, in Raul Hilberg, *Documents of Destruction* (Chicago: Quadrangle Books, 1971), p. 20. By permission of Franklin Watts, Inc.

58. A PRAYER BEFORE KOL NIDRE: Leo Baeck, in Nahum N. Glatzer, op. cit., pp. 613 ff. See item 14.

59. I SHALL REQUIRE COURAGE: Anne Frank, *The Diary of a Young Girl* (New York, 1952), pp. 221–22. Copyright 1952 by Otto H. Frank. By permission of Doubleday & Company, Inc.

60. A GHETTO IN OCCUPIED POLAND: von Unruh, in Raul Hilberg, op. cit., p. 40. See item 57.

61. JEWISH CULTURAL LIFE IN THE GHETTOS OF POLAND: Emanuel Ringelblum; 62. OUR TOWN IS BURNING: Mordecai Gebirtig; 63. A PROTEST AGAINST THE INDIFFERENCE OF THE WORLD: Samuel Zygelbojm; 64. POLISH FRIENDS: "Wladka." Quoted in Jacob Glatstein, Israel Knox, and Samuel Margoshes, eds., *An Anthology of Holocaust Literature* (Philadelphia, 1969), pp. 336–39 (abridged); pp. 38–39; 329–31; pp. 364–69 (abridged). Copyright © 1969 by the Jewish Publication Society of America and reprinted by permission of the society.

65. MORDECAI ANILEWICZ: COMMANDER OF THE WARSAW GHETTO UPRISING: Emanuel Ringelblum, in *They Fought Back*, ed. and trans. by Yuri Suhl (New York: Crown Publishers, 1967), pp. 85–91 (abridged). Copyright 1967 by Yuri Suhl. Reprinted by permission of Yuri Suhl.

66. THE LAST WISH OF MY LIFE: Mordecai Anilewicz, in Glatstein-Knox-Margoshes, op. cit., pp. 334–35. See item 61.

67. A MANIFESTO OF THE JEWISH RESISTANCE IN VILNA: Quoted in Glatstein-Knox-Margoshes, op. cit., pp. 332–33. See item 61.

68. THE LAST DAYS OF THE WARSAW GHETTO: Ziviah Lubetkin,

Commentary, vol. 3. no. 5 (1947), pp. 401–11. Trans. from the Hebrew by Shlomo Katz. Copyright © by the American Jewish Committee. By permission of *Commentary* and Ziviah Lubetkin.

69. THE JEWISH COUNCILS: Yehuda Bauer, *They Chose Life* (New York, 1973), pp. 38–42 (abridged). Copyright © 1973 by the American Jewish Committee and reprinted by its permission.

70. THE MEANING OF RESISTANCE: Abraham Foxman, in Glatstein-Knox-Margoshes, op. cit., p. 92. See item 61.

71. THE SANCTIFICATION OF LIFE: Yehuda Bauer, op. cit., pp. 32–33. See item 69.

72. NEVER SAY THAT THERE IS ONLY DEATH FOR YOU: Hirsch Glick; and 73. I BELIEVE. Quoted in Glatstein-Knox-Margoshes, op. cit., p. 349; p. 623. See item 61.

74. LIBERATED—AT LAST: Simon Wiesenthal, in *The Murderers Among Us: The Simon Wiesenthal Memoirs*, ed. and with an introductory profile by Joseph Wechsberg (New York, 1967), pp. 45–56 (abridged). Copyright © 1967 by Opera Mundi, Paris. By permission of McGraw-Hill Book Company.

75. THE INDICTMENT OF ADOLF EICHMANN: Gideon Hausner, in *6,000,000 Accusers*, trans. and ed. by Shabtai Rosenne (Jerusalem, 1961), pp. 29 ff. and 173 ff. (abridged). Copyright by Minister Gideon Hausner and used by his permission.

76. THE SHOCK OF THE HOLOCAUST: H. H. Ben-Sasson, in *Jewish Society Through the Ages*, ed. by H. H. Ben Sasson and S. Ettinger (New York, 1972), pp. 342 ff. Copyright 1969 by UNESCO. By permission of Schocken Books, Inc.

77. THE VOW: Abraham Shlonsky, in Jacob Sonntag, *Jewish Writing Today* (London, 1974), p. 62. Trans. by S. J. Goldsmith. Copyright © 1974 by The Jewish Quarterly. By permission of Vallentine, Mitchell & Co., London.

78. THE AWAKENING: Moses Hess; and 79. AUTO-EMANCIPATION: Leo Pinsker, in Arthur Hertzberg, *The Zionist Idea* (New York, 1960), pp. 119 ff. (abridged); pp. 182–98 (abridged). Copyright © by Arthur Hertzberg. By permission of Rabbi Hertzberg and Doubleday & Co.

80. THE MANIFESTO OF THE BILU: Quoted in Walter Laqueur, ed., *A Documentary History of the Middle East Conflict* (New York, 1970), pp. 3–4. Copyright © 1969, 1970 by B. L. Mazel, Inc. By permission of Bantam Books, Inc.

81. THE JEWISH STATE: Theodor Herzl, *The Jewish State*, in Ludwig Lewisohn, *Theodor Herzl: A Portrait for This Age* (Cleveland and New York, World Publishing Co., 1955), pp. 233–55 (abridged);

trans. by S. d'Avigdor and revised by Ben Halpern and Moshe Kohn. Copyright © 1955 by the Theodor Herzl Foundation. By permission of the foundation.

82. THE ZIONIST PROGRAM: First Zionist Congress, 1897, in Walter Laqueur, op. cit., pp. 11–12. See item 80.

83. THE AIMS OF ZIONISM: Richard Gottheil, *The Aims of Zionism* (New York, 1898), (abridged).

84. A SPIRITUAL CENTER: Ahad Ha-Am, from "A Spiritual Center," in Ahad Ha-Am, *Essays, Letters, Memoirs* (Oxford, 1946), p. 204; trans. and ed. by Leon Simon. By permission of East and West Library, London.

85. MY FIRST MEETING WITH LORD BALFOUR: Chaim Weizmann, op. cit., pp. 109–11. See item 37.

86. THE BALFOUR DECLARATION: quoted in Adam Rutherford, *Anglo-Saxon Israel or Israel-Britain*, published by the author (London, 1934), p. 164.

87. DEFINITIONS AND STATEMENTS: Chaim Weizmann, in Sam E. Bloch, ed., *Chaim Weizmann: Excerpts from His Historic Statements, Writings and Addresses* (New York, 1962), pp. 41, 19, 45. By permission of Sam E. Bloch and World Zionist Organization, American Section.

88. PEOPLE AND LABOR: Aaron David Gordon, "People and Labor," in Arthur Hertzberg, op. cit., pp. 372–74 (abridged). See item 78.

89. THE UNITED NATIONS DECIDES ON A JEWISH STATE; and 90. THE UNITED STATES RECOGNIZES THE STATE OF ISRAEL: Chaim Weizmann, op. cit., pp. 457–59; pp. 477–79. See item 37.

91. STATE OF ISRAEL PROCLAMATION OF INDEPENDENCE; and 92. THE LAW OF RETURN: quoted in Walter Laqueur, op. cit., pp. 125–28; p. 129. See item 80.

93. HEBREW THE NATIONAL LANGUAGE OF THE STATE: Chaim Rabin, "The Revival of Hebrew," in *Israel Today*, no. 5 (Jerusalem, 1958), pp. 6–10, 112–14 (abridged). By permission of Israel Digest, World Zionist Organization.

94. A GENERAL SPEAKS AFTER THE SIX-DAY WAR: Yitzhak Rabin (Jerusalem: Hebrew University, 1967). By permission of Prime Minister Rabin.

95. SOLDIERS TALK ABOUT THE SIX-DAY WAR: From Henry Near, ed., *The Seventh Day* (London: Andre Deutsch, 1970), pp. 19–20, 32–33, 124, 131–32. Copyright © 1967 by Siach Lochamim. English version Copyright © 1970 by Henry Near and used by his permission.

96. RESOLUTION ON THE MIDDLE EAST: The Security Council of the
    United Nations; and 97. THE SEVEN POINTS: Al Fatah. Quoted in
    Walter Laqueur, op. cit., pp. 373–74, 379–80. See item 80.

98. ISRAEL AFTER THE YOM KIPPUR WAR: Hanoch Bartov, *Commen-
    tary*, vol. 57, no. 3 (1974), pp. 41–45. Copyright © by the American
    Jewish Committee. By permission of *Commentary* and Hanoch
    Bartov.

99. INVITATION TO WEEPING: Arnon Lapid, in *Hadassah Magazine*,
    September 1974, trans. from the Hebrew by Moshe Kohn. By
    permission of Hadassah Magazine.

100. THE ISRAEL-ARAB CONFLICT: TWO VIEWPOINTS: Albert
    Hourani, "Palestine and Israel," in the *Observer* (London), Sep-
    tember 3, 1967, and J. L. Talmon, "Israel and the Arabs," in the
    Observer, September 10, 1967. By permission of the Observer,
    London.

101. TO BIGOTRY NO SANCTION: Hebrew Congregation of Newport,
    R.I., letter to George Washington, in Irving J. Sloan, ed., *The Jews in
    America, 1621–1970* (Dobbs Ferry, N. Y., 1971), p. 95. Copyright ©
    1971 by Oceana Publications and reprinted by their permission.

102. INHERENT NATURAL RIGHTS: George Washington; 103. STATE
    AID TO PAROCHIAL SCHOOLS: Congregation Shearith Israel;
    104. AID TO NEEDY IMMIGRANTS: Circular. In Morris U. Schappes,
    ed., *A Documentary History of the Jews in the United States* (1971),
    pp. 80 f.; pp. 126 f.; pp. 198 ff. (abridged). Copyright © 1950, 1971 by
    Morris U. Schappes. By permission of Schocken Books, Inc.

105. ARARAT, A CITY OF REFUGE: Mordecai Manuel Noah, in A. B.
    Makover, *Mordecai M. Noah* (New York, 1915), pp. 48–47 (abridged).
    Copyright 1915 by Bloch Publishing Co. and used by their per-
    mission.

106. THE JEWS AND SUNDAY LAWS; 107. ESTABLISHING JEWISH
    CEMETERIES; 108. SETTLING IN CALIFORNIA. Quoted in Morris
    U. Schappes, op. cit., pp. 279 ff. (abridged); p. 293; pp. 441 ff.
    (abridged). See item 102.

109. FROM A RESOLUTION DURING THE CIVIL WAR: Hebrew Congre-
    gation of Shreveport, La., in Irving J. Sloan, op. cit., pp. 97 f.
    (abridged). See item 101.

110. A GERMAN IMMIGRANT IN THE SOUTH: Oscar Solomon Straus, in
    Jacob Rader Marcus, *Memoirs of American Jews, 1775–1865*
    (Philadelphia, 1955), vol. 2, pp. 289–300 (abridged). Copyright 1955
    by the Jewish Publication Society of America and reprinted by their
    permission.

111. I DISCOVER AMERICA: Abraham Cahan, *The Rise of David*

Levinsky (New York, 1945), pp. 85–91. Copyright © 1960 by John Higham, 1917, 1945 by Abraham Cahan. By permission of Harper & Row, Publishers.

112. THE STREET OF PEDDLERS AND PUSHCARTS: from *New York Tribune*, September 15, 1898. By permission of Whitney Communications Corporation, New York.

113. BEGINNINGS: LIFE IN THE NEW COUNTRY: Jacob Riis, "The Home—A Workshop," in Jacob Riis, *How the Other Half Lives* (New York, 1957), p. 80. Copyright © 1902, 1957 by Hill and Wang. By permission of Farrar, Straus and Giroux, Inc. "Health in the Tenements," and "Morals and Family Life," in Jacob A. Riis, *The Children of the Poor* (New York, 1892), pp. 39–40, 42–44. By permission of Charles Scribner's Sons.

114. ADJUSTING TO THE NEW WORLD: from *New York Tribune*, August 16, 1903 (abridged). See item 112.

115. PHILANTHROPISTS AND IMMIGRANTS: Boris D. Bogen, in Harold U. Ribalow, ed., *Autobiographies of American Jews* (Philadelphia, 1973), pp. 398 ff. (abridged). Copyright © 1965 by the Jewish Publication Society of America and used by their permission.

116. SWEATSHOPS: WHAT IS THE SWEATING SYSTEM?: John R. Commons, "U. S. Industrial Commission Reports," 1901, quoted in Allon Schoener, ed., *Portal to America: The Lower East Side, 1870–1925*, pp. 58 f. Copyright © 1967 by Allon Schoener. By permission of Holt, Rinehart and Winston, Publishers.

117. CHILDREN IN SWEATSHOPS: Edwin Markham, *Cosmopolitan Magazine*, January 1907, quoted in Allon Schoener, op. cit., pp. 162 f. By permission of Cosmopolitan Magazine.

118. FACTORY SYSTEM INSTEAD OF TASK WORK: Ernest Pole, "The Outlook," November 21, 1903, quoted in Allon Schoener, op. cit., pp. 169–71. See item 116.

119. ACHIEVEMENTS: Abraham Cahan, op. cit., pp. 374, 442–44 (abridged). See item 111.

120. THE BIRTH OF THE JEWISH UNIONS: Morris Hillquit, *Loose Leaves from a Busy Life* (New York, 1934), pp. 15–36. Copyright, 1934, by Vera Hillquit. By permission of Macmillan Publishing Co., Inc.

121. BECOMING A LABOR LAWYER: Louis Waldman, *Labor Lawyer* (New York, 1944), pp. 19–38 (abridged). Copyright © 1944 by Louis Waldman, renewal © 1972 by Louis Waldman. Reprinted by permission of the publishers, E. P. Dutton & Co., Inc.

122. BECOMING AMERICANIZED: Hutchins Hapgood, *The Spirit of the Ghetto: Studies of the Jewish Quarter in New York*. New edition, preface and notes by Harry Golden (New York, 1965), pp. 28–29, 32,

44–45. Copyright © 1902, 1965 by Funk & Wagnalls Co., Inc., and used by their permission.

123. YIDDISH NEWSPAPERS: Hutchins Hapgood, op. cit., p. 186. See the preceding item.

124. WHAT THE YIDDISH PRESS TAUGHT ME: Morris R. Cohen, *A Dreamer's Journey* (Glencoe, Ill., 1949), pp. 219 f. (abridged). Copyright 1949 by The Free Press. By permission of Macmillan Publishing Co., Inc.

125. FROM "BINTEL BRIEF": *Jewish Daily Forward*, in Isaac Metzker, ed., *A Bintel Brief* (New York, 1971) (selections). Translation and Introduction, copyright © 1971 by Isaac Metzker. Reprinted by permission of Doubleday & Company, Inc.

126. BECOMING A SCULPTOR: *Epstein: Autobiography* by Sir Jacob Epstein (New York, 1965), pp. 1–8 (abridged). Copyright © 1955, 1963 by the Executors of the Late Sir Jacob Epstein. Reprinted by permission of the publishers, E. P. Dutton & Co., Inc.

127. BECOMING A PHILOSOPHER: Morris R. Cohen, op. cit., pp. 65–95 (abridged). See item 124.

128. BECOMING A WRITER: Maurice Hindus, *A Traveler in Two Worlds*, (Garden City, N.Y.: Doubleday & Co., 1971), pp. 40–61, 315–17 (abridged). Copyright © 1971 by Frances McClerman Hindus and reprinted by permission of Mrs. Hindus.

129. A CHAMPION OF JEWISH RIGHTS: Louis Marshall, *Champion of Liberty: Selected Papers and Addresses*, ed. by Charles Reznikoff (Philadelphia, 1957), vol. 1, pp. 376–80. Copyright © 1957 by The American Jewish Committee and The Jewish Publication Society of America and reprinted by their permission and by courtesy of James Marshall, family custodian of the Marshall Papers.

130. THE JEWISH TASK: Louis Dembitz Brandeis, "The Jewish Problem and How to Solve It," quoted ·in Arthur Hertzberg, op. cit., pp. 517–23 (abridged). See item 78.

131. THE SUBURBAN JEW: Marshall Sklare, Joseph Ringelblum, and Benjamin B. Ringer, *Not Quite at Home: How an American Jewish Community Lives with Itself and Its Neighbors* (New York, 1969), pp. 80–85. Copyright © 1969 by the American Jewish Committee and reprinted by its permission.

Index